Dictionary of English Idioms

Viva

Dictionary of English Idioms

JOHN O. E. CLARK

Viva Books

New Delhi | Mumbai | Chennai | Kolkata | Bengaluru | Hyderabad | Kochi | Guwahati

This edition first published
in 2010 by

Viva Books Private Limited
4737/23, Ansari Road, Daryaganj
New Delhi 110002
Tel: 011-4224 2200, Fax: 011- 422 2240
E-mail: vivadelhi@vivagroupindia.net
http://www.vivagroupindia.com

Reprinted 2011

ISBN: 978-81-309-1248-6

Printed in India by Anand Sons, Delhi.

Preface

Idioms are the stuff of conversation, and it can be argued that their foundation in the spoken word places them in the forefront of a language's evolution. Like a living organism, a language has to adapt to survive, or it is in danger of becoming extinct. Idioms are among the chief means by which such adaptation occurs. But what are idioms?

When literal meanings are applied to individual words in a combination of words, and the intended meaning of the combination does not emerge, we are usually dealing with an idiom. Put another way, an English idiom cannot generally be translated literally into another language and preserve its meaning. Idioms are illogical and few follow the rules of English grammar, let alone that of another language. For instance, somebody familiar with idiomatic English would understand what is meant if a person is described as a "dark horse " or a "queer fish". Obviously no person is literally a horse or a fish - of any colour or strangeness. Yet the expressions "dark fish" and "queer horse" are not accepted idioms. Only certain combinations of words are acceptable, and these have to be learned.

Also slight differences in phrasing can make a great difference to meaning. For instance, there is a lot of difference between a "dark horse" and a "horse of another colour", and the meanings of "settle down", "settle on" and "settle up" are very different. But these subtleties too have to be learned.

It is the purpose of this book to assist in the learning process. It contains more than 10,000 idioms and idiomatic sayings in current English usage. Each is defined, and each has at least one sentence that provides an example of how the idiom is used. Each idiom is listed under a key word that forms a part of it. If more than one word can be regarded as a key word, the idiom is assigned to one of them and included as a cross-reference under the others. Thus "mad as a March hare" is defined under "hare", but included also as a cross-reference under "mad" and "March".

Under each key word, idioms are listed alphabetically. Alternative words or phrases are separated by an oblique stroke. Optional words or phrases, in brackets, are ignored for the purposes of alphabetization.

John O. E. Clark

Preface

A

aback

to be taken aback = surprised
"I was taken aback when she suddenly screamed."

abeyance

be in/fall into abeyance = be waiting or in suspense
"The decision is in abeyance until he returns from holiday."

abide

abide by = comply with, remain faithful to
"There will be no trouble as long as you abide by the rules."
abide by the consequences = endure the result
"If you do insist on going you must realize that you will have to abide by the consequences."
cannot abide = cannot tolerate
"I cannot abide his annoying habit of sniffing."

about

about to = just going to
"I'm glad we happened to meet, I was about to write to you."
how about?/what about? = what do you think about?
"How about going for a walk?"
"What about a cup of tea?"
out and about = active, moving around out of doors
"My mother says that she doesn't get out and about much these days."
up and about = out of bed (after and illness)
"The doctor says she should be up and about next week."
See also: be (about) the size of it.

above

above all = most important, more than anything else
"He's a good footballer and, above all, a great sportsman."
above and beyond = in addition, more than necessary
"She stayed behind to help with the cleaning, which is above and beyond her regular work."
above asking = too proud to ask
"He seems so self-sufficient but fortunately he's not above asking for help when he needs it."
above oneself = self-satisfied, conceited
"He got above himself after he was nominated for the award."
above suspicion = known to be too honest to be suspected of wrong-doing
"Whoever took the money it wasn't Christine ñ she's above suspicion."
not above = not too honest/proud to
"He's not above taking paper and envelopes from work for his own use at home."
See also: above board; above one's station; above par; rise above oneself.

abuse

terms of abuse = bad/uncomplimentary language
"He had no convincing reply to my argument, so resorted to terms of abuse."

accent

accent you could cut with a knife = strong, noticeable accent (in speaking)
"The Frenchman had lived in England for more than ten years but he still had an accent you could cut with a knife."
See also: broken accent/English.

accident

accidentally on purpose = deliberately but underhandedly
"He got his revenge by spilling his drink over the other man accidentally on purpose."

chapter of accidents = succession of misfortunes/mistakes
"I ran out of petrol, had a broken windscreen, and then got a flat tyre ñ the whole trip was a chapter of accidents."

accommodate

accommodate with = supply, lend
"Could you please accommodate me with five pounds."

accord

according to = as said by
"According to her the party was a failure."

of/on one's own accord = voluntarily
"I didn't make him go ñ he went of his own accord."

with one accord = unanimously, with everyone's agreement, simultaneously
"He had only just started to sing when with one accord they left the room."

account

account for = explain
"A stone in his shoe accounts for why he was limping."

an account to settle = grudge to avenge
"Ever since the day he insulted me I've had an account to settle with him."

be accountable for = be responsible for
"We warned him that he would be accountable for his actions."

by all accounts = according to popular opinion
"The Grand Hotel is the best in town by all accounts."

by one's own account = according to what one says
"Lionel was accused of shoplifting but by his account he has never even been in the shop concerned."

call to account = require someone to justify his or her actions
"One day he'll be called to account for his bad timekeeping."

doctor the accounts = falsify accounts (usually to make them appear better/worse than they are).
"He avoided paying tax for three consecutive years by doctoring his accounts."

give a good account of (oneself) = do/perform well
"There was stiff competition but she nevertheless gave a good account of herself."

keep an account of = keep a (written) record of
"Please keep an account of how long the job takes."

no accounting for taste = a preference the speaker does not agree with
"Have you seen her new dress? It's purple with yellow flowers on it ñ still, there's no accounting for taste."

of no account = worthless, of no importance
"Don't worry about that mistake, it's of no account."

on account = towards (in part payment of) a debt
"He owes me fifty pounds and gave me ten on account last night."

on account of = because of
"He didn't go on account of his illness."

on no account/not on any account = in no circumstances

"On no account should you ever put a knife blade in the toaster."

on one's own account = for oneself

"She's gone into business on her own account."

on somebody's account = on behalf of somebody, for somebody's sake

"I only went on his account, I didn't really want to go."

on that account = for that reason

"It was raining and on that account I wore a hat."

put/turn to (good) account = use to (personal) advantage

"He turned the delay to good account by catching up on some other work."

settle/square an account (with somebody) = settle a real or figurative debt, avenge oneself

"He deliberately insulted me but I'll square accounts with him one day."

take account of/take into account = include (in one's judgement)

"The speaker failed to take account of the age of her audience and so many of her remarks were too difficult for them to understand."

See also: blow-by-blow account.

ace

ace in the hole = resource or riposte held in reserve

"His remarkable ability to always score the last point in the match is his team's ace in the hole."

it's ace! = it is the best!

"Have you heard their new record? It's ace!"

play one's ace = use one's most powerful resource

"The general decided to play his ace and send in the tanks."

trump somebody's ace = counter an opponent's move by an even more powerful one

"He did not invite me to his party but I trumped his ace by holding one on the same night ñ and everybody came to mine."

(come) within an ace of = (be) very close to

"She came within an ace of winning first prize."

See also: black as the ace of spades; have an ace up one's sleeve; hold all the aces.

ache

See: one's heart aches/bleeds for somebody.

Achilles

See: Achille's heel.

acid

acid test = crucial test or trial

"Can Jones beat Smith? That's the acid test."

come the old acid = (try) to deceive somebody

"I don't believe you, so don't come the old acid with me."

acquaint

acquaint one with = make one aware of

"He refused to acquaint me with his reasons for declining my offer."

be acquainted with = know

"I'm not acquainted with the finer points of football."

acquaintance

have a nodding acquaintance with = know somebody/something only slightly

"No, I don't know the name of Everton's captain; I've only a nodding acquaintance with football."

make the acquaintance of = to get to know or meet
"Who, Mary Smith? I've never made her acquaintance."
scrape up an acquaintance with = deliberately try to make friends with somebody (usually for one's own advantage)
"I scraped up an acquaintance with the secretary and got him to propose me for membership of the club."

acquire
acquired taste = liking/preference for the unusual, obtained gradually
"I like jam with cheese, but it's an acquired taste."

acquit
acquit oneself = behave (as required/ expected)
"She was nervous about meeting the duke, but she acquitted herself well."

across
get/put something across = make one's (possibly difficult) meaning clear
"The difficulty in selling this item is getting across to the potential customer that the higher quality justifies the higher price."
See also: across the board.

act
act a part = hide one's real feelings
"He pretended to be impressed by their new car but he was only acting a part."
act of God = unforeseen and damaging event, or favourable divine intervention
"It was an act of God: the river broke its banks and they were flooded out."
"Nobody was hurt in the bus crash ñ it must have been an act of God."
act on/upon = take action because of (something known)
"He suggested what I should do and I acted on his advice."
act up = misbehave or malfunction
"My car wouldn't start again this morning ñ it's always acting up lately."
catch somebody in the act = come across somebody while he/she is doing something wrong
"I went back unexpectedly and caught him in the act of searching my personal papers."
get in on the act = intrude, or copy somebody, for a hoped-for advantage
"They were doing well in their new shop until her mother got in on the act and drove away much of their custom."
get/put one's act together = become organized
"His lecture was going badly until he got his act together and by the end they were all very impressed."
old pal's act = favouritism to a friend (especially in business)
"I put in the lowest price but he gave the contract to his friend's firm ñ a typical example of the old pal's act."
put on an act = pretend (ostentatiously)
"He appeared to be upset with her but he was only putting on an act."
See also: act/be one's age; play/act the fool; read the riot act.

action
actions speak louder than words = deeds are more effective than mere talk
"Actions speak louder than words when it comes to tidying up the village."

action stations = be prepared immediately
"Action stations! Here comes the boss."

go into action = start working (vigorously)
"He's reluctant to begin, but when he does you should see him go into action."

out of action = not working (of a machine), indisposed (of a person)
"My washing machine has been out of action since last Monday."
"I'm sorry not to have called round earlier, but I've been out of action with the flu."

piece of the action = part in (an undertaking)
"She's starting a new business and has promised me a piece of the action."

actress

as the actress said to the bishop = emphasizing a (usually suggestive) double meaning
"That's a big one, as the actress said to the bishop."

Adam

Adam's ale = water
"You can't beat a drink of Adam's ale when your throat is dry and you are really thirsty."

Adam's rib = woman(kind) (equated with Eve)
"The origin of the human race owes more to Adam's rib than to Adam."

not known from Adam = completely unknown
"Who's that? He greeted me, but I don't know him from Adam."

add

add up = make sense
"I understand; it all adds up now."

See also: add insult to injury.

addition

in addition (to) = as well as
"He's bad tempered, in addition to being unreasonable."

address

address oneself to = direct one's effort/attention to
"When I've finished painting the house I'll address my attention to doing the garden."

address the ball (at golf) = line up the club before making a shot
"The short putt was so easy that he didn't even bother to address the ball."

admiration

See: lost in admiration.

advance

in advance of = before (in time)
"The cooks arrived on camp in advance of the main party."

make advances to = try to establish a friendship with
"This awful man made advances to me on the train."

advantage

have the advantage of = be in a better/superior position than, or know something that somebody else does not
"She was younger than her opponent but had the advantage of more experience."
"You seem to know my name but you have the advantage of me, because I

something to one's advantage = something that benefits one (usually financially)
"Please come to my office next Monday when you may hear something to your advantage."
take advantage of somebody = profit by somebody else's ignorance/innocence
"She knows very little about cars and the salesman really took advantage of her."
to advantage = in a beneficial way
"The plain vase shows off the flowers to advantage."
turn to advantage = make beneficial
"He had to stay at home but turned it to his advantage by catching up on his reading."
See also: set something off to advantage.

advocate
See: devil's advocate.

affair
affair of the heart = love affair
"Her relationship with Peter is an affair of the heart."
have an affair with = have an emotional/sexual relationship with
"My wife has accused me of having an affair with my secretary."
hole-and-corner/hole-in-the-corner affair = secret (and possibly sordid) relationship
"They spent the odd night away together in his caravan ñ it was a real hole-in-the-corner affair."

afoot
something afoot = planned (secretly)
"I hear there's something afoot about changing the management structure of the company."

afraid
be afraid = be sorry
"I'm afraid I've spilled my coffee."

after
after all = in spite of everything
"He had a runny nose and a sore throat, but he didn't get flu after all."
be after somebody = pursue, want to catch
"The police are after him."
be after something = desire, want to obtain
"What I'm really after is a new car."

again
come again? = pardon? (what did you say?)
"Come again? I didn't hear you properly."
now and again = occasionally
"I only go there now and again."

age
act/be one's age = behave in an adult manner
"Don't cry. It's time you started acting your age."
"Be your age! Remember, you're sixteen now."
age before beauty = older people should take precedence over younger ones (meant sarcastically)
"The boy was here first, but age before beauty!"
age of consent = 16 years for a girl in Britain (over which age a man can legally have sexual relations with her)
"She's going on holiday with her boyfriend ñ well, she's over the age of consent."
ages since = a long time
"Hello! It's ages since I saw you."
an age/for ages = for a long period (of time)

"I wish the bus would come; I've been waiting here for ages."
"It seems an age since I last had a decent meal."

at an advanced age = very old
"Even at his advanced age he still went for a bicycle ride every day."

at an awkward age = at any difficult stage of life, usually adolescence or the menopause
"He's at that awkward age; always hanging around on street corners."
"My mother has become very moody ñ but she's at an awkward age."

come of age = reach the age of being legally responsible for one's actions (eighteen years for most purposes in Britain)
"She signed her own hire purchase agreement now that she's come of age."

look/show one's age = appear to be as old as one really is
"He's nearly seventy, but doesn't look his age."
"She's nearly sixty, and beginning to show her age."

of tender age/years = young/immature
"She is still of tender age and much too young to get engaged."

ripe old age = very old
"Did you hear that William died last week? Still, he lived to a ripe old age."

under age = below a legally required age
"He started drinking in pubs when he was still under age."

agony

agony column = letters to a newspaper/magazine from readers with problems that are answered by the publication's resident expert
"The agony column is my favourite part of the magazine."

pile on the agony = deliberately make somebody's pain, discomfort or disappointment seem worse
"I told him I'd lost my job and he piled on the agony by saying that I'll probably never get another one."
"Our opponents scored the first goal and then piled on the agony by scoring five more."

agree

agree to differ = agree (amicably) to a difference of opinion
"I though it would take three weeks, she said four, so we agreed to differ."

one-sided agreement = agreement that favours one party but not the other
"It was a one-sided agreement: he got the right of way over my land but I was still forbidden to cross over his fields."

aid

in aid of = for the help/benefit of
"What's that new machine in aid of?"
"I'm collecting money in aid of starving children."

air

airs and graces/put on airs = affectation/adopt an affected manner
"I cannot stand his airs and graces ñ he is, after all, just an ordinary person like us."

airy-fairy = dreamy but impractical
"He was supposed to give us advice, but all he came up with were airy-fairy ideas."

(you could) cut the air with a knife = there was an atmosphere of tension/resentment
"After he told the meeting that he

would no longer give his support to the project, you could cut the air with a knife."

dance/walk on air = be in a state of ecstasy
"When I heard that I had got the job I could have walked on air."

give oneself airs = show off, try to impress/claim to be what one is not
"He's not really that good ñ he's only giving himself airs."

go up in the air = become very angry
"When she saw the damage to her car she went right up in the air."

have a hangdog air = appear to be shame-faced
"I wanted to tell him off, but he had such a hangdog air I just couldn't do it."

hot air = bluster, unsubstantiatable claim
"I know he says he can run a mile in under four minutes, but that's all hot air."

(up) in the air = undecided/unresolved
"We thought we were going to Spain next week, but because of the seamen's strike that is all up in the air."

into thin air = emphasizes disappearance
"I searched for the ball for ten minutes, but it had vanished into thin air."

make the air turn blue/turn the air blue = swear, blaspheme
"When he saw what she had done, he made the air turn blue."

out of thin air = (apparently) from nowhere
"The magician produced a rabbit out of thin air."

something in the air = rumour/suspicion that something is about to happen
"I have a feeling that he's going to leave us ñ there is something in the air."

take the air = go/walk out of doors
"There's nothing better when on holiday than to take the air before breakfast each day."

See also: air a grievance; clear the air; free as the air/wind/a bird; fresh-air fiend; walk on air.

Aladdin

Aladdin's cave = repository of expensive/good things
"To the poor peasant, the supermarket was an Aladdin's cave."

alarm

false alarm = something, although expected, that does not happen/an unnecessary warning
"The sky went very dark and we thought it was going to rain but it was a false alarm."
"Martin said the boss was going to make a surprise visit, but it proved to be a false alarm."

ale

See: Adam's ale.

Alec(k)

smart Alec(k) = somebody who claims (conceitedly) to know everything
"He keeps telling the instructor what to do ñ the smart Alec."

alert

on the alert = prepared and ready for anything
"Keep on the alert, we're due for an inspection."

alive

alive and kicking = aware and active
"Despite his great age, George is still alive and kicking."

alive with = crowded/infested with

"The town square was alive with people."
"The poor dog was alive with fleas."

be alive to a situation/the fact that = be aware of something
"Jane's husband is being unfaithful but she doesn't seem to be alive to the situation."

all

all along = all the time/from the beginning
"I knew that all along."

all and sundry = everyone
"On the day of the birth of his first child, he was giving cigars away to all and sundry."

all at once/all of a sudden = suddenly
"Then all at once there was a crash of breaking glass."
"The window caved in all of a sudden."

all for something = be enthusiastically in favour of something
"Let shops open on Sundays? I'm all for it."

all for the best = ultimately for the good
"Don't be upset that you can't go with them, it's probably all for the best."

all in = exhausted, or inclusive (of extras)
"When I finally got back from the long walk I was all in."
"The cost of accommodation was only ten pounds a night all in."

all in all = taken as a whole
"There were some slightly cloudy days, but all in all the weather was good."

all of = at least, fully
"It took all of three days to do."

all one = immaterial, makes no difference
"He can protest if he wants to, it's all one to me."

all out = with maximum effort
"They are making an all-out attempt to climb to the top."

all over the place = to many destinations, or drunk/incompletely done
"Every year she travels all over the place."
"When he finally left the pub he was all over the place."
"Brian tried to build a shed but it was all over the place and fell down within a few weeks."

all round = various
"He is good at quizzes because he has an all-round knowledge."

all rounder = somebody with various skills
"She's equally good at running and jumping and is one of the team's best all rounders."

all set = in a state of readiness
"We're all set for the trip tomorrow."

all the best = farewell (i.e. may you fare well)
"All the best, I'll see you next week."

(not) all there = (not) clever/sane
"She's all there; she will soon work out how to do it."
"You can't expect him to be able to do it, he's not all there."

all the same = nevertheless
"All the same, I still think you are wrong."

all the same to = makes no difference to
"I'll have a glass of beer, if it's all the same to you."

all things considered = after everything has been taken into account
"The dealer has offered you a hundred pounds for the furniture and, all things considered, it's probably a fair price."

all told = in total

"There were only nine people there all told."

all up with = ended (of life/prospects)
"Once the diagnosis was confirmed, it was all up with her."

all very well = as far as something goes
"Your apology is all very well, but what about some compensation for the damage you have caused?"

at all = in the smallest way
"I do not like it at all."

for all I care/know = as if I care (expressing indifference or ignorance)
"He can wait for ever, for all I care."
"For all I know, she's going out with somebody else by now."

for all that = nevertheless, despite the circumstances
"She was unkind to him but he still loves her for all that."

get away from it all = escape from everyday responsibilities
"What I'd like is a fortnight in Greece where I can get away from it all."

not all that = not as believed/expected/suggested
"The food was expensive and not all that good."

not at all = not (emphatically)
"I didn't think ne knew I was going to be there, but he was not at all surprised when I arrived."

on all fours = on hands and knees
"He was so drunk he could only cross the room on all fours!"

one and all = everyone
"Here's good luck to you, one and all."

when all's said and done = when everything is taken into consideration
"When all's said and done, your injuries could have been worse."

See also: above all; all ends up; all in a day's work; all in good time; all of a sudden; all over; all ship-shape and Bristol fashion; at all costs; be all and end all; on all fours.

alley

blind alley = something with no prospects or likelihood of a result
"We then tried tracing the fault in the machine's wiring, but it turned out to be yet another blind alley."

allowance

make allowance(s) for = take into account
"They asked too much of him and made no allowance for his inexperience."

alone

go it alone = act on one's own, independently of others
"Nobody would help me, so I decided to go it alone."

let alone = without even considering
"He's the best shot in the world, let alone in England."

leave/let well alone = add/do nothing else (for fear of spoiling something)
"You've persuaded your father to agree to one of your requests so I should let well alone in case he changes his mind."

along

all along = all the time
"Why look so surprised? You knew that would happen all along."

along with = together with
"She came to dinner along with her boyfriend."

go along with = agree (but perhaps deceitfully)
"It suits my immediate needs so I'll go

along with his suggestion for the time being."

See also: all along the line.

also

also-ran = loser

"He tried for the job but was among the also-rans."

amends

make amends (for) = make up (for), compensate

"I'm sorry I'm late, but perhaps a good meal will make amends for my keeping you waiting."

angel

guardian angel = protector (who seeks no reward)

"She will not accept anything for looking after my father when he was ill; she has been a real guardian angel to him."

like an angel = with purity and/or innocence

"Despite his bad reputation, he behaved like an angel at the school party."

on the side of the angels = in favour of what is correct/moral

"In any dispute, he always comes down on the side of the angels."

See also: angel of mercy; fools rush in where angels fear to tread.

anger

See: more in sorrow than in anger.

angle

angle for = try to obtain something using hints

"He asked me how work was going but he was really angling for

animal

rare animal = somebody of unusual ability/talent, or with an unusual combination of abilities

"He's that rare animal, a professional musician and a scientist."

behave like an animal = (of people) behave in an inhuman or very antisocial way

"The crowd behaved like animals, pushing and fighting among themselves."

dumb animals = animals, emphasizing their non-human status and inability to speak for themselves

"You mustn't be cruel to dumb animals."

lower/worse than animals = (of people) inhuman or very antisocial

"I have no sympathy for football hooligans ñ they are worse than animals."

answer

answer back = reply cheekily

"Be quiet! I've told you not to answer back."

answer for (something) = be responsible/blamed for (something)

"Get it wrong and you'll answer for the consequences."

answer to the name of = acknowledge the name of, be called

"The new girl answers to the name of Ethel."

be answerable for = accept responsibility for

"If you don't stop it, I won't be answerable for my actions."

know all the answers = be adept/well informed (possibly in a conceited way)

"He thinks he knows all the answers,

straight answer = unambiguous reply, without being devious
"The trouble is, whatever you ask, he will never give you a straight answer."
the answer's a lemon = a non-answer to a long involved/boring question
"I can't remember every detail of what you said, but I suspect the answer's a lemon!"
See also: answer by return; not to take no for an answer.

ants
See: have ants in one's pants.

anybody
anybody's guess = uncertain/cannot be predicted
"When he'll finally turn up is anybody's guess!"

anything
anything but = not in the least, far from
"The task looked simple, but it turned out to be anything but easy."

apart
tell apart = distinguish (between)
"The twins are so alike, it's impossible to tell them apart."
See also: joking apart.

apology
an apology for = poor example/sample of
"The animal is bald and mangy; it's an apology for a dog."

appear
appear for = represent in court
"He is the barrister who will appear for the defence."
keep up appearances = outwardly maintain a status that may not be
"With little or no income, he is finding it increasingly difficult to keep up appearances."
make/put in an appearance = attend
"The chairman has arrived ñ it's about time he put in an appearance at one of these functions."
to all appearances = apparently, seemingly
"She kept smiling and to all appearances was enjoying herself."

appetite
See: put an edge on one's appetite.

apple
apple of one's eye = favourite person, one who is loved best
"Grandfather always made the most fuss of Gillian; she was the apple of his eye."
apple-pie bed = bed with the sheet folded in such a way that one cannot get in it
"For a prank, they made apple-pie beds for all the new student nurses."
apple-pie order = neat and tidy
"This room must be in apple-pie order before the tour of inspection."
rotten apple (in the barrel) = bad person among many good ones
"He let down the whole group, but there always seems to be one rotten apple."
upset the apple-cart = spoil somebody's plans
"He wanted to go away, but all leave has been cancelled. That's upset his apple-cart."

approval
on approval = returnable if not satisfactory
"I wasn't sure whether the red

cushions would match my settee, so I bought one on approval."

April

April fool = somebody on whom a joke is played on 1 April (before noon)
"I've put salt instead of sugar in your tea. April fool!"

apron

tied to one's mother's apron strings = totally dependent on one's mother
"He's over twenty and lives at home, still tied to his mother's apron strings."

area

no-go area = place that is unsafe (because of military, terrorist or criminal activity/presence)
"The continuing violence between rival gangs of youths has made a large part of the housing estate a no-go area."

See also: grey area.

argue

argue somebody down = reduce somebody to silence through vigorous argument
"He kept saying he didn't want to go, but eventually she argued him down."

argue something out = keep talking until agreement is reached
"So far we disagree; let's argue it out over a drink."

argue the toss = questioning (often unreasonably), argumentative
"Don't let us argue the toss over who is going to pay for the meal."

ark

out of the ark = very old
"He never buys anything new; even his car came out of the ark."

arm

arm of the sea = narrow inlet
"We found a secluded sandy beach along an arm of the sea."

arm twisting = pressurizing (by persuasion or threat)
"She didn't want to go, but with a good deal of arm twisting I finally persuaded her."

chance one's arm = take a (calculated) risk
"The car was so cheap there was probably something wrong with it, but I still chanced my arm and bought it."

give one's right arm (for) = pay any price, make a sacrifice (for)
"I'd give my right arm for that last stamp I need to complete the set."

keep/hold at arm's length = keep remotely formal, distant
"The landlord prefers to keep new customers at arm's length until he knows what they are really like."

long arm of coincidence = however unlikely, coincidences can happen
"On holiday in Hongkong, thousands of miles from home, I bumped into my next door neighbour ñ talk about the long arm of coincidence!"

long arm of the law = inescapable police detection or justice
"He was arrested six years after he had committed the crime ñ you can't escape the long arm of the law."

(my) right arm = good friend and supporter
"When I was ill and out of work, Charles was my right arm and helped me over the worst time of my life."

take up arms = become involved in a conflict
"The unions have threatened to take up arms against the government's proposed wages policy."

twist somebody's arm = put pressure on/ persuade somebody to force him/her to do something
"I didn't really want to go out tonight but, since you're going to pay for the drinks, you've twisted my arm."
up in arms = angrily protesting
"She told she didn't want to work late ñ she was really up in arms about it."
with one arm tied behind one's back = very easily
"I could bake a better cake with one arm tied behind my back!"
with open arms = enthusiastically and without hesitation
"When I said I would go back and work for him, he welcomed me with open arms."
See also: babe/baby in arms; brothers in arms; one-armed bandit; strong-arm tactics.

armchair
armchair traveller = somebody who reads or watches films about overseas places but does not actually visit them
"He pretends to know about the best restaurants in Athens, yet he's really only an armchair traveller."

armour
See: chink in somebody's armour.

army
you and whose army? = you and who else?
"You think you can beat me at chess? You and whose army?"

around
to have been around = to be experienced, worldly-wise
"You can't fool her easily, she's been around too long."
See also: (all) around/round the houses.

arrears
in arrears = behind with payment(s)
"I don't know how I'm going to pay ñ I've been in arrears with my rent for three months now."

arrest
(under) house arrest = being compelled (by official order) to remain in one's home
"The police did not take her away, but she was put under house arrest until the time of her trial."
under arrest = in police custody
"They put him under arrest and took him to the police station, where they charged him with stealing a car."

arrive
arrive at = reach by a process of thought, deduce
"I thought it over for several days before finally arriving at a decision about the job offer."

art
off to a fine art = (be able to do something) to perfection
"After only a few day's instruction, she got typing off to a fine art."
See also: black art/magic; state of the art; work of art.

article
article of faith = deeply-held conviction
"It's an article of faith among West Indians that they have the best test cricket team in the world."

as

as for one = as far as one is concerned
"Daniel wants to bring his girlfriend, but as for her I would rather she stayed away."

as it is = in the present circumstances
"I wanted to buy another car but as it is I'll have to keep the old one a bit longer."

as it were = metaphorically speaking
"When he said that, she went for him like an angry bull, as it were."

as you were = return to your previous position/state
"Please go over to the other side of the room. No ñ sorry, as you were ñ please go back."

See also: as yet.

ascendant

(one's star is) in the ascendant = rising in influence/popularity
"They take a lot more notice of him now that his star is in the ascendant."

ash

See: rake over the ashes

ask

ask after somebody = enquire about somebody's health/happiness
"Mary asked after you and your husband."

ask for it = deserve/invite unpleasantness
"Do you really want to know what I think about your new hair style? Well, you've asked for it!"

asking price = price/value put on something by the seller
"The clock is worth three times the asking price."

for the asking = freely available
"Go down to the timber yard, there's plenty of scrap wood there for the asking."

if you ask me = in my view/opinion
"She's the best typist of the lot, if you ask me."

See also: above asking; ask a silly question; ask for trouble.

askance

See: look askance at.

ass

make an ass of oneself/somebody = make oneself/somebody look foolish
"I made an ass of myself at the party by dropping cake all over their new carpet."

astray

go astray = become misplaced/stolen
"Every time I buy a new pen, it goes astray within a couple of days."

See also: lead somebody astray.

at

at it = doing something
"He still washing his car ñ he's been at it all day."

at that = thus far and no further, or as well
"It's probably all right to buy her a drink, but you had better let it go at that."
"He says he is going to invite her out and he probably will, at that."

See also: at a (single) stroke; not at all.

attach

See: with no strings attached.

attack

blunt the attack = reduce the effect of an aggressive act

"George was strongly critical of my behaviour, but I was able to blunt his attack by reminding him about his own behaviour last time."

make a full-blooded attack (on) = attack strongly/wholeheartedly
"He made a full-blooded attack on Labour's defence policy."

attendance
See: dance attendance on.

attention
call/draw attention to = bring to somebody's notice
"The guide drew our attention to the magnificent carved panelling."

pay attention (to) = be attentive (to)
"Children, pay attention to what I have to say."

rivet one's attention = apply/hold all one's attention
"The cat riveted its attention on the hole into which the mouse had disappeared."

attitude
holier-than-thou attitude = (unjustified) stance of being better/more virtuous than everyone else
"I could put up with his specific criticisms if it were not for his holier-than-thou attitude."

auction
See: Dutch auction.

aunt
Aunt Sally = deliberate target of abuse/ridicule (to make a point)
"The BBC has become the Aunt Sally of every extremist point of view."

my giddy/sainted aunt = exclamation of surprise
"My giddy aunt! Haven't you finished yet?"

autumn
autumn of somebody's life = past the age of maturity, after one's "best" years
"It's amazing what somebody can still contribute to society even in the autumn of his life."

avail
avail oneself of = make use of
"Only residents may avail themselves of the hotel's facilities."

of/to little/no avail = with hardly any/no result
"I tried to borrow some money but to little avail."
"I tried to persuade him to come, but to no avail."

avenue
explore every avenue = make every possible enquiry
"We must explore every avenue before coming to the final decision."

aversion
pet aversion = somebody/something specially disliked
"Spiders are my pet aversion."

awakening
rude awakening = sudden unpleasant discovery
"We had an enjoyable time at the theatre, but then to find my car had been stolen came as a rude awakening."

away
do away with = dispose of, abolish, or kill

"We decided to do away with our old cooker and buy a new one."
"Did you hear about Elizabeth? She tried to do away with herself."

get away with = do without being discovered or, if discovered, without being punished
"I parked my car on a double yellow line for nearly an hour but got away with it."

See also: edge away; get away from it all; straight away.

axe

have an axe to grind = pursue a personal and private aim (often leading to a biased point of view)
"It was unlike him to agree so readily, I suspect he's got some axe to grind."

to be axed = to lose one's job
"I used to work in a supermarket but was axed when the firm had a bad trading year."

B

baby

babe/baby in arms = somebody who is immature/naive
"He believes anything he's told, just like a babe in arms."

cry baby = somebody who weeps or complains for the most trivial of causes
"Don't be a cry baby. That tiny scratch can hardly hurt at all."

left holding the baby = left to take the blame for something
"We were taking apples in the orchard when Tony saw the farmer coming, ran away, and left me holding the baby."

throw out the baby with the bath water = lose something that is very useful when getting rid of something that is apparently of no use
"He lost a brand-new set of spanners when he let the scrap dealer clear out the contents of his garage; it was a case of throwing out the baby with the bath water."

wet the baby's head = celebrate the birth of a baby by having a drink (with the parent)
"My brother's wife has just had a baby and I'm meeting him tonight to wet the baby's head."

back

at the back of = ultimately responsible
"There's something sinister at the back of that series of crimes."

back and forth = from one place to another and back again
"I spend more than three hours a day going back and forth to the office."

back-breaking task/work = demanding or exhausting task/work
"Digging that clay soil is back-breaking work."

back down = give in, relinquish any claim to something
"He was threatening legal action but he soon backed down when he got that letter from my solicitor."

back-fire = go wrong (resulting in the opposite of what was intended/required)
"Our plans back-fired because of the rail strike and we had to drive all the way to Scotland instead of taking the train."

back number = out-of-date issue of a newspaper or magazine, or something that is outmoded
"I didn't buy the magazine last month; I must try to get hold of a back number so that I can catch up on the articles I missed."
"The dress Pat wore to the disco was a real back-number."

back of beyond = remote, inaccessible
"He's bought a ruined cottage at the back of beyond."

(at the) back of one's mind = remaining (but not prominently) in one's thoughts
"I've always had it at the back of my mind to learn to play chess one day."

back out (of) = withdraw (from an agreement/contract/promise)
"I know I said I would come but my husband is ill and so I'm afraid I shall have to back out."

back-pedal = withdraw (after having expressed interest in something)
"Paul agreed to help but now he's back-pedalling because he says he's too busy."

back-room boys = anonymous people who develop/plan a project
"The new model has been a great success but we must not forget the back-room boys who made it possible."

back to the drawing-board = return to the beginning (and re-plan)
"The furniture won't all fit in that way so I'm afraid it's back to the drawing-board."

back to the wall = in difficulties with no retreat
"They made more than ten objections but William overcame them all; he always fights best when his back's to the wall."

back up = support somebody/something
"Fred told them and I backed up everything he said."

behind one's back = without one's knowledge
"They waited until I left the room and then discussed it behind my back."

break the back of = complete the larger part of
"If we work a couple of extra hours this evening we shall break the back of this job."

by the back stairs = in an unofficial way, indirectly
"My uncle is a manager at my new place of work and so I was able to get the job by the back stairs."

get off somebody's back = stop harassing somebody
"I wish you would get off his back, he's not doing you any harm."

get one's back up = anger/annoy one
"His constant sniffing gets my back up."

get/put somebody's back up = provoke somebody to anger, annoy
"His condescending attitude really gets my back up."

glad to see the back of somebody/something = be pleased when somebody/something leaves or finishes
"My mother has been so demanding while staying with us I shall be glad to see the back of her."
"We'll be glad to see the back of our old car, it keeps breaking down."

go back on = change one's mind, contradict
"He promised to help and then went back on his word and said he was too busy."

hang back = be reluctant to go forward
"Catch up with the others Jenny; don't keep hanging back."

have a broad back = be able/willing to accept blame for the errors of others
"Don't worry; tell them I did it, I have a broad back."

have no backbone = lacking courage
"It's no use asking Roger to come water skiing, he hasn't the backbone for it."

like the back of a bus = ugly
"She has a nice figure but she's got a face like the back of a bus."

like the back of one's hand = intimately
"She knows the layout of the back streets like the back of her hand."

make a rod for one's own back = cause trouble for oneself by one's actions
"I didn't know when I volunteered to help with the old people's club that I was making a rod for my own back ñ it now takes up nearly all of my free time."

on one's back = harassed by, or bedridden (through illness or disability)
"She's keeps nagging me, she's always on my back."

"It's good to go for a walk again; I've been on my back with flu for a week."

pat on the back = congratulate/praise (mildly)

"He's worked better than usual this week, I think he deserves some sort of pat on the back."

put one's back into = make a strenuous effort

"You'll finish the job much quicker if you put your back into it."

see the back of = be finished with

"I hope we'll see the back of this bad weather before I start my holiday."

stab in the back = betrayal

"I was stabbed in the back by my assistant who got promotion in preference to me because he told them about my forthcoming divorce."

take a back seat = adopt an inconspicuous/inferior position or role

"It's about time you took a back seat and let your son run the business."

talk through the back of one's neck = talk nonsense

"She was talking through the back of her neck when she said I was going to resign from my job."

through the back door = in an unofficial way, indirectly

"They were so involved with the main issues that I was able to slip in my amendment through the back door."

to the backbone = absolutely, unquestioningly

"He'll never give credit to a Lancashire team ñ he's a Yorkshireman to the backbone."

turn one's back on = abandon, deliberately ignore

"Although you disapprove of Mary's behaviour, you can't turn your back on the fact that she's still your daughter."

when one's back is turned = when one is not looking or absent

"I told you not to use the cooker, yet as soon as my back was turned you were frying eggs and bacon."

with one hand tied behind one's back = very easily

"I could bake a better cake than that with one hand tied behind my back!"

you scratch my back and I'll scratch yours = you do me a favour and I will do you one in return

"If you give me a hand clearing the rubbish from my garden I'll help you to paint your house ñ you scratch my back and I'll scratch yours."

See also: answer back; back-/left-handed compliment; back the wrong horse; fall off the back of a lorry; fed up (to the back teeth); get one's own back; go back to square one; in by the back door; like water off a duck's back; scratch somebody's back.

background

keep/remain/stay in the background = be deliberately inconspicuous

"Although he finances most of the club's events he keeps mainly in the background."

back seat

take a back seat = remove oneself from a position of authority/power

"Albert has decided to take a back seat now that his son is old enough to run the family business."

See also: back-seat driver.

backward

bend/lean over backwards = take great trouble to be accommodating or helpful

"The examination candidates were not very good but the examiner bent over backwards to let as many pass as possible."

not backward in coming forward = attention-seeking, not shy
"There she goes, making eyes at the boss; she's certainly not backward in coming forward."

See also: know something backwards.

bacon

bring home the bacon = succeed in a (difficult) enterprise
"We had to work hard to get an order out of the Americans but finally we were able to bring home the bacon."

save somebody's bacon = rescue somebody (who is in a difficult situation)
"Thanks for your prompt payment of my bill, it saved my bacon with the bank manager."

bad

bad blood (between people) = ill feeling
"I'm not surprised they fought each other last night, there has always been bad blood between them."

bad debt = money owing that is written off (and never paid)
"My business is in financial trouble because of a series of bad debts."

bad egg/hat/lot = somebody of bad character/reputation
"I'd advise you not to associate with him, he's a bad lot."

bad language = swearing, blaspheming
"I will not tolerate bad language in this house."

bad light/odour = bad/unfavourable reputation
"The report showed the government in a bad light."
"The government is in bad odour with the public because of the contents of the report."

badly off = poor, not wealthy
"We were so badly off when I was a child that we had a meat dish for dinner only on a Sunday."

bad patch = difficult/unfavourable situation
"My business has been through a bad patch recently and I have been unable to maintain a reasonable profit margin."

come to a bad end = finish in unpleasant/criminal circumstances (possibly by dying)
"He's already been caught shoplifting; that boy will come to a bad end."

go from bad to worse = deteriorate (gradually)
"The service in this hotel goes from bad to worse."

in a bad way = critically ill (of a person), or in a very poor state (of a thing)
"I hear that Brian is in a bad way after his accident."
"The canal is now in a very bad way through neglect."

in bad taste = ill-mannered/offensive
"I thought the remarks she made about royalty in front of the Duchess were in very bad taste."

in somebody's bad books = be in disfavour with somebody
"She refuses to talk to me but I don't know why I'm in her bad books."

not (so/too) bad = comparatively good
"Have you tried the new restaurant yet? It's not too bad."

too bad = unfortunate
"It's too bad that the sale of your house has fallen through."

See also: bad faith; good/bad form; in bad odour; look bad; (using) bad/strong language; with bad/good grace.

badger
badger somebody = pester, make continual demands
"I wish she'd stop badgering me for a new coat."

bag
bag and baggage = with all one's possessions
"I packed up and left, bag and baggage."
bag of bones = very thin (person or animal)
"Look at that dog, the poor thing is only a bag of bones."
bag of tricks = complete set of accessories/equipment
"Please may I borrow your bag of tricks so that I can service my car at home."
in the bag = successfully concluded, or as sure as if concluded
"We've completed the task ñ it's in the bag."
"My application for promotion is in the bag."
mixed bag = varied collection
"The new intake of students appears to be a very mixed bag."
pack one's bags = leave (in anger)
"She tried to put up my rent yet again so I packed my bags and went somewhere else."
See also: bag/bundle of nerves; let the cat out of the bag

bait
jail bait = precocious young (under age) woman
"Be careful about getting involved with her, she's only fifteen and typical jail bait."
rise to the bait = to react in a hoped-for way to a hint or stimulus
"She always rises to the bait when I deliberately provoke her with unkind remarks about her favourite pop group."

baker
See: baker's dozen.

balance
in the balance = unresolved
"I don't know whether I'll be able to come, it's still in the balance."
(catch) somebody off balance = at a disadvantage
"I caught him off balance at the meeting and got my argument in first."
on balance = considering every aspect
"On balance, I think I would rather not commit myself to going with you."
strike a balance = compare things to find their worth
"We have to strike a balance between the extra cost of a new microcomputer and the extra convenience of a new photocopier."
See also: tip the balance.

bald
bald as a billiard ball/coot = completely bald
"He's only forty years old and already he's as bald as a billiard ball."

ball
ball of fire = somebody who is very energetic
"Get John to help you, he's a regular ball of fire."
ballpark figure = rough estimate
"I don't need an accurate quotation yet; just give me a ballpark figure."
have a ball = have a very enjoyable time
"The holiday was wonderful ñ we had a ball."

have the ball at one's feet = be in a position to make the next move
"We'll have to wait and see what Sheila has to say, the ball's at her feet."

have the ball in one's court = have to make the next move
"The ball's in his court and we can only wait for him to give a decision."

keep one's eye on the ball = be alert, continue to pay attention to something
"The work passes through this office so quickly that you have to keep your eye on the ball to make sure nothing gets missed."

keep/set/start the ball rolling = continue/ begin doing something
"I shall be a bit late for the party so would you please keep the ball rolling until I arrive."

new ballgame = totally different set of (competitive) circumstances
"They have asked us to change the specification, but then it would be a completely new ballgame."

on the ball = alert, well informed
"Jane will probably know, she's always on the ball."

play ball with somebody = co-operate with somebody
"He is very helpful and it is easy to play ball with him."

See also: address the ball.

balloon

(when) the balloon goes/went up = moment of crisis/trouble
"Wait till she finds out ñ then watch the balloon go up."

bamboo

See: bamboo curtain.

banana

underdeveloped nation
"There's no point in putting in a big export effort just to sell a few goods to some remote banana republic."

be/go bananas = lose one's temper
"He went bananas when he saw the damage to his wife's car."

slip on a banana skin = make a gaffe.
"The Foreign Secretary slipped on a banana skin when he accidentally referred to foreigners as wogs."

band

beat the band = be extreme (in some respect)
"His lawnmower makes enough noise to beat the band."

one-man band = work by oneself (with no helpers)
"It's amazing how many items he makes in a day considering he's only a one-man band."

bandit

one-armed bandit = fruit machine (gambling)
"I won six pounds on the pub's one-armed bandit."

bandwagon

climb/jump on (board) the bandwagon = support somebody/something that looks like being a success (for personal gain)
"Trust him to climb on the bandwagon and join the Alliance now that they look like winning in this constituency."

bang

bang goes something = something has suddenly gone
"If I don't get paid for that job soon, bang goes my holiday in France."

bang on = exactly what is required
"Those gloves you gave me are bang on ñ the right size and the right colour to match my new shoes."
go with a bang = go very well
"Once the music started to liven up the party went with a bang."
See also: gang bang.

bank
bank on = depend on
"George will definitely come, you can always bank on him."
break the bank = use up all one's available funds, or have a landslide win at gambling
"That new outfit I bought broke the bank and I cannot get anything else until pay day."
"Donald won nine consecutive times at roulette and broke the bank at the casino."

banner
carry the banner for = support
"I've written a letter of complaint to British Rail; somebody has got to carry the banner for better standards of service."

baptism
See: baptism of fire.

bar
all over bar the shouting = finished apart from the final throes or official announcement
"The score is three-nil and there goes the final whistle; it's all over bar the shouting."
bar none = without exception
"She is the best writer in the world bar none."
called to the bar = made a barrister
"Belinda spends most of her time in court since she was called to the bar last year."
colour bar = (unlawful) regulation that excludes coloured people from certain activities
"Bring along your Jamaican friend; there's no colour bar in this club."
prop up the bar = frequent a particular pub
"You can usually find Jack propping up the bar at his local."

bare
bare bones = essential/most important features
"The bare bones of the scheme are its cheapness and simplicity."
bare-faced lie = shameless/impudent lie
"I saw him down the road last week and yet he says he's been away in Italy for more than a month; it is obviously a bare-faced lie."
with one's bare hands = without using a tool or weapon
"If he says that again I'll kill him with my bare hands!"

bargain
bargain for = prepare for, expect
"We ran out of food at the party because I didn't bargain for so many people turning up."
drive a hard bargain = insist on harsh terms in an agreement
"I am happy to let Marilyn negotiate for us because she can drive a hard bargain."
into the bargain = as well, in addition
"It was not only cold but started to snow into the bargain."
make the best of a bad bargain/job = cheerfully accept bad luck/adversity

"By the time we got there they only had blue ones left, but we made the best of a bad bargain and bought them anyway."

strike a bargain = finally reach an agreement

"We finally struck a bargain after half an hour of wrangling over who should pay the bill."

bargepole

wouldn't touch somebody/something with a bargepole = would avoid at all costs

"That builder uses inferior materials and I wouldn't touch him with a bargepole for any building work of mine."

bark

bark up the wrong tree = suffer under a misapprehension

"She thought I'd made the report to the police, but she was barking up the wrong tree."

one's bark is worse than one's bite = the (apparent) threat is worse than the (real) action

"Don't worry about his grumpy expression, his bark is worse than his bite."

See also: don't keep a dog and bark yourself.

barrack-room

barrack-room lawyer = somebody (typically a serviceman) who quotes the rule book to annoy/discomfit his superiors

"He's a typical barrack-room lawyer and I only wish he'd put as much effort into doing his job properly as he does into applying the fine points of the rules."

barrel

over a barrel = in an indefensible position, helpless

"I had to comply; she knew about my indiscretion and she had me over a barrel."

scrape the (bottom of the) barrel = be forced to use the (poor) remnants of something

"Everyone else was off sick so we had to give the job to Ted ñ that's really scraping the bottom of the barrel."

See also: bad/rotten apple (in the barrel).

base

get to/make first base = successfully complete the first stage

"She was lucky even to get to first base with that crazy scheme of hers."

bash

have a bash at something = make an attempt at

"Come on. Let's have a bash at climbing to the top of the hill."

basinful

have a basinful (of) = endure (more than enough of) something unpleasant

"I've had a basinful of his insults, and next time I'll tell him so."

basket

put all one's eggs in one basket = commit all one's expectations/resources to a single plan

"Although she's a freelance, she has put all her eggs in one basket and works five days a week for just a single client."

basting

give somebody a (thorough) basting = thoroughly beat

"Martin had beaten me at chess two weeks running but last night I gave him a thorough basting."

bat

be/have bats in the belfry = mad

"You can't believe a word she says because she is bats in the belfry."

blind as a bat = totally blind

"Didn't you see the car coming? You must be as blind as a bat."

carry one's bat = be present for the whole of an activity, right to the end

"David helped to survey the site, organized the workforce, and carried his bat to be present at the opening ceremony."

like a bat out of hell = at high speed

"The motorbike came round the corner like a bat out of hell."

off one's (own) bat = independently, without help/prompting

"I didn't have to ask her, she volunteered off her own bat."

play a straight bat = be honest, undeceitful

"Frank plays a straight bat and you can always rely on him."

See also: not bat an eyelid.

bated

See: with bated breath.

bath

blood bath = carnage, bloody battle

"When armed riot troops arrived to break up the demonstration it turned into a blood bath."

battle

battle of the bulge = slimmer's fight against being overweight

"I find that eating low-fat spread instead of butter helps in the battle of the bulge."

battle royal = intense fight involving everyone

"The two opposing groups and the police clashed, resulting in a battle royal."

fight a losing battle = continue to resist, even though the outcome will inevitably be unfavourable

"He keeps trying new hair lotions to stave off baldness but I'm afraid he's fighting a losing battle."

half the battle = good way towards achieving success, great help

"Once we had prepared the site and laid the concrete for my new garage, it was half the battle."

pitched battle = contest with both sides totally committed

"Each side committed its reserves and a pitched battle followed."

running battle = drawn-out dispute or contest

"I'm getting tired of the running battle between the employers and the unions."

bay

at bay = cornered (by enemies) and made to defend oneself

"The robbers set off the alarm and found themselves at bay inside the bank when the police arrived and surrounded it."

hold/keep at bay = hold off, keep at a distance

"I paid in a cheque for a hundred pounds to keep the bank manager at bay."

be

be-all and end-all = whole of something

"Learning how to dance is not the be-all and end-all of social achievement."

be that as it may = yet, even so

"I know you don't like him but be that as it may, you can at least be polite to him."

let it be = leave it alone

"Don't touch that wasp, let it be."

bead

See: draw a bead on.

beam

broad in the beam = having wide hips

"She's got a fairly nice figure but she is a bit broad in the beam."

off (the) beam = lacking precision, off course

"Your answer to the sum is way off beam."

on one's beam ends = in a desperate situation

"Please can you lend me twenty pounds? I'm on my beam ends."

bean

full of beans = energetic, lively, high-spirited

"Albert has been walking for almost six hours and he is still full of beans."

haven't a bean = penniless

"I cannot afford to go because I haven't a bean."

know how many beans make five = be worldly wise, shrewd

"You won't deceive her easily, she knows how many beans make five."

not worth a bean = worthless

"Don't take any notice of his opinion, it is not worth a bean."

spill the beans = be indiscreet, confess

"Trust her to spill the beans, she never could keep a secret."

bear

bear/lead a charmed life = be very lucky (in avoiding misfortune)

"He got out of the crash without a scratch; he must bear a charmed life."

bear down on/upon = approach purposefully or in a threatening way

"I was about to drive off when I saw this huge lorry bearing down on me."

bear enquiry/investigation = favourably withstand close examination

"I only hope that his business accounts will bear investigation."

bear in mind = remember (with caution)

"You must bear in mind that many of those solvents are poisonous."

bear on/have a bearing on = be relevant to

"Your comments bear on/have bearing on the central issue of the arguments."

bear oneself = behave

"Despite being heckled by the crowd, the leader bore himself with dignity."

bear out = confirm

"She recently won a beauty contest, which bears out the fact that she is one of the prettiest girls in town."

bear up = tolerate difficulty/pain with fortitude

"I don't know how she continues to bear up under the strain of having to look after her invalid mother."

bear with = be patient/sympathetic towards somebody

"Please bear with me while I finish attending to this other customer first."

(like a) bear with a sore head = bad tempered

"I shouldn't talk to him this morning ñ he's like a bear with a sore head."

bear witness = be a witness to something, prove

"The farmer's weather-beaten face bore witness to his years spent outdoors."

grin and bear it = (cheerfully) endure difficulty/hardship

"He doesn't want to work late next

week but he'll just have to grin and bear it."

See also: bear a grudge; bear fruit; bear garden; bear one's cross; bear the brunt of; grin and bear it.

bearings

find/get one's bearings = locate/orientate oneself

"I only started my new job yesterday and I haven't yet had time to get my bearings."

lose one's bearings = get lost, become disorientated

"It's so easy to lose one's bearings in the underground passages between the terminals at the airport."

beard

See: beard the lion in his den.

beat

beat about the bush = prevaricate, avoid a direct answer

"Don't beat about the bush, tell me truthfully what happened."

beat a path to somebody's door = repeatedly visit somebody

"Her local admirers beat a path to her door."

beat a (hasty) retreat = run away

"We saw a bull enter the field we were in so we decided to beat a hasty retreat."

beat down = force/persuade somebody to lower the price of something

"He wanted a hundred pounds for it but I managed to beat him down to seventy-five."

beat hollow = completely defeat

"Our team beat them hollow by four clear goals."

beat it = run away

"Come on, let's beat it before we are discovered in here."

beat one's brains out = think very hard to (try to) solve a problem

"I beat my brains out trying to think of a way of getting round the difficulty."

beat somebody to it = do something first (before anyone else can)

"There was only one vacant space in the car park and Nigel beat me to it."

beat to a pulp = badly injure through beating

"Before we could drag him off he'd beaten his poor victim to a pulp."

if you can't beat them, join them = if they will not change their minds, you must change yours

"I tried for years to get them to take up chess but they insisted on playing cards, and in the end I joined in and played cards with them ñ if you can't beast them, join them."

off-beat = unusual, unconventional

"Such a combination of colours is really too off-beat for an old people's home."

off the beaten track = difficult to get to, away from main roads

"I know of an unspoiled old pub off the beaten track in the wilds of Essex."

take a lot of/some beating = difficult to better

"She scored 47 at her first attempt, and that will take a lot of beating."

See also: beat the band; beat the drum for; beat the living daylights out of somebody; dead beat.

beauty

beauty is in the eye of the beholder = preference (in terms of somebody's appearance) is a personal one

"She seems very plain but he dotes on

her, but beauty is in the eye of the beholder."

beauty is only skin deep = somebody/something that is superficially attractive is not necessarily all good
"Although she looks pretty I'm not sure she has the strength of character for the job ñ remember, beauty is only skin deep."

the beauty of it (is) = the best/most satisfying aspect (is)
"The beauty of my new car is that it only needs servicing every ten thousand miles."

See also: age before beauty; beauty is only skin deep; get one's beauty sleep.

beaver

beaver away = work long and industriously
"She beavers away for hours knitting jumpers for her favourite charity."

See also: eager beaver

beck

at somebody's beck and call = constantly dominated by somebody
"I'm tired of being at my mother's beck and call."

become

become of = happen to
"What became of that Alsatian you had?"

bed

bed of nails/thorns = annoying, embarrassing or painful situation
"Our marriage has become a bed of nails since my mother-in-law came to live with us."

bed of roses = easy/luxurious situation
"Compared with my life, his has always been a bed of roses."

bed sitter = single room used as a bedroom and a living room
"My student son is looking for a bed sitter within walking distance of his college."

get into bed with = enter into a business agreement/contract with
"The only way he could share the contract was to get into bed with an American company."

get out of bed (on) the wrong side = be disagreeable/grumpy
"She's in a bad mood this morning. She must have got out of bed on the wrong side."

good bedside manner (of a doctor) = way of dealing with a patient that reassures and inspires confidence
"All of her patients agree that she has a good bedside manner."

go to bed with = have sexual intercourse with
"She had only known him a few days before she went to bed with him."

make one's bed and (must) lie in it = face the consequences of one's actions
"We did warn him what would happen if he went ahead, and having made his bed he must now lie in it."

See also: apple-pie bed; feather bed.

bee

bee in one's bonnet = obsessive idea
"He has a bee in his bonnet about women wearing trousers in the office."

bee-line = straight line between two points
"As soon as we got there he made a bee-line for the bar."

bee's knees = the best (person), expert
"Ask Sarah if you want to know anything about the new machine, she's the bee's knees."

busy as a bee = very (and continuously) busy
"I've been as busy as a bee all day doing my spring cleaning."

beef
beef about = complain
"Take no notice; he's always beefing about something."

beer
all beer and skittles = amusing, lacking seriousness
"He has no responsibilities or money problems; to him, life is all beer and skittles."
small beer = something that is unimportant
"Don't worry about giving me the change, it's small beer anyway."

before
before long = soon
"I hope the bus comes before long, I'm getting cold waiting."

beg
beg, steal or borrow = obtain by any means
"I needed a special spanner and I couldn't beg, steal or borrow one anywhere."
beg the question = assume the truth of something that can in fact be disputed
"You haven't even asked her yet so assuming that she will accept is begging the question."
beg to differ = disagree
"You may think that football is better to watch than cricket, but I beg to differ."
go begging = left because unwanted
"Few people turned up and much of the food that was provided went begging."

beggar
beggars can't be choosers = the needy have to take what is available
"I really wanted a pink one but they only had blue ones in my size and beggars can't be choosers"
See also: beggar description.

begin
to begin with = firstly
"I have several choices what to do. To begin with, I could do nothing!"

behalf
on behalf of = representing, in place of
"I'm asking you on behalf of my sister."

behind
behind the scenes = privately, secretly
"I got his agreement behind the scenes before we went into the public meeting."
behind the times = old-fashioned, out-of-date
"He gained little support because his ideas on the subject are now well behind the times."
come from behind = achieve success although initially at a disadvantage
"Up to the week of the election the Labour candidate was expected to win, but at the last minute the Liberal came from behind and won a majority of votes."
get/fall behind = become late, get in arrears
"I was buying a car on hire purchase, but after six months I fell behind with the payments and the company repossessed it."
put something behind one = deliberately try to forget (something unpleasant)
"I had a difficult time following my

divorce but I have now put all that behind me."

See also: behind one's back.

being

for the time being = temporarily

"She is running the shop for the time being, while the manager is away."

belfry

See: bats in the belfry.

belief

beyond belief = unbelievable

"How insulting! His insolence is beyond belief."

to the best of one's belief = in one's honest view

"To the best of my belief he has never been in trouble before."

believe

believe one's ears/eyes = accept as true what one hears/sees

"When I saw how she was dressed, I could hardly believe my eyes!"

make believe = imagine/pretend

"Let's make believe we're twenty years younger again."

bell

clear/sound as a bell = in excellent health/condition

"He went for a medical examination and the doctor said he was as sound as a bell."

ring a bell = remind one

"I can't remember her name but her face rings a bell."

saved by the bell = rescued from unpleasantness at the very last minute

"He angrily demanded an explanation but I was saved by the bell when his wife came in and insisted on talking about her garden."

belly

belly-ache about = complain naggingly

"I wish he'd stop belly-aching about his children's behaviour."

have a bellyful = have more than enough

"He said he'd had a bellyful of his partner's lack of help and was thinking of ending the association between them."

have eyes bigger than one's belly = overeat, be greedy

"I'm sorry I can't finish my pudding; my eye's are bigger than my belly."

belt

below the belt = unfair

"You should not have used what you know of his past against him ñ that was below the belt."

belt along/away = travel fast

"We belted along the motorway for nearly a hundred miles, and then had to travel at a crawl along the minor roads."

belt up = stop talking

"Oh belt up, I'm tired of your moaning."

pull one's belt in/tighten one's belt = spend less, make economies

"I'll have to tighten my belt now that I can get no more overtime working."

under one's belt = to have as an achievement or experience

"Janet has four A-levels under her belt."

bench

on the bench = serving as judge or magistrate

"Mr Justice Watson has recently retired after sixty years on the bench."

bend

bend the rules = cheat, or ignore a regulation

"Gerald bent the rules and carried an extra club in the golf competition, but nobody noticed."

"She was only one day over the age limit so the organizers bent the rules and accepted her entry."

catch someone bending = have an advantage over somebody by surprising him/her

"The vicar caught me bending when he called unexpectedly while I was decorating the kitchen ceiling and covered in paint."

on one's bended knees = in a very submissive way

"I wouldn't change my mind even if he came to me on bended knees."

round the bend = insane, mad

"Don't take any notice of her ramblings, she's completely round the bend."

See also: bend/lean over backwards; bend somebody's ear; lift/bend the elbow.

beneath

beneath contempt = not even worth an expression of disapproval

"The thugs who rob old people are beneath contempt."

benefit

benefit of the doubt = assumption of innocence, without proof

"Jones said that his train had been delayed; the foreman gave him the benefit of the doubt and did not reduce his pay for being late."

bent

bent upon = determined

"She was bent upon getting married before she was twenty-five."

hell bent (on) = very determined

"He was hell bent on not getting married before he was thirty."

berth

give a wide berth (to) = avoid

"He's so boring that I always give him a wide berth at parties."

beside

beside the point = irrelevant

"The cost is beside the point; what about the quality?"

beside oneself = irrational, very emotional

"She was beside herself when she heard that her cat had been run over by a car and killed."

best

at best = the best that can be expected in the circumstances

"The painting is not as valuable as you think; at best it will fetch a hundred pounds at auction."

at the best of times = even when circumstances are better

"I don't like Chinese food even at the best of times."

(the) best part (of) = most

"It was the best part of a week before the weather improved."

do one's (level) best = try hard

"He seems to be doing his level best to annoy me."

(all) for the best = leading to a favourable outcome, if unpromising now

"We couldn't go away because the car wouldn't start, but it turned out to be for the best when a good friend arrived from abroad unannounced."

get/have the best of both worlds = have the advantages from two different situations
"He's not married yet he lives with a girl who cooks his meals and does his washing ñ he's got the best of both worlds."
have the best of it = win an argument/ contest
"Linda was losing at first but eventually got the best of it after her opponent made several silly mistakes."
make the best of (a bad job) = obtain the best result possible in difficult circumstances, compromise
"It started to rain so we couldn't have a picnic, but we made the best of a bad job and went for a walk anyway."
past it/past one's best = too old (for a particular activity)
"He's past it, he can't keep swimming for more than an hour any more."
"She's still very attractive to men, although she claims she is past her best."
put one's best foot forward = make an extra effort, walk quickly
"Come on; put your best foot forward and we'll be home before dark."
(come off) second best = (be) loser in a contest between two
"The challenger fought such a good match that the champion came off second best."
six of the best = six strokes of the cane
"When I was at school such behaviour would be punished by six of the best."
Sunday best = best clothes
"They all came in their Sunday best and I felt out of place in my casual clothes."
to the best of one's ability/belief/ knowledge = as well as one is able/ knows
"James always does the work to the best of his ability."
"To the best of my knowledge. Nicolas is under twenty-five."
(up) with the best = as good as anyone else
"She hardly seems to try sometimes and yet she's always up with the best."
See also: all for the best; may the best man win; to the best of one's belief.

bet

bet one's bottom dollar/bet one's life = be almost certain
"It's a public holiday tomorrow and you can bet your bottom dollar it will rain."
"I'd bet my life that it was Richard I saw in the distance."
hedge one's bets = reduce the chances of being wrong by opting for two different choices simultaneously
"If I were you I'd hedge my bets and apply for both jobs at the same time."
I/you bet = I am/you can be certain
"You bet I'll be there."

better

better half = wife, partner
"Let me introduce you to my better half."
better late than never = more satisfactory that something happens, even if late, than that it never happens at all
"I finally got reimbursed after waiting for more than six months; it was better late than never, I suppose."
better off = more wealthy/more advantageous
"Now that my older brother's children have left home he is much better off than me."

"A car is expensive to run and difficult to park ñ you'd be better off with a motorbike."

for better or (for) worse = whatever happens

"We may be lost but, for better or worse, I'm going to chose the left-hand road."

get the better of = beat

"Our boxer seemed to be losing but he finally got the better of his opponent in the last round."

go one better (than) = supersede (with an improvement)

"I bought an MG but he had to go one better and get a Jaguar."

have seen better days = worn, showing its age

"The cinema is run down and has seen better days."

know better = be less foolish

"Don't do that, you ought to know better at your age."

no better than = the same as

"The new pens are no better than the old ones."

think better of somebody = think of somebody in a more favourable way

"I've thought better of him since he did that voluntary work."

think better of something = reconsider

"I was going to come but then I thought better of it."

See also: best/better part of

between

between the devil and the deep blue sea = with a choice between two equally undesirable alternatives

"After my car broke down I didn't know whether to stay with it in case the AA or RAC came along or to walk to the next garage; I was caught between the devil and the deep blue sea."

between these four walls = confidentially (and privately)

"Between these four walls I think the new man is no good."

between two stools = failing to meet either of two (conflicting) requirements

"The book falls between the two stools of authority and popularity."

between you and me/ourselves = confidentially

"Between you and me I hope he fails."

between you, me and the bedpost/gatepost = confidentially (and privately)

"I know he has got it wrong before, but that's between you, me and the gatepost."

betwixt and between = mid way, neither one nor the other

"That's a strange creature; it looks somewhere betwixt and between a horse and a dog."

few and far between = rare, scarce

"These days decent restaurants are few and far between."

read between the lines = detect an unstated but implied meaning

"Reading between the lines I think she's unhappy despite her jolly manner."

bewitched

bewitched, bothered and bewildered = totally confused

"The question took me by surprise and I was bewitched, bothered and bewildered."

beyond

beyond compare/measure = inestimable, very much

"The value of one's health is beyond measure."

beyond one's grasp/reach = unattainable

"Quantum physics is quite beyond Norman's reach."

beyond one's ken = outside one's experience/knowledge

"I can't repair a car engine, it's quite beyond my ken."

beyond the pale = unacceptable (socially), ill-mannered

"Robert's behaviour last night was beyond the pale."

See also: above and beyond; back of beyond; beyond belief; beyond price; beyond recall.

bias

on the bias = obliquely, diagonally

"A square of cloth cut on the bias does not stretch in either dimension."

bib

best bib and tucker = best clothes

"We must wear our best bib and tucker to go to the firm's annual dinner."

bid

bid fair = look promising

"The signs bid fair for a profitable deal."

bid farewell/welcome (to) = say goodbye/hello (to)

"The time has come to bid you farewell."

"You bid them welcome while I make us all a cup of coffee."

make a bid for freedom = try to escape

"As soon as the door is left ajar the puppy makes a bid for freedom."

straw bid = worthless bid

"He's going to the auction but can only make a straw bid for the painting."

bide

bide one's time = wait for a good chance

"I'm bound to win a prize eventually, I'm just biding my time."

big

be big of somebody = generous (often sarcastic)

"He said he'd donate five pounds to the restoration fund ñ that's big of him!"

Big Apple = New York

"I'm going to the Big Apple for my holiday."

Big Brother = dictatorial authority

"Now that they have installed closed-circuit TV I can't help thinking that Big Brother is watching me all the time."

big fish/noise/shot/wheel = important person

"Fanshaw is a big fish in merchant banking."

"Just because he's got a company car he thinks he's some sort of big shot."

big guns = most important/senior people (in a particular group)

"We'd better tidy up, the big guns from head office are coming tomorrow."

big head = somebody who is conceited

"I'm getting tired of Gerald telling us how he won his school's sports cup; he's becoming a big head."

big time = best/highest reaches of an activity

"Now that her record has sold a million copies she is ready for the big time."

go down/over big with = be impressive

"It's worth taking John along because he always goes over big with overseas clients."

in a big way = enthusiastically

"He's gone in for gardening in a big way."

talk big = boast

"Simon's always talking big about his prowess on the golf course."

too big for one's boots/shoes = conceited

"Ever since she got that manager's job she has been too big for her boots."

See also: big daddy; big deal; big hand.

bile

full of bile = bitter and resentful

"It's difficult talking to him these days; he seems full of bile since his wife left him."

get one's bile up = arouse bitterness/ resentment in one

"It gets my bile up to be treated in such an inconsiderate way."

bill

bill and coo = caress and talk in a loving way

"It makes me happy to see young lovers billing and cooing as they stroll through the park."

clean bill of health = declared completely fit

"The doctor gave me a clean bill of health after my medical."

fill the bill = be exactly right for what is needed

"He should fill the bill for the extra mechanic we've been looking for."

foot the bill = pay for (somebody else)

"We all went out for a meal and fortunately my father-in-law footed the bill."

top the bill = be the best

"Among all the engineers in the company, Peter tops the bill."

"When it comes to food, a plain grilled steak tops the bill for me every time."

See also: bill of fare.

bind

in a bind = in difficulty or trouble

"After that incident in the car park I was in a bit of a bind with the police."

bird

able to/can charm the birds from the trees = be very persuasive, so charming that almost anybody complies with one's wishes

"Tell Maria to ask the boss if we can go home early on Friday ñ she can charm the birds from the trees."

a little bird told me = I will not say who told me

"A little bird told me that you are getting engaged next week; is it true?"

bird brain(ed) = fool(ish)

"Don't ask that bird brain, he knows nothing."

bird has flown = person has disappeared/ escaped

"We tried to find him at his last known address but the bird had flown."

bird in the hand (is worth two in the bush) = actual possession is better than mere promises

"Mike said he would give me fifteen pounds for it next week but Arthur offered me twelve pounds immediately, so I took the bird in the hand."

bird of ill omen = carrier of bad news

"Douglas told us that he had witnessed another motorway crash; he seems to be a bird of ill omen."

bird of passage = somebody who is passing through and has no permanent home

"He's a bird of passage and is only staying with us for a couple of nights on his way to America."

birds and the bees = fundamental knowledge about (human) sexual relations

"It's about time we told our daughter about the birds and the bees."

bird's eye view = view from a high vantage point

"From the top of the church tower you can get a bird's eye view of the whole town."

birds of a feather = people of similar temperament/views

"They're birds of a feather ñ they both like football, snooker and drinking beer."

early bird = somebody who gets up or arrives early

"I'm an early bird and prefer to catch the first train in the morning."

for the birds = trivial, of little worth

"I can't be bothered saving waste paper, that's for the birds."

free as a bird = completely free and without responsibilities

"At last I am free as a bird and can go anywhere I want to."

give somebody the bird = show disapproval vocally (by hissing or booing)

"The comedian told only old jokes and the audience soon gave him the bird."

kill two birds with one stone = obtain two results with a single action

"I had to go to Coventry on business so I thought I'd kill two birds with one stone and visit my sister who lives nearby."

like a bird = problem-free

"My car goes like a bird now that it's been serviced."

odd bird = strange person

"He's an odd bird; he always wears his slippers to go down to the pub."

rare bird = unusual person (with two conflicting interests)

"James is a rare bird ñ his record collection consists mostly of Palestrina and heavy metal."

birthday

birthday suit = nude

"I had just stepped out of the shower and the maid walked in and caught me in my birthday suit."

biscuit

take the biscuit = be the worst/most extreme possible

"Susan always wears outrageous hats but her latest one takes the biscuit."

bishop

See: as the actress said to the bishop.

bit

bit between one's teeth = eager but out of control

"She's a very enthusiastic member of the team but you have to watch the quality of her work when she gets the bit between her teeth."

bit by bit = little by little, gradually

"He said I could pay off the debt bit by bit."

bit much = more than one would like, excessive

"I thought it was a bit much when she threw her empty cigarette packet out of the window."

(a) bit of = some, rather

"She's bringing her children and they can be a bit of a nuisance."

bit of a lad = man who is somewhat lecherous

"James is a bit of a lad ñ he has a new girlfriend every week."

bit of all right = attractive/pleasing person or thing

"You should see his new girlfriend, she's a bit of all right."

bit of skirt/stuff = young woman (regarded sexually)

"Look at that bit of skirt over there."

bit on the side = extramarital partner

"He goes down to Brighton every other weekend to see his bit on the side."

bits and bobs/pieces = odds and ends

"I made it from some bits and pieces I found in the shed."

champing at the bit = eager to go/start

"He's champing at the bit to begin his new job next week."

do one's bit = make a contribution

"Albert helped them clear up afterwards ñ he likes to do his bit for the youth club."

every bit as = equally as, just as

"She says the new shop is every bit as good as the old one."

not a bit (of it) = not at all

"He didn't seem to care, not a bit of it."

thrilled to bits = very pleased

"He's thrilled to bits with his new fishing rod."

See also: a bit of the other.

bite

biter bit = deceiver deceived

"She went there to try to sell some plastic cups and things to the shopkeeper and ended up buying a new set of saucepans ñ it was a case of the biter bit."

bite off more than one can chew = undertake more than one can accomplish

"Ian said he would get it done by next Monday but I suspect he has bitten off more than he can chew."

bite one's lip = fail to talk or suddenly stop talking (through embarrassment or annoyance)

"I decided to bite my lip and refrain from telling her what I thought of her."

bite the hand that feeds one = be very ungrateful (to a benefactor)

"My bank manager approved my overdraft so I sent him a box of cigars ñ I've no intention of biting the hand that feeds me!"

once bitten, twice shy = be extra cautious after having had an unpleasant experience

"I'm sure the shopkeeper gave me too little change so I am going to check it carefully next time ñ once bitten, twice shy."

put the bite on = borrow money from

"She put the bite on me so that she could buy some new shoes."

what's biting somebody? = what is upsetting somebody?

"She refuses to talk to anyone; what's biting her?"

See also: bite/snap one's head off; bite the bullet; bite the dust; (mere) flea bite; one's bark is worse than one's bite; take two bites of the cherry.

bitter

bitter as gall = very bitter

"My Aunt Martha thought that she was done a terrible injustice when she was jilted as a young woman and she's been as bitter as gall ever since."

bitter pill (to swallow) = something that is difficult/painful to accept

"He found being made redundant a very bitter pill to swallow."

See also: to the bitter end

black

black and blue = badly bruised
"I slipped and rolled down the bank; the next day I was black and blue all over."

black art/magic = devil worship
"Many years ago people practised black magic in those caves."

black as the ace of spades = completely black
"We have a new kitten and it's as black as the ace of spades."

black box = small piece of electronic equipment
"Investigators searched around the crashed plane for the black box flight recorder."

blacken somebody's name = spoil/ruin somebody's reputation
"After the company dismissed him for misappropriation of funds, they effectively blackened his name throughout the profession."

black goods/services = refuse to deal with goods/services on the instruction of a trade union
"All cargoes from Dover are blacked until the dockworkers' strike there has been settled."

black-leg labour = extra (non-union) workers brought in by an employer during a strike
"They managed to maintain nearly fifty per cent of their normal production during the strike by employing black-leg labour."

black list = list of names of non-favoured/unsuitable people
"That woman never pays her bills; I'll have to put her on my black list."

black look = angry/bad-tempered expression
"He gave me a black look when I suggested that he was being unfair to his son."

black market = source of illicit goods (which should be rationed or unobtainable)
"Good quality jeans are only available on the black market in Russia."

black mood = angry/ill-tempered disposition
"I'd be careful what you say to Barbara today ñ she's in one of her black moods."

black out = lose consciousness
"I felt dizzy and then I blacked out."

black sheep (of the family) = somebody who does not conform to the family's wishes
"Sheila ran off with a married man, but then she always has been the black sheep of the family."

black spot = place that is notorious (for accidents/crime)
"That road junction is a well-known accident black spot."

in black and white = printed
"If you don't believe me, look it up in the book and read it for yourself in black and white."

in somebody's black books = out of favour
"I must be in his black books because he keeps deliberately avoiding me."

in the black = in credit (at the bank)
"We've just paid a fairly large cheque into the bank so we should be in the black for a while."

little black book = confidential/private record (of names)
"I think I have her phone number in my little black book."

not so black as one is painted = better than one is reputed to be

"He's never caused me any trouble and I don't think he's as black as he is painted."

swear black is white = tell a gross lie

"He would swear black is white if he thought it would further his career."

two blacks don't make a white = a second wrong does not remedy the first

"There's no point in letting down his tyres just because he scratched your car; two blacks don't make a white."

See also: black day; black economy; black eye; black ice.

blame

shoulder the blame/responsibility = accept the total blame/responsibility

"She shouldered the blame for all that had gone wrong that day."

blank

blank look/stare = empty facial expression

"He obviously didn't recognize me because he merely gave me a blank look when I walked up to him."

mind be a blank = have no memory of

"My mind's a total blank about the events immediately following the accident."

See also: blank cheque; draw a blank.

blanket

blanket bath = all-over wash given to a bed-ridden patient

"He broke his thigh-bone and was put into traction, so that a nurse had to give him a blanket bath every day."

blanket term = all-embracing description

"Cancer is a blanket term for several quite different disorders."

on the wrong side of the blanket = out of wedlock, illegitimate

"He thinks he owes the whole world a grudge because he was born on the wrong side of the blanket."

wet blanket = somebody who spoils one's amusement (by being miserable)

"We went to the fair but she wouldn't go on the roundabouts or try her hand on the shooting gallery ñ she was a right wet blanket."

blarney

full of blarney = a flattering, persuasive talker

"Don't pay any attention to Patrick, he's full of blarney."

blast

at full blast = at maximum speed/ strength

"No wonder it's hot in here, you've got your fire going full blast."

blaze

blaze a trail = pioneer, be first to do something

"Alan blazed a trail to the new picnic area and we all followed."

go like blazes = go very quickly

"Tom's new motorbike goes like blazes."

bleed

bleed (somebody) white = extort all of somebody's money

"The tax man is trying to bleed me white."

one's heart bleeds for somebody = one is very sorry for somebody (often sarcastically)

"He's down to his last hundred thousand pounds ñ my heart bleeds for him!"

blessing

blessing in disguise = hidden benefit (thought at first to be unlucky)

"We missed the bus but it turned out to be a blessing in disguise because it was later involved in a collision with a lorry."

count one's blessings = recognize favourable factors (among unfavourable ones)

"You had a bad bout of flu but you can count your blessings it didn't turn into pneumonia, like mine did."

give one's blessing to = approve of

"The chairman has given his blessing to Neil's plan for expanding production."

mixed blessing = something with both good and bad aspects

"Moving house was a mixed blessing; we've got a bigger garden but I've got farther to travel to work."

blind

blind drunk = very drunk

"He had six pints of beer and was blind drunk by the time he went home."

blind impulse = sudden, irrational/ illogical act

"We were not going to take a holiday this year but we were passing the travel agents and on a blind impulse went in and booked a fortnight in Thailand for next month."

blind somebody with science = deliberately confuse somebody by talking about technicalities

"The printing was poor and he tried to blind me with science by saying that it was the fault of the paper and not his machine."

in the country of the blind (the one-eyed man is king) = in a situation where somebody has a little ability/ knowledge (he/she has an advantage over people with no ability/ knowledge)

"Sylvia's rudimentary knowledge of chess was more than enough to beat Peter, who had seldom played the game before; in the country of the blind .Ö"

none so blind (as those who cannot see) = nobody is less persuadable than somebody who refuses to listen to argument

"There's none so blind as Terry when it comes to praising the work of modern artists."

swear blind = be adamant (even if lying)

"She swore blind she wasn't at the show and yet I saw her there."

the blind leading the blind = the uninformed attempting to inform others

"He said he knew the way and would lead us there, but he didn't; it was a case of the blind leading the blind."

See also: a nod is as good as a wink to a blind horse; blind alley; blind as a bat; blind date; blind spot; rob somebody blind; turn a blind eye to.

blink

in the blink of an eye/eyelid = instantly

"I'll be ready in the blink of an eye."

on the blink = (of machine) with an intermittent fault

"I haven't been able to hoover the carpet because my vacuum cleaner is on the blink."

block

mental block = obstruction to a thought process

"I get a mental block every time I try to do sums in my head."

put one's head on the block = deliberately make oneself vulnerable
"You tell the boss about the mistake; I'm not going to put my head on the block!"
See also: chip off the old block; stumbling block.

blonde
dumb blonde = pretty but unintelligent girl
"She's a typical dumb blonde ñ good looks but stupid!"

blood
after/out for one's blood = seeking revenge on one
"Ever since I accidentally backed into his car he's been after my blood."
blood and thunder = melodramatic/ sensational (of an entertainment medium)
"I like those early western films ñ all blood and thunder."
blood brother = very close friend
"Bob's like a blood brother and would do anything for me."
blood is thicker than water = relations come before (mere) friends
"Never mind what your friend at work would like, your sister could have that last ticket ñ remember, blood is thicker than water."
blood letting = disagreement in which someone suffers badly
"There will be some blood letting at the board meeting when the directors meet to discuss how all those stores went missing."
blood money = favour/reward made to somebody who betrays somebody e! e
"I didn't mean to let slip that Peter had been convicted of a crime many years ago; I don't want your thanks and I don't want your blood money."
blood on one's hands = be guilty of harming somebody
"The headquarters staff planned the action in which so many of our men were killed or wounded; the generals all have blood on their hands."
blood relation/relative = somebody ultimately descended from the same man or woman as oneself
"Many societies prohibit marriages between blood relatives."
blood sport = sport in which an animal is deliberately killed
"I abhor fox hunting and other blood sports."
blood sucker = blackmailer/extortionist
"That loan company charges 40 per cent interest on all money borrowed, the blood suckers."
blood will tell/out = inherited tendencies will eventually make their presence known
"He was brought up by a distant cousin in the city but was never happy until he went to work on a farm, as his father used to; blood will out."
blue blood(ed) = (of) aristocratic or noble origin
"When Malcolm takes charge his blue blood begins to show."
cause bad blood between people = make people dislike each other
"The two brothers fell in love with the same girl, which caused bad blood between them."
draw blood = hurt/injure
"Ruth's insulting remarks about Angela really drew blood."
first blood = first success/win
"Tottenham scored after only two minutes and it was first blood to them."
fresh blood = new member(s) of a group

"Many of the players are getting sluggish and what this team needs is some fresh blood."

get blood out of a stone = try to do the impossible

"The Inland Revenue have sent me a tax bill for more than a hundred pounds, but they can't get blood out of a stone because I just haven't got the money."

having one's blood up = being angry/excited

"I shouldn't have done it but my blood was up and I hit him."

in cold/hot blood = calmly and coolly or angrily and bad tempered

"The officer slowly took aim and shot the prisoner in cold blood."

"She didn't really mean to insult you; she lost her temper and said it in hot blood."

in the blood = inherited/innate

"All my family like sailing, it's in the blood."

make one's blood boil = make one very angry

"Every time I see somebody hitting a child it makes my blood boil."

make one's blood run cold = frighten, make one apprehensive

"Every time the new manager stares at me he makes my blood run cold."

out for blood = determined to beat somebody/to succeed

"The tennis champion was obviously out for blood and she beat her opponent in two straight sets."

runs in one's blood = is inherited

"His father was a farmer and he prefers the outdoor life; it runs in his blood."

shed/spill blood = injure or kill

"They didn't intend to spill blood but the situation got out of hand and some people were hurt quite badly."

sweat blood = work very hard

"I sweated blood on that job yet he didn't even thank me!"

taste blood = be encouraged/stimulated by an initial success

"She's passed one exam and she'll try even harder now that she's tasted blood."

young blood = (new) younger members of a group

"The team needs some young blood to make it more competitive."

See also: bad blood; blood bath; bloody somebody's nose; chill one's (the) blood; let blood; make a full-blooded attack; new blood; one's own flesh and blood; red-blooded; stir the blood.

bloom

(first) bloom of youth = youthful beauty

"In the first bloom of youth, she looked beautiful at her sixteenth birthday party."

past one's bloom = past one's best (in age)

"I used to have many men friends but there are fewer now that I'm past my bloom."

bloomer

make a bloomer = make a silly mistake

"He made a bloomer by starting the food mixer without its lid on, spraying egg all over the kitchen."

blossom

blossom out into = finally develop into

"He started by mending bicycles but now his business has blossomed out into one that employs several mechanics doing major car repairs."

blot

blot on the landscape = eyesore

"That new factory chimney is a blot on the landscape."

blot out = obliterate

"I just want to blot out the memory of the whole unhappy affair."

See also: blot one's copy book.

blow

blow a gasket/one's top = lose one's temper

"When mother saw the mess on the new carpet she blew a gasket."

"When father came home and saw it I thought he was going to blow his top."

blow-by-blow account = detailed sequential description

"He bored us all with a blow-by-blow account of what he did on holiday."

blow hot and cold = be alternatively enthusiastic/friendly and then the reverse

"One day she talks to you and the next day she ignores you ñ always blowing hot and cold."

blow/let off steam = release pent-up feelings

"Don't apologize for shouting at them, it does you good to blow off steam occasionally."

blow one's own trumpet = boast

"He blew his own trumpet and told us how he won first prize."

blow one's top = lose one's temper

"If your mother sees what you have done she will blow her top."

blow out = large or expensive meal

"You should have seen the blow out we had for Christmas dinner."

blow over = subside, fade away

"I hope Margaret's bad mood soon blows over."

blow someone's mind = cause hallucinations

"Kevin was very ill after he took those pills that blew his mind."

blow the expense = never mind the cost

"I'm going on a fortnight's holiday to America and blow the expense!"

blow the gaff/whistle on somebody = reveal somebody's guilty secret

"He'd have got away with it if his brother hadn't blown the gaff to the police."

"My brother blew the whistle on me and told the police."

blow up = exaggerate

"The minister made a fairly innocent comment but the newspapers blew it up out of all proportion."

strike a blow for/against = lend one's support/act to oppose

"The crowd pulled down the barriers and struck a blow for freedom."

"The authorities put up barriers and struck a blow against freedom."

See also: blow something wide open; blow up in somebody's face; see which way the wind blows.

blue

blue film/magazine/video = pornographic film/magazine/video

"They showed some blue videos at Joe's stag party."

(in a) blue funk = afraid like a coward

"Just the thought of travelling by air puts me in a blue funk."

(until one is) blue in the face = without result indefinitely

"You can ask to go until you're blue in the face ñ but you're not going!"

blue one's money = be (uncaringly) extravagant
"I won ten pounds on the first race and blued it all on the second."
blue pencil = (figurative tool of) censorship
"The script was a bit racy until the producer wielded his blue pencil."
blue stocking = prude, woman who values learning above amusement
"She's a blue stocking and all she talks about is books when we go out together."
(scream) blue murder = (create an) angry/violent scene
"I only jostled her accidentally in the crowd yet she screamed blue murder."
feel/look blue = be sad
"Those old weepy movies always make me feel blue."
have the blues = be depressed
"I'm sorry I was poor company last night ñ I had the blues for some reason."
once in a blue moon = very seldom
"Barry only visits his parents once in a blue moon."
out of the blue = unexpectedly
"They wrote and offered me a job out of the blue."
See also: black and blue; blue blooded; blue-eyed boy; bolt from the blue; make the air turn blue; till one is blue in the face; true blue Conservative.

bluff

call somebody's bluff = challenge somebody whom one thinks is lying
"Keith claims to know the managing director; the way to call his bluff is to see if he can describe him, because that particular director is actually a woman!"

blush

at (the) first blush = on first consideration
"Judy's ideas looked excellent at first blush."
spare somebody's blushes = withhold praise so as not to embarrass somebody
"I'll spare your blushes and not tell the others how helpful you have been throughout the project."

board

above board = honest, in the open
"Mary says she'll join in the scheme as long as everything is above board."
across the board = in every way, affecting everyone equally
"The union negotiated a five per cent pay rise for all its members across the board."
go by the board = be forgotten/ignored
"They started jostling for food and good manners went by the board."
stiff as a board = rigid/very stiff
"I hung out the washing to dry on a frosty day and when I went to take it in it was as stiff as a board."
sweep the board = win everything
"The vicar's wife swept the board at the flower show and won every class."
take on board = accept an idea/proposal
"I find it difficult to take on board the chairman's plans for reorganization."

boat

burn one's boats/bridges = take an irrevocable step
"David got tired of working in London so he burned his boats and moved up to Scotland and bought a small hotel there."
(all) in the same boat = in similar (difficult) circumstances

"I don't know why you're complaining that you have to pay more, we're all in the same boat."

miss the boat = miss an opportunity

"John offered me a share in the venture but I couldn't raise the money in time and I missed the boat."

push the boat out = celebrate (with drinks)

"Now that we know we have got that new contract, let's go down the pub and push the boat out."

rock the boat = interfere in an undertaking so as to jeopardize its success

"We'll have enough trouble finishing on time without June rocking the boat."

Bob

Bob's your uncle = that is what was wanted

"You just go straight along the road for a mile, turn left, and its first on the left ñ and Bob's your uncle!"

body

body and soul = completely

"He committed himself to the task body and soul."

body-blow = damaging/severe set-back

"The withdrawal of the subsidy dealt a body-blow to the club's plans for larger accommodation."

have/have no body = have/lack substance

"I prefer a red wine with plenty of body."

keep body and soul together = sustain life

"I earn so little money that I find it difficult to keep body and soul together these days."

See also: dog's body; over my dead body; own somebody body and soul.

bog

get bogged down = become stuck, reach a deadlock/impasse

"The negotiations got bogged down in an argument about overtime rates."

boil

boil down to = amount to

"When it comes to buying a car it all boils down to price in the end."

boil over = lose one's temper

"Elizabeth seems to boil over for the slightest reason these days."

come to the boil = reach a critical/significant state

"That project we postponed has finally come to the boil and we must start work on it next week"

See also: a watched pot never boils; make one's blood boil; off the boil.

bold

See: bold as brass; make so bold as to.

bolster

bolster up = give (moral) support

"I need some more examples to bolster up my theory."

bolt

bolt from the blue = total surprise

"My father's redundancy came as a bolt from the blue."

bolt upright = exactly perpendicular

"It annoys me if a lamppost is not bolt upright."

shoot one's bolt = commit irrevocably and unsuccessfully

"Bill regretted talking to the foreman like that but he had shot his bolt and was sacked immediately afterwards."

See also: nuts and bolts.

bomb

come as a bombshell = come as a complete (unpleasant) surprise
"The news of his death came as a complete bombshell"

cost a bomb = be very expensive
"Those new houses they are building farther up the hill cost a bomb."

go down (like) a bomb = be very popular/successful
"The Scottish comedian went down a bomb with the audience."

go like a bomb = move very fast, or sell very well
"Harry's new car goes like a bomb."
"Small packets of nuts would go like a bomb if only the shop would stock them."

light/put a bomb under somebody = to stimulate/urge somebody (to do something)
"I had to put a bomb under her to get her to agree to start the job tomorrow."

See also: earn a bomb.

bone

bone dry = completely dry
"Make sure you hair is bone dry before you go out into the cold weather."

bone-headed (from the neck up) = stupid
"There's no point in asking her, she's bone-headed from the neck up."

bone idle = very lazy
"David is bone idle; he stood and watched while the rest of us carried all the chairs in from the garden."

bone to pick (with somebody) = issue to accuse somebody of
"I've a bone to pick with her ñ she didn't finish the job properly."

bone up on = learn or revise a subject
"My pen friend from Paris is coming to stay so I had better bone up on my French."

cut to the bone = minimize, make as little as possible
"We cut our prices to the bone but still couldn't sell enough to recover our costs."

dry as a bone = totally dry
"We badly need some rain, my garden is as dry as a bone."

feel in one's bones = intuition/ premonition
"I think our bid will be successful, I can feel it in my bones."

lazy bones = idle person
"Come on, lazy bones; come and help us clear up."

make no bones about it = be candid/ frank
"She made no bones about it and told him exactly what she thought of him."

make old bones = live to a great age
"I've a strange feeling that I'll never make old bones."

near the bone = bordering on indecency/ risqué
"Some of his jokes were a bit near the bone."

See also: bag of bones; bare bones; bone of contention.

bonnet

See: have a bee in one's bonnet.

book

booked for speeding (of the driver of the vehicle) = stopped by the police and charged with exceeding the speed limit
"Wendy passed her driving test and was booked for speeding the very next day."

book in = register (at a hotel)
"We have to book in before twelve o'clock, or the hotel will let the room go to somebody else."
bring somebody to book = find evidence to arrest/try/punish somebody
"It's about time those muggers were caught and brought to book."
by/according to the book = following the rules (often strictly or fastidiously)
"Charles sometimes takes a long time to complete a job because he does everything by the book."
closed book = something of which one is ignorant
"Nuclear physics is a closed book to me."
in one's bad/good books = disliked/liked
"She won't speak to me; for some reason I am in her bad books."
"He has a lot of influence so it's worth keeping in his good books."
in one's book = in one's own opinion
"In my book Walter is the best assistant we've ever had."
one for the book = something worth noting/recording
"Maria arrived on time today. That's one for the book!"
open book = something that is easily understood, unconcealed
"I have no secrets; my life is an open book."
read somebody like a book = be fully aware of somebody's unexpressed thoughts
"I know what he'll probably do ñ I can read him like a book."
suit one's book = agree with one's own interests
"It suits Henry's book to work late and travel home after the rush hour."
take a leaf out of somebody's book = copy somebody's example
"Why don't you take a leaf out of Anne's book and have your hair cut shorter?"
throw the book at = make as many accusations as possible
"If he gets caught with a bald tyre on his car, the police will discover all the other faults and throw the book at him."
See also: cook the books; turn up for the book(s).

boot

(car) boot sale = sale of small secondhand items that the sellers take in the boots of their cars
"I bought an old box camera for fifty pence at a car boot sale."
(tough as) old boots = resilient and hard to harm
"Freda won't mind the cold weather, she's as tough as old boots."
die with one's boots on = die at work
"He had a massive heart attack in the office and died with his boots on."
hang up one's boots = retire
"Jim's nearly seventy and it's about time he hung up his boots."
have one's heart sink into one's boots = be in despair/dismay
"When I saw all the mess I had to clear up my heart sank into my boots."
lick somebody's boots/shoes = fawn, flatter somebody for personal gain
"I wish he wouldn't lick the manager's boots; it's obvious he's just seeking favours."
like old boots = vigorously
"She was working like old boots to finish the task before the end of the day."
order of the boot = sack (from a job)
"He came back drunk after lunch so

the boss gave him the order of the boot."

pull oneself up by one's bootstraps = make a conscious effort to improve one's situation (unaided)

"Janice lost her job but she pulled herself up by her bootstraps and started her own business."

put the boot in = further harm somebody who is already distressed or harmed

"His wife left him and then his firm put the boot in by making him redundant."

the boot's on the other foot = the other person now has the advantage

"At first he was quicker than me but I've been practising and now the boot's on the other foot."

to boot = also/in addition

"My new house has a garage, greenhouse and garden shed to boot."

See also: too big for one's boots.

bore

bore somebody stiff/the pants off somebody/somebody to tears = be very boring

"I had to sit through three hours of Welsh folk singing ñ I was bored stiff."

"He's a dreadful lecturer; he bores the pants off all his students."

"Judy's boyfriend took her to a cricket match last Saturday; she says it bored her to tears."

born

be born before one's time = anticipate later ideas/opinions

"Leonardo designed flying machines before anyone had invented engines to power them; he was born before his time."

born with a silver spoon in one's mouth = born with inherited privilege/wealth

"She was born with a silver spoon in her mouth and has never had to do a day's hard work in her life."

in all one's born days = ever

"In all my born days I've never seen a dog with green eyes."

not born yesterday = not a fool/ inexperienced person

"Don't try to tell me that's the way to Brighton; I wasn't born yesterday, you know."

borrow

borrowed plumes = inappropriate or unofficially used symbols of position/ status

"He wore his brother's evening dress to the function but looked very uncomfortable in his borrowed plumes instead of his usual jeans and tee shirt."

borrowed time = unexpected extension of life

"She's been terminally ill for several months and I'm afraid she's only living on borrowed time."

See also: beg, steal or borrow

bosom

bosom friend/pal = very close friend

"Bill and Ben always go round together ñ they've been bosom pals all their lives."

bosom of one's family = immediate family (parents, brothers and sisters)

"He's twenty-one yet still lives in the bosom of his family."

both

be unable to have something both ways = be unable to make two (equally attractive) choices when only one is actually possible

"You want to go to the pictures with Edna and at the same time stay at home and watch football on television; well, you can't have it both ways."

play both ends against the middle = risky sharp practice (in which one person tries to take advantage of two other participants by setting them against each other and hopes to profit from their conflict)
"It was a dubious deal and I might have got away with it if I hadn't tried to play both ends against the middle."

bottle

be on the bottle = be a regular drinker
"Jack's been on the bottle ever since he came back from working abroad."

bottle up = hold in (emotions/feelings)
"In spite of the cruel things she said to him, he bottled up his feelings and displayed no emotion at all."

hit the bottle = drink excessively
"After Wendy's husband left her she began to hit the bottle."

See also: crack a bottle; lose one's bottle.

bottom

at the bottom of = ultimately responsible for
"I suspect that somebody in the stores is at the bottom of these mysterious thefts of stock."

bottom fall out of = collapse
"The value of the shares tumbled when the bottom fell out of the market."

bottomless pit = hell
"May he burn in the bottomless pit!"

from the bottom of one's heart = very sincerely
"We all thank you from the bottom of our hearts."

get to the bottom of = discover the truth about
"Somebody broke that table and I'm determined to get to the bottom of the matter."

knock the bottom out of = demonstrate that something has no value
"His pithy comments knocked the bottom out of my argument."

rock bottom = lowest point possible
"His success depends on buying at rock bottom prices and then selling quickly at a slight profit."

touch bottom = reach the lowest point
"Share prices touched bottom at about noon and then rose slightly before the market closed."

See also: bet one's bottom dollar; bottom drawer.

bound

bound for = going towards
"We're off on Sunday, bound for the seaside."

bound to = sure to/must
"It's bound to rain on Sunday."
"I feel I'm bound to keep my promise."

bound up in = involved with
"We seldom see Pamela these days because she's so bound up in writing her new book."

bound up with = associated with
"He's bound up with the grocery trade in some way or another."

I'll be bound = I'm sure
"England will beat Australia, I'll be bound."

out of/within bounds = outside/inside permitted limits
"The headmaster's garden is out of bounds to all pupils."
"You can play records as long as you keep the noise within bounds."

within the bounds of possibility = possible (just)
"Cutting ten minutes off the journey time is within the bounds of possibility."

bow

another/two string(s) to one's bow = additional attribute/talent
"Louise studied architecture and mathematics so she's got at least two strings to her bow."

bow and scrape = fawn/be servile
"I don't care what he says, I'll not bow and scrape to any man."

bowed down with = troubled/worried by
"He was bowed down with grief after the death of his friend."

bow to somebody's better/superior judgement/knowledge = accept that somebody knows better
"She knew the names of all the plants we came across and I had to bow to her superior knowledge."

bow to the inevitable = accept that something is unavoidable
"I cannot run as fast as I used to but I'm now nearly forty and so I suppose I should bow to the inevitable."

bow out = resign
"Now that I'm over sixty it's time for me to bow out and make way for a younger person."

shot across the bows = warning
"The boss said that she would do something about it if our time keeping didn't improve and that we should take her remarks as a shot across the bows."

bowl

bowl a fast one = trick/be deceitful
"We were sharing the work quite well until he bowled a fast one and left me with all the messy jobs while he did the paper work."

bowl along = go at a fast, easy pace
"The car bowled along and we got to the coast in under an hour."

bowl of cherries = ease and luxury
"Unfortunately life is not a bowl of cherries and you have to work hard for your living."

bowl over = surprise completely
"I was bowled over by their generosity towards me."

box

box clever = be crafty
"I'll have to box clever if I'm going to beat her at chess."

box number = number that identifies an advertiser (in a newspaper etc.) who does not want to reveal his address; replies sent to the box number at the paper are passed on to the advertiser unopened
"I don't want my neighbours to know I'm selling my car so I've advertised it under a box number."

box the compass = name the (32) points of the compass in correct sequence
"Everyone who takes up sailing should learn to box the compass."

See also: black box; box somebody's ears; get on one's soap box.

boy

blue-eyed boy = a favourite
"He seems to be able to do what he likes because he's the teacher's blue-eyed boy."

boy racer = teenager on a small motorcycle or in an old (slow) car
"I wish those boy racers' motorbikes made less noise."

boys in blue = policemen
"Look out! Here come the boys in blue."

boys will be boys = childish behaviour (in men and boys) is to be expected
"Look at those grown men paddling in rock pools looking for crabs! Oh well, boys will be boys."

golden boy = young man showing exceptional promise, and idolized because of that
"The young German player is the golden boy of tennis."

jobs for the boys = favours for friends/ relations
"You won't get any work off him unless he already knows you; it's strictly jobs for the boys."

mother's boy = spoiled son
"Jeremy still lives at home and his mother cooks all his favourite meals for him; he's a typical mother's boy."

nancy boy = man who is effeminate/gay
"Here comes Jeremy with his latest friend, a right nancy boy!"

new boy = new employee
"Can you please tell me where the accounts department is; I'm a new boy here."

old boy network = informal association of professionals, typically ex-public school or ex-army
"I heard on the old boy network that there will soon be a vacant seat on the board of a leading merchant bank."

one of the boys = accepted member of a group
"You can always trust Arthur ñ he's one of the boys."

See also: back-room boys; fancy boy; happy as a sand boy; man and boy; old boy/girl; whipping boy.

brace

brace yourself = be prepared for unpleasantness
"Brace yourself and I'll tell you how much the repair will cost you."

brain

brainchild = one's own idea
"It was my brainchild and I'd like to see the job through to the end."

brain drain = drift of graduates (particularly scientists/technicians) from Britain to the United States
"Angela got her degree in computer science and decided to join the brain drain and go and work in California."

brains trust = discussion group of experts
"We've decided to form a brains trust of all the section chiefs so that we can discuss each other's problems."

have a brainstorm = have an uncontrolled emotional outburst
"The news of his son's death caused him to have a brainstorm."

have a brainwave = have a sudden inspiration
"I've had a brainwave. Why don't we move the table under the window, out of the way?"

have something on the brain = be obsessed/preoccupied with something
"His only interest is football ñ he's got football on the brain."

hare-brained (scheme) = impractical/ stupid (plan)
"Julian came up with another of his hare-brained schemes for raising money."

make one's brain hurt/reel = be very difficult to grasp (mentally), or be incredible
"The details of quantum physics make my brain hurt."

pick somebody's brains = seek particular information from somebody with the necessary knowledge

"I hope you don't mind my picking your brains, but can you please explain how to propagate strawberries?"

rack one's brains = try very hard to remember/think of something

"I've racked my brains all day and I still can't remember who was Prime Minister in 1952."

scatter brain = somebody who is careless/disorganized in thinking

"He's a scatter brain in the office; he often forgets to post the letters, and when he does he usually forgets to put stamps on them."

turn one's brain = make one go mad

"The atrocities he saw during the war eventually turned his brain."

See also: beat one's brains out; cudgel one's brain.

branch

branch out = develop into/become independent of

"I'm tired of working for other people and so I've decided to branch out on my own."

offer/hold out an olive branch = want to make peace

"We've disagreed violently for months, but I've held out an olive branch and it's now up to him to respond."

brass

brass hat = high-ranking officer/official

"Decisions about policy are made by the brass hats."

bold as brass = shamelessly self-assured

"He walked in, bold as brass, wearing nothing but his underpants."

get down to brass tacks = reduce an argument/discussion to the fundamental issues

"Never mind the side-issues, let's get down to brass tacks and thrash out a basic agreement."

have the brass neck to (do something) = be bold/shameless enough to (do something)

"I lent him his bus fare and then he had the brass neck to ask me for a lift home."

top brass = senior management/officers

"We'd better get the place tidied up, the top brass are coming tomorrow."

brave

put on a brave face = pretend that the situation is better than it really is

"The strikers got none of their demands and all they could do was to put on a brave face and return to work."

See also: brave the elements.

breach

fill/step into the breach = deputise for somebody/substitute for something

"The leading man got laryngitis but his understudy stepped into the breach and gave an excellent performance."

"A wood screw will fill the breach until you can buy the proper bolt for the job."

heal the breach = end a serious disagreement

"I've at last been able to heal the breach between my father and me."

bread

best thing since sliced bread = something (new) that is very well liked

"My mother thinks that her new dishwasher is the best thing since sliced bread."

bread and butter = living, basic daily work
"Routine office work is my bread and butter."

breadwinner = wage-earner for a family
"After Frank's father died he became the breadwinner for his mother and young sisters."

cast one's bread on/upon the waters = speculate (with little hope of reward/ success)
"Mine must have been only one of hundreds of applications for that job in America; I've cast my bread upon the waters and must now wait and see what happens, if anything."

have one's bread buttered on both sides = have an easy/effortless existence
"He was already a successful businessman when his father died and left him a fortune, so he's now got his bread buttered on both sides."

know which side one's bread is buttered = be aware of where one's best interests lie
"She'll accept that new job if she knows which side her bread is buttered."

on the bread line = extremely poor
"He was out of work for three years and did not qualify for state aid, so that he was practically on the bread line."

take the bread out of somebody's mouth = prevent somebody from earning a living
"The man in the local shop is worried that the new supermarket will take the bread out of his mouth."

See also: one's daily bread.

break

bad/lucky break = bad/good luck
"I've had a series of bad breaks recently and it's about time my luck changed for the better."

break a fall = prevent injury (in a fall)
"She slipped over the edge but some bushes broke her fall and she was hardly hurt at all."

break a habit = cease to do something habitually
"I've tried to give up smoking several times but I find it impossible the break the habit."

break a journey = interrupt a journey
"We thought we'd break our journey at Canterbury and take a look at the cathedral before going on to Dover."

break a leg = good luck/do well (in a performance)
"This is your big chance. Go on out there and break a leg!"

break a/the record = do better than a/the previous performance
"The West German athlete is expected to break the record for the high jump."

break cover = to suddenly emerge from hiding
"The deer broke cover and ran across the open ground."

break down/up (emotionally) = lose control of one's emotions
"When she heard the news she broke down and cried."

break even = make neither a profit nor a loss
"I got a new car for the same price as I sold my old one, so I broke even on the deal."

break in on = interrupt
"Barbara is always breaking in on our private conversations."

break in the weather = change (for the better) in the weather
"We're waiting for a break in the weather so that we can dig the garden."

break into = begin vocalizing, or force an entry, or make an abrupt start
"The whole audience broke into laughter."
"Their house was broken into while they were away on holiday."
"Suddenly the leaders broke into a gallop."

breakneck speed = very fast pace
"The car skidded round the corner at breakneck speed."

break new ground = pioneer, make a discovery
"Her research is breaking new ground in biochemistry."

break of day = dawn
"We had a long drive ahead of us so we got up at break of day to make an early start."

break off = stop suddenly
"The speaker broke off in the middle of a sentence with a fit of coughing."

break one's neck (for) = be in a great hurry (to do something)
"Oh good, there's a pub; I'm breaking my neck for a drink."

break/keep a promise = fail to keep a promise
"Stephen broke his promise and refused to help us after all."

break out (in a rash) = appear (suddenly)
"The child broke out into a rash five days after being exposed to infection."

break out into a cold sweat = be suddenly afraid/apprehensive
"I break out into a cold sweat merely thinking about snakes."

break ranks = move out of position (in disorder)
"The soldiers broke ranks and scattered when they heard the aircraft approaching."

break service = win a point against the server (in tennis etc.)
"He's two games behind and needs to break service twice to win the set."

break somebody's heart = cause somebody (deep) distress
"It broke his heart to see the old family home pulled down."

break something down = separate something (into its components)
"The best way to clean the machine is to break it down into its component parts and clean each piece individually."

break the ice = strike up an acquaintance after overcoming initial shyness
"I offered her a cigarette to break the ice, and we were soon in conversation."

break the news = convey information
"I don't know how to break the news to him about the change in plans."

break the thread = interrupt a line of reasoning/thought
"Where had we got to? That phone call has broken the thread."

break through = force an opening in an obstruction
"You can see where the fox broke through the wire to get at the chickens."

break wind = release gas from the stomach or bowel
"I'm told that in some Arab countries it is considered polite to break wind after a meal."

break with = sever connections with
"I've decided to break with Silvia once and for all."

make a/the break = leave
"I've decided to make the break and go and work for somebody else."

See also: break/get out of the habit; break/keep one's word; break one's duck; break the back of; break the bank; make or break.

breakfast

See: donkey's breakfast

breast

beat one's breast = greatly regret an error
"Anybody could easily have made a similar mistake, so there's no need to beat your breast about it."

make a clean breast of = confess fully
"I've decided to make a clean breast of it and tell you that it was me who broke the window."

breath

breath of fresh air = refreshing development
"His ideas about revitalizing the company's activities are like a breath of fresh air."

hold one's breath = wait (in anticipation) for something to happen
"She said she might decide to go out with me but I'm not holding my breath!"

in the same breath = simultaneously
"Jill said she couldn't afford new clothes yet in the same breath described the new outfit she'd just bought."

out of/short of breath = breathless
"By the time I'd reached the top of the hill I was completely out of breath."

save your breath (to cool your porridge) = I do not want hear your comments
"I don't care what you think; save your breath to cool your porridge!"

take one's breath away = astonish/give intense pleasure to/surprise one
"The beautiful view from the top of the mountain took my breath away."

under one's breath = in a whisper
"His suggestion was so outrageous, I couldn't help commenting under my breath."

waste one's breath = talk when nobody heeds or is listening
"I told them how to do it but I was wasting my breath; they went and tried it their way ñ and failed!"

with bated breath = anxiously, in anticipation of something (unpleasant)
"We waited for the judge's decision with bated breath."

with one's last breath = until one dies
"I shall still disagree with him with my last breath."

breathe

breathe again = recover/relax
"We're over the worst part of the trip, we can breathe again now."

breathe down somebody's neck = watch somebody (too) closely
"I wish the foreman would stop breathing down my neck."

breathe easily/easy/freely = to be relieved
"You can breathe easy now, the inspector's gone."

breathing space = pause (for recovery)
"I'm looking forward to a breathing space when my children go back to school."

breathe life into = provide the inspiration/vital force
"Then Jan joined the team and breathed new life into the project."

breathe one's last = die
"He'll maintain that point of view until he breathes his last."

not to breathe a word = not to tell
"I'll tell you how I did it if you promise not to breathe a word to the others."

take a breather = take a rest (from vigorous activity)
"I've mowed the front lawn, and I'm just taking a breather before tackling the back lawn."

brick

a (gold/regular) brick = a (very good) friend
"Throughout all my difficulties she's been a brick and helped me willingly."

like a ton of bricks = firmly/heavily
"She's a very strict teacher; as a soon as a child does the slightest thing wrong she's down on him like a ton of bricks."

like talking to a brick wall = wasting time trying to convince somebody who is bigoted/obstinate
"Trying to get Paul to agree to spend more money on amenities is like talking to a brick wall."

make bricks without straw = make something without the essential materials
"I'll do my best with the ingredients you happen to have, but I can't make bricks without straw."

See also: bang/knock one's head against a brick wall; drop a brick/clanger.

bridge

burn one's boats/bridges = make an irrevocable decision
"I wasn't sure about removing that tree, but I've burned my bridges and chopped it down now."

cross that bridge when one comes to it = do not worry unnecessarily about a difficulty that may never arise
"Don't worry about how we're going to pay for a new machine, we'll cross that bridge when we come to it."

See also: water under the bridge.

brief

hold no brief for = have nothing to say in favour of
"I hold no brief for Janet; you must decide for yourself whether to trust her."

bright

bright and breezy/bright-eyed and bushy-tailed = cheerful and happy
"She's always bright and breezy, even first thing on a Monday morning."

bright and early = very early in the morning
"Let's get up bright and early and drive down to Devon."

bright idea = clever original thought (sometimes used sarcastically)
"Dad had the bright idea of making a serving hatch in the wall between the kitchen and the dining room."
"Half the wall has collapsed. Whose bright idea was it to make a hole in it?"

bright lights = entertainment district
"I'm bored with staying in the country. Let's go off to the bright lights and see a film or a show."

bright spark = clever person
"Nora's a bright spark; she found a way of re-using old paper in the copying machine."

look on the bright side = be optimistic
"No matter what happens, Gill always looks on the bright side."

See also: bright as a button

bring

bring about/to pass = make happen
"The chairman is trying to bring about some long overdue changes in company policy."

bring back to life = revive

"The business had declined over the years but the new manager soon brought it back to life."

bring down = cause something to end
"Failure to win a vote of confidence could bring down the government."

bring down the curtain on = put an end to
"Lack of volunteers brought down the curtain on plans to form a local youth club."

bring forth = produce
"Henry's new methods brought forth nothing but trouble."

bring home to one = make one realize
"A trip through the shanty town brought home to me just how poor the people are."

bring in = introduce, or yield
"The council is to bring in new rules about trading on a Sunday."
"The investment brings in a hundred pounds interest every month."

bring into line = cause to conform
"We need to modify that plan somewhat to bring it into line with the others."

bring into play = cause to start functioning
"The defenders were doing reasonably well until the attackers brought their tanks into play."

bring into the world = give birth to/be a parent of
"We decided not to have children because we think it irresponsible to bring a child into the world when the future is so uncertain."

bring off = succeed in doing something
"Try to sell them our most profitable product and let's hope you can bring off a deal."

bring on = cause
"The high pollen count will probably bring on my hay fever."

bring oneself to = persuade oneself
"I can never bring myself to eat snails."

bring out = demonstrate/reveal, or publish
"A difficult challenge brings out the best in her."
"I hope to bring out my new book in the spring of next year."

bring round/to = restore somebody to consciousness
"My sister fainted and it was a minute or two before we could bring her round."

bring somebody down to earth = make somebody aware of practicalities (rather than dreams/fanciful ideas)
"Her ambition was to be a top photographic model, but having to go out and find any sort of a job immediately to pay the rent soon brought her down to earth."

bring somebody up short = make somebody stop what he/she is doing
"I thought the plan would succeed but was brought up short when Bernard pointed out how much it would really cost."

bring something to a head = precipitate a crisis in order to get action
"To bring matters to a head I threatened to resign, and they finally listened to my complaints about the working conditions."

bring something to light = ensure that something is noticed, or to reveal something
"The investigation brought to light a discrepancy in the accounts."

bring the house down = gain an audience's whole-hearted approval
"The joke about the elephant brought the house down."

bring to a close = conclude (formally)
"There was no other business so the

chairman brought the meeting to a close."

bring to bear = employ/put to use
"If it won't move you'll have to bring more force to bear on it."

bring to light = reveal
"New evidence has brought to light his involvement in the crime."

bring to mind = cause to recall
"That tune always brings to mind a holiday I once spent in Greece."

bring to pass = cause to happen
"After trying for weeks to close the deal we finally brought it to pass."

bring up = raise (a topic), or rear (a child), or vomit
"I'd like to bring up the subject of my expenses."
"It is difficult for an unmarried mother to bring up her child on her own."
"The shellfish must have been bad because I brought up the whole of my dinner."

bring up the rear = come in last place/ position
"My wife went first, followed by the children, and I brought up the rear."

bring word = convey information/news
"I've just been brought word that Tim's in hospital."

See also: bring down/fall about somebody's ears; bring home the bacon; bring into contempt; bring (carry) into effect; bring somebody down to earth; bring to book.

bristle

bristle with = be full of
"I'm worried about the new scheme; it seems to be bristling with difficulties."

Bristol

all ship-shape and Bristol fashion = properly organized and tidy
"She keeps everything on her desk all ship-shape and Bristol fashion."

broad

as broad as it's long = either way is as good as the other
"Either you come and collect me or I'll pick you up. It's as broad as it's long to me."

See also: broad hint; broad in the beam; have broad shoulders; in broad daylight.

broken

broken accent/English = imperfect speech/English
"One could tell immediately she was from abroad because of her broken accent."

broken home = family in which the parents no longer live together
"Her Probation Officer suggests that her insecurity stems from the fact that she comes from a broken home."

broken reed = supporter who has failed
"He let me down at the last minute and turned out to be a broken reed."

broken-winded (horse) = breathless/ exhausted
"We'd only gone about half a mile before he was panting like a broken-winded horse."

See also: stony broke.

broker

honest broker = trustworthy and impartial intermediary
"We need an honest broker to negotiate with the terrorists who are holding the hostages."

broom

new broom = somebody (eager) who is newly appointed

"What this department requires is a new broom to liven everyone else up."

brother

brotherhood of man = whole of human society

"International co-operation should take advantage of the selflessness of the brotherhood of man."

brothers in arms = comrades (in adversity)

"As brothers in arms we should all make it clear to the authorities what our demands are."

See also: Big Brother; blood brother.

brow

by the sweat of one's brow = through one's own hard work

"He became a success entirely by the sweat of his own brow."

See also: knit one's brows

browned

browned off = bored/disenchanted

"I'm browned off with watching the same old programmes on television every week."

brunt

bear the brunt of = receive (and withstand) the main thrust of an attack

"Peter didn't come to support me at the meeting and I had to bear the brunt of the opposition's attack."

brush

brush aside/to one side = ignore (objections to something)

"James made some adverse criticisms of the plan but I was able to brush them aside."

brush up on = revise/refresh one's

"I'll have to brush up on my French if Jean-Luc is coming to stay."

brush with danger/death/the law = come close to/into conflict with danger/death/the law

"The motorcyclist had a brush with danger as he skidded round the bend."

"The only time I had a brush with the law was when I was falsely accused of taking away a car without the owner's consent."

give somebody the brush-off = terminate a friendship with somebody

"He'd let me down more than once so the next time he asked me for a favour I gave him the brush off."

tarred with the same brush = assumed to have the same (bad) qualities as one's associates

"She's a friend of that liar Jane and is probably tarred with the same brush."

See also: brush/sweep something under the carpet/rug; daft as a brush.

brute

brute force = (excessive) physical force

"When he can't argue his way out of a difficulty he usually resorts to brute force and hits somebody!"

buck

buck up = hurry

"Buck up! We'll be late if you don't get a move on."

pass the buck = pass on responsibility (for something one does not want to be held responsible for)

"When things get difficult he's too ready to pass the buck."

the buck stops here = I/we are ultimately responsible

"Any problem must be dealt with in this department, because the buck

bucket

kick the bucket = die

"I hear poor old John's kicked the bucket."

rain (in) buckets = rain very heavily

"We were there for a fortnight and it rained buckets every day."

See also: cry/weep buckets.

buckle

buckle down/under = get down to hard work/submit

"The only way we'll meet the schedule is to buckle down and get on with the job."

"I don't see why I should have to buckle under every time he makes an unreasonable demand."

bud

budding talent = emerging ability

"We must make best use of any budding talent and encourage the young members of the group."

nip in the bud = forestall/frustrate a scheme/plan (before it can be implemented)

"Any ill-feeling has to be nipped in the bud before it develops into open revolt."

bug

bitten by a bug = become addicted to/ enthusiastic for something

"After I took him to see the model railway exhibition he got bitten by the bug and took up the hobby himself."

bugged room = room having electronic devices that detect and transmit (to an outsider) any conversation

"The Russian embassy believe that the ambassador's room has been bugged by the CIA."

bug somebody = (deliberately) annoy somebody

"It really bugs me the way he keeps drumming his fingers on the table."

computer bug = error in a computer program

"I couldn't run the program because it contained a bug that I could neither identify nor cure."

debug a (computer) program = find and remove an error in a computer program

"The new computer has a debug routine that sorts out any errors in the program."

litter bug = somebody who (knowingly) drops/scatters litter

"The worst kind of litter bug is the person who throws sweet papers out of the window of a moving car."

See also: snug as a bug in a rug.

build

big build up = accumulation of interest/ resources before an event

"The circus act came as an anticlimax after the big build up given by the ring master."

"Intelligence reports indicate that there is probably a big build up of troops at the eastern end of the front line."

bulk

in bulk = in large quantity

"We buy potatoes in bulk and share them and the total cost with our neighbours."

the bulk = most

"Unfortunately it rained on the day of the fete and the bulk of the people who came went home early."

bull

like a bull at a gate = very forcefully

"The deal required a gentle, subtle

approach but he went for the other side like a bull at a gate."

like a bull in a china shop = in an awkward/clumsy manner

"The flower border required careful weeding with a trowel but he attacked it with a spade like a bull in a china shop."

like a red rag to a bull = certain to anger/very provocative

"To my father the sight of a punk hair-do is like a red rag to a bull."

score a bull's eye = have a spectacular (but unlikely) success

"In spite of the scruffy way he dresses, he scored a bull's eye with Mabel and she's agreed to go out with him."

take the bull by the horns = take bold action to overcome a difficulty

"I couldn't afford the travelling expenses to work when the fares were increased so I took the bull by the horns and asked my boss for a rise in pay."

bullet

bite the bullet = take on a challenge, or persevere (unwillingly)

"We must bite the bullet now the other company is not bidding and go for the contract."

"It was a long and uninteresting task but I had to bite the bullet and get on with it until it was finished."

bullet with one's name on = inevitable hit

"There is no point in taking cover; if the bullet has your name on it, you will be hit what ever you do."

give somebody the bullet = to dismiss somebody (from employment)

"The boss caught Ted stealing so he gave him the bullet."

bump

bump into = meet unexpectedly

"I bumped into Jones the other day."

bump off = kill

"Last night I dreamt I'd bumped off my mother-in-law."

bump up = increase/raise

"The florists always seem to bump up their prices just before Mother's Day."

bun

bun in the oven = pregnant

"My neighbour's got a bun in the oven again; that will make her fifth child."

bunch

bunch of fives = punch (with a clenched fist)

"You say that again and I'll give you a bunch of fives."

bundle

bundle of energy = full of vigour

"That child is a bundle of energy; no wonder she sleeps so well."

bundle of nerves = very nervous

"I was a bundle of nerves just before I took my driving test."

go a bundle on = be enthusiastic about

"I don't go a bundle on her new dress."

bunk

do a bunk = abscond/go away suddenly

"He ran up a large bill at the hotel and then did a bunk without paying."

buoy

buoy up = give (encouraging) support to

"The cut in bank rate is expected to buoy up the economy."

burden

burden of one's song = (repeated) main point/message

"Despite all the rhetoric the real burden of his song concerned the plight of the unemployed."

white man's burden = colonial responsibility

"Developing roads and railways in Africa was all part of the white man's burden."

burglar

cat burglar = thief who climbs up the outside of a building to gain access (through a window)

"The cat burglar must have climbed up that drainpipe."

burn

burn a hole in one's pocket = have more money than one is accustomed to, and be eager to spend it

"The Christmas bonus was burning a hole in my pocket so I went and bought myself a new suit."

burning question = vital issue

"He has a good reputation for originality and quality, but the burning question is can he do the job on time?"

burn one's fingers/get one's fingers burned = suffer having made a bad decision

"I only tried the stock market once, but I got my fingers burned and I haven't bought any shares since."

burn the candle at both ends = be active night and day

"On holiday we explored the countryside during the day and went to nightclubs for most of the night ñ we really burned the candle at both ends."

burn the midnight oil = work until very late

"By burning the midnight oil I managed to finish the job on time."

burn to a frazzle = burn (food) completely

"She forgot to watch the frying pan and the bacon was burned to a frazzle."

burnt offering = food spoiled by burning

"We left the meat in the oven but we were delayed in traffic and it was a burnt offering by the time we got back."

money to burn = have more money than is essential for one's needs

"Why don't you ask Sir William for a donation? He's got money to burn."

See also: burn one's boats/bridges; have one's ears burning.

burst

burst a blood vessel = lose control of one's temper

"When I told him what his daughter had said I thought he'd burst a blood vessel."

burst at the seams = be uncomfortably (over)full

"I ate so much I thought I'd burst at the seams."

burst into tears/laughter, or burst out crying/laughing = suddenly express extreme sadness/happiness

"I broke the news to her and she burst into tears."

"When he fell into the pond I couldn't help but burst out laughing."

bury

bury one's head in the sand = deliberately ignore something that is obvious (but unpleasant)

"It's no use burying your head in the sand you will have to face facts, even if they do show that you've been a fool."

See also: bury the hatchet/one's differences; dead and buried.

bus

busman's holiday = time off work during which one does much the same as if one were still at work
"I went and had a look round Kew Gardens with the botanist Joyce Singleton; it was a bit of a busman's holiday for her."

miss the bus/boat = miss an opportunity
"I couldn't decide whether to apply for the job and by the time I did I had missed the bus because they had already appointed somebody else."

See also: like the back of a bus.

bush

beat about the bush = prevaricate
"Don't beat about the bush, just tell me exactly how much do you want for it?"

bush telegraph = method of (unofficially) spreading news/rumour by word of mouth
"I hear on the bush telegraph that the manager has resigned."

take to the bush = go into hiding
"An enemy patrol was approaching so the platoon took to the bush until they had passed."

bushel

hide one's light under a bushel = conceal one's talents
"You should have told them at the interview that you've got experience with every type of machine ñ there's no point in hiding your light under a bushel."

business

bad business = troublesome/unsavoury affair
"Did you hear about the thefts from the storeroom? It's a bad business, and everybody is suspect."

be business-like = be efficient/organized
"I admire her business-like approach to everything she does."

be in business = be able to proceed
"All we need is one more to make up a foursome and then we're in business."

be no business of somebody's = of no concern to somebody
"It's no business of yours what I do in my free time."

business end (of something) = operative part (of something)
"Be careful with that soldering iron, the business end is very hot."

funny business = dubious/illegal activity
"I'm going to leave you two alone in the house and I want no funny business."

get down to business = reduce (a discussion) to its essentials
"After the introductions we immediately got down to business and reached an agreement within an hour."

go out of business = fail (of a business, because of financial difficulties)
"He only traded for a few months and went out of business because he was undercapitalized."

have no business (to) = have no authority/right (to)
"Why don't you tell her that she has no business to interfere in your affairs."

like nobody's business = very well
"I only met her that morning but we got on like nobody's business."

make it one's business (to) = deliberately undertake (to)
"Nobody seemed to know what was going on so I made it my business to find out."

mean business = to be taken seriously
"He's brought his own darts to the pub so he obviously means business."
mind one's own business = not become involved
"Peter's always prying into my private life; I wish he'd mind his own business."
send somebody about his/her business = refuse unsolicited offers of advice/help
"He came to the door and tried to sell me an encyclopaedia but I soon sent him about his business."
the business/works = exactly what is required
"A ten pound donation to the fund? That's just the business!"
to mean business = to take something seriously
"You could tell he meant business by the expression on his face."
See also: monkey business.

bust
bust a gut = try one's utmost (to the point of exhaustion)
"Take your time; there's no need to bust a gut."
fit to bust/burst = with utmost vigour
"We worked fit to bust to tidy the house before my mother-in-law arrived."
go bust = fail in business
"The company went bust soon after the striking men returned to work."

but
anything but = emphasizing the opposite
"I'll be hours yet, I'm anything but finished."
but for = if it was not for
"But for the rain, we would have finished that roof by now."
no buts about it = without (any) doubt
"There's no buts about it, Paris is a more beautiful city than London."
See also: all but.

butt
butt in = interrupt
"I'm sorry to butt in, but I have to disagree with you."

butter
(fine words) butter (me) no parsnips = do not try to hide the truth with clever words
"Butter me no parsnips and tell me exactly what happened."
butter somebody up = flatter somebody (while seeking a favour)
"It's no use buttering me up, you're having no more pocket money this week."
butter wouldn't melt in his/her mouth = he/she appears to be innocent/naive (although probably is not)
"She claims she couldn't have done it ñ but then, butter wouldn't melt in her mouth."
spread the butter too thick = over-flatter somebody
"Arnold kept telling her how attractive she was, but he spread the butter on too thick and she was unimpressed."
See also: bread and butter; have one's bread buttered on both sides; know which side one's bread is buttered.

butterflies
butterflies in one's stomach/tummy = state of anticipation/nervousness
"I always get butterflies in my stomach before I go to the dentist."

button
bright as a button = clever/intelligent
"You only have to tell her once, she's as bright as a button."

button-hole somebody = detain somebody for a (private) conversation
"I finally button-holed the boss and told her about the holes in the car park."

button one's lip = remain silent
"Despite what she said I buttoned my lip and refused to be provoked."

have something buttoned/sewn up = with all preparations made/complete
"I've got that new job buttoned up and I'll finish it well on time."

press the button = = activate/give the order to proceed
"Everything's ready, we're just waiting for you to press the button."

buy

buy a pig in a poke = buy something unseen
"Don't buy a pig in a poke ñ go and see the books they're advertising before you send any money."

buy somebody off = pay somebody to desist/go away
"He was going to complain but I bought him off with a couple of drinks."

buy out = purchase a rival's business
"Our competitors must be worried by our new product because they offered to buy us out."

buy up = purchase as much as possible
"He bought up all the spare building land in the district and can now charge what he wants for it."

(a) good buy = (a) bargain
"The record player was a good buy because it included twenty pounds' worth of free records."

by

by and by = soon
"I know it's been a long trip but we'll get there by and by."

by and large = taken as a whole
"By and large the extra effort seems to have been worthwhile."

by oneself = alone
"Please go away, I want to be by myself."

by the by/by the way = incidentally
"By the way, what did you say that new girl's name was?

by the same token = as well
"You want your wife to give up smoking but then, by the same token, so should you."

bygones

let bygones be bygones = forget former differences
"Why don't you let bygones be bygones and ask him round for a drink?"

byword

become a byword = become proverbial/standard
"Her name has become a byword for integrity."

C

Cain

raise Cain = be very angry and likely to cause a scene
"I hope Mother doesn't see the chip in that vase ñ its her favourite and she'll raise Cain if she does."

cake

go/sell like hot cakes = to sell quickly
"If you could get a shop to stock those jumpers they would sell like hot cakes, and you'd soon get somebody interested in your designs."

have one's cake and eat it = be able to choose both of two desirable, but mutually exclusive, options
"He had to choose between the two girls in the end, although he wanted to have his cake and eat it by going out with both."

icing on the cake = additional unexpected perk
"Getting the manager to accept our new plans in addition to implementing our original ones was really the icing on the cake."

piece of cake = easy task
"My new job is a piece of cake ñ one of the easiest I've ever had."

slice of the cake = share of the benefit/ profit
"Harry's bound to want a bigger slice of the cake after doing most of the work on that job."

that takes the cake! = exclamation of disbclicf/incredulity
"You don't mean to say she's going to her ex-husband's wedding ñ that takes the cake!"

calf

calf/puppy love = adolescent love
"I don't think she'll take long to get over the break-up with her boyfriend, it was only calf-love."

kill the fatted calf = welcoming hospitality after an absence
"We're going to kill the fatted calf for Alfred when he comes back from his expedition."

call

call a halt = put an end to
"They decided to call a halt to the match when they found the ground was waterlogged."

call a spade a spade = be blunt/ forthright
"You must remember that when you ask him his opinion, he calls a spade a spade and will tell you exactly what he thinks."

call a thing one's own = have exclusive possession of something
"Who's taken my pencil? You can't call a thing your own in this house!"

call away = be asked to attend somewhere else
"The estate agent had been called away on other business when I phoned."

call down = invoke
"Every time I don't go to church on a Sunday I have a guilty feeling that I'm going to call down the wrath of God."

call for = to collect, or require as necessary, or demand
"I'll call for the old clothes for the Jumble Sale tomorrow."
"It called for all his patience when he looked after Tommy."
"The extension to the local library will call for a great number of new books."

call in/into question = express doubts about
"The decision by the headmaster was called into question by some of the teachers who thought it unnecessarily harsh."

call it a day = bring to an end for the time being
"When the rain became too heavy to continue, the players decided to call it a day and continue the tennis match the following week."

call it a night = end an activity in the evening/night
"Shall we call it a night for now and continue our discussion tomorrow?"

call it quits = the advantage is now even
"I'll give you my new record instead of the money I owe you, and then we can call it quits."

call names = insult
"The boys were calling the old lady names as she hobbled up the street."

call off = cancel/postpone indefinitely
"My brother and his girlfriend decided to call off their wedding until they had saved more money towards their mortgage."

call on/upon = require, or appeal to, or visit
"He will have to call upon all his experience to complete the new work on time."
"The charity had to call on many well-known people for donations to raise the enormous amount of money they needed."
"Perhaps you would call on my mother while you are passing and tell her I'll see her later this evening."

call out = cry/shout out loud
"The sudden blow to her leg made her call out in pain."

call the shots/tune = be in charge of, make the decisions
"Barry is calling the shots while the district manager is on holiday."

call to mind = remember
"I am sure I know her but I can't quite call to mind where I have seen her before."

call to order = restore order
"The chairman had to call the meeting to order after the ribald comments of one of the members caused uproar among the others."

call up = summon, or telephone
"Sue has been called up to the manager's office."
"I'll call her up and ask her if she wants to come with us."

no call to = no need/reason to
"There was no call to shout at him like that, he didn't know about the damage to your car."

not called for = not necessary (although acceptable)
"Their attack went well and the reserves were not called for."

on call = be available if required
"Alan was the vet on call last night."

pay a call = to visit somebody
"They decided to pay a call on their friends while they were in the area."

uncalled for = unwanted and unnecessary
"Walter's spiteful remarks were quite uncalled for."

See also: call/draw attention to; called to the bar; call of nature; call off the dogs; call somebody names; call somebody's bluff; call something into question; call to account.

calm

calm before the storm = a period of (relative) peace before a crisis or uproar

"Laying the tables in the canteen before the dinner break is just the calm before the storm."

See also: calm as a millpond.

camel

the last straw that breaks the camel's back = something that exceeds the limit of endurance/tolerance

"After all the expense I've had recently, the final demand for payment of the gas bill was the last straw that broke the camel's back."

camp

camp-follower = hanger-on

"He became the pop group's camp-follower after he went to see them in concert a year ago."

camp it up = to act in an over-effeminate manner

"Brian was always camping it up and pretending to be queer to make us laugh."

enter the enemies' camp = enter the premises/inner sanctum of a rival

"The director sent one of his employees into the enemies' camp to try to get a preview of their new designs."

See also: strike camp.

can

(one) can keep it = remark used by somebody who is unimpressed or disgusted

"If that's all he can manage for amusement in his new Youth Club, he can keep it!"

can of worms = troublesome matter

"My father opened a real can of worms when he took over the ailing company and tried to get it doing business again."

in the can = completed (of a task), or in prison

"That's the first stage of the project in the can, now let's get on with the second."

"Mike was convicted of burglary and put in the can for a year."

See also: carry the can.

candle

cannot/not fit to hold a candle to somebody = cannot be favourably compared with somebody

"Pete cannot hold a candle to Donald when it comes to real expertise."

not worth the candle = the effort/trouble is not justified by the result

"That job of his is so poorly paid it's just not worth the candle."

See also: burn the candle at both ends; hold a candle to the devil.

cannon

cannon fodder = soldiers (of inferior rank) who are deliberately put into the front line to become inevitable casualties in a war

"The infantry were cannon-fodder in the attack that was bound to fail."

canoe

paddle one's own canoe = be completely unaided

"You have to paddle your own canoe when you are a student and living away from home."

cannot

cannot but/cannot help but = be bound to/must

"I couldn't help but remark about the poor service in the restaurant."

canvas

under canvas = in a tent

"We were living under canvas for the whole two weeks of our holiday."

cap

go cap in hand = to beg, ask humbly

"Hilda had to go cap in hand to the boss for yet another day off when her mother really was ill."

if the cap fits, wear it = recognise one's shortcomings

"Michael was not talking about you when he said that a person he knew was extremely untidy ñ but if the cap fits, wear it."

pass/send/take the cap round = ask for donations (by circulating a cap or any container)

"They passed the cap round at our club last night to get a retirement present for one of the committee members."

put on one's thinking cap = think hard/ seriously about something

"He's good at dressing shop windows but he really had to put his thinking cap on when they asked him for an idea for a carnival float."

set one's cap at = try to gain the affections of

"Dave has set his cap at the new typist."

that caps it all! = exclamation of disbelief/incredulity

"They're getting divorced after all the trouble they had adopting that baby ñ well that caps it all!"

to cap/top it all = to better/crown an achievement

"He won the school finals and then, to cap it all, went on to win the County Championships."

See also: Dutch cap; feather in one's cap; mad cap.

capital

make capital of/out of = turn a situation to good account or advantage

"Roy made capital out of the bus strike by charging people a pound to take them to the station in his car."

captain

captain of industry = industrial tycoon

"British manufacturing would be in a better state today if the captains of industry had reinvested some of their profits in new factories and machines."

captive

captive audience/market = a lack of choice on the part of the consumer

"Commuters are a lucrative captive market for British Rail."

card

(quite) a card = a joker/prankster

"My daughter is quite a card, although her father didn't think so when she tied his shoelaces together while he was asleep in the chair."

ask for/get one's cards = resign/get dismissed from one's employment

"If he's caught taking those tools home from work he's going to get his cards."

have a card up one's sleeve = to have something unexpected in reserve

"Sidney doesn't seem to be very worried about the fact his wife is threatening to leave him, he says he has a card up his sleeve that will sort everything out and change her mind."

hold all the cards = be in a position of control/power

"When I'm chairman of the club I'll hold all the cards and Bert will have to abide by the rules."

house of cards = inherently unstable plan/structure
"Regional government depends on local government, local government depends on the councils, councils depend on committees, and committees depend on the conscientiousness of their individual members, the whole idea is a house of cards!"

lay/put one's cards on the table = be frank/honest
"I don't want to hide anything from you so I'll put my cards on the table and tell you everything."

one's best/leading/trump card = something that one is particularly good/strong at
"Experience is Adrian's leading card, and easily makes up for his lack of theoretical knowledge."
"They were uncertain whether to award us the contract until we played our trump card and offered them earlier delivery than our competitors."

on the cards = very likely to happen/can be foreseen
"Stella thinks she's staying in that job indefinitely but its on the cards that she'll get the sack."

play one's cards close to one's chest = be secretive about one's (real) intentions
"I never know what he's planning to do because he plays his cards so close to his chest."

play one's cards right/well = act/behave/plan to one's best advantage
"Why don't you go and talk to Susan? If you play your cards right she might let you take her to the party."

reveal/show one's cards = declare one's intentions
"It's usually best to show your cards when dealing with Anthony; he responds well if you take him into your confidence."

show the red card = dismiss somebody from work
"He arrived back drunk after lunch and the boss showed him the red card."

show the yellow card = give a warning
"The boss showed him the yellow card after he'd been late for work three days running."

stack the cards against somebody = impede somebody's plans/progress
"My rival got in first and by the time I came to make my bid the cards were stacked against me."

care

have a care! = be careful!
"Have a care! That's my best china you're knocking about."

take care of = look after, or be careful with
"Would you mind taking care of my cat while I'm away on holiday?"
"Take care of those loose floorboards."

See also: for all I know/care; not care a tinker's cuss/damn; not care tuppence.

career

chequered career = work record that includes many changes (for better and worse)
"He had a chequered career in his early days but seems to have settled down now that he's joined the police force."

carpet

brush/sweep something under the carpet/rug = deliberately forget/hide something that is to one's disadvantage
"Let's sweep the whole unfortunate incident under the carpet and never refer to it again."

on the carpet/mat = being disciplined (by a superior)
"Jack's on the carpet for breaking that machine."

(roll out the) red carpet = (give somebody an) elaborate/formal welcome
"My mother-in-law is coming from Canada to stay with us so I suppose we'll have to roll out the red carpet."

carrot

a stick or a carrot = a threat or an inducement
"Valerie won't be forced to do anything ñ a carrot is much more effective than a stick in her case."

carrot to a donkey = inducement/ temptation
"Colin will come to the party; the chance of a free drink is like a carrot to a donkey to him!"

carry

carried away = lacking self-control
"Don't get carried away! You've seen a pretty girl before!"

carry all before one = be highly successful/beat all rivals
"Sean carried all before him in our club's tennis tournament and won the champion's trophy."

carry a torch (for somebody) = have (unreciprocated) love for somebody
"He still carries a torch for Judith although she's married somebody else."

carry off (a situation) = overcome a disadvantage/succeed
"My brother forgot to buy his wife a birthday card but managed to carry it off by taking her out for an expensive meal."

carry on = display emotion out of proportion to its cause
"Don't carry on so, she's only broken a cup ñ she could have cut herself badly."

carry on with = have an affair with
"I hear that James is carrying on with his secretary."

carry out = do/execute
"The well-disciplined soldiers carried out their orders without question."

carry over = postpone
"There wasn't time to finish all the games last night and so some have had to be carried over until next week."

carry the can = accept blame/ responsibility
"I don't see why I should carry the can for his mistakes as well as my own."

carry the day = win
"Our team got off to a poor start but eventually carried the day and won by two clear goals."

carry through = complete (in spite of difficulties)
"There's no point in starting the task unless you're prepared to carry it through to the end."

carry weight = have influence
"He may be the boss at work but his wishes seem to carry very little weight at home."

carry (along) with = persuade
"As long as we can carry the others along with us we'll make an unbeatable combination."

See also: carry conviction; carry one's bat; carry the banner for.

cart

put the cart before that horse = do something in the wrong order
"You've put boiling water in the teapot before putting the tea in ñ that's putting the cart before the horse!"
See also: clever as a cartload/wagonload of monkeys; upset the apple-cart.

case

as the case may be = whichever (of several choices) applies
"I don't mind; I'll have tea or coffee, as the case may be."
case in point = pertinent example
"My daughter likes to wear blue; her new skirt is a case in point."
(no) case to answer for = action/ behaviour that needs (no) justification
"No matter what Herbert says about your involvement with our competitors I don't think you have a case to answer for."
cast-iron case = irrefutable argument
"If your typewriter was stolen while you were away, why don't you claim on the insurance? You have a cast-iron case."
hard case = somebody who is tough (with criminal/violent tendencies)
"Guy has turned into a really hard case since he's been in prison."
in any case = whatever else is considered/happens
"You may keep the goods, have something in exchange, or have your money back; in any case, you can't lose."
in case = as a precaution
"Take your umbrella in case it rains."
in case of = in the event of
"The police soon arrive in any case of trouble."
in that case = in the event/that being so
"Howard has declined to come, and in that case we can ask somebody else."
is/is not the case = is true/false
"If what you say is really the case I believe your excuse."
"I was angry when I discovered it was not the case and she'd been lying."
make out a case for = provide an argument in favour of
"Even the whites find it difficult to make out a case for apartheid."
open and shut case = situation of predictable/sure outcome
"She's the only applicant for the job, so she's bound to be appointed ñ it's an open and shut case."
See also: meet the case.

cash

cash and carry = retail outlet that supplies goods (often in bulk) at lower than normal prices on condition that the purchaser provides carriage (for delivery)
"You can buy cases of canned beer far cheaper at the cash and carry than at the off licence in town."
cash down = immediate payment for (possible part of) goods or services
"That will cost you 20 pounds cash down and 80 pounds over 12 months."
cash in on = take advantage of
"She cashed in on her knowledge of French and got a job as a courier."
cash in one's chips = die
"He liked flying micro-light aircraft but cashed in his chips when the machine's main structure failed."
cash on the nail = cash (coins/

banknotes) as opposed to cheques, credit cards, promissory notes etc
"If its cash on the nail you can have the car for 600 pounds."

hard cash = coins/banknotes (as opposed to less negotiable cheques etc.
"You have to pay with hard cash at the discount store they won't accept credit cards or cheques there."

cast

cast about = look/seek for
"The personnel manager has been casting about for somebody who can act as receptionist."

cast adrift = abandon(ed)
"After John's involvement with the police he has been cast adrift by nearly all of his friends."

cast anchor = end a voyage (lower the anchor)
"We were at sea for five weeks before we cast anchor near one of the Pacific islands."

cast an eye over = make a cursory inspection
"Tom, cast your eye over that new stock and make sure that it is all there."

cast a shadow over = have a dampening/ dispiriting effect on
"On the last night of our holiday we went to a party, but the knowledge that we were going home the next day cast a shadow over the whole evening."

cast aside = discard (as of no relevance/ value)
"You must cast aside all doubts and tackle the job with confidence."

cast a spell over = exert a controlling influence (by no obvious means)
"Tina seems to able to cast a spell over Terry and get him to do anything she wants."

cast aspersions on = make unfavourable comments about
"You're always casting aspersions on Graham's ability; don't you like him?"

cast doubts on/upon = introduce doubt about
"The lack of facilities for elderly People has cast doubts on the whole of the redevelopment scheme."

cast down = miserable/unhappy
"Sylvia's been cast down ever since her mother became so ill."

casting vote = deciding vote made (by the chairman of a meeting) when a previous vote is tied (with equal numbers of votes on each side)
"There are equal numbers of Conservatives and Socialists on our council, but the Chairman is a Conservative and so his party always wins if it comes to a casting vote."

cast in one's lot = agree to share the fate of somebody else
"I was getting nowhere on my own so I decided to cast in my lot with Hal and now we're successfully in business together."

cast lots = settle an issue by means of a lottery
"Nobody wanted to walk back to the village in the rain so we cast lots ñ and I lost and had to do it!"

cast light upon = reveal information about something
"Can anybody cast light upon how this chair got broken?"

cast off = release a vessel's moorings before sailing, or throw away
"Most of the crew are going to their bunks early tonight because we cast off at dawn tomorrow."
"It's about time you cast off that

feeling of gloom and began to enjoy yourself."

cast out = expel from
"Anybody who dared to oppose the new dictatorship was cast out of his own country."

cast the net = make a wide search
"The police cast the net far and wide in an attempt to find the murderer."

See also: cast in the same mould; the die is cast.

castle

an Englishman's home is his castle = privacy and security are guaranteed in one's own home
"The encyclopaedia salesman seemed determined to come in and I was just as determined he wouldn't ñ an Englishman's home is his castle."

castles in Spain/the air = a dream of (non-existent) wealth and happiness
"My plans for what I shall do after I retire from work are only castles in the air."

cat

a cat may look at a king = all people are equal, irrespective of their social backgrounds
"His arrogant manner with his staff is highly objectionable; he should remember that a cat may look at a king!"

be a copycat = imitate
"That pattern you've drawn is the same as Mabel's; don't be a copycat ñ make up a design of your own."

bell the cat = risk a confrontation with an opponent for the common good
"Everybody was unhappy with the new rates of pay and so I decided to bell the cat and take it up with the

cat and mouse game = activity involving continuous manoeuvring for supremacy
"The employers and the unions played a cat and mouse game over the proposed pay increases."

cat get one's tongue = be rendered speechless
"Come on, speak up ñ or has the cat got your tongue?"

cat's pyjamas/whiskers = the best
"My new car is just the cat's whiskers."

cat that swallowed the cream = self-satisfied person
"Ever since she qualified she's been like the cat that swallowed the cream."

curiosity killed the cat = warning not to be inquisitive/nosy
"Please stop prying into my private life. Remember, curiosity killed the cat."

enough to make a cat laugh = very funny
"When he slipped on a banana skin it was enough to make a cat laugh."

fight like cat and dog = be continually quarrelling
"There's never any peace in our house because my two daughters fight like cat and dog."

grin like a Cheshire cat = grin widely
"When we turned up at father's house unexpectedly he grinned like a Cheshire cat and welcomed us in."

lead a cat and dog life = continually quarrel
"Mark and Linda lead a cat and dog life, and I shouldn't be surprised if they split up soon."

let the cat out of the bag = unintentionally reveal a secret
"We were going to throw a surprise

the cat out of the bag and he knew all about it beforehand."

like a cat on hot bricks = fidgety, restless, uneasy

"Keep still, Emily, you're like a cat on hot bricks."

like something the cat brought in = dishevelled/untidy

"After trudging home across the moors in the rain we looked like something the cat brought in."

make a cat's paw of = dupe/exploit

"They wanted me to take the matter up with the boss but I refused to be made a cat's paw of."

no/not enough room to swing a cat = confined/cramped for space

"Our new kitchen is tiny, with not enough room to swing a cat."

not a cat in hell's chance = no chance

"Chelsea haven't a cat in hell's chance of winning the league this season."

put the cat among the pigeons = (deliberately) cause an uproar

"Julia told Arthur's wife where he was on Monday night and that really put the cat among the pigeons."

run around like a scalded cat = bustle/run around busily (but often unnecessarily)

"Fiona is always running round like a scalded cat yet she seems to get very little work done!"

when the cat's away (mice will play) = people will take advantage of any lack of supervision

"Colin has been to the pub every night since his wife's been in hospital; still, when the cat's away!"

which way the cat jumps = probable outcome, dependent on preceding events

"I don't know whether I can have holiday this year; I must wait and see which way the cat jumps."

See also: play cat and mouse with; rain cats and dogs.

catch

catch a cold = make a bad choice/purchase

"That lawnmower I bought in the jumble sale turned out to be useless; I really caught a cold with that one!"

catch a glimpse/sight of = see very briefly

"I was at the back of the crowd and so I only caught a glimpse of the Duke when he drove past."

catch cold = become chilled

"Put your coat on before you go out or you'll catch cold."

catch hold of = grasp

"Catch hold of this rope when I throw it to you."

catch it = get into trouble

"You're late! You'll catch it when you get home!"

catch on = understand, or become fashionable/popular

"We only have to tell Sylvia once; she soon catches on."

"The skate-board caught on for a few months, but then dropped out of fashion."

catch one's breath = take a brief rest

"Let's sit down a minute to catch our breath."

catch penny = cheap/tawdry

"They were giving away plastic toys as a catch penny to get people to go into their shop."

catch phrase = commonly used expression

"Bugs Bunny's catch phrase is ëWhat's up, Doc?'"

catch red-handed = discover somebody in the act of doing something wrong
"The children were stealing apples when the farmer arrived and caught them red-handed."
catch somebody bending/napping/on the hop = take somebody unawares/ unprepared, or at a disadvantage
"You mustn't be caught bending when Debbie's around or she'll quickly seize the advantage."
"Please wait for me; you've caught me on the hop and I must change my clothes before I come out with you."
catch somebody's eye = gain somebody's attention
"A new dress caught my eye in Harrod's window."
catch somebody out = discover somebody making an error/ misdemeanour, or trick somebody
"I tried to slip off early from work, but the boss caught me out and even made me stay an extra half hour."
"See if you can catch Michael out with that double-headed coin."
catch somebody with his/her fingers/ hand in the till = discover somebody in the act of stealing (money)
"Bill lost his job because he was caught with his hand in the till."
catch somebody with his pants/trousers down = discover somebody at an extreme disadvantage
"I was imitating the supervisor's strange way of talking when he walked in and caught me with my pants down."
catch up = get level with
"Don't dawdle, Bobby. Come on, catch up at once!"
catch up on = do something that has been postponed
"Now that I have finished that typing job I can catch up on my housework."
Catch-22 situation = inescapable dilemma (whichever course of action is taken)
"If I speak she says I'm overbearing and if I remain silent she accuses me of sulking; it's a Catch-22 situation."
See also: catch a crab; catch fire; catch one's death; catch somebody in the act; (catch) somebody off balance.

cause

good cause = undertaking that deserves support (because of its altruistic/ charitable nature)
"I don't mind giving money to them because I know it's for a good cause."
lost cause = undertaking that is bound to fail
"His attempt to row across the Atlantic in a bath was a lost cause right from the start!"

caution

be a (real) caution = be amusing/popular (for flouting convention)
"Uncle Albert's a real caution ñ always teasing my mother about her teenage sweethearts."
throw caution to the winds = behave with extreme rashness
"It was foggy on the mountain but the climbers threw caution to the winds and set off for the summit."

cave

See: Aladdin's cave.

cease

See: wonders will never cease.

centre

centre of attraction/attention = somebody/something that holds most attention

"Amy is always the centre of attraction at parties."

ceremony

stand on ceremony = behave in an over-formal manner

"The chairman would like to see you. Just go to his office and walk in ñ we don't stand on ceremony in this company."

certain

for certain = assuredly, inevitably

"Look at that sky! It's going to rain for certain."

moral certainty = very probable

"Arnold ran so well in the heats that it's a moral certainty he'll win the final race."

of a certain age = middle-aged (or older)

"Women of a certain age always fall for Graham's charm."

See also: dead certainty; in an interesting/certain condition.

chain

chain of events = (inevitable) sequence of happenings

"I only intended to go to the drama group meeting once to see what it was like, but I soon got caught up in a chain of events and a couple of months later I was appearing in their Christmas production."

chain letter = (usually anonymous) letter requesting the recipient to send several copies of it to other people, with a view to bringing good luck or obtaining money for the originator.

"I think that chain letters are a confidence trick and should be made illegal."

chain reaction = a result which brings about another similar result which, in turn, causes another, and so on

"The lorry ran into the back of the rearmost car in the queue which bumped into the car in front, which then hit the next one, and so on in a chain reaction."

chain store = one of a group of similar shops under the same ownership

"One advantage of most chain stores is that goods purchased in one of the shops can usually be returned to one of the others if there is any problem."

chair

address the chair = direct one's comments to the chairman (as is required in a formal meeting of, for example, a committee)

"Councillor Jones, I must remind you to address your remarks only to the chair, and not to other members of this committee."

appeal to the chair = request the formal protection/support of the chairman (of, for example, a committee)

"I appeal to the chair to censure Councillor Jones for his objectionable and personal remarks about my integrity."

fall off one's chair = be very surprised

"When she said she was engaged to be married I nearly fell off my chair."

take the chair = act as chairman (of, for example, a committee)

"The Mayor didn't arrive and the meeting voted to ask Councillor Jones to take the chair."

chalk

by a long chalk = by a wide margin

"The fielder threw the ball but missed the wicket by a long chalk."

chalk something up to experience =

(stoically), while intending to avoid it in future
"I paid fifty pounds in the market for a so-called bargain piece of porcelain which turned out to be worthless; I'll just have to chalk it up to experience."

chalk up = record, score
"Liverpool chalked up yet another home victory against Arsenal."

different as chalk and/from cheese = entirely different
"Although they are twins, temperamentally they are as different as chalk and cheese."

champ

champ at the bit = be (very) impatient
"By the time my wife had done her hair and got dressed, I was champing at the bit in case the party was all over by the time we got there!"

chance

cat's/snowball's chance in hell = even the remotest chance (of all)
"She hasn't a snowball's chance in hell of persuading her boyfriend to take her to Hawaii for a holiday."

chance in a million = very remote chance, virtual impossibility
"She has only a chance in a million of getting the job."

chances are = (the) probability is
"I shouldn't look forward too much to seeing Grace at the party; chances are she won't come anyway."

chances are even/against it = it is equally possible/unlikely
"The chances are even that Grace will come to the party."
"If you're wondering whether Grace will come to the party, I think the chances are against it."

(no) earthly chance/fat chance = (not even) the remotest chance
"You've no earthly chance of driving from London to Bristol in under an hour."
"Fat chance you have of driving from London to Bristol in under an hour."

even chance = equal probability
"There are only two contestants in the race so that, in theory at least, each has an even chance of winning."

eye on/to the main chance = alert for an opportunity for personal gain
"Although I act as Oscar's agent, I always keep an eye on the main chance in case I can do some business of my own."

fancy one's chances = be (over)confident that one will succeed
"Ann really fancies her chances of promotion to the vacant job of chief supervisor."

fighting/sporting chance = fair/ reasonable chance
"I think the Tory's have a fighting chance of winning the next election."
"Priscilla won't even give me a sporting chance of saying sorry for what I did the other day."

game of chance = dependent on luck (as opposed to choice/skill)
"Cynics believe that finding a good husband these days is a game of chance."

ghost of a chance = even the remotest chance
"You haven't a ghost of a chance of driving from London to Bristol in under an hour."

on the off chance = in case, in the hope
"I'm glad I found you at home; I just called round on the off chance that you'd be in."

stand a good/fair chance of = be fairly likely to

"Why don't you enter the competition? I think you stand a good chance of winning a prize."

take a chance/take no chances = risk/not risk something

"I won't take a chance on a July holiday in Britain ñ it always rains!"

"I take no chances and spend my holidays abroad, where it seldom rains."

See also: chance one's arm; dog's chance; fat chance.

change

change hands = change ownership

"According to the official record, that car has changed hands five times in the last four years!"

change of air = different environment/ climate

"I've been sitting at this desk for five hours; I think I'll go out for a change of air."

change of heart = change in one's feelings (often leading to a change of mind)

"I didn't intend to go to the football match because our side has been playing badly, but I had a change of heart and went and cheered for them as usual."

change of life = menopause

"Many women are affected emotionally by the hormonal changes that accompany the change of life."

change one's tune = change one's mind

"He wanted to come on the trip but he soon changed his tune when I told him how much it was going to cost."

get no change out of = fail to get help/ satisfaction from

"There's no point in asking Owen to help with the preparations ñ you'll get no change out of him!"

ring the changes = vary

"Alan always goes to the same pub at lunchtimes, but I like to ring the changes and try a different one occasionally."

small change = low-value coins

"The trouble with the new pound coins is that you think you've only got a pocketful of small change but in fact it's worth several pounds."

See also: a change is as good as a rest; change the subject.

chapter

quote chapter and verse = provide evidence for one's statements (often to a boring extreme)

"Alright, I believe you! There's no need to quote chapter and verse."

See also: chapter of accidents.

character

in/out of character = as/not as expected from a somebody's usual behaviour

"I was surprised when Louise lost her temper ñ it's quite out of character."

charge

charge an arm and a leg = charge very high prices, overcharge

"They charge you an arm and a leg for a bowl of soup in that new restaurant."

charge with = entrust with/make responsible for

"I'm charging you with making sure that this mess is cleared up before you go."

charged with = filled with

"The air was charged with emotion when the aging actress made her final appearance on stage."

in charge of = responsible for

"Pilfering has stopped entirely since they put Angus in charge of the stores."

trump up a charge = invent an accusation
"Sylvia does not get on with the supervisor and the danger is that he will trump up some charge to discredit her."

charity

charity begins at home = one's family should have first claim to one's kindness/resources
"It's all very well giving up all your free time to the youth club, but your family hardly ever sees you; charity begins at home, you know."

cold as charity = callous/unsympathetic
"There's no point in asking him for help, he's as cold as charity."

Charlie

proper Charlie = a fool
"I hate fancy dress parties; they make me feel a proper Charlie."

charm

go/work like a charm = function very well
"We have had no problems with our new computer, it works like a charm."

lead a charmed life = run risks with impunity
"Glen leads a charmed life ñ he's had three motorbike accidents without being injured."

See also: bear/lead a charmed life.

chase

chase (after) rainbows = dream/think about the unobtainable
"Neil's always chasing after rainbows and never comes up with a really practical idea."

chase up = try to make something happen more quickly
"If the goods I ordered don't arrive tomorrow, I'll have to contact the supplier and chase them up."

wild goose chase = useless journey/search
"Lois said she knew the way so we followed her car, but she took us on a wild goose chase all round the country lanes instead of taking the direct route along the main road."

chat

chat up = talk to somebody persuasively for one's own gain
"Lionel is very good at chatting up strange girls and getting them to go out with him."

cheap

cheap as dirt/dirt cheap = very cheap
"That new shop in the high street is selling pocket calculators dirt cheap."

on the cheap = at minimum cost
"I go abroad on the cheap by getting a lift from a lorry driver who's crossing on the ferry."

check

check into/up on = examine for accuracy/truthfulness
"The police checked up on his story and found he was telling the truth."

check in/out = begin/end one's stay at a hotel
"The hotel insists that guests check out of their rooms before 11 o'clock in the morning."

check off = account for items (on a list)
"I have to work late at the shop tomorrow to check off articles on display as part of the stock take."

hold/keep in check = restrain
"I find it difficult to keep my spending in check when I'm on holiday."

keep a check on = examine/record routinely
"Make sure you keep a check on what you spend on company business."

cheek

cheek by jowl with = (very) close to
"It's the company's policy to have only one canteen so that the managers eat cheek by jowl with the shop floor workers."

cheek of the devil = (insolent) audacity
"Tina had the cheek of the devil to ask the landlord for free drinks because it was her birthday."

give somebody cheek = show lack of respect to somebody senior/superior
"Eat your supper and go to bed ñ and don't give me any of your cheek!"

have a/the cheek to = be impertinent/insolent
"I didn't have the cheek to tell her that, at her age, she looked ridiculous in such a short skirt."

turn the other cheek = ignore a slight/violence against oneself
"She was quite insulting to Barry but he turned the other cheek and let her get on with it."

See also: have/with one's tongue in one's cheek.

cheer

cheer up = adopt a happier manner
"Cheer up! I'm sure you'll feel better tomorrow."

See also: cup that cheers.

cheese

big cheese = somebody in authority/of importance
"Let's get the place cleaned up, the boss is bringing round a couple of big cheeses tomorrow."

cheesed off = bored/disgruntled
"I'm cheesed off with having to mow the lawn every week."

hard cheese! = bad luck! (usually meant in sympathy)
"You missed the last bus? Oh, hard cheese!"

cheese paring = mean(ness)
"He's renowned for his cheese paring even after you have quoted him your lowest possible price for the job."

cheque

blank cheque = permission to do anything one likes
"The manager gave her a blank cheque to reorganize the department in any way she thought fit."

cheque-book journalism = purchase by a newspaper at a high price of the (exclusive) rights to a person's" story" to gain advantage over its competitors
"Rewarding a criminal by paying him for an exclusive account of his crime is one of the worst forms of cheque-book journalism."

cherry

take two bites at the cherry = make two attempts at doing something that should be achievable in one attempt
"I made a mistake the first time I tried to do the task but was lucky and, given two bites of the cherry, I got it right the second time."

Cheshire

See: grin like a Cheshire cat

chest

get something of one's chest = confess, say something one has been suppressing for a time
"I finally told her what I'd done and I was really gla'l to get it off my chest."

hold/play one's cards/hand close to one's chest = be secretive
"You never know Kirsty's opinion because she holds her cards very close to her chest."
See also: put hairs on somebody's chest.

chestnut

old chestnut = worn-out joke/statement (and thus lacking credibility)
"He gave as his excuse for being late that old chestnut about the train being delayed."
pull the chestnuts out of the fire = to (take a risk to) help somebody in difficulty
"The last batsmen played some risky strokes to pull the chestnuts out of the fire and score the winning run."

chew

chew something over = think about something at length
"Please chew over my offer and let me know next week whether you're interested."
chew the cud = consider carefully, ponder
"I chewed the cud for a couple of days before deciding to refuse your offer."
chew the fat = talk at length (but usually inconsequentially)
"We hadn't seen each other for ages and we chewed the fat all night, reminiscing about old times."

chicken

chicken feed = paltry amount/sum
"I wouldn't work for them; they're only paying chicken feed for a very demanding job."
chicken hearted/livered = cowardly
"Don't be chicken hearted, have a go ñ you stand as good a chance as anyone else."
chicken out = lose one's nerve
"Jamie was going to walk along the top of the wall but he chickened out at the last minute."
don't count one's chickens (before they're hatched) = don't count on the outcome of something before it has happened
"Don't count your chickens and buy that new outfit until you're sure the bonus has been paid."
no (spring) chicken = no longer young
"She's no chicken and shouldn't be riding on the back of a motorbike at her age."
tender as a chicken = soft
"He's as tender as a chicken and not up to hard manual work."

chief

too many chiefs and not enough Indians = too many people in a supervisory role, and too few workers to implement their instructions
"That company's overheads cost 70 per cent of their turnover; the trouble is, there are too many chiefs and not enough Indians."

child

child bride = woman who marries when she is considered to be too young (immature) for marriage.
"My sister was a child bride; she married when she was only seventeen, but next year will be her silver wedding anniversary."
child of nature = somebody with (genuine) naivety
"Alison spent the first sixteen years of her life in a small Wiltshire village before she came to London; she's a real child of nature."

child's play = very easy challenge/task
"Assembling that do-it-yourself furniture was child's play ñ as long as you read the plans correctly!"
latch-key child = (young) schoolchild who has a key to the family home, to gain access before the parent(s) return after work
"She says that much of her self-sufficiency derives from being a latch-key child when she was young."
love child = child born to a couple who are not married
"Mary was a love child whose father left her mother before she was born."
second childhood = child-like behaviour in middle/old age
"John is a grandfather yet he's been in his second childhood since he bought that sports car."

chill
cast a chill over = have a saddening/ depressive influence on
"My mother-in-law always seems to cast a chill over the proceedings when she arrives."
chilled to the bone/marrow = very cold
"We went to build a snowman but before it was half finished I was chilled to the bone."
chill one's blood = cause terror
"That new horror film is enough to chill your blood."
take the chill off = make warmer
"Let's light the fire and take the chill off the room."
See also: catch a chill/cold; send chills up somebody's spine.

chime
chime in with = inject one's remarks into those already stated
"We had all agreed, then Mabel chimed in with her personal objections."

chimney
smoke like a chimney = smoke (cigarettes) excessively
"No wonder her fingers are stained brown, she smokes like a chimney."

chin
have a chin-wag = have a prolonged conversation
"I only see my sister about twice a year but when I do we have a good chin-wag."
keep one's chin up = remain cheerful (in adversity)
"No matter what happens to him, Leo always seems to keep his chin up."
lead with one's chin = make an attack without defending oneself
"Halfway through the meeting he questioned my point of view and I made the mistake of leading with my chin, whereupon he was able to demonstrate that I had totally reversed my stance since the last discussion."
take (it) on the chin = courageously accept adversity/punishment
"Robert was made redundant after twenty years with the same firm, but he took it on the chin and found another job within a week."

china
See: not for all the tea in China.

chink
chink in one's armour = a (little-known) weakness that makes one vulnerable (to attack)
"If he questions the total, ask him to calculate the figures; he's no good at

adding up ñ and that's the chink in his armour."

chip

blue chips = highly valued (and low-risk) investment

"A safe investment is blue chips or, better still, gilt-edged securities."

chip in = contribute to, or interrupt

"When you're collecting for charity, you can always rely on Reg to chip in a few pounds."

"When you're trying to explain something to somebody, you can always rely on Reg to chip in with his opinion."

chip off the old block = child that resembles a parent

"Simon's a chip off the old block ñ he's got ginger hair, just like his father."

chip on one's shoulder = embittered/bigoted attitude

"She's had a chip on her shoulder ever since the firm wouldn't meet her expenses claim for travelling to and from work."

have one's chips = be dead/finished

"After what she did yesterday she's had her chips as far as I'm concerned."

when the chips are down = at the critical/crucial point

"James always appears to be undecided, but when the chips are down he makes up his mind and unswervingly acts on his decision."

chisel

chisel somebody = cheat somebody

"I tried to do him a favour and he chiselled me out of ten pounds."

chock

chock-a-block = crowded/packed together

"The town centre was chock-a-block with tourists."

"When the bus finally came it was chock-a-block and we had to wait for the next one."

choice

Hobson's choice = no choice at all

"By the time we got to the bar it was Hobson's choice ñ white wine or nothing."

spoiled for choice = with a wide range of choices

"When we got to the bar we were spoiled for choice: four kinds of beer, six types of wine, and all the spirit drinks you could think of."

choose

See: choose/draw the short straw.

chop

chop and change = keep changing (one's choice/mind)

"June says that, rather than two or three dresses, she prefers to have several blouses and skirts so that she can chop and change to create many different outfits."

give somebody the chop = dismiss/get rid of somebody

"They caught him pilfering stock from work so they gave him the chop."

give something the chop = destroy/discontinue/dispose of something

"I used to go to pottery classes but they took up too much time so I decided to give them the chop."

"My cheap watch never kept good time so I gave it the chop and bought a new one."

lick one's chops = relish (in anticipation of food/pleasure/satisfaction)

"Mick licked his chops when I told him Wendy was coming to the party."

chord

strike a chord = trigger a memory
"I can't remember her name but her face strikes a chord."

touch a chord = stimulate an emotion
"Every time I smell wood smoke it touches a chord and I remember my childhood in the country."

chorus

chorus of approval = general/unanimous approval
"Henry's suggestion that we should all contribute a pound to the fund was met by a chorus of approval."

in chorus = in unison
"Following Henry's suggestion we all replied ëYes' in chorus."

chuck

chuck away = carelessly throw away
"If the old jacket I gave you doesn't fit, just chuck it away."

chuck something in = stop doing something
"I used to go swimming every week, but then I decided to chuck it in."
"Stop fighting, you boys. Chuck it in!"

chuck out = expel, throw away/out
"We cleaned the cupboard and chucked out years of accumulated rubbish."

chuck up = vomit
"He had so much to drink that he chucked up in the car on the way home."

chum

chum up with = make (close) friends of
"I notice it didn't take Julian long to chum up with the new secretary."

chump

off one's chump = mad
"His actions are so irrational that I think he must be off his chump."

church

go into the church = become a priest
"His mother wanted him to go into the church, but he went his own way and became a professional wrestler."

poor as a church mouse = very poor
"I don't know how they manage to bring up four children ñ they're as poor as church mice."

Cinderella

Cinderella of something = least admired/favoured
"Rifle shooting is the Cinderella of Olympic sports, attracting little in the way of sponsorship or public support."

circle

come full circle = return to the starting point
"Once more fashion has come full circle and long skirts are popular again."

dress circle = balcony immediately above the stalls in a cinema or theatre
"For an anniversary present Stuart took me to the opera and we had seats in the dress circle."

go round in circles = keep moving (literally or figuratively) but make no progress
"We've argued this point for nearly two hours and we're just going round in circles."

run round in (small) circles = be very busy (but often ineffectively)
"I seem to have been running round in circles all day and yet I've got no progress to show for it."

square the circle = attempt the impossible
“Trying to find a solution to our company’s financial problems is like trying to square the circle.”
vicious circle = sequence of problematic events in which the result of one only worsens the cause of the next, and so on, until the final outcome exacerbates the first
“He drinks to forget his problems, which centre on being in debt, but the money he spends on drink only gets him deeper in debt, and so on ñ it’s a vicious circle.”

circumstance
circumstantial evidence = evidence which gives an indication of somebody’s involvement (in a crime, for example), but which does not constitute direct proof
“Just because you saw my car outside the pub doesn’t prove I was inside ñ that’s only circumstantial evidence.
extenuating circumstances = acceptable excuse
“There are extenuating circumstances why I was late: the intercity train broke down and we had to wait more than an hour for a replacement.”
in/under the circumstances = taking into account the conditions or the situation
“She was only fifteen and in the circumstances the policeman let her off with a warning.”
victim of circumstances = somebody who suffers through no fault of his/her own
“Born into a very poor family in a slum area and lacking any formal education, he grew up a victim of circumstances among the most underprivileged section of society.”
See also: in easy circumstances.

circus
three-ring circus = noisy confused place
“The hall was like a three-ring circus until the police arrived to restore order.”

civil
civil tongue (in one’s head)= politeness
“You may have cause for complaint but at least you could keep a civil tongue in your head.”

civvy
Civvy Street = not in the armed forces
“Gordon found it strange going back to Civvy Street after spending the previous twelve years in the RAF.”

claim
stake a claim = (make a) claim
“You stake a claim on that table while I go to the bar and get us some drinks.”

clamp
clamp down (on) = impose (even more stringent) restrictions (on)
“The Government announced that it is going to clamp down on people who avoid paying their television licence fees.”

clam
clam up = become silent
“She clams up every time I bring up the question of marriage.”

clanger
drop a clanger = make a blunder
“I dropped a real clanger when I started talking about premature baldness in men ñ I didn’t know Ron

clap

clap eyes on = see, catch sight of
"I fell in love with Liza the first time I clapped eyes on her."

clapped out = worn out
"We must get a new kettle, Stephen, this one's clapped out."

clap-trap = inconsequential/worthless talk
"Most of the politician's speech was a load of clap-trap."

like the clappers = very fast
"That new turbo-charged Ford goes like the clappers."

class

class of one's/its own = without equal
"As an opera singer, Caruso was in a class of his own."

bottom/top of the class = best/worst in a group
"Among cricketers, Ian Botham has to be top of the class."

claw

get one's claws into = display jealousy (through sarcasm/insult), or entrap (into marriage)
"Since Kathy got promotion her younger sister's really got her claws into her."
"Hal had better watch out now that Pam's got her claws into him ñ she's the marrying kind!"

clay

feet of clay = weakness of character in somebody previously thought to be worthy of respect
"The cabinet minister had to resign after being caught having an affair with his secretary. Like some of his predecessors, he was found to have feet of clay."

clean

clean as a whistle = veıy clean(ly)
"I want you to wash these dishes until they're as clean as a whistle."
"The nurse took some tweezers and pulled out the splinter as clean as a whistle."

clean bill of health = fit
"I just had a medical and the doctor gave me a clean bill of health."

clean-cut = sharply/unambiguously defined, or of healthy appearance
"I want a fair, clean-cut decision in writing."
"The typical Western hero is slim, bronzed and clean-cut."

clean down = rub/scrub until totally clean
"I want you to clean down the top of that wooden table until I can eat my dinner off it."

clean out = empty something, or take all of somebody's money
"We have finally cleaned out all the rubbish from the cupboard under the stairs."
"I was playing poker with the usual crowd but they cleaned me out after only five hands."

clean sheet/slate = unblemished record (of behaviour)
"Gary came out of the navy with a clean sheet."

clean through = right through, without obstruction
"The bullet passed clean through his chest."

clean up = make a substantial gain
"Humphrey bought all the available shares in the company and cleaned up when he sold them a week or so later."

come clean = confess
"It's obvious you did it so you might as well come clean."

keep one's nose clean = stay out of trouble
"It's alright here as long as you keep your nose clean; if you don't, they treat you badly."
live a clean life = be blameless/moral
"He's lived a clean life and as a result his conscience is completely untroubled."
make a clean breast of = confess
"I've decided to make a clean breast of it and tell you exactly what happened that night."
make a clean sweep = dispose of (everything)
"My roses got some sort of fungus infection so I decided to make a clean sweep and replace the lot with new healthy plants."
one's hands are clean = one is blameless/innocent
"I'm not worried about the investigation because my hands are totally clean."
show a clean pairs of heels = outrun (one's pursuers)
"The prisoner eluded his escort and showed them a clean pair of heels as he ran through the back streets of the town."

cleaners
taken to the cleaners = have all one's money taken (through gambling or deception)
"I thought it was a friendly game of cards for small stakes but they really took me to the cleaners."

clear
clear as crystal/crystal clear = perfectly clear/plain
"Thanks for the explanation; it's all

clear as mud = obscure
"His explanation was as clear as mud ñ I still don't understand!"
clear away = remove
"Please clear away all that rubbish."
clear conscience = feeling of blamelessness/innocence
"I had nothing to fear when the customs official questioned me because I had a clear conscience."
clear-cut = clearly/unambiguously defined
"The question is very complicated and I'm afraid I cannot yet give you a clear-cut answer."
clear of = free from
"When I make that final payment I shall be clear of all debts."
clear off = go away
"The children soon cleared off when they saw the farmer approaching with his dog."
clear out = clean/empty, or go away
"It's about time we cleared out the attic, it's full of junk."
"Clear out! And don't come back!"
clear the air = have a frank discussion to eliminate any misunderstanding
"We talked it over for about an hour and really cleared the air, so that we're good friends again now."
clear the way = remove obstructions
"Satisfactory answers to these questions should clear the way for an immediate decision."
clear up = tidy, or become fine (of weather), or make plain
"I wish you would clear up that mess."
Do you think the weather will clear up by this evening?"
"I'd like to clear up any misgivings you may have."
coast is clear = there is nobody to

"Wait until the coast is clear and then climb in through my window."

in the clear = free from debt/suspicion

"Now that Gus has accounted for his movements on the night of the crime he's in the clear."

steer clear of = avoid

"I should steer clear of Edward ñ he can be a bad influence."

See also: clear/sound as a bell; clear somebody's name; clear the decks; see one's way clear.

cleft

cleft stick = dilemma

"I'm in a cleft stick: I don't know whether to spend my bonus on a holiday or on a new set of clothes."

clever

See: clever dick.

cliff

cliff-hanger = happening/story with an unpredictable ending

"The election will be a cliff-hanger this time, with both major parties attracting equal support."

click

click into place = suddenly become clear (in understanding)

"Once I'd got the last piece of data the whole problem clicked into place."

click with somebody = spontaneously become firm friends or lovers

"Tina and Paul seemed to click the first day they met."

climb

climb down = withdraw (an untenable opinion/statement)

"In the face of the new evidence he had to climb down and admit he had

social climber = somebody who advances his/her position by associating with people of influence

"Caruthers cultivates the friendship of anybody in the aristocracy; he's the worst sort of social climber."

See also: climb/jump onto the bandwagon.

clinch

clinch a deal = finalize an agreement

"We were able to clinch the deal by offering to deliver the goods a week earlier than our competitors."

cling

cling on like a limpet/grim death = hold on to something with determination

"I finally got a free pass to the ground and I'm going to cling on to it like grim death."

clip

clipped speech = staccato way of talking

"I could tell from her clipped speech that she probably learned her English in South Africa."

clip the wings of somebody = curtail/limit somebody's powers

"The new manager alienated all the staff with his rearranged schedules, but the production director soon clipped his wings and put us back on the old ones."

clip somebody's ear = slap somebody on the side of the face (literally or figuratively)

"He was so over-confident of his ability that he needed a good clip round the ear to remind him of his inexperience."

cloak

cloak and dagger = secret/surreptitious

"I believe Karen did some sort of cloak and dagger work for the Foreign Office when she was younger."

under the cloak of = under the pretence of

"Under the cloak of bidding for a contract, I was able to find out quite a lot about their future business plans."

clock

against the clock = under time pressure

"We worked all night against the clock to finish the job on time."

beat the clock = finish a task earlier than expected

"The work went well and we beat the clock, finishing nearly two hours before the deadline."

clock on/off = record the time of arrival at/departure from work

"We have to clock on by half past seven and can't clock off before five o'clock."

like clockwork = smoothly, without a hitch

"They took us to the airport, whisked us straight on a plane, and had a car waiting for us at the other end; the whole operation ran like clockwork."

put/set/turn the clock back = return to former (often outmoded) ways

"I wish I could put the clock back and re-live my schooldays; I regret not having tried harder and passed more exams."

round the clock = without break for 24 hours

"The whole group worked round the clock to complete the order on time."

watch the clock = keep a close watch on the time so as not to work any longer than absolutely necessary

"Nigel watches the clock and always leaves work at exactly 5.30, whether or not he has completed his day's allocation."

See also: regular as clockwork.

close

at close quarters = near

"The car looked fine until I saw it at close quarters, when the rust marks were clearly visible."

close call/shave = near miss

"Joe had a close call when his motorbike nearly collided with a lorry."

closed book = unknown, undiscovered

"Nuclear physics is a closed book to me."

close down = shut (for good)

"Our local cinema is closing down at the end of the week, and is going to be turned into a Bingo hall."

close-fisted = mean

"There's no point in asking Horace for a donation; you know how close-fisted he is."

closed shop = place of work at which employees have to belong to a trade union as a condition of employment

"You can't get a job at the new factory unless you hold a union card ñ it's a closed shop."

close in (up)on = surround

"It was horrible to see the mob close in upon their victim."

close on = very nearly

"His new house must be worth close on 200,000 pounds."

close ranks = act together defensively

"The trade unions closed ranks and agreed to co-operate to oppose the new legislation."

close season = time during which fishing/hunting for certain species is not allowed, extended to mean also the period of the year during which a

"He plays international football for England and cricket for a minor county during the close season."

close up = move nearer together, or shut (as a verb); or near (hyphenated, as an adjective)
"Those pictures over the fireplace look better now you've closed them up."
"Please put those things away and close up the cupboard doors."
"I took a wonderful close-up photograph of a butterfly."

close with = grapple with
"He turned and closed with his assailant, and eventually disarmed him."

See also: behind closed doors; close the door to; close to home.

cloth

cloth ears = said of somebody who ignores/refuses to listen
"Come on, cloth ears, that's twice I've asked you to help."

respect for the cloth = respect for the clergy
"The vicar addressed the crowd but they showed no respect for the cloth and heckled him just as much as the other speakers."

man of the cloth = member of the clergy
"The priest offered his help in an informal capacity, not as a man of the cloth."

sackcloth and ashes = state of remorse/penitence
"Jacob will have to go to his wife in sackcloth and ashes and apologize for his behaviour the other day."

clothing

wolf in sheep's clothing = somebody who appears to be harmless but is in fact dangerous
"He joined the party and turned out to be a wolf in sheep's clothing because he was sent to infiltrate our group for the extreme right wingers."

cloud

cloud cuckoo land = ideal/perfect dream world
"Wendy never makes a practical suggestion; she seems to live in cloud cuckoo land."

be/have one's head in the clouds = day-dreaming
"It's about time Leonard got his head out of the clouds and did some work!"

cast a cloud over = have a depressing influence on
"His miserable manner cast a cloud over the whole proceedings."

every cloud has a silver lining = consolation can always be found in every misfortune
"I was sorry to hear you'd been ill, but remember every cloud has a silver lining."

on cloud nine = in a state of euphoria/happiness
"Maria's been on cloud nine ever since she got engaged."

under a cloud = under suspicion/distrusted
"I hope they soon find out who's been stealing stock; the whole department feels under a cloud at the moment."

wait till the clouds roll by = wait until circumstances improve
"We'll have to wait until the clouds roll by before we can afford another holiday."

clover

in clover = happy and prosperous
"If only I could win the lottery I'd be in clover for the rest of my life!"

club

club together = combine finances/ resources

"The staff clubbed together to buy the canteen manageress a leaving present."

in the (pudding) club = pregnant

"Jane's only been married a couple of months and she's already in the club."

join the club! = expression of sympathy in mutual adversity/bad luck

"You failed your driving test? Join the club! I failed mine twice."

clue

have no/not a clue = have no idea/ inkling

"My car has broken down and I haven't a clue what's wrong with it."

clutch

clutch at a straw/straws = make a desperate (and usually unsuccessful) attempt

"Jim's making one last attempt to raise enough funds to save his business, but I'm afraid he's only clutching at straws and will not be successful."

coach

drive a coach and horses through = discredit/evade easily

"The new licensing regulations are very loosely defined, you can easily drive a coach and horses through them."

slow coach = somebody who is reluctant/tardy

"Come on, slow coach; catch up with the others!"

coals

carry coals to Newcastle = take something to where it is superfluous

"Vincent has such a good stock of wine that taking a bottle when you visit him is like carrying coals to Newcastle."

haul over the coals = discipline/rebuke for a wrongdoing

"The boss hauled me over the coals for that mistake I made last week."

coast

See: coast is clear.

coat

be dragged by one's coat tails = be forced to do something (reluctantly)

"I was dragged by my coat tails and made to go to see the new film, even though I knew I wouldn't enjoy it."

cut one's coat according to one's cloth = do only what one has the resources for

"I could only afford to buy a three-year-old car, but you have to cut your coat according to your cloth."

hang on somebody's coat tails = associate with a successful colleague in order to further one's own progress

"By hanging on to the manager's coat tails she was able to get the job of supervisor."

trail one's coat = try to pick a quarrel with somebody

"Mike is always trailing his coat in an attempt to have a showdown with William."

cobwebs

blow the cobwebs away = refresh oneself (in the open air)

"I've been sitting at this desk for five hours. I think I'll go for a walk around the block to blow the cobwebs away."

cock

be cock-a-hoop = exultant/triumphant

"Janice has been all cock-a-hoop since she passed her final exams."

cock and bull story = unbelievably exaggerated account
“Victor arrived late and told us some cock and bull story about his train catching fire.”
cock a snook = disdainfully defy
“Peter is probably an anarchist at heart ñ he’s always cocking a snook at authority.”
cock-eyed = illogical/impractical
“Anthea had this cock-eyed scheme for raising money by holding a balloon race.”
cock of the rock/walk = somebody who (arrogantly) dominates others
“Julia has been cock of the rock ever since she got her promotion.”
cocksure = (over)confident
“My father is so cocksure, he won’t even admit he’s capable of making a mistake.”
cock up = bungling error
“Terry made a right cock up of painting his house ñ it looks a mess.”
go off at half cock = begin before everything is ready
“John went off at half cock and started unloading the van before we had cleared space to put the things in.”
knock into a cocked hat = be much better than
“Mary is so proud of her new car but Janet’s knocks it into a cocked hat.”
live like fighting cocks = live well (on good food)
“The Jones family live like fighting cocks ever since he got that new well-paid job at the ministry.”
take a cockshot at = make a wild throw at
“That white cat was scratching around in my onion bed again and so I took a cockshot at it with a lump of earth.”
See also: cock an eye at.

cockles
warm the cockles of one’s heart = make one feel warm (emotionally or physically)
“I like a good brandy ñ it warms the cockles of your heart.”
“It warms the cockles of my heart to see how well the children get on with each other.”

cocktail
Molotov cocktail = (home-made) petrol bomb
“The local people attacked the enemy tanks in the streets using Molotov cocktails.”

coffin
coffin nail = cigarette
“Anybody got a spare coffin nail? I’m desperate for a smoke.”
nail in one’s/somebody’s coffin = one of several cumulative mistakes that contributes to one’s/somebody’s downfall
“I missed the deadline again last week; I suppose that’s another nail in my coffin.”
“That drunk-driving charge will drive another nail into his coffin, and his job must really be threatened now.”

cog
cog in the machine = somebody who makes an apparently insignificant contribution to a large scheme/organization
“I’m one of dozens of people working in the stores at one of ICI’s factories, and just a cog in a very big machine.”

coil
shuffle off this mortal coil = die
“I’d like to go to Rome at least once before I shuffle off this mortal coil.”

coin

coin a phrase = invent an expression, or more usually to draw attention to a well-worn one

"Don't worry, every cloud has a silver lining, to coin a phrase."

coin it = make (much) money quickly

"Brian works overtime and has an evening job; he must be coining it."

other side of the coin = opposite aspect/ point of view

"The new houses are fine but the slums that still exist are the other side of the coin."

pay back in the same coin = reply/ retaliate in the same manner

"If he persists in making personal remarks I shall pay him back in the same coin."

coincidence

See: long arm of coincidence.

cold

cold all over/cold sweat = fright

"Her driving always brings me out in a cold sweat."

blow hot and cold = alternate between enthusiasm and disinterest

"I wish he'd make up his mind whether or not to support the new scheme, but he's still blowing hot and cold about the idea."

cold comfort = little or no satisfaction

"I've been off sick for two weeks and it's cold comfort to know that it will be another two before I'm completely recovered."

cold light of day = common sensical/ logical analysis

"Our enthusiasm for the plan faded in the cold light of day and we realized how impractical it really was."

cold shoulder = deliberately avoid

"I don't know what I've done to offend Doreen but she gave me the cold shoulder when we met accidentally in town."

cold steel = edged weapons

"We fixed bayonets and the enemy soon ran off at the sight of cold steel."

cold storage = safe keeping

"We had to put our holiday plans in cold storage until we could afford the air fare."

cold war = non-violent but hostile relationship between nations

"There are signs of an approaching end to the cold war between the United States and the Soviet Union."

in cold blood = deliberately, callously

"The bank robber drew a gun and shot the guard in cold blood."

leave one cold = be unaffected by (emotionally)

"He has a good voice but his new record leaves me cold."

left out in the cold = excluded/ignored

"Poor Alice, she always seems to be left out in the cold at parties."

pour/throw cold water onto something = be unenthusiastic about something

"The chairman poured cold water onto all our suggestions for fund raising."

stone cold = very cold

"Drink your coffee before it goes stone cold."

See also: get cold feet; make one's blood run cold; out in the cold.

collar

collar somebody = detain somebody

"Old Watson collared me on the way to the station and I had to talk to him for ten minutes before I could get away."

feel somebody's collar = make an arrest
"He's a right villain; the police have felt his collar more than once!"
hot under the collar = angry
"He gets very hot under the collar whenever he hears about cruelty to animals."
white-collar worker = office worker/ professional
"Comparatively few white-collar workers belong to a trade union."
See also: dog collar.

collision
head-on collision = collision in which a vehicle runs into the front of a vehicle approaching it
"Paul was badly injured when his car was in head-on collision with a bus."

colour
false colours = pretence
"He applied for the machinist's job under false colours because he has absolutely no experience of handling machine tools."
give/lend colour to = corroborate/ support
"You can never reach him by phone at home these days, which probably lends colour to the rumour that he has left his wife."
local colour = background knowledge
"The description of the town lacked any local colour that would have let you know what it's like to live there."
nail one's colours to the mast = commit publicly (to a point of view)
"He decided to make politics his career and nailed his colours to the mast of Socialism."
off colour = unwell
"I'm sorry not to have contacted you sooner but I've been off colour for the last few days."
paint in glowing colours = exaggerate the advantages/benefits of something
"Her account of her trip was painted in glowing colours but it couldn't have been all that pleasant because it rained the whole time she was there."
see the colour of (somebody's) money = insist on a down payment or proof that money is available before supplying goods/services
"If David is buying your car I suggest you see the colour of his money before parting with it."
show oneself in one's true colours = reveal oneself as one really is
"Although he pretends to be well-bred he showed himself in his true colours the other day when he dropped that weight on his foot and swore like a trooper."
with flying colours = in triumph/very successfully
"Thora passed all her exams with flying colours."
See also: colour bar.

column
dodge the column = avoid duty/work
"I've noticed that Sam always dodges the column when the nasty jobs come round."
fifth column = group of collaborators/ saboteurs
"There seems to be a fifth column within the party which leaks its plans to the opposition."
See also: agony column.

comb
go through something with a fine-tooth comb = thoroughly examine/search something

"The customs men went through our luggage with a fine-tooth comb."

come

come about = happen/occur
"I don't know how it came about but I've got a dent in the rear of my car."

come across = find/meet (accidentally)
"We were feeling thirsty when we came across this charming little café alongside the river."

come again = pardon
"Come again, I didn't hear what you said first time."

come along = hurry up
"Come along, children, you will be late for school."

come away = break off/dislodge
"The handle of the cup came away in my hand."

come away empty handed = achieve nothing
"He asked for a donation but went away empty handed."

come back = remember, or return
"I remember, it all comes back to me."
"Thanks for visiting me, and please come back soon."

come-back = return to fame/prominence
"She retired from the stage ten years ago but is making a come-back in the new production at the Globe theatre."

come by = acquire/obtain
"Where did you come by that new coat?"

come down = reduce (verb), or loss of position/status (noun)
"They now put fewer biscuits in the packet so what it really comes down to is a hidden price increase."
"He used to be Managing Director of his own company so it must be quite a come down for him to go and work for somebody else."

come down on = discipline/rebuke
"The only way to treat vandals is to come down on them hard."

come forward = volunteer
"Will anybody who is willing to help please come forward."

come good = prove (eventually) to be helpful/talented/successful
"Our team was struggling, but the strikers came good in the second half and scored three goals."

come hell or high water = no matter what happens
"Don't worry; I'll be there, come hell or high water."

come hither = flirtatious/seductive
"Did you see that come hither look she gave me?"

come in for = become subject to/receive
"The plan for a new ring road has come in for a lot of criticism."

come in handy = prove to be useful
"I should keep those pieces of wood, they may come in handy."

come into = inherit
"Charles will come into a lot of money when his father dies."

come into force = become operational
"The new regulations come into force next week."

come into one's own = show at one's best
"The two cars were equally matched at first but once they went onto rough ground the vehicle with the four-wheel drive came into its own."

come of = result from
"It's hard to predict what will come of these modifications."

come off = succeed
"It's difficult to guarantee that the trick will come off every time."

come off badly/well = fail/succeed
"The champion came off badly in his first match with the new player."

"All our theatre club's productions usually come off well."

come off second best = lose

"He played Tony at darts but came off second best."

come on to = begin/start to

"We'd better hurry, it's coming on to snow."

come out with = say

"Rose comes out with the strangest remarks at times."

come over = affect, or become, or make an impression, or visit

"Something came over him and he behaved most irrationally."

"It was stuffy in the room and I came over all faint."

"Adrian comes over very well as a salesman."

"Why don't you come over to our place next weekend."

come right = have a happy/successful outcome

"The characters in the film disliked each other at first but it all came right in the end."

come round/to = regain consciousness

"He received a blow on the head and it took him several minutes to come round."

come to an arrangement = agree

"Don't worry about price ñ I'm sure we can come to some sort of arrangement."

come to blows = fight

"They were shouting insults at each other and it wasn't long before they came to blows."

come to grief = meet a disaster

"The racing driver was going too fast and he came to grief on the second bend."

come to light = be discovered/revealed

"Once the police began to look into her past, all sorts of things came to light."

come to pass = happen

"The plan has been approved but goodness knows when it will come to pass."

come to terms with = accept

"It has taken Arthur a long time to come to terms with his disability."

come true = actually occur

"I won 25,000 on the Premium Bonds ñ it's like a dream come true."

come under = classified with, or subordinate to

"Lions come under the cat family."

"Now he's my boss yet he came under me at our last job."

come unstuck = fail, or encounter an unexpected problem

"Lionel drives far too fast and one of these days he's going to really come unstuck."

come upon = find

"We turned a corner and came upon an old country inn."

come up to = equal

"Her new record doesn't come up to her last one."

come up to scratch = meet a standard

"He's a very personable young man but his work doesn't really come up to scratch."

come up with = get level with, or produce/suggest

"The car came up with the lorry as it climbed the steep hill."

"Peggy has come up with this fantastic idea for a party."

come what may = no matter what

"I don't care if it does rain, I'm going come what may."

have it coming to one = deserve what is about to happen

"Somebody finally got fed up with

Micky's insults and punched him on the nose; he's had it coming to him for years."

how come? = how did that occur?
"How come you never learned to read properly?"

if it comes to that = in that event
"If it comes to that I can always service my car myself."

it comes to this = summarized
"Basically it comes to this: how much will it cost?"

not know whether one is coming or going = be confused
"I had so many queries at once yesterday that I didn't know whether I was coming or going."

See also: come back to earth; come down; come home to roost; come of age; come out in the wash; come out on top; come to nothing; come to rest; come/turn up trumps; coming; easy come, easy go.

comedy

black comedy = drama/story that has a comic treatment of a tragic theme
"The Life of Brian was a black comedy about the life of Christ."

comfort

comfort station = public lavatory
"Please stop the car at the next comfort station we come to."

creature comforts = food, clothing, and other providers of physical (as opposed to emotional) well-being
"Diana's new flat has a washing machine, waste disposal, dish washer, microwave oven, central heating and all the creature comforts."

crumb of comfort = slight consolation
"England's win at cricket was the only crumb of comfort in a week of consistently bad news for British sport."

comforter

Job's comforter = somebody whose advice/comments make one feel worse rather than bring comfort in adversity
"I was out of work and the man at the Job Centre told me that unemployment is likely to continue to rise in this area ñ he's a right Job's comforter."

coming

have something coming to one = about to experience something (deserved/ inevitable)
"They're going to charge Peter with falsifying his accounts, but he's had it coming to him for years."

not know whether one is coming or going = be in a state of great confusion/uncertainty
"I'm trying to do three things at once and I don't know whether I'm coming or going."

command

at one's command = within one's grasp/ knowledge
"The Vicar can always find an apt quotation because he's got the whole Bible at his command."

comment

no comment = I do not wish/refuse to say anything
"The Prime Minister's standard reply to controversial questions is No Comment."

commentary

running commentary = "live" account/ commentary made while a (sporting) event is actually taking place

"Raymond Glendenning had the remarkable ability of remembering every player's name while giving a running commentary on a football match."

commission

kick-back commission = (monetary) reward given as an inducement for placing a contract/work with an associate

"The managing director promised that if I place the work with his company he'll give me a generous kick-back commission."

in/into commission = become functional/ operational

"The journey to York is much quicker now that the new high-speed trains have come into commission."

on commission = (earnings) for sales made/services rendered

"Door-to-door salesmen usually have a low basic wage and earn most of their money on commission."

out of commission = not operational

"My car has been out of commission for a week while being repaired."

common

by common consent = by a majority agreement

"By common consent the staff agreed to complain about the working conditions in the new offices."

common as muck = with very poor manners

"You shouldn't be surprised at Sheila's impolite behaviour ñ she's as common as muck."

common ground = area of agreement/ mutual interest

"Bill and Ben never get into a prolonged discussion because there is no common ground between them."

common knowledge = something that is generally/widely know

"It's common knowledge that our boss is having an affair with his typist."

common or garden = very ordinary

"Jason prepares all his accounts using a microcomputer but I do mine with common or garden pencil and paper."

common origin = single source

"It's interesting that the words guardian and warden have a common origin."

common parlance = ordinary manner of speaking

"The local council are advertising for a Rodent Operator, which in common parlance means a rat catcher."

common touch = behaviour similar to that of ordinary people

"Although she married an earl, Susan never lost the common touch and still calls round occasionally for a chat and a cup of tea."

in common = of mutual interest, or similarity

"These modern pop tunes have nothing in common with the old music hall songs we used to sing when I was a girl."

in common with = like/in agreement with

"I must say, in common with Helen, that I strongly oppose the proposal."

company

bad company = disreputable associates

"He goes round in bad company and one day he'll be in trouble with the police."

good company = somebody who is entertaining/pleasant to be with

"I like going out with Hal because he's such good company."

having company for dinner = entertaining guests for a meal
"Janice says she can't come on Sunday because they've got company for dinner."

in company with = like/in agreement with
"I hate snakes, in company with bats and spiders."

keep company with = be the regular (sexual) partner of
"Anne now keeps company with Roger, although he is not yet divorced from his legal wife."

keep somebody company = remain with somebody who would otherwise be alone
"Alice came round to keep me company while my husband was out fishing."

know a person by the company he/she keeps = judge somebody by his/her associates
"Mick goes round with a group of leather-jacketed bike riders, and you can always know somebody by the company he keeps."

part company = leave/separate
"We were listening to some music and I didn't part company with Len until after midnight last night."
"I'll have to get my briefcase mended, the handle has parted company with the rest of it."

present company excepted = excluding those present
"I think that most people are politically naive, present company excepted of course."

See also: two's company (but three's a crowd).

compare

beyond compare = unequalled
"Her writing ability is beyond compare."

compare notes (with) = talk to somebody else about matters of common interest
"Why don't you compare notes with William before you go to Paris? He's just been there and knows all the best places to visit."

in comparison with = compared with
"I don't know what you're complaining of ñ you're rich in comparison with most people in Africa."

complete

complete with = including
"He bought the whole machine, complete with spares, for under fifty pounds."

complex

Oedipus complex = sexual love of a boy/man for his mother
"He's always buying his mother expensive gifts, and I'm beginning to wonder if he's got an Oedipus complex."

compliment

back-/left-handed compliment, or a two-edged compliment = ironical comment that sounds like a compliment but is not
"The manager said that any company would be lucky if they could get me to work for them ñ a back-handed compliment if ever I heard one!"

complimentary tickets = free tickets (to a theatre, etc.)
"Jack's got two complementary tickets for the Cup Final, so guess where we're going next Saturday!"

compliments of the season = Christmas greetings

"May I wish you the compliments of the season and a Happy New Year."

fish for compliments = solicit favourable comments

"There's no need to fish for compliments ñ I really do like your new hair style."

give one's compliments = express one's good wishes

"Give your father my compliments the next time you see him."

pay a compliment = praise, or show appreciation/respect

"She paid me the compliment of saying that I was the best dancer there."

return the compliment = offer back a favour in return for one received

"Thank you for inviting us round for dinner, we really enjoyed ourselves. We would like to return the compliment, and ask you to come to us next Saturday."

compound

compound the felony = make a difficulty even worse

"I ran out of petrol and then, to compound the felony, I found that I'd got a flat tyre."

computer

See: computer bug.

concern

as far as I am concerned = in my opinion, which I know you will ignore/not take into account

"You go into business with him if you like, but as far as I'm concerned the man is not to be trusted."

going concern = fully operational business

"Dad's decided to get rid of his shop and sell it as a going concern."

conclusion

arrive at/come to the conclusion = decide (having weighed the evidence)

"I've known Steve for a year now but I have reluctantly come to the conclusion that he's a fool."

foregone conclusion = predetermined outcome (but often only in the opinion of the speaker)

"It was a foregone conclusion that Newcastle would beat Chelsea in the Cup Final."

jump to a conclusion = prematurely decide the outcome/significance of something

"My car just happened to be parked outside Belinda's flat and you immediately jumped to the conclusion that I was seeing her without my wife's knowledge."

condition

in condition = fit/healthy

"You have to be in condition to play any sport seriously these days."

on condition that = based on the agreement/restriction that

"I'll help you paint your house on condition that you help me dig my garden."

out of condition = unfit

"I'd willingly come on a five-mile walk with you but I'm afraid I've been out of condition since my accident."

See also: in a delicate condition; in mint condition.

conference

round-table conference = discussion that involves everybody with a relevant point of view

"Before we decide where to go for the outing let's have a round-table conference with all the members of the club."

confess

I must confess = I freely admit
"I don't know the way to the hotel, but I must confess this is the first time I've been to Plymouth."

confidence

confidence trick = deception that takes advantage of somebody's belief in the honesty of the deceiver
"The second-hand car I bought from the dealer down the road looked fine but turned out to be unroadworthy; I was yet another victim of a confidence trick."

in (strict) confidence = on condition that one does not reveal what one is told
"I'll tell you in strict confidence that Roger and Gill are going to get divorced."

take into one's confidence = trust somebody with a secret
"Frank took me into his confidence before he resigned and told me he was thinking of changing his job."

See also: vote of confidence.

conjure

conjure with = become involved with/ consider/conceive
"Higher mathematics is something I'd rather not conjure with."
"Nobody in his right mind would conjure with the prospect of a Communist government in Britain."

name to conjure with = name of somebody important
"After the ceremony we are invited to lunch with the Archbishop of Canterbury ñ and there's a name to conjure with!"

connection

in connection with = concerning
"The travel agents wrote to us in connection with our holiday booking."

in that connection = referring/relating to something (specified)
"Yes, I know quite a lot about the history of bicycles and I'm glad you've asked me to help in that connection."

fail to make/miss the connection = fail to appreciate an association (of ideas/ thoughts)
"I didn't realize he'd suffered during the war; he told us he was born in the early 1940s and lived in France, but I failed to make the connection."

conscience

conscience money = payment/reward given to somebody who has betrayed a principle/trust
"He's a member of the other team and secretly let us know who his side were going to field against us at the next match, so we gave him ten pounds conscience money."

have on one's conscience = retain guilt about
"I have to admit that once I stood back and let somebody else take the blame for one of my mistakes, but I've had it on my conscience ever since."

in all conscience = to be completely honest
"Thanks for your generous offer, but in all conscience I can't accept more than the going rate for the job."

consent

See: age of consent.

consequence

of little/no consequence = ignorable/ unimportant
"Don't worry what the neighbours will think, it's of no consequence."

of some consequence = important
"Since he gained a seat on the board,

Charles has become a man of some consequence."

take the consequences = accept the blame/results

"If you will experiment with soft drugs you must take the consequences."

See also: abide by the consequences.

Conservative

true-blue Conservative = somebody committed (to the point of bigotry) to the politics/policies of the Conservative Party

"Fanshawe is a true-blue Conservative ñ he'd vote for Mrs Thatcher even if she threatened to nationalize golf!"

consideration

in consideration of = taking into account

"They paid me a small bonus in consideration of my years of service with the company."

small consideration = insignificant fee

"It's very cheap staying in Tunis; for a small consideration you can hire a guide for half a day, and he'll show you round the whole of Carthage."

take into consideration = allow for/take account of

"She's done very well really, when you take her age into consideration."

under consideration = being thought about

"Your proposal is under consideration by the committee, and we will let you know what it decides."

construction

put a false construction on = lie about/ misinterpret (deliberately)

"I told the authorities what happened, but they put a false construction on my statement and had me charged with shoplifting."

contact

come in(to) contact with = encounter/ meet

"You seldom come into contact with Scotsmen in this part of the country."

contempt

bring into contempt = fail to show (due) respect for

"What really annoys me about the behaviour of British football hooligans when they're abroad is the way they bring the whole of our country into contempt."

contempt of court = failure to obey, or interference with the running of, a court of law

"After twice warning a heckler in the public gallery, the judge convicted him of contempt of court."

familiarity breeds contempt = a long friendship can develop into acrimony/ disrespect

"They had been partners for so long that they began to take each other for granted and eventually began to disagree on important issues; still, they say that familiarity breeds contempt."

hold in contempt = show a disrespectful attitude towards

"When a newly introduced piece of legislation is held in contempt by the general public, one is entitled to ask whether it is good legislation."

content

to one's heart's content = as much as one desires

"We went fruit picking and we could eat strawberries to our heart's content."

contention
bone of contention = subject that always leads to an argument
"The right of access between our houses has been a bone of contention between my neighbour and me ever since I moved in."

contractor
cowboy contractor = tradesman who uses unskilful methods and substandard materials
"We had these cowboy contractors to paint the outside of the house, but it needed doing again within a few months."

contradiction
contradiction in terms = conflicting/ illogical statement
"You can't call a hedgehog cuddly ñ that's a contradiction in terms!"

contrary
contrary to expectations = not what was expected
"Contrary to expectations, Glen remained sober for the whole of the party."
on/to the contrary = it is the opposite
"Don't think we don't want to come ñ on the contrary, we'd love to but we have a previous engagement."

convenience
all modern conveniences (sometimes abbreviated to all mod cons) = appliances/facilities that allow a high standard of living
"Their new flat has central heating, a washing machine, fitted kitchen ñ in fact, all the modern conveniences."
at one's convenience = whenever it suits one
"Please call round at your convenience and we'll discuss the matter."
at one's earliest convenience = as soon as it suits one
"I'm quite willing to discuss the matter at your earliest convenience."
make a convenience of = take advantage of/use (for selfish purposes)
"It's obvious she wasn't really fond of you, she was just making a convenience of you because you drove her to and from work each day."
public convenience = public lavatory
"What this town lacks is a public convenience in the shopping centre."

conversation
conversation piece = unusual object that stimulates discussion
"Ed had a large portrait of a nude over his fireplace which he could always rely on to be a conversation piece with anybody who came to visit him."

converted
preach to the converted = put a point of view to somebody who already holds it
"You don't have to tell the Welsh about the attractions of rugby football ñ you're preaching to the converted!"

conviction
carry conviction = be convincing/ persuasive
"The councillor's proposal didn't succeed because his argument failed to carry conviction."
have the courage of one's convictions = have unshakeable belief in one's point of view
"You must have the courage of your convictions and tell your father that you think he's making a mistake."

cook
cook somebody's goose = spoil somebody's chances of success
"I'll soon cook his goose if he thinks he's going to the boss behind my back."
cook the books = falsify the accounts
"By cooking his books Jim didn't pay any corporation tax at all last year."
cook up = invent
"She cooked up some story about having to stay at home to look after her aged mother."
what's cooking? = what is happening?
"I've heard rumours about a take-over bid; do you know what's cooking?"

cookie
that's the way the cookie crumbles = that is the inevitable (undesirable) result
"I'm afraid it's your turn to work late again, but that's the way the cookie crumbles."

cool
cool as a cucumber = calm/self-assured
"You can always rely on Louise in an emergency; no matter what happens, she stays as cool as a cucumber."
cool, calm and collected = in total control of one's feelings
"No matter what happens, when other people begin to panic Walter always stays cool, calm and collected."
cool down = become less angry/emotional
"Cool down; there's no need to lose your temper over such a trivial matter."
"I thought you'd never cool down after what Harold said to you."
cool it = become less angry/emotional immediately
"Stop fighting you boys! Now cool it!"
cool one's heels = be kept waiting
"I had to cool my heels for nearly an hour before the boss would see me."
keep a cool head/keep one's cool = remain calm
"It's a distinct advantage around here to keep a cool head when things begin to go wrong."
"I try to keep my cool even when the people around me are hurling insults at each other."
See also: cool customer; cool hand; lose one's cool/rag/wool; play it cool.

coop
fly the coop = escape
"The police are searching the moors for three prisoners who flew the coop yesterday."

cop
cop it = get into trouble (for a misdemeanour)
"You'll cop it when your father finds out what you've done."
cop shop = police station
"I've got to go down the cop shop and show them my driving licence."
fair cop = just arrests/discovery (of a wrongdoer)
"Glen was stopped by the police for speeding but it was a fair cop because he was doing over 90 at the time."
not much cop = not very good/not worthy of its reputation
"Jan tells me that the new disco is not much cop."

copy
See: fair copy.

copybook
blot one's copybook = make a serious blunder (which affects one's record/reputation)

"You really blotted your copybook when you accused the manager of being a fool."

core

hard core = unshakeable central group
"We hope to be able to change the regulations despite a hard core of objectors who want to leave things as they are."

to the core = thoroughly
"Many of the men in the new revolutionary government are dishonest to the core."

corn

tread on somebody's corns = usurp (somebody's authority/position)
"It was difficult to go in and sort out their management's inefficiencies without treading on somebody's corns."

corner

all the corners of the earth = everywhere
"Interpol have searched all the corners of the earth for the elusive hijackers."

corner the market = buy/control the major source of supply of a commodity
"Alex bought the ailing company's entire stock of screwdrivers and cornered the market ñ now every retailer has to buy from him."

cut corners = achieve a required result by making economies in materials/ time
"Our competitors must be cutting corners somewhere to produce the goods for less than we can."

drive somebody into a corner = force somebody into a situation from which he/she cannot retreat
"At the next meeting I intend to drive the treasurer into a corner and then ask him to account publicly for the overspend on his expenses allowance."

in a tight corner = in an awkward situation (from which it is difficult to escape)
"I got into a tight corner financially and had to sell my car to pay back what I owed."

knock the corners off somebody = show somebody how to correct his/her ineptitude/inexperience
"I've told the new lad to go and work with Arthur, who will soon knock the corners off him."

out of the corner of one's eye = (looking at something) indirectly/ surreptitiously
"I entered the room behind him, but he must have seen me out of the corner of his eye because he immediately turned round and called me over to him."

round the corner = nearby
"Let's go to the Red Lion, it's only round the corner."

turn the corner = begin to improve
"My mother's been very ill but she turned the corner last week and is now recovering fast."

See also: hole-and-corner/hole-in-the-corner affair.

corner-stone

lay the corner-stone = establish
"The dictator used military discipline to lay the corner-stone of a new police system."

corrected

stand corrected = admit a mistake
"Thank you for pointing out I was wrong; I stand corrected."

cost

at all costs = no matter what the price
"We've got to finish this job by tomorrow at all costs!"

at the cost of = at the expense/loss of
"We went the long way round to see some of the countryside at the cost of an extra hour's travelling time."

count the cost = estimate the likely cost (in terms of risk/time, etc.) of an undertaking
"She didn't count the cost before agreeing to the plan, and now she regrets her decision."

to one's cost = to one's loss
"It was a very unsound investment, as he's now found out to his cost."

See also: cost a packet.

cottage

cottage hospital = small (country) hospital with very limited facilities
"They took him first to the cottage hospital but they had to no heart unit and he had to be transferred by ambulance to the main hospital in the county town."

cottage industry = small-scale manufacturing/production (typically in somebody's home)
"The Robertsons started making pottery as a cottage industry but their business has now expanded so much they have had to hire several workers and rent premises on the industrial estate."

cotton

cotton on to = understand
"Angela soon cottons on to each new job you explain to her."

wrap somebody (up) in cotton wool = be overprotective
"There's no harm in letting Jimmy go out to play in the snow ñ you can't wrap him up in cotton wool all his life!"

cough

cough up = pay (a debt)
"It's about time Terry coughed up for a round of drinks, he hasn't bought any all evening."

cough it up = speak out
"Come on, cough it up! What are you trying to say?"

cough to = admit (a misdemeanour/mistake)
"When the police arrested Bill for housebreaking he coughed to five other burglaries he'd done."

counsel

keep one's own counsel = keep one's views to oneself
"I tend to keep my own counsel until I know what everybody else thinks."

count

count against = be disadvantageous
"Her prison record is bound to count against her when she applies for a job."

count for = be worth
"All that extra effort counts for nothing now that they have cancelled the whole project."

count me in/out = include/exclude me
"If you're organizing a trip to the pop festival you can count me in."
"No thanks, count me out; I've had enough to drink."

count on = rely on
"You can always count on Maria to lay on an excellent meal."

does not count = should be/is excluded/

"The value of my company pension depends on my years of service, although the time I was away in the forces doesn't count."

out for the count = deeply asleep/unconscious

"I was so tired after all that gardening that I was out for the count for ten whole hours last night."

See also: count for nothing; count one's blessings; count the cost; stand up and be counted.

countenance

keep one's countenance = not betray one's feelings/remain calm

"Tony's talk was well received and he was able to keep his countenance even after he realized that his flies were undone."

counter

over the counter = from stock at a retailer/shop

"The difficulty with maintaining an old car is that so few spare parts are available over the counter."

run counter to = disagree with

"I agreed to take part in the scheme, although its objectives run counter to what I really believe to be best."

under the counter = secretly/surreptitiously (of something not openly available)

"Those cigars I prefer are still in short supply and I can't buy them anywhere locally, although my father was able to get me some under the counter."

country

appeal/go to the country = seek re-election (of a government)

"A proposal for a change in the law was defeated in Parliament, and so the Government decided to go to the country and let the electorate indicate its views about the issue."

country cousin = (unsophisticated) person who lives in the country

"The disco is always crowded on a Saturday night when those country cousins come into town from the surrounding villages."

in one's line of country = within one's competence/experience

"I'll willingly help you; painting walls is just in my line of country."

courage

muster/pluck/screw/summon up one's courage, or take one's courage in both hands = force oneself to attempt something (that one feels incapable of doing or that involves danger/risk)

"I hate heights but I screwed up all my courage and walked across the new suspension bridge over the River Humber."

"I really lack sufficient experience, but I took my courage in both hands and applied for the vacant manager's job."

See also: Dutch courage; have the courage of one's convictions.

course

adopt a course (of action) = commit to (a way of) doing something

"The unions have adopted a course that's bound to bring them into conflict with the management."

change course = alter one's direction

"We've got to pursue the plan, and anyway it's too late to change course now."

continue/embark on a course (of action) = pursue/decide on a way of doing something

"If the company continues on this course it's heading for financial trouble."
"He's so obstinate that, having embarked on a course of action, he'll never change his mind no matter what happens."
crash course = intensive programme of training
"I must take a crash course in German before I go on holiday."
in (the) course of = being/in process of
"The shop will remain open while it is in the course of redecoration."
in due course = eventually
"I've ordered the goods and the shopkeeper says he'll put through a request and have them in stock in due course."
run its course = proceed to its inevitable/logical conclusion
"There's no treatment for that virus infection, the doctor can only let it run its course."
stay the course = endure/persist
"That new labourer is not very strong and I doubt if he'll stay the course."
See also: as a matter of course; par for the course; steer a middle course.

court
laughed out of court = ridiculed
"Any request for more funds will be laughed out of court."
hold court = converse with less important people
"The supervisor holds court to all the trainees at the beginning of each working day."
pay court to = solicit attention/favours
"It's sickening the way Judy pays court to the managing director all the time."
put oneself out of court = take an action that excludes one from consideration
"At the job interview I admitted that I haven't any formal qualifications and immediately put myself out of court."
See also: have the ball in one's court; kangaroo court; rule something out of court.

cousin
See: country cousin.

Coventry
send somebody to Coventry = refuse to speak to somebody (as a punishment for a misdemeanour)
"Ian was sent to Coventry by his workmates for refusing to join the union."

cover
cover one's tracks = hide/remove incriminating evidence
"I regretted sending that memo to the boss but was able to cover my tracks by removing it from his in-tray before he got to work."
cover up = hide (something incriminating)
"The authorities were able to cover up what really happened at the incident."
take cover = seek protection
"It rained so hard we had to take cover in a shop doorway."
under cover = indoors/protected
"It looked like rain so the committee decided to hold the baby show under cover."
"It's advisable to stay under cover when hundred of starlings start forming flocks at dusk."
See also: break cover; cover a lot of (the) ground; cover/include a multitude of sins.

cow

milch cow = source of easy profit
"Too many people regard the Social Security as a milch cow from which they can get an inexhaustible supply of money without having to work for it."

sacred cow = something held in high esteem and beyond criticism
"The Public School system is often seen to be the sacred cow of the upper classes."

till the cows come home = for ever
"You can wait till the cows come home but I won't change my mind!"

crab

catch a crab = make a clumsy rowing stroke by dipping the oar too deep in the water
"The two boats were level until one of the Oxford crew caught a crab and let Cambridge into the lead."

crack

crack a bottle = open a bottle and drink the contents
"It's my birthday; let's crack a bottle of champagne."

crack a crib = break into a house to steal
"The lads say they're going to crack a crib on that new expensive housing estate."

crack of doom = end of the world
"I bet you that Steve will still be wearing that old jacket at the crack of doom."

crack the whip = apply authority (severely/vigorously)
"The captain will have to crack the whip if his side's performance is to improve enough to win the match."

crack up = break down/deteriorate mentally, or praise highly
"Cyril is going to crack up if he doesn't stop working so hard."
"In my opinion that new Japanese car is not all it's cracked up to be."

drive somebody crackers = make somebody go mad
"Turn down that radio! It's driving me crackers."

fair crack of the whip = fair opportunity/share
"All I want is a fair crack of the whip so that I can demonstrate what I can do."
"The new pay scales don't give the unskilled workers a fair crack of the whip."

get cracking = hurry up (and start)
"If we get cracking we'll finish mowing the lawn by the time the pub opens."

have a crack at = make an attempt (to)
"I'm not very good at snooker but I'm willing to have a crack at it if you want a game."

not what it's cracked up to be = not as good as is claimed
"We tried the new supermarket last week, but it's not what it's cracked up to be."

paper over the cracks = make a temporary/insubstantial repair (only to obvious defects)
"The whole system needed reorganizing, but all we could do in the time was to paper over the cracks."

See also: crack a joke.

cradle

cradle snatcher = somebody who has as a partner or who marries somebody much younger than himself/herself
"She's got a son older than her present lover, the cradle snatcher!"

from the cradle = since early childhood
"I've been able to ride a bike from the cradle."

cramp
cramp somebody's style = restrict somebody's room to demonstrate his/her ability
"The opposition spokesman is a very persuasive talker but we'll only let him speak for five minutes ñ that should cramp his style."

crash
crash out = fall (deeply) asleep
"I was so tired after working all night that I just crashed out in a chair."
See also: crash course.

crazy
be crazy about = like very much
"Linda is crazy about David Bowie."

cream
cream off = take the best part
"The company failed to grow because the directors creamed off the profits to pay themselves high salaries."
the cream of = the best of
"The cream of Britain's youth was killed in the trenches in the First World War."

create
create a stink/merry hell = make a (big) fuss
"Your mother will create merry hell if she sees that mess."

credit
a credit to = somebody whose achievements reflect favourably on somebody else
"You must be proud of your daughter's examination successes ñ she's a real credit to you."
get/take the credit for = be held (favourably) responsible for
"Thanks for your kind words, but the whole team should get the credit."
"He has an annoying habit of taking the credit for other people's achievements."
give credit for = acknowledge somebody's ability
"I'm surprised you thought the watch could be any good at that price; I gave you credit for having more common sense."
give credit to = acknowledge somebody's contribution to/praise
"I'll give all credit to them; we couldn't have done it without their help."

creek
up the creek (without a paddle) = in difficulties
"We had a puncture on the motorway and we were not carrying a spare wheel, so we were right up the creek."

creeps
give one the creeps = make one feel abhorrent/fearful
"There's something about that old tramp that gives me the creeps."
make one's flesh creep = cause a feeling of abhorrence
"Some of these new horror films make my flesh creep."

crest
on the crest of a wave = euphoric/successful
"Bernard is on the crest of a wave because he's just won the football pools."

crew

skeleton crew = minimum number of people to perform a task (that normally requires more)
"Many of the staff were off sick with the flu but we managed to keep the project going with a skeleton crew."

crib

See: crack a crib.

cricket

not cricket = dishonourable/unfair
"One of our competitors tried to sabotage our vehicles ñ and that's just not cricket."

chirpy/merry as a cricket = very lively/ jaunty
"Old Henry has been as chirpy as a cricket since he married that young girl."

crock

crock of gold = unattainable reward
"He's spent all his life searching for a crock of gold, but he'll never find it."

old crock = battered old car, or an old person
"I see you've got another car. At least you didn't have to pay much for that old crock!"
"I'm beginning to suffer from rheumatism, and at times I feel like a right old crock."

crocodile

crocodile tears = insincere sorrow/ sympathy
"I don't know how Nancy can shed crocodile tears about Philip's accident ñ she's been looking for an excuse to stop seeing him for weeks now."

Croesus

See: rich as Croesus

crop

crop up = happen/occur (unexpectedly)
"Let's take a trip to the coast and see what crops up."

come a cropper = have an accident (involving a fall), or suffer a misfortune
"Lloyd came a cropper on his bicycle and broke his leg."
"Barbara came a cropper when her business failed."

cross

bear one's cross = tolerate sorrow/ suffering
"Pat was born deaf but she bears her cross cheerfully."

have one's cross to bear = carry a heavy responsibility/sorrow
"I have to look after my aged mother, but then everybody has a cross to bear."

See also: cross one's mind; cross-purposes; cross somebody's palm with silver; cross somebody's path; cross swords with somebody; get/have one's wires crossed; keep one's fingers crossed.

cross-roads

at the cross-roads = at a point of decision
"I was at the cross-roads when I left university. I didn't know whether to follow an academic career or go into industry."

crow

as the crow flies = in a direct line
"We're only five miles from the coast as the crow flies, although it is nearly ten by the road."

crow about/over = boast
"I'm tired of hearing her crow about

winning the cup at the club's tennis tournament."

crow's feet = lines round the eyes
"She's developed a double chin and crow's feet, and is really beginning to look her age."

See also: stone me/the crows.

crowd

follow the crowd = do what everybody else does
"When it comes to fashion she just follows the crowd."

crown

crown it all = finally/in addition to everything
"We were hopelessly lost, tired, hungry and, to crown it all, it started to rain."

cruel

cruel to be kind = help somebody by using unpleasant methods
"I had to be cruel to be kind and warn him that he'd lose his job if he didn't improve his performance."

crumpet

bit of crumpet = sexually attractive young woman
"Cor! Look at that bit of crumpet who's just come in."

crunch

come to the crunch = reach the testing point
"When it comes to the crunch, you can always rely on Colin to remain calm and do exactly the right thing."

crush

have a crush on somebody = be infatuated by somebody
"My teenage daughter has got a crush on the singer George Michael."

crust

earn a crust = earn a living
"He earns a crust by writing detective stories."

upper crust = aristocracy/high ranks of society
"Her ambition is to marry a member of the upper crust."

cry

be crying out for = be in obvious need of
"This room is crying out for a new carpet."

cry down = speak badly of, disparage
"I don't think Joe is trustworthy, but I wouldn't cry him down in front of his friends."

far cry = long way
"My new flat is all right but it's a far cry from luxury."

cry for the moon = wish for the unattainable
"If you want a knighthood you might as well cry for the moon."

crying need = something needing urgent attention
"The Ethiopians have a crying need for more food immediately."

crying shame = great shame
"I think it's a crying shame that hospitals have to close some of their wards through lack of staff."

cry off = cancel a previous commitment
"Jack said he would play for our team at the weekend but he cried off at the last minute."

cry one's eyes/heart out = cry copiously
"She cried her eyes out when she heard her dog had been killed by a car."

cry out for = appeal (passionately) for/ need (desperately)
"It's a shame that, even in our affluent society, charities have to cry out for funds."

cry over spilt milk = continue to regret something that cannot be reversed
"You dropped your ring into the sea and you'll never find it now, so there's no use crying over spilt milk."

cry stinking fish = speak unfavourably about one's associates
"I didn't expect him to cry stinking fish and run down his own family like that."

cry/weep buckets = cry profusely
"When she heard about her brother's death she cried buckets."

cry wolf = call for help unnecessarily
"Susan is always crying wolf when the slightest thing goes wrong."

for crying out loud! = exclamation of annoyance/surprise
"For crying out loud! Aren't you ever going to be ready to go out?"

in full cry = at the most vigorous part of the action
"The Labour candidate will take some beating in the election now that his supporters are in full cry."

See also: cry baby; hue and cry; voice crying in the wilderness.

crystal

crystal ball = something that enables one to predict the future
"I haven't got a crystal ball so I do not know which horse is going to win the Derby."

See also: clear as crystal.

cuckoo

cuckoo in the nest = interloper, somebody who takes advantage of a friendship for personal gain
"I didn't realize when I befriended him that he'd turn out to be a cuckoo in the nest and steal my wife's affections."

See also: in cloud cuckoo land

cucumber

See: cool as a cucumber.

cudgel

cudgel one's brains = think very hard (in an attempt to remember something)
"I've cudgelled my brains all day and I still can't remember that chap's name."

take up the cudgels = lend strong support to (a cause)
"She was getting very little support for her charity until we took up the cudgels on her behalf."

cue

take one's cue from = follow somebody else's example
"If you don't know which knife and fork to use just take your cue from me."

cuff

off the cuff = unrehearsed
"He is good at giving an entertaining speech completely off the cuff."

cup

another cup of tea = a totally different matter
"I don't mind giving money towards the scheme but if you want me to help with the actual digging that's another cup of tea."

cup that cheers = alcoholic drink
"Let's go out at lunch time and round to the pub to sample the cup that cheers."

in one's cups = drunk

"Barry was really in his cups at the party last night."

nice (old) cup of tea = difficult situation
"The car has broken down again ñ that's a nice cup of tea."

not one's cup of tea = not what one likes/ prefers
"Sally wants me to go with her to a rock concert but that's definitely not my cup of tea."

one's cup is full = one is feeling very emotional/happy
"All five of my grandchildren came to see me on my birthday and my cup was full."

cupboard

cupboard love = simulated affection for personal gain
"It's all cupboard love ñ she only embraces me when she wants to borrow some money."

skeleton in the cupboard = shameful secret
"She never refers to her childhood; I wonder if she has a skeleton in the cupboard?"

cupid

play cupid = introduce a couple in the hope that they will become close friends/fall in love
"I wish my mother would stop playing cupid and inviting me round to her house to meet all the eligible bachelors of the neighbourhood."

curate

See: like the curate's egg.

cure

kill or cure = take extreme action that either resolves a difficulty or makes it much worse
"I can't get that stain out of the carpet so I think I'll try soaking it in petrol ñ it will be a case of kill or cure."

curiosity

See: curiosity killed the cat.

curl

curl up = recoil in abhorrence
"It makes me curl up whenever I see somebody picking his nose."

have somebody by the short and curlies = put somebody in an indefensible position
"The policeman had followed me down the motorway at 90 miles an hour for three miles, so that when he finally stopped me he had me by the short and curlies."

See also: make one's hair curl.

currency

acquire/gain/obtain currency = become widely known
"I'd like to know how the rumour about redundancies gained currency among the staff."

curry

curry favour = be obsequious in order to gain approval
"There's no point in trying to curry favour with the new boss, she judges everybody strictly on his or her merits."

curtain

bamboo curtain = barrier to diplomatic relations/trade between China and the Western world
"One way of increasing exports to Asia is for British companies to penetrate the bamboo curtain."

curtains for somebody = somebody's death/demise

"If Smith doesn't change his attitude and continues to insist on a confrontation with the management, then it will be curtains for him."

curtain raiser = short preliminary to the main event

"An unknown comedian did his act as a curtain raiser and I thought he was better than the main show."

draw a curtain over = hide/make secret

"I'd rather draw a curtain over what I got up to in my youth."

iron curtain = barrier to diplomatic relations/trade between the Soviet Union and the Western world

"If the Soviet Union's desire to abolish nuclear weapons is genuine, it could raise the iron curtain for evermore."

ring down the curtain = bring to an end/ conclude

"The closure of Croydon airport rang down the curtain on a historic phase in British civil aviation."

cuss

not to care a tinker's cuss = not to care at all

"I'm tired of Pat's tantrums; I don't care a tinker's cuss whether she goes out with me or not."

customer

cool customer = somebody who is aloof/ self-assured

"Anthony is a cool customer; he asked the bank manager to double his overdraft ñ and the bank agreed!"

queer/rum customer = somebody who is strange/unpredictable

"Old Tom's a rum customer, you never know what he's thinking."

rough/ugly customer = somebody with an aggressive/threatening manner

"I'd be very careful not to annoy Harry ñ he can be an ugly customer."

slippery customer = somebody who is elusive or reluctant to make a commitment

"Garfield is a slippery customer, he's twice escaped from police custody."

"You can never pin down Wendy to an exact time and place to meet, she's such a slippery customer."

tough customer = somebody with great emotional/physical strength, or who is difficult to deal with

"You have to be a tough customer to be a professional boxer."

"Their new sales manager is a tough customer, so I was particularly pleased to negotiate such a favourable price."

cut

be cut, or half cut = drunk, or nearly drunk

"It's no good trying to do business with Algernon after lunch because he's nearly always half cut by then."

cut above the rest = superior

"I prefer chateau-bottled wines because they're nearly always a cut above the rest."

cut across = contradict

"I refuse to condone fox hunting because it cuts across everything I believe about the rights of animals."

cut a dash/figure = have an (ostentatiously) elegant/fashionable appearance

"Jerry thinks he cuts quite a dash with the ladies in his new mohair suit."

cut and dried = predetermined/ unalterable

"There's no point in trying to change the arrangements ñ they're all cut and dried, as usual."

cut and run = abandon something/ escape/leave hurriedly

"Most of the demonstrators cut and ran as soon as they saw the police approaching."

cut and thrust = competitive aspects of a situation

"I really enjoy the cut and thrust of good argument about politics."

cut back = make economies

"The Government announced that it is going to cut back its spending on defence."

cut both ways = affect both aspects of something equally

"Any increase in personal taxation cuts both ways: the government collects more in direct taxes but gets less from indirect taxation because people have less to spend on goods and services."

cut down to size = reduce somebody's arrogance/superiority

"He was boasting as usual about his prowess on the tennis court, but Pam soon cut him down to size by beating him effortlessly in straight sets."

cut fine = complete just in time

"Your train leaves in half an hour and you're still not dressed; that's cutting it a bit fine, isn't it?"

cut in = interrupt, or take over somebody else's dancing partner

"I'm sorry but I must cut in and remind you that you're quoting the wrong statistics."

"Excuse me, may I cut in and dance with Carol?"

cut it out! = stop doing that!

"Cut it out! You know I'm ticklish."

cut off = break in a telephone conversation (because of equipment malfunction)

"I was talking to Hilda on the phone but we were cut off before she could tell me all the latest gossip."

cut off without a penny/shilling = disinherit

"My father was so furious when I refused to go into the family business that he cut me off without a penny."

cut one's own throat = take self-damaging action

"Sheila cut her own throat by leaving her job before she'd found another one."

cut one's teeth on = learn about initially/ have fundamental knowledge of

"When the mechanic asked me what was wrong with the car he didn't realize that I'd cut my teeth on repairing engines of all types."

cut out = exclude, or stop working (of a machine)

"It was obvious that Charlie wasn't welcome in the group when they kept cutting him out of the conversation."

"The plane was coming into land when one of its engines suddenly cut out."

cut out for = have a natural ability for

"I think I'm going to resign; I'm just not cut out for this job."

cut somebody dead = deliberately ignore somebody (in public)

"Smythe has cut me dead ever since that unfortunate affair with the club funds."

cut short = curtail/interrupt

"The master of ceremonies cut short the preliminaries so that we could get on with the meal."

"Councillor Jones was droning on and eventually the chairman had to cut him short to give somebody else a chance to speak."

cut the ground from under somebody/ somebody's feet = anticipate/refute an opponent's arguments, so leaving him/ her with no case

"When he brought up the matter of travelling expenses I cut the ground from under his feet by pointing out that he had a free meal on the company every day he was away."

cut the (Gordian) knot = take quick, bold action to resolve a difficulty
"The old stock had deteriorated and was all mixed up so the manager decided to cut the Gordian knot, sell it all as scrap, and re-stock with new materials."

cut to the quick = very hurt (emotionally)
"Her insulting remarks cut me to the quick."

cut up = feeling great sorrow
"Brian was terribly cut up when his father died."

cut up nasty/rough = become aggressive/ angry
"The other driver began to cut up rough when I refused to admit the collision was my fault."

short cut = more direct/quicker way
"We'll have to take some short cuts if we're to finish this job on time."

See also: cut a long story short; cut corners; cut loose; cut no ice; cut off in one's prime; cut one's coat according to one's cloth; cut one's losses; cut off one's nose to spite one's face; cut the air with a knife; cut to the bone.

cut-off

cut-off point = point (usually in time) beyond which no further action is taken
"The cost of the project keeps increasing but there has to be a cut-off point when we will just have to say that there is no more money available."

cut-throat

cut-throat competition = viciously aggressive/restrictive
"It is extremely difficult to launch a new product in the face of cut-throat competition from rival producers."

cylinder

firing on all cylinders = functioning perfectly
"I haven't been firing on all cylinders since I had that bout of flu."

D

dab
be a dab hand at = be adept/expert at
"Ian is a dab hand at the oriental art of origami."

dabble
dabble in = take a passing interest in
"I dabble in writing poetry but I do it only for my own pleasure, not for publication."

daddy
daddy of them all = best/largest example
"I've seen some big spiders, but the one I found in the bath last night was the daddy of them all."
big daddy = authoritarian father/leader
"Keith wanted to ask June for a date but was wary of the disapproving glare of big daddy."
sugar daddy = mature/elderly man who lavishes attention/gifts on a young woman
"Because of the age difference, Rosemary's older companion had the reputation of being a sugar daddy."

daft
as daft as a brush = very silly/stupid
"You must be as daft as a brush to pay a hundred pounds for that worm-eaten old chair."

daggers
at daggers drawn = prepared for a confrontation/fight
"The leader of the opposition and the prime minister are at daggers drawn over the unemployment issue."
look daggers at = look with a piercing and disapproving stare
"The headmaster looked daggers at the two boys who were talking during assembly."

daily
daily dozen = regular (daily) physical exercises
"Workers at the Japanese car factory were required to do their daily dozen at the beginning of each shift."
one's daily bread = one's living
"I earn my daily bread by working in a supermarket."

daisy
push up the daisies = be dead
"I'll be pushing up the daisies long before the new by-pass is finished."
See also: fresh as a daisy.

damage
what's the damage? = how much do I owe you? (to pay for goods/services)
"Thank you for getting us here so quickly. What's the damage, driver?"

damn
damn all = nothing at all
"You've contributed damn all to the fund and now you expect to benefit from it!"
damn well = expression used for emphasis
"When I give you an order, you damn well carry it out!"
"You know damn well I don't like cauliflower!"
damn with faint praise = disguise criticism/disapproval with insincere praise
"The disappointed runner-up in the beauty contest damned with faint praise the newly crowned queen."
do one's damnedest = do one's best

"Harry said he'd do his damnedest to get my car finished by this evening."

I'll be damned if = I would rather go to hell than to

"I'll be damned if I'll tidy your room; do it yourself!"

not care/give a damn = not care at all

"When asked her views about shops opening on Sundays, the woman said she didn't care a damn either way."

not worth a damn = totally worthless

"Don't trust him. His promises are not worth a damn."

damp

damp down = discourage/suppress

"The authorities decided to damp down the dissidents' activities by imposing a curfew."

damp squib = expected success that turns out to be a failure

"The pop concert went off like a damp squib when the main act failed to appear."

put a/the damper on = discourage/counteract an (expected) effect

"A death in the family put a damper on our Christmas celebrations."

dance

dance attendance on = fawn on/pamper

"The Chairman expects the entire staff to dance attendance on him when he deigns to visit our office."

lead somebody a (merry/pretty) dance = deliberately mislead somebody/waste somebody's time

"The boys led the farmer a merry dance; he was searching for them in the orchard when all the time they were hiding in the barn."

See also: dance/walk on air; make a song and dance about something.

dander

get one's dander up = become (very) angry

"There's no need to get your dander up, just because you've lost a game of chess."

Darby

Darby and Joan = devoted and elderly married couple

"Having been together for more than 60 years, Eric and Betty were regarded as the Darby and Joan of the village."

dare

dare devil = somebody who takes excessive (and unnecessary) risks

"The pilot was a dare devil to fly his small plane upside-down under Tower Bridge."

how dare you! = how can you say that/be so rude

"You called me a wally. How dare you!"

I dare say = I suppose/venture to say

"I dare say it will rain on Monday because I'm beginning my holiday."

(just) you dare = do not (with great emphasis)

"You dare play with matches while I'm out."

dark

dark horse = somebody of unknown (and possibly dubious) character

"Jack is a dark horse, he never says much and you don't know what he's thinking."

in the dark = in ignorance/not knowing

"The union was kept in the dark about the management's redundancy plans."

keep it dark = keep it secret/to yourself

"I've just had a tip that number five

will win the next race, but keep it dark."

leap/shot in the dark = an attempt that has little chance of success/a guess
"Jane's attempt to find her lost ring in the long grass was just a shot in the dark, and nobody was surprised when she failed to find it."

whistle in the dark = encourage with (false) optimism
"After the heavy snowfall the groundsman was whistling in the dark when he promised that the pitch would be clear for a three o'clock kick-off."

See also: dark days.

darling

mother's darling = spoiled (male) child
"Robert was often teased at school for being a mother's darling."

dash

cut a dash = impress by one's dress
"Jake thinks he cuts a dash in his new cowboy boots."

dash off = hurry away, or do something quickly/superficially
"Must you dash off? Why not stay for a cup of tea?"
"I dashed off two more drawings before lunch today."

dash somebody's hopes = disappoint/ disillusion somebody
"The general's hopes of victory were dashed when enemy reinforcements arrived."

date

blind date = prearranged meeting between strangers (usually a man and a woman)
"My wife and I first met on a blind date arranged by her sister."

date somebody = arrange to go out with somebody (of the opposite sex)
"I've been dating Diana regularly since last November."

make a date with somebody = arrange to meet somebody
"I've made a date with Harold for next Thursday. Will you be able to come to the meeting?"

out of date = behind the times/out of fashion
"Throw away that railway timetable, it's months out of date."
"In these days of electronic calculators, the slide rule is out of date as a mathematical aid."

up to date = modern/in fashion
"Julia keeps up to date with all the latest pop record releases."

to date = up to now
"To date we have no news from the disaster area."

daughter

See: daughter language.

daunted

nothing daunted = irrespective of any difficulty
"The child was just adding the tenth brick to the tower she was building when it collapsed, but nothing daunted she started to build it all over again."

David

David and Goliath situation = confrontation in which the person with less ability/experience/strength wins
"It was a David and Goliath situation and yet remarkably the subsidiary company made a successful take-over bid for the large holding company."

Davy Jones

Davy Jones' locker = the (bottom of the) sea

"The Captain recited a prayer as the bosun's body was committed to the sea on its way to Davy Jones' locker."

dawn

dawn on = become aware/enlightened

"I was working away at the office when it suddenly dawned on me I had forgotten to go and meet the boss at the station."

day

all day long = continuously/without a break for a whole day

"The police searched the common all day long, but failed to find the murder weapon."

all in a day's work = within one's duties/ obligation

"The old lady thanked the firemen for getting her cat down out of a tree but to them it was all in a day's work."

any day (now) = soon

"Mary's baby is expected any day now."

any day of the week = at any time

"I don't like coffee; I'd rather have a cup of tea any day of the week."

as happy as the day is long = very happy

"Give my mother a comfortable chair and a television set and she's as happy as the day's long."

black day = bad/disastrous event

"It was a black day for the aircraft workers when the government announced it was cancelling its contract for a new fighter."

carry/win the day = gain a victory

"Kevin scored a goal during the last minute of the game and carried the day for his side."

dark days = troubled times

"The political turmoils of the 1930s were dark days for the Spanish."

day after day/day in day out = continuously (and monotonously) for several days

"The weather was awful; it rained day in day out for a whole week."

day dream = lose oneself in one's imagination

"The student was unable to answer the question because he had spent most of the lecture in a day dream."

day of reckoning = time when one has to account for past actions

"The shoplifter's day of reckoning came when he was charged with 22 cases of theft."

days of old/yore = in (distant) historical times

"In days of yore it was usual for cavalrymen to wear suits of armour."

days to come = the future

"In days to come it may be possible to travel beyond the Solar System."

every dog has its day = eventually everyone achieves success

"After five attempts, Carol finally passed her driving test ñ after all, every dog has its day."

fall on evil days = suffer unfortunate circumstances

"Bernard has fallen on evil days since he lost his job and his wife left him."

for days on end = for many consecutive days

"It rained for days on end during our holiday."

from day to day = as time progresses (daily)

"The bank manager said he would monitor the account from day to day and make his decision about a loan at the end of the month."

good old days = earlier times (remembered with fondness)
"The two farmers reminisced about the good old days before the EEC agricultural policy."

have one's day = have a time when one is prosperous/successful
"William has retired from competition now, but he had his day when he won the all-England championships."

livelong day = all day long
"Please be quiet. You've been nagging me the livelong day."

make a day of it = spend all day doing something enjoyable
"I had to go to London for an early morning meeting so I decided to make a day of it and see some of the sights."

make somebody's day = give somebody a welcome surprise
"It made my day when I received a £500 tax rebate."

name the day = announce the date of a forthcoming wedding
"David produced a diamond ring and asked Dawn if they could name the day."

not one's day/one of those days = time when things do not go as planned
"It just wasn't my day: the car wouldn't start, I was late for the meeting, and to top it all I laddered my tights!"
"I knew it would turn out to be one of those days when I overslept."

not to have all day = to have only a limited time
"Hurry up! We haven't got all day, you know!"

off day = day when things do not go well/to form
"Although favourite to win the race, the champion jockey had an off day and was unplaced."

old/olden days = distant past
"In the old days you could get a pint of beer for a shilling."

one of these (fine) days = at some time in the future
"Perhaps one of these fine days you'll get to work on time."

one's days are numbered = one's time is limited
"She has made so many mistakes her days must be numbered in that job."

open as the day = totally honest
"I'd trust her with my life's savings ñ she's as open as the day."

palmy days = time of prosperity
"Britain enjoyed palmy days in the early sixties when the country was booming."

red letter day = memorable date/event
"Yesterday was a red letter day for Julie; she passed the last of her exams and heard that she had been accepted for university."

salad days = time of youthful inexperience
"Although still in his salad days, Mark was showing great promise on the cricket field."

save the day = prevent a failure
"I left my wallet at home but Jock saved the day by lending me ten pounds."

the other day = one day recently
"The other day I saw a squirrel in my garden."

to have seen better days = to be past its best/have outlived its usefulness
"I need a new coat, this one has seen better days."

that will be the day! = that is very unlikely!
"My husband, get up before eight o'clock? That'll be the day!"

See also: at the end of the day; call it a

day; daily round; day's grace; dog days; early days; every dog has its day; have a field day; have seen better days; in all one's born days; in broad daylight; (a bit) late in the day; man of his day; nine days' wonder; one of these fine days; pass the time of day; roll on the day; save something for a rainy day; tomorrow is another day.

daylight

beat the living daylights out of somebody = beat severely/knock senseless
"At the end of the film, the hero beat the living daylights out of the villain."

daylight robbery = flagrant over-charging
"A charge of £1.20 for a cup of coffee is daylight robbery."

frighten/scare the living daylights out of somebody = terrify somebody
"That horror film we saw last night scared the living daylights out of me."

in broad daylight = in full view during the day
"The car was stolen in broad daylight."

see daylight = perceive an eventual solution to a problem
"After puzzling for hours I finally saw daylight and found the answer."

dead

dead and buried = (long) forgotten
"Linda and Tina were again on speaking terms, their disagreement dead and buried."

dead as a dodo = extinct/obsolete
"As a mode of transport the sedan chair is as dead as a dodo."

dead as a doornail/mutton = (emphatically) dead
"He drove into a tree at over a hundred miles an hour and is as dead as a doornail."

dead beat = exhausted
"The long-distance runner was dead beat as he crossed the finishing line."

dead certainty = absolute certainty
"It's a dead certainty that the Tories will be re-elected."

dead drunk = very drunk (to the point of unconsciousness)
"I don't know how Ann stands for her husband's behaviour; he comes home dead drunk nearly every night."

dead from the neck up = foolish/stupid
"My new girlfriend may have a nice figure but unfortunately she's dead from the neck up."

dead heat = race in which two (or more) contestants are exactly level at the finish
"After the stewards' enquiry, the result of the 3.15 was declared a dead heat."

dead loss = total loss/useless
"That new film is a dead loss; it's a waste of money going to see it."

dead man's shoes = job opportunity provided by somebody's death or retirement
"The junior executive was impatient for promotion but knew that he would only get it by stepping into a dead man's shoes."

dead of night = darkest part of the night
"They ransacked the old lady's house in the dead of night."

dead-pan = lacking any expression
"You need a dead-pan face to be a successful poker player."

dead ringer (for somebody) = a double/somebody who looks exactly the same
"That man on the other side of the road is a dead ringer for Ronald Reagan."

dead to the world = fast asleep/unconscious
"Exhausted by their exploits that day the two boys had supper and fell asleep, dead to the world."

dead wood = useless appendage/person
"The management decided to economize by cutting the dead wood from the workforce, thus reducing the wages bill."

drop dead! = go away!
"You're not coming with us, so drop dead!"

enough to wake the dead = very loud
"The music at the disco was enough to wake the dead."

go dead = cease working
"I was talking to my brother on the telephone when suddenly the line went dead."

make a dead set at = purposefully attack/approach
"Norman made a dead set at me as soon as I entered the room and gave me some very interesting news."

over my dead body = only if my most vigorous opposition fails
"What do you mean your mother is coming to stay for a week? Over my dead body she is!"

refuse to/wouldn't be seen dead in = be too ashamed/embarrassed to do something
"What an old-fashioned coat! I wouldn't be seen dead wearing that."
"I refuse to be seen dead with my brother after what he has done."

See also: be in (deadly) earnest; cut somebody dead; dead duck; dead end; dead-end job; dead to rights; dead men tell no tales; play dead/possum; stone dead; stop dead.

deadline

meet a deadline = have something ready on time
"I must have the results first thing on Monday morning if we are to meet the deadline."

deaf

deaf as a post = (very) deaf
"I had to shout at the old man before he heard me; he must be as deaf as a post."

turn a deaf ear to = deliberately ignore
"The vicar turned a deaf ear to Michelle's bad language because he knew it was out of character."

See also: fall on deaf ears; stone deaf.

deal

big deal! = I'm totally unimpressed
"So your father has bought a new car. Big deal! Mine has just bought an aeroplane!"

fair deal = a substantial amount/quality, quite a lot
"We've had a fair deal of snow already this winter, and it's still only December."

it's a deal = it is agreed
"It's a deal then? You'll pay me two thousand pounds for the car."

raw deal = unfair treatment
"The soldier thought he'd been given a raw deal when assigned to guard duty for the third time running."

square deal = fair/reasonable agreement
"The workers were offered a square deal of a 35-hour week and guaranteed overtime."

dear

oh dear! = expression of (anxious) surprise
"Oh dear! Is it time to go already?"

death

be the death of (somebody) = be the cause of (somebody's) death, or cause great amusement, or annoyance/ trouble
"Abolishing subsidies could well be the death of the farming industry in this country."
"Charlie was fooling around as usual ñ one day that man's antics will be the death of me!"
"Those children will be the death of me with their continual quarrelling."

catch one's death = catch a chill/very bad cold
"Put on a coat if you're going out in the snow or you'll catch your death."

death trap = place in which one is in danger of being seriously injured/ killed
"That old car of his is a death trap: the steering is faulty and the brakes are non-existent."

do to death = overdo/overexpose
"The television companies have done to death the coverage of the election, I'm tired of it already."

feel like death warmed up = feel exhausted/ill
"I was at a party till three o'clock this morning and I still feel like death warmed up."

in at the death = present at the very end
"I've worked on this project for nearly three years and with only two weeks to go I'm determined to be in at the death."

pale as death = very pale
"The two hostages looked as pale as death when they were released by the terrorists after being held for six months."

sick to death of = thoroughly fed up
"June was trying to do her homework but was sick to death of the constant interruptions."

sign somebody's death warrant = action that results in somebody's death or downfall
"Finding his fingerprints on the murder weapon signed his death warrant."

tickled to death = highly amused
"We were all tickled to death at the antics of the clowns."

to the death = until somebody is defeated or killed
"With only two rounds to go, both boxers were determined to fight to the death."

work something to death = force something to work excessively, or overexpose something
"The engine had been worked to death and was in need of major repairs."
"The new Superman film has received so much media coverage that it is in danger of being worked to death."

See also: at death's door; cling/hold on like grim death; dice with death; fate worse than death; jaws of death; kiss of death.

debt

be in somebody's debt = owe somebody (often gratitude)
"Thank you for rescuing my cat, I shall always be in your debt."

get into debt = owe money
"I can't seem to live on my salary without getting into debt at the end of each month."

See also: bad debt.

deck

clear the decks = prepare for action
"Let's clear the decks everyone and get ready to start the next job."

sweep the deck = beat everybody and win all the stakes
"I had a very lucky time playing poker yesterday evening; by nine o'clock I had swept the deck and won all their money."

declare
declare war = give formal notice of intent to fight
"The police have declared war on drivers who persistently exceed the speed limit."

deep
in deep water = in trouble
"William is in deep water; apparently the bank has threatened to evict him unless he pays his mortgage arrears by the end of the month."
See also: deep game; dive/throw somebody in at the deep end; still waters run deep.

default
in default of = in the absence of
"In default of a proper stretcher they carried the victim on a tightly held blanket."
win by default = win because the opponent does not compete
"Our side won the final game by default after our opponents failed to turn up because their coach was involved in an accident."

defensive
on the defensive = in a state of defence
"If you believe in a cause, speak up for it; don't always be on the defensive."
throw somebody on the defensive = put somebody in a situation in which he/she has to defend himself/herself
"Liverpool's first all-out attack put Arsenal on the defensive and they never regained the initiative throughout the rest of the game."

deference
in deference to = because of respect for
"We always stand when the National Anthem is played in deference to the Queen."

degree
by degrees = gradually
"We have a lot of work to do to make the company profitable again, but we're getting there by degrees."
one degree under = unwell
"I feel one degree under this morning; it must have been that curry I had for supper last night."
third degree = persistent/brutal interrogation
"The accused refused to confess despite being subjected to the third degree for two whole days."
to a degree = to some extent/in a way
"I think the general public will favour your policy to a degree, but you must make more radical reforms to gain their wholehearted support."

delicate
in a delicate condition = pregnant
"Ann Smith phoned to say she can't come pony trekking after all because she's in a delicate condition."

deliver
See: deliver the goods

delusion
delusions of grandeur = belief that one is more important than one actually is
"Some local government officials

have delusions of grandeur far in excess of their actual value to the community."

demand

in demand = (very) popular
"Soft drinks are much in demand this hot weather."

make demands on = continually require/put pressure on
"I find that running the youth club makes more and more demands on my free time."

on demand = when(ever) asked
"He has promised to repay the loan at any time on demand."

demon

demon for = very enthusiastic/have a deep commitment for
"Barry is a demon for snooker, and plays at every opportunity he gets."

the demon drink = habitual drinking/alcohol(ism)
"James never has any money because of the demon drink."

den

den of thieves = group of criminals, or derogatory term for a group of like-minded people
"When all my wife's friends come round for a coffee morning it's like a den of thieves."

lion's den = enemy territory/dangerous situation
"The young constable looked around him and realized he had strayed into a lion's den of pimps and prostitutes."

dent

make a dent in = reduce/lessen
"Buying that new carpet has made a big dent in our savings."

depart

new departure = change of course/method
"Creating children's books is a new departure for this publishing company."

the (dear) departed = somebody who is dead
"And let us remember the dear departed, who cannot be with us today."

depend

depend upon it = be sure/beyond doubt
"It's the annual fete tomorrow and it is bound to rain, you can depend upon it ñ it always does!"

that depends on = is conditional on
"Whether you go to the disco this evening depends on what your father says."

depth

out of/beyond one's depth = in difficulty (because of overstretching one's ability/knowledge)
"She thought that the Open University course would be easy, but now has to admit that she's out of her depth."

plumb the depths = reach the lowest level
"Immediately after my wife's death I plumbed the depths of sorrow."

in depth = in great detail/thoroughly
"The professor has carried out an investigation in depth, and intends to publish his findings soon."

description

beggar description = be indescribable (because of its greatness)
"The rubbish left behind by the Cup Final crowd beggars description."

deserts

receive one's just deserts = get what one deserves
"He was fined for shoplifting but only received his just deserts."

deserve

richly deserve = be (rightly) entitled to
"Walter has been with this company for more than forty years and richly deserves a long and happy retirement."

design

by design = according to a plan/ deliberately
"Wendy wore a low-cut dress by design because she knew it would make her the centre of attention."

have designs on = wish to take/own
"Half the men in the office have designs on my secretary."

desire

See: leave a lot/much to be desired.

desk

desk general = commander with no battle experience
"The Sales Director is a desk general ñ he's asking us to increase sales yet he's never made a single sale himself."

despair

give way/yield to despair = give up hope
"Even through all her family and financial troubles, Margaret never gave way to despair."

device

leave somebody to his/her own devices = leave somebody alone
"Now that the children are older, we can leave them to their own devices to amuse themselves."

devil

be a devil = be bold/take a risk
"Go on, be a devil. Try a whiskey for a change."

be a devil for = be very fond of
"My children are devils for ice cream."

better the devil you know = the bad thing you are aware of is better than another of which you are unaware
"The disheartened crew heard that they were to get a new captain and were pleased until somebody reminded them: better the devil you know."

between the devil and the deep blue sea = in a dilemma/with a choice between two equally unpleasant alternatives
"I must move to a larger house or spend money extending this one; either will be expensive so I'm between the devil and the deep blue sea."

devil-may-care = wildly reckless
"He drives that sports car of his in a devil-may-care manner."

devil in disguise = somebody/something apparently good but actually bad
"A few drinks may seem harmless but beware: alcohol is a devil in disguise."

devil take the hindmost = I do not care what happens to others
"I'm going to make sure that he first pays what he owes me, and the devil take the hindmost."

devil's advocate = somebody who ensures that the unfavourable aspects of a decision/situation are taken into account
"We were excited about our planned trip to the States, but Ron played devil's advocate by making us take out

extra medical insurance and warning us to be on our guard against muggers."

hold a candle to the devil = play safe by keeping on good terms with both sides in a dispute

"Although he was a member of one of the most notorious gangs in London, he held a candle to the devil by giving the police the occasional tip-off."

play the very devil with = make worse/ misbehave

"The damp weather plays the very devil with my rheumatism."

"Our new puppy played the very devil with me, he's been trying to chew the furniture all day."

speak/talk of the devil = said of somebody who appears just as he/she is being talked about

"I wish the tea lady would bring round the drinks trolley ñ speak of the devil, here she is."

the devil looks after/takes care of his own = bad people seem to succeed (in preference to good ones)

"The devil certainly looks after his own ñ the man who stole all that money has just won first prize on the Premium Bonds!"

the very devil = mischief-maker/nuisance

"My young son is the very devil; he's asleep all day but cries and keep us awake all night."

See also: dare devil; give the devil his due; needs must (when the devil drives); the devil/hell to pay; the devil's own job.

dialogue

dialogue of the deaf = discussion in which neither side acknowledges/ agrees the opinions of the other

"It is expected that no agreement will be reached in the new round of arms talks because both countries are engaged in a dialogue of the deaf."

diamond

diamond cut diamond = contest between equally determined and well-matched opponents

"The two cats challenged each other for the disputed territory ñ it was a case of diamond cut diamond."

rough diamond = somebody who is (apparently) brash/unsophisticated but is nevertheless good-hearted

"I know he looks a bit of a rough diamond in his tattered jeans, but apparently he does a lot of good work for local charities."

diarrhoea

verbal diarrhoea = wordy but insubstantial speech

"The cabinet minister's speech was regarded by the pressmen present as so much verbal diarrhoea."

dice

dice with death = take a (severe) risk

"If you comment about Dad's bald patch, you're dicing with death ñ he's very touchy about it."

no dice = definitely not

"We asked the bank for more time to pay but no dice, they refused."

the dice are loaded = the odds are against/there is no chance of success

"I ran all the way to the station but the dice were loaded against me because the train had been cancelled anyway."

dick

clever dick = a know-all

"All right, clever dick, what's the capital of Cyprus?"

See also: any/every Tom, Dick and Harry.

die

be dying for = have a great desire for
"After hours of working in the hot sun, the men were dying for a cold beer."

be dying from/of = be approaching death because of
"The grass on my lawn is dying from lack of water."

be dying to do something = be very keen to do something
"I've been dying to go and see the Summer Exhibition at the Royal Academy."

die away/down = fade/gradually diminish
"After the initial cheers, the noise of the crowd began to die away as the group started playing."
"Unrest appears to have died down after an appeal for order from the President."

die in harness/with one's boots on = die while still at work
"Poor old Jones had a heart attack in the office, but at least he died in harness and not in some hospital bed."

die laughing = be highly amused/laugh to the point of exhaustion
"You should have seen Peter Sellers in that film last night ñ you would have died laughing."

die off = die one by one
"Unless the starving people get food immediately, they will die off within a week."

die out = become extinct
"The wolf died out in Britain hundreds of years ago."

never say die = do not give in
"The attitude of the British people during the Second World War was never say die."

straight as a die = totally honest
"You can trust Jimmy to come to a fair arrangement, he's as straight as a die."

the die is cast = the outcome is inevitable/it is too late to change one's mind
"The die is cast now, but I still say they were too young to get married."

See also: die like a dog; do or die; what did your last servant die of?

differ

See: agree to differ; beg to differ.

difference

make all the difference = have a great effect on
"The salesman said it would make all the difference to our heating bills if we installed double glazing."

sink one's differences = forget past disagreements
"It's nearly two years since they fell out; it's about time they sank their differences a˙ 1 became friends again."

split the difference = compromise between two close amounts/quantities
"I'm asking £1200 for the car and you're offering £1000; why don't we split the difference and call it £1100?"

See also: bury the hatchet/one's differences.

dig

dig in = begin energetically
"Come on, dig in; there's plenty of food for everybody."

dig oneself in = secure one's position
"Once I've dug myself in on the management committee, I'll try and get some changes made around here."

dig one's feet/heels/toes in = be resolute/ stubborn

"The old lady dug her heels in and refused to sell her house to the developers ñ at any price."

dig somebody in the ribs = poke somebody in the side of the chest

"Look what Malcolm is doing! Give him a dig in the ribs and stop him."

See also: dig one's grave; gold-digger.

dignity

stand on one's dignity = be pompous/ insist on respect

"Don't stand on your dignity, come in and meet the boys."

dilemma

on the horns of a dilemma = faced with two equally unpleasant alternatives

"The patient's condition was critical and she needed an operation but there was no guarantee that she would survive the anaesthetic; the surgeon was on the horns of a dilemma."

dim

take a dim view of = disapprove of, or be unimpressed

"The farmer naturally took a dim view of the council's plans to build a new road across his land."

din

din into = force somebody to accept/ learn something (by repeating it)

"I just can't din into my son that it is important to pass exams and get qualifications."

dinner

dog's dinner = an (untidy) mess

"Vera came to the party dressed up like a dog's dinner in a punk outfit and with her hair dyed pink."

dint

by dint of = by means of

"Peter was able to get us good seats by dint of his membership of the entertainment committee."

dip

dip into = examine superficially, or use part of a reserve

"I've only dipped into the book, but from what I've seen it is well written."

"I shall have to dip into my savings to pay for the car repairs."

dip into one's pocket = spend money

"The group was surprised to see Patrick dip into his pocket and offer to buy a round of drinks."

diplomacy

wrist-slap diplomacy = demonstration of a minor disagreement between countries at diplomatic level

"Because of the border incident, a measure of wrist-slap diplomacy was employed and the trade secretary cancelled the proposed visit."

direction

See: step in the right direction.

dirt

pay dirt = soil (from a mine) containing precious metal or precious stones

"The prospector yelled with delight when he hit pay dirt."

See also: dirty game; eat dirt; treat somebody like (a piece of) dirt.

dirty

dirty look = disapproving/hostile stare

"Two women wearing identical dresses gave each other dirty looks across the dance floor."

dirty money = money obtained dishonestly
"The trouble dealing with him is you don't know if you're being paid with dirty money."
dirty trick = dishonest/unfair means
"The salesman used some dirty tricks to improve his monthly sales figures."
dirty weather = stormy/wet weather
"The dirty weather caused the cancellation of a whole day's play at Wimbledon."
dirty weekend = weekend spent together by an unmarried couple or one having an illicit (extramarital) affair
"Judging by the number of Smiths registered here, this is obviously a popular hotel for a dirty weekend."
dirty work = criminal activity, or unpleasant task
"He had made so much money from crime that he could afford to pay others to do his dirty work, and thus he avoided any risk of getting caught."
"We've got to wash down the paintwork and scrub the floor. Have you noticed how Brian is always missing when there's dirty work to be done?"
do the dirty on = betray/play a mean trick on
"I crept into work late unnoticed until the supervisor did the dirty on me and told the boss."
See also: dirty dog; dirty/rough end of the stick; dirty old man; dirty/soil one's hands.

discount

at a discount = at a reduced price
"All our goods may be purchased at a discount of ten per cent until the end of the week."

discretion

discretion is the better part of valour = it is wiser to be safe than to indulge in risky heroics
"When I spun round angrily and then saw the size of the chap who had nudged me in the back I decided that discretion was the better part of valour and apologised."
reach the age of discretion = (of a woman) be legally old enough to have sexual intercourse
"I've not discouraged my daughter from going on the pill now that she's reached the age of discretion."

discussion

open to discussion = arguable/negotiable
"We're in broad general agreement although the final details of the terms are still open to discussion."

disguise

See: blessing in disguise.

dish

dish out = give out/distribute
"To help promote the new range of products the company propose to dish out a free gift to each customer."
dish up = present food/information
"Take your places at the table, children, I'm just dishing up."
"I predict the Chairman will be dishing up his usual repertoire of boring jokes at the Christmas party."
what a dish! = what an attractive girl!
"Have you seen the new secretary? What a dish!"

disorderly
disorderly house = brothel
"Be careful how much you drink in the red light district or you may wake up in a disorderly house!"

dispose
be disposed to = be willing to
"I am disposed to make a substantial contribution if you can convince me that the money will be well spent."
be indisposed = be unwell
"Theo phoned to say he's indisposed and won't be coming to work today."
be well disposed towards somebody = think well of/be friendly with somebody
"I think we should ask for a loan while the bank is well disposed towards us."
dispose of = get rid of/kill, or complete/deal with
"The revolutionaries' main ambition is to dispose of the present head of state."
"The committee quickly disposed of the final items on the agenda and adjourned to the bar."

distance
keep one's distance = not be too familiar/personal
"The other girls told me about the office Romeo and advised me to keep my distance from him."
within spitting/striking distance = very close
"Hard luck! You came within striking distance of beating the record."

ditch
last ditch effort = final attempt
"The crew made a last ditch effort to put out the blaze before finally abandoning ship."
last ditch stand = final resistance (from a point of no retreat)
"The opposition made a last ditch stand to try to get the government to change its policy."
See also: dull as ditchwater.

dive
See: dive/throw somebody in at the deep end.

divine
divine right = God-given privilege (of kings/queens to rule)
"Everybody was annoyed at the German tourists who seemed to think they had some divine right to the best positions around the swimming pool."

do
anything doing? = is anything happening?
"Anything doing at the village hall tonight?"
could do with = need
"We could do with a new carpet, this one's nearly worn out."
do away with = abolish/destroy/kill
"A recent press leak about plans to do away with income tax has been strongly denied by the government."
"He's been unhappy for months and in a fit of depression he finally did away with himself."
do duty for = act on behalf of/substitute for
"Mr Rogers will do duty for me while I'm away next week."
"In an emergency, a tightly tied woman's stocking can do duty for a car's fan belt so that you can drive it to a garage."

do for = cause harm to somebody
"I'll do for you if I catch you on my property again!"

do me a favour! = I do not believe you!
"Do me a favour! You can't expect me to believe that you bought your new hi-fi for only fifty pounds."

done in = exhausted
"After a twenty-mile walk we were all done in."

done to a turn = cooked to perfection
"That chicken was delicious; it was done to a turn."

do or die = be determined to succeed at all costs
"We've got to get the roof finished before it rains or we'll all get soaked; it's a question of do or die, I'm afraid."

do somebody in = kill somebody
"They tried to do him in by giving him a poisoned drink."

do something for = improve the appearance/appeal of
"That new hair style really does something for you, it looks great."

do up = make improvements/repairs
"John says he's going to do up his old car and sell it."

have done with = finish/have no further connection with
"The machine has caused us nothing but trouble; let's get a new one and have done with it."

have to do with = have relevance, or be associated with
"You say you don't want to go because it's on a Tuesday, but what has that got to do with it?"
"He's a bit of a bully and my advice is to have nothing to do with him."

it (just) isn't done = it is socially unacceptable
"At dinner the port should never be passed to the right ñ it just isn't done."

that will do = that is enough
"I'll just have a half pint, that will do."
"That will do! Stop playing around at once!"

that's done it! = it has happened and there will be trouble
"That's done it! Wait until father finds out."

well done! = congratulations!
"Well done! You've beaten the previous record by ten seconds."

you do that! = you carry on (I don't care)
"If you want to make a fool of yourself, you do that!"

See also: do justice to; do one's bit; do one's nut; do somebody proud; do the dirty on; do the trick; do to death; hard done by; (well) I never did; make do; nothing doing.

dock

in dock = undergoing repair, or in hospital
"Can you please give me a lift? I'm afraid my car's in dock."
"I've got to go into dock next week to have an operation."

put somebody in the dock = on trial/ under examination
"The scientist was put in the dock to explain the reasoning behind some of his theories."

doctor

doctor something = interfere with/ modify something
"He was sick after somebody doctored his drink."

family doctor = general practitioner
"Our new family doctor is a woman."

have an animal doctored = have a male animal castrated
"Our cat comes home at night now that we've had him doctored."

(just) what the doctor ordered = exactly what is required
"That meal was just what the doctor ordered, I hadn't eaten a thing all day."

See also: doctor the accounts.

dodo

See: dead as a dodo.

dog

call off the dogs = end a search
"The police have decided to call off the dogs in their hunt for the missing diamonds because they've almost certainly left the country by now."

die like a dog = have a shameful/ undignified death
"None of the enthusiastic volunteers realized that they would die like dogs in the trenches of the Somme."

dirty dog = somebody who is underhanded/unscrupulous
"Professor Moriarty could be described as the dirty dog of the Sherlock Holmes stories."

dog collar = (priest's) clerical collar
"Our vicar often leaves off his dog collar and comes to the discos at the youth club."

dog days = hottest time of the year
"The summers are getting colder. What ever happened to the dog days I remember from my youth?"

dog-eared = with frayed/tattered edges
"We must get some new books for the English class because the old ones are getting very dog-eared."

dog eat dog = ruthless competition
"You need a strong character to survive the dog eat dog of big business."

dog fight = aerial combat between fighter aircraft, or general meleé
"The plane may be slightly slower but it can turn in a much tighter circle ñ a big advantage in a dog fight."

(in the) dog house = (in) disgrace (particularly a husband with whom his wife is displeased)
"No thanks, I won't have any more to drink or I'll be in the dog house when I get home."

dog in the manager = somebody who spoils somebody else's pleasure (although not wanting to participate himself/herself)
"Just because you don't want to go to the party there's no need to be dog in the manger and prevent me from going."

dog Latin = incorrect Latin
"That strange new religious sect conducts its services in dog Latin."

dog's body = general assistant/helper
"The foreman said he wanted a general dog's body to help out on the site."

dog's breakfast/dinner = a mess
"You've made a right dog's dinner of painting that door."

dog's chance = remote chance of success
"I wouldn't risk my money on that horse, it hasn't a dog's chance of winning."

dog tired = exhausted
"I'm dog tired, I've worked overtime every night this week."

don't keep a dog and bark yourself = do not employ somebody to do a job and then do it yourself
"Don't keep a dog and bark yourself ñ your secretary should do that filing, you've got better things to do."

every dog has its day = everyone eventually gets a favourable opportunity

"After trying for five years I eventually won the bridge tournament; it just goes to show that every dog has its day."

gay dog = somebody who is overtly carefree

"Graham is a bit of a gay dog with the women; I wonder if his wife knows?"

give a dog a bad name = a bad reputation is remembered

"I got into trouble with the law several years ago and now when anything goes missing I automatically come under suspicion; no wonder they say give a dog a bad name."

go to the dogs = decline/be ruined

"Our local pub has gone to the dogs since they put in the snooker tables and video juke boxes."

hair of the dog (that bit you) = drink similar to that which gave one a hangover

"My stomach still feels wobbly; let's go over to the pub and have a hair of the dog."

lead a dog's life = have an unpeaceful/worrying life

"Poor Mike, his wife leads him a dog's life with her incessant nagging."

let sleeping dogs lie = do not disturb a situation that is finally calm after being troubled

"He wanted to talk again about the strike we had last year, but I decided to let sleeping dogs lie and changed the subject."

let the dog see the rabbit = give the participants a chance

"Move back, it's Tony's go. Let the dog see the rabbit."

lie doggo = remain in hiding

"The escaped prisoners lay doggo in a haystack until the searchers had gone away."

like a dog with two tails = ecstatic/very happy

"The old lady was like a dog with two tails when her son and his wife came home from Australia with the grandchildren she'd never seen before."

lucky dog = somebody who has good fortune (often said with envy)

"Ian is a lucky dog; his wife has just inherited a small fortune."

shaggy dog story = drawn-out joke (with a weak ending)

"He spent the whole lunchtime telling this interminable shaggy dog story about an actress and a bishop."

sly dog = somebody who is crafty/secretive

"I saw Sam out with that barmaid the other day; the sly dog never even mentioned that he was dating her!"

tail wagging the dog = minor factor controlling a major one

"Because the boss bought a cheap lot of dark green paint, they have painted all the offices with it. It's a depressing environment to work in and a typical case of the tail wagging the dog."

throw somebody to the dogs = condemn somebody to an unpleasant fate

"If any of the junior ministers makes a mistake the prime minister does not support them but throws them to the dogs."

top dog = champion/somebody in the most superior position

"After winning four major international events he's the top dog among formula one motor racing drivers."

treat somebody worse than a dog = behave towards somebody with total insensitivity/no respect

"Because Captain Bligh treated the crew of HMS Bounty like dogs, they eventually mutinied."

underdog = somebody who is inferior/on the losing side

"As the only non-graduate applicant, he knew he was the underdog and unlikely to get the position."

work like a dog = work very hard (for little reward)

"I work like a dog all week and the taxman takes most of my pay before I even see it."

you can't teach a old dog new tricks = elderly/experienced people find it difficult to adjust to new ideas

"My secretary has been using that old manual typewriter for more than twenty years and I cannot get her to change to a word processor; it seems you can't teach an old dog new tricks."

See also: dog's dinner; every dog has his day; have a hangdog air; love me, love my dog; rain cats and dogs; sick as a dog; there's life in the old dog yet.

doing

See: do.

doldrums

in the doldrums = in a state of (enforced) inactivity

"During the spring and summer the restaurant was always crowded, but in late autumn it found itself in the doldrums."

doll

doll up = dress in one's finery

"We went to the theatre all dolled up but most of the audience were in casual clothes."

dollar

feel/look like a million dollars = feel/look very attractive

"In your new evening gown you look like a million dollars."

the 64 million dollar question = a very difficult/unanswerable question

"We can only speculate on the answer, but who really did build Stonehenge? That is the 64 million dollar question."

See also: bet one's bottom dollar.

done

See: do.

donkey

donkey's breakfast = straw-filled mattress, or wood-chip wallpaper

"At transit camp we had to sleep in a tent on a donkey's breakfast."

"The walls of the house were so uneven we papered them with donkey's breakfast and then painted them with emulsion paint."

donkey work = menial/routine tasks

"While the chef created culinary masterpieces his assistants did all the donkey work for him."

for donkey's years = for a very long time

"Joe has been the gardener at the mansion for donkey's years, and the place will never be the same now that he's retired."

talk the hind leg off a donkey = talk incessantly (to the point of boredom)

"Even though James retired from politics ten years ago, he can still talk the hind leg off a donkey."

doom

See: the crack of doom.

doomsday

till doomsday = for ever
"It will take us till doomsday to clear up all this mess."

door

at death's door = on the point of death
"My mother would never let us stay home from school unless we were practically at death's door."

behind closed doors = in secret
"The board of directors met the major shareholders behind closed doors to discuss the take-over bid."

close the door to = exclude
"The committee voted to set the subscription rate high in order to close the door to time-wasters and people they regarded as undesirable."

have a foot in the door = gain access to a (difficult-to-enter) group/ organization
"He hoped he had a foot in the door of journalism by getting an article published in the local paper."

in by/through the back door = secretly/ without (formal) permission
"The importing of tortoises is now officially banned, but some still seem get in by the back door and find their way into pet shops."

keep the wolf from the door = ensure that one has enough money for basic necessities (such as food and shelter)
"I have a spare-time job in the evenings and do overtime most weekends, which all helps to keep the wolf from the door."

lay at somebody's door = blame somebody
"The cause of the recent chaos on the railways has been laid at the door of the trade unions, who insist on working to rule."

leave the door open = provide a possibility for the future
"The recent tax cuts have left the door open for job creation and new investment in industry."

lock the stable door after the horse has bolted = take precautions after the event
"The jeweller had been burgled twice in a year before he decided to install extra security devices, but it was a case of locking the stable door after the horse has bolted."

next door to = almost the same as
"The judge remarked that omitting to tell the truth was next door to lying as far as the law is concerned."

on one's doorstep = close to where one lives
"Our new house was a bit expensive, but we save money on travelling because the main shops and my office are right on our doorstep."

show somebody the door = ask/tell somebody to leave
"The drunk was upsetting all the other customers and the landlord decided it was time to show him the door."

shut/slam the door in somebody's face = refuse to talk to somebody
"The management repeated their previous offer and then slammed the door in the union's face; a strike now seems inevitable."

See also: open door policy; open the door to.

dose

like a dose of salts = very quickly
"Good Lord! The children have gone through that packet of biscuits like a dose of salts."

See also: dose/taste of one's own medicine.

dot the i's and cross the t's = pay attention to/complete the details
"The proposal was nearly ready to be put before the board for consideration, it was just a matter of dotting the i's and crossing the t's.
on the dot = exactly on time
"The headmaster wants to see you at nine o'clock on the dot."
sign on the dotted line = write one's signature (on a binding/formal document)
"The car will be yours, sir, as soon as you sign on the dotted linc."
See also: the year dot.

double
be somebody's double = to resemble somebody very closely
"She looks so much like Jane Fonda she could be her double."
double-back = retrace one's steps
"This isn't the right way; we'll have to double back to the crossroads and try again."
double-barrelled name = hyphenated surname
"Gordon's surname is Flint-Johnson, which is a combination of the surnames of his father and his mother after she remarried."
double-cross = betray a trust/break a promise
"The art dealer agreed to sell me the painting, but then double-crossed me when somebody else offered to pay more for it."
double-dealing = using deceptive/ underhanded business practices
"The property tycoon was double-dealing by offering the farmer much less than the market price for the land, knowing full well that he could easily sell it at a vast profit."
double-dyed = stained with guilt
"Jacob is a double-dyed scoundrel who would rob his own mother!"
double-edged = dual/double-purpose
"Famine is the double-edged result of poverty and lack of resources."
double-quick = very quick
"You'll have to get to the bank in double-quick time if you want to get there before it closes."
double talk = ambiguous statement (intended to mislead)
"The newspaper article condemned the minister's reply as so much double talk, and demanded straight answers to the key questions."
double time = fast marching pace, or twice the usual rate of pay
"The platoon will have to march in double time to get back to base before nightfall."
"Anybody who volunteers to work overtime this weekend will be paid double time."
double up = increase twofold, or do duty for two things
"To finish the wall by Friday we'll have to double up on the number of bricklayers."
"If necessary, my waterproof cape doubles up as a groundsheet."
in double harness = in partnership with
"Laurel and Hardy were in double harness throughout most of their film careers."
seeing double = having double vision (usually through the action of alcohol), or mistaking two very similar things as being the same
"After nine pints of beer John had great difficulty putting the key in the lock because he was seeing double."
"When I see you and your twin sister together I think I'm seeing double."

See also: double Dutch.

doubt

beyond/without (a shadow of a) doubt = certainly
"On such damning evidence the outcome of the case is beyond doubt."
"Dave Foster is without doubt the biggest man I've ever seen."

doubting Thomas = somebody who always expresses doubt
"I didn't bother to tell Hannah about the good news; she's such a doubting Thomas, she probably wouldn't have believed me anyway."

give somebody the benefit of the doubt = accept somebody's word if it cannot be proved wrong
"At first I didn't know whether to accept his excuse about the train being delayed, but in the end I decided to give him the benefit of the doubt."

in doubt = questionable/uncertain
"I'm still in doubt as to whether we'll have enough funds to carry out the expansion programme."

no doubt = certainly
"No doubt you know how much it is going to cost you."

dove

dove of peace = symbol of peace
"At last there is a chance that the hawks of war will be replaced by doves of peace."

See also: gentle as a dove.

down

be/feel down = feel depressed
"I'm sorry I was grumpy yesterday, I was feeling down for some reason."

do somebody down = abuse/slander somebody
"I hate to do anybody down, but I do think that Malcolm is a right prat."

down and out = knocked down and unconscious/with no fight left, or (somebody) with no means of (financial) support
"After successfully fighting off two take-over bids, the third one found the tycoon down and out."
"Lack of cheap temporary accommodation has led to an increase in the number of down and outs who have to sleep on city streets at night."

down-at-heel = poor/poverty-stricken
"Although he was down-at-heel, he still had his pride and was determined not to accept any form of charity."

down-hearted = dispirited/depressed
"Sheila felt down-hearted when she failed to pass her audition."

down in the mouth/dumps = miserable/unhappy
"Brian came home looking very down in the mouth after receiving his redundancy notice."

down under = Australia (and New Zealand)
"My mate Bruce comes from down under."

down with! = away with!
"Down with drink! It's an evil influence on society!"

have a down on somebody = treat somebody unfairly/wish somebody harm
"French wine producers tend to have a down on their Italian counterparts because they regard them as a threat to their long-established markets."

See also: down on one's luck; down-to-earth; down tools; go down the drain; hit somebody when he/she is down; run somebody down; suit somebody down to the ground; talk down to somebody.

dozen

baker's dozen = thirteen

"I go to the florists on the corner, because if you pay for twelve roses they always give you a baker's dozen."

dozens of = many

"We couldn't make up our minds which wallpaper to buy, there were dozens of patterns to choose from."

talk nineteen to the dozen = talk rapidly

"Sports commentators have to be able to talk nineteen to the dozen when the action gets fast and furious."

See also: six of one and half-a-dozen of the other.

drab

See: dribs and drabs.

drag

be in/wear drag = (of a man) wear women's clothes

"Dave wore drag to the fancy dress party."

drag in/up = bring an unnecessary/unwanted topic into a discussion

"The issue is quite complicated enough, without dragging in the argument about the possible effects on wildlife in the twenty-first century."

"As soon as it became known that he was standing for parliament, the newspapers were quick to drag up references to the scandals which dogged the very early days of his career."

drag on = go on so long as to cause boredom

"The sermon began to drag on, and the congregation fidgeted nervously."

drag out = prolong (unnecessarily), or to extract information (from somebody who is reluctant to give it)

"The film director had tended to drag out the plot with too many bedroom scenes."

"Rachel didn't want to tell me about her new boyfriend but eventually I was able to drag it out of her."

drag somebody through the mire/mud = dishonour/shame somebody

"By the time the press had dragged him through the mud he had to stand down as presidential candidate."

See also: drag one's feet.

drain

go down the drain = go to waste/be lost

"John had spent hours keying data into the computer, but it all went down the drain when a power cut erased the machine's memory."

See also: brain drain; laugh like a drain.

draught

on draught = available from a barrel (as opposed to bottles)

"Let's go to the Bolton Arms; I believe they have Guinness on draught there."

See also: feel the draught/pinch.

draw

draw a bead on = aim at

"He carefully drew a bead on the rogue elephant and shot it dead."

draw a blank = fail to find something

"I've searched the entire office for the missing file but I've drawn a blank."

draw a veil over = say no more about something

"I think it best if we draw a veil over what happened last night."

draw away/back = recoil/retreat

"We tried to help fight the fire but had to draw away from the heat of the flames."

draw in = shorten, or arrive/stop
"After the summer solstice the days begin to draw in."
"The train drew into the station."

draw lots = take part in a lottery (to select somebody for something)
"It was pouring with rain so we used the playing cards to draw lots to see who would go and get the fish and chips for supper."

draw on = take from (reserve)
"Andy can always draw on his working knowledge of the process to solve any problems."

(long) drawn out = extended/prolonged
"The autobiography is quite interesting apart from the long drawn out section that deals with the author's schooldays."

draw near = approach
"You can tell when Christmas draws near because the shops are full of decorations."

draw off = decant/siphon or divert the flow of (a liquid)
"The flight engineer knew that if the plane wasn't refuelled soon he would have to draw off fuel from the reserve tanks."

draw on = allure/entice, or take from
"You hide up that tree with the rifle and I'll let the leopard get my scent and draw it on ñ but make sure you don't miss!"
"I would like to draw on your extensive local knowledge, please."

draw out = extend/prolong, or extract information, or withdraw money
"As usual the minister's speech, although drawn out, contained nothing new."
"The interrogators used threats and torture to draw out a confession from the spy."
"He planned to draw out $500 from his current account."

draw somebody aside = take somebody from a group for a private conversation
"During the meeting the boss drew me to aside to ask me what I thought the outcome would be."

draw somebody's fire = tactically allow oneself to be attacked
"The Captain says that we must draw the fire of the shore battery in order that the landing party can get to the beach unopposed."

draw to an end = bring/come to a conclusion
"I knew the film must be drawing to an end because the hero had just been killed."

drawn game = contest that ends with both sides even
"The union won the concession over tea breaks and the management got its way about piecework rates, so the meeting was judged to be a drawn game."

draw up = compile, or arrive
"I will draw up the itinerary for the Queen's visit and we'll discuss it at the next meeting."
"The Queen's coach drew up at the entrance to Westminster Abbey."

draw upon/on = take from reserves/ resources
"They had sufficient food for only two more days and if the weather didn't improve they would have to draw on their emergency rations."

good draw = popular attraction
"Topless waitresses are always a good draw in the gentlemensí club on Friday nights."

on the drawing-board = at the design/ planning stage

"The new model won't be available for several years ñ it's still on the drawing-board."

quick on the draw = quick to react

"The contestants on the television quiz show had to be quick on the draw because they were allowed only ten seconds to answer a question."

See also: call/draw attention to; back to the drawing-board; choose/draw the short straw; draw a parallel; draw blood; draw/pull in one's horns; draw the line (at).

drawer

bottom drawer = household articles collected by a girl before she gets married

"I bought you some table mats when I was on holiday. If you don't use them now, you can always put them in your bottom drawer."

(not) out of the top drawer = (not) of a high social position

"You have to be out of the top drawer to get a management position with that company."

dream

beyond one's wildest dreams = much better than one could expect/imagine

"I had hoped to win the football pools one day but to get this much was beyond my wildest dreams."

dream up = devise/invent

"I had to dream up a convincing story about why I was late for work this morning."

(go) like a dream = work perfectly, as hoped/planned

"The car had been laid up all winter but when I turned on the ignition it started first time and went like a dream."

not dream of = not occur to one

"Although the door was open, I wouldn't dream of going in unless invited."

sweet dreams = sleep well

"Good night, my darling. Sweet dreams."

See also: day dream.

dress

dress down/give a dressing down = give somebody a severe reprimand

"The butler gave the maid a dressing down for not cleaning the silver properly."

dress to kill/up to the nines = dress to attract attention

"Nora arrived at the party dressed to kill, causing every head to turn in admiration."

dress up = wear one's best clothes, or don a costume, or decorate something (to improve its appearance)

"We shall have to dress up in evening clothes to go to the gala performance."

"Good, it's a costume party ñ I love to dress up."

"The Christmas tree is a bit spindly but it will look fine when it's dressed up with all its decorations."

drib

dribs and drabs = small scattered amounts/quantities

"He paid me back the money I lent him in dribs and drabs, but I got it all eventually."

drift

catch/get the drift of = understand

"It seems the project is going to cost more than we thought, if I get the drift of what you're telling us."

drink

drink like a fish = drink heavily/to excess
"Tom used to drink like a fish ñ eight pints a night was quite usual for him."

drink in = absorb (eagerly)
"He has a fund of interesting experiences and I can drink in anything he says."

drink on the house = complimentary drink (from the landlord/proprietor)
"Malcolm offered his regular customers a drink on the house on his birthday."

drink to = to toast
"Let's all drink to the success of the project."

in/into the drink = in/into the water
"I tried to regain my balance but I fell off the jetty and into the drink."

See also: drink (take) one's fill; drink somebody under the table; spike a drink; the demon drink.

drive

back-seat driver = somebody who offers unwanted advice to the person in charge
"My assistant has become a bit of a back-seat driver and it's getting on my nerves."

drive at = imply/suggest
"I could now see what the detective was driving at: he was trying to establish my whereabouts on the night of the crime."

drive away/off = repel/discourage
"The owners of the mansion had installed an electric fence and several large dogs to drive away any intruders."

drive somebody mad/round the bend/round the twist/to drink = severely anger/annoy/frustrate somebody
"The noise of that machinery is driving me round the bend!"
"The children's incessant quarrelling was enough to drive their parents to drink."

in the driver's seat = in control
"While the manager is on holiday his assistant will be in the driver's seat."

what are you driving at? = what are you implying/trying to say?
"What are you driving at? Are you implying that I don't know what I'm talking about?"

See also: drive a hard bargain; drive somebody up the wall; drive/hammer something home; pure as the driven snow.

drone

drone on = talk incessantly and monotonously
"I hate these political documentaries; they drone on about the same thing time after time ñ they never change."

drop

drop a brick/clanger = make a blunder (in conversation)
"I dropped a brick when I told that joke about the pope ñ I didn't realize that Alex was a staunch Roman Catholic."

drop a hint = make a subtle suggestion
"I will drop the boy a hint and suggest that the might find it easier to find a job if he got rid of the green punk hair style."

drop a line = write a letter
"During our first day at summer camp we were told to drop a line to our parents to tell them that we had arrived safely."

drop behind = get farther (back) from the leader

"After leading for most of the race, the favourite dropped behind as an outsider sprinted past him to win by two lengths."

drop in = call on/visit
"Please drop in any time you are passing this way."

drop in the bucket/ocean = insignificant amount/quantity
"Our Solar System is a drop in the ocean when compared to the infinite expanse of the universe."

drop off = fall asleep, or decline
"My grandfather sits in his chair after lunch and drops off for a couple of hours."
"Sales of ice cream have begun to drop off significantly now that summer is over."

drop out = reject convention (and join the alternative society)
"When I was a student I dropped out of university and went to live in a hippie community, but I regret it now."

fit/ready to drop = exhausted
"The drill sergeant took the men on a ten-mile march and they were all fit to drop by the time they got back to barracks."

have a drop too much = be drunk
"At the end of the party Gill was all right but her husband had had a drop too much."

have the drop on somebody = have the advantage over somebody
"He asked about exports and had the drop on me because he had access to all the latest government statistics."

See also: at the drop of a hat; drop dead; drop/give/throw a hint.

drown

drown one's sorrows = drink in order to (temporarily) forget one's troubles
"Alex lost a hundred pounds at the dog track and decided to go home and drown his sorrows."

drug

See: drug on the market.

drum

beat the drum for = be an enthusiastic supporter of
"Jeremy never misses an opportunity to beat the drum for the Social Democrats."

drum up = assemble/organize
"The whole family arrived unexpectedly but mother drummed up a meal for them somehow."
"We must go round knocking on doors if necessary to drum up more support for the cause."

drummed out = expelled in disgrace
"He was drummed out of the service for conduct unbecoming of an officer."

drum something into somebody = make somebody learn something (by repetition/indoctrination)
"I constantly drum it into my children not to accept lifts from strangers."

See also: jungle drums.

drunk

See: blind drunk; dead drunk.

dry

dry as dust = parched/very dry, or very uninteresting
"I could do with a drink, my throat is as dry as dust."
"I find his early novels as dry as dust."

dry up = be unable to talk/stop talking, or dry dishes (after washing up)

"When it came to my turn to speak I just dried up."
"He's been talking for a quarter of an hour; I wish he'd dry up and then we could all go home."
"If you wash the dishes I'll dry up for you."

dry out = stop drinking (alcohol)
"June was in danger of becoming an alcoholic and so she's gone to a special nursing home to dry out."

See: bone dry; cut and dried; high and dry; dry run.

duck

break one's duck = score/succeed (after having failed previously)
"Somebody has finally bought one of my paintings ñ at least I've broken my duck!"

dead duck = something that is finished/ over with
"After women obtained the right to vote, the suffragette movement became a dead duck in Britain."

lame duck = something that needs (financial) support
"The ailing motor industry is a lame duck that the government has helped in the past."

like a dying duck (in a thunderstorm) = sad and weak
"Come on, cheer up! You look like a dying duck in a thunderstorm."

like water off a duck's back = without having any effect
"To the seasoned campaigner, the remarks of hecklers were like water off a duck's back."

lovely weather for ducks = wet weather
"You're lucky it's sunny in Scotland; it's lovely weather for ducks down here."

make a duck = score zero (at cricket)
"Much to his embarrassment, the captain made a duck in each innings."

sitting duck = easy target
"Parking offenders are sitting ducks for the police; I wish they would leave us alone and go and arrest some muggers instead."

take to something like a duck to water = be completely at ease in a new situation
"Even after years of using a mechanical typewriter, my secretary has taken to her new word processor like a duck to water."

ugly duckling = somebody who is unattractive/unpromising when young
"You'd never believe it, but that beauty used to be an ugly duckling when I knew her at school."

due

give somebody his due = give somebody the credit he/she deserves
"His work isn't brilliant but, give him his due, he is conscientious and loyal."

give the devil his due = acknowledge a good aspect in somebody one dislikes
"Give the devil his due, our boss pays well even if he does work us extremely hard."

dull

dull the edge of = make less effective
"I wish I hadn't eaten that ice cream, it's dulled the edge of my appetite for lunch."

dull as ditchwater = very dull
"I tried to read her latest book but found it as dull as ditchwater."

dumb

our dumb friends = animals (stressing their non-human nature)

"We should all remember our dumb friends on Guy Fawkes night, and shut them indoors away from the sound of fireworks."

See also: dumb animals; dumb blonde.

dummy

like a tailor's dummy = lacking animation

"Don't stand there like a tailor's dummy, come in and join the dancing."

dumps

(down) in the dumps = depressed/ miserable

"I'm feeling down in the dumps these days, I think I need a holiday."

duration

for the duration = for as long as something lasts

"Blackout regulations were in force for the duration of the Second World War."

dust

bite the dust = die/cease to exist

"The cavalry commander predicted that many Sioux would bite the dust if they attacked the fort."

"Oh well, another good idea bites the dust."

like gold dust = extremely rare

"I'm looking for a first edition of the book but they're like gold dust ñ I can't find one anywhere."

not so dusty = quite good

"In spite of his age his piano playing is still not so dusty."

not to see somebody for dust = unable to see somebody because he/she has left in a hurry

"When I told the spectators the beer tent was open you couldn't see them for dust."

shake the dust from one's feet = move away

"The family decided to shake the dust from their feet and emigrate to Australia."

throw dust in somebody's eyes = confuse/ mislead somebody

"The accused had thrown dust in the eyes of the police by giving them a false alibi."

when/after the dust has settled = when the situation is calm again

"Now that the strike is over, we must form a management-staff committee when the dust has settled."

See also: dry as dust.

Dutch

double Dutch = nonsense

"I do wish this contract was written in plain English; all this legal jargon is double Dutch to me."

Dutch auction = auction at which the bidding starts with a high price, which is gradually reduced until somebody is willing to pay it

"We held a Dutch auction for charity and people were paying tens of pounds for worthless junk."

Dutch cap = (contraceptive) diaphragm

"The Dutch cap is not as reliable as the oral contraceptive pill."

Dutch courage = confidence that results from having an alcoholic drink

"I had to have a drink to give me Dutch courage before my wedding."

Dutch treat = occasion on which everybody pays for himself/herself

"It was near the end of the month and we were all hard up, so we decided to have a Dutch treat and each buy our own drinks."

go Dutch = share the cost (equally)
"I took Mary out to lunch and she insisted on going Dutch."

*I'm a Dutchman if.*Ö = phrase that emphasizes the improbability of a statement
"She says she's only 45, but if she's a day under 50 then I'm a Dutchman."

talk to somebody like a Dutch uncle = give severe but friendly advice
"Because it was the youth's first offence, the police sergeant spoke to him like a Dutch uncle and warned him not to get into any more trouble."

duty

duty bound = have a moral/personal obligation
"Having witnessed the accident I felt duty bound to make a statement to the police."

See also: do duty for; in the line of duty.

dwell

dwell on = talk about at length
"I'm still annoyed about it, but we won't dwell on that subject any longer."

dye

dyed-in-the-wool = fixed/inflexible (in one's views)
"Farmer Jones was a dyed-in-the-wool traditionalist; he would never use any modern pesticides."

of the deepest dye = extreme/fanatic (in one's views)
"He was a supporter of the deepest dye, and had been a member of the movement for more than forty years."

See also: double-dyed.

dying

See: die

E

eager

eager beaver = somebody who is enthusiastic/overzealous
"Ask young Harry to do it ñ he's still an eager beaver and wants to impress by his willingness."

eagle

eagle eye = keen/vigilant sight
"John said that his daughters could have a party on Saturday night, but warned them that he would be keeping an eagle eye on the proceedings."

ear

about one's ears = all around one
"I regret getting involved with my daughter's marital problems; all it's done is to bring trouble about my ears."

an ear for = an appreciation of
"Gary quite likes pop music, but has an ear for the classics as well."

be all ears = listen attentively
"The children were all ears as the old man told them a fairy story."

bend somebody's ear = talk (boringly) to somebody
"My mother bent my ear for nearly an hour about the problem she's having with her neighbours."

box somebody's ears/give somebody a thick ear = slap somebody on the side of the head
"If you don't behave yourselves I'll box your ears!"
"My father gave me a thick ear when he heard I'd been playing truant."

cauliflower ear = injury caused by repeated blows/pressure to the ear
"That cauliflower ear is a sure sign that he was once a professional boxer."

come to/reach one's ears = be made aware of
"It has come to my ears that some members of staff are leaving work early; this practice must stop forthwith."

coming out of one's ears = in great excess
"The Duke and Duchess were so wealthy that they seemed to have money coming out of their ears."

ear-splitting = excessively loud/shrill
"There was an ear-splitting roar as the Red Arrows display team flew overhead."

flea in the ear = a scolding
"The gardener sent the boy off with a flea in his ear and told him not to walk on the flower beds again."

gain the ear of = get somebody to listen to one
"We'll only get our proposal considered if can gain the ear of the managing director."

give ear to = listen/pay attention to
"The press gave ear to the chancellor's warning of a possible rise in interest rates."

give one's ears for = make great personal sacrifice for/pay any price for
"I'd give my ears for a chance to fly on Concorde."

grate on the ear = sound harsh/unpleasant
"The constant whine of the electric drill was beginning to grate on my ears."

have a word in somebody's ear = speak to somebody privately
"When you have time would you come to my office, I'd like to have a word in your ear."

have long ears = be inquisitive/nosey
"Brenda has long ears; one of these days, she's going to hear something that will upset her."

have one's ear to the ground = be alert to the situation
"Keep your ears to the ground; I've heard a rumour that there is going to be a surprise budget to increase the rate of VAT."

have one's ears burning = be the subject of conversation
"No, we weren't talking about you. Why, were your ears burning?"

have the ear of = have access to a (higher) source of information
"What he says is probably true because he has the ear of the Queen."

I'm all ears = I am listening intently
"Tell me what she said next ñ I'm all ears."

in one ear and out of the other = not remembered/ignored
"The doctor advised the patient to cut down on her drinking but he could tell that it was going in one ear and out of the other."

lend an ear = listen (attentively)
"If you would lend an ear for a couple of minutes you might learn something to your advantage."

no ear for music = non-musical
"The band doesn't sound out of tune to me, but then I've no ear for music."

play by ear = play a musical instrument without using printed music
"I can play the piano by ear, but I regret now that I never learned to read music properly."

play it by ear = see how a situation develops and react accordingly/improvise
"My solicitor advised me to take no action immediately but play it by ear until we could prove that the hotel was legally responsible for my accident."

prick up one's ears = suddenly start listening carefully
"He wasn't paying much attention then pricked up his ears when he heard that the terms included the use of a company car."

throw somebody out on his/her ear = forcibly eject somebody
"The drunk was making a nuisance of himself and so the manager threw him out on his ear."

unable to believe one's ears = amazed/astounded
"I was unable to believe my ears, the language she used was so disgusting."

up to one's ears in = overwhelmed with/submerged in
"They've borrowed so much money that they're up to their ears in debt."
"I'm sorry, I'll have to cancel lunch today because I'm up to my ears in paper work."

reach somebody's ears = come to somebody's attention/notice
"It's reached my ears that you were seen going into the pub last night."

set somebody by the ears = lead to disharmony among people
"Trying to agree where to go on holiday set the family by the ears."

wet behind the ears = inexperienced/naive
"Many of these youngsters know the job in theory but they're still wet behind the ears when it comes to putting it into practice."

within earshot = within hearing distance (that is, relatively near)
"Don't wander off too far, children; I want you to remain within ear-shot."

See also: dog-eared; fall on deaf ears; make a pig's ear of something; make a silk purse out of a sow's ear; pin back one's ears; turn a deaf ear to; walls have ears.

early

bright and early = first thing in the morning
"We must get up bright and early in the morning, we've got a long drive ahead of us."

early days/early in the day = too soon to be sure
"I'd like to think that they might get married eventually, but it's early days yet."

See also: early bird.

earn

earn a bomb = earn much money
"Fred is only a waiter but he earns a bomb because of all the tips he receives."

See also: earn a crust; turn an honest penny.

earnest

be in (deadly) earnest = be very serious
"The gangster was in deadly earnest about his threat to burn down the club unless the protection money was paid."

earth

bring somebody down to earth = make somebody face up to reality
"The bank manger said that, in order to bring me down to earth and control my spending, I would have no overdraft facility and my cheque card would be withdrawn."

come back to earth = face reality
"We've had a wonderful holiday, but now we must come back to earth and get ready to go to work tomorrow."

down-to-earth = basic/practical
"I don't need a luxury car, just a down-to-earth and reliable means of transport."

ends of the earth = remotest parts of the world
"You could go to the ends of the earth before you'd find a better man for the job."

go to earth = go into hiding
"There were no clues to his whereabouts, the fugitive had obviously gone to earth."

have not an earthly = have no chance whatever
"He hasn't an earthly of getting there in under an hour."

like nothing on earth = incomparably/indescribably bad
"The smell from that drain is like nothing on earth."

move heaven and earth = go to any lengths/do everything possible
"I would move heaven and earth to be near my parents if I thought they needed me."

no earthly good/use = useless
"It's no earthly use crying, I've made up my mind and I won't change it."

no earthly reason for = no justification for
"There's no earthly reason for not getting here on time, you only live round the corner."

pay the earth for = pay a very high price for
"Her husband must have paid the earth for that ring Wendy's wearing."

run somebody/something to earth = find somebody/something that is elusive/hidden

"I looked everywhere for that invoice and finally ran it to earth among the sales receipts."

salt of the earth = somebody who is very good/worthy

"He's the salt of the earth, he'd do anything to help anyone in trouble."

what on earth? = exclamatory question of surprise

"What on earth have you done with my glasses? I can't find them anywhere!"

wipe off the face of the earth = destroy completely

"We shall not rest until we have wiped the disease off the face of the earth."

See also: all the corners of the earth; how on earth?; like heaven on earth.

ease

ease up = slow down/relax

"Remember to ease up as you approach the bridge, oncoming traffic has the right of way."

put/set somebody's at his/her ease = make somebody feel relaxed

"I felt nervous when I went to see the managing director, but he immediately put me at my ease with his open and friendly manner."

easy

easier said than done = harder to do than to talk about

"To reach the tree-house you have to climb a rope ladder ñ which is easier said than done."

easy as pie = very easy

"Learning to drive these latest automatic cars is as easy as pie."

easy come, easy go = something (money) that is easily obtained can be lost/parted with casually

"I won five pounds on the fruit machine, but lost it all when I played again; oh well, easy come, easy go!"

easy-going = relaxed/undemanding

"My Mum won't mind you coming back for tea, she's very easy-going about visitors."

easy meat/touch = somebody who is easy to dupe/take advantage of

"Old-aged pensioners are easy meat for some of these door-to-door salesmen."

easy money = money obtained with little effort

"The man in the club said that if I wanted to earn some easy money all I had to do was take a package to an address in London."

easy on the eye = pleasant to look at

"We painted our living room in pastel colours to make it easy on the eye."

go easy on somebody = be lenient with somebody

"The judge decided to go easy on the youth because it was his first offence."

go easy on/with something = do not be (over) generous with

"I'll have a gin and tonic please, but go easy on the tonic."

I'm easy = I don't mind/I'm agreeable

"Yes, I'm easy; I'll work late tonight."

in easy circumstances/on easy street = financially secure/well off

"Now that we've inherited my father's money we can live in easy circumstances."

on easy terms = easily/in a relaxed manner, or on credit/hire purchase

"One of the best qualities of our management is that you can always talk to them on easy terms."

"The bank said that I could pay back the loan on easy terms over the next two years."

take it easy = relax/slow down

"The doctor told me to take it easy or I might have a heart attack."
See also: ill at ease.

eat

eat away/into = erode/consume gradually
"I must repair the boot of my car because rust is eating away the metal."
"They had to eat into their savings to pay for their daughter's wedding."

eat dirt = tolerate insults/humiliation
"Just let me hear him say that and I'll make him eat dirt!"

eat humble pie = apologise meekly (when proven wrong)
"Edward had to eat humble pie when it became obvious that his wife was right all along."

eat like a horse = eat a lot
"My teenage son eats like horse ñ the fridge is always empty."

eat one's head off = eat greedily
"They obviously hadn't tasted such good food before and they all ate their heads off."

eat one's heart out = make one envy/grieve/pine
"Roger will eat his heart out when he sees my new Mercedes."
"It eats my heart out to see all those abandoned animals at Battersea dogs' home."
"She ate her heart out while her boyfriend was away in Germany."

eat one's words = deeply regret what one has said
"I wanted to eat my words when I found out that she had painted the picture I criticized so caustically."

eat somebody out of house and home = eat more than one's host can afford/provide
"I just don't know where those children put it all, they're eating me out of house and home."

have somebody eat out of one's hand = gain somebody's complete confidence/have control over someone
"She certainly knows how to deal with men, she's got that one eating out of her hand."

make somebody eat his/her words = make somebody retract/withdraw a statement
"I said that my wife would never pass her driving test, and when she did she made me eat my words."

what's eating you? = what are you bothered/worried about?
"What's eating you? You 've hardly said a word to me since you arrived this morning."

See also: dog eat dog; eat one's hat; have one's cake and eat it; the proof of the pudding is in the eating.

ebb

See: at (a) low ebb.

economy

black economy = unofficial business ventures that evade tax
"A recent report suggests that many self-employed and part-time workers are contributors to the black economy."

suitcase economy = economic system that is subject to high inflation
"Many debt-ridden countries of the Third World have suitcase economies."

edge

edge away = gradually move away
"The tugs took up the strain and the ocean liner edged away from the quayside."

edge somebody out = gradually get rid of somebody

"With no real reason to sack him, all we can do is to edge him out by by degrees."

give somebody the rough edge of one's tongue = scold/reprimand somebody
"Roy hasn't tidied up his room as I asked ñ he'll get the rough edge of my tongue when he comes home."

have the edge on = have the advantage
"If we launch our new model a few weeks before the motor show we'll have the edge on our competitors."

not get a word in edgeways = be unable to interrupt somebody who is talking continuously
"My wife never stops talking. If I wanted to tell her that the kitchen was on fire I wouldn't be able to get a word in edgeways!"

on edge = nervous/tense
"Dad arrived home in a bad mood and put the whole family on edge."

put an edge on one's appetite = make one hungry
"That long walk has put an edge on my appetite."

set one's teeth on edge = make one cringe/feel uncomfortable (as a result of a grating sound)
"Whenever the chalk skids across the blackboard it sets my teeth on edge."

take the edge off = make less severe/ stringent
"Some people like to take the edge off their beer by adding a small amount of lemonade."

See also: dull the edge of; on the razor's edge; thin edge of the wedge.

educate

educated guess = answer given on the basis of knowledge/past experience
"I don't know the exact population of London but at an educated guess I'd

eel

slippery as an eel = difficult to catch/pin down
"The chancellor was as slippery as an eel in managing to evade all questions about the forthcoming budget."

effect

bring (carry) into effect = put into operation
"If Britain were to be attacked, the Prime Minister would immediately bring into effect retaliatory measures."

for effect = in order to impress
"For extra effect, the pop star added a laser display to his act."

in effect = in fact/effectively
"Although nominally a monarchy, the Netherlands is in effect a republic."

of/to no effect = useless(ly)
"I argued with them for nearly an hour, but to no effect."

take effect = happen/come about
"The decrease of two per cent in income tax will take effect on the 6th April."

to that effect = confirming that
"You still owe me a hundred pounds, and I have your promissory note to that effect."

to the effect that = that states/confirms
"I have a note to the effect that you owe me a hundred pounds."

with effect from = to commence on/from
"With effect from 2nd April your rent will be increased to £30."

effort

Herculean effort = maximum (physical) effort
"The two men made a Herculean effort to lift the fallen tree off the victim's car."

See also: last ditch effort.

egg

don't put all one's eggs in one basket = do not commit all one's resources at once
"You should diversify your assets. Put some into property, some in gilt-edged stock, and the rest in a high-interest account; that way you don't put all your eggs in one basket."

egg-head = somebody of superior intellect
"Although characterized as an egg-head, our professor has the remarkable ability of being able to explain difficult concepts in a simple way."

egg somebody on = encourage somebody
"The marathon runner was near to exhaustion when he entered the stadium, but the crowd egged him on to the finishing line."

good egg = somebody who is likeable/popular (usually because he/she is accommodating/amenable)
"Charles is a good egg, he will always find time to make up a fourth at bridge."

have egg on one's face = be embarrassed/humiliated
"I was struggling with a puzzle when my seven-year-old daughter came along and did it immediately ñ did I have egg on my face!"

kill the goose that lays the golden egg = forego/relinquish a source of income/wealth (through greed)
"They're our main client and we could increase our profit margin on their work, but we mustn't kill the goose that lays the golden egg."

like the curate's egg = good in parts
"I showed the drawing to the art buyer who was clearly not impressed when he said it was like the curate's egg."

nest egg = savings (for the future)
"The interest on that investment should provide a substantial nest egg for when we retire."

sure as eggs is eggs = absolutely certain
"I've just put my washing out to dry and so you can be as sure as eggs is eggs that it will rain within the hour!"

tread on eggs = proceed with great caution
"The reporters were aware hat they were treading on eggs when they asked the terrorist leader about the alleged atrocities committed by his troops."

See also: bad egg/hat/lot; put all one's eggs in one basket; teach one's grandmother to suck eggs.

ego

ego trip = self-indulgent activity
"Few film stars would pass up the chance of going on an ego trip to the United States to collect an Oscar."

eight

See: figure of eight; one over the eight.

elbow

at one's elbow = close at hand
"The new work benches are well planned; you never have to move from your seat because everything is at your elbow."

elbow grease = manual effort/energy
"Dad said we must use more elbow grease to get a really good shine on the car."

elbow one's way = force one's way (through a crowd)
"The faction from the extreme left is trying to elbow its way into power by short-cutting the democratic process."

elbow room = enough space to move in

"Stop crowding round. Give me some elbow room so that I can attend to the victim."

give somebody the elbow = get rid of somebody

"Maria gave her boyfriend the elbow after he twice failed to keep a date."

lift/bend the elbow = drink (regularly)

"Reg calls in the Rose and Crown every evening to lift the elbow with a few friends."

more power to his elbow = may he succeed/good luck to him

"If he's trying to change the law so that shops can open on Sundays, more power to his elbow."

out at the elbows = tattered/worn-out

"Although he's a rich man, every time I've seen him at weekends he's been wearing a jacket out at the elbows."

up to one's elbows = very busy

"What a day! I'm up to my elbows in housework, the children are off school and my mother is coming to stay!"

See also: up and down like a fiddler's elbow.

element

brave the elements = go out in bad weather

"I think I'll brave the elements and take the dog for a walk."

in one's element = doing what one best likes doing/at home

"My wife loves to entertain and she's in her element when called upon to do her party piece."

out of one's element = in an unknown/unnatural situation

"He had only played in small provincial theatres and was completely out of his element among the glamour of Broadway."

elephant

memory like an elephant = very good memory

"Even though I hadn't seen her for thirty years she still remembered the names of my children ñ she must have a memory like an elephant."

pink elephants = hallucinations symptomatic of dipsomania (chronic alcoholism)

"It's time you cut down on your drinking. If you keep on like this you'll be seeing pink elephants next."

rogue elephant = an elephant which splits away from the herd and becomes a dangerous nuisance, hence somebody who is rebellious/anti-authoritarian

"The Polish authorities probably regard the Solidarity leaders as rogue elephants."

white elephant = useless/unwanted object

"The council had built an elaborate memorial in the town square and the local press severely criticized them for spending rate payers' money on a white elephant."

eleven

eleventh hour = very last minute

"He was about to be led to the scaffold when at the eleventh hour a messenger arrived with a pardon."

else

or else = or you will regret it

"Tidy your up room, or else."

empty

empty-handed = carrying/with nothing

"The Artful Dodger sent Oliver out to pick a few pockets, and told him not to come back empty-handed."

empty-headed = not very bright (mentally)
"The boy I interviewed this morning seemed somewhat empty-headed; he could answer hardly any of my questions, even the simplest ones."

on an empty stomach = without having eaten
"It is not good for you to take vigorous exercise on an empty stomach."

end

all ends up = completely
"I played my niece at chess and she beat me all ends up."

at an end = completed/exhausted/over
"On November 11th 1918 the First World War was finally at an end."

at one's wits' end = out of patience/in a state of despair
"I'm at my wits' end with that son of ours, he's been in trouble with the police again."

at the end of one's rope/tether = limit of one's patience
"Thank goodness you're home. You can put the children to bed, I've had them all day and I'm nearly at the end of my tether."

at the end of the day = finally, when everything has been taken into account
"Rates of production are bound to vary but what matters at the end of the day is to complete the contract on schedule."

be the end of = cause the demise/death of
"His heavy drinking will be the end of him one day."

come to a sticky end = die/end in a very unpleasant situation
"Most gangsters come to a sticky end

dead end = situation from which no progress can be made
"My job is a dead end; I just work in the stores and there's absolutely no prospect of promotion."

dive/throw somebody in at the deep end = tackle a new situation with its most difficult aspect
"The whole company needed sorting out so he dived in at the deep end and started with the management structure."

end for end/end over end = in a reverse position
"If you turn the bench end for end it will be facing the way you want."

end it all = commit suicide
"Some days I get so depressed I really consider ending it all."

end of the line/road = enforced conclusion/limit
"The scientists have reached the end of the road and can only continue the research if they receive more government funding."

end on = with the end facing in the principal direction
"I meant you to join the pieces of wood end on, not side by side."
"Oliver always tackles a problem end on ñ not the most subtle approach but often effective."

ends of the earth = any extreme
"She would go to the ends of the earth to make a better life for her family."

end up = finally arrive/become
"We drove around at random and ended up by the lake."
"If you don't eat less you'll end up looking like a whale!"

in the end = finally
"Most Western films are predictable: the villain is killed and the hero wins the girl in the end."

keep one's end up = do one's share
"As long as you keep your end up we should finish within the hour."

make (both) ends meet = have enough money to live on
"It was very difficult for Arthur to make ends meet when his factory was put on a three-day week during the recession."

no end of = a lot/very much
"Your sister will make no end of a fuss if she finds out you've borrowed her lipstick without asking."

not know one end of something from the other = know nothing about something
"It's no use asking Barry to help mend a car, he doesn't know one end of a spanner from the other."

not look beyond the end of one's nose = make only a superficial search
"The book you want is over there; your trouble is you don't look beyond the end of your nose."

not see beyond the end of one's nose = be narrow-minded, with no imagination/vision
"Gerald couldn't see beyond the end of his nose; everyone else knew that his wife only married him for his money."

not the end of the world = the situation is not as bad as it seems
"Just after the opening of the village fete there was a sudden downpour, but it was not the end of the world because business was booming in the beer tent."

on end = continuously/without a break
"It has been raining for days on end because of a static depression over the North Atlantic."

on the receiving end = get something (usually unpleasant)
"Why do I always seem to be on the receiving end when there are rotten jobs to be done?"

put an end/stop to = destroy/finish
"The police raid put an end to the drug dealing operation."

the (absolute) end = the ultimate limit
"That man is the absolute end. You wouldn't believe what he's just done!"

the end justifies the means = the method employed is acceptable if the result is what is desired
"He is not always honest in his dealings but he makes a lot of money and claims that the end justifies the means."

thin end of the wedge = the (insignificant in itself) beginning of something that eventually leads to a major difficulty
"I don't mind if you stay out late for once, but you must understand that it's not the thin end of the wedge and won't become a regular thing."

tie up the loose ends = put the finishing touches to something
"The parties have agreed in principle to the new contract, and they only have to tie up a few loose ends before signing."

to no end = with no result/without success
"I tried to get Tony to change his mind, but it was to no end."

to the bitter end = to the finish, regardless of the cost or consequences
"The small resistance group were determined to fight to the bitter end to free their country from occupation."

(get hold of the) wrong end of the stick = misunderstand
"The shopkeeper got hold of the wrong end of the stick; I asked him for two dozen six-inch nails and he

gave me six dozen two-inch nails!"
See also: at a loose end; be-all and end-all; come to a bad end; dead-end job; dirty/rough end of the stick; draw to an end; fag end; for days on end; go off the deep end; in at the deep end; make one's hair curl/stand on end; never hear the end of something; no end of; odds and ends/sods; on one's beam ends; see the light at the end of the tunnel; think no end of.

enemy
be one's own worse enemy = contribute to one's own failings
"I'm trying to lose weight but I'm my own worst enemy because I cannot resist eating chocolates."
how goes the enemy? = what is the time?
"How goes the enemy? It must be nearly lunch time."
sworn enemies = irreconcilable opponents
"My dog and the neighbour's cat are sworn enemies."

English
broken English = English spoken by somebody with an incomplete knowledge of the language
"I could tell he was a foreigner because he spoke broken English."
plain English = straightforward/uncomplicated language
"Never mind the tortuous explanation; tell me in plain English, are you coming or not?"

enlarge
enlarge on = expand an explanation
"You say that the car is economical, would you mind enlarging on that?"

enough
curiously/remarkably/strangely/oddly enough = actually (although you would not expect it to be true)
"I know I'm nearly sixty but oddly enough I feel as fit as I did at forty."
enough and to spare = more than is needed
"Of course you must stay for lunch, we've enough and to spare."
enough is enough = I can tolerate no more
"You've come in late once too often. Enough is enough and I'm going to make you stay at home in the evenings for the rest of the week."
enough to wake the dead = very loud/noisy
"Turn that radio down, it's enough to wake the dead."
fair enough = I'm in agreement
"Fair enough, I think that's a very reasonable price."
sure enough = as expected
"I hadn't been to my home town for twenty-five years but sure enough it still looks the same."
that's (quite) enough = that is sufficient/stop
"That's quite enough fooling around, somebody might get hurt."
See also: enough is as good as a feast.

enquiry
searching enquiry = in-depth investigation
"The Ministry of Transport made a searching enquiry to discover the cause of the plane crash."

enter
enter a protest = make a protest
"The Russian team entered a formal

protest against the tactics of the American side."

enter into = involve oneself/engage in, or sympathize with, or form part of

"The minister refused to enter into discussions before the debate in Parliament."

"He's always miserable at parties, he won't enter into the spirit of the thing."

"The possibility of bad weather didn't even enter into our plans."

enter (up)on = begin

"You are about the enter upon a new phase in your life."

enter somebody's head = occur to somebody

"He stepped straight out without looking and it didn't even enter his head that there might be a car coming."

entry

make an entry = record in a log/register etc., or arrive in a ceremonious manner

"The captain made an entry in the ship's log that they had sighted their first landfall for sixty days."

"The film star made a grand entry into the room, knowing that everyone would stare at her."

envy

be the envy of somebody = be envied by somebody

"Their new swimming pool is the envy of all their neighbours."

green with envy = very envious

"The other girls were green with envy when she told them that her new boyfriend owned a Ferrari."

equal

all/other things being equal = everything being taken into consideration and found not to matter

"The champion has a great deal of experience and all things being equal should win easily."

be/feel equal to = feel adequate for

"I really don't feel equal to listening to my mother's complaining for yet another hour."

err

err on the right side = deliberately overestimate a requirement

"I don't know how much copier paper we need, but it's best to err on the right side and order a couple of extra reams rather than run out altogether."

errand

See: fool's errand.

error

clerical error = mistake in typing/writing

"The typist made a clerical error and gave the date as the 31st June."

See also: trial and error.

escape

See: narrow escape/squeak.

estate

the fourth estate = the press

"American presidential candidates have to be aware of the tremendous influence of the fourth estate."

esteem

hold in high esteem = regard with (great) respect

"Mother Teresa was held in high esteem throughout the world for her selfless dedication to the poor people of Calcutta."

estimate

rough estimate = broad indication/ calculated guess
"The builder said that at a rough estimate the job would take about a fortnight to complete."

eternal

eternal city = Rome
"You mustn't go to Italy without visiting the eternal city."

eternal triangle = sexual association of two women and a man (or two men and a woman)
"Glen has got himself involved in an eternal triangle that will probably result in divorce."

eternity

for (an) eternity = for ever/a very long time
"I missed the express and the journey by stopping train seemed to go on for an eternity."

even

be/get even with = take revenge on
"The sheriff vowed to get even with the outlaws for killing his deputy."

even so = all things considered
"There will probably be many people after the job but even so I'd still apply for it if I were you."

even Stephen(s) = equal/level
"We've both scored ten points so we're even Stephens."

even up = equalize
"We need one more player to enter and even up the numbers to prevent somebody from having a bye in the first round."

See also: break even; even chance; even keel; even money.

event

at/in all events = whether or not that is so
"It isn't certain if we'll complete the job tomorrow. At all events it has to be finished by the end of the week."

be wise after the event = know too late what one should have done
"I shouldn't have put that extra spoonful of curry powder in this meal, but I suppose we can all be wise after the event."

happy event = birth of a baby
"Hello, Mary, when's the happy event? It can't be long now."

in any event = anyway/regardless of what happens
"In any event I'm going to the disco tonight whether you want to come with me or not."

in the (normal) course of events = as things (usually) happen
"There is a very mixed entry for the competition this year, but in the normal course of events the best two players finish up in the final."

in the event = as things transpired
"I thought Bill was going to be there but in the event he had to go and see his mother."

in the event of = if something should happen
"In the event of a power failure the emergency lighting comes on automatically."

ever

am/do I ever = emphatically yes
"Do I want a drink? Do I ever!"
"Was I enjoying myself? Was I ever!"

did you ever? = expression of puzzled surprise
"Did you ever hear of anybody making such a mess of it as that?"

ever so = very
"I was ever so pleased to hear that you're expecting a baby."

ever such a = a very
"Have you seen Tom Smith's conker? He's got ever such a big one!"

for ever and a day = for ever/a very long time
"The council said they would come and repair the road but it looks as though it will be for ever and a day before it gets done."

for ever and ever = eternally
"Robert swears he will love me for ever and ever."

every

every man jack (of them) = all (of them)
"They're a bunch of crooks, every man jack of them."

every now and again/then, every so often = occasionally
"Every now and again I like to spend a few days in the country to get away from the bustle of London."

every other = alternate
"The nurse was told to take the patient's temperature every other hour."

See also: at every turn.

everything

everything but the kitchen sink = an (unnecessarily) large number of objects
"When we came to move house our garden shed contained everything but the kitchen sink."

hold everything! = stop everything (you are doing)!
"Hold everything! There's been yet another change of plan!"

See also: everything comes to he/him who waits.

evil

put off the evil hour/moment = postpone something unpleasant
"I don't really want another confrontation with my ex-wife about the divorce settlement, and so I've put off the evil hour until next week."

See also: fall on evil days; give somebody the evil eye.

example

make an example of somebody = reprimand/punish somebody as a deterrent to others
"The headmaster decided to make an example of the two boys and so he caned them in front of the whole school."

set somebody a (good) example = behave in a way that encourages others to copy
"Behave yourself. You should be setting your sister a good example."

exception

take exception to = be offended by/ object to
"I take exception to being addressed by my surname, I consider it bad manners."

the exception that proves the rule = a general principle is proved to be valid if it cannot be applied to a particular instance
"The fact that Wendy keeps failing her driving test is the exception that proves the rule that most women make good drivers."

exchange

exchange words = argue/quarrel
"When she gave me a parking ticket I exchanged a few well chosen words with the traffic warden."

fair exchange is no robbery = nobody loses if things exchanged have the same value
"I'll let you borrow my lawn mower if I can use your electric drill; after all, fair exchange is no robbery."

excuse
lame excuse = unconvincing reason
"Missing the train is a lame excuse for getting to work late; you should have left home earlier."

exercise
exercise one's power = use one's authority
"The Speaker of the House of Commons exercises his power to bring members to order in debates in Parliament."
object of the exercise = aim/purpose
"The sales director told the design team that the object of the exercise was to produce a more attractive product."

exhibition
make an exhibition of oneself = behave in a (very) foolish manner
"My husband got drunk at the wedding and made an exhibition of himself by proposing to the vicar's wife."

expect
be expecting = pregnant
"I'm soon to be a grandmother ñ my daughter's expecting."
expect me when you see me – be unable/unwilling to specify when one will be somewhere
"I don't know what time I'll get home tonight because of the train strike, so expect me when you see me."

expense
at one's/somebody's expense = to one's/somebody's disadvantage
"I think it is cruel to make jokes at somebody else's expense."
at the expense of = by causing harm to
"We can only increase productivity at the expense of quality, which could ruin the company's reputation."
go to the expense of = spend money (to impress/achieve something)
"The council have gone to the expense of repainting the entire town hall in preparation for the Queen's visit next month."
put somebody to expense = cause somebody to spend money
"It was a marvellous meal; I hope I didn't put you to too much expense."
See also: blow the expense.

explain
explain away = give a satisfactory excuse
"After their row and his wife had stormed upstairs, he explained away her absence to his guests by saying that she had a bad headache."

explore
See: explore every avenue.

expression
holier-than-thou expression = facial expression that is self-satisfied, smug, superior
"It annoys me when Philip adopts that holier-than-thou expression with his sons; he forgets that he was just as bad as them when he was their age."

extent
to a certain extent, to a considerable/large extent = partly, mostly

"You must take responsibility for the accident to a certain extent, because you were not paying full attention."
"The success of the new product was to a large extent due to a nationwide advertising campaign."

extreme

go to extremes = do more than is necessary
"Don't bother to spring clean the whole house just because my mother is coming ñ there's no need to go to extremes."

go to the other extreme = take an opposite view/course of action
"Ned used to be a scuba diver and now he's gone to the other extreme and taken up hang gliding."

eye

all eyes = very attentive
"When she walked into the room wearing nothing but a bikini I was all eyes."

before one's (very) eyes = in one's direct vision
"He claimed he had given up smoking, but later he lit a cigarette before my very eyes."

black eye = bruising of the eye socket caused by a blow to the eye
"When his mother asked Trevor where he got his black eye he told her that he'd walked into a door."

cast/run an eye over = look at quickly/superficially
"During the course of her everyday work the Prime Minister receives many letters and she likes to cast her eye over as many as she can."

clap/set eyes on = see/notice
"I haven't clapped eyes on brother for weeks now."

cock an eye at = give a knowing glance
"Mike was telling his wife that this was his first visit to the pub for several weeks, when the landlord cocked an eye at him and so he quickly changed the subject."

eye for an eye = take revenge by doing to an enemy what he/she did to you
"The supporters of capital punishment for murderers argue that it is society's way of taking an eye for an eye."

eye-opener = revelation
"I called early and saw the beauty queen with her curlers in ñ it was a real eye-opener."

eye somebody (up and down) = view somebody with doubt/suspicion
"My mother always eyes my boyfriends up and down before she lets me go out with them."

eye-wash = nonsense
"The press report of the incident was a load of eye-wash ñ I should know, I was there."

get one's eye/hand in = become familiar with a situation
"The whole process is changing over to a computerized system; once you've got your eye in you should find it much easier to work with."

give somebody the evil eye = give somebody a threatening/malicious look
"The two wrestlers were giving each other the evil eye across the ring before the start of the contest."

give somebody the glad eye = flirt with somebody
"When I met the new girl in the office she smiled and gave me the glad eye, and made me think that it wasn't such a bad place to work after all."

have a (good) eye for = be a good judge of something's qualities

"Barny has a good eye for a greyhound and very often picks the winner."

have/keep an eye on the main chance = take a mercenary view/be alert for ways of turning things to one's own advantage

"You have to keep an eye on the main chance if you want to get on in this firm."

have a roving eye = habitually look at (and try to form associations with) attractive women

"They're planning to get married soon, but he's always had a roving eye and I don't know how long it will last."

have/keep an eye on = keep a close watch on

"She had to go out unexpectedly and asked her husband to keep an eye on the dinner in case it burned."

have eyes bigger than one's belly/ stomach = greedy

"The woman scolded the boy for taking two pieces of cake, telling him that he had eyes bigger than his stomach."

have eyes in the back of one's head = be aware of something that one should apparently not know about

"How did Mum know we were doing that? She must have eyes in the back of her head!"

have one's eye on = notice/take a liking to

"I'm going to the antique shop to buy a vase I've had my eye on for some time."

have one's eyes about one = be alert/ watchful

"The platoon leader warned the men to have their eyes about them and beware of booby traps."

in one's mind's eye = in one's imagination

"We bought a run-down old house but in my mind's eye I could see what it would be like when it was restored."

in the eyes of = from the point of view of (the church/law etc.)

"Driving without due care and attention is a crime in the eyes of the law."

in the public eye = famous/well-known, subject to public scrutiny

"Members of the Royal Family are often in the public eye and appreciate their rare moments of privacy."

keep an eye open/out for = watch out for

"I've just put my washing out to dry, would you please keep an eye out for rain and bring it in if necessary."

keep a weather eye open = be alert for any changes

"He asked his broker to keep a weather eye open for any significant change in the price of gold as he was considering another purchase."

keep one's eye in = remain in form/ practice

"Even when he's not playing in competitions, Jack still has a game of darts in his local pub to keep his eye in."

keep one's eyes open/peeled/skinned = remain alert

"Alfred Hitchcock always made a brief appearance in his own films, so keep your eyes peeled and see if you can spot him in this one."

make (sheep's) eyes at = flirt/make appealing glances at

"Don't deny there's nothing between you, I saw you making eyes at my husband at the party last night!"

meet somebody's eyes = look at somebody face to face

"I could tell that he wasn't being

truthful because he wouldn't meet my eyes when he answered the question."

more than meets the eye = more than is immediately obvious
"Why should the robbers take the painting but leave behind the cash and jewellery? There's more to this case than meets the eye."

naked eye = unaided vision (without the use of an optical instrument)
"Bacteria are so small that it is impossible to see them with the naked eye."

not to be able to take one's eyes off somebody/something = be unable to stop looking at somebody/something
"She was a stunning girl. I couldn't take my eyes off her."

not to believe one's eyes = doubt the credibility of something unusual
"I couldn't believe my eyes when I saw him driving a Rolls Royce ñ two years ago he was a labourer on a building site."

one in the eye for = a come-down/rejection
"Fred thought that Susan was attracted to him, so it was one in the eye for him when she said she preferred me."

out of the corner of one's eye = at the edge of one's vision
"I was about to cross the road when out of the corner of my eye I saw a motorbike coming round the bend."

private eye = private detective
"She hired a private eye to investigate whether her husband was involved with another woman."

pull the wool over somebody's eyes = deceive somebody
"It's no good trying to pull the wool over Harold's eyes, he's far too perceptive."

score/hit a bull's eye = achieve sudden success
"In the pop music world, if you have a good sound, the right image and a tough manager you may hit the bull's eye."

see eye to eye = agree/share the same point of view
"The World Health Organization and various national governments see eye to eye about the need to step up research to combat the spread of AIDS."

see with (only) half an eye = notice something that is obvious
"I could see with half an eye that the deal would be detrimental to the company."

see with one's own eyes = witness personally
"I tell you it's true ñ I saw it with my own eyes."

sight for sore eyes = pleasant surprise
"You're a sight for sore eyes, I haven't seen you for ages."

through the eyes of = from somebody else's viewpoint
"Cats are warm and affectionate creatures to us, but viewed through the eyes of birds and mice they are vicious predators."

turn a blind eye to = deliberately ignore/pretend not to see
"It pays to turn a blind eye to some of things that go on around here."

up to one's eyes = very busy
"We're up to our eyes in work and so all the machinists are being offered as much overtime as they want."

view with a beady eye = observe with caution
"The teacher viewed several of the students with a beady eye in case they tried to cheat during the examination."

with an eye to = with an eventual aim
"He bought an old barn with an eye to converting it to a restaurant."

with one's eyes open = fully aware of the likely consequences
"Clive lost a fortune on the stock market, but he went into it with his eyes open and remains quite philosophical about it."

with one's eyes closed/shut = very easily
"This cake tastes awful, I could make a better one myself with my eyes closed."

worm's eye view = very low viewpoint
"When I look out of my basement window I get a worm's eye view of the passers-by."

See also: apple of one's eye; bird's eye view; catch somebody's eye; cry one's eyes/heart out; eagle eye; easy on the eye; eye on/to the main chance; eye witness; hawk eyed; in the blink of an eye; in/a twinkling of an eye; keep one's eye on the ball; lynx-eyed; open one's eyes to; remove the scales from somebody's eyes; shut one's eyes to; smack in the eye; throw dust in somebody's eyes; twinkle in somebody's eye.

eyeball

eyeball to eyeball = in direct conflict
"The union and the management were eyeball to eyeball across the negotiating table, with neither side willing to make any concessions."

eyebrow

raise one's eyebrows = be mildly shocked/surprised
"The managing director raised his eyebrows when I handed him my resignation after twenty years with the company."

eyeful

an eyeful = attractive/pleasing to look at
"The blonde was a real eyeful as she reclined on the beach in her skimpy bikini."

eyelid

not bat an eyelid = be impassive/show no reaction
"My husband must have been in a good mood yesterday, he didn't bat an eyelid when I told him I'd dented the car."

eye teeth

See: give one's eye/back teeth for something.

F

face

blow up in somebody's face = be violently changed/ended
"The architect's over-elaborate presentation blew up in his face when his client refused to pay for it."

face down = with the front or upper surface downwards
"The gunmen made the guards lie face down on the floor."

face (the) facts = acknowledge the truth
"The time has come to face facts and admit that you're not as young as you used to be."

face it out = maintain a falsehood
"I've told the boss it wasn't my fault even though it was and now I'll just have to face it out."

face the music = submit to discipline/punishment
"John's wife phoned and told him she knows what he's been up to ñ he'll have to face the music when he goes home tonight."

face to face = in the presence of, or person to person
"We passed through the shanty town and it was the first time I had come face to face with real poverty."
"We've written to each other for more than a year and at last we meet face to face."

face up = with the front or upper surface upwards
"The box contains cream cakes so it's important to carry it face up."

face up to = accept (a challenge) without weakening
"Just my luck! I've got to face up to the reigning champion in the first round of the golf tournament."

face out = defy/refuse to admit a mistake
"The controversial candidate in the election has faced out all attempts by his party to get him to stand down."

face value = apparent worth
"Robert is a real cynic; he won't accept anything or anyone on face value."

face with = confront
"Sue is helpless when faced with even the simplest maths calculation."

fall flat on one's face = make a blunder
"Terry was overconfident and it serves him right that he fell flat on his face on the first day in his new job."

fly in the face of = vigorously oppose
"James refuses to wear a suit, even in the office; he's always flown in the face of convention."

give something a face-lift = improve the (outward) appearance of something
"My company bought an old building, gave it a face-lift, and converted it to offices."

have a red face = be embarrassed
"Did I have a red face when the maid walked into my hotel room as I was changing."

have the face to = be bold enough to
"I don't know how she has the face to wear such short skirts with legs like hers."

his/her face fell = he/she expressed disappointment
"Andrew's face fell when he was told he couldn't go on the trip."

in the face of = when confronted by
"A good soldier remains calm even in the face of danger."

keep a straight face = not show one's feelings (especially when amused)
"When I saw her new punk hair-do I didn't know how to keep a straight face."

let's face it = let us be honest
"Let's face it, you're getting too old to go hang gliding."

long face = gloomy/miserable expression
"There's no need to walk round with a long face all the time; things are bound to improve for you soon."

look somebody in the face = look unflinchingly at somebody
"I don't know how she can look me in the face after what she said to me yesterday."

look/stare one in the face = be very obvious
"I wouldn't know an original Renoir from a copy if it looked me in the face."

lose face = lose respect
"It's difficult to admit one is wrong without losing face."

make faces = grimace
"The children were making faces at the teacher behind her back."

not just a pretty face = somebody who is more intelligent than it might appear
"Linda has got a degree in physics and a higher degree in mathematics, so she's not just a pretty face."

one's face is one's fortune = one's good looks are one's chief advantage
"She should succeed as a photographic model because her face is her fortune."

on the face of it = apparently/based on the available evidence
"On the face of it you have as good a chance as anyone of getting Valerie to go out with you."

poker/straight face – expression that reveals no emotion
"He maintains a poker face and you can't even guess what he's thinking."

put a brave/bold/good face (up)on it = remain outwardly cheerful in adversity
"Gavin put a bold face on it when the doctors told him that he would never completely recover from his illness."

put a new face on it = alter the situation
"I was going to write to my MP about the lack of facilities for young people, but it puts a new face on it now that the council has announced that it is going to open a youth club."

put one's face on = apply make-up
"I won't be a minute, darling, I'm just going to put my face on."

save face = retain respect
"There was no way Philip could save face after he was convicted of fraud."

set one's face against = refuse to accept
"You'll never convince Harold to support the scheme now that he's set his face against it."

show one's face = attend/be present only briefly
"The Managing Director showed his face at the office party for a few minutes and then left us to get on with it."

shut your face = shut up/be quiet
"Oh, shut your face; you're always moaning about something."

staring one in the face = very obvious
"I couldn't find my comb yet it was on the dressing table, staring me in the face all the time."

throw something in somebody's face = forcibly remind somebody of something (disadvantageous to him/her) that he/she would rather forget
"Every time the subject of my motoring conviction comes up my wife can't help throwing it in my face."

till one is blue in the face = endlessly
"I've told Chris till I'm blue in the face to wipe his feet before he goes indoors."

to one's face = honestly/openly
"If he has a complaint I wish he'd make it to my face, and not hint about it to other people."
See also: bare-faced lie; blue in the face; have a face like a fiddle; have/pull a long face; have egg on one's face; laugh in somebody's face; plain as the nose on your face; pull a face; shut/slam the door in somebody's face; was somebody's face red!; wipe the grin/smile off somebody's face.

fact
facts of life = knowledge of sex, or truth of a situation
"My parents didn't tell me the facts of life until I was well into puberty."
"You're too trusting; it's one of the hard facts of life that not everybody is as honest as you are."
facts and figures = data, statistics, and so on
"I cannot comment on the company's profitability until I've had an opportunity to study all the facts and figures."
hard facts = undeniable truth
"Unemployment has become one of the hard facts of contemporary society."
in (actual) fact = actually/in truth
"I told the man on the door that I'm over eighteen although in fact I've only just turned seventeen."
See also: as a matter of fact; face the facts; matter of fact; matter-of-fact.

fag
fag end = last part/remnant
"We're right at the fag end of the job and should finish it easily by next week."
fagged out = exhausted
"I'm fagged out after all that gardening."
too much fag = too much trouble
"You'll have to go to the pub on your own tonight; I'm not coming ñ it's too much fag in this weather."

fail
failing that = if that does not apply/happen
"I'll meet you at lunch time or, failing that, after work."
without fail = for certain
"We'll dispatch your order today, Madam, without fail."
See also: words fail me.

failure
(nearly) have heart failure = be very surprised
"I nearly had heart failure when that policeman shone his torch into the back of our parked car."

faint
have not the faintest idea = have no knowledge of whatsoever
"Sorry, I haven't the faintest idea where the Public Library is."
See also: damn with faint praise.

fair
all's fair in love and war = vigorous competition is acceptable in emotionally-charged situations
"He started shouting insults at me so I told everybody about his prison record ñ all's fair in love and war."
fair and square = honest(ly), or exactly on target
"I like doing business with that new firm because they are fair and square in all their dealings."

"A custard pie hit the clown fair and square in the face."

fair copy = good likeness, or clean/uncorrected version of a text

"He demonstrated his artistic talents by making a fair copy of the Mona Lisa."

"Miss Smith, I have amended that letter; would you please make a fair copy and bring it to me for signature."

fair do's = be fair

"Fair do's, you said you would give me half but you've kept most of it for yourself."

fair enough = accepted/agreed

"Fair enough, you bring the drinks and I'll provide the food."

(by) fair means or foul = (by) any method, honest or not

"Smith is determined to get on in this world, by fair means or foul."

fair sex = women

"I prefer the company of the fair sex to that of men."

fair's fair = be fair/honest

"Give me some of yours; fair's fair, your piece of cake is much bigger than mine."

fair to middling = average, not good and not bad

"How am I feeling today? Oh, fair to middling."

go a fair way towards = be nearly enough

"That two-hundred pound bonus will go a fair way towards paying for my holiday."

See also: bid fair; fair cop; fair deal; fair game; fair-weather friend; play fair.

fairy

fairy godmother = benefactor

"Aunt Joan was a fairy godmother to our family when mother was ill; she came and cleaned the house and did all the cooking."

See also: airy-fairy.

faith

bad faith = lack of trust

"There was always bad faith between the couple and no one was surprised when they split up."

breach of faith = broken promise

"The firm switched the order to our main competitor at the last minute; it was a breach of faith for which I'll never forgive them."

in bad faith = dishonestly

"He knew the machine was faulty when he sold it so he accepted the money in bad faith."

in (all) good faith = honestly (but often with a problematic outcome)

"I lent him the money in all good faith but didn't know he had no intention of paying me back."

pin one's faith on/put one's faith in = rely (completely) on

"It's no good pinning your faith on winning the football pools, you'd better go out and find a job."

shake one's faith = undermine one's beliefs

"The activities of muggers and vandals begin to shake my faith in the goodness of human beings."

shatter one's faith = destroy one's beliefs

"The circumstances of my parents' divorce shattered my faith in the sanctity of marriage."

See also: article of faith.

fall

easy as falling off a log = very easy

"Roger can solve quadratic equations as easy as falling off a log."

fall about (laughing) = laugh uncontrollably
"The antics of the monkeys at the zoo made everyone fall about."

fall astern/behind = get/lag behind
"The Russian athlete made a break for the lead and the rest of the runners soon fell behind."
"The hire purchase company repossessed my car because I fell behind with the payments."

fall away/off = decline
"Attendance at meetings seems to have fallen off lately."

fall back = retreat
"The enemy fell back to its second line of defence before we could surround them."

fall back on/upon = resort to
"I like to keep some money in a savings account to fall back on in an emergency."

fall between two stools = fail to meet either of two requirements (because of a reluctance to commit to one of them)
"The book falls between two stools because it is too difficult for children and not sophisticated enough for adults."

fall by the wayside = fail to complete something
"There was a plan to put more buses on the route but that fell by the wayside when economies were made."

fall flat = fail to interest/succeed
"She was feeling miserable and all my attempts to cheer her up fell flat."

fall for = become in love with
"My mother and father fell for each other when they were still at school."
"I fell for this house as soon as I saw it."

fall/run foul of = quarrel with
"I wouldn't like to fall foul of Alfred's wife when she's in a temper."

fall into arrears = get behind with payments owed
"I've had so little income during the last six months that I have fallen in arrears with my rent."

fall into place = become clear/understandable
"I was puzzled by the problem until I realized I had previously missed out one vital factor ñ then suddenly everything fell into place."

fall into line/step = agree with
"Spain must fall into step with the rest of Europe if it is to become a member of the Common Market."

fall in with = adopt/comply with (something already existing)
"They already had a method of doing the job when I took it over, and it was easier to fall in with their scheme than to impose a new one of my own."

fall on/upon = come across, or attack/seize
"I fell on that old lamp in a junk shop in town."
"Alistair was walking through an alleyway when he was fallen on by two muggers."
"I happened to mention that I am an amateur artist and the foreman fell upon the fact and made me paint the doors and windows."

fall on bad times = become impoverished
"I fell on bad times after I lost my job and it has taken me two years to recover."

fall on deaf ears/on stony ground = be (deliberately) ignored
"I went to see the boss but my request for a pay rise fell on deaf ears."

fall on one's feet = be very lucky (to survive a risk)

"Christine resigned from her job in a fit of pique and got another one the very same day; she always seems to fall on her feet."

fall out = cease to be friends/disagree

"No, you keep the change; we're not going to fall out for twenty pence!"

fall over backwards = make every effort to do something

"He said he'd fall over backwards to help, if only he had the time."

fall over oneself = be overeager to please

"I hate that new typist; she fell over herself to impress the boss, and now he's made her his secretary."

fall short = fail to meet a specified amount/quantity/standard

"The money we collected for charity fell just short of a thousand pounds."

"That new microcomputer may be cheap, but its features fall short of what we have come to expect from today's personal computers."

fall through = fail to happen

"We were going to buy a new house but the sale of ours fell through, so we'll just have to wait a bit longer."

fall to one's lot = become one's duty/ responsibility

"We had an official visit to the factory the other day and it fell to my lot to introduce the mayor to the rest of the managers."

fall under = be included in/with

"Assault falls under the category of crimes against the person."

"Marvin was a good lad until he fell under the influence of those Mods and Rockers."

fall upon somebody's neck = fawn, be obsequious

"Just watch her fall on the manager's neck when she wants something."

fall within = lie between

"Debbie's new party dress hardly falls within the limits of decency."

"The car's top speed falls within the range 120 to 125 miles per hour."

ride for a fall = take a course that is likely to lead to disaster

"In my opinion, anyone who invests money in that new company is riding for a fall."

See also: come/fall apart at the seams; fall flat on one's face; fall from grace; fall guy; fall into the habit; fall off; fall off the back of a lorry; fall sick; fall to pieces; his/her face fell.

false

false pretences = deliberate deception

"The actress got the part by false pretences because she said she had played the role before when in truth she hadn't."

false start = beginning that falters and has to be repeated

"The amateur pianist made one or two false starts before finally playing the piece right through."

false step = misdemeanour/mistake

"They're very strict at our school; one false step, and you're disciplined."

strike a false note = appear not to be genuine

"I wasn't surprised when he turned out to be an impostor; something about his manner struck a false note with me."

See also: false alarm; put a false construction on.

familiarity

See: familiarity breeds contempt.

family

family feud = long-standing family quarrel

"Because of a family feud, the two brothers haven't spoken to each other for ten years."

family tree = ancestry/genealogy

"I cannot trace my family tree back farther than my great-grandparents."

in the family way = pregnant

"John will have to marry Janet now that he's got her in the family way."

person of (some) family = somebody who is high born

"I believe Robinson is a person of some family, although you wouldn't think so to look at him today."

run in the family = be an inherited characteristic

"Both of my daughters have black hair and blue eyes; it is an unusual combination but it runs in the family."

See also: family doctor; family man.

fan

fan the flames = make a difficulty even worse

"The Government's policy would appear to be to fan the flames between the employers and the unions."

fancy

catch/take/tickle somebody's fancy = stimulate somebody's desire for/ interest in something

"I looked in the window of the antique shop and a pair of china dogs immediately caught my fancy."

footloose and fancy-free = carefree, with no responsibilities

"I think I'll go hiking in Europe for my holidays; I'll probably go on my own, footloose and fancy-free."

fancy boy/man = (male) lover

"Have you seen Penny's new fancy man? He's young enough to be her son!"

fancy one's chances = be (over)confident

"I fancy my chances today so I've put a large bet on a horse in the Grand National."

fancy oneself = be conceited

"Malcolm really fancies himself in his new outfit."

fancy price = over expensive

"I don't like that new restaurant; they charge fancy prices for mediocre food and poor service."

fancy somebody = be sexually attracted to somebody

"Tony says he fancies that girl in the red dress."

fancy that! = I am surprised!

"Fancy that! We've gone three whole weeks without a drop of rain."

fancy woman = (female) lover

"Bill neglects his wife and spends all his spare money on presents for his fancy woman."

just fancy! = just imagine!

"Just fancy! A rich husband, a car of your own, and ten thousand pounds a year just to spend on yourself."

take a fancy to = take a liking to

"We've taken a fancy to Greek food after having spent our holiday in Crete."

See also: flight of fancy.

Fanny

(sweet) Fanny Adams = nothing at all

"I helped him move all the furniture and filing cabinets up two flights of stairs to the next floor, and what did he give me for helping him? Sweet Fanny Adams!"

far

as far as in one lies = as much as one is able

"As far as in one lies I'll do everything

I possibly can to help."

as/so far as one can tell = apparently
"As far as one can tell she's gone back to live with her ex-husband."

by far/far and away = absolutely/without equal
"There were five acts in the cabaret and the comedian was the best by far."
"There were five acts in the cabaret but far and away the best was the comedian."

far and near/wide = over a large area
"I've searched far and wide for my umbrella and I still can't find it."

far be it from me = presumptuous and self-denigrating remark
"Far be it from me to tell you how to run your life, but I think you should get divorced."

far-fetched = exaggerated/lacking credibility
"He told be some far-fetched story about climbing the Matterhorn when he was only fifteen."

far-flung = distant
"Hong Kong is last far-flung outpost of the old British Empire."

far from/not far from = distant/close
"I'm afraid her explanation is far from the truth."
"Your offer is not far from the price I'm willing to accept."

far from it = by no means/not at all
"She didn't seem pleased to see me, far from it."

far gone = in need of repair (of a thing), or not totally conscious through drink/drugs (of a person)
"My old jacket is pretty far gone and I'll have to buy another one."
"He's been smoking pot all afternoon and he'll be far gone for the rest of the day."

go far = be successful (in one's career)
"She's got a good education and a charming personality and she should go far."

go too far = be excessive in one's behaviour/be impolite
"You've gone too far this time and I'm going to leave you for good!"

so far, so good = up to this point everything is satisfactory (although it may not continue to be so)
"We've covered the first half of the course without mishap and so far, so good."

See also: far cry from; far out; few and far between.

fare

bill of fare = menu, or list of things available/to be done
"Let's look at the bill of fare and decide what we're going to eat."

farm

farm out = make something somebody else's responsibility, to subcontract
"We were able to farm out the children with my parents and go away for the weekend on our own."
"We've got so much work to do that we've had to farm some of it out."

farthing

not give a brass farthing = not care (in the slightest)
"I don't give a brass farthing for what you think, I'm going to do it anyway."

fashion

after a fashion = in an approximate sort of a way (intended as a veiled criticism)
"My daughter made the dinner last night and it was all right, after a fashion."

all the fashion = (very) popular

"Short spiky hair is all the fashion with the girls in my class at school."

See also: all ship-shape and Bristol fashion; like it's going out of fashion.

fast

fast and furious = quick(ly) and vigorous(ly)

"The mob made a fast and furious attempt to break down the barriers."

not so fast = wait a minute

"Not so fast, I haven't accepted the first part of your argument yet."

play fast and loose = deceitfully/ selfishly change one's attitudes

"Mark is not serious about Angela and is only playing fast and loose with her affections."

pull a fast one = cheat/deceive

"I paid for the goods with a ten pound note but the shop assistant pulled a fast one and only gave me change for a fiver."

stand fast = remain still, unmoving/ unyielding

"Even when confronted with new evidence to the contrary, he stood fast and would not change his opinion."

See also: make fast.

fasten

fasten on to = grasp

"Maria is remarkably quick at fastening on to new ideas."

fasten your seat belts! = hold on!/be prepared for a (pleasant) surprise

"Fasten your seat belts! I've got some wonderful news ñ we've won first prize on the football pools!"

fat

fat chance = very unlikely

"Will I go fishing with you on Saturday? Fat chance, my wife wants me to take her shopping."

fat lot of = very little

"Fat lot of good that will do, trying to paint a whole wall with a one-inch brush."

live off the fat of the land = live in luxury

"Trevor has been able to live off the fat of the land since he inherited his father's fortune."

the fat is in the fire = an action has caused trouble

"When your mother finds out what you've done the fat will really be in the fire."

See also: chew the fat; kill the fatted calf.

fate

as sure as fate = inevitably

"You can't keep on shoplifting; as sure as fate you'll be caught one day."

fate worse than death = something that is most undesirable, or (of a woman) unwilling participation in sex

"I would regard having to commute fifty miles to work each day as a fate worse than death."

"Victorian women were brought up to regard sex as a fate worse than death."

seal somebody's fate = guarantee future unpleasantness for somebody

"The police found her fingerprints at the scene of the crime, and that sealed her fate."

tempt fate = take a risk

"Walking through that field with the bull loose is just tempting fate."

father

father and mother of = extreme version of

"I woke up this morning with the father and mother of a headache."

father figure = man regarded with affection/respect, as a child might show to a father
"The boss is a father figure to all the staff where I work, and morale is very high."
like father, like son = people usually behave like their parents
"His father was a chess champion and he is also very good at the game: like father, like son."
his father's son = resembles his father
"Simon is his father's son all right ñ same ginger hair and violent temper!"
how's your father = improper (often sexual) activity
"On the way back from the party, my girlfriend and I had a bit of how's your father on the back seat of my car."
on the father's side = inherited through the father
"Gill has always seemed a bit strange, but I believe there's a history of insanity on the father's side."
the father of = founder/inventor
"Priestley has been called the father of modern chemistry."
when father turns, we all turn = father is the absolute authority in our family
"Although we wanted to go to the zoo, Dad wanted to go to the beach and that's where we went ñ when father turns, we all turn."
See also: the mother and father of.

fault

fault on the right side = flaw which is to somebody's credit, not discredit
"Ann's naivety is at least a fault on the right side."
find fault with = be (over)critical of
"No matter how hard I try, that teacher always finds fault with my work."
to a fault = to excess
"Jack would give you his last shilling ñ he's generous to a fault."

favour

do me/us a favour! = you cannot expect me to believe that!
"Do us a favour! You can't have bought that car for only a hundred pounds!"
find favour = receive approval
"I hope your proposal finds favour with the committee."
in high favour = well thought of
"Jan should get a good rise this year, she's in high favour with the management."
in somebody's favour = to somebody's advantage
"The referee always seemed to make decisions in the champion's favour, never the challenger's."
See also: curry favour.

fear

for fear of = in case
"I dare not go with you for fear of my father finding out."
in fear (and trembling) = very apprehensive(ly)/anxious(ly)
"My wife always goes to the dentist in fear and trembling."
never fear = do not worry
"Never fear, we'll all be there to back you up if there's any trouble."
no fear! = no I will not!
"Go sailing with you? No fear! I can't swim!"
put the fear of God into = frighten/terrify
"I've got no head for heights. Just the thought of climbing a ladder puts the fear of God into me."
there's not much fear of = it is extremely unlikely that (something will happen)
"There's not much fear of rain so

we're going to have a barbecue."

without fear or favour = in a totally fair/unbiased manner
"The Ombudsman investigates complaints about misuse of authority without fear or favour."

feast

enough is as good as a feast = sufficient is as good as a large amount/quantity
"No you can't go to the pictures. You've been once already this week, and enough's as good as a feast."

feast one's eyes on = enjoy looking at
"Come and feast your eyes on this beautiful view."

feather

be spitting feathers = be very angry/thirsty
"Len was spitting feathers when he saw what some vandal had done to his new car."
"We had trekked five miles across the moors and I was spitting feathers when fortunately we came across a small country pub."

feather-bed = spoil
"His mother has feather-bedded him all his life and he's quite unfit to go and live on his own."

feather-brained = impractical/lacking in common sense
"They had some feather-brained scheme to float a pontoon bridge across the Channel."

feathered friends = birds
"We mustn't forget to put out food for our feathered friends in frosty weather."

feather in one's cap = attainment/honour
"Sir Joseph's knighthood was the final feather in his cap after years of dedicated service to the community."

feather one's nest = selfishly (and possibly dishonestly) further one's own interests
"The Chairman is taking money out of the company to feather his own nest, rather than re-invest it to help the business grow."

in fine feather = happy/healthy
"You're in fine feather this morning, Barry; had a win on the football pools?"

make the feathers fly = provoke a fierce struggle
"She's just spotted her husband drooling over that blonde ñ that will make the feathers fly!"

show the white feather = display cowardice
"The challenger showed the white feather as soon as he stepped into the ring with the champion."

smooth somebody's (ruffled) feathers = calm somebody down
"Marian was obviously annoyed by Peter's remarks but I smoothed her ruffled feathers and she began to talk to him again."

you could have knocked me down with a feather = I was taken totally by surprise
"You could have knocked me down with a feather when the doorman casually mentioned that he had a degree is astrophysics."

See also: birds of a feather; ruffle somebody's feathers.

fed

fed up (to the back teeth) = (very) bored/tired
"I'm fed up to the back teeth with modern pop records ñ they all sound tne same to me."

feed
See: chicken feed.

feel
feel for = have (great) sympathy for
"I really feel for him in his grief, but I don't know how to console him for her death."
feel free = do not hesitate/do as you please
"It's very hot in here, do feel free to take your jacket or tie off if you want to."
"I don't want to go but feel free! You don't have to do everything I do."
feel like = experience emotionally
"You can't know what I feel like, having to stay indoors every day."
feel out of it = feel excluded from something
"There are so many youngsters at parties these days, I feel out of it."
feel the draught/pinch = experience difficulty (because of lack of money)
"Jack has been out of work for six months now and he's really feeling the pinch."
feel up to it = be inclined/well enough to do something
"I don't think i'll go to work today, I don't feel up to it."
get the feel of = become accustomed to
"My new sewing machine is an electric one, it seemed strange at first but it's quite all right when you get the feel of it."
not to feel oneself = to feel unwell
"I don't feel myself this morning, I'll go and have a lie down."
See also: feel at home; feel in one's bones; feel/look blue; feel small.

feeler
put out feelers = make (discreet) enquiries
"The management put out feelers to find out what sort of catering the staff really wanted for the new canteen."

feeling
cause/create bad feelings = offend
"I'm sorry you think you have been insulted; I didn't mean to cause bad feelings."
feeling for somebody = affection for somebody
"I've always had a feeling for Barbara, ever since we first met."
feeling for something = aptitude for/be in sympathy with something
"My son's good at driving; he seems to have a feeling for it."
"It's no use trying to learn ballet unless you have a feeling for music."
fellow feelings = sympathy
"A good doctor combines reassurance with fellow feelings for his or her patients."
get the feeling that = come to the conclusion that, or feel
"Do you ever get the feeling that you're not wanted?"
have mixed feelings about = be ambivalent/have neither good nor bad feelings about
"My wife definitely wants to go to North Africa for a holiday this year, but I've got mixed feelings about it."
I know the feeling = I think/have experienced the same thing
"You don't like classical music? I know the feeling, I find it boring as well."
no hard feelings = no offence/no feeling of bitterness
"I accept your apology and I can assure you that there are no hard feelings on my part."

play on somebody's feelings = deliberately manipulate somebody's emotions
"Walter is not really starved of affection; he's just playing on your feelings of sympathy by pretending to be unloved."
sinking feeling = feeling of (great) apprehension
"Every time I go to the dentist I get a sinking feeling as soon as I enter the waiting room."
vent one's feelings on = release anger/ frustration (caused by one thing) by attacking something else
"Whenever I have a quarrel with my wife I vent my feelings on the overgrown part of the garden."
See also: Monday morning feeling.

feet
at somebody's feet = under somebody's influence (because of his/her attractiveness/talent, etc.)
"That new typist has all the single men at her feet."
cut the ground from under somebody's feet = nullify somebody's argument/ effectiveness
"I was just persuading the board to accept my proposal when the Chairman cut the ground from under my feet by saying that the firm couldn't afford it."
drag one's feet = move slowly
"The job's behind schedule because the machinists have been dragging their feet."
feet first/foremost = dead/unconscious
"The most common way of coming back from the trenches in World War I was feet first."
find one's feet = become accustomed to a new situation
"Don't worry about starting the new job ñ you'll soon find your feet."
get back on one's feet = return to normal health after an illness, or return to prosperity after being in debt
"Take these tablets the doctor prescribed and you'll soon be back on your feet."
"My divorce cost me a fortune and it took three years to get back on my feet."
get cold feet = go back on a commitment because of fear/nervousness
"I volunteered to do a parachute jump to raise money for charity but I got cold feet at the last minute and didn't go through with it."
have both feet on the ground/keep one's feet on the ground = take a practical/ realistic view
"Joan is a bit of a dreamer whereas her sister Margaret keeps her feet firmly on the ground."
have one's feet under the desk/table = be settled in a job/somebody else's family
"Naturally I feel a bit strange at first at my new job but I'll be all right once I get my feet under the desk."
"Robert had nowhere to live so he went to stay with his girlfriend's parents and he's really got his feet under the table."
have the world at one's feet = be well-placed to succeed
"I envy you! You 've got your brillaint qualifications and a well-paid job with good prospects of promotion ñ you've really got the whole world at your feet."
have two left feet = be inept at anything requiring skilled footwork
"There's no point in asking me to dance ñ I've got two left feet."

keep one's feet = maintain one's balance/ upright posture
"It was so windy I could hardly keep my feet."

not let the grass grow under one's feet = waste no time
"Linda was only out of work for a week before she found another job; she certainly doesn't let the grass grow under her feet."

on one's feet = standing
"I must take my shoes off; I've been on my feet all day."

put one's feet up/take the weight off one's feet = take a rest (by lying/sitting down)
"You've been working hard in the garden all morning; why don't you put your feet up for half an hour?"

run/rushed off one's feet = very busy
"I'm sorry I didn't phone earlier but I've been rushed off my feet today."

set somebody on his/her feet = provide help in getting somebody established
"Theo was very lucky; his father gave him five thousand pounds to buy a partnership and set him on his feet."

sit at somebody's feet = remain with an expert/master in order to learn
"He's the self-declared authority on Baroque music and expects everybody to sit at his feet."

stand on one's own (two) feet = be independent
"It's about time you left home and stood on your own two feet."

sweep somebody off his/her feet = make a very favourable impression, or make somebody fall in love with one
"Wendy had this German student staying with her and he swept her completely off her feet."

think on one's feet = be mentally agile/ think quickly
"There's no time to consult reference books, you have to think on your feet in this job."

throw oneself at somebody's feet = ask in a very humble manner/beg for mercy
"I threw myself at her feet and asked her to forgive me."

under one's feet = in one's way
"Get out from under my feet you children, I've got work to do."

vote with one's feet = move elsewhere to register disapproval
"The service in the restaurant was so poor that we voted with our feet and went to the one round the corner."

walk off one's feet = tire by excessive walking
"We went Christmas shopping in London yesterday and my wife walked me off my feet."

with one's feet up = inactive/resting
"After dinner John sat there with his feet up and let his wife do all the washing up."

See also: foot; crow's feet; fall on one's feet; feet of clay; have the ball at one's feet; land on one's feet; shake the dust from one's feet.

fell

at one fell swoop = very quickly/all at once
"I put a plate of biscuits on the table and the three children ate them at one fell swoop."

fellow

hail-fellow-well-met = very (and often insincerely) friendly
"Most car salesmen are hail-fellow-well-met, but I suppose it's the way they're told to do their job."

See also: fellow feelings.

fellowship

extend the hand of fellowship = wish to make friends
"Since its change of leadership the Soviet Union has extended the hand of fellowship to the West."

fence

rush one's fences = act carelessly and quickly
"You'd make fewer mistakes if you took your time and didn't rush your fences."

right/wrong side of the fence = socially acceptable/unacceptable
"I can't get proposed for membership of the golf club because I'm from the wrong side of the fence."

sit on the fence = be undecided/hedge
"Many politicians sit on the fence when it comes to controversial issues like capital punishment and immigration control."

fend

fend for oneself = look after/provide for oneself
"I'm looking forward to the time when my children leave home and begin to fend for themselves."

ferret

ferret out = (deviously) seek
"See if you can ferret out any information about his past that we can use to discredit him."

fetch

fetch and carry = perform menial tasks for somebody
"She took me on as her personal assistant but all I seem to do is fetch and carry for her."

fetch up = arrive at
"We set off in the car with no particular destination in mind and fetched up at the beach."

fettle

in fine fettle = in good health (mentally and/or physically)
"I feel in fine fettle after my two weeks' holiday."

fever

at fever pitch = very excited
"By the time the pop group went into the finale of their act, the audience was at fever pitch."

few

a few too many = too much to drink
"Give me a hand with Wendy, I'm afraid she's had a few too many."

a good few = many
"A good few people came to watch the game."

few and far between = extremely rare
"Really good restaurants are few and far between these days."

have a few = have several (too many) drinks
"He was staggering across the room and had obviously had a few."

See also: a man/somebody of few words; precious few/little; quite a few.

fiddle

be on the fiddle/work a fiddle = do something dishonest for gain
"He earns the same as me but he's always got plenty of money ñ he must be on the fiddle."

fiddle about = spend time on trifles/mess about
"Stop fiddling about with the car and come in and have your dinner."

fiddle while Rome burns = be inactive

during an emergency/while something significant is happening
"While the country's leader was away cruising on his yacht there was a military take-over of the government ñ a typical case of fiddling while Rome burns."

have a face like a fiddle = be visibly miserable/unhappy
"What's the matter with you? You 've got a face like a fiddle."

play second fiddle = take a minor/secondary role
"They wanted to bring in a new man as general manager over me but I refuse to play second fiddle to anyone and so I've resigned."

up and down like a fiddler's elbow = move repeatedly (and often ineffectively)
"Why don't you sit still for a while? You're up and down like a fiddler's elbow!"

field

back/play the field = take advantage of every available opportunity
"Gwyneth doesn't have a regular boyfriend; she plays the field and goes out with a different man every time."

have a field day = derive great pleasure from doing something
"A sack of grain fell off the trailer and burst, and all the birds had a field day, eating as much as they could."

field of view/vision = range of sight
"From my hotel window there were seven church towers within my field of view."

take the field = enter a place of competition/contest
"The opposition party has made much of the running so far but just wait until our candidate takes the field."

See also: play the field.

fiend

fresh-air fiend = somebody who (sometimes antisocially) insists on having windows open/taking long walks in the open air
"It's always cold in my office in the winter because I have to share it with a fresh-air fiend."

fifty

go fifty-fifty with = share (the cost) equally
"I couldn't afford to pay for both of us so we went fifty-fifty."

fig

not care/give a fig = not care at all
"I don't give a fig what he thinks, I'm going to do it anyway!"

not worth a fig = worthless
"You can forget his offer of help, it 's not worth a fig."

fight

fight it out = continue a (not necessarily physical) contest until there is a clear winner
"I'm sorry, I won't take sides; if you and your sister both want to use the hair drier at the same time you'll have to fight it out between you."

fight like cat and dog = quarrel repeatedly and vigorously
"My parents used to fight like cat and dog yet paradoxically they still loved each other."

fight shy of = avoid/be reluctant to
"He accused Malcolm of being devious, but fought shy of actually calling him a liar."

fight to a standstill = engage in combat/a contest until one is totally exhausted
"Both contestants fought to a standstill and the referee had to declare that the match was a tie."
knock/take the fight out of somebody = reduce somebody's aggressiveness or will to survive/win
"A drunk tried to start an argument with Mark, but a few well chosen words soon took the fight out of him."
look/spoil for a fight = actively seek an argument/challenge
"Be careful: the boss is in a bad mood this morning and he's spoiling for a fight."
plenty of fight left in one = with plenty of reserves of energy
"Don't worry about how the Chairman might react to the take-over bid; there's plenty of fight left in him."
put up a good fight = react well to a challenge
"The challenger put up a good fight but eventually the champion's skill and experience won her the match."
running fight = contest that continues for a long time
"For three years, there's been a running fight between the Tory and Labour members of the Housing Committee about raising council house rents."
show fight = react aggressively to a challenge
"If I were you I wouldn't accept such criticism without making a reply; why don't you show some fight?"
three-cornered fight = contest between three contestants
"At the last general election only the Tories and Labour contested the seat, but the Lib Dems also entered a candidate for the by-election, making it a three- cornered fight."
See also: dog fight; fight tooth and nail; live like fighting cocks.

fighting
hand-to-hand fighting = combat not involving weapons
"The infantry attacked the enemy position in an action that was soon reduced to hand-to-hand fighting."
See also: fighting/sporting chance; fighting fit.

figment
figment of one's imagination = something that is totally imaginary
"Was that girl wearing no blouse or was it a figment of my imagination?"

figure
cut a good/pretty or a poor/sorry figure = make a good/bad impression
"The British trade stand cut a poor figure among the lavish displays of the Americans and the Japanese."
figurehead = somebody with a high position but no real authority
"The mayor is just a figurehead; it's the council that makes all the real decisions."
figure of eight = pattern in the shape of the figure eight
"Returning honey bees dance a figure of eight on the honeycomb to communicate a source of pollen to other members of the hive."
figure of fun = somebody who is ridiculed
"The teacher severely punished a group of children who made a figure of fun of the disabled boy in their class."
figure of speech = usage of words (such as idiom and metaphor) which gives

them a recognized, but non-literal, meaning
"Word Wise is a dictionary of idioms, which are among the most common figures of speech."

figure out = calculate, resolve a problem
"It took me nearly an hour to figure out how to do that puzzle."

in round figures = approximately, to the nearest round number
"In round figures, there must have been 50,000 spectators at the match."

that figures! = that is what I would have expected/thought
"They have again forecast rain for the Bank Holiday. That figures!"

See also: ballpark figure; facts and figures; father figure.

file

in Indian file = in a line, one behind the other
"The undergrowth was so thick that we had to force our way through in Indian file."

rank and file = ordinary people
"To retain credibility, the government has to convince the rank and file that its policies are best for them."

fill

drink (take) one's fill = drink as much as one wants
"On the landlord's birthday he said he would pay for all the beer and invited us to drink our fill."

fill an office = take up an (official) appointment
"While the manager was off sick, his deputy successfully filled his office until he returned to work."

fill in for = deputize for
"The manager's deputy filled in for her while she was off sick."

fill out = become fatter
"My daughter's face has begun to fill out now that she's recovered from her illness."

fill somebody in = provide somebody with missing information
"Can you please fill me in on what has happened since I've been away?"

fill somebody's shoes = take over somebody else's job/role
"Thomas is leaving next month and the company is going to find it very difficult to get somebody to fill his shoes."

See also: fill the bill.

filthy

filthy lucre = money
"You can't bribe me; I don't want your filthy lucre."

filthy rich = very wealthy
"He's filthy rich: he has a mansion in the country with stables, a swimming pool and a Rolls Royce in the garage."

final

final touch = last contribution (to complete something to perfection)
"Your new black evening gown is beautiful and that gold brooch adds the final touch."

See also: have the final/last word.

find

find fault with = discover a flaw in
"I can't find fault with the new restaurant: the food is good and the service is excellent."

find guilty = convict
"The jury took only four minutes to find the accused guilty."

find oneself = be (at/in a particular place/ situation)

"We were lost for an hour or so and then suddenly found ourselves on the road to Brighton."

"Your remarks were so unexpected that I find myself at a loss for words."

find out = make a conscious effort to discover something

"Can anyone find out when Stephen's birthday is?"

find out the hard way = learn something without outside help

"Today's children are allowed to use pocket calculators in maths lessons, but in my day we had to do it the hard way and learn our multiplication tables."

find something heavy going = have difficulty doing something

"Madge is trying to study algebra but she's finding it very heavy going."

take us as you find us = accept us as we are if you arrive unexpectedly

"You're welcome to call round and see us at any time but you'll have to take us as you find us."

See also: find/get one's bearings; find it in one's heart; find one's tongue.

fine

(draw a) fine distinction = (indicate) a slight difference

"He is able to draw a fine distinction between very good wine and excellent wine."

fine and dandy = satisfactory

"We've finished decorating the living room and it all looks fine and dandy."

get something down to a fine art = be very proficient at something

"Barry will service your car in less than an hour ñ he's got it down to a fine art."

not to put too fine a point on it = to be candid/frank

"I don't like your attitude and, not to put too fine a point on it, I won't tolerate it in future."

one of these fine days = one day soon

"One of these fine days, my boy, you're going to find out what it's like to have to get up every morning and go to work."

finger

at one's fingertips = well within one's competence/knowledge

"She's got the names of all the Beatles records at her fingertips."

all fingers and thumbs = clumsy

"That's the second glass I've dropped; I seem to be all fingers and thumbs today."

burn one's fingers/get one's fingers burnt = suffer (as a result of poor judgement)

"I tried investing in stocks and shares but I burned my fingers and lost a lot of money."

can count on the fingers of one hand = there are very few

"You can count the number of black policemen in London on the fingers of one hand."

crook one's little finger/snap one's fingers = demand/get attention

"Tony is infatuated with Louise; she only has to snap her fingers and he comes running."

green fingers = skill at gardening

"My mother's got green fingers and she can grow anything in her small garden."

hang on by one's fingernails = make a desperate effort to retain something

"Tottenham were by far the best team, but Arsenal managed to hang on by their fingernails and the game ended in draw."

have a finger in = have an interest in
"I believe Margot's got a finger in that new boutique in the High Street."

have a finger in every pie = be simultaneously involved in many activities
"Hal buys and sells antique books, helps run a wine bar, and plays in a rock band in the evenings ñ he's got a finger in every pie."

have itchy fingers = be very eager
"When our young son is struggling with a jigsaw puzzle my husband always has itchy fingers and wants to take over and finish it."

have light/sticky fingers = have a reputation as a thief
"I'd be careful about putting him in charge of the petty cash, he's got sticky fingers."

have more (of something) in one's little finger than somebody else has in his/her whole body = be much better than somebody else
"He has more ability as a painter in his little finger than his father has in his whole body."

keep one's fingers crossed = wish for good fortune
"Good luck with your exams. I'll keep my fingers crossed for you."

keep one's finger(s) on the pulse = remain informed about something
"The secret of good management is to keep your finger(s) on the pulse and to know exactly what is happening day by day."

lay a finger on somebody = harm somebody (usually physically)
"If you lay a finger on my son you'll regret it!"

lift/stir a finger = make an effort to do something
"The rest of the family spent nearly all day working in the garden but my father just sat in a chair and didn't lift a finger to help."

point the finger at = accuse/blame
"When the money went missing the real thief pointed the finger at me."

pull/take one's finger out = stir from complacency/inactivity (and do something)
"It's about time you pulled your finger out and gave us a hand with this work!"

put one's finger on = identify
"We'd been arguing the point for several minutes when Mabel came in and put her finger on the real cause of the problem."

put the finger on = inform on somebody to the police
"Most petty criminals support each other in any dealings with the police but they will not hesitate to put the finger on a child molester."

slip through one's fingers = miss an opportunity
"I had a chance of a bargain at the sale but I let it slip through my fingers."

twist somebody round one's little finger = get somebody to do anything one wishes
"Tony would do anything for Louise because she can twist him around her little finger."

work one's fingers to the bone = work very hard
"I've worked my fingers to the bone for years and yet I've been unable to save any money."

See also: catch somebody with his/her fingers/hand in the till; snap one's fingers at.

finish

finish with someone = end an association/friendship
"Linda and Robert have been going out together for nearly a year but she says she's decided to finish with him."

See also: finishing touches.

fire

baptism of fire = unpleasant first experience of something
"The first time I went sailing we got caught in a gale ñ it was a real baptism of fire."

between two fires = being attacked from both/two directions
"In family quarrels I'm often between two fires ñ the children crying at me one side and my husband shouting at me on the other."

catch/take fire = begin to burn
"An oil tanker caught fire and burned for several days."

fire away = begin
"Fire away, ask me anything you like."

fire bug = arsonist
"The police forensic expert said that the blaze was started by a fire bug."

fire up = become angry and indignant
"Charles becomes all fired up if you mention women drivers, ever since he had that collision with one."

go through fire and water = tackle any difficulty (to do something)
"I'd go through fire and water to get a chance to see the Wimbledon tennis finals."

hang fire = be delayed
"The opening of the new hotel has hung fire because the decorators haven't yet finished painting it inside."

have several irons in the fire = be involved with several activities (simultaneously)
"I don't care too much if this plan doesn't succeed because I've got several more irons in the fire."

in the line of fire = at risk because one is between two opposing forces
"Whenever my parents start arguing I try to keep out of the line of fire."

jump out of the frying pan into the fire = move from one difficulty to an even worse one
"I got bored with my job so I left and moved to a different firm up the road; but the work there is even more tedious ñ I jumped out of the frying pan into the fire.

like a house on fire = very quickly/well
"Mike's new motorbike goes like a house on fire."
"We only met last week and already we get on like a house on fire."

play with fire = take an extreme (and unnecessary) risk
"I wouldn't tease that bull terrier if I were you, that's playing with fire."

pull the chestnuts out of the fire = rescue somebody from a difficult situation
"It was impossible living in a one-roomed flat after we had the baby but Dad pulled the chestnuts out of the fire by lending us the deposit for a house."

set the Thames on fire = cause a sensation
"Fiona has enough talent to become a competent professional musician, but she won'tset the Thames on fire."

spread like wild fire = spread rapidly
"The disease was practically unknown ten years ago but then it flared and spread like wild fire until it reached epidemic proportions."

there's no smoke without fire = a rumour is usually based, however remotely, on fact

"The directors have denied that there is any truth in the rumour that the company is about to be taken over, but there's no smoke without fire."

under fire = being criticised/held responsible
"The management is under fire for not anticipating that the new overtime rates would not be well received by the staff."

See also: ball of fire; baptism of fire; draw somebody's fire; firing on all cylinders; open fire; the fat is in the fire.

first

at first hand = directly from the source
"I got the information at first hand from the person who decided to make it public."

at first sight = as seen initially (without any detailed examination)
"At first sight your estimate for painting my house seems very reasonable."

first and foremost = before any other consideration
"Some tourists do visit Southampton but the city is first and foremost a port, not a resort."

first and last/from first to last = completely
"Angus always finished his work on schedule because he is first and last a professional."

first class = best/excellent
"We stayed at a four-star hotel where the food and service were both first class."

first come, first served = precedence will be given to the first arrival(s)
"I'm sorry, all tickets for front-row seats have been sold; it was the usual case of first come, first served."

first light = dawn
"I like nothing better in the summer than taking the dog out for a walk at first light."

first-night nerves = nervousness felt before doing something for the first time
"Don't worry about starting your new school, you'll be all right; it's just a question of first-night nerves."

first off = before something else
"First off, you've got to make sure you know the way."

first thing = as early as possible in the day
"I'll start doing the garden first thing tomorrow, as long as it doesn't rain tonight."

first things first = put things in their correct order of priority
"I know you want to put up some pictures, but first things first we must re-paint the wall."

get a first = win first prize, or be awarded a first-class degree at a university
"My mother entered the local flower show just for fun and got a first."
"Samuel went on to university after school and got a first in chemistry at Cambridge."

in the first place = initially/to begin with
"What do we need to take for the trip? In the first place we must make sure we have enough food and drink."

of the first magnitude/order/water = of the best quality
"Nigel helped me through my financial problems ñ he's a friend of the first order."

See also: at the first blush; first blood; not know the first thing about.

fish

big fish = somebody important
"The boss is coming this afternoon to show some big fish around the factory."

big fish in a small pond = somebody who is important only among a small group
"Just because Bill is treasurer of our pub's Christmas savings club he thinks he's a financial wizard, but he's only a big fish in a small pond."

cold fish = somebody who is unemotional/unsympathetic
"Sue is a cold fish; she showed absolutely no reaction to those awful pictures of starving children."

feed the fishes = drown
"Make sure you wear your life jacket, otherwise ñ if you fall overboard ñ you'll end up feeding the fishes."

fish for compliments = seek praise
"It annoys me the way that new girl is always fishing for compliments when she talks to the men."

fish in troubled waters = interfere/get involved in an unpleasant situation
"Both partners now resent your interference; that's what you get when you fish in the troubled waters of marital strife."

have other fish to fry = have alternative/ more important matters to attend to
"I don't care that my bid to buy those few shares failed ñ I've got plenty of other fish to fry."

like a fish out of water = lacking experience and thus ill-at-ease
"I knew nobody at all on my first day there and I felt like a fish out of water."

neither fish nor fowl = neither one thing nor the other
"The cross between North American English and the British version ñ called mid-Atlantic ñ is neither fish nor fowl and should be banned."

(fine/pretty) kettle of fish = confused/ difficult situation
"So now you think you are going to be prosecuted for careless driving; that's a fine kettle of fish youíve got yourself into."

queer fish = somebody who is eccentric/ strange
"John's a queer fish, he nearly always wears odd socks."

small fish = somebody who is relatively unimportant
"I work for a large company but I'm only a small fish, one of twenty looking after the stock ordering."

smell something fishy = be suspicious
"He said he couldn't come into work because he was ill, but I smell something fishy and think he went to see the last day of the Test Match at Lords."

there are plenty more fish in the sea = there are numerous other people to meet
"My boyfriend and I have split up but I don't care ñ there's plenty more fish in the sea."

See also: cry stinking fish; drink like a fish.

fist

iron fist = firmness, or harsh discipline
"Our old form teacher used to rule the class with an iron fist."

mailed fist = military power
"The Hungarian revolutionaries were unable to resist the mailed fist of the Soviet Union."

See also: hand over fist; shake one's fist.

fit

fighting fit = in the peak of health
"I feel fighting fit after my holiday."

fit in with = be accommodating/comply with
"You organize the meeting and I'll fit in with your plans."

fit like a glove = fit snugly/perfectly
"I bought a new skirt in a sale and it fits like a glove."

fit of nerves = short period of anxiety/nervousness
"I had a fit of nerves just before my driving test but I was all right once the actual test began."

fit the bill = meet the requirement
"We need some new curtains and I've seen some inexpensive material in the sale that exactly fits the bill."

fit to bust = excessively/very much
"The young child was obviously lost and crying fit to bust."

fit to drop = exhausted
"The PE instructor kept us doing exercises until we were fit to drop."

fit to wake the dead = very loud
"The noise of music from my neighbour's party was fit to wake the dead."

fit up/out = do/make/supply something to meet a requirement
"Can you fit me up with a new handle for my case?"
"Harvey has fitted up a darkroom in his garden shed."
"I had my workroom fitted out with new lighting and electrical wiring."

have/throw a fit = be angry/excited
"Your mother would have a fit if she could see you now."

in fits and starts = intermittently/spasmodically
"My car is a nuisance in the winter; the engine only runs in fits and starts until it has really warmed up."

not fit to hold a candle to = very inferior to
"Today's so-called champions are not fit to hold a candle to the winners of ten or twenty years ago."

see/think fit = consider sensible/wise
"I'll leave it to you. You decide where we should go as you see fit."

fix

fix on = decide
"We've finally fixed on next May the third as our wedding day."

fix up = arrange for
"Could you please fix up a taxi for after the show?"

in a fix = in difficulty
"I'm in a fix. Can you please lend me five pounds until the end of the week."

flag

flag down = stop (a vehicle)
"Our car ran out of petrol on the moors but fortunately we were able to flag down a passing motorist who took us to the nearest garage."

flag of convenience = foreign flag of registry of a ship (used as a method of tax avoidance)
"The tanker was flying a Liberian flag I think ñ or some other flag of convenience."

hang/put the flags out = celebrate
"If you pass your exams I'll put the flags out."

hoist/show/wave the white flag = surrender
"Martin is very good at chess. We had played only about twenty moves when I had to hoist the white flag and resign."

keep the flag flying = (work to) maintain the existing situation
"I stayed behind to keep the flag flying at the office in London while the rest of the staff went to man our company's stand went to man our company's stand at a trade fair in Birmingham."
show the flag = demonstrate (and defend) one's position
"Several show business personalities came to the rally and showed the flag, lending their support to the cause."

flake
flaked out = exhausted
"I don't know how you can keep going, I'm flaked out."

flame
add fuel to the flames = make a difficulty even worse
"The management's refusal to meet representatives of the trade union merely added fuel to the flames of dissatisfaction among the workforce."
old flame = ex-boyfriend or ex-girlfriend
"I was in a pub with my wife the other evening when I met an old flame and the three of us got on remarkably well together."
shoot down in flames = destroy
"At the meeting Smith made some feeble objection to my plan which I was able to shoot down in flames with no trouble."

flare
flare up = break out/erupt
"An epidemic of swine fever has flared up in Wiltshire."

flash
flash in the pan = something that is short-lived/unique
"I managed to win the darts tournament this time but it was a flash in the pan and I'm very unlikely to get past the first round next time."
in a flash = in a moment
"The clown could change his expression from sadness to happiness in a flash."
quick as a flash = very quickly
"The striker got the ball and quick as a flash it was in the back of the net."

flat
be caught flat-footed = caught unprepared/taken by surprise
"We were all caught flat-footed when the Colonel made a surprise inspection."
fall flat = fail
"She was in a miserable mood and all my attempts to cheer her up fell flat."
flat as a flounder/pancake = completely flat
"Most of the landscape in the Fens is as flat as a pancake."
flat broke = having no money
"I can't come out with you tonight because I'm flat broke."
flat denial = complete denial/refusal
"When accused of robbing a shop in Maidstone he made a flat denial and said he'd never even been to the town."
flat out = at maximum speed, or asleep/unconscious
"My car will only go at 65 miles an hour when it's flat out."
"Martin came home at dawn after an all-night party and when I came down this morning I found him flat out on the settee."

flat spin = panic/state of great agitation
"Reg is in a flat spin; his wife is coming back from a trip a day earlier than expected and he hasn't done any cleaning or washing up for a week."

that's flat! = that is my final word!
"I don't care whether you go on the outing, but I'm not, and that's flat!"

flatter

don't flatter yourself! = don't think so well of yourself!
"Don't flatter yourself! You 're not the only one who's asked me to go out with him."

flea

(mere) flea bite = insignificant amount/quantity
"We raised nearly a hundred pounds at the church jumble sale but it's only a flea bite compared with the amount we need to renovate the church roof."

flea market = place that sells only second-hand articles
"I bought some old 78-rpm records at a flea market in the village hall."

flea pit = run-down cinema or theatre
"What's showing at the flea pit this week? Another forty-year-old film, I bet."

sent somebody off/away with a flea in his/her ear = dismiss somebody after a rebuff/scolding
"That spotty teenager had the cheek to ask me for a dance so I sent him away with a flea in his ear."

flesh

flesh out = expand/extend
"Sheila's face is beginning to flesh out now that she's passed through the growth spurt of puberty."
"This essay is far too short; I'll have to think of some way to flesh it out."

flesh pots (of somewhere) = place that provides luxurious living "He has lived in Mayfair and various other flesh pots of Europe."

have/get one's pound of flesh = be determined to obtain one's total entitlement
"The building society had to have its pound of flesh and foreclosed on my mortgage when I was only a few months in arrears with the repayments."

in the flesh = in person
"I was walking past the stage door when I saw the star of the show in the flesh."

more than flesh and blood can stand = beyond human endurance
"My husband's snoring is more than flesh and blood can stand."

neither flesh/fish/fowl/nor good red herring = neither one thing nor the other
"The combination of the modern-style extension and the original Victorian building is neither flesh, nor fowl nor good red herring."

one's own flesh and blood = one's family
"He took his father's watch and sold it ñ he even robbed his own flesh and blood."

thorn in one's flesh = persistent source of irritation
"My younger brother is always trying to scrounge money; he's been a thorn in my flesh for years."

See also: goosc flcsh/pimplcs; go thc way of all flesh; make one's flesh creep.

flies

See: fly.

flight

flight of fancy = a dream/imaginary situation
"My ambition is to become a film star, but it's probably just a flight of fancy."

in the first/top flight = among the leaders
"His performance at the concert last night proved that he is in the top flight of international pianists."

put somebody to flight = make somebody run away
"The bully ambled over but Winston stood up to him and soon put him to flight."

take flight = run away
"The demonstrators took flight when the police horses arrived."

fling

fling oneself at somebody = make an obvious and strenuous attempt to gain somebody's affections/attention
"It's degrading the way Caroline is flinging herself at that older man."

have one's fling = (take a final opportunity to) do as one pleases
"I've had my fling; now I'm going to settle down and get married."

flip

flip through = look at in a casual way
"I had a quick flip through the book and it looked very interesting."

flip over = change, or somersault
"Depending on who he is talking to, Harry can flip over from a Cockney accent to a posh cultured one."
"The aircraft appeared to flip over in the air before it crashed to the ground."

flit

See: do a moonlight (flit).

float

float a company = raise the finance to launch a new company
"I'm thinking of floating a company to import Turkish carpets."

float an idea = bring an idea to the notice of others
"We didn't know what to do at the weekend and Betty floated the idea of taking a trip to Canterbury to see the cathedral."

flock

like a flock of sheep = in an easily-led group, with no will of its own
"Tom decided he was going to strip off and jump in the lake for a swim, and the others all followed him like a flock of sheep."

flog

flog a dead horse = persist in doing something that cannot produce the desired result
"You'll be flogging a dead horse if you keep trying to get Walter to make a contribution, you know how mean he is."

flog (a topic) to death = persist in discussing something until everybody is bored with it
"Not the story about the time you met Prince Charles ñ you've flogged that one to death."

flood

flood tide = high tide/high water
"The ship was so large that it could only cross the outer sandbank and enter the harbour safely on the flood tide."

before the Flood = a very long time ago
"Old William has been coming to this

pub every night since before the Flood."

See also: open the flood gates.

floor

fall through the floor = be extremely surprised

"I haven't seen my sister for more than twenty years and when she walked into the room I nearly fell through the floor."

get in on the ground floor = be in at the beginning of something

"One of the best ways to succeed in a small company is to get in on the ground floor and prosper as the company expands."

floor somebody = knock somebody down, or defeat in argument

"The challenger was much lighter but he floored the champion with a single blow to the chin."

"Councillor Jones promised to spend more on welfare services if he was re-elected but he was completely floored when I asked him how he was going to pay for it."

shop floor = working environment of manual workers, or the workers themselves

"The trouble with our boss is that he's never worked on the shop floor and cannot appreciate a worker's problems."

"We have an enlightened management that consults the shop floor about all major issues."

sink through the floor = fall steeply and rapidly

"If the Russians release their stocks of tin onto the world market the price of the metal will sink through the floor."

sweep/wipe the floor with = defeat convincingly and easily

"In the latest series of chess games the challenger was no match for the champion, who wiped the floor with him nearly every time."

take the floor = stand up to speak, or begin to dance

"And now, Ladies and Gentleman, it is my pleasant duty to ask our distinguished guest speaker to take the floor."

"My parents were first to take the floor at the dance given to celebrate their silver wedding anniversary."

See also: hold the floor.

flower

flower people = people who advocate non-violence and oppose materialism/militarism

"The flower people take a very moral attitude, but what would they do in the event of a threatened nuclear attack?"

in the flower of one's youth = at one's physical best

"She looks very attractive in that dress, considering she's not in the flower of her youth."

See also: (as) welcome as the flowers in May.

flutter

cause a flutter = cause excitement/a stir

"The director's threat to resign caused a flutter of speculation among the shareholders."

flutter one's eyelashes at somebody = catch the attention of somebody of the opposite sex

"Flutter your eyelashes at the barman, Peggy, and ask him to serve us with drinks."

have a flutter = make a (modest) bet

"I always have a flutter on the Grand National."

fly

couldn't/wouldn't hurt a fly = very feeble, or very gentle
"I shouldn't worry about Barry's threats, he couldn't hurt a fly even if he tried."
"You can trust David to handle a young puppy with care, he wouldn't hurt a fly."

fly a kite = release an idea/information in order to gauge people's opinions about it
"The minister said that the government was considering increasing VAT, but he was probably only flying a kite."

fly at somebody = attack somebody (physically or verbally)
"I merely mentioned to my wife that, because of pressure of work, we may have to cancel our planned weekend away and she flew at me."

fly-by-night (operator) = operating for only a short time (and then doing so in an untrustworthy way)
"I never buy goods from the fly-by-night operators at the market, you can never find them again if the goods are faulty."

fly in the ointment = something that mars/spoils something else
"It was a very good party. The only fly in the ointment was that the host got drunk and started abusing everybody!"

fly off at a tangent = digress
"It is difficult to have a sensible discussion with my mother because she's always flying off at a tangent and talking about something else."

fly off the handle = burst into anger
"I'm sorry I accidentally spilled your drink, but there's no need to fly off the handle."

fly on the wall = eavesdropper
"I wish I could be a fly on the wall at the management meeting that decides our new rates of pay."

let fly = harangue/scold severely
"Karen had her hair cut short and dyed pink and you should have heard how her mother let fly at her."

like flies = in very large numbers
"I went shopping on Christmas Eve and the people were like flies."

make the fur/sparks fly = precipitate a fierce row
"The supervisor has told the typists that she wants less talking and more typing: that should make the fur fly!"

no flies on him/her = he/she is no fool
"You won't catch Tina with that double-headed coin; there are no flies on her."

pigs might fly! = that is most unlikely!
"You might be getting a knighthood? Pigs might fly!"

See also: as the crow flies; fly in the face of; fly the coop; time flies.

flying

flying feet = ability to run fast
"Our wing forward can always rely on his flying feet to avoid a tackle."

flying high = (successfully) holding a position of importance/power
"James is flying high now that he's got his directorship."

flying pickets = secondary pickets brought from elsewhere during a strike to supplement the local pickets
"The police stopped and turned back a bus load of flying pickets who were on their way to the strike-bound factory."

flying start = very good beginning
"The extra injection of cash meant that the new venture got off to a flying start."

flying visit = very brief visit
"It's only a flying visit and I can't stop for more than five minutes."
send flying = knock over
"He accidentally kicked the table and sent all the glasses flying."
with flying colours = with distinction/merit
"My daughter took her final exams and passed them with flying colours."

foam
foam at the mouth = be very angry
"Some of Anthony's stupid comments make me foam at the mouth."

fob
fob off = (try to) pass off a substitute for the thing required
"Can I have a fresh loaf, please; I've no wish to be fobbed off with one of those stale ones."

fog
in a fog = confused (mentally)
"Tell me again how you work this machine, I'm still in a fog about it."
not the foggiest (idea) = not an inkling
"Don't ask me where they are, I haven't the foggiest."

fold
fold up = collapse/close
"The business folded up after only six months' trading."
return to the fold = go back to a group (after an absence)
"Jack has taken up his old job again; he's come back to the fold after working for somebody else for a couple of years."

follow
follow one's bent = do what one is best at/use an inborn ability
"Jan moved on into educational publishing but Val followed her bent and remained in teaching until she retired."
follow one's nose = go directly ahead
"Turn left at the crossroads and then just follow your nose."
follow one's own devices = improvise
"I hadn't got the right materials so I followed my own devices and used some odd bits of wood to finish the job."
follow suit = copy/do the same as somebody else
"Phil decided to go into town and the rest of us followed suit."
follow the dictates of one's heart = do what one instinctively wants to
"If you feel you can't marry him because of his religious views you must follow the dictates of your heart."
follow up = take action using information provided/progress already made
"The salesmen make most sales by following up leads provided by customers' enquiries."
follow-up = something that comes after something else/a sequel
"He's writing a book on China as a follow-up to his first one about Japan."
See also: follow/tread in somebody's footsteps.

food
food for thought = something worthy of careful consideration
"The solicitor's advice gave me food for thought."
off one's food = lacking an appetite
"I've been off my food ever since I had the flu last month."

fool

fool around = behave in a foolish way, or have an affair with

"Come here, children; stop fooling around with empty tins."

"It's rumoured that Malcolm is fooling around with a married woman."

fool for one's pains = somebody whose effort/help is rewarded by ingratitude

"I worked all weekend to finish the job and didn't get so much as a word of thanks; I was a fool for my pains."

fool's errand = pointless task

"They sent me all the way to Brighton to buy some special component, but it turned out to be a fool's errand because they were out of stock."

fool's gold = iron pyrites (an ore of iron that outwardly resembles gold)

"The old miner thought he'd struck it rich but all he'd found was fool's gold."

fool's paradise = illusory happiness

"She thinks they can get married on his earnings of only fifty pounds a week but she's living in a fool's paradise."

fools rush in (where angels fear to tread) = people take action without thinking through the consequences

"Everybody bought some just because the goods were cheap; but they turned out to be faulty ñ they say fools rush in."

make a fool of somebody = make somebody look foolish

"I turned up at the wrong meeting and made a right fool of myself."

more fool you = you behaved foolishly

"If he already owes you money and you've lent him another ten pounds, more fool you."

nobody's fool = somebody who does not lack common sense/intellect

"Pam is no fool, she'll master her new job in a couple of days."

play/act the fool = behave in a foolish manner

"John often plays the fool so it is difficult to know when to take him seriously."

not suffer fools gladly = be intolerant with people who lack common sense/are slow to learn

"He doesn't suffer fools gladly so he's hardly the best person to be instructor on the beginners' course."

See also: April fool.

foot

catch somebody on the wrong foot = catch somebody off balance

"The boss caught me on the wrong foot when he asked where I was yesterday when I should have been at work."

follow/tread in somebody's footsteps = do the same as one's predecessor

"Peter is following in his father's footsteps and going into banking."

foot the bill = pay for something

"The celebration cost hundreds of pounds; I wonder who's going to foot the bill?"

gain a foothold = gain possession of small part of something

"His technique is to purchase a few shares to gain a foothold and then quietly buy up enough stock until he can make a take-over bid for the whole company."

get/have a foot in the door = gain acceptance/admission to an organization etc.

"Once you can get a foot in the door by persuading them to order a small amount it is often possible to go on and sell them large quantities."

get/start off on the right/wrong foot = begin well/badly

"When we assemble the unit we must first read the instructions to make sure we start off on the right foot."

"Henry started off on the wrong foot by being late on his first day at work."

have a foot in both camps = deal with both parties in a dispute

"The gun runner has a foot in both camps; he sells arms to both the Arabs and the Israelis."

keep/miss one's footing = remain upright/stumble

"I don't know how you keep your footing on this rocky slope."

"Harold missed his footing in the dark and sprained his ankle."

my foot! = certainly not!

"You think Yorkshire is the best cricket side? My foot!"

not put a foot wrong = never make a mistake

"He's not put a foot wrong during all the ten years he's worked here."

on a firm footing = on a secure basis

"Let's draw up a contract and put our relationship on a firm footing."

on a friendly footing = in a friendly way

"In dealing with clients I like to keep the meetings on a friendly footing."

one foot in the grave = very ill/old

"He's much too old to go skiing, he's got one foot in the grave!"

on foot = walking

"The temple is so remote that the only way to get there is on foot."

put one's best foot forward = begin to do something purposefully

"Come on chaps. Put your best foot forward and we should be back at camp in time for supper."

put one's foot down = insist

"My husband wanted to buy a puppy, but I would have to look after it so I put my foot down and said No."

put one's foot in it = unintentionally do or say something distressing/insulting

"My new son-in-law's name is John, but I put my foot in it by calling him Roger, which was the name of my daughter's ex-husband."

set foot on = go somewhere (for the first time)

"We went to Tunis for a holiday and it was the first time we had set foot on African soil."

stamp one's foot = display anger

"When her husband told her what he had done she stamped her foot and threatened to divorce him."

See also: feet; have a foot in the door; tread under foot; wait on somebody hand and foot.

football

political football = issue that is an object of contention between political parties

"The plight of the old-age pensioners has become a political football in the run up to the election."

for

for all one is worth = with the utmost effort

"All he could do when the bull turned nasty was to run for all he was worth."

for it = due for a scolding

"You'll be for it when your mother finds out what you've done."

for what it is worth = if you think it is worth anything

"Well that's my opinion, for what it's worth."

"She studied for six years and finally got a degree in political science, for

what it's worth."
See also: but for; for effect; for show.

forbid

forbidden fruit = unattainable desire
"I'm very attracted to my neighbour's wife, but that's forbidden fruit."

God forbid = I hope not
"It might pour with rain on Cup Final day, God forbid."

force

by force of circumstances = by circumstances out of one's control
"I had to sell my house by force of circumstances; my company moved me to their office up north."

come into force = take effect
"The new regulations come into force next month."

driving force = somebody whose enthusiasm/influence stimulates others to act
"My father used to try to get me to study harder but the real driving force was my mother."

force of habit = habitual
"You don't really need three spoonfuls of sugar in your tea, it's just force of habit."

force one's way = attain something/reach somewhere by using force
"I had to force my way through the crowd to get to the exit."

force somebody's hand = compel somebody to do something
"I didn't want to say this but you've forced my hand and I must point out that you have falsified several of the figures in your report."

force the pace = (bring pressure to bear) to speed something up
"There's no point in trying to force the pace, we're already working as fast as we can."

join forces = combine with others for a common purpose
"If our two companies were to join forces we could undercut all out competitors."

join the forces = enlist in military service
"Martin isn't sure what he'll do when he leaves school, but he's thinking of joining the forces."

use brute force (and ignorance) = try to do something (in an unsubtle way) merely by using force
"There's no point in using brute force on a nut that has jammed ñ you're likely to shear off the bolt."

fore

come to the fore = become prominent
"When Gill is doing the monthly accounts, her mathematical ability comes to the fore."

foreign

foreign body/substance = object that should not be present/impurity
"Waiter! There's a foreign body in my soup!"
"The trouble with cheap wine is that it may be contaminated with foreign substances."

on foreign soil = abroad
"We went for a day trip to Calais and it was the first time we'd set foot on foreign soil."

forget

forget it = never mind
"I'm sorry for what I said." "Forget it, I can't remember anyway."

forget oneself = behave in a disrespectful/ill-mannered way

"You must be forgetting yourself ñ you don't eat peas with a knife!"

forgive

forgive and forget = discount any previous disagreements/differences
"Let's forgive and forget and co-operate to make the new venture a success."

fork

fork in the road = point/moment of decision
"On my fortieth birthday I had reached a fork in the road, and I decided to give up working for somebody else and start my own business."
fork out = pay
"It's bad enough having to pay for the food, but I was expected to fork out for the drinks well!"
See also: speak with a forked tongue.

forlorn

forlorn hope = undertaking with very little chance of success
"The Liberals have put up a candidate in the Prime Minister's constituency, but it must be a forlorn hope."

form

good/bad form = socially acceptable/ unacceptable behaviour
"At least Jeremy had the good form to go back and apologize."
"The members of my club regard it as terribly bad form to query the bill, even if it's obviously wrong."
in the form of = taking the appearance/ shape of
"The money will be sent to you each week in the form of a cheque, not cash."
matter of form = for the sake of convention
"You have already got the job but I must interview the other candidates as a matter of form."
off form = not up to one's best
"I'm sorry I'm so slow today but I'm feeling a bit off form."
on form = at one's best
"Our darts captain is unbeatable when he's on form."
(run) true to form = (happen) as expected/predicted
"Brian ran true to form ñ he had a few pints of beer and then fell asleep."

formula

face-saving formula = scheme that prevents somebody from being criticized/embarrassed
"The government's plan to increase prescription charges met with a storm of protest until the minister came up with the face-saving formula of saying that it was only a temporary measure."

fort

hold the fort = take care of something while the person responsible is absent
"Will you please hold the fort, Judy, while I go out for a sandwich."

forth

hold forth = speak (pompously)
"This chap at the zoo was holding forth about the habits of various animals, but he obviously knew very little."

fortune

make a fortune = earn a lot of money
"He made a fortune by buying buttons in large quantities and selling them a few at a time at a large profit."

small fortune = a lot of money
"He owns his own business and has a house and a yacht; he must be worth a small fortune."
soldier of fortune = a mercenary
"Many of the professional troops in the Angolan conflict were soldiers of fortune."

forty
forty winks = nap/short sleep
"I'm just going to take forty winks before I go out later this evening."

forward
look forward to = anticipate with pleasure
"Hello there! We've been looking forward to you coming for weeks."
See also: not backward in coming forward.

foul
See: fall/run foul of; foul one's (own) nest; foul play.

found
all/everything found = (of a job) including food and accommodation as well as pay
"As a member of the army I get regular pay and everything found."

foundation
foundation garment = corset, roll-on or the like
"My sister works in a shop selling foundation garments."
shake somebody to the foundations = greatly frighten/surprise somebody
"When the dealer told me how much the painting was worth it shook me to the foundations."

fountain
fountain head = origin/source
"They believe that their god is the fountain head of all truth."

four
four-letter word = obscenity/swearword
"I wish he wouldn't use so many four-many words when he is talking to women."
four-square to = directly facing
"The new bingo hall stands foursquare to the old town hall."
make up a four = join three others to play cards
"If Terry will make up a four we can have a game of bridge."
make a foursome = combine to make four people
"The two couples made a foursome and went on holiday together."
on all fours = on hands and knees/on four feet
"Sandy was crawling about on all fours looking for her missing contact lens."
"Although baboons can walk upright, they move much quicker on all fours."

fowl
dress a fowl = remove the entrails of poultry before cooking
"Very few women today know how to dress a fowl; it's all done for them before the chickens are frozen."

fox
be foxed = be puzzled
"I enjoy word games but The Times crossword puzzle usually foxes me."
cunning as a fox = very cunning
"Be careful in your dealings with Sammy, he's as cunning as a fox and

old/sly fox = somebody who is cunning
"You old fox, you talked her into selling the car for less than it's worth."
See also: run with the fox/hare and hunt with the hounds.

frame

frame of mind = mental attitude
"I have to be in the right frame of mind to play chess."
frame-up = arrest/conviction based on falsified evidence
"He was arrested for burglary but claimed it was a frame-up and that he was innocent."

fraught

fraught with danger = full of risk
"The trek through the jungle is fraught with danger for all but the most experienced."

fray

in the thick of the fray = at the centre of the action
"We're very busy getting the orders out and the manager's there in the thick of the fray, wrapping parcels and licking stamps."

free

free and easy = relaxed/unhampered by responsibilities
"I wish I was a bachelor like you, Mark; you're free and easy and can do anything you want."
free as the air/wind/a bird = completely free
"Now that I've got my divorce I feel as free as a bird."
free-for-all = contest in which everyone has an equal chance of winning
"Instead of there being an orderly it turned into a free-for-all with everyone pushing and shoving to get his first."
free from/of = without
"What everybody desires is a world free from war or want."
"Thank goodness that sandwiches to take away are still free of VAT."
free, gratis and for nothing = totally free
"He gave me two Cup Final tickets free, gratis and for nothing."
free hand = unrestricted authority to act
"Roy is the expert so they gave him a free hand to sort out the problem."
free-hand = made without the aid of drawing instruments
"He has the amazing skill of being able to draw a perfect circle free-hand."
freelance = somebody who is employed for a particular task and not as a regular member of the workforce
"I prefer to work at home as a freelance, doing jobs for several people at the same time."
free translation = approximate interpretation
"Never mind the exact technical specification, just give us a free translation of what the machine can do."
make free with = make use of somebody else's property
"He won't lend anybody his equipment yet he's always ready to make free with my tool kit."
scot free = completely free
"The police stopped him when he was doing 90 miles an hour and yet they let him off scot free."
set free = release
"I think all caged birds should be set free."

French

pardon my French = forgive my bad language

"I think he's a prat, pardon my French."

take French leave = abscond/go away without permission

"He got tired with his job so he took French leave and had a prolonged holiday for three months."

See also: French letter.

fresh

fresh as a daisy/fresh as (new) paint = very fresh

"This fruit was picked only yesterday, it's as fresh as a daisy."

"The children looked as fresh as new paint after their bath."

See also: fresh-air friend.

Friday

girl/man Friday = general assistant/helpmate

"We've advertised for a girl Friday to provide general help in the office."

friend

bosom friend = close friend

"We've been bosom friends since we were at school together."

fair-weather friend = somebody who is friendly only when one is having good fortune

"Sally is a typical fair-weather friend: she's very pally when I have plenty of money but doesn't want to know me when I haven't.

friend at court = associate in a position of importance/power

"Be careful what you say to the supervisor, she's got friends at court."

make friends with = become (closely) acquainted with

"We only moved into our new house ten days ago and already my wife has made friends with half the women in the street."

our dumb friends = animals

"I abhor any kind of cruelty to any of our dumb friends."

we're just good friends = we have no sexual involvement

"I took my secretary to the theatre last night. I know what you're thinking, but we're just good friends."

your friend and mine = somebody we all/both know and like

"And who should I meet there but your friend and mine, the vicar."

See also: feathered friends.

frills

without frills = plain/unelaborate

"We had a simple room with no frills, just a bed and a chest of drawers."

fringe

lunatic fringe = people with an extreme point of view

"The average trade union member is a reasonable man; the trouble is the lunatic fringe of Communists and militants."

frog

frog in the throat = hoarseness

"Pardon me if I sound gruff, I've got a frog in my throat this morning."

frog march = manhandle somebody by grabbing his collar and the seat of his trousers

"The landlord grabbed the troublemaker and frog marched him out the door."

front

in front of = in somebody's hearing
"Please don't swear in front of the children."
See also: front man.

frown

frown on = disapprove of
"My father frowns on all but the most conventional of dress."

fruit

bear fruit = produce (good) results
"It's about time that investment bore fruit and earned me some interest."
See also: forbidden fruit.

fry

small fry = somebody who is insignificant
"When you go there make sure you deal with the sales manager, not any of the small fry who work for him."

full

be full of oneself = boastful/conceited
"Philip is full of himself ever since he got that new car."
in full = complete(ly)
"This is to acknowledge receipt of your letter; I shall reply in full as soon as possible."
know full well = definitely know
"You knew full well my mother was coming yet you came home late."
in the fullness of time = eventually
"Don't worry, you'll get another chance in the fullness of time."
See also: full house; full steam ahead; (at) full tilt; have one's hands full.

fun

for the fun of it = for amusement
"Those horrible boys were throwing stones at the seagulls just for the fun of it."
fun and games = amusement
"We had some fun and games last night going through some old family photographs."
like fun = very quickly/vigorously
"My old washing machine rattles like fun when I put it on maximum spin speed."
make fun of/poke fun at = cruelly derive amusement from/ridicule
"It's wrong to make fun of people just because they're old."
See also: figure of fun.

funeral

that's your funeral! = you must take the consequences!
"You have no knowledge of cars but if you want to dismantle the engine, that's your funeral!"

funk

in a blue funk = very afraid/terrified
"I was in a blue funk in case my wife found out what I'd done."

funny

funny business = deceit/trickery, or sexual activity
"He was involved in some funny business over missing petty cash."
"Yes, you two can stay home and watch television while we're out, but I want no funny business!"

furniture

part of the furniture = somebody who is unnoticed (because he/she is nearly always present)

"Our doorman has worked for the company for years and has become part of the furniture."

fury

like fury = very quickly/vigorously
"Glen drives like fury in that new sports car of his."

fuss

make a fuss = complain
"Don't make such a fuss about a little scratch."

make a fuss of = be overattentive/spoil
"When my husband comes home, he makes a big fuss of the dog before even talking to me."

future

in future = from now on
"In future I want everyone to get to work on time."

in the future = some time yet to come
"I hope we'll have shorter working hours in the future."

G

gab

gift of the gab = ability to talk convincingly and easily
"Colin should make a good salesman, he's got the gift of the gab and persistence."

gaff

blow the gaff = inform (on somebody to the authorities)/reveal a (guilty) secret
"Joe blew the gaff on the bank robbers and now he's afraid they might seek revenge."

gall

gall and wormwood = reason for bitterness
"Harsh conditions and long working hours were gall and wormwood to early trade unionists."

have the gall to = have the cheek/ impudence to
"He began by making personal remarks about my family and then he had the gall to ask me to lend him some money."

See also: bitter as gall.

gallery

play to the gallery = show off to gain popularity
"Even in what is meant to be the discussion of a serious political issue, the Labour candidate plays to the gallery in an attempt to win votes."

See also: rogue's gallery.

gambit

opening gambit = opening move (seeking an advantage)
"Peter's usual opening gambit is to buy a girl a drink, so that she immediately thinks she owes him something."

game

beat/play somebody at his own game = compete successfully with somebody in their own area of expertise
"Stewart is always quoting scraps of Shakespeare, so I beat him at his own game the other day and quoted Cervantes ñ in the original Spanish!"

deep game = secret/devious ploy
"Although Gerald offered his wholehearted support, I can't help feeling he's playing some deep game of his own."

dirty game = activity in which people do not always act in an honest/moral way
"People say that party politics, even at local level, can be a dirty game."

fair game = somebody/something that may be justifiably attacked
"Some actors complain about the power of the critics, but I think that anybody who charges other people to see him perform is fair game."

game of chance = gambling game (usually a card game played for money)
"Would any of you gents care to join us in a little game of chance?"

game, set and match = total defeat
"And my ace of trumps wins the thirteenth and final trick; game, set and match, I'm afraid."

game to the end = continuing to try (even in adversity) until one can continue no more
"My Uncle William passed away last week; he was ninety, and game to the end."

give the game/show away = inadvertently reveal a secret

"We were going to throw a surprise party for my wife's birthday, but my daughter gave the game away so we all went out to dinner instead."

know what somebody's game is = discover what somebody's (devious) intentions are

"Arthur has suddenly got very friendly, but I know what his game is ñ he's trying to get somebody to propose him for membership of the golf club."

losing game = activity which one cannot succeed at

"We're playing a losing game by trying to undercut our competitor's prices all the time."

mug's game = activity which only a fool would expect to succeed at

"Betting on horses is a mug's game ñ nobody ever wins in the long term."

name of the game = crucial/important factor

"The name of the game in pop music is originality."

off/on one's game = not performing/ performing at one's best

"I'm sorry I keep making mistakes; I seem to be off my game this morning."

on the game = earning money as a prostitute

"She may be a famous model now, but she was on the game for years before some fashion photographer discovered her."

play a waiting game = delay making a commitment until the situation is more advantageous

"They've both asked her to go out with them, but Vera is playing a waiting game until she finds out which one of her suitors has the most money!"

play the game = behave in an honourable way

"There is a lot of money at stake in Melvin's take-over bid, but you can always rely on him to play the game."

put somebody off his game = distract somebody while playing a game

"Phil will never make a pro-fessional snooker player because the slightest noise from the audience puts him completely off his game."

so that's your game = so that is what your intention is

"I see, so that's your game: you're going to paint the windows before the doors."

the game is not worth the candle = the result is not worth the effort needed to achieve it

"I've decided to give up my job because it is so poorly paid that the game's not worth the candle."

the game is up = you are discovered (committing a crime/deception)

"The store detective told the shoplifter that the game was up and that there was no point in making any fuss."

two can play at that game = I can also be as deceitful/unpleasant/etc. (as somebody else)

"I discovered that my husband was having an affair ñ well, two can play at that game!"

what's the game? = what is going on?

"What's the game? Why is everybody looking at me like that?"

what's your game? = what are you doing?

"What's your game? What are you doing in my garden?"

winning game = game in a series that decides the overall result/winner

"This could be the winning game for the challenger, who only needs two more points for the championship."

gang

gang bang = multiple rape
"According to the newspapers the four boys subjected the girl to a gang-bang."

gang up on somebody = combine to harm somebody
"The victim had no chance when four or five thugs ganged up on him."

press-gang somebody = force somebody to do something (against his/her wishes)
"The Vicar has pressed-ganged me into organizing the Christmas jumble sale."

garden

bear garden = noisy and chaotic gathering
"After everybody had been drinking for a while, the party turned into a bear garden."

everything in the garden is lovely = everything is satisfactory
"I've got a loving wife, two beautiful children and a good job; everything in the garden's lovely."

(lead somebody) up the garden path = deceive somebody
"He led her up the garden path: he told her that he was only thirty-five and that he'd never been married before."

gasp

at/on/with one's last gasp = at the point at which one must finish (because of exhaustion or death)
"With his last gasp, he murmured the name of the person who shot him."

gate

gate-crash = attend a party uninvited
"If Jeremy is not holding his own party on a Saturday night he usually goes and gate-crashes somebody else's."

like a bull at a gate = in a clumsy/impetuous way
"Take it gently; why must you go at everything like a bull at a gate?" See also: open the flood gates.

gate-post

between you, me and the gate-post = confidentially
"Between you, me and the gate-post, John and I are going to get engaged next week."

gauntlet

run the gauntlet = be exposed to criticism/danger/etc.
"I've had my hair dyed and tomorrow I'll have to run the gauntlet of all the comments from the people at work."

throw/fling down the gauntlet = issue a challenge
"Our competitors have thrown down the gauntlet and challenged us to make a product as good as theirs at a cheaper price."

take up the gauntlet = accept a challenge
"We have taken up the gauntlet and are redesigning the product using cheaper materials to undercut our competitors."

gen

gen up on = (fully) inform oneself about
"You'd better gen up on roses if we're going to visit my father ñ he's a very keen gardener."

gentle

the gentle sex = women
"You don't expect to hear such bad language from the gentle sex."

gentle as a dove = very gentle/tender
"Although a vicious hunter, the lioness was as gentle as a dove when playing with her cubs."

gentleman

gentleman's agreement = unwritten agreement kept to because of the integrity of the parties concerned
"I've no signed contract with him but we've got a gentleman's agreement, and that's good enough for me."

get

be getting on for = approaching/close to
"It must be getting on for dinner time."

get about = move/travel
"I don't get about much since my arthritis got worse."
"It's amazing how quickly bad news gets about."

get ahead = succeed (in one's career)
"Come on, do your homework. You'll have to pass your exams if you want to get ahead."

get a load of something = look at something (expressing approval/surprise)
"Get a load of that car Jean's driving!"
"You think your desk is a mess! Get a load of mine!"

get along with you!/get away (with you!) = you don't say! (= I can hardly believe what you are telling me)
"Get away! Are you really going to Tibet for your honeymoon?"

get a move on = hurry up
"Get a move on or we'll miss our train."

get at somebody = provoke/needle somebody
"The boss keeps finding fault with my work; for some reason he's been getting at me all day."

get at something = tamper with something
"My desk wasn't like this when I left it; I think it's been got at."

get away from it all = remove oneself from the pressures of everyday life
"I'm tired of travelling in and out to work everyday in the rush hour; I'd like to buy a cottage in the country and get away from it all."

get away with = fail to be caught out (in a crime/deception/mistake)
"My seventeen-year-old daughter is so small that she can get away with paying half fare on the buses."

get by = (just) manage
"I've had to take a cut in pay but I suppose I'll get by."

get cracking/going/weaving = begin doing something (vigorously/with a will)
"Henry, it's about time you got cracking and re-decorated the living room."

get down to it = tackle a task in earnest, or reduce something to basics
"It's nearly bed time, shouldn't you be getting down to your homework?"
"When you get down to it, playing the piano is only a question of putting the right fingers on the right keys for the right length of time."

get even with = take revenge on
"She may have beaten me today but I'll get even with her eventually."

get hold of = grasp/obtain somebody/something, or contact somebody
"This beggar came up and got hold of my sleeve."
"It took me ages to get hold of the spare part I needed to mend my vacuum cleaner."

"I've been trying to get hold of you all morning but every time I phoned you were out."

get into = become interested in

"I like his short stories but I find it very difficult to get into the full-length novels."

get it = understand

"I don't get it. How do migrating swallows know their way to Africa?"

"The red wire goes to the positive terminal. Get it?"

get it in the neck = be punished/scolded

"Did I get it in the neck from my wife when I got home late after the office party."

get lost! = go away!

"Get lost! And don't come round here annoying me again."

get off = avoid a reprimand/punishment

"He was stopped for speeding, but he said he was taking his pregnant wife to hospital and he got off."

get off to a bad/good start = begin promisingly/unpromisingly

"Ann took me home to meet her parents and I got off to a bad start by spilling my tea on their new carpet."

"Well, men, we've made a good start; let's see if we can keep up the pace."

get off with somebody = form a (sexual) relationship with somebody

"Mark is trying hard to get off with the new typist."

get on = succeed (in one's career)

"Fiona has studied hard and has all the qualifications required, so she should get on."

get oneself up = dress extravagantly/formally

"They have asked me to their wedding so I'll have to get myself up for the occasion."

get one's eye in = attain one's standard of ability

"The new job was a bit daunting at first but it was all right once I'd got my eye in."

get one's own back = take revenge

"Ray took my place in the car park but I got my own back by parking behind him so that he can't get out."

get on one's bike = go away

"I don't want to hear any more of your complaining about it, so get on your bike!"

get on one's high horse = take offence (because of hurt pride)

"I never said a word against your family, so don't get on your high horse with me."

get on with somebody = have a friendly relationship with somebody

"I find it easy to make friends with most people, but I just can't get on with Tyrone."

get on with something = (start to) do something

"I suppose I should get on with the washing up."

"Well, if you're going to leave, get on with it!"

get on with you! = I don't believe you! (jokingly)

"Get on with you! They couldn't have said all those nice things about me!"

get out of hand = become out of control

"At first it was only horseplay but it soon got out of hand and developed into a full-scale fight."

get out of something = avoid blame/a duty/punishment, etc.

"I was supposed to stay in after school but I got out of it by saying that my mother was ill and I was needed at home."

get over = recover

"I'm feeling a bit weak because I've just got over flu."
"My daughter is heartbroken because she has just split up with her boyfriend, but she'll soon get over it."

get rid of = dispose of
"I wish you'd get rid of that old jacket, it's full of holes."

get round = cajole/persuade
"I'd like a new coat; I must see if I can get round my husband to pay for it."

get round to = find time to
"I must get round to mowing the lawn this weekend."

get something across/over = communicate information/make something understood
"Ted knows all about servicing cars but he can't seem to get it across to others."

get something going = begin an undertaking, or start a machine
"Fred has applied for several jobs and I believe that at last he's got something going with the firm down the road."
"My car stands outside all night and I can never get it going these damp mornings."

get the better of = defeat
"It took me an hour to finish the crossword puzzle but I was determined that it wouldn't get the better of me."

get the wind up = become afraid
"We were going to take a short cut across the top of the cliffs but Nigel got the wind up and said we'd be safer walking the long way round along the road."

get the wrong end of the stick = misunderstand/miss the point
"No, you've got the wrong end of the stick. I said I would pay the musician not play the musician."

get through to = make contact with
"I've been trying all afternoon to get through to the station on the telephone."

getting at = insinuating/meaning
"I'm sorry, I don't understand; I don't know what you're getting at."

get together = meet
"It's about time we got together for a chat."

get up to = do (in the sense make mischief)
"What have you been getting up to while I've been away?"

get under somebody's skin/get up somebody's nose = annoy/irritate somebody
"Penny's condescending manner really gets under my skin."

get well oiled = become drunk
"We stayed in the pub until closing time and we all got well oiled."

get wind of = hear about
"I hope Terry doesn't get wind of the surprise party we've organized for him."

how are you getting on? = how are things progressing/prospering?
"How are you getting on with your new puppy?"

tell somebody where to get off = reprimand somebody
"The greengrocer tried to sell my wife some overripe fruit, but she soon told him where to get off."

See also: don't get me wrong; get away with murder; get off somebody's back; get somebody's goat.

ghost

ghost of a chance = little or no chance
"If he thinks he can beat me at darts he hasn't a ghost of a chance."

ghost town = town that is abandoned/ very quiet
"The place has been like a ghost town since they built the new by-pass round it."

give up the ghost = die
"She was very ill for weeks before she finally gave up the ghost."

look like a ghost/as if one's seen a ghost = appear very pale
"She looked like a ghost and said she was feeling faint."

gift

think one is God's gift to = conceitedly (and mistakenly) believe that one is very highly regarded
"The trouble with Graham is that he thinks he's God's gift to women."

See also: gift of the gab.

gild

gild the lily = add unnecessary extra ornament to something that is already beautiful/ornamental
"Don't put any more decorations on the Christmas cake, that would be gilding the lily."

gilt

gilt-edged investment = reliable/safe investment
"I prefer the small but safe return on gilt-edged investments to the higher but riskier profit from speculative ones."

take the gilt off the gingerbread = remove the attractive part of something
"I like best the atmosphere at a live pop concert, and merely listening to a recording at home takes the gilt off the gingerbread."

ginger

ginger group = group of activists (within a larger organization)
"Those who want to repeal the latest trade union legislation have formed a ginger group within the TUC."

ginger up = enliven
"I'll put on some records we can bop to ñ that should ginger up the party!"

gird

gird up one's loins = prepare for action
"The boss has called me to his office. I'd better gird up my loins and go and see what he wants."

girl

bachelor girl = unmarried woman
"I haven't met the right man yet, but I don't intend to be a bachelor girl all my life."

bunny girl = scantily-clad hostess at a night club
"They're opening a new club in town with bunny girls as waitresses."

good-time girl = woman who very much likes to enjoy herself (and is not too concerned how she does it)
"Before I met Michael I was a typical good-time girl, but now that we're engaged I've settled down a lot."

See also: girl/man Friday.

give

don't give me that = do not expect me to believe that
"Don't give me that. You plead poverty and yet you drive around in a new car."

give a bad/good account of oneself = perform badly/well
"She was competing against more experienced people but she still gave a good account of herself."

give and take = fair compromise (for mutual benefit)
"A happy marriage depends largely on give and take."

give as good as one gets = be able to meet an attack with an equally effective counterattack
"I enjoy listening to Harold in an argument because he always gives as good as he gets."

give away = betray/reveal
"I shouldn't really be at this party because I didn't receive an invitation, but please don't give me away."

give-away = incontrovertible evidence (of guilt)
"Somebody took the cold meat, and the cat's paw prints on the table were a right give-away."

give birth to = originate
"It is said that James Watt's observation of steam issuing from a kettle gave birth to the idea of the steam engine."

give chase = chase
"The robbers drove off at high speed and a police car gave chase."

give in = surrender/yield
"The defenders were outnumbered and had to give in."

give it a miss = not do something
"I usually go to the match on Saturdays but I think I'll give it a miss this week."

give it a rest/give it up = take a break from or stop doing something
"Amy has been playing her radio all morning. I wish she'd give it a rest."
"You know that smoking is bad for you, why don't you give it up?"

give me (a) something = I like something best
"My wife prefers continental cooking but give me roast beef and three veg any day."

give off = emit
"Without a sufficient draught of air, a coke fire can give off poisonous fumes."

give oneself away = (accidentally) reveal one's guilt
"He claimed he hadn't been drinking but the smell of his breath gave him away."

give oneself up = surrender
"The escaped prisoner was exhausted after being on the run for three days and he decided to give himself up."

give or take = except for/approximately
"There must have been two hundred people there, give or take a few."

give out = become exhausted
"We had a wonderful time on holiday until our money gave out."

give rise to = generate/produce
"The rubbish tip gives rise to an awful smell."

give somebody away = hand over the bride in marriage, or reveal a secret about somebody
"Ethel's father died when she was a child and so she's asked her uncle to give her away when she gets married."
"I went to a stag party last night but I told my wife I was working late, so for goodness' sake don't give me away!"

give somebody a wide berth = avoid somebody
"Barry can be quite nasty when he's had a drink, I'd give him a wide berth if I were you."

give somebody/something a miss/the go-by = avoid
"No thanks, I won't come to the pub this evening, I think I'll give it a miss."
"Ever since some oysters made me ill I've given all shellfish the go-by."

give somebody his/her head = allow somebody to do as he/she pleases, without restraint
"You're the expert; we'll give you your head to solve the problem and then we'll do anything you recommend."

give somebody what for = thoroughly castigate/punish somebody
"You wait till your father gets home ñ I'll give him what for!"

give up = surrender, or yield
"Throw down your weapons and come out! The building is surrounded, so you might as well give up now."
"Gradually the archaeologists made the ancient site give up its secrets."

I give up! = I cannot guess what happens next, or exclamation of frustration
"I give up! What happened after you went back to his flat?"
"Oh, I give up! I can never do these stupid puzzles!"

not to give a brass farthing/tuppeny damn = not to care
"I don't give a brass farthing what you do at home, in my house you do as I say."

what gives? = what is happening?
"What gives? Why are all the lights off?"

See also: give a dog a bad name; give ear to; give ground; give in one's notice; give notice; give place to; give somebody a piece of one's mind; give somebody enough rope; give somebody the elbow; give somebody the evil eye; give somebody the glad eye; give somebody the works; give the game away; give way (to).

given

"You can rely on Jill, she's not given to making mistakes."

gizzard

something that sticks in one's gizzard = something that annoys one intensely
"What sticks in my gizzard is the way he steals everyone else's ideas and then claims them as his own."

glad

be glad to see the back of somebody = be pleased when somebody leaves
"My uncle is staying with us for a while but he's such an old bore that I shall be glad to see the back of him."

glad rags = best clothes
"Let's put our glad rags on and go to town for a meal."

See also: give somebody the glad eye.

glance

at first glance = at the first brief look
"I haven't studied the plan thoroughly but at first glance it seems exactly what we want." glance at/over = look briefly at
"I happened to glance at the weather forecast and I believe it said it is going to rain."

glass

glass jaw = weakness that makes a boxer very vulnerable to blows on the chin
"He would have been world champion if he hadn't got a glass jaw."

people who live in glass houses (shouldn't throw stones) = critics should be wary of criticism
"She's always finding fault with other people's work and yet makes plenty of mistakes herself; people who live in glass houses shouldn't throw stones!"

See also: raise one's glass to

globe

four corners of the globe = throughout the world

"People from the four corners of the world attended the festival."

globe trotters = regular international travellers

"The book is aimed at globe trotters rather than the one-trip-a-year holiday traveller."

glory

glory hole = cupboard or small room containing discarded items

"Just leave your boots in the glory hole under the stairs."

glory in = take pride/self-satisfaction in

"The new president addressed the crowd and gloried in their enthusiastic cheers."

in all one's glory = dressed in one's best/finery

"I wore my evening suit and turned up in all my glory, only to find that everyone else was casually dressed."

gloss

gloss over = deliberately ignore/take only superficial notice of

"The main points of the plan seem fine and I think we can gloss over the details for now."

glove

hand in glove with = in inseparable association with

"Drug trafficking goes hand in glove with other sorts of crime."

iron hand/fist in a velvet glove = firmness concealed behind apparent gentleness

"The boss always appears kind and sympathetic but in fact rules with an iron fist in a velvet glove."

with kid gloves = with extreme gentleness

"He's an extremely touchy character and you have to handle him with kid gloves."

with the gloves off = earnestly and without mercy

"After the polite preliminaries were over, the two speakers attacked each other's policies with the gloves off."

See also: fit like a glove.

glutton

glutton for punishment = somebody who does not mind difficult/unpleasant tasks etc.

"That's the third time you've worked late this week for no extra pay ñ you seem to be a glutton for punishment."

gnomes

gnomes of Zurich = Swiss bankers influential in the world money market

"The Chancellor of the Exchequer doesn't only have to convince the cabinet that his budget is sound, he has to convince the gnomes of Zurich."

go

at one go = with only one attempt

"She blew out all the candles at one go."

be on the go = be active/busy

"I seem to have been on the go all day."

from the word go = from the beginning/start

"David has been working for this company right from the word go."

go after/for = attack, or attempt to get/chase

"They're advertising a cashier's job at Smith and Company; why don't you go after it?"

"When Bill made that remark Angela really went for him."

go against the grain = oppose natural tendencies
"It goes against the grain for me to accept money merely for giving somebody a helping hand."

go ahead = carry on/continue, or go before
"You can go ahead and start the engine now."
"You go ahead and we'll follow in a few minutes."

go as you please = do as you wish
"What I like about where I work is you can go as you please as long as you complete your job on time."

go at something bald-headed = do something impetuously
"You always go at a job bald-headed. Why don't you stop and think first?"

go a long way towards = approach closely to
"This bonus will go a long way towards paying off my overdraft."

go along with = agree/comply with
"I pretended to go along with his plan in order to find out more about it."

go back on = break (an agreement/promise)
"You can't go back on the deal now, I've started the work."

go begging = be left over
"Can I have the last biscuit if it's going begging?"

go-between = intermediary
"Jim and his wife haven't been talking for months and their poor daughter has to act as a go-between."

go bust = become bankrupt/insolvent
"The company I worked for went bust last year and it took me months to find a new job."

go-by = action to avoid something
"We usually go away for Easter but we decided to give it the go-by this year and stay at home."

go by the board = be ignored
"There are unwritten rules about doing business but these sometimes go by the board when competition in fierce."

go downhill = decline/worsen
"My mother's health has gone steadily downhill since she had pneumonia."

go down with = become ill with
"Mary won't be able to come on Saturday because she's gone down with the flu."

go fifty-fifty/halves = share equally
"I can only afford to go out with you if we go halves with the bill."

go for a Burton = die/cease to be of any use
"I haven't got my old Morris Minor car any more, it went for a Burton last year."

go for nothing = be given away (free)
"The stall-holder couldn't get anybody to buy that old cutlery we gave him and it went for nothing in the end."

go for somebody = attack somebody
"I thought Wendy was so quiet, but when Martin made that comment she really went for him."

go-getter = somebody who is ambitious/forceful at his/her job
"That new salesman is a real go-getter; he's brought in four new orders already this week."

go great guns = perform well
"Our runner was going great guns until he tripped and fell."

go in for = enter (a competition)/participate in
"I'm getting too old to go in for these vigorous sports."
"Janice is thinking of going in for bee-

keeping when she moves to the country."

go into something = investigate something
"I'm sure this bank statement is wrong; I'll have to go into it with my accountant."

go it alone = do something without outside help
"I was tired of working for other people so I decided to go it alone and set up my own business."

go off = become bad
"We haven't a fridge and the milk goes off within a day in hot weather."

go off one's chump/head/rocker = go mad/lose all control (temporarily)
"Mick has just bought a job lot of 2,000 World War II gas masks; he must have gone off his rocker, what's he going to do with them all?"

go off somebody = become less friendly with somebody
"I soon went off John when I found out that he smokes in bed."

go off the deep end = become suddenly angry
"It's only a minor scratch on your car ñ there's no need to go off the deep end."

go on = continue/proceed
"Go on, what happened next?"
"You go on and we'll follow later."

go one better = outdo
"I was pleased to be able to buy a new Ford but my neighbour had to go one better and get a Mercedes."

go on the stage = become an actor/actress
"My teenage daughter wants to go on the stage."

go out of one's way = take extra trouble to do something
"Val is always being insulting and I don't see why I should go out of my way to be pleasant to her."

go over to the other side = change one's allegiance/loyalty
"One of our key supporters deserted and went over to the other side."

go over the ground = examine fundamental aspects of something
"We've already discussed the details of the proposal; surely we don't have to go over that ground again?"

go phut = cease to function/work
"That's the third light bulb that has gone phut this week!"

go round = avoid/detour
"We'll get there quicker if we go round all the large towns along the route."

go straight = be law-abiding (after having broken the law)
"After her release from prison, Judy promised faithfully that she would go straight in future."

go through fire and water = overcome extreme difficulty/hardship (to achieve something)
"Peter has really fallen for Belinda; he'd go through fire and water to give her anything she wanted."

go through the motions = pretend to do something (without actually doing it properly)
"I didn't really want to play a hard game of tennis with my son, so I went through the motions and let him win the first two sets."

go through with = fulfil a commitment
"I said I would go out with Mike tomorrow, but I don't think I'll go through with it."

go together = complement/match
"The carpet and curtains are similar colours and go together quite well."

go to one's head = make one become

conceited/over-confident
"We think you are a most valuable member of the team, but don't let it go to your head."

go to pieces = lose control of one's behaviour/emotions
"Poor Lionel went to pieces after his wife died."

go to pot/to the dogs = deteriorate, or become disorganized/out of control
"The whole factory has gone to pot since the general manager left."
"There is increasing crime and unemployment all the time; I think the country is going to the dogs."

go to sea = enlist in the navy
"My son has decided he'd like to go to sea when he leaves school."

go to sleep = become numb
"I've been sitting awkwardly and my leg has gone to sleep."

go to the country = seek re-election (of a government)
"The government were defeated over the issue of capital punishment and so they have decided to go to the country."

go to the wall/go under = become bankrupt/insolvent
"Several small companies have gone to the wall since the government raised the rate of corporation tax."

go to town = be extravagant/lavish
"Dan really went to town on his daughter's wedding reception."

go to war = engage in warfare
"There is a possibility that the two countries will go to war over the fishing rights in their disputed territorial waters."

go west = cease to exist/die
"The town's last remaining cinema went west last year and it's now a bingo palace."

go with a bang = be a (spectacular) success
"I was a bit worried about asking my boss to dinner, but the whole evening went with a bang."

go without = have none
"If you don't like what I've cooked you for dinner you can go without!"

go without saying = be self-evident/need not be mentioned
"And of course I will help to pay for it, that goes without saying."

have a go = make an attempt
"I've never eaten snails before, but I'll have a go at anything once."

here we go again = the same thing is happening again
"Here we go again, yet another quiz programme on television."

make a go of something = do something successfully
"Neil is starting a minicab business; I do hope he makes a go of it."

it's no go = it cannot be done
"Sorry, it's no go; I cannot give you any more pocket money until the end of the week."

See also: go Dutch; go easy on somebody; go easy on/with something; going concern; go to earth; here goes; there you go.

goat

act/play the goat = behave foolishly
"Glen is always acting the goat, I never know when to take him seriously."

get somebody's goat = (severely) annoy somebody
"What gets my goat is the way he always accepts a drink but never buys you one back."

sort out the sheep from the goats = determine what is useful/valuable from among what is not
"The management is asking everyone to produce ten more items each day; that should sort out the sheep from the goats."

God

by God!/good God! = exclamation of surprise
"By God! You said that without moving your lips!"
"Good God! You can 't charge that much for apples this time of year!"

for God's/goodness' sake! = exclamation of annoyance/surprise
"For God's sake, you should have realized that crocodiles bite!"

God forbid/please God = I hope it is not so/I hope it may it never happen
"I hear that Jan has been involved in a car crash? God forbid that she's injured."" .ÖPlease God she isn't injured."

God knows/goodness knows = nobody knows
"God knows how the cat got up on the roof."

honest to God! = in all truth!
"Honest to God, that is exactly what she said!"

little tin god = somebody with an inflated opinion of his/her own importance
"Most of the bank's junior employees think they're little tin gods."

in the lap of the gods = subject to chance/fate
"I did my best and now it's in the lap of the god's whether or not I pass the exam."

put the fear of God into somebody = frighten somebody
"I have no problem riding my moped, but that 750 cc motorbike puts the fear of God into me."

the gods = uppermost balcony in a theatre
"I like the bird's-eye view you get from the gods."

think one is God's gift to = have a conceited belief as to one's worth
"Look at the way Roy is behaving with those girls! His trouble is he thinks he's God's gift to women."

ye gods! = exclamation of surprise
"Ye gods! You're not going out in those clothes are you?"

See also: act of God; fairy godmother; the mills of God grind slowly (but they grind exceedingly small).

goes

here goes = let us see what happens
"I've never drunk brandy before. Here goes ñ let's have a glass and see what it tastes like."

how goes it (with you)? = what is happening (with you)?/what progress has been made?
"How goes it? Do you think you will have finished the job by Friday?"

that's how/the way it goes = these are the (usually unpleasant) circumstances
"I'm sorry you didn't recover your investment, but that's the way it goes when you speculate on the stock market."

going

easy going = friendly/undemanding
"You'll have no trouble with Mark, he's so easy going since he got married last year."

get going = begin/start
"I find it very difficult to get going these wintry mornings."

"My petrol lawn mower may be old, but at least it's easy to get going."

going concern = thriving business
"Arthur has greatly increased the turnover of his shop and he's decided to sell it as a going concern."

going for = priced at/sold for
"How much are these houses going for nowadays?"

going strong = flourishing/thriving
"My father is ninety next birthday and he's still going strong."

hard/heavy going = difficult/hard work
"Doris take a long time to complete a job because she makes such heavy going of it."

how are things going?/how's it going? = general enquiry about what has been happening/what progress has been made
"We haven't met for ages; how are things going with you?"
"How's it going with that new project?"

to be going on with = for the time being
"I'll pay you most of the money on Friday to be going on with, and the rest next week."

while the going is good = while the opportunity exists
"I don't like the look of those rain clouds and think we should return home while the going is good, before it rains and we get soaked."

See also: go; have a lot going for one.

gold

as good as gold = very well behaved
"We took the children to a restaurant for a meal and they were as good as gold."

gold-digger = young woman who forms an association with men merely to obtain money from them
"In three years Pam has been engaged four times; she only does it so that the boyfriends give her money and presents, the gold-digger."

gold mine = very profitable (retail) business
"Our corner shop charges high prices and is open all hours; it must be a gold mine for its owners."

worth one's weight in gold = highly valued as an employee/member of a team, etc.
"I'm glad we took on that new girl to help in the shop, she's very willing and worth her weight in gold."

See also: crock of gold; have a heart of gold; like gold dust.

golden

golden boy = talented young man who is expected to become successful
"The young German player was the golden boy of Wimbledon and is expected to win the championship within the next few years."

golden days = pleasant/prosperous time in the past
"I used to see three films a week in the golden days when cinemas were flourishing."

golden handshake = (large) payment made to an employee who leaves a job prematurely
"Henry's company asked him to retire early but he was able to pay off his mortgage with the golden handshake they gave him."

golden opportunity = very favourable chance
"I'm glad your father is coming to dinner, it will be a golden opportunity for me to ask his advice."

golden rule = basic principle (which should always be adhered to)

"Remember, when driving a car the golden rule is never take both hands off the steering wheel."

golf

golf widow = wife who is often left alone while her husband is playing golf
"Since Brian retired he has been playing a round of golf with his friends at least three times a week and I've become a golf widow."

gone

dead and gone = dead for some time
"Most of my contemporaries are dead and gone, but I suppose that's what happens when you are in your eighties."

far gone = drugged/drunk (of somebody), or old/worn out (of something)
"After six pints of beer he's so far gone he can't even remember his address."
"I'll have to buy some new shoes, these are far gone."

gone on somebody/something = very attracted to somebody/something
"My son is completely gone on the girl who has just come to live next door."
"My daughter is totally gone on heavy metal music."

good

a good job = fortunate
"It's a good job your mother can't see you now."

all in good time = eventually
"Yes, dear, I will get round to painting the garden fence all in good time."

all well and good = acceptable (but with nagging doubts)
"You're going to bring all the food and drink. That's all well and good, but what happens if you don't turn up?"

as good as = equivalent to/very nearly
"I bought a second-hand chair which is as good as new."
"At the end of the interview he as good as said I had got the job."

be so good as to = kindly/please
"Would you be so good as to pass me the mustard?"
"Richard was so good as to drive me home in his car."

do somebody (a power of) good = improve somebody's behaviour/manner/health etc.
"Come on, take this medicine; I know it tastes nasty but it will do you good."

do somebody a good turn = be helpful to somebody
"I was going to buy some bedding plants at the supermarket but Roy did me a good turn and told me about a garden centre where I could get them much cheaper."

for good (and all) = for ever
"Louise is determined to stop smoking for good and all."

for good measure = as an extra
"I asked the florist for ten roses and he gave me a dozen for good measure."

good and ready = completely ready
"Don't rush me; I'll come when I'm good and ready."

good for nothing = worthless
"That watch hasn't worked for years; it's good for nothing, why don't you throw it away?"

good for you! = congratulations!
"Good for you! You've passed all your exams."

good gracious!/good grief! = exclamation of surprise

"Good gracious! Is that the time? I'm going to miss the last train if I don't hurry."

good Samaritan = somebody who takes much trouble to help others
"My neighbour was a good Samaritan when I sprained my ankle. She did all my shopping and took the dog for a walk every day."

good turn = favour
"You did me a good turn when you suggested that I apply for a rise; I went and saw the boss, and he agreed to increase my wages from next month."

good while = long time
"It's been a good while since we had kippers for breakfast."

give as good as one gets = to be as effective as the other person in a contest
"You don't have to worry about Tina in an argument with somebody, she can give as good as shc gets."

have a good time = enjoy oneself
"Did you have a good time on holiday?"

in good time = with time to spare
"There's no need to hurry, we will get to the airport in good time."

in somebody's good books = favoured by somebody/well thought of
"Our supervisor is all right as long as you keep in her good books."

make good = repair damage, or succeed
"We will have to make good those cracks in the ceiling before we paint it."
"Ian started by selling fruit off a barrow, but he made good and now he owns two shops."

make good time = do something in less time than expected
"We made good time and drove to the coast in under two hours."

not good enough = not acceptable
"It's too enough; that's the second time this week you've been late."

on good terms = friendly
"I'm on good terms with my local MP and he's promised to look into the matter."

on to a good thing = in a favourable situation
"You're on to a good thing if your job offers unlimited voluntary overtime ñ you can virtually earn as much as you like."

put in a good word for = recommend
"If they want some more people to go on the trip, put in a good word for me."

take in good part = accept cheerfully
"We often tease John about his bald head but he takes it in good part."

that's a good one! = I do not believe you!
"You won the snooker tournament? That's a good one! You'll be telling me you beat Steve Davis next!"

to the good = to an advantage/profit
"I may have ordered too many bricks, but that's all to the good; we can use any left over to build a garden wall."

up to no good = committing a crime/ making mischief
"Those children are very quiet; I bet they're up to no good."

See also: as good as gold; good egg; good old days; in good hands; it's a good thing; my good man.

goodness

See: for God's/goodness' sake; God/ goodness knows

goods

deliver the goods = do something effectively/as promised

"If Helen says she will complete the job on time you can always rely on her to deliver the goods."

have the goods on somebody = know something incriminating about somebody
"The crime syndicate has the goods on the governor and are blackmailing him."

See also: black goods/services.

goose

goose flesh/pimples = bumpy skin caused by cold or fear
"Merely the thought of holding a snake makes me come out in goose flesh."

kill the goose that lays the golden egg = destroy/spoil one's chief source of profit
"They regularly buy large quantities from us, so we should not put up our prices too much; we don't want to kill the goose that lays the golden egg."

say "boo" to a goose = frighten somebody
"The boss may look a bit fierce, but in fact he wouldn't say ëboo' to a goose."

what is sauce for the goose is sauce for the gander = something that applies to one partner should also apply to the other
"George likes to have a drink with his friends but objects when his wife goes round to her mother's; what's sauce for the goose is sauce for the gander."

See also: cook somebody's goose; wild goose chase.

gooseberry

play gooseberry = be an unwanted third person with an (established) couple
"Janet and John have asked me to go round for the evening but I don't want to play gooseberry."

gospel

take as gospel = believe to be absolutely true (without question)
"You can take it as gospel that the Smiths are going to sell their house and live in a caravan."

got

have got to = must
"I've got to get some cigarettes on the way home."

grab

how does that grab you? = what do you think of that?
"I've decided to increase your pocket money to two pounds a week. How does that grab you?"

up for grabs = available to anyone
"Has that car been sold or is it still up for grabs?"

grace

day's grace = extra day (in which to pay a bill etc.)
"My rent was due yesterday; I must take it to the landlord today because I only get a day's grace."

fall from grace = lose favour
"The cabinet minister fell from grace when the newspapers published a report about his extramarital activities."

get into somebody's good graces = wheedle oneself into favour
"I'm meeting my girlfriend's parents at the weekend; I suppose I must get into their good graces if I'm going to ask her to marry me."

grace and favour = describing something bestowed (free) by the monarch

"The Dowager Duchess lives in a grace and favour apartment at Hampton Court."

grace note = in music, a short note that embellishes a main note of a melody (usually played immediately before it)
"Her harpsichord performance of a simple tune was fussy and spoiled for me by her overuse of grace notes."

grace with one's presence = attend (formal, or sarcastic)
"We had a family reunion and my sister ñ whom I haven't seen for years ñ graced us with her presence."

saving grace = good quality among bad ones
"The resort had little or no entertainment and nowhere good to eat, but one saving grace was that it didn't rain all week."

with bad/good grace = unwillingly/ willingly
"I asked him three times and he finally did it, but with bad grace."

See also: airs and graces.

gracious
See: good gracious!

grade
make the grade = attain a required standard
"Margaret had a natural aptitude for cooking and, with proper training, should be able to make the grade as a qualified chef."

grain
See: go against the grain

grandmother
teach one's grandmother to suck eggs = inform somebody who is better informed than oneself
"Trying to tell Harold anything about pistols is like teaching your grandmother to suck eggs."

granted
take somebody for granted = assume somebody is content without asking him/her
"I don't mind helping out every week but I don't want to be taken for granted."

take something for granted = assume something is true
"I took it for granted that the garage would sell me the right part for my car but when I got home I found that it wouldn't fit."

grape
sour grapes = bitter feeling resulting from disappointment
"James says he would hate to have my new job, but he applied for it himself unsuccessfully, so it's probably just sour grapes on his part."

through the grape-vine = a rumour
"I've heard through the grape-vine that our local cinema is going to close."

grasp
grasp the nettle = tackle a difficult/ unpleasant task with determination
"The worst thing about a party is clearing up afterwards, but if we grasp the nettle we can get it all done in a hour."

grass
grass on somebody = inform on somebody to the police/authorities
"The police wouldn't have known of Terry's involvement if his brother hadn't grassed on him."

grass roots = ordinary but influential members of a group/organization
"The grass roots of the party are bitterly opposed to legislation to reduce the power of the trade unions."

grass widow = woman whose husband is away
"My husband is going on a business trip to Germany so I'll be a grass widow for a week."

let the grass grow under one's feet = procrastinate/waste time
"Have you finished that job already? You certainly don't let the grass grow under your feet."

put/send out to grass = make somebody retire (from work)
"I'm 63 and I've been given early retirement and put out to grass."

See also: be (as) green as grass; not let the grass grow under one's feet; snake in the grass.

grate

See: grate on the ear.

grave

dig one's own grave = be in difficulty because of one's own (misjudged) actions
"If you give up this job before you've found another one you might be digging your own grave."

goose/somebody walking over one's grave = feeling of uneasiness that causes one to shiver
"I shivered but I'm not cold ñ somebody must have walked over my grave."

make somebody turn in his/her grave = bad enough to anger somebody who is dead if he/she were still alive
"Listen to that awful music. It's enough to make Beethoven turn in his grave!"

See also: have one foot in the grave; silent as the grave.

gravy

get on/join the gravy train = become wealthy
"It is worth investing all one's money in property, if only to get on the gravy train."

See also: share of the gravy.

grease

grease somebody's palm = bribe/tip somebody
"Bill has some complimentary tickets and if you grease his palm he'll probably let you have a couple."

grease the wheels = make things run smoothly
"I gave the removal men some money for a drink to help grease the wheels."

like greased lightning = very quickly
"We were enjoying ourselves so much the time just went like greased lightning."

smell of the grease-paint = performing in a circus/theatre
"I gave up acting ten years ago but I still long for the smell of the grease paint."

See also: elbow grease.

great

no great shakes = not much good
"I'm disappointed with her new record ñ it's no great shakes."

that's great! = that is excellent!
"You're going to get married? That's great!"

the great I am = person who thinks he/she is very important

"Here comes the supervisor; the great I am is going to tell us all how to do our jobs."

See also: go great guns; great minds think alike.

Greek

all Greek to me = too difficult to understand/unknown

"My son is studying physical chemistry but it's all Greek to me."

green

be (as) green as grass = naive/inexperienced

"Give the new lad a hand if he needs it, he's as green as grass."

green about the gills = looking as if one is about to vomit (because of excess drink, motion sickness, shock, etc.)

"Is Maria all right? She's had a lot to drink and is looking a bit green about the gills."

green-eyed monster = jealousy

"If you think your husband's secretary is too attractive, beware of the green-eyed monster."

green fingers = talent at gardening

"My mother's really got green fingers; if she planted a pencil it would grow!"

green light = approval/permission to start, a go-ahead

"The government has given the green light to the channel tunnel project."

not to be as green as one is cabbage-looking = not to be as stupid as one appears

"Sell you my car for five hundred pounds? It's worth twice that and I'm not as green as I'm cabbage-looking."

See also: green with envy.

grey

grey area = something that is imprecisely defined/known

"Regarding the contract, the schedule is clear enough but I'm worried about the grey area concerning who pays for any price rise of the raw materials."

grey-beard = elderly man

"I expected the sports master to be a young man so you can imagine my surprise when I was introduced to this grey-beard who must have been at least sixty."

grey matter = brain/intellect

"She may be getting old but there's nothing wrong with her grey matter."

grief

come to grief = be damaged/destroyed, have an accident

"You were cycling downhill far too fast and I'm not surprised you came to grief."

See also: good grief!

grievance

air a grievance = make known that one feels unfairly treated

"You should wait until we have a staff meeting; that's the time to air any grievance you may have."

nurse a grievance = retain a feeling of bitterness because of (supposed) unfair treatment

"You were found guilty in a fair trial and you've served your sentence; there's no point in nursing a grievance."

grill

grill somebody = interrogate somebody

"The police grilled him for four hours before they released him from custody."

grim

cling/hold on like grim death = hold something tenaciously

"She slipped half way down the cliff and then hung on like grim death until help arrived."

grin

grin and bear it = suffer without making a complaint

"My boss sometimes makes insulting remarks but I just grin and bear it rather than risk losing my job."

See also: wipe the grin/smile off somebody's face.

grind

grind somebody down = oppress somebody

"For years, the landowners have ground down the peasants and exploited them."

grind to a halt = gradually stop

"If the buses and underground go on strike, business in London will grind to halt."

keep one's nose to the grindstone = work long and hard

"I'll have to keep my nose to the grindstone if I'm to finish this project on time."

the daily grind = daily work

"I need a holiday as a relief from the daily grind."

See also: have an axe to grind; the mills of God grind slowly (but they grind exceedingly small).

grip

come/get to grips with = deal with

"My eyes were bandaged for three weeks and I had to get to grips with the problem of blindness, even though I knew it was only temporary."

get a grip on oneself = get oneself under control

"Get a grip on yourself and stop crying at once."

in the grip of = in the control/power of

"The whole of London was in the grip of an flu epidemic."

lose one's grip = lose control

"The trouble with being parents of teenage children is that once you lose your grip, they can make life miserable for everyone."

grist

all grist to the mill = everything has some value

"So you didn't get as much as you would have liked when you sold your car, but never mind, it's all grist to the mill."

groove

be/get into/run in a groove = be in a routine/unchanging job or way of life

"My life seems to be in a groove, I do the same things day after day."

ground

break new ground = do/find something new

"The book breaks new ground by acknowledging that men, as well as women, may have hormonal problems at middle age."

common ground = area of mutual experience/interest

"My father and my new boyfriend have cricket and beer drinking as common ground, so they should get on well with each other."

cover a lot of/the ground = deal with a wide range of topics

"We covered a lot of ground at the meeting, leaving only one thing to discuss tomorrow."

down to the ground = appropriate/ suitable for somebody

"That new car is Graham down to the ground ñ all bright and flashy."

gain ground = advance/progress

"Labour gained ground mainly from the Alliance in the run-up to the election."

get off the ground = initiate/put into action

"The chief difficulty with such projects is getting them off the ground, although once they're started they tend to keep going."

give ground = (be forced to) retreat/yield

"Raymond will never give ground in a debate, even when he knows he's technically in the wrong."

go to ground = hide (to evade pursuers/ searchers)

"The escaped prisoner must have gone to ground somewhere because an extensive search failed to find him."

groundswell of opinion = views of the majority (of ordinary people)

"Despite the decision about capital punishment taken in Parliament, the groundswell of opinion seems to be in favour of reintroducing it."

hold/stand one's ground = be firm/ unyielding

"The opposition attacked the government's employment policy, but the Minister stood his ground and pointed out that unemployment is steadily falling."

let somebody in at/on the ground floor = allow somebody to join a company on the same terms as its founders

"The business was sound but undercapitalized and so, in return for a substantial investment, the directors let me in on the ground floor."

on one's home ground = where one has the advantage of local knowledge/ personal experience

"The interview was fairly difficult until they asked me about car maintenance, where I was on my home ground and could impress them with the extent of my knowledge."

rooted to the ground = immobile/fixed in one spot

"Sammy stood rooted to the ground, bewildered by all that was happening around him, and wouldn't come although we called and called."

run somebody to ground = find somebody (who has been evasive)

"I had been trying to contact Albert all week and I finally ran him to ground at his club."

shift one's ground = change one's opinion/viewpoint

"When I asked Emma about her views on the new town hall she shifted her ground and said she liked it, although previously she had said she thought it was a monstrosity."

stamping ground = somebody's favourite haunt

"I know the Red Lion; it was on my stamping ground when I lived on the other side of the town."

suit somebody down to the ground = totally meet somebody's needs/ requirements

"My new job pays a bit more and is located much nearer where I live: it suits me down to the ground."

thick/thin on the ground = common/ uncommon

"It took us a long time to find somewhere to live, but five-bedroomed houses are not very thick

on the ground in this district."
"Reliable plumbers are thin on the ground these days."
See also: cut the ground from under somebody's feet; get in on the ground floor; ground rules; have one's ear to the ground; have one's feet on the ground; lose ground.

grow
growing pains = difficulties that occur during the initial stages of a development
"Apart from a few growing pains with the heating controls, the new printing machine has functioned very well."
grown-up = adult
"As you have no school tomorrow you can stay up late and watch the midnight movie on television with the grown-ups."
grow on one = become slowly acceptable/likeable
"I didn't like that new record at first but it grows on you the more you hear it."
grow out of = become too large/mature for
"My daughter has grown out of her school uniform in only six months."
"My son's only interest seems to be motorbikes, but I suppose he will grow out of it."
grow up = behave like an adult
"You're eighteen now and it's about time you grew up."
See also: money doesn't grow on trees.

growth
cancerous growth = something bad which spreads out of control
"Vandalism is increasing on the large housing estates like a cancerous growth."

grudge
bear a grudge = retain feelings of bitterness (because of unfair treatment)
"Penny always avoids Peter; she's borne him a grudge ever since he got her dismissed from her previous job five years ago."

guard
catch somebody off his/her guard = take somebody by surprise (unprepared to meet an attack)
"The best way to ask the boss for a rise is to catch him off his guard and just slip it into the conversation."
drop/keep up one's guard = be unprepared/prepared to meet an attack
"The interviewer asked some very searching questions but the government spokesman didn't drop his guard for a second."
guard against = beware of
"The company has had a good year but we must guard against complacency."
off/on one's guard = unprepared/ prepared to defend oneself
"I'm always on my guard when people ask my views about whether Britain should stay in the Common Market."
See also: old guard.

guardian
See: guardian angel.

guess
guessing game = situation of (very) uncertain outcome
"The company seems to have no policy for future development ñ what it is likely to do next is a guessing game."

guess what = here is a surprise
"Guess what! Trelawny and I have exactly the same birthday."
your guess is as good as mine = I know as little about it as you do
"I don't know the time of the last train ñ your guess is as good as mine."
wild guess = haphazard guess
"I didn't really know your age, it was just a wild guess."
See also: anybody's guess; educated guess.

guest
be my guest = (feel free to) do as you please
"If you want to borrow the car, be my guest."

gum
up a gum tree = in a difficult/untenable position
"The salesman had been briefed only about the overall design and appeal of the machine, but the purchaser asked searching questions about its construction and maintenance, which left the salesman up a gum tree."
See also: gum up the works.

gun
big guns = important/powerful people
"We had better tidy the place up, the big guns from head office are coming tomorrow."
give something the gun = test something to its maximum potential
"Why don't you take your new car down the motorway and give it the gun to find out how fast it can go?"
go down with all guns blazing/firing = lose while still fighting
"Mike refused to accept overall responsibility for his department's poor performance and was subsequently demoted ñ but at least he went down with all guns firing."
go great guns = be successful/do well
"Since the change in the regulations about corporation tax, our company has been going great guns."
gun for somebody = seek somebody in order to do him/her harm/mischief
"I would advise you to be wary of Kevin; he's been gunning for you since you stole his girlfriend."
spike somebody's guns = anticipate and counter criticism
"The boss is bound to question the cost of the food for the office party, so let's spike his guns by pointing out that he's getting the drinks very cheaply."
stick to one's guns = hold fast to one's principles
"In spite of the change in the political climate, he sticks to his guns about the need for trade union reform."
See also: jump the gun; son of a gun.

guts
hate somebody's guts = have a strong dislike for somebody
"Basically I hate his guts but I try not to show it when doing business with him."
have the guts to = have the courage to
"After what he said to my wife, I was surprised that he had the guts to come round and apologize."
See also: slog one's guts out.

gutter
gutter press = lower (sensation-seeking) forms of journalism
"The cabinet minister's indiscretion

might have been overlooked if the gutter press had not found out about it."

out of the gutter = from a deprived/very humble background
"Sir Jasper took her out of the gutter and made her into the toast of London society."

guy

fall guy = a dupe, somebody who is left to take the blame/punishment for somebody else's misdeeds
"The gang ran off and left their lookout as a fall guy."

wise guy = somebody who thinks he/she knows everything
"Bob pretends to be such a wise guy, but we all know he's not as clever as he thinks."

H

habit

break/get out of the habit = break/ change a routine
"In order to lose weight Jane tried to get out of the habit of taking sugar in her coffee."

creature of habit = somebody who always follows the same predictable pattern of behaviour
"Jack was a creature of habit ñ he always ate lunch at exactly 12.30 every day."

deep-rooted habit = long-standing pattern of behaviour
"I have often tried to give up smoking but it is such a deep-rooted habit after twenty years that I have yet to succeed."

fall into a/the habit = acquire the habit
"It's very easy to fall into the habit of smoking, but extremely difficult to stop."

from force of habit = because of (a need to conform to) a long-standing pattern of behaviour
"Although he had been retired from the army for seven years, from force of habit the major always got up at 6 o'clock in the morning."

make a habit of = adopt as routine behaviour
"I make a habit of walking to work now instead of taking the bus."

hackles

make one's hackles rise = make one (angrily) defensive
"It really made my hackles rise when I was refused entry to the club, especially when the doorman said it

hail

hail-fellow-well-met = (over)friendly
"Have you noticed that Jones is always hail-fellow-well-met when he wants something, but off-hand when he doesn't?"

hail from = be born at/come from
"That's not a local accent. Where do you hail from?"

hair

don't loose your hair over it/keep your hair on = do not overreact/do not worry needlessly
"I know you've got your driving test tomorrow but don't lose your hair over it, you can always take it again if you do not pass."

get in somebody's hair = annoy somebody (by getting in his/her way)
"I'm glad the new trainee is keen but I wish he'd stop hanging around my bench and getting in my hair."

get/have somebody by the short hairs = have somebody at a total disadvantage
"We'll have to agree to their terms because we owe them a lot of money and they have us by the short hairs."

hair-raising = frightening/terrifying
"My wife lets out a hair-raising scream when she finds a spider in the bath."

hair's breadth = very small distance
"The stuntman flew the aircraft upside-down within a hair's breadth of the rooftops."

harm a hair of somebody's head = harm somebody even slightly
"You'll have me to answer to if you harm a hair of her head."

let one's hair down = relax and enjoy oneself
"You've been working very hard lately

out more and let your hair down occasionally?"

make one's hair curl/stand on end = cause deep fear/revulsion
"A man accepted a bet to sleep for a night in a pit full of snakes. The very thought of it makes my hair curl!"
"The scene in the horror film where the cannibals dismembered the missionary left me with my hair standing on end."

not turn a hair = remain calm
"I accused him of incompetence but he didn't even turn a hair."

put hairs on somebody's chest = make somebody manly/virile
"Try some draught Guinness, it'll put hairs on your chest."

split hairs = be (over)fastidious/argue over trifles
"You think it happened last June and I think it was July; let's not split hairs and say it was some time last summer."

tear one's hair out = be very frustrated/ worried
"He had been puzzling all day for the answer to the last clue in the crossword and was about to tear his hair out when his wife told him the correct answer."

wear a hair shirt = be penitent
"When my wife finds out about where I was last night I'll have to wear a hair shirt for a week."

without turning/not turning a hair = be calm/unaffected
"The wine tasted like vinegar, yet Norman drank a large glass of it without turning a hair."

See also: hair of the dog (that bit you); keep one's hair/shirt on; neither hide nor hair of.

half

at half-mast = falling down (of trousers, etc.)
"Pull your socks up, Patrick; they look untidy at half-mast."

by half = by too much
"Go on, try it! You're too cautious by half."

by halves = incompletely
"Whenever Mary and David disagree they finish up shouting and yelling at each other ñ they don't do things by halves."

go halves = share (equally)
"Neither of us had much money so we decided to go halves on a take-away pizza."

half a loaf is better than none/no bread (at all) = be grateful for what one has, even if it is not everything that one wants
"Your company's profits are down and they have stopped all overtime. But at least you still have a job, and half a loaf is better than none."

half a moment/tick = a very short time
"I'll be with you in half a moment."

half-and-half = equal(ly)
"After the debate, the audience were divided half-and-half for and against the motion."

half-baked = ill-conceived/incomplete (of a thing), or feeble-minded (of a person)
"I refuse to put money into some half-baked plan to grow pineapples in Iceland."
"Pay no attention to Billy; I think he's a bit half-baked anyway."

half-hearted = unenthusiastic
"I was feeling a bit tired and made only a half-hearted attempt at doing the housework."

half seas over = fairly drunk

"Greg apologized for his behaviour and gave as his excuse that he was half seas over at the time."

half-way house = mid-point

"Spending money on a complete overhaul of the machine is a half-way house between buying a new one and continuing to pay for minor day-to-day repairs."

half-witted = stupid/mentally unsound

"Everyone thought that John's plan to have a barbecue in the middle of January was a half-witted idea."

have half a chance = a small chance/opportunity

"Given half a chance I'd give up my present job and join a circus."

have half a mind = inclination

"It's such a nice day I've half a mind to take the afternoon off work."

how the other half lives = how people less/more fortunate than oneself live

"We're going to spend a few days in Monte Carlo; it will be interesting to see how the other half lives."

meet somebody half way = (agree to a) compromise

"You want £1,200 for the car and I only want to spend £1,000. Why don't you meet me half way and accept £1,100?"

no half measures = no compromise

"I want all the existing paint stripped off and new undercoat and gloss applied. I want a thorough job, with no half measures."

not half = very definitely

"Did I enjoy the show? Not half!"

one's better/other half = one's husband/wife

"I don't know whether I'll see you tonight; it depends if my better half has made any other plans."

something and a half = good/large example of something

"That's a marrow and a half. How did you grow one that big?"

the half of it = (only) part

"When you saw Sue talking to Mr Jones, that was only the half of it; later I saw them holding hands."

See also: go off at half cock; half the battle; see with (only) half an eye.

hallmark

have the hallmark of = be characteristic of/have the (outward) signs of

"The plan has all the hallmarks of being a total failure."

halt

See: call a halt; grind to a halt; halt/pause/stop in midstream.

ham

ham-fisted/-handed = clumsy

"Although thrilled at the birth of his baby daughter, David was afraid to hold her because he said he was so ham-fisted he might hurt her."

hamlet

like Hamlet without the Prince (of Denmark) = without the chief participant

"The last night of the Proms without Land of Hope and Glory would be like Hamlet without the Prince."

hammer

give somebody a hammering = beat somebody soundly

"I played my niece at chess and she gave me a right hammering."

hammer away/out = keep working until a result is reached

"The committee spent hours trying to

agenda before finally reaching agreement."

hammer something home = get somebody to realize/understand something through persistent/vigorous reasoning
"I can't seem to hammer home to my daughter the importance of passing her maths and English exams."

like hammer and tongs = very enthusiastically/vigorously
"Our team went like hammer and tongs in the piano-smashing contest and easily won first prize."
"I knew it was only a matter of time before they got divorced because they were always arguing like hammer and tongs."

under the hammer = put up for sale at auction
"The contents of the late duke's house are due to come under the hammer next week."

hand

accept with both hands = accept eagerly/enthusiastically
"When the sales director offered me the chance of representing the company at the world fair in New York I accepted with both hands."

all hands to the pumps = everybody must help
"We had only a few days of fine weather to complete the harvest so it was a question of all hands to the pumps until the work was done."

at/on hand = readily available
"We always keep a good stock of drink on hand in case we have unexpected visitors."

baby, although I only have the news at second-hand."

at/in the hands of = the responsibility of
"Security for the Queen's visit will be in the hands of the Special Branch and members of the police force."

big hand = enthusiastic applause
"When the ageing actress stepped forward to receive her award, the whole audience gave her a big hand."

bite the hand that feeds one = return kindness with hostility/ingratitude
"If you're going to complain to the boss about working conditions, make sure you don't bite the hand that feeds you."

bound/tied hand and foot = totally helpless/restricted
"The priest was bound hand and foot by the confidentiality of the confessional and was unable to help the police in their enquiries even though he knew the identity of the man they were seeking."

by hand = manually, or personally
"That is a pretty jumper; did you knit it by hand?"
"The post is unreliable so I'll deliver the contract by hand."

clean hands = blameless
"The accused came away from the trial with clean hands after the judge declared there was no case to answer."

close at/to hand = nearby
"It doesn't matter where you live in England there is usually a Chinese take-away restaurant close at hand."
"When on safari in Africa I used to sleep with my rifle close to hand because lions would sometimes stray into the camp looking for food."

"The sergeant is a cool hand; shells were exploding close to our position but he just continued to read his book and sip his tea."

dirty/soil one's hands = be involved with something dishonest
"I don't care how much money there is to be made, I wouldn't soil my hands by getting involved in that sort of business."

do a hands turn = work
"Nigel is a lazy so-and-so; he hasn't done a hand's turn for months now."

(at) first hand = from somebody with personal knowledge
"I learned about the incident first hand because I know one of the policemen who worked on the case."

from hand to hand = from one person to another
"I was sitting at the end of the row and my drink had to be passed from hand to hand until it eventually reached me."

from hand to mouth = in poverty
"During the Depression, formerly rich people were bankrupted and found themselves living from hand to mouth."

gain/have the upper hand = gain the advantage/lead
"Manchester United gained the upper hand over Arsenal by scoring two penalty goals in the first five minutes."

gain/have the whip hand = be in a position of control/domination
"Adolf Hitler had the whip hand over the German people and the government after his spectacular rise to power in the 1930s."

give one's hand to = accept an offer of marriage (very formal)
"I will consent to my daughter's giving her hand to you only on receipt of the agreed dowry."

give somebody the glad hand = welcome warmly
"I was unsure how I would be received by the new chairman, but he gave me the glad hand and invited me to join him for a drink."

great hand (at something) = adept/expert (at doing something)
"Jim's a great hand at organizing barbecues, but he often drinks too much and then burns the steaks."

hand down = bequeath/pass on as an inheritance
"This gold watch has been handed down from father to son for three generations."

hand in hand = associated/united (with), or holding hands
"Drug pushing usually goes hand in hand with other forms of organized crime."
"At the end of the film the lovers walked off into the sunset hand in hand."

hand it to someone = give (due) credit
"I've got to hand it to you, Bill; I didn't think you would last five minutes in the army and now you tell me you've been offered a commission."

hand on heart = honestly/sincerely
"The politician stated hand on heart that the newspaper's allegations were totally untrue."

hand over = concede/pass on/surrender
"The terrorists agreed to hand over the hostages in return for safe passage out of the country."

hand over fist = quickly, or in quantity
"The corner shop is open fifteen hours a day. The owner must be making money hand over fist."

hand over hand = (climbing etc.) using first one hand and then the other
"The pot-holers left the cave by climbing up a rope hand over hand."

hands off = leave alone, or remote(ly)
"Keep your hands off those cakes ñ you can't have any until tea time."
"The government has decided on a hands off policy and let individual companies negotiate their own terms with the trade unions."

have a hand in = be involved in/with
"Although the surgeon was directly responsible for performing the heart transplant operation, all the theatre staff had a hand in its success."

have one's hands full = be very busy/ fully occupied
"I will really have my hands full on Saturday; we're having a dinner party and the whole family is coming."

have one's hands tied = be restricted (by regulations/rules)
"I would like to accept your offer, but I still have three months to run on my present contract, so my hands are tied for the time being."

have only one pair of hands = have too much work to do
"The boss wants me to do Joe's work as well as my own. Doesn't he know I've only got one pair of hands?"

have something on one's hands = be in possession of something
"My father has plenty of time on his hands now that he has retired."

heavy hand = authoritarianism/severity
"Children in Victorian England were often brought up with a heavy hand and as a result had more respect for people and property than many of today's children."

high-handed = arrogantly/selfishly
"He scolded the waitress in a high-handed manner for spilling wine on the table cloth."

hold somebody's hand = accompany somebody
"My wife is so afraid of going to the dentist that I have to go along and hold her hand or she would never go."

in good hands = well cared for
"Don't worry about going to hospital ñ you'll be in very good hands."

(well) in hand = being done, or under control
"The repair won't take long, we've got the job in hand now."
"After a scuffle in the stands, the police soon had the crowd well in hand and the match continued without further interruption."

in the hands of = in the possession of
"The company has debts of over a million pounds and is now in the hands of the official receiver."

keep in hand = retain a stock/store of
"We always keep a good supply of paper in hand in case we suddenly have a lot of photocopying to do."

lay hands on = find
"If I could lay my hands on some extra cash I'd buy a car."

left hand doesn't know what the right hand is doing = lack of communication between two parts of the same group/organization
"The Prime Minister said he would not call an election until next year, whereas the party chairman said an election was imminent. The press report concluded that the left hand didn't know what the right hand was doing."

lend a hand = help
"The vicar asked the congregation for volunteers to lend a hand with the preparations for the Harvest Festival."

lift/raise one's hand against = threaten
"The president stated that his country would not tolerate anybody who raised a hand against their allies."

off hand = casual, or unprepared/without notice
"She threw the dart in an off-hand manner and it landed in the treble twenty."
"I don't really know off hand, but I'll probably arrive at about ten o'clock."

off one's hands = no longer one's concern/responsibility
"Both my children start at boarding school next week, so they'll be off my hands and I'll have much more free time."

old hand/stager = somebody who is experienced
"Bill is an old hand at the building trade and he can still lay nearly a thousand bricks a day."

on all hands/on every hand = in every direction/surrounding
"The patrol got lost and the leader suddenly realized that the enemy were on all hands."

on one's hands = in one's possession
"Business is poor at present and I've got a lot of stock on my hands which I can't sell."

on one's hands and knees = in a begging manner
"I shall have to go to the bank manager on my hands and knees and see if I can get a loan."

(on the one hand).Ö (and) on the other hand = alternatively
"On the one hand you could get £60,000 for your house if you sell it now, on the other hand if you wait six months you would probably get another £5,000 the way house prices are rising around here."

open hand = generosity
"Whenever I was short of money I could always rely on my father to offer an open hand."

out of hand = out of control
"The Home Secretary stated that the overcrowding in Britain's prisons was getting out of hand and that new prisons would be built to ease the situation."

out of one's hands = out of one's possession/responsibility
"Your request for more funds has been referred to head office so I'm afraid it's now out of my hands."

overplay one's hand = overconfident to the point that puts one at a disadvantage
"The marathon runner raced ahead in the early stages of the race but he had overplayed his hand and had to drop out exhausted with only three miles to go."

play into somebody's hands = do exactly what somebody else wants one to do
"We pretended to withdraw so that the enemy followed, and they played right into our hands by walking into the ambush we had set up."

put one's hand in one's pocket = pay
"The trouble with owning an old car is that you seem always to be putting your hand in your pocket for repairs."

reveal/show one's hand = reveal one's intentions
"There are rumours of tax cuts, but the Chancellor refuses to show his hand until the budget."

right-hand man = principal assistant
"If you require further details ask Stephen, he's my right-hand man."

second hand = not new (in the possession of the second owner)
"I bought this dress second hand

because I could never afford anything of this quality new."

shake hands on it = make an agreement
"The salesman drove a hard bargain but I finally managed to bring down the price by ten per cent and we shook hands on it."

sit on one's hands = be idle/unoccupied, or (deliberately) take no action
"We couldn't go out because it was raining and there was nothing to do in the hotel, so we just sat on our hands all day."
"The union threatened to strike, but the management sat on its hands because it's policy was not to negotiate unless there had been an official strike ballot of all the workers."

sleight of hand = deviousness/trickery
"The company's directors were unaware of the possibility of a take-over bid until they discovered that by some sleight of hand a rival firm had bought forty per cent of their shares.

stay one's hand = hold back/take no action
"The general was unaware of the enemy's intentions so he chose to stay his hand and consolidate his position."

strong hand = firmness/resolution
"The Speaker of the House of Commons often has to maintain order with a strong hand."

take a hand in = be involved in/take part in
"I took a hand in organizing the Christmas play last year and the vicar has asked me to do the same this year."

take in hand = take charge of
"The headmaster asked for volunteers to take in hand the training of the junior rugby team."

take something off somebody's hands = relieve somebody of possession/ responsibility
"The dealer said he didn't really want to buy my car but that he would give me a hundred pounds to take it off my hands."
"I have run the play school for two years now and I wish I could find somebody to take it off my hands so that I can devote more time to my own children."

throw in one's hand = give up/resign
"After spending a lifetime trying to construct a perpetual motion machine, the eccentric inventor threw in his hand because he had finally proved it was impossible."

try one's hand at = make an attempt to
"After the magician had finished his act, he invited members of the audience to join him on stage and try their hands at some simple conjuring tricks."

turn one's hand to = (be able to) adapt one's skills to
"My husband is quite clever really, he can turn his hand to most do-it-yourself jobs around the house."

wait on somebody hand and foot = satisfy somebody's every need (in a servile manner)
"The Sultan was a powerful man with a retinue of servants to wait on him hand and foot."

wash one's hands of = dissociate oneself from
"I'll wash my hands of that boy if he gets into any more trouble, even if he is my own son."

win hands down = defeat effortlessly
"I played chess with an old man who beat me hands down; I later discovered he was a grand master."

work hand in hand with = co-operate, work closely with
"The Admiral said that the fleet would be working hand in hand with the US Air Force on the NATO exercise."
See also: at first hand; be a dab hand at; bird in the hand; bite the hand that feeds one; blood on one's hands; catch somebody with his/her hands in the till; change hands; empty-handed; extend the hand of fellowship; force somebody's hand; free hand; go cap in hand; hand in glove with somebody; get one's eye/hand in; have somebody eat out of one's hand; have the whip hand; hold/play one's cards/hand close to one's chest; iron hand/fist in a velvet glove; keep one's hand in; live from hand to mouth; many hands make light work; near at hand; raise one's hand against; ready to hand; rub one's hands; show of hands; with one hand tied behind one's back; with one's bare hands.

handle
give/put a handle to = give a name to
"I remember her face but I can't put a handle to it."
handle to one's name = a title
"Do not call me Jones; my name has a handle to it, and so please call me Mister Jones in future."
too hot to handle = too risky to possess
"The newspaper would not print the story because it was too hot to handle and might have attracted the attention of the intelligence department."
"Nobody would take the stolen painting from the thief because it was too hot to handle."
See also: fly off the handle.

handshake
See: golden handshake.

hang
get/lose the hang of = become familiar/unfamiliar with
"I have never driven an automatic car before and I keep trying to change gear, but I expect I'll soon get the hang of it."
"You never lose the hang of riding a bicycle once you have learned properly."
hang about/around = wait a moment, or loiter
"Hang about, I'll just put the car away and then I'll help you make the dinner."
"There should be more places for young people to go so that they don't have to hang around street corners."
hang back = hesitate
"Knowing the press were waiting outside, the film star hung back for several minutes before emerging from the court building where she had just appeared on a drugs charge."
hang by a thread = be in a precarious position
"The survival of the woodland is hanging by a thread; the developers are due to destroy it in two days time if we cannot get a court order to stop them."
hang heavy = pass slowly (of time)
"Time hangs heavy when you're out of work and looking for a job."
hang in = persevere
"When things get difficult the trick is to hang in until they get better."
hanging matter/offence = (action that is regarded as a) serious misdemeanour
"Don't let your mother see you using

her best perfume ñ that's a hanging offence!"

hang in the balance = be in a state of indecision (regarding a situation that could get better or worse)

"After six hours discussion the jury could still not agree and the fate of the accused remained hanging in the balance."

hang it = mild expletive

"I'm supposed to be on a diet but hang it, I will have a piece of cake!"

hang (up)on = depend (up)on

"Our daughter would like to go to university but it all hangs on her A-level results."

hang one's head = be ashamed

"The little boy hung his head when his mother caught him teasing the cat."

hang on somebody's lips/words = listen attentively

"When grandfather tells a ghost story all the children hang on his every word."

hang out = to frequent

"I haven't seen you in this pub for ages. Where do you hang out these days?"

hang together = be complete/consistent, or share the responsibility

"This grand scheme will never hang together, and the board would not agree to the cost anyway."

"I got you into this mess in the first place, so we'll hang together and try to find a solution."

hang up = terminate a telephone call

"If you don't want to talk to him when he phones you, why don't you just hang up?"

have something hanging over one's head = be under a threat (of unpleasantness)

"I wish the company would reveal their plans; I hate having the threat of redundancy hanging over my head."

hung up on = obsessed with

"It's about time Harry made some new women friends, but I'm afraid he's still hung up on his ex-wife."

I'll be hanged = expression of disbelief/surprise, or of resoluteness

"Well I'll be hanged, I didn't expect to see you again until next month."

"I'll be hanged if you think that I'm going to tolerate that sort of behaviour in my house."

let it all hang out = do as you like

"After a week's hard work I like nothing better than going to a party and letting it all hang out."

there by hangs a tale = there is more to this matter, but it is best left unsaid

"Judy said she was staying at home last evening but I saw her car parked outside the night club, and thereby hangs a tale."

See also: have a hangdog air; hang fire; hang/put the flags out; hang up one's hat; one might as well be hung for a sheep as a lamb.

happen

happen one's way = become available to one (by chance)

"I wasn't looking for a new job, it just happened my way and I took it."

happen what may = whatever happens

"Happen what may, she's determined to marry that good-for-nothing Jones boy."

it's all happening = there is much activity

"Why don't you come to the new sports centre with me? That's where it's all happening now."

See also: worse things happen at sea.

happy

go to the happy hunting ground = die
"My aunt has been a widow for ten years, ever since uncle went to the happy hunting ground."

happy as a dog with two tails/lark/ sandboy/Larry = very happy
"Give my husband an old motorbike to tinker with and he's as happy as a dog with two tails."
"The children are as happy as Larry playing on the beach all day."

happy-go-lucky = carefree
"I envy Gary; he approaches life's challenges in a happy-go- lucky way and never seems to come to any harm."

happy hunting ground = place where one finds pleasurable/profitable pursuits
"The underground stations in the summer are a happy hunting ground for pickpockets."

happy landings! = (goodbye and) good luck!
"I hope you have an enjoyable time on holiday. Happy landings!"

happy medium = sensible compromise (between two extremes)
"You must find a happy medium between going out every night of the week and living the life of a recluse."

trigger-happy = too ready to employ violence
"Thank goodness the new Soviet premier is not as trigger-happy as his predecessor."

See also: as happy as the day is long; happy event; many happy returns.

hard

be hard on somebody = be overcritical/ unfair to somebody
"She's new at the job and bound to make a few mistakes, so don't be too hard on her."

be hard put to do something = have difficulty/trouble in doing something
"David has applied for a new position but I think he'll be hard put to meet the required standard."

go hard with somebody = be to somebody's disadvantage
"There is an undefendable case against you so you might as well plead guilty; it will only go hard with you if you don't."

hard and fast = firm/immovable
"The Prime Minister stuck hard and fast to her policy of no U-turns in the government's economic plans."

hard at it = working busily
"The teacher arrived at the classroom five minutes late and was surprised to find the children hard at it reading their history books."

hard-bitten = inflexible/tough
"His experiences in Vietnam have left him really hard-bitten."

hard-boiled = unemotional/tough
"It's no good appealing to the bank manager for yet another loan; he's much too hard-boiled to be influenced by your pleas of poverty."

hard by = close/very near
"I'll meet you in the car park hard by the station."

hard cash = money (coin and banknotes only)
"The plumber offered me a ten per cent discount if I paid him in hard cash."

hard done by = receiving bad/poor treatment
"So you didn't get a big rise this year. But you've still got a company car and an expense account, so you're not hard done by."

hard drinker = somebody who drinks (spirits) habitually
"Tom's a hard drinker and it will affect his health and his job if he's not careful."

hard-earned = gained through much effort
"Because of the hazardous nature of their work, North Sea divers deserve every penny of their hard-earned pay."

harden one's heart = feel little emotion/sympathy
"When people come round to the house collecting for charity I just harden my heart and give them nothing."

hard-faced/hard-featured/hard-nosed = grim/tough, unsympathetic
"The extreme left-wing faction are hard-nosed exponents of the socialist doctrine."

hard-headed = practical/sensible, unemotional
"She was a hard-headed woman who was determined to succeed against her male rivals."

hard hit = adversely affected
"Exports are being hard hit by the strength of the pound against foreign currencies."

hard-hitting = of great impact
"Mrs Mandela frequently risks arrest by making hard-hitting criticisms of the Apartheid system in her country."

hard/tough nut to crack = difficult problem/person
"I'll get the information from him eventually but he's a hard nut to crack and it may take a long time."

hard of hearing = partially deaf
"You have to raise your voice when you speak to grandfather because he's a bit hard of hearing."

hard on the heels of = close behind
"The Spring Bank Holiday will fall hard on the heels of Easter this year."

hard put to it = find it difficult to do something
"Thanks for the loan, but you ought to know that I'll be hard put to it to repay you before the end of the month."

hard stuff = spirit drink (as opposed to beer or wine)
"If you don't want another pint, why don't you have a drop of the hard stuff?"

hard times = difficult/worrying situation
"The people who lived in London during the blitz certainly experienced hard times."

hard up = without much money
"We're a bit hard up this year so we won't be going on holiday after all."

hard words = critical/scolding comments
"She had a few hard words to say about the way her daughter behaved."

play hard to get = try to make oneself more attractive/wanted by being difficult to contact
"The best way of getting Malcolm to ask you out is to play hard to get."

take a hard line = be firm/uncompromising
"The local justices are taking a hard line with people who drink and drive."

take something hard = be upset by something
"Seth really took it hard when his old dog died."

See also: die-hard; drive a hard bargain; hard as nails; hard case; hard cheese; hard core; hard facts; hard lines/luck; hard luck story; (hard) pressed for; hold hard; no hard feelings.

hare

hare-brained = foolish/irresponsible
"Whose hare-brained idea was it to padlock the fire exits?"

mad as a March hare = silly/mentally unstable
"Tony is trying to break the record for walking backwards from Land's End to John O'Groats ñ he must be as mad as a March hare!"

run with the hare and hunt with the hounds = simultaneously support both sides in a dispute
"You can't run with the hare and hunt with the hounds: you say that you're against capital punishment and yet you also think that the punishment should always fit the crime."

hark

hark back = refer back
"If you hark back to Victorian times I'm sure you'll have to admit that the working man is much better off today."

harm

out of harm's way = in safety
"I told the boys that they shouldn't play football in the street but go to the park out of harm's way."

See also: harm a hair of somebody's head.

harness

in double harness = working as a pair
"Each man will work with a trainee in double harness for the next two weeks."

in harness = at work
"I was in harness at the factory for twenty years before it shut

See also: die in harness/with one's boots on.

harp

harp on = keep talking about (to the point of boredom)
"No I don't want to visit your mother today ñ I'm tired of listening to her harping on about her operation."

Harry

See: any/every Tom, Dick and Harry.

harvest

reap a barren/rich harvest = get no/much reward
"That company is in severe financial difficulties. If you invest money in its shares you will reap a barren harvest."
"If you study hard and pass all your exams you will reap a rich harvest later in life."

hash

make a hash of = do something badly
"I asked the office girl to sort those papers into alphabetical order and she's made a complete hash of it."

settle somebody's hash = neutralize a trouble-maker
"If Micky starts talking to you like that again I'll soon settle his hash."

haste

more haste, less speed = a quick approach to a task often results in carelessness/mistakes
"Take your time and make sure you put the machine back together; remember ñ more haste, less speed."

hat

at the drop of a hat = at once/without

"If somebody offered me a trip to Bermuda I'd be off at the drop of a hat."

brass hat = high-ranking (army) officer
"We had to paint nearly everything in the camp just because some brass hats were coming to make an inspection."

eat one's hat = admit one is wrong
"England has a very poor side this season, and if they win the World Cup I'll eat my hat!"

(perform the) hat trick = succeed in scoring/winning three times in succession
"Having won in the British and American Open Championships, the German golfer was favourite to make his hat trick in the European Cup."

hang one's hat up (in a house) = make oneself at home
"Do come again, you're very welcome to hang your hat up here at any time."

hang on to one's hat = cling/hold on, or be ready for something unusual
"Hang on to your hats, here comes the water splash!"
"I've got some marvellous news, so hang on to your hats."

keep something under one's hat = keep a confidence/secret
"I hear that John and Mary are getting a divorce, but keep it under your hat."

old hat = out-of-date/old-fashioned
"The sixties expressions cool, hip and far-out are now old hat."

pass/send/take the hat round = collect money
"Claire has had an accident and is in hospital so I suggest we pass the hat round to buy her some flowers to cheer her up."

raise/take off one's hat to = admire/express approval for
"You've lost two stone since you started your diet; I didn't think you would persevere and I take my hat off to you."

talk out of/through (the top of) one's hat/head = talk nonsense
"Don't talk out of your hat! You couldn't possibly have got here in only half an hour."

throw one's hat into the ring = issue a challenge
"I threw my hat into the ring and said I could do the job faster than anyone else."

tip one's hat to somebody = (respectfully) acknowledge somebody's ability/superiority
"The last runner to finish in the local marathon was sixty-five years old, and I tip my hat to her."

wear two different hats = do two different jobs at once
"I'm wearing two different hats at the moment: I'm a mother to my children and nurse to my husband who is in bed with the flu."

See also: bad egg/hat/lot; knock into a cocked hat; put the (tin) lid/hat on.

hatch

batten down the hatches = anticipate/prepare for trouble
"The threat of inflation has made many city institutions batten down the hatches and not take risks in the stock market."

down the hatch! = cheers! (said to somebody taking a drink)
"Down the hatch! Here's success to temperance!"

hatches, matches and dispatches = (announcements of) births, marriages and deaths (in a newspaper)

"The best way of keeping up with what's happening in the town is to read the hatches, matches and dispatches every week."

See also: don't count one's chickens (before they're hatched).

hatchet

bury the hatchet/one's differences = agree to forget a former disagreement
"We decided to bury the hatchet and forget what happened between us last year."

do a hatchet job on = attack/discredit
"The opposition leader tried to do a hatchet job on the Chancellor's budget plans by claiming that they were inflationary."

hatchet man = somebody who is employed to perform an unpleasant task (relating to others)
"The management have employed a hatchet man to reduce the staff by making a third of thc workforce redundant."

hate

blinded by hatred = letting hatred interfere with one's better judgement
"She was so blinded by hatred that she would not admit that her ex-husband was proposing generous terms for the divorce settlement."

hate somebody's guts = have an absolute dislike of somebody
"I can't understand why they ever went into partnership, it's obvious they hate each others' guts."

pet hate = a particular annoyance
"My pet hate is having to get out of a nice warm bed on a freezing cold morning."

hatter

as mad as a hatter = quite mad (= anything from mildly eccentric/silly to mentally deranged)
"He's as mad as a hatter; he's trying to cross a tomato with a potato to make pink mash to go with sausages and beans."

haul

long haul = protracted/tiring task
"It's been a long haul, but at last we have completed the job."

See also: haul over the coals.

have

have a go = make an attempt/try, or attack (verbally or physically)
"Can I have a go in your new car tomorrow?"
"The boss had a go at me for leaving work early."

have a head like sieve = be (habitually) forgetful
"I can never remember names because I've got a head like a sieve."

have an ear to the ground = remain alert for new information/news
"I have an ear to the ground and I have learned that there could be some major changes in the cabinet."

have anything or something to do with = be concerned with/involved in
"I hear the police have been round. Has it anything to do with that riotous party you had on Saturday night?"

have a way with = have a natural flair for
"I must say Gill seems to have a way with dogs, they seem to respond to every word she says."

have been around = to be experienced
"Sir Gerald has been around; after more than twenty years in the

diplomatic corps he knows exactly how to deal with these strange requests from abroad."

have done (with) = be finished (with)
"Have you done with my lawn mower yet? I'd like to have it back to mow my own lawn."

have enough/a lot on one's plate = undertake sufficient/much to do
"No, I'm sorry, we can't service your car by next Tuesday ñ we've got enough on our plate already."
"The captain of an ocean liner has a lot on his plate: he's responsible for the safety and well-being of the ship, the crew, and the passengers."

have had it = have died/failed/lost/missed an opportunity
"I think this old car has finally had it and I'll have to get another one."
"If you don't get good exam results these days you've had it as far as a decent job is concerned."
"I'm afraid you've had it; it's past time and they've stopped serving drinks."

have it away/off = have sexual intercourse
"His main hope was that she would let him have it away in the back of his car."

have it/what's coming to one = to deserve what happens to one
"You'll have what's coming to you if you're not better behaved!"

have it in for somebody = intend to cause somebody harm/trouble
"The corporal seems to have it in for me; that's the third time he's put me on a charge this month."

have it in one = have the ability/skill
"I hear you've won a scholarship to university. Well done, I didn't think you had it in you."

"I'm going to see Ron and have it out with him; this dispute has gone on long enough."

have no time for = dislike/not tolerate
"I've got no time for all this metric nonsense; give me feet and inches any day."

have somebody on = trick somebody
"Don't take any notice of Marilyn; she's only having you on."

have (somebody) up = prosecute somebody
"George has been had up for not paying maintenance to his ex-wife."

have something on = be occupied, be wearing something
"I'm sorry I can't come on Saturday, I already have something on."
"She was about twenty years old and had on a red and white dress."

have it taped = have control of a situation/solution to a problem
"I'm going to have to rearrange the schedule for the extra people, but give me half an hour and I'll soon have it taped."

have/want nothing to do with = dissociate oneself from
"You can do what you want, but I want nothing to do with it."
"I've had nothing to do with him since he upset my wife."

have (got) to = must
"I have to go now, Dad says I have to be home by ten-thirty."

have to do with = affect, concern/be relevant to
"The doctors do not know what causes the disease but suspect that it has to do with mineral deficiency."

have/keep up one's sleeve = keep concealed until needed
"The troops thought the initial

they could rely on the general to keep something up his sleeve."

have what it takes = possess what is needed to successfully do something
"Susan really has what it takes to be a fashion photographer."

have wind of = hear a rumour of
"The stock market got wind of a possible take-over bid and share prices soared."

let somebody have it = attack somebody (physically or verbally)
"If he comes back and says that again I'm going to let him have it!"

what have you = and so on/anything else
"The shed was full of old shoes, tyres, broken plant pots and what have you."

See also: have a screw loose; have/keep an eye on; have it both ways; have one's eye on; have no/not a clue; have not an earthly; have one's hands full; have one's head screwed on; have one's work cut out; have the advantage of; have the edge on.

havoc

play havoc with = cause damage to/ disrupt
"I don't want to go out in this strong wind, it will play havoc with my new hair-do."

hawk

hawk-eyed = with very keen eyesight
"We seldom misbehaved under the hawk-eyed gaze of our teacher."

See also: watch somebody like a hawk.

hay

go haywire = go out of control
"My model aircraft transmitter failed and the plane went haywire and crashed into a tree."

hit the hay = go to bed/sleep
"I'm feeling tired; if you'll excuse me I think I'll hit the hay."

make hay while the sun shines = make the best of an opportunity
"I've been offered a lucrative contract in the States; it's only for six months but I might as well make hay while the sun shines."

haystack

look/search for a needle in a haystack = try to find something (small) that is lost among many other things
"Trying to find a pen that works in this house is like trying to find a needle in a haystack."

head

above/over one's head = beyond one's level of understanding
"The only magazine in the waiting room was a scientific journal full of technical jargon way above my head."

bang/knock one's head against a brick wall = do something to no avail
"I've tried five times to explain how to use the machine but he still cannot do it ñ I'm just banging my head against a brick wall."

bang/knock somebody's heads together = threat to put an end to a dispute
"If you two boys don't stop quarrelling immediately, I'll bang your heads together."

bite/snap somebody's head off = answer angrily/curtly
"I only asked what time dinner would be ready, there's no need to bite my head off."

bring/come to a head = bring to a point where action is needed
"The long-standing dispute about working conditions finally came to a

head when the workforce voted for strike action."

by a short head = by a (very) small margin

"The two candidates were well matched, but Jones had slightly more experience and got the job by a short head."

some/enter into one's head = occur to one

"I remember seeing the man on the park bench but I thought he was sleeping; it didn't enter my head that he might be dead."

come to/reach a head = reach a critical stage

"Barry and Anne were always bickering, but things have now really come to a head and I fear that their marriage is about to break up."

count heads = count the people present

"On a rough count of heads I'd say there were about two hundred people there last night."

get one's head down = go to bed (and sleep)

"I've been travelling for nearly twenty hours and I can't wait to get my head down."

get something into one's head = grasp an idea, or learn/memorize

"Can't you get it into your head that it is dangerous to ride a motorbike without wearing protective clothing."

"I have difficulty learning French irregular verbs; I just can't seem to get them into my head."

give/let somebody have somebody his/her head = allow somebody freedom to act as he/she wishes

"We'll give young Jones his head and let him write the press releases for a while."

go off one's head = go mad/lose control of one's reason

"When I told my husband cost of my new coat he said I must have gone off my head to spend that much."

go to one's head = make one arrogant/conceited, or make one (slightly) drunk

"Jane's promotion has gone to her head. Now she's a member of the salaried staff she insists on being called Miss Jones."

"Don't drink too much of that special brew lager or it'll go straight to your head."

go over somebody's head = contact somebody's superior

"Apparently Maria went over the supervisor's head and complained directly to the department manager."

have a good head on one's shoulders = be clever/sensible

"My daughter's fiancé seems to have a good head on his shoulders ñ he's going to night school to improve his qualifications."

have a head for = have the ability/flair for

"Jason should go in for accounting because he has a good head for figures."

have a (good) head for heights = be untroubled by heights

"I've been watching the steeplejacks at work. I couldn't do their job, I haven't a head for heights."

have a swollen head = be conceited

"Doreen really annoys me. Just because her husband has been on television a few times it's given her a swollen head."

have one's head in the clouds = be daydreaming

"You won't get much sense from Janet now that she's fallen for Mister

Wonderful, she's going around with her head in the clouds."

have one's head screwed on (the right way) = be capable/shrewd
"I don't worry too much about my wife being on her own while I'm away, she's got her head screwed on and can take care of herself."

head and shoulders above = very much better than
"When Jack's painting won first prize in the competition, the judge said it was head and shoulders above the other entries."

head off = divert/intercept
"The sheriff said that the posse could head off the outlaws at the pass."

head of the family = senior member of a family
"My mother has been head of the family since my father's death."

head on = in direct confrontation
"The car skidded on some ice and collided head on with an approaching lorry."
"The unions seem to be seeking a head on conflict with the management."

head-over-ears/heels = completely/ totally
"Now that I've paid the tax demand and the children's school fees, I'll be head-over-heels in debt for the next six months."

heads I win, tails you lose = I win, no matter what the outcome
"If I work late they don't pay me overtime, and if I don't finish a job by the end of the day they reduce my pay; it's a case of heads I win, tails you lose."

heads or tails? = which side of a coin will show after it has been tossed?
"You call, heads or tails? That will decide who pays for the drinks."

head start = initial advantage (over competitors)
"Wendy did have a bit of a head start when she joined this company ñ her father is one of the major shareholders."

heads will roll = somebody will be in grave trouble
"As a result of the leak to the press, heads will roll in Whitehall."

hold a pistol to somebody's head = threaten somebody
"I didn't want to go to the club with him but he held a pistol to my head and said he'd tell my wife that I went last week if I didn't go again."

hold one's head high/up = be proud/ unashamed
"Now that the case against me has been dismissed, I can once again hold my head up in public."

keep a level head/keep one's head = remain calm
"An essential quality for members of the bomb disposal squad is to be able to keep a level head at all times."

keep one's head above water = remain out of debt
"With high interest rates and a wages freeze, many householders are only just managing to keep their heads above water."

keep one's head down = remain inconspicuous, or keep working (busily)
"The sergeant is looking for volunteers for guard duty, so I'd keep my head down for a while if I were you."
"The job has got to be done so you might as well keep your head down until it's finished."

make neither head nor tail of something = not understand something
"I don't know why they don't write legal documents in plain English, I can't make head nor tail of this one."

make one's head spin = confuse one
"All these metric units make my head spin ñ why couldn't we stick with feet and inches?"

need one's head examined = be foolish/slightly mad
"What! You paid five hundred pounds for that wreck of a car? You need your head examined!"

not know whether one is on one's head or one's heels = be completely confused
"It was hectic at work today. I had so many phone calls and queries to answer that I didn't know whether I was on my head or my heels."

off/out of one's head = very foolish/mad
"She must be off her head to leave her children on their own for so long."

off the top of one's head = without thinking
"I don't know the exact number of people who have been invited but off the top of my head I should think there will be about forty."

old head on young shoulders = (uncharacteristic) wisdom in youth
"Young Mark seems very knowledgeable and experienced for his age ñ definitely an old head on young shoulders."

on one's (own) head = one's (own) responsibility
"I don't approve of your getting married so young, but if you're determined to do so it's on your own head."

on your own head be it = you will be responsible (for any trouble)
"The boss is in a bad mood today but if you insist on going to see him to complain, on your own head be it."

put something into somebody's head = suggest something
"No you can't stay out all night. Whoever put that idea into your head?"

put one's head in(to) a noose/on the block = court disaster
"Graham was out with his girlfriend last night and he asked me to tell his wife that he spent the evening with me. But I don't see why I should put my head in a noose to conceal his affair."

put one's head in the lion's mouth = take a grave risk (by putting oneself at the mercy of somebody else)
"I know the kidnappers said that you had to go entirely alone to deliver the ransom money, but isn't that putting your head in the lion's mouth?"

put one's heads together = discuss something between/among oneselves
"I don't know as much about the theoretical side as you do, I'm more of a practical person. But if we put our heads together we should be able to find a solution to the problem."

put something out of one's head = deliberately forget
"I was considered becoming a model, but I soon put that idea out of my head when I got married and started a family."

raise/rear its ugly head = (re)appear (of something unpleasant)
"The scandal involving the cabinet minister has reared its ugly head again ñ it's headline news once more."

soft/weak in the head = foolish/slightly mad
"I must have been soft in the head to

refuse to buy those shares for twenty pence each ñ they are now worth nearly two pounds."

standing on one's head = effortlessly/ with ease
"It's your best subject and you should be able to pass the exam standing on your head."

swollen-headed = conceited
"Dora has been so swollen-headed since she won that scholarship."

take something into one's head = (foolishly) decide to do something
"My husband has never indulged in physical exercise but he's just taken it into his head to go jogging every day."

talk somebody's head off = talk so much that one makes somebody bored/ weary
"The trouble with Julian is that once he gets you on the phone he talks your head off."

turn somebody's head/brain = make somebody conceited
"She sat next to the Duke at the charity dinner, and it's turned her head ñ anyone would think she was an aristocrat herself!"

two heads are better than one = two people co-operating have a better chance of solving a problem that one person by himself/herself
"I've been trying for ages to make these figures tally ñ see if you can find any errors. After all, two heads are better than one."

See also: bury one's head in the sand; eat one's head off; empty-headed; enter somebody's head; hard-headed; hang one's head; have a roof over one's head; have a tongue in one's head; have eyes in the back of one's head; hit the nail on the head; lose one's head; need something like a hole in the head; price on somebody's head; put one's head on the block; right in the head; scratch one's head; shake one's head; short head; shout one's head off; snap one's head off; talk out of/through (the top of) one's hat/head; trouble one's head with.

headache

be a headache = cause difficulty/ problems
"Now that our boys are growing up, the constant need for new clothes for them is getting to be a real headache."

headlines

hit the headlines = make news
"Farmer Jones hit the headlines when he found dozens of ancient gold coins while ploughing a field."

headway

make headway = make progress
"It has taken some time to organize the new subsidiary company but a modest first year profit shows that at last we're making headway."

heap

See: strike somebody all of a heap.

hear

fair hearing = impartial assessment
"The judge is aware of the extenuating circumstances and you'll definitely be given a fair hearing."

hear from = receive a communication from
"I've heard from our agent in New York that sales there are proving to be very profitable."

hear! hear! = exclamation of agreement
"You're going to buy another round of drinks? Hear! hear! I'll drink to that!"

hearing things = hear something that is not there/was not said
"I didn't say that ñ you must be hearing things."

hear of = be informed of
"Yes, we are moving soon, but how did you hear of it?"

I've heard that one before! = I do not believe you
"There's no point in asking for a day off to go to your grandmother's funeral. I've heard that one before!"

I've never heard of such a thing = how extraordinary/unusual
"He rode a bicycle along the top of the wall? I've never heard of such a thing."

lose one's hearing = become deaf
"All human beings lose their hearing to some extent as they grow older."

out of hearing = beyond audible range
"I've got some useful information for you, Inspector; let's go where we'll be out of hearing."

unheard of = extraordinary/unique
"It's unheard of for somebody so young to get a place at university."

will not hear of = refuse to accept/allow
"I offered to pay the bill but she wouldn't hear of it."

See also: hard of hearing; never hear the end of something.

heart

after one's (own) heart = of the kind one likes
"I see you prefer French cooking ñ you're a man after my own heart."

allow one's heart to rule one's head = let one's emotions override common sense
"Gill's relationship with a married man is bound to end in unhappiness, but I'm afraid she's letting her heart rule her head."

at heart = mainly/really
"I don't enjoy soccer ñ I'm a rugby man at heart."

break one's heart = cause one (great) sorrow
"It breaks my heart to think of all the money we spent on our son's education and all he wants to do is work in a dreary factory."

change of heart = change of attitude/view point
"I was going to report you to the head teacher for insolence, but I've had a change of heart and I'll give you a detention instead."

close/near to one's heart = among things that most affect/concern one
"Because of their selfless dedication and bravery, the volunteer lifeboat men have always been close to my heart."

do one's heart good = make one glad/happy
"It does my heart good to see the blossom on the trees after that awful winter we've just had."

find it in one's heart = convince/persuade oneself
"I know he's been naughty but I can't find it in my heart to punish him."

from the bottom of one's heart = most sincerely
"I would like to thank all the hospital staff from the bottom of my heart for the way they cared for my mother when she was ill."

give one/have heart failure = be greatly shocked
"That tremendous clap of thunder nearly gave me heart failure."

have a heart! = be reasonable!
"Have a heart! It will take me all day

to address those envelopes; can't somebody else do some of them?"

have a heart of gold = be very considerate/kind
"Our platoon sergeant has a heart of gold ñ he looks after us as if we were his own sons."

have a heart of oak = be loyal/trustworthy
"Edward can always be relied on when you need him, he has a heart of oak."

have a heart of stone = be totally unfeeling
"I haven't a heart of stone but if that cat has any more kittens then I'm afraid I'll have to drown them."

have no heart = be insensitive/unsympathetic
"I don't know how you can support fox hunting, have you no heart?"

have no heart for/not have the heart for = be unenthusiastic
"I should do some gardening this weekend but I haven't the heart for it."

have one's heart (sink into)/in one's boots = be in a state of despair
"I thought for a moment that I'd won the football pools, then my heart sank into my boots when I realized that I hadn't posted the coupon."

have one's heart in one's mouth = be very apprehensive
"My heart was in my mouth when I saw the child run out into the road."

have one's heart in the right place = be kind/sincere (despite appearances to the contrary)
"The two boys who offered to clean my car had their hearts in the right place, but it is a pity they hosed it down with the windows open!"

heart and soul = totally/with maximum effort
"Janet always puts herself heart and soul into everything she does."

heart goes out to = feel sympathy for
"My heart goes out to all those people who were made homeless by the hurricane."

heart of the matter = the fundamental/main point
"Let's get down to the heart of the matter and leave the details until later."

heart-rending = distressing
"Do you remember the heart-rending scene in the film where the hero says his final farewells to his dying wife?"

heart-to-heart talk = frank discussion
"The constable said he would not press charges against the young offender but that the chief inspector wanted to see him for a heart-to-heart talk."

in good heart = cheerful/happy
"Everyone in the office was in good heart today because we were given our annual bonus."

in one's heart of hearts = in all honesty
"He made a reasonable recovery from the operation but his mother knew in her heart of hearts that he was far from well."

know/learn (off) by heart = know from memory/memorize
"Can I help you with the machine? I know the instructions off by heart."
"I think every child should be made to learn multiplication tables off by heart, before they are allowed to use electronic calculators."

not have the heart to = be unwilling to
"The old lady was so pleased to be going on holiday for a few days that I hadn't the heart to tell her that her cat had been run over."

not have one's heart in it = be unenthusiastic

"I've started the housework but I haven't my heart in it and I'd rather sit in the garden reading a book."

one's heart aches/bleeds for somebody = one feels great sympathy for somebody (usually meant sarcastically)

"You've only got a twenty per cent pay increase? My heart bleeds for you!"

one's heart goes out to somebody = one feels great sympathy for somebody (usually meant sincerely)

"My heart goes out to poor Emma; she's expecting a baby in two weeks time and her husband has just been killed in a car crash."

one's heart stands still = one is (very) afraid

"I hate flying; my heart stands still every time we go through turbulence and the plane rocks about."

pour one's heart out = confide one's troubles (to a sympathetic hearer)

"Thanks for letting me pour my heart out to you. I feel much better now that I've told somebody."

pull/tug one's heart strings = stimulate feelings of pathos/sympathy

"Those old Lassie films always pull my heart strings."

put (fresh) heart into = encourage/ stimulate

"The junior team is a bit demoralised after a succession of defeats. We must find a way of putting fresh heart into them."

set one's heart upon = desire intensely

"I want to buy a new car this year, and I've set my heart on a Mercedes."

sick at heart = thoroughly dejected/ dispirited

"I was sick at heart when the foreman wouldn't let me have the afternoon off because I was looking forward to going to my son's school sports day."

steel one's heart against = suppress one's natural emotions

"The doctor steeled his heart and told the couple in a matter-of-fact way that they would never be able to have children."

take heart = receive encouragement/ moral support

"You lost in the second round of the competition, but you can take heart from the fact that the person who beat you eventually became champion."

take somebody to one's heart = accept somebody lovingly

"My George has a soft spot for animals, he's really taken that stray cat to heart."

take something to heart = take seriously, or be upset/offended by

"If you take my advice to heart you'll alter your approach and be less aggressive in your dealings with people."

"At the audition today Tina wasn't chosen for a part in the school play and she's really taken it to heart."

wear one's heart on one's sleeve = display one's feelings openly

"My daughter seems to have a succession of disastrous love affairs, but that's what happens when you wear your heart on your sleeve."

win the heart of = gain the admiration/ love of

"The young boy's successful struggle with a crippling disease won the hearts of the whole country when his story was told in the newspapers."

with a heavy/sinking heart = with a feeling of sadness

"I returned home with a heavy heart after my father's funeral."

with a light heart = with a feeling of happiness

"The seasoned golf professional accepted his defeat by the young player with a light heart ñ after all, he had coached her."

with all one's heart (and soul) = most enthusiastically/sincerely

"I would like to thank everybody with all my heart for the splendid retirement present you have given me."

See also: down-hearted; eat one's heart out; harden one's heart; have heart failure; lose heart; lose one's heart; open one's heart; steal somebody's heart; to one's heart's content; warm the cockles of one's heart; young at/in heart.

heat

at fever heat/pitch = at maximum activity/enthusiasm

"The boat was taking water rapidly, and the crew worked at fever pitch to stop it sinking."

in the heat of the moment = while excited/emotionally aroused

"He heard the child's screams and in the heat of the moment jumped off the bridge into the river to save her."

turn on the heat = (cruelly) put pressure on somebody

"If the suspect doesn't confess soon we may have to turn on the heat."

See also: dead heat.

heave

give somebody/something the (old) heave-ho = get rid of somebody/something

"This car is worn out and I'm going to have to give it the heave-ho."

heave in/into sight = come into view

"We knew there was another ship nearby, and when the fog lifted it hove into sight."

make one heave = make one disgusted

"The way Michael fawns on the boss makes me heave."

heaven

for heaven's sake = exclamation of mild annoyance

"For heavens sake, do you have to have the radio on so loud?"

good heavens/heavens above = exclamation of surprise

"Good heavens! Where did you get that outfit?"

heaven forbid = may it not be so

"Heaven forbid! I'd be the last person to say anything like that about you."

heaven only knows = I do not know/nobody knows

"Heaven only knows what has upset her, she's been in a bad mood all day."

in heaven's name = exclamation of annoyance/surprise (in a question)

"In heaven's name, what do you think you are doing with that knife?"

like heaven on earth = idyllic/perfect

"The Mediterranean island we visited on holiday was like heaven on earth."

manna from heaven = sudden source of comfort/relief

"Sir William's offer to pay the balance of the money needed to repair the village hall came like manna from heaven."

move heaven and earth = do everything in one's power

"I'd move heaven and earth to get a date with Andrew."

seventh heaven = state of extreme happiness

"Sit him down with some cans of beer in front of the television set when there's football on and he's in his seventh heaven."

smell/stink to high heaven = have an offensive smell

"I phoned a plumber to clear the drains because they were beginning to stink to high heaven."

thank heavens = expression of gratitude/ relief

"Thank heavens you're not hurt."

the heavens opened = it poured with rain

"We just started to lay out the picnic and the heavens opened."

heavy

lie heavy on = be a burden/worry to

"His dishonest dealings lay heavy on his conscience."

make heavy weather of = have (unnecessary) difficulty with

"He was making heavy weather of cutting the lawn because the mower blades needed sharpening."

time hangs heavy = time passes slowly

"Time hangs heavy when you're out of work and have nothing to do all day."

See also: hard/heavy going; heavy hand; with a heavy heart.

hedge

See: hedge one's bets.

heel

Achilles' heel = weak/vulnerable point

"He would have made a good pilot but his drinking habit was his Achilles' heel."

bring somebody to heel/make somebody come to heel = make somebody comply obediently

"The police used a water cannon on the rioters and soon brought them to heel."

(hard) on the heels of = be immediately behind

"The lioness bounded across the plain, hard on the heels of a terrified gazelle."

set somebody by the heels = imprison somebody

"The assailant was set by the heels awaiting trial."

set somebody (back) on his/her heels = shock/surprise somebody

"It really set her back on her heels when I told her how much the repairs to her car would cost."

take to one's heels = run away

"The villagers had to take to their heels as the molten lava poured down the mountainside."

tread on somebody's heels = compete with somebody (for his/her job/ position)

"Martin's work has improved tremendously since he's had that new assistant treading on his heels."

turn on one's heel = turn (and walk) away

"When I asked him for the money he owes me he just turned on his heel and walked away."

well-heeled = wealthy

"He must be well-heeled, he works for a firm of stockbrokers in the city and drives a new Porsche."

See also: cool one's heels; dig one's feet/ heels/toes in; down-at-heel; head over heels; kick one's heels; show a clean pair of heels.

hell

all hell breaks loose = a state of chaos ensues

"All hell broke loose at the Women's

Institute meeting when a mouse ran across the floor."

come hell or high water = what ever happens/at whatever cost

"The cab driver promised to get me to the airport on time come hell or high water."

for the hell of it = (just) for fun

"I've never acted before but I thought I'd give it a try just for the hell of it."

frighten/scare the hell out of = terrify

"It would scare the hell out of me to ride that bike as fast as he does."

give somebody hell = make life very unpleasant for/punish somebody

"The kidnappers gave him hell for the six months they held him captive."

"Mum will give me hell when she finds out I've broken her best vase."

go to hell = go away

"You tell him from me to go to hell; I'm not going to apologise, because it wasn't my fault."

hell-bent on = determined

"The yachtsmen were hell-bent on winning the America's Cup for Britain."

hell for leather = recklessly fast

"The hounds were only a few yards behind the fox, which was running hell for leather in its bid to escape."

hell to pay = serious consequences/ trouble

"My solicitor warned me that there would be hell to pay if I don't turn up for the court case tomorrow."

like (merry) hell = enthusiastically/ vigorously, or emphatically not

"The rescuers worked like hell to free the man from the wrecked car."

"You want me to give up my holiday? Like hell I will!"

not have a hope in hell = have no hope at all

"You've left it too late. You haven't a hope in hell of catching the twelve o'clock train now."

play (merry) hell with = make worse, or severely damage/disrupt

"I find that damp weather plays hell with my rheumatism."

"These atmospheric conditions are playing merry hell with VHF reception tonight."

raise hell = create a great fuss/noise

"Father will raise hell when he sees what you've done to his precious rose bushes."

to hell with = I do not care at all

"He's got no right to be jealous. To hell with him, I'll go out with who I like."

until hell freezes over = for ever

"Jeremy will be my friend until hell freezes over."

what the hell = it does not matter, or whatever

"I paid fifty pounds for a pair of shoes, but what the hell ñ it's only money!"

"What the hell do you think you are doing?"

when the hell = whenever

"When the hell are you going to mend that broken window?"

where the hell = wherever

"Where the hell is that taxi? I ordered it half an hour ago."

who the hell = whoever

"Who the hell does he think he is, telling me what to do?"

See also: cat's/snowball's chance in hell; like a bat out of hell.

helm

at the helm = in charge/control

"Mr Jones is at the helm in our

London office, if you'd like to contact him I'm sure he can help."

take the helm = take charge/control

"The vice president will take the helm while I'm away at the summit meeting in Geneva."

help

help oneself to = freely take

"Refreshments will be available all day long so just help yourself when you're hungry."

not if I can help it = only without my agreement

"My daughter won't be riding on the back of her boyfriend's motorbike, not if I can help it."

hem

hem in = confine/trap

"I couldn't get my car out of the drive because somebody had parked across the end and hemmed me in."

hen

hen-party = all-female gathering

"Mary is getting married at the weekend and has invited all her girlfriends to a hen party on Friday."

hen-pecked = dominated by one's girlfriend/wife

"I don't know how George tolerates his wife, he's hen-pecked from morning to night."

like a hen with one (only) chicken = overprotective of an only child

"She never lets her son go out on his own, she's like a hen with only one chicken."

mother hen = woman who constantly fusses (over her children)

"Look at the way she's watering those seedlings! She fusses over them like a mother hen."

here

be up to here = have more than one can do/tolerate

"I can't come out to lunch because I'm up to here with work."

"I'm up to here with my wife's incessant nagging."

here and now = at this present time

"If we are to complete the job on time, you must decide here and now to make a start."

here and there = in various places

"The car is basically in good condition, it just needs a touch of paint here and there."

here goes = said before doing something difficult/risky/unpleasant

"Well here goes, I've never tried driving a combine harvester before."

"This medicine smells awful but I've got to drink it ñ here goes."

here's to.Ö = toast to success

"Here's to Nancy, may all her troubles be little ones."

here, there and everywhere = everywhere

"Tina, go and tidy your room. There are clothes and make- up here, there and everywhere."

here today and gone tomorrow = (only) temporary

"None of today's youngsters seem able to stand the pace in industry, they're here today and gone tomorrow."

neither here nor there = irrelevant/trivial

"It doesn't matter which day you come to repair the fence, it's neither here nor there to me."

See also: here we go again.

hero

hero's welcome = enthusiastic welcome

winning the European Cup they were given a hero's welcome."

herring

red herring = deliberately misleading factor
"The information about increased development costs was merely a red herring to divert attention from the fact that the initial budget was wrongly estimated."

hide

neither hide nor hair of = no trace of
"Terry said he would see me at the station but I could find neither hide nor hair of him."

on a hiding to nothing = situation in which one must lose
"If you think the bank will lend you yet more money you're on a hiding to nothing."

tan somebody's hide = beat/smack somebody
"I'll tan your hide if I catch you doing that again."

See also: hide one's light under a bushel.

high

all-time high = (world) record achievement
"His total of thirty-four is an all-time high for the number of raw eggs eaten in one minute."

blow something sky high = prove something to be wrong
"The idea that men are somehow superior to women was blown sky high years ago."

for the high jump = about to be disciplined/punished (for a misdeed)
"You'll be for the high jump if you get caught cheating."

high and dry = stranded/in a very difficult situation
"My traveller's cheques were stolen and I was left high and dry in the middle of my holiday."

high and mighty = arrogant/self-opinionated
"I worked my way up the firm the hard way; nowadays it seems that any high and mighty university type can enter the company straight at the top."

high as a kite = intoxicated (with drink or drugs)
"He offered me these strange-smelling cigarettes and within twenty minutes I was as high as a kite."

high days and holidays = special occasions
"I only wear my best suit on high days and holidays ñ it should last for ever!"

high-falutin(g) = pompous/pretentious
"Refuse disposal operatives is our council's high-faluting name for dustmen."

high-flown = extravagant
"He has some high-flown scheme for heating his house using solar power."

high-flyer = somebody who is ambitious
"Hal's a real high-flyer; he started his own business when he was only in his twenties and he was a millionaire before his fortieth birthday."

high life = luxurious (way of) life
"Now that he's been made bankrupt he has had to abandon the high life and live much more frugally."

highly-strung = very nervous/tense
"Thoroughbred horses are highly-strung animals and do not like loud noises or sudden movements."

high-minded = (very) moral/strict
"My father was very high-minded; he would not let me wear make-up until I was sixteen years old."

high places = superior/upper levels of a group
"It seems that the only way to get on these days is to have friends in high places."
high-sounding = pompous/pretentious
"She may have married a lord and have a high-sounding name now, but I knew her when she was plain Miss Jones from Clapham."
high spot = main attraction/feature
"The high spot of the show was a display by the Red Arrows."
high table = raised table (at dinner) for important/senior people
"His appointment was formalized when he was invited to take his place at the high table."
hightail it = run away
"We'd better hightail it out of here ñ the police are coming."
high tea = small meal eaten in late afternoon/early evening
"The vicar's wife has asked us round to high tea on Thursday."
high time = enjoyable time, or time to do something that is late/overdue
"Once I'm on holiday I like to relax and have a high time while I've got the chance."
"The sergeant-major told the recruit it was high time he had a haircut."
hunt/search high and low = make a thorough search
"I don't know where I've left my car keys, I've searched high and low for them."
in high dudgeon = feeling offended
"I told her not to speak to me like that and she left the room in high dudgeon."
run high = be intense
"Cases of cruelty to children always make feelings run high."
See also: high-handed; live high off the hog; on one's high horse; riding high; search high and low.

highway
highway robbery = exorbitant charge/price
"Fifty pence for a can of lemonade is highway robbery, yet that is what the street vendors charge."
Queen's highway = public road
"The Member of Parliament for Oxbridge was fined fifty pounds for unlawful obstruction of the Queen's highway."

hill
old as the hills = very old
"Where did you get that dress? From the style, it must be as old as the hills."
over the hill = past its/one's best
"Nowadays, computer programmers are over the hill at thirty years old."
up hill and down dale = everywhere
"I've searched up hill and down dale but still can't find that piece of paper with your address on it."

hilt
up to the hilt = to the maximum
"I would like to build an extension to my house, but I'm up to the hilt on my mortgage so I'll have to leave it a few years."

hindmost
See: devil take the hindmost.

hinge
hinge upon = depend on
"My son has a place at Eton, although of course it still hinges on the result of his entrance examination."

hint

broad hint = obvious clue

"When my elder brother brought his girlfriend round to meet all the family, he gave a broad hint that they were to become engaged quite soon."

drop/give/throw a hint = give a (casual) clue

"The vicar dropped a hint that volunteers were still wanted to help with the Jumble Sale."

hip

shoot from the hip = react quickly

"Many interviewers have been surprised at the chancellor's ability to shoot from the hip."

history

ancient history = familiar story/stale news

"Yes, I do know that Angela has been married before ñ it's ancient history."

go down in history = be remembered

"Last week's earthquake in South America will go down in history as one of the world's worst natural disasters."

make history = do something that will be long remembered

"If he wins the Grand National, he will make history as the youngest jockey ever to do so."

hit

hit-and-run = fail to stop after causing injury when driving

"The police say the injured man was the victim of a hit-and-run accident."

hit back = retaliate/defend oneself

"To survive in big business you have to be prepared to hit back at your critics."

hit below the belt = use unfair tactics

"Most people agreed that the newspaper was hitting below the belt when it tried to discredit the cabinet minister by detailing some of her childhood misdeeds."

hit hard/hard hit = harmed by misfortune

"The company was hit hard by the recession and is only now beginning to recover."

hit it off = become friends

"Wendy and I never really hit it off and we seldom see each other these days."

hit-or-miss = lacking in organization/ careless

"It was a very hit-or-miss affair, totally lacking any kind of organization."

hit somebody when he/she is down = take advantage of somebody who is in trouble

"I don't want to ask him for the money he owes me because he's still out of work, and you can't hit a man when he's down."

hit the deck = (deliberately) fall to the floor/ground

"When the soldiers heard the shells coming they hit the deck."

hit the headlines = become public knowledge/make news

"Share prices are bound to tumble when the take-over bid hits the headlines."

hit the nail on the head = make a (very) accurate description/guess

"You hit the nail on the head when you said I was unhappy with my job."

hit the road/trail = begin a journey

"I had better hit the road if I'm to be back home before dark."

hit the roof = (suddenly) lose one's temper

"My husband hit the roof when he found out that my boss had taken me to dinner last night."

hit upon = make an (unexpected) discovery

"The author hit upon the idea for a new book when he overheard two people talking in a restaurant."

make a hit = meet with approval/ friendliness

"David's proposal made a hit with the other members of the committee."

smash hit = big success

"That new video game was a smash hit with the children ñ it's kept them quite for hours."

See also: hit man; hit the hay; hit the jackpot; hit the sack.

hive

hive off = pass on to somebody else

"The chocolate factory would often hive off some of its production to a sub-contractor during the busy period before Christmas."

hobby

hobby horse = favourite subject

"Is Sam boring you again with his hobby horse about the Earth being colonized by creatures from outer space?"

rich man's hobby = expensive (self-) indulgence

"Costs have risen so much in recent years that ocean sailing has become a rich man's hobby."

ride a hobby horse (to death) = constantly refer to a favourite subject

"No I don't want to talk to Sam. I can't stand another minute of him riding his hobby horse about invaders from space."

Hobson's

See: Hobson's choice

hog

go the whole hog = do something completely

"A trip to Australia is a once-in-a-lifetime opportunity, so I might as well go the whole hog and fit in a trip to New Zealand at the same time."

live high off the hog = have a luxurious lifestyle

"We lived high off the hog for two whole weeks while we were on holiday."

See also: road hog.

hoist

hoist with one's own petard = caught in one's own trap

"I thought I would embarrass the financial director by revealing his next month's projection but I was hoist with my own petard when the leak was traced back to me."

hold

get hold of = obtain (something), or contact (somebody)

"I managed to get hold of a set of encyclopaedias for half price."

"Oh there you are. I've been trying to get hold of you all day."

have a hold over somebody = have somebody in one's power

"I don't know why she doesn't leave him ñ he must have some sort of hold over her."

hold all the aces = be in control

"I tried to get them to change their minds but the opponents to the proposal held all the aces and I was outvoted."

hold back = delay/restrain
"Hold back the front page! News has just come in of a plane crash at Gatwick."
"I find it difficult to hold back my anger when he starts arguing in favour of Apartheid."

hold cheap = consider worthless/of low esteem
"Shoddy goods imported from the Far East are held cheap by British importers."

hold dear = value highly
"The work of Professor Jones is held dear by the world's scientific community."

hold forth = speak at length (publicly)
"Jane is always holding forth about the rights of women."

hold good = remain valid
"The basic design of the Mini has held good for more than twenty-five years."

hold hard = delay/stop
"Hold hard! You're going the wrong way."

hold (oneself) in = restrain oneself
"We couldn't hold ourselves in while watching the antics of the monkeys at the zoo."

hold it! = stop!
"Hold it! There's a car coming."

hold it against somebody = blame/have a low opinion of somebody
"I have done quite well in my career, but it's still held against me that I didn't have a university education."

hold off = fail to arrive
"We need the bad weather to hold off for another day or so until we have finished the work outside."

hold on = wait
"Hold on for a minute, I've just got to put on my make-up."
"Mr Jones is talking on the other line; would you like to hold on for a minute and I'll put you through as soon as he's available."

hold one's own = maintain one's advantage/position, compete successfully
"Although she was only sixteen years old, she could hold her own against players twice her age."

hold one's peace/tongue = keep silent
"I held my piece, even though I wanted to tell her exactly what I thought."

hold out = retain one's position/survive, or extend
"The strikers are holding out for more money and will not return to work until they get it."
"The pilot said he could hold out for another hour before he would have to ditch the plane because of lack of fuel."
"We can hold out no hope that anybody has survived the crash."

hold over = postpone/retain for later
"The remaining three items on the agenda will be held over until next week's meeting."

hold somebody to something = make somebody keep a promise/follow a set of rules
"You said you'd pay me back by next Monday and I'm going to hold you to it."
"Servants in the Royal Household are held to a strict code of protocol."

hold sway = have superiority
"The meeting was divided about the issue but at the final vote the moderates held sway."

hold the floor = speak at/dominate a meeting etc.
"As usual the chairman held the floor

for most of the debate."

hold together = remain firm/united, or be complete/consistent

"I've repaired the break and it should hold together until you can buy a new one."

"I'm afraid your argument just doesn't hold together."

hold-up = delay, or raise, or support

"An accident caused a hold-up on the motorway."

"Hold up your hand if you know the answer to the question."

"The medieval barn is held up by oak beams made from old ships' timbers."

hold water = be correct/withstand investigation

"When you look into the costings, that scheme of yours just doesn't hold water."

hold with = agree

"I don't hold with the theory that there could be intelligent life on Mars."

no holds barred = total freedom of choice/method (without conforming to established rules)

"When Lord Jones makes a take-over bid there are no holds barred."

there's no holding somebody = it is difficult/impossible to restrain somebody

"Ann used to be frightened of water, but now that she's learned to swim there's no holding her and she goes swimming nearly every day."

See also: cannot/not fit to hold a candle to; hold a pistol to somebody's head; hold court; hold/keep at bay; hold everything!; hold/keep in check; hold in contempt; hold/stand one's ground; hold on like grim death; hold somebody to ransom; hold the fort; hold your horses; keep/hold at arm's length.

hole

be in a hole = be in difficulties

"I'm in a bit of a hole because my mother-in-law is coming for a visit and I've just broken the vase she gave us as a wedding present."

like the Black Hole of Calcutta = very crowded and hot

"It was like the Black Hole of Calcutta on the underground this morning."

make a hole in = use the largest part of

"That last round of drinks made a large hole in ten pounds."

need something like a hole in the head = not need something at all

"I need extra work today like I need a hole in the head."

nineteenth hole = bar (in the club house of a golf course)

"It is very cold today. Let's skip the golf and go straight to the nineteenth hole."

pick holes in = criticize/find fault with

"Why must you pick holes in everything I say?"

square peg in a round hole = somebody who is unsuited to his/her job/position

"I've declined the invitation to the Royal Garden Party; I'd just be a square peg in a round hole among all those posh people."

See also: ace in the hole; burn a hole in one's pocket; glory hole; hole and corner affair.

holiday

See: busman's holiday.

hollow

have a hollow ring = appear insincere/untrue

"I'm afraid your promise never to do it again has a hollow ring to it."

hollow laugh = unamused laughter

"The children gave a polite but hollow laugh to the head teacher's feeble jokes."

hollow promise = promise that will not be kept

"Some observers think that the Soviet Union's offer to reduce spending on armaments is just a hollow promise."

See also: beat hollow.

holy

holy of holies = most revered/special place (within a building)

"We visited a stately home and the guide showed us nearly everything except one room, which he said was the owner's holy of holies."

holy terror = child who is badly behaved

"I like having my niece staying with me but she's a holy terror when it comes to bed time."

See also: holier-than-thou attitude; holier-than-thou expression.

homage

do/pay homage to = acknowledge the superiority of/revere

"The Queen paid homage to the victims of two world wars by laying a wreath on the Cenotaph."

home

at-home = occasion on which one receives any guests/visitors to one's home

"The vicar and his wife are holding an at-home on Saturday and we ought to call and pay our respects."

bring something home to somebody = make somebody aware of (an unpleasant truth)

"My trip to Calcutta brought home to me that some people have to live in the most appalling conditions."

close to home = uncomfortably near the truth

"His comment about people over claiming on expenses came a bit too close to home."

come home to roost = return of unpleasantness as a result of a previous (antisocial) action

"You should not have sold the car in that unsafe condition; sooner or later your misdeeds will come home to roost."

drive/hammer something home = try to get somebody to accept/understand something (using forceful/repeated argument)

"It took me a long time to drive home the fact that their grand schemes would cost a great deal of money."

feel at home = feel comfortable/relaxed

"Although I've never worked for a bank before, I feel quite at home there because I used to work for an accountant and I'm used to dealing with figures."

get something home to = make something clear/obvious to

"I can't seem to get it home to my son that extra time spent studying now will pay off in the future."

home and dry = safe/successful

"With only two minutes to go before the end of the game, Chelsea had a three-goal lead and were virtually home and dry."

home from home = place where one feels as comfortable/relaxed as in one's own home

"The small guest house we stayed in was just like home from home."

home in on = aim for/be drawn to

"Among all those figures, the auditors homed in on the ones concerning directors' expenses."

home is where the heart is = wherever one's family/partner lives is equivalent to home
"Although I come from the country, I enjoy sharing a flat in London with Gill ñ after all, home is where the heart is."
last home = final resting place/tomb
"The World War II bomber found a last home in the Hendon aircraft museum."
make oneself at home = be as comfortable/relaxed as if one were in one's own home
"Pull up a chair and have a drink ñ make yourself at home."
nothing to write home about = unremarkable
"I've had a look at the dresses in the new boutique, but they're nothing to write home about."
romp/waltz home = win easily
"The extra training paid off, and she romped home in record time."
See also: bring home the bacon; broken home; charity begins at home; eat somebody out of house and home; home truth; romp home; strike home; till the cows come home.

homework
do one's homework = make adequate preparation
"That last candidate impressed me with his knowledge of the company's activities, he has really done his homework."

honest
earn an honest penny = make money honestly
"Although Bill has been in trouble with the police, he earns an honest penny these days by driving a van."
See also: honest broker; make an honest woman (out) of.

honey
be as sweet as honey = be very pleasant (in order to gain an advantage)
"Jeff is usually an abrasive character, but he can be as sweet as honey when he wants something."

honeymoon
the honeymoon is over = end of a peaceful period at the beginning of a new venture
"We knew the honeymoon was over when the new manager started to make sweeping changes to increase efficiency."

honour
debt of honour = debt that has no legal obligation
"I told him I'd repay his kindness to me and I will ñ I regard it as a debt of honour."
do the honours = act as host/hostess
"We'll go to the Red Lion for lunch and if you'll do the honours and get the first round of drinks, Peter, I'll organize some food for us all."
honour bound = having a moral obligation
"Her father was a good friend of mine, and I felt honour bound to help her when she was in trouble."
honours are even = each side has achieved equal success
"The duellists had shot each other in the arm, so honours were even and they parted on good terms."
in honour of = as a sign of esteem/respect
"It is my pleasure to unveil this plaque in honour of the great man who was born here."

point of honour = matter of (moral) principle
"I regard it as a point of honour always to keep my promises."

there's no honour among thieves = dishonest people cannot trust each other
"James told the police that it was his brother who stole the car, which goes to show that there's no honour among thieves."

hook

by hook or by crook = by any means (fair or foul)
"That's the second time he's beaten me at chess this week; I'll win next time by hook or by crook."

be hooked on = be addicted to
"Children as young as eight years old can get hooked on heroin, according to a recent report."

hook line and sinker = completely
"The girl at the party really believed me when I said I worked for MI5, she swallowed the story hook, line and sinker."

let somebody off the hook = allow somebody to escape from a difficulty/problem
"The teacher let me off the hook but said she would report me to the headmaster the next time I forgot to hand in my homework."

sling one's hook = go away
"It was obvious I wasn't wanted so I just slung my hook."

hoop

be put/go through the hoop = have to suffer unpleasantness
"The authorities put the dissident author through the hoop by denouncing him as an enemy of the state and putting him under house arrest."

See also: be cock-a-hoop.

hoot

not to care two hoots = not to care at all
"I don't care two hoots if the record is top of the charts, it's much too loud so turn it down."

hop

hop it = go away
"Hop it, and don't come back!"

hopping mad = very angry
"My Dad's hopping mad because the dog has just chewed up his Cup Final ticket."

See also: catch somebody bending/napping/on the hop.

hope

fond hope = a genuine wish for something that is unlikely to happen
"All we can do is to entertain the fond hope that they will find a cure for the disease before it cripples him."

I hope you feel proud of yourself! = I hope you are pleased (although I think you should not be)
"That's the second glass you've broken this evening. I hope you feel proud of yourself!"

hope against hope = keep hoping (but with little chance of fulfilment)
"We were hoping against hope that our son was among the survivors."

pin one's hopes on = (optimistically) rely on
"The opposition party are pinning their hopes on a massive swing away from the government in the next election."

raise somebody's hopes = increase somebody's expectations that something will happen
"The manager raised our hopes by saying that there is a chance of a bonus if we finish the job on time."

some hopes! = there is no point in being hopeful (because what you desire is very unlikely)
"My daughter wants to marry a millionaire. Some hopes!"

(great) white hope = somebody/something on whom/which a group depends for success
"The manufacture of synthetic protein is the great white hope for solving the world food crisis."

See also: dash somebody's hopes.

horizon

on the horizon = within view
"Company profits have declined over the last three years but there are signs of an upturn on the horizon."

hornet

bring a hornet's nest about one's ears = do something to precipitate trouble
"For goodness' sake don't remind him of the unfortunate business that happened last year or you'll bring a hornet's nest about our ears."

stir up a hornet's nest = create trouble
"I've decided to send in an agent to gather intelligence, but if he gets caught it will stir up a hornet's nest on the diplomatic front."

horns

draw/pull in one's horns = act with more restraint
"The landowner wanted to divert the river to irrigate his land but drew in his horns when an armed band of villagers arrived to express their disapproval."

lock horns with somebody = argue/fight with somebody
"I argued with Councillor Jones for more than half an hour. I've no wish to lock horns with him again."

See also: on the horns of a dilemma; take the bull by the horns.

horse

back the wrong horse = put one's faith/trust in somebody who later loses, or something which fails
"Despite his criminal record I still gave him a job, but I backed the wrong horse because he's just been convicted of shoplifting."

(straight) from the horse's mouth = direct from a (reliable) source
"I have it straight from the horse's mouth that Jones Incorporated have had a very good year and now is the time to buy some of their shares before the figures are announced."

hold your horses! = wait a minute!/slow down!
"Hold your horses! I can't come yet, I haven't finished doing my hair."

horses for courses = everybody has his/her own special attributes
"I like being the member of a crew on a sailing boat, but I haven't got the ability to sail single-handed ñ after all, it's horses for courses."

horse laugh = loud/raucous laugh
"At the end of the joke she gave a horse laugh that could be heard a street away."

horse of a different/another colour = somebody/something of a different type
"Normally, men who are not wearing a tie are not admitted to the club, but

as you've only come to read the electricity meter that's a horse of a different colour."

horse sense = common sense

"It's all very well having a university degree, but you cannot succeed in life without horse sense as well."

horse-trading = hard bargaining

"After a great deal of horse trading, I finally bought the car for a reasonable price."

old war horse = veteran fighter/soldier

"The major is an old war horse who'll bore you with tales of his wartime exploits, if you let him."

stalking horse = somebody who is employed to stimulate action in others

"Although he has asked me to put in a price for the job, he's just using me as a stalking horse to get better prices from his own estimators."

swap/change horses in midstream = change allegiance/tactics in the middle of a project

"The United manager was worried about the strength of their opponent's attack, so he swapped horses in midstream, brought on two substitutes and instructed them to play a defensive game."

you can take a horse to water (but you cannot make it drink) = you can encourage somebody to do something, but you cannot force him/her

"I agreed to take the children to the fair, but I refused to ride on the big dipper no matter how much they tried to persuade me; after all, you can take a horse to water but you cannot make it drink."

Trojan horse = apparent asset that turns out to favour a competitor

"The senior civil servant they arrested for spying turned out to be a Trojan horse, planted by enemy intelligence twenty years previously."

white horses = white-topped waves at sea

"We went down to the beach and the sea was very rough, with white horses rolling in and breaking on the rocks."

wild horses wouldn't (make one do something) = nothing would (make one do something)

"The newspaper reporters wanted to know why I had resigned from the cabinet but wild horses wouldn't drag it out of me."

willing horse = somebody who is (always) willing to help

"John's a willing horse but he always seems to get the rotten jobs."

See also: a nod is as good as a wink to a blind horse; dark horse; eat like a horse; flog a dead horse; high horse; lock the stable door after the horse has bolted; look a gift horse in the mouth; one horse race; put the cart before the horse; ride a hobby horse (to death); work like a horse/Trojan.

hot

be hot on = be keen on, or be very knowledgeable about

"I think my daughter is hot on the boy next door."

"Vic is very hot on any question to do with sport."

feel/look not too hot = feel/look unwell

"I don't feel too hot today, do you mind if I go home from work early?"

hot and bothered = flustered

"I stalled the car in the middle of a roundabout, but my driving instructor told me not to get hot and bothered and to relax."

hot-blooded = emotionally volatile

"Mediterranean peoples have a

reputation for being hot-blooded."

hot favourite = the one most likely to succeed
"Mildred is hot favourite for promotion to the supervisor's position."

hot-headed = likely to act irrationally/in anger
"I fear that Vincent is too hot-headed to be made responsible for dealing with customers' complaints."

hot line = direct communication link (for emergencies)
"If the situation is that serious I'll have to use my hot line to the chairman of the company."

hot stuff = somebody with great ability
"You want to watch out for the other team's centre forward ñ he's hot stuff."

in hot water = in trouble
"You'll be in hot water when your mother finds out what you've done."

in the hot seat = in a difficult/ responsible position
"I'll be in the hot seat when the boss finds out what went wrong."

make it hot for somebody = put somebody in a difficult situation
"The police say they'll make it really hot for Barry if they catch him a second time driving his car without tax."

piping hot = very hot
"There is nothing as good as a piping hot cup of cocoa on a cold winter's evening."

See also: blow hot and cold; go like hot cakes; hot air; hot potato; hot seat; hot under the collar.

hour

after hours = after the time that a public house/shop usually closes
"The landlord was fined for allowing people to drink after hours."

(till/until) all hours = very late (at night)
"Linda stays up until all hours watching television."

hour of need = when one is in great need of help
"I was in debt with the bank and the building society, but my father helped me in my hour of need and made me an interest-free loan."

keep regular hours = sleep/work to a regular routine
"I wouldn't want to do shift work as Colin does, I like to keep regular hours."

rush hour = peak period of commuting traffic
"I had hoped to finish my shopping by three o'clock but by the time it was done I got caught in a traffic jam during the evening rush hour."

(wee) small hours = very early in the morning
"I hadn't seen my brother for years and when he came to stay we talked about old times until the small hours."

witching hour = midnight
"I was so engrossed in my book that I only went to bed when the chiming of the church clock reminded me it was the witching hour."

zero hour = time at which something is due to happen/start
"Get your equipment ready, it's coming up to zero hour."

See also: eleventh hour.

house

(all) around/round the houses = in a roundabout manner
"She obviously wanted to tell me, but went all round the houses before finally admitting she did it."

bring the house down = cause much applause/laughter
"My husband drank a bit too much at the party and did his Elvis Presley impersonation ñ it really brought the house down."

empty house = very poorly attended cinema/theatre
"Perhaps because of lack of publicity, the company's production of a science fiction version of Othello played to empty houses all week."

free house = public house that is not tied to one particular brewery
"Let's go to the Crown for a change, it's a free house and they sell eight different kinds of draught beer."

full house = cinema/theatre that is full, or a hand at poker that contains three cards of the same rank and two other cards of the same rank
"The full house signs were up every night that Jaws II was shown at our local cinema."
"I'd been losing steadily at poker all evening and when I finally got a full house it was beaten by a straight flush."

half-way house = something that is intermediate between two extremes
"The trouble with many modern pubs is that they are a half-way house between a disco and a fast-food shop."

house of cards = impractical scheme (which is sure to fail)
"The company's financial affairs were in a disastrous state, and the business was a house of cards that could fail at any time."

house of ill-fame/ill-repute = brothel
"Mrs Jones was to appear in court charged with running a house of ill-repute and living off immoral earnings."

house-to-house = calling at every house
"The police made a house-to-house search for the escaped prisoner."

house-warming = party to celebrate moving into a new home
"We decided to have only a small house-warming and more than fifty of our friends turned up."

in the best houses = among high-born/wealthy people
"They started a business as freelance butlers and now they have clients in the best houses throughout the country."
"There is now little stigma attached to becoming pregnant before marriage; it happens in the best houses."

keep open house = always make casual visitors welcome
"My new neighbours seem very friendly, they said they keep open house and I could call round at any time."

like the side of a house = very large
"My wife has gone like the side of a house since she stopped smoking."

on the house = free (of drinks/food provided by the host)
"It was the pub landlord's silver wedding anniversary the other day and he gave all his regular customers a drink on the house."

put/set one's house in order = arrange one's affairs in an orderly way
"Peter questioned my wisdom in buying a car on hire purchase, yet he has several large outstanding debts; he should put his own house in order before criticizing other people."

rough house = brawl/fight
"The British sailors had claimed the bar as their own and when the Americans came in it quickly turned into a rough house."

safe as houses = very safe/secure
"You should put your money in a bank or building society account where it will be as safe as houses, rather than in one of these dubious high-interest investments."

shout the house down = shout very loudly
"My Dad shouted the house down when our dog walked across the wet cement he had just laid."

the House of God = a church/place of worship
"The vicar went up to the tourist and asked him to refrain from smoking in the House of God."

See also: disorderly house; drink on the house; eat somebody out of house and home; (in the) dog house; like a house on fire; (under) house arrest.

household

head of the household = senior member of the family
"Thank you for asking us to come and see you on Saturday. I've still got to ask the head of the household but I'm sure he'll agree."

household name = somebody who is very well known
"Patrick Moore is a household name, familiar to millions of television viewers as the man who presented the Sky at Night series for more than twenty years."

household word = word that is very well known
"Hoover has become a household word for a vacuum cleaner throughout the world."

how

and how! = emphatically yes
"Did she smack him? And how!"

any old how = in a careless manner
"I asked her to put her clothes away tidily but she just threw them in the corner any old how."

how about? = would you consider/think about?
"How about a Chinese meal for a change?"

how come? = why?
"How come you're not at work today?"

how do you do? = formal greeting made when one is introduced to somebody (and not requiring an answer)
"How do you do? I have been looking forward to meeting you for some time."

how come? = why is it so?
"How come it always seems to rain as soon as I have finished washing my car?"

how on earth.Ö? = however. Ö?
"How on earth did the cat manage to get on that roof?"

how's that for.Ö? = what do you think of that as an example of.Ö?
"How's that for a good shot? Double twenty with the first dart."

See also: how goes it (with you)?; how's tricks?

hue

hue and cry = great/loud commotion, public outcry
"The lenient sentence passed on the rapist caused such a hue and cry that questions were asked in the House of Commons and many people demanded a change in the law."

huff

huff and puff = appear confused (pompously)

"Never mind huffing and puffing, just give me a straight answer to my question."

in a huff = having taken offence/grumpy
"She asked me what I thought of her new skirt, and when I told her she stalked off in a huff."

hum

hum and haw = dither/hesitate
"Don't sit there humming and hawing, you promised to take me out to dinner so get changed and let's go."

make things hum = make things happen (effortlessly and quickly)
"I'll be glad when Julia gets back from holiday because she seems to be the only person who can make things hum around here."

humble

See: eat humble pie.

humour

dry humour = subtle (and often sarcastic) sense of fun
"I prefer the dry humour of situation comedy to the slapstick of circus clowns."

out of humour = ill-tempered/irritable
"Old Joe's out of humour tonight ñ he went to the races and lost a hundred pounds on the horses."

sick humour = joke that is in bad taste
"I don't like the sick humour of some of today's comedy entertainers; I prefer the straightforward approach of a stand-up comedian."

hump

over the hump = past a critical/maximum point
"We're over the hump at work although we've still got several back orders to catch up on."

hundred

a hundred and one = very many
"Betty gave me a hundred and one reasons why she couldn't come out with me this evening."

not a hundred miles away = very close
"I won't say who made the mistake, but he's sitting not a hundred miles away from me."

hungry

hungry as a hunter = very hungry
"What's for dinner? I'm as hungry as a hunter after doing all that gardening."

hunt

hunt down = continue searching until one finds somebody/something
"It took me ages to hunt down a pair of shoes to match my new dress."

hunt high and low = make a thorough search
"I've hunted high and low for my lipstick and I still can't find it."

hunt up = look/search for
"I'm going to the reference library to hunt up some information for my school research project."

pot hunter = somebody who enters competitions merely for the prize money and not for entertainment
"I used to enjoy dog showing, but now that the prize money is so much higher it attracts pot hunters and everybody takes it too seriously."

run with the fox/hare and hunt with the hounds = try to be on both sides of a contest at the same time
"You shouldn't cheer on the home side when they are winning and then

support their opponents if they get in the lead; your trouble is you want to run with the fox and hunt with the hounds."

hunting-ground
See: happy hunting-ground

hurdle
first hurdle = initial obstacle
"I have the money to build an extension to my house but the first hurdle is to get the plans passed by the council."

hush
hush-hush = secret
"Martin has taken a hush-hush job at a department of the Ministry of Defence."
hush money = money paid to somebody to ensure his/her silence (about a misdeed/potential scandal)
"The man admitted in court that he had been given hush money to say nothing about the stolen diamonds."
hush up = conceal/suppress, or be quiet
"The government has hushed up its plans for more pit closures until after the by-election."
"Will you children hush up, I'm trying to listen to the radio."

I

i

dot the i's and cross the t's = take care of the (minor) details
"Broadly speaking James does adequate work, but somebody else still has to follow behind him to dot the i's and cross the t's."

ice

black ice = thin invisible film of ice
"Motorists are warned to take extra care this morning because there is black ice on many roads."

break the ice = lessen shyness (by initiating a conversation) when meeting somebody for the first time
"I broke the ice with the new girl in the office by offering her a cup of coffee and introducing her to a few of the others."

cut no ice = fail to have an effect
"Flattery cuts no ice with Alison, she's far too shrewd."

put on ice = postpone
"The council has put its road-widening scheme on ice until it has the money to pay for it."

skate/tread on thin ice = take an (unnecessary) risk
"He seemed satisfied with my description of how the machine works, but I was skating on thin ice because I don't really know much about it myself."

See also: icing on the cake

iceberg

tip of the iceberg = relatively minor factor that represents something much larger
"The cases of rape reported to the police are only the tip of the iceberg; it is almost certain that many more cases go unreported."

icing

the icing on the cake = decorative (but unnecessary) addition
"The basic car is adequate and the special wheel trims and two-tone paintwork are just icing on the cake."

idea

half-baked idea = impractical/ incomplete plan
"Jim's got some half-baked idea about converting his garage into a sauna."

moth-eaten idea = old-fashioned/ outmoded plan
"His proposals consisted of a mixture of trivial details and moth-eaten ideas."

not have an/the foggiest idea = have no knowledge at all
"I haven't the foggiest idea when the next train is due."

not one's idea of = opposite to what one believes/thinks
"Watching twenty-two grown men kicking a ball about is not my idea of a Saturday afternoon's entertainment."

put an idea into somebody's head = suggest something to somebody
"No you can't have a motorbike. Whoever put that idea into your head?"

run away with an idea = assume
"Don't run away with the idea that you can call me up at any time of the day or night."

that's the idea! = you are nearly correct
"That's the idea! Now try it with three balls at once and you'll soon be a juggler."

the very idea! = I do not agree with you

"Go to Cornwall on the back of a motorbike? The very idea! I'm much too old for that."

toy with an idea = consider a plan/proposal
"I'm toying with the idea of going to China for my holiday this year."

what's the big idea? = What do you think you are doing?
"What's the big idea? That's my beer you're drinking."

idle

See: bone idle.

ilk

of that ilk = of the same name
"I think he's Smith's brother or one of that ilk."

ill

diplomatic illness = feigned illness as an excuse not to do something
"The boss is coming round on an inspection tomorrow. I think I'll have a diplomatic illness and report sick."

go ill with somebody = end in trouble for somebody
"It will go ill with him if he doesn't admit he was in the building when the crime took place."

ill-at-ease = uncomfortable (because of the circumstances/situation one is in)
"He's so aggressive I always feel ill-at-ease in his company."

ill-gotten gains = money obtained dishonestly
"The bank robbers went to Brazil to live on their ill-gotten gains."

it's an ill wind = an apparently unfavourable situation has its good aspects
"It now takes me an hour on the train to travel to work, but at least I can catch up on my leisure reading; it's an ill wind.Ö"

speak ill of = slander/say uncomplimentary things about
"You shouldn't speak ill of Mabel, remember she has been kind to you in the past."

illusion

be under no illusion = be fully aware of the truth
"He's under no illusion and knows that the job will only last for six months."

image

the (spitting) image of = very like/similar to
"My husband is the image of his brother."

imagine

by no stretch of the imagination = it is extremely unlikely that
"By no stretch of the imagination will you ever become the world's greatest tennis player, even if you practice all day."

(just) imagine that! = expression of surprised disbelief
"Imagine that! Dad actually did the washing up!"

See also: figment of one's imagination.

immemorial

from time immemorial = from before anybody can remember
"There have been ponies on Dartmoor from time immemorial."

impression

be under the impression that = to believe/think that
"I was under the impression that you were not coming until tomorrow."

create/give a false impression = mislead
"Wearing those clothes gives people a totally false impression of what you are really like."
create/make a good impression = appear at one's best/be regarded favourably
"Wearing a suit at an interview usually makes a good impression."

impulse
See: blind impulse.

in
fall in = realize/understand
"They were making obscure references to my new hair style and it was several minutes before I fell in."
have it in for somebody = be waiting for a chance to harm somebody
"The boss criticizes whatever I do; he really seems to have it in for me lately."
in and out of = continually in a certain place
"I've caught a chill, and I seem to be in and out of the toilet all day."
in for = about to happen
"Let's hope we're in for a few weeks of sunny weather."
in for it = about to be in trouble
"You'll be in for it if your wife finds out."
in keeping with = appropriate/corresponding to, matching
"Arthur wore a dark suit, in keeping with the solemnity of the occasion."
in (right) lumber = in trouble
"The police caught me driving with no car insurance and now I'm in right lumber."
in on = be a party to/informed about
"Mike is a nosey chap, he always wants to be in on everything."
ins and outs = details
"Ask Brenda, she knows all the ins and outs of how the photocopier works."
(well) in with = be friendly/in association with
"It pays to keep in with Jerry, he knows everything that goes on around here."
nothing/not much in it = (very) little difference, no/little truth in the case in point
"I've compared the price of the camera in two shops and there's not much in it."
"Don't take any notice of what she told you, there's nothing in it."
See also: in double harness; in harness.

inch
every inch a = a complete
"When it comes to consideration for others, Wilfred is every inch a gentleman."
give somebody an inch and they'll take a mile = make somebody a concession and he/she will take advantage and seek even more
"I let Judy go home early a couple of times but the trouble with her is that if you give her an inch she takes a mile: she goes home early every day now."
within an inch of = very close to
"My brother had hard luck in the snooker tournament, he came within an inch of winning the cup."
within an inch of one's life = to be dangerously close to death
"The muggers beat up the old man within an inch of his life."

incline
be inclined to = be slightly in favour of doing something

"If I were you, I'd be inclined to wait and see what happens."

incumbent

incumbent upon one = my duty/responsibility to
"Gentlemen, it is incumbent upon me today to give you some bad news."

industry

key industry = industrial activity that is important/significant in national terms
"It is time that the government realized that electronics, not shipbuilding, is one of Britain's key industries."
See also: captain of industry; cottage industry.

inference

draw an/the inference = conclude
"From what she said, I drew the inference that she would rather run her own small team than deputize for the leader of a large one."

influence

under the influence = drunk
"He made some very rash promises, but we have to remember that he was under the influence at the time."

information

fish for information = try to find out about something (in a subtle/surreptitious manner)
"Lionel asked me how things were going at work, but I suspect he was just fishing for information that might be helpful to his own company."

iniquity

den/sink of iniquity = place where wrong-doers gather
"The snooker room at the back of the pub is a right den of iniquity on Saturday nights when all the local tearaways gather there."

initiative

on one's own initiative = on one's own, without authorization/prompting
"Nobody in authority was available to take advantage of the offer of a reduced price for a bulk order, so I ordered twice our normal requirement on my own initiative."
take the initiative = adopt the role of leader/decision-maker
"The sergeant was injured and so the corporal took the initiative and led the platoon out of the danger area."

innings

have a good innings = live for a comparatively long time
"Old George died last week at the age of seventy-nine, but he had a good innings."

inroad

See: make inroads into.

inside

know something inside out = know everything about something
"Judy knows astronomy inside out."

insolence

dumb insolence = refusal to comply with regulations/rules etc., but without saying anything at all
"I would rather somebody who is forthright and argues with me than somebody who resorts to dumb insolence."

instance

in the first instance = initially/at first
"You made several mistakes. In the first instance, you forgot to turn on the power supply any of the machines."

insult

add insult to injury = add offensive/unkind behaviour to the harm that one has already done to somebody
"And as if stealing the contract from us wasn't enough, they added insult to injury by saying that we probably couldn't have fulfilled it anyway."

intent

to all intents and purposes = as far as is important/significant
"Several countries have entered the contest but to all intents and purposes only the United States and the Soviet Union have any chance of winning."

interest

in an interesting/certain condition = pregnant
"I hear the Richard's girlfriend is in an interesting condition."

in the interest of = for/in order to have
"The press weren't told about the meeting in the interest of secrecy."

pay back with interest = make the punishment exceed the harm that invoked it
"The bully punched the young lad in the back, who turned round and paid him back with interest by knocking him out."

interim

in the interim = meanwhile
"The general manager is leaving and in the interim his deputy will take over until a successor is appointed."

into

be into something = be enthusiastic/knowledgeable about
"My daughter is into rock music, but I cannot stand it myself."

iota

one iota = the smallest part
"I'm afraid I don't have one iota of respect for the man who is taking over from the general manager."

iron

iron fist/hand in a velvet glove = ruthlessness that is disguised by an outward appearance of gentleness
"Many of the so-called liberal dictators of African nations rule using an iron hand in a velvet glove."

iron out = resolve/remove
"Let us meet tomorrow to iron out any difficulties in the final agreement."

have several irons in the fire = be involved in several activities at once
"Don't worry about the failure of Gerald's company, he has several other irons in the fire."

strike while the iron is hot = take an opportunity while it presents itself
"He wanted a quick decision so I decided to strike while the iron was hot and told him I accepted his terms."

with an iron hand = ruthlessly
"Kevin rules his family with an iron hand and even his wife seems afraid of him at times."

See also: iron curtain; man of iron/steel; rule with a rod of iron.

issue

at issue = under dispute
"Don't change the subject, that's not the point at issue."

confuse the issue = introduce

irrelevances/divert attention from the main point
"Let us first decide where we are going for a holiday; don't confuse the issue by discussing whether we are going by road or rail."

force an issue = bring a dispute to a decision point
"They couldn't agree whether to have the office redecorated in yellow or green so I forced the issue by saying that if they didn't decide today it would stay as it is."

side issue = something of secondary importance
"The committee met to discuss the organization of this year's carnival but they spent most of the time debating the side issue of whether to start it at two o'clock or three o'clock."

take/join issue with somebody = disagree with somebody
"The minister joined issue with the opposition spokesman on the question of the government's attempts to reduce unemployment in the northern counties."

it

this is it = this is what you have been expecting, or this is the critical point/ stage
"This is it: the Grand Canyon in all its splendour."
"We've worked on the car for weeks and this is it ñ will the engine start?"

itch

have an itching palm = want/be greedy to obtain money
"Be careful when you do business with Patrick, he has an itching palm."

ivory

ivory tower = protected/unrealistic way of life
"Academics in their ivory towers have no idea what it is like to earn one's living in industry or commerce."

J

jack

before you can say Jack Robinson = very quickly

"As I walked into the kitchen the cat jumped out of the window before you could say Jack Robinson."

cheap-jack = inexpensive but poorly made/shoddy

"The British market is flooded with cheap-jack goods from Asia."

every Jack has his Jill = for every man there is a woman partner somewhere

"Don't worry, Tyrone, you'll get a girlfriend one day ñ remember, every Jack has his Jill."

I'm all right, Jack/pull up the ladder, Jack = I am in a happy/satisfactory position (and I do not care about anybody else)

"The conductress could see I was running for the bus but she deliberately rang the bell and off it went ñ a typical case of I'm all right, Jack."

jack-in-office = pompous/self-important person in a position of authority/ power

"If I were you I'd deal with the appropriate government department, not some jack-in-office on the local council."

jack in (something) = give up/stop doing (something)

"I used to work nights but I had to jack it in because I couldn't sleep during the day."

jack-in-the-box = somebody who fidgets/does not sit still

"Sit still, Valerie, you're up and down like a jack-in-the-box."

Jack is as good as his master = a labourer/servant is as worthy as the person who employs him/her

"The directors have just increased their salaries and the workers want a pay raise as well; they think that Jack is as good as his master."

jack of all trades = somebody who can do various kinds of jobs (but does none exclusively)

"This chap is a jack of all trades; he wired in a new power point, plumbed in the washing machine and re-tiled the kitchen ñ all in one day and for a very reasonable price."

Jack Tar = sailor (in the Royal Navy)

"He was a Jack Tar at the start of the Second World War and he saw action for the whole six years."

jack up = increase

"In the budget the chancellor is bound to jack up the price of cigarettes."

See also: every man jack (of them).

jackpot

hit the jackpot = gain/win a lot of money/success

"Marcia hit the jackpot when she opened her antique shop; she's so successful she's thinking of buying another one."

jail

jail-bird = somebody who has been in prison (habitually)

"I was sentenced to five days for contempt of court and now everybody thinks I'm a jail-bird."

See also: jail bait.

jam

in a jam = in difficulty

"I'm in a bit of a jam; can you lend me ten pounds until tomorrow?"

jam on it = extra benefit in an already

favourable situation
"You have a well-paid job and a company car, and now you're asking for travelling expenses. What do you want, jam on it?"
money for jam/old rope = money obtained very easily
"My job is money for jam ñ the pay is good and I don't have to work very hard."

Jane
plain Jane = woman who is not particularly attractive
"The new receptionist is a bit of a plain Jane but she's very efficient at her job."

jaw
jaw away = talk incessantly
"Whenever my wife and her mother get together they jaw away for hours."
jaws of death = place/point at which one is in danger of dying
"After Doris had her accident, it was only the skill of the surgeons that saved her from the jaws of death."
set one's jaw = adopt an attitude of grim determination
"They told her that she would never make a good lorry driver but she set her jaw and worked at it until she was."
sock on the jaw = sudden setback/shock
"I didn't realize Christopher was trying to discredit me and his accusation came as a sock on the jaw."
take it on the jaw = accept a setback/punishment without complaint
"Norman had misbehaved and, as a punishment, his mother wouldn't let him go on the outing, but he took it on the jaw."
See also: glass jaw.

jay
jay-walker = pedestrian who wanders into the road in front of moving traffic
"I hate driving into town at Christmas time because the roads are full of jay-walkers."

Jekyll
Jekyll and Hyde personality = character that has two opposite sides to it
"He loves his dog and yet he's unkind to his children; he must have a Jekyll and Hyde personality."

jib
jib at = baulk at/be unwilling to do something
"I don't mind painting the doors but I jib at hanging wallpaper."
the cut of somebody's jib = somebody's overall appearance
"You could tell the old man was once in the services by the cut of his jib."

jinks
high jinks = boisterous fun
"The students always have high jinks at their parties."

Joan
See: Darby and Joan.

job
axe a job = stop the work on a job/task
"Tom was working on the excavations for the new swimming pool but the council decided to axe the job and now he's out of work again."
bad job = (very) unfortunate event
"That motorway pile-up was a bad job."

boot somebody out of a job = dismiss somebody/make somebody redundant
"I hear Harry has been booted out of his job for consistently bad time-keeping."

dead-end job = job with no prospects of promotion
"My salary is quite good but it's a dead-end job and I shall have to move if I want to get a higher position."

do a job = commit a crime (usually robbery)
"I've heard a rumour that Spike did that job on the industrial estate last week."

give something up as a bad job = stop doing something that looks as though it will end in failure
"I tried three times to persuade Mary to come to the party and in the end I gave it up as a bad job."

good job = fortunate/just as well
"It's a good job your father doesn't know what you're doing."

hatchet job = ruthless action
"When the company was taken over the new managing director did a hatchet job and fired half the staff."

have a job to = have difficulty in
"My garage contains so much rubbish that I have a job to get the car in."

inside job = crime that involves an employee of the organization affected
"Somebody supplied the robbers with a key to factory so it must have been an inside job."

Job's comforter = somebody who does not comfort at all
"Roy is a Job's comforter: I sprained my ankle and couldn't walk and he offered to lend me his bicycle!"

job lot = miscellaneous collection
"I bought that jug as part of a job lot at the church jumble sale."

jobs for the boys = situation in which contracts/jobs are obtained by people who are associated with those who make the decision to place the work
"It's no good bidding for that contract; its jobs for the boys and the work is already promised to the sales director's nephew."

land a plum job = obtain a good contract/job
"John has landed a plum job with a computer firm in London."

make a good job of = do something well
"Please tidy your bedroom ñ and make sure you make a good job of it.

make the best of a bad job = compromise/get some benefit from an unfavourable situation
"It rained when we got to Brighton so we made the best of a bad job by going to see a film instead of sitting on the beach."

on the job = at work/while working, or having sexual intercourse
"The best way to learn about car maintenance is on the job."
"Dave is so promiscuous ñ he's on the job with a different girl practically every night!"

put-up job = contrived scheme (designed to deceive)
"He claimed that his car had been stolen but it was a put-up job because he had really sold it to a scrap merchant."

the devil's own job = great difficulty
"I had the devil's own job finding your road on this vast housing estate."

try the patience of Job = test even somebody with unlimited patience
"I've checked six pages of figures

three times looking for the one error; it's enough to try the patience of Job."

See also: just the job/thing/ticket.

jockey

jockey for position = manoeuvre into a position (of advantage)

"It's amusing to see all the middle managers jockeying for position to try to get the vacant general manager's job."

jog

jog along = proceed gently/unhurriedly

"My father is over seventy now but he still jogs along in much the same way as he always did."

jog a person's memory = remind somebody

"I'm afraid I can't remember your wife's name, you'll have to jog my memory."

joint

See: put somebody's nose out of joint.

joke

beyond a joke = no longer funny

"The state of the wall where people have scribbled on it is beyond a joke."

corny joke = well-known joke

"The comedian failed to entertain us, with his corny jokes and awful singing."

crack a joke = tell a joke/funny story

"You can rely on Colin to crack a joke when things get tense in the office."

it's no joke = it is serious

"It's no joke when your brakes fail on the motorway."

joking apart = seriously

"You must have felt foolish when you fell off the horse but, joking apart, I hope you weren't hurt."

practical joke = prank that makes fun at somebody else's expense

"Charles likes playing practical jokes on other people but he doesn't like them played on him."

sick joke = remark intended to be funny but made in (very) bad taste

"And then he told a sick joke about two people in wheelchairs."

standing joke = something that is always humorous even when repeated often

"Edward's imitation Scots accent is a standing joke around here."

take a joke = accept in good humour a joke/trick played on one

"You have to be able to take a joke to work with some of the pranksters in our office."

that's a joke!/you must be joking! = I do not believe what you say

"A thousand pounds for that wreck of a car? You must be joking!"

Jones

keep up with the Joneses = ensure that one's social standing is equal to that of one's neighbours

"My son-in-law has bought a second car, but it's merely to keep up with the Joneses because his wife can't even drive."

See also: Davy Jones' locker.

jot

jot down = make a note of

"I'll just jot down your address so that I can send on the details you asked for by post."

jot or tittle = smallest amount/quantity

"I want this place cleaned so that there is not one jot or tittle of dust or dirt anywhere."

not to care a jot = not to care at all

"I don't care a jot what he wants, I'm going to do what I want for a change."

jowl
cheek by jowl = (very) close
"One interesting thing about these receptions is that you find yourself cheek by jowl with people from all over the world."

joy
full of the joys of spring = very happy
"Jill has been full of the joys of spring since she got her new job."
get no joy = fail to obtain what one seeks
"It's no good asking Thora for a contribution, you'll get no joy from her."
wish somebody joy = hope that somebody will enjoy doing something (while being glad that one does not have to do it oneself)
"Malcolm said that he was going pot-holing in the Pennines and I wished him joy."
See also: pride and joy.

judge
See: sober as a judge.

judgement
against one's better judgement = regretfully (= now I regret it)
"My wife is going to the opera on Saturday and against my better judgement I've agreed to go with her."
sit in judgement = adopt the role of arbiter/critic (often without the right or necessary ability)
"He criticises the way I dress, but who is he to sit in judgement on me?"
snap judgement = quick decision
"I nearly always regret it if I make a snap judgement when buying a pair of shoes."

jugular
go for the jugular = take aggressive action
"The tennis match was quite even until the last set, when the champion went for the jugular and won easily."

juice
stew in one's own juice = suffer because of one's own foolishness
"He knew he'd be in trouble with the bank if he overspent again; I've helped him before but this time I'm leaving him to stew in his own juice."

jump
be one jump ahead = anticipate what is likely to happen (and be ready for it)
"You have to be one jump ahead to survive in this business."
for the high jump = about to be punished/reprimanded
"You'll be for the high jump when the boss finds out what you've done."
go take a running jump (at yourself)! = go away!
"I definitely don't want to see him. Tell him to go take a running jump."
jump at = eagerly seize an opportunity
"Pete offered to sell me his car for only five hundred pounds so I jumped at it."
jump bail = forfeit bail by failing to appear for trial
"The robbers jumped bail and fled to South America."
jump down somebody's throat = talk to somebody in an abrupt/angry way
"I heard you. There's no need to jump down my throat."
jumping-off place = point of departure
"If all three cars are going to travel

together we might as well use my house as a jumping-off place."

jump out of one's skin = be frightened
"I didn't hear you come into the room and you made me jump out of my skin."

jump the gun = be too eager/hasty
"Roy jumped the gun and started building an extension to his house before he had planning permission, and now he's furious because the local council have made him pull it all down."

jump the queue = fail to wait one's turn (and move ahead of others who are waiting)
"Dozens of people were waiting to get the star's autograph but Louise knows the stage doorkeeper and was able to jump the queue."

jump to it = act quickly
"Come on, you men, line up in threes ñ and jump to it!"

See also: climb/jump onto the band wagon; jump to a conclusion.

jumper

shove it up one's jumper = do whatever one likes with it
"I told him I didn't want his old bicycle and he could shove it up his jumper."

jungle

law of the jungle = rules (or lack of them) that apply to a fierce contest which is outside civilized control
"In the battles for ownership of newspapers the law of the jungle often prevails."

just

just about = almost/nearly
"It's just about twelve o'clock."

just a minute/moment/second/tick = please wait for a very short while
"Just a moment, I'll be ready almost immediately."

just as well = fortunate/for the best
"I had a puncture so it was just as well I was carrying a spare wheel."

just in case = to allow for the event that
"Take your umbrella just in case it rains."

just so = neat and tidy, or precisely
"Everything has to be just so for the governor's inspection."
"You think that muggers should be punished more severely? Just so, I'm in total agreement."

just the job/thing/ticket = exactly what is required
"If you want a small screwdriver I've got just the thing here."

justice

do justice to = treat fairly/reveal the merit of
"Only the best wine can do justice to this excellent meal."

do somebody/something justice = present somebody/something fairly/to best advantage
"To concentrate on the few minor faults and not mention the overall soundness of the plan would not be doing it justice."

poetic justice = accidental but appropriate reward for goodness or retribution for wrongdoing
"He pushed several other runners to get to the front so it was poetic justice when he tripped and fell."

rough justice = over harsh punishment
"The men who refused to go on strike will have to face the rough justice of the union's disciplinary committee."

K

kangaroo

kangaroo court = body which (without formal/judicial power) passes judgement
"To the people who refused to go on strike, the most difficult part of their decision was the possibility that they would later be subject to the union's kangaroo court."

keel

keel over = suddenly fall over
"A tower crane keeled over and crushed some temporary buildings, but fortunately nobody was hurt."

on an even keel = balanced/calm
"Norma is a good influence on the rest of the staff because she keeps on an even keel no matter what happens."

keen

See: keen as mustard; sharp/keen as a razor.

keep

for keeps = for ever/permanent(ly)
"Just remember, in theory the marriage contract is for keeps."

in keeping with = (as is) appropriate/ suited to
"I would appreciate it if you would extinguish your cigarettes, in keeping with the solemnity of the occasion.

keep abreast of = keep up with/maintain one's position (in a competitive situation)
"One of the difficulties of researchers in a fast-moving area like computer science is keeping abreast of current developments."

keep aloof = deliberately remain remote (from everyday/practical things)
"Maggie used to do the shopping for her mother every week but she keeps aloof now she's married Algernon, insists on being called Margaret, and has servants to buy the food for the household."

keep an/one's eye on = watch carefully
"I've put the vegetables on to cook; please keep an eye the potatoes while I go to the corner shop for some ice cream."

keep a stiff upper lip = remain calm and unemotional (in adversity)
"Nigel always keeps a stiff upper lip, so that it's impossible to know what he really feels about anything."

keep a straight face = deliberately fail to laugh, even though one is amused
"She put pink and green stripes in her hair and looked rather like a Neapolitan ice cream. I couldn't keep a straight face when she asked me what I thought about it."

keep at it = persevere
"The only way to succeed in business these days is to keep at it."

keep at arm's length = remain remote from
"The boss can be a bit familiar but he's all right if you keep him at arm's length."

keep back = retain, or restrain
"I shall be late arriving so would you mind keeping back some food for me."
"The police had great difficulty keeping back the crowd."

keep company with = associate with (often referring to a sexual relationship/courtship between a man and a woman)
"I hear Hilda is keeping company with the man from number fifteen."

keep cool/keep one's head = remain calm
"One of Hal's great strengths is the ability to keep cool when things start to go wrong."

keep going = continue (to function)
"This illness makes me feel so tired that some days I don't know how to keep going."

keep in touch = remain in communication
"I hope you make a success of your new life in Canada ñ and don't forget to keep in touch."

keep in with somebody = maintain an association/friendship (for one's own advantage)
"It's worth keeping in with June because she knows all the latest gossip round here."

keep it dark = preserve a confidence/secret
"I'm thinking of changing jobs, but please keep it dark for the moment."

keep it to yourself = do not tell anyone
"I hear that Sandra is going to have a baby, but I don't know if she's told her parents yet so keep it to yourself."

keep it up = carry on (doing something)
"The first two or three days of a slimming diet are not difficult, but then I always find it hard to keep it up."

keep off = avoid
"The doctor has told me to keep off cigarettes and alcohol."

keep on (at somebody) = nag
"I'd like my wife a lot better if she didn't keep on at me all the time."

keep one's (own) counsel = keep a confidence/secret
"The journalist asked me what was going to happen to the staff when the factory closes, but I kept my own counsel."

keep one's distance = not get too close/friendly
"I would like to get to know Janet better but she always keeps her distance."

keep one's end up = maintain one's contribution/share (in an activity)
"Vic is still a useful member of the team although he's finding it increasingly difficult to keep his end up now that he's over thirty-five."

keep one's eyes peeled/skinned = be alert/on the watch
"There should be a bus along soon. Keep your eyes peeled and let me know when it's coming."

keep one's feet = maintain one's balance/upright posture
"The sea was so rough that even the crew found it difficult to keep their feet."

keep one's fingers crossed = wish for success
"Good luck with the exams. I shall be keeping my fingers crossed for you."

keep one's hair/shirt on = remain calm/not lose one's temper
"Keep your shirt on! There's no need to get so upset."

keep one's hand in = practice (to maintain one's skill at something)
"George doesn't play darts professionally any more but he still keeps his hand in by having an occasional game at the local pub."

keep one's head above water = remain financially solvent
"With costs continuing to rise, people on fixed incomes are finding it increasingly difficult to keep their heads above water."

keep one's nose clean = stay out of trouble
"That short prison sentence has done

Wilfred good. He's come out determined to keep his nose clean in future."

keep one's word = keep a promise
"He kept his word and paid me the money he owed me exactly on time."

keep out = exclude
"The club has raised its entrance and membership charges in an attempt to keep out undesirable people."

keep out of the way = stay away
"Your father is going to paint the staircase so you children had better keep out of the way."

keep something back = fail to be completely frank
"She told me about what happened on holiday, but I've got a feeling she's keeping something back."

keep something from somebody = be secretive/fail to tell somebody something
"Brian has been acting in a strange way recently, and I think he's keeping something from me."

keep the ball rolling = maintain the momentum/progress (of an activity)
"I'll make the first four or five pieces and then it's up to you to keep the ball rolling."

keep the peace = maintain tranquillity/prevent fighting
"My girlfriend keeps on nagging me to get a haircut so I finally had one today; it was worth it if only to keep the peace."

keep (oneself) to oneself = be retiring/inclined to introversion
"He comes into the pub most evenings but always sits in the corner and keeps to himself."

keep to the straight and narrow (path) = obey the law
"Elizabeth was fined for her first offence but she's learned her lesson and swears she's going to keep to the straight and narrow in future."

keep/loose track of = follow/fail to follow
"Please ask if you cannot keep track of what I'm telling you."
"The music has so many melodic lines occurring simultaneously that it is easy to lose track of any particular one of them."

keep up with = maintain the same rate of progress/position as
"My daughter is very good at maths and I find it increasingly difficult to keep up with her."
"After six miles of their marathon race, only a handful of runners were keeping up with the leader."

worth its/one's keep = worth the cost of maintenance
"My dog just lies around all day, and doesn't even bark when strangers knock on the door ñ he's not even worth his keep."

you can keep it! = I don't want it!
"If that's what pernod tastes like you can keep it!"

See also: have/keep something up one's sleeve; keep a low profile; keep a tight rein on; keep/lose track of something; keep on an even keel; keep one's eye on the ball; keep one's options open; keep pace with; keep/set/start the ball rolling; keep something under wraps; keep tabs on; keep up with the Joneses.

ken
See: beyond one's ken.

kettle
a different kettle of fish = something that is very different

"He's very good at arithmetic and anything to do with figures but he can't spell ñ that's a totally different kettle of fish."

fine/pretty kettle of fish = confused situation/mess/muddle
"This is a pretty kettle of fish; how are we going to explain what happened?"

See also: pot calling the kettle black.

key

get/have the key to the door = reach the age of majority (currently eighteen in Britain, formerly twenty-one)
"Will you come to my party next Saturday? I'm getting the key of the door."

(all) keyed up = agitated/anxious/excited
"I always get keyed up before an examination."

key position = important/principal job/position
"Workshop foreman is a key position in this factory."
"The press photographers arrived early so that they could take up key positions overlooking the route of the procession."

key to a problem = aspect of a problem that, if dealt with, leads to a solution
"The country desperately needs more houses and the key to the problem, as usual, is money."

low key = quiet/without emphasis
"We plan to make an official announcement next month but for the time being we're keeping it very low key."

skeleton key = composite key that will open many different locks
"There is no sign of a break-in so the burglars probably used a skeleton key."

kick

for a kick off = first/to start with
"You can give me back my spanners for a kick off!"

for kicks = for fun/thrills
"He's the sort of person who would pull the wings off a fly just for kicks."

kick-back = commission/reward for a favour paid out of the receipts that result from that favour
"I have recommended that Martin be given the contract and if he is, he's promised me a kick-back."

kick off = begin(ning)/start
"Yes, I would like to go to the concert with you tomorrow evening. What time does it kick off?"

kick one's heels = be kept waiting
"The boss kept me kicking my heels for half an hour before he would see me."

kick over the traces = behave unconventionally/break the rules
"All teenagers kick over the traces at some time."

kick somebody in the teeth = cause somebody great discouragement/disappointment
"They kicked me in the teeth by not giving me the job even after they had already promised it to me."

kick somebody upstairs = promote somebody in order to vacate his/her job
"They decided to kick him upstairs and appoint a younger man to take his place."

kick somebody when he/she is down = add to the misfortunes of somebody who is already in an unfortunate situation
"Bill owes me fifty pounds but he's been out of work for weeks, so I don't

like to kick him when he's down and ask for the money back."

kick up a fuss = create a disturbance
"My steak is a bit tough but please don't kick up a fuss and call the waiter."

kick up one's heels = depart
"I'm thoroughly tired of the British winters so I've decided to kick up my heels and go to live in Australia."

See also: alive and kicking; kick the bucket.

kid

kid's stuff = very easy/simple
"He has a marvellous understanding of words and the Times crossword puzzle is kid's stuff for him."

with kid gloves = (very) gently
"Marty can be a bit moody and you have to learn to handle her with kid gloves."

you're kidding! = I don't believe you!
"You're kidding! You can't have finished all that work already."

See also: whiz kid.

kill

dressed to kill = dressed in one's best/to impress
"Betty came to the party dressed to kill and she certainly was the centre of attention."

in at the kill = present at the end
"I've worked on the project for nearly three years and I'm determined to be in at the kill when it is finished next month."

(could) kill oneself = greatly regret something
"I bought a new watch and could have killed myself later when I saw an identical model for sale in another shop at only half the price I paid."

kill oneself laughing = be very amused
"I killed myself laughing when I saw that old Chaplin film on television last night."

kill time = occupy oneself while waiting
"It's a hour before our train leaves so let's have a look round the shops to kill time."

kill two birds with one stone = (take the opportunity to) do two things simultaneously
"If we've got to go to Exeter to see your father we could kill two birds with one stone and visit the Ship Museum as well."

kill with kindness = be over kind
"She gives that child everything he asks for. She will kill him with kindness if she's not careful."

make a killing = make a large profit
"Howard tells me he made a killing on the stock market last week."

See also: kill or cure; kill the fatted calf; kill the goose that lays the golden egg.

kin

kith and kin = family/relations
"I'm not going away for Christmas; I prefer to stay at home with my own kith and kin."

next of kin = nearest relative/person who legally inherits from one (in the absence of a will to the contrary)
"Since I got divorced my mother has been my next of kin."

kind

in kind = in the same way, or in goods rather than in cash
"She complimented me on my hair style and I replied in kind."
"When I do odd jobs for the local farmer he always pays me in kind; last week he gave me some a dozen eggs,

a lump of cheese and a box of apples."

two of a kind = two people/things that are very similar
"Ann and Michael are two of a kind: they both like rock music, old cars and Indian food."

See also: cruel to be kind; nothing of the kind/sort.

kindly

not take kindly to = be annoyed by/not like
"Your father won't take kindly to the fact that you've walked on his flower beds."

kindred

kindred spirits = people with the same attitudes/points of view
"We were on the moors miles from anywhere when we met these kindred spirits who also like walking, so we teamed up and walked on together."

king

a cat may laugh/look at a king = a humble/ordinary person has every right to look at an important person
"The new president didn't want any of the peasants at his inauguration but a cat may look at a king and his advisors persuaded him to change his mind."

fit for a king = luxurious/of the best quality
"We hadn't been home for several months and when we did go my mother made us a meal fit for a king."

king of the castle = (the) most important person
"We take our orders from the area manager ñ he's the king of the castle around here."

king's ransom = very high price
"I bought a leg of lamb in the supermarket and it cost me a king's ransom."

kingdom

send to kingdom come = destroy/kill
"There is an ants' nest under my kitchen doorstep. I must get some poison and send them to kingdom come."

until kingdom come = for a very long time/for ever
"If you miss the nine-forty train you have to wait until kingdom come for the next one."

kiss

kiss of death = something that brings about ruin
"Bad reviews can be the kiss of death to a new West End play."

kiss of life = mouth-to-mouth resuscitation
"A rescuer gave the drowning man the kiss of life until the ambulance came."

kiss somebody/something goodbye = never expect to see again
"If you've lent Frank a saw you can kiss that goodbye ñ he never gives anything back."

kitchen

if you don't like the heat get out of the kitchen = if you cannot stand the pace/pressure required to do something, then you should stop doing it
"We have all got to work extra hard and long hours to finish this contract on time, and if you don't like the heat get out of the kitchen."

See also: everything but the kitchen sink.

kite

fly a kite = make a suggestion merely in order to gauge people's reaction to it

"I was only flying a kite when I started the rumour that the firm might be moving premises to a site in Scotland."

See also: high as a kite.

kitten

have kittens = be very anxious/nervous

"My boss invited my wife and me round for a drink at his house. As we were sitting there I saw this huge spider crawling across the floor, and I was having kittens because my wife would have screamed if she had seen it."

See also: nervous as a kitten; weak as a kitten.

knee

bring somebody to his/her knees = make somebody feel defeated/humble

"His company was doing well until lack of capital brought him to his knees."

on (one's) bended knees = humbly/like a beggar

"I've asked him on bended knees but my father still won't let me go on the school trip to Austria."

See also: weak-kneed.

knickers

get one's knickers in a twist = become excited/panic

"I promise I won't spend more than a hundred pounds in the sales so don't get your knickers in a twist."

knife

get one's knife into somebody = bear a grudge against/be persistently hostile to somebody

"For some reason he's got his knife into me, although I don't know what harm I ever did him."

on a knife-edge = finely balanced

"The project is on a knife-edge between success and failure."

put the knife in = add to somebody's sufferings

"I lost my job and my health began to suffer, when my wife put the knife in by saying that she was leaving me to go and live with my best friend."

under the knife = undergoing surgery

"Before antiseptic surgery as many soldiers died under the knife as in battle."

you could cut the air with a knife = you could detect an emotionally-charged/smoky atmosphere

"John and Gill had obviously been quarrelling; when we walked into their flat you could cut the air with a knife."

See also: accent you could cut with a knife.

knight

knight in shining armour = benefactor/somebody who helps one when in trouble

"While I was establishing the business the bank manager really was a knight in shining armour."

knit

knit one's brows = frown/think hard

"He knit his brows as he considered my request."

knob

with knobs on = (that is) even better/more

"I don't care if your Mum has got a

new vacuum cleaner ñ we've got one with knobs on."
"And the same to you with knobs on!"

knock

knock-about = boisterous/informal
"We sometimes have a knock-about game of football, but nobody takes it very seriously."

knock about with = associate with
"I think she knocks about with that dark-haired chap from down the road."

knock back = drink quickly
"Tony must have been thirsty, he's knocked back three pints in half an hour."

knock-down price = cheap, bargain price
"It was the last one they had and they sold it me at a knock-down price."

knocking shop = brothel
"The red light district is full of seedy clubs and knocking shops."

knock into a cocked hat = beat/be better than
"I have good LPs of the Beethoven symphonies but the new CD recordings knock them into a cocked hat."

knock it off! = stop it!
"Knock it off, you lot, I'm trying to get some rest."

knock off = cease work, or steal
"We usually knock off at about five o'clock."
"You must be careful what you buy from somebody in a pub because you don't know if it's been knocked off."

knock over = complete (quickly)
"Mike can knock over three or four of those simple drawings in a day."

knock something down = offer/sell something cheaply, at a bargain price
"The shop in the High Street has knocked down its summer dresses to make way for its winter stock."

knock something on the head = cancel/stop doing something
"I used to go out nearly every night but I decided to knock it on the head because I couldn't really afford it."

knock the bottom out of = reduce/undermine the worth of
"This sudden cold spell has knocked the bottom out of the market for seasonal items like ice cream and suntan oil."

knock spots off/the living daylights out of/the stuffing out of somebody = soundly beat/thrash somebody
"My new washing machine knocks spots off the old one."
"The unseeded player has no chance; the champion will knock the living daylights out of her."

knock together/up = improvise/make hurriedly
"See if you can knock together some sort of box to put it in."

take a knock = suffer (a setback)
"The sales of large cars have taken a knock since the increase in the price of petrol."

See also: knock somebody for six; knock somebody into the middle of next week.

knot

at a rate of knots = very quickly
"A motorbike roared round the corner at a rate of knots."

tie somebody (up) in knots = confuse somebody
"The more Brian tried to explain why he was late the more he tied himself in knots."

tie the knot = get married
"I was pleased to hear you'd got

engaged. When are you going to tie the knot?"

See also: cut the (Gordian) knot.

know

for all I know = I do not know (and do not care) but

"For all I know she may have emigrated to Outer Mongolia."

have known better days = not to be as good/wealthy as formerly

"My old typewriter has known better days, it's about time I bought a new one."

"Charles has known better days and finds it difficult to live on only his pension."

I don't know about you = I don't care what you think/want

"I don't know about you, but I think it's very cold in this room."

I knew it = I was certain (that something would happen)

"I knew it, that branch wasn't strong enough to hold you."

in the know = in possession of information/knowledge

know a thing or two (about) = have a good knowledge (of), or show good common sense

"David certainly knows a thing or two about car engines."

"Mary knows a thing or two and won't buy clothes unless she has tried them on."

know all the answers/a thing or two = be well informed

"Peter knows a thing or two about what happened but he's not telling."

know somebody by sight = recognize somebody but not know his/her name

"I know him by sight but I can't remember where we met."

know something backwards/inside out = know something very well

"She's studied the American constitution until she knows it inside out."

know the ropes = be experienced

"If you want to know anything about the process ask Gloria, she knows the ropes."

know the score = be aware of the true situation

"I wasn't at the meeting but Jim was ñ ask him, he knows the score."

"Robin is usually in the know, let's ask him."

not know one is born = not to have encountered any trouble in life

"He still lives at home and has a large allowance from his rich grandfather ñ he doesn't know he is born."

not know the first thing about = know nothing about

"Do you think you could help me change my sparking plugs? I don't know the first thing about cars."

not know when one is well off = not realize how fortunate one is

"You've got a good job and a lovely wife ñ you don't know when you're well off."

not that I know of = not as far as I am aware

"She's not been to America that I know of."

you know = remember

"You know that red car we used to have? I saw it on the motorway yesterday."

you never know = perhaps/possibly

"You never know, it may stop raining by this evening."

See also: don't know somebody from Adam; know one's place; know one's stuff; know something straight off; know what one is talking about; not know one end of something from the other.

knowledge

come to one's knowledge = be told about/find out

"It has come to my knowledge that train fares are going to be increased again."

knuckle

knuckle down to something = begin working in earnest at something

"You left school four months ago. It's about time you knuckled down and found yourself a job."

knuckle sandwich = a punch (to the face) with a closed fist

"This chap deliberately jostled Wally so he turned round and gave him a knuckle sandwich."

knuckle under = give in/submit

"You shouldn't knuckle under all the time; your wife can't always be right."

near the knuckle = bordering on the indecent

"The comedian's jokes were too near the knuckle for most of the women in the audience."

rap somebody on the knuckles = reprimand/scold somebody

"The boss rapped me on the knuckles for failing to spot the mistake."

L

labour

black-leg labour = people employed (by the management) when the regular workers are on strike
"The pickets tried to block the road to prevent buses carrying black-leg labour from entering the factory gates."

labour a point = make a point (of discussion) (too) frequently
"All right, that's the fourth time you asked if you can go out tomorrow night. There's no need to labour the point."

labour in vain = work but with no result
"I tried to teach him chess but I was labouring in vain, he just doesn't seem to be able to get the hang of it."

labour of love = task done for no reward, just one's own satisfaction
"I don't mind arranging the flowers for the church every Sunday, it's a labour of love."

labour under a delusion = be under a misapprehension
"Bill took ages to do the job because he was labouring under the delusion that every part had to be painted three times, not just the once that was required."

lace

lace a drink = add a spirit (brandy, rum etc.) to a non-alcoholic beverage (coffee, tea etc.)
"The best treatment for a cold is black coffee liberally laced with rum."

See also: strait laced.

lad

See: bit of a lad.

ladder

top (rung) of the ladder = highest position in a career
"Sir Arnold has been at the top of the ladder for nearly twenty years and he's finally decided to retire and make way for a younger person."

See also: pull up the ladder, Jack.

lady

ladies' man = man who likes (and seeks) the company of women
"Mark has always been a bit of a ladies' man; it will be interesting to see if he settles down now that he's got married."

Lady Bountiful = rich/generous woman (usually pejorative)
"We work hard for the old people all the time, but Mrs Harrington-Jones only comes round once a year at Christmas to play the Lady Bountiful."

lady in waiting = woman who is pregnant
"I haven't seen Cindy for a few months and didn't realize that she is a lady in waiting."

lady killer = man popular with women
"Keith is a right lady killer, he has a new girlfriend every week."

lady of the town = prostitute
"Be careful of the ladies of the town when you spend that weekend in Amsterdam."

one's good lady = one's wife
"Morning, George, and how's your good lady today?"

the old lady of Threadneedle Street = the Bank of England
"It is no good the government trying to bring down inflation if they don't get the co-operation of the old lady of Threadneedle Street."

laid

get laid = have sexual intercourse
"I've been on my own for five weeks, so I'm going out tonight to get laid."

laid back = (very) relaxed
"The boss was angry with Wendy, but she's so laid back she wasn't at all troubled."

laid up = out of commission (through disrepair or illness)
"My car has been laid up for nearly a week now."
"I've been laid up with a stomach complaint for nearly a week."

lamb

go like a lamb (to the slaughter) = do something meekly/without resistance
"There goes Jones to the headmaster's study like a lamb to the slaughter. I wonder if he realizes he's going to be punished?"

one might as well be hung for a sheep as a lamb = if punishment is due, one might as well do something really bad and enjoy it while one can
"I'm an hour late going home already so I think I'll have another drink; I might as well be hung for a sheep as a lamb."

mutton dressed up as lamb = describing an older woman who dresses and behaves as if she were much younger
"At first sight I thought she was attractive but in a better light I realized she was mutton dressed up as lamb."

See also: in two shakes (of a lamb's tail).

lame

See: lame duck; lame excuse.

land

be landed with = end up with
"My daughter has just got engaged and I suppose I shall be landed with the cost of the wedding."

in the land of Nod = asleep
"By nine o'clock all young children should be in the land of Nod."

in the land of the living = active/alert
"After being off work for a week with a bad cold it's good to be back in the land of the living again."

land of milk and honey = fertile region
"By using irrigation, the Israelis have turned parts of the Negev Desert into a land of milk and honey."

land of the midnight sun = northern Norway and other places north of the Arctic Circle where the sun never sets (even at night) during summer months
"We spent our honeymoon in the land of the midnight sun."

land on one's feet = be fortunate/lucky
"Out of nearly fifty applicants Rick was chosen for the job, but then he always lands on his feet."

land somebody with something = pass a difficult/unpleasant task to somebody else
"They landed me with the task of breaking the bad news to the staff."

land up = finish at
"We were looking for this country park but took the wrong turning and landed up in Milton Keynes."

lie of the land = situation as it applies (before doing something)
"According to the lie of the land we can either make a start on the job or wait until more people arrive tomorrow."

no man's land = neutral ground between opposing forces
"My application is lost somewhere in the no man's land between the planning office and the rates department."

see how the land lies = analyse the situation (before doing something)
"I don't know whether we will start the job or not until I see how the land lies."
See also: happy landing; live off the fat of the land; spy out the land.

landscape
See: blot on the landscape.

landslide
landslide victory = overwhelming win
"The Conservatives gained a landslide victory and were returned for a second term of government."

lane
go down memory lane = indulge in nostalgic memories
"The old Bing Crosby record certainly took me down memory lane."

language
daughter language = language derived from another (earlier) one
"In many ways Italian is a daughter language of Latin."
dead language = language that is no longer spoken in everyday use
"A small band of dedicated people are doing their best to stop Cornish from becoming a dead language."
murder a language = speak a language very badly
"She thinks she can speak French but all she does is to murder the language."
pick up a language = acquire the ability to speak a language (without formal tuition)
"Mike has a good ear for accents and can pick up most European languages quite easily."
second language = language (that is spoken/understood) other than one's mother tongue
"English is spoken as a second language in many parts of India."
speak/talk the same language as somebody = share the same views as somebody
"My wife and I speak the same language when it come to music."
See also: (using) bad/strong language.

lap
drop/land in one's lap = occur without one having to try
"Belinda was thinking of changing jobs when this chance of promotion dropped in her lap, so she took it and stayed on at a much higher salary."
in the lap of the gods = dependent only on chance
"We've organized everything but the weather ñ and that's in the lap of the gods."
lap of luxury = luxurious situation
"Sally did well for herself: she married an earl and now lives in the lap of luxury."

large
at large = free
"The police recaptured one of the escaped prisoners after he had been at large for only two hours."
larger than life = with an exaggerated character
"The people in Westerns are nearly always depicted larger than life, usually either totally good or totally bad."

lark
happy as a lark = very happy
"I was as happy as a lark just strolling

along the lanes and looking at the flowers."

lark about/have a lark = fool about/play the fool

"Stop larking about, children, and settle down to do your homework."

rise/get up with the lark = rise very early in the morning

"I always get up with the lark when I'm on holiday to make the most of every single day."

lash

lash out = hit out, or spend lavishly

"The cat was injured and lashed out at anybody who went near it."

"Stephen is bound to lash out at his only daughter's wedding."

last

at (long) last = in the end

"Thank goodness, here's the train at last."

at/with one's last gasp = with one's last (dying) breath

"With his last gasp, the hero named the man who had shot him."

last but not least = said of the best item on a list that is deliberately left until last

"And now, last but not least, the star of our show: Bendy Wendy."

last out = endure/last

"Do you think the sugar will last out until I go shopping on Saturday?"

last straw = final factor that, in addition to others, makes a situation impossible

"I was in a hurry to get ready and I broke a nail and laddered my tights; then when I lost an ear-ring it was the last straw."

on one's last legs = near to breakdown/collapse

"I'll soon have to scrap this lawn mower, it's beyond repair and on its last legs."

stick to one's last = not depart from what one is best at

"That electrician should stick to his last and not keep trying to tell the plumber how to do his job."

the last = the least likely/wanted

"Now it's started to rain. That's the last thing we need!"

"The last thing I expected was that you would come on the early train."

the last word = very up-to-date

"His car has the last word in stereo equipment."

See also: see the last of somebody.

latch

latch on to = grasp (an idea/object), or join

"Martin soon latched on to the rules of backgammon."

"Linda seems to have latched on to that gang of youngsters who hang around the shops."

See also: latch-key child.

late

at the latest = by a certain time (and preferably sooner)

"The job has got to be finished by Friday night at the latest."

better late than never = a late occurrence is preferable to one that doesn't happen at all

"By the time the trolley gets here the tea has gone cold, but better late than never I suppose."

(a bit) late in the day = too late

"It's a bit late in the day to say you don't really want to start a family yet ñ you've been pregnant for six months!"

of late = recently

"Have you noticed that Alice has been

a bit depressed of late?"

sooner or later = eventually

"We'll surround the place. They will have to come out sooner or later when they run out of food and water."

lather

in a lather = agitated/upset

"The boss always gets in a lather during stocktaking time."

Latin

See: dog Latin.

laugh

don't make me laugh! = I don't believe you!/that is ridiculous!

"Don't make me laugh! You paid two hundred pounds for a scruffy mongrel like that?"

have the last laugh = be finally proved right

"We went the long way round and they took a short cut, but we had the last laugh because they got lost!"

have the laugh on somebody = be able to make fun of somebody

"We had the laugh on Peter: we tied his shoelaces together when he was asleep and, of course, as soon as he tried to walk he fell over."

laughing stock = object of ridicule

"You're not coming out with me dressed like that, you'll make me a laughing stock with all the neighbours."

laugh like a drain/laugh one's head off = laugh very loudly/for a long time

"My daughter laughed her head off when she saw photographs of me when I was a child."

laugh in somebody's face = regard somebody with total scorn

"If I were to ask the boss for a rise he'd probably just laugh in my face."

laugh on the other side of one's face = have apparent happiness/success turned to disappointment/failure

"Enjoy the meal while you can; you'll laugh on the other side of your face when you get the bill."

laugh something away/off = regard difficulties as being unimportant

"Albert just laughed it off when I told him they were putting up the price of petrol yet again."

laugh something out of court = scornfully dismiss/disregard something without even considering it

"A proposal for a tunnel under the Thames between the House of Commons and Fullers Brewery was laughed out of court."

laugh up one's sleeve = laugh in secret, or laugh inwardly without showing amusement

"The committee appeared to take my tunnel proposal seriously, but I suspect that they were really laughing up their sleeves all the time."

no laughing matter = serious matter

"It's no laughing matter when you lose your job at my age."

you're laughing = you will have nothing to worry about

"If he will pay you five hundred pounds for that wreck of a car, you're laughing."

See also: die laughing; hollow laugh; horse laugh; kill oneself laughing; laughed out of court; laughter is the best medicine; raise a laugh.

launch

launch out = begin (something expansive/grand)

"You only have to mention the price of petrol to Harold and he launches out into a harangue about the government and its financial policies at home and abroad."

laurels

look to one's laurels = make sure one continues to perform as well as in the past

"You'll have to look to your laurels if you don't want that new chap to be promoted before you are."

rest on one's laurels = rely on one's past reputation to maintain one's position (without making any further effort)

"It's about time Justin made a practical contribution to the running of this firm; he's been resting on his laurels for too long."

law

beyond the law = outside the jurisdiction of the courts

"Some senior members of the police force think that they're beyond the law and shouldn't get fined for parking or speeding like us ordinary motorists."

call in the law = call the police

"Break it up, you two, or I'll call in the law."

have the law on somebody = ensure that the police/courts take legal action against somebody

"If you let your dog dig up my flower bed again I'll have the law on you."

in the eye(s) of the law = from a strictly legal point of view

"Parking with your car bumper overhanging the pavement may seem trivial to you, but in the eyes of the law it is still an offence."

law-abiding = honest/upholding the law

"Why don't the police go and chase a few burglars instead of pestering law-abiding citizens about their car tax and dog licences."

law unto himself = describing somebody who rejects convention or the usual rules

"Terry has always been a law unto himself; he even refused to wear uniform when he was at school."

lay down the law = state something forcefully and without heed of any objections

"My father has been laying down the law about me coming home late, so I'll have to stay in for a few evenings until he calms down about it."

Murphy's/sod's law = adage which states that if anything can go wrong it will

"I needed one more bolt to finish the job, but nobody around here had the right type in stock and I had to order one from Manchester ñ sod's law applies again!"

Parkinson's law = adage which states that a task tends to expand to take up the time available for it

"It is no good allocating an extra day in the hope of increasing production; Parkinson's law will apply, we will get the same number of items made, and they will have cost more!"

take the law into one's own hands = obtain what one regards as justice without using the legal process

"When a group of us caught the man who had been peeping into our bedroom windows we took the law into our own hands and gave him a good thrashing."

unwritten law = accepted, but not formal, rule/code of behaviour

"It's an unwritten law around here that everyone fetches his own coffee, even the managers."

See also: long arm of the law; law of the jungle.

lawyer

barrack-room lawyer = somebody who is always seeking an argument

"Colin is a right barrack-room lawyer; he'll argue about anything just for the sake of it."

lay

lay a bet = make a wager

"Are you going to lay a bet on the Derby?"

lay about one = strike out in all directions

"I was outnumbered so I just lay about me until I could break free and run away."

lay about/into somebody = belabour/berate somebody

"My father came home a little drunk and my mother really laid into him."

lay aside = postpone/put to one side

"I got stuck with that jigsaw puzzle so I've laid it aside for the time being."

lay bare = expose

"The article in the Sunday newspaper laid bare corruption in parts of local government."

lay emphasis/stress/weight on = emphasize

"And I cannot lay enough stress on the fact that this behaviour has got to stop!"

lay hold of/one's hand on = obtain

"Do you think you can lay hold of some cheap whiskey for me?"

"It is very difficult to lay one's hands on cheap whiskey these days."

lay in/up = put in store

"We mustn't forget to lay in some logs for the winter."

lay it on thick/with a trowel = exaggerate/flatter

"I thought you laid it on a bit thick when you said that Ann's was the best painting you've ever seen."

lay low = flatten, or make ill

"The blast of the explosion laid low trees and houses for miles around."

"I've been laid low with flu for the last couple of weeks."

lay off somebody = stop annoying/harming somebody

"Lay off him, Johnny, he's not hurting you."

lay on = provide

"I like going to their parties, they always lay on good food."

lay oneself open (to) = be vulnerable to

"Remember to keep accurate records of all expenditure; you don't want to lay yourself open to charges of fiddling the accounts."

lay open = expose/uncover

"Huge excavators removed the topsoil to lay open the seam of coal beneath."

lay out = arrange a corpse after death

"An undertaker's first job is to lay out the body and prepare it for burial."

lay somebody off = (temporarily) end somebody's employment

"They have laid off twenty workers at the mill because of lack of orders."

lay somebody to rest = bury somebody (after death)

"Our dog was twelve years old when she died, and we laid her to rest in the orchard."

lay something at somebody's door = blame/make somebody responsible for something

"Somebody has been smoking in here and if I can lay it at your door I'll report you."

lay waste = completely destroy (over an area)

"Continual shelling laid waste vast areas of farmland all along the front line."

See also: lay at somebody's door; lay down the law; lay one's cards on the table.

lead

give a lead = give an indication for others to follow
"The others think that the water is too cold but if you give a lead and jump in first, they will all follow."

lead a double life = have two different lifestyles simultaneously
"The ferry captain was leading a double life; he had two wives, one in Calais and one in Dover!"

leading light = somebody who is highly regarded/influential
"The theatre club has gone from strength to strength since William became its leading light and raised financial support from local businessmen."

leading question = question whose phrasing anticipates/provokes the required answer
"The defence objected to the prosecution asking a leading question and had it changed from ëIs that the man you saw?' to ëIs the man you saw present in this room?'"

lead nowhere = fail/make no progress
"All this arguing is leading nowhere; let's change the subject."

lead off = speak angrily (and at length)
"I know you are annoyed but there's no reason to lead off like that."

lead somebody astray = tempt somebody into wrongdoing
"I was only going to have one drink but the chaps in the pub led me astray and I stayed and had several."

lead somebody by the nose = force somebody to submit to what one wants
"With regard to staff requirements, our boss's secretary can lead him by the nose."

lead up to = gradually prepare for
"The crescendo in the last movement leads up to a grand climax and a repeat of the main theme."

swinging the lead = avoiding work/ malingering
"Ron is always swinging the lead and leaving us to do most of the hard work."

take the lead = play the leading part
"Charlton Heston took the lead in many films of stories from the bible."

See also: lead a dog's life; lead somebody a (merry) dance; lead the way; (lead somebody) up the garden path; put lead in one's pencil.

leaf

leaf through = quickly turn the pages (of a book)
"It says the book is illustrated but I've leafed through it and can find only one or two pictures."

shake like a leaf = tremble, be very cold/ frightened
"Gill shook like a leaf when she heard the footsteps behind her in the dark."

take a leaf out of somebody's book = follow somebody's example
"Why don't you take a leaf out of David's book and keep your room tidy as well?"

turn over a new leaf = start behaving in a better way
"I used to go out every evening but I've decided to turn over a new leaf and stay at home more to concentrate on my studies."

See also: loose-leaf(ed).

league

bottom/top of the league = worst/best

"The Kings Arms is the bottom of the league as far as local pubs are concerned."

"Well done, Linda. Your painting is top of the league."

in league with = allied/associated with (often for no good purpose)

"Be careful what you say to Martin, I think he's in league with the opposition."

not in the same league as = not as good as

"Shop cakes are all right, I suppose, but they're not in the same league as the ones my mother makes."

leak

leak out = be known/revealed

"We've no idea how the news of our impending divorce leaked out, we were trying to keep it secret."

lean

lean on somebody = depend on somebody, or persuade somebody using slight pressure

"My father is marvellous, I can always lean on him if I'm in trouble."

"Bill still hasn't paid me that money he owes me; I think I'll have to lean on him a bit."

See also: bend/lean over backwards; lean/thin time.

leap

by leaps and bounds = very quickly

"Janet has grown by leaps and bounds since her eleventh birthday."

leap in the dark = action of uncertain outcome

"To many couples nowadays, marriage is a leap in the dark which all too often ends in divorce."

learn

learn something by heart = memorize something (so that it can be instantly recalled)

"In the days before electronic calculators all children had to learn their tables by heart."

learn a lesson = learn how to/not to do something (often after a mishap/ mistake)

"Leroy used to steal apples from our neighbour's orchard but he learned his lesson after being forced to stay up a tree for hours by the farmer's dog."

learn something the hard way = learn something through one's own (bitter) experience

"I learned to drive the hard way on a car with a crash gearbox ñ there were no synchromesh or automatic gearboxes when I was a lad."

learn the ropes = learn the details/ procedure of a craft/undertaking

"It is your first day here but you'll soon learn the ropes if you watch the others closely."

you live and learn = one learns through experience

"I tried to take a short cut through the back streets and got hopelessly lost. Oh well, you live and learn ñ I should have stayed on the main road."

lease

new lease of life = opportunity for an extra period of active/useful life

"Repairing the rust and repainting my car has given it a new lease of life."

leash

straining at the leash = eager/impatient

"The photographers were straining at

the leash to take photographs of the Miss World contestants."

least

in the least = at all

"The children were not in the least impressed at my attempts to build a snowman."

least of all = particularly not

"I don't take kindly to bigots ñ least of all religious bigots."

least said, soonest mended/the least said the better = saying as little as possible is the best policy in a difficult situation

"We had a bitter argument and although I still thought I was right, I decided that least said, soonest mended and changed the subject."

not least = particularly

"The whole meal was excellent, not least the fresh strawberries they served for dessert."

to say the least = without overstatement

"When I returned the ring she had lost, she was grateful to say the least."

leather

hell for leather = as fast as possible

"We heard the bus coming as we approached the corner so we ran hell for leather and just caught it."

leave

beg one's leave of somebody = ask somebody if one might leave

"I'm afraid I must beg my leave of you now if I'm to be in time to catch the last bus home."

leave a lot/much to be desired = be undesirable/unsatisfactory

"The cottage is very old and the sanitary arrangements leave a lot to be desired."

leave a nasty taste in one's mouth = leave one with feelings of bitterness/ regret

"We finally settled our differences, but some of the things she had said left a nasty taste in my mouth."

leave in the lurch = abandon

"We were having a meal when he met some of his old friends and went off with them, leaving me in the lurch to pay the bill."

leave it at that = say no more (about something)

"We have both had our say so let's leave it at that."

leave it out! = don't do/say that!

"Leave it out! You cant have got here from London in less than an hour."

leave no stone unturned = make a (very) thorough search

"The police say they will leave no stone unturned until they find the murderer and his accomplice."

leave of absence = permission not to attend/be present

"Jones has asked for a week's leave of absence to go to see his sick father in America."

leave off = stop

"We leave off work early at half past four on a Friday."

"Leave off! You'll break it if you're not careful!"

leave one cold = not affect/impress one

"I used to like him as a singer but his new record leaves me cold."

leave oneself wide open = be vulnerable/ have no defence

"I thought I had explained away the discrepancy but he had the actual figures and so I left myself wide open to a charge of telling lies."

leave out = omit

"Say that again, but this time leave out the swear words."

leave over = stop, or postpone
"Leave over, you're hurting me!"
"We'll never finish the job tonight so we'll have to leave part of it over until tomorrow."

leave somebody at the post = leave somebody way behind
"Lester left everybody at the post when it came to learning the new techniques."

leave somebody to it = let somebody continue on his/her own
"You obviously don't need any help so I'll leave you to it."

leave standing = be superior to
"Marilyn is a pretty girl but the new barmaid at our local pub leaves her standing."

leave well alone = avoid/make no change
"She's in one of her moods; I'd leave well alone, if I were you."
"These machines can be temperamental and the secret is, once they're running smoothly, leave well alone."

leave word = leave a message
"John was here earlier and he left word that he'll be at the club from nine o'clock onwards."

take it or leave it = please yourself, or you can have it only under these conditions
"I'm sorry you don't like eating fish but that's all there is ñ you must take it or leave it."
"The price for the car is ten pounds; so make up your mind ñ take it or leave it."

take leave of one's senses = go (slightly) mad
"If you paid a hundred pounds for that dress you must have taken leave of your senses!"

without so much as a by your leave = without comment/permission
"She stormed in, grabbed her books and stormed out again without so much as a by your leave."

See also: leave somebody to his/her own devices; leave the door open; left holding the baby; left on the shelf; take French leave.

leech

cling/stick like a leech = remain adhered/very close to
"My son has a new puppy and it clings to him like a leech wherever he goes."
"This new adhesive plaster sticks like a leech."

leeway

make up leeway = regain lost distance/time
"We must make up quite a lot of leeway if we're to finish the job on schedule."

left

have two left feet = move clumsily
"I never learned to dance because I've got two left feet."

left, right and centre = in large quantities and in all directions
"Colin was slightly drunk and hurling insults left, right and centre."

leg

find/get one's sea legs = become accustomed to travelling on a boat/ship
"It was a bit choppy on the cruise but I was all right once I found my sea legs."

give a leg up = help somebody to reach a higher level

"Give me a leg up and I'll climb over the wall."

"Clive's father gave him a considerable leg up when he appointed him a director of the family firm."

have no/not enough legs = not be going fast enough (to reach a particular place)

"The golfer putted the ball in exactly the right direction but it hadn't enough legs to reach the hole."

leg it = run away/fast

"We heard a police patrol approaching so we had to leg it."

leg-pull = prank/joke

"Just for a leg-pull, let's tell Arthur we've all got to work on Christmas Day."

not have a leg to stand on = have no excuse/justification for one's actions/ views

"Once the police proved that I had confused my whereabouts on the two dates, I hadn't a leg to stand on."

pull somebody's leg = jokingly try to lie to somebody

"You're pulling my leg; I haven't really got a big spider crawling up my back, have I?"

shake a leg! = hurry up!

"Shake a leg! We won't get back before dark if we don't hurry."

show a leg! = wake up!

"Show a leg! It's time you were all up and about ñ breakfast is in five minute's time."

stretch one's legs = go for a walk (after a time of inactivity)

"I've been sitting at this desk for over five hours; I think I'll just go outside and stretch my legs."

walk somebody off his/her legs = make somebody walk farther than he/she can go without becoming (very) tired

"I took the children to the zoo and they walked me off my legs."

See also: cost an arm and a leg; on one's last legs; talk the hind leg off a donkey; with one's tail between one's legs.

leisure

at one's leisure = when one has time

"I'd like to see you in my office but there's no hurry ñ call in at your leisure."

lemon

See: the answer's a lemon.

lend

lend itself to = be usable on

"I like this black dress, it lends itself to almost any occasion."

lend one's name to = allow one's name to be associated with something

"The proposal will get a better reception if we can find somebody important to lend his name to it."

See also: give/lend a (helping) hand; lend an ear.

length

at (great) length = for a long time/in detail

"The Chairman spoke at great length about the change in the company's fortunes over the last year."

"He explained at length why we hadn't made a profit."

go to any lengths = do anything (regardless of the consequences)

"She said she would go to any lengths to get her children back."

See also: keep/hold at arm's length.

leopard

a leopard never changes its spots = somebody's basic nature cannot be changed
"Christine has twice been fined for stealing so I would be very cautious about employing her ñ remember, a leopard never changes its spots."

lesson

let that be a lesson (to you) = learn from your (recent) mistake
"Let that be a lesson to you. Never trust anyone who offers you something for nothing."

object lesson = classic/clear example
"Their faultless performance was an object lesson in how to dance the tango."

teach somebody a lesson = reprimand/punish somebody in order to discourage bad behaviour
"You do that again and I'll teach you a lesson you'll never forget!"

let

let alone = not including
"There were two hundred adults there, let alone the children."

let blood = injure/wound
"The challenger seemed to be out-classed, although he was the first to let blood."

let-down = disappointment
"The star attraction didn't turn up and the whole show was a big let-down."

let drop/fall/slip = (accidentally) reveal
"I was talking to the boss and she let drop that there are going to be some major changes around here."

let fly = speak out angrily
"When he called her stupid she really let fly at him."

let off = (allow to) explode
"Terrorists let off a car bomb in a crowded shopping centre."

let off steam = give vent to pent up feelings (in angry words/vigorous activity)
"Whenever I become frustrated I let off steam with a hard game of squash."

let on = disclose (a secret)
"I hear they're going to throw a surprise party for Gill, but don't let on."

let oneself go = take no trouble about one's appearance, or behave without restraint
"It's all too easy to let yourself go when you're old and live on your own."
"Come on, it's your birthday; why don't you let yourself go for once?"

let out = allow somebody/something to escape/leave
"Have you let the cat out?"
"Harry won't be let out of prison for at least six years."

let somebody down = disappoint somebody/fail to keep an appointment/promise
"I'm sorry to let you down but I can't come tomorrow after all."

let somebody have it = make a vigorous attack on somebody
"If he doesn't stop nagging soon I'll really let him have it!"

let somebody in = allow somebody to enter
"Let me in! It's freezing out here!"

let somebody in for something = cause somebody to become involved in difficulty/unpleasantness
"The supervisor has let Mary in for a hard time by transferring her to the night shift."

let somebody in on something = share

something (a secret/undertaking) with somebody
"I've only let you in on the plans, and nobody else, so please don't tell anybody else."

let somebody loose on = allow somebody a free hand (to do as he/she wishes)
"I let that new hairdresser loose on my hair and look what she did!"

let somebody off = waive a punishment
"The police stopped Mike for speeding but let him off with a caution."

let something (well) alone = avoid changing something
"That dog looks vicious; I should let it alone, if I were you."

let something pass = allow something to be said/occur without comment
"I overheard what you said about my new outfit, but I'll let it pass."

let something slide = allow something to become late/worse
"Roy has really let his business slide since he's taken an interest in hang gliding and vintage cars."

let up = diminish
"I wish this rain would let up and then we could go for a drive."

See also: blood letting; let bygones be bygones; let one's hair down; let sleeping dogs lie; let the cat out of the bag; not let the grass grow under one's feet; let something rip.

letter

French letter = condom, contraceptive sheath
"They say that wearing a French letter is the best defence against catching AIDS."

to the letter = exactly
"You must follow the directions to the letter whenever you take any kind of medicine."

within the letter of the law = exactly in accordance with written instructions/ regulations (if not necessarily the spirit of them)
"We have completed the contract within the letter of the law, although we could do a slightly better job if we had more time."

See also: red letter day; man of letters.

level

find its own level = settle at its natural position/rank
"With a mixed age group of children to teach, it is often best to let them find their own level to start with."

keep a level head = remain calm/sensible
"You can always rely on Flavia to keep a level head when everybody else is panicking."

level pegging = having equal ability/ score
"After four sets and ten games in the final set the two players are still level pegging."

on the level = fair/honest
"I shouldn't do business with Dennis unless you think he's on the level."

See also: do one's (level) best.

liberty

take liberties = behave with a lack of respect
"Our boss will come and have a drink with the staff occasionally but he doesn't like anyone taking liberties."

take the liberty = do something without permission
"I took the liberty of putting your milk in my fridge while you were out because it was standing in full sunshine."

licence

licence to print money = very profitable venture
"He says he'll pay me ten pounds an hour whether or not I can fix his machines; it's a licence to print money."

lick

lick and a promise = quick (cursory) wash
"Hurry up, a lick and a promise will do because you had a bath only an hour ago."

lick one's wounds = comfort oneself (immediately) after suffering discomfort/pain
"I was bitterly disappointed not to get that job but I suppose I'll be all right once I've licked my wounds."

lick something into shape = make something better/more perfect
"That new trainer should soon lick our team into shape."

See also: lick somebody's boots/shoes; lick/smack one's lips.

lid

blow/lift/take the lid off = disclose
"The Sunday newspaper's campaign has finally taken the lid off corruption on the Oxbridge council."

flip one's lid = go mad (with anger)
"When I saw what they had done I nearly flipped my lid."

put the (tin) lid/hat on = bring something to an end (in an unpleasant way)
"It started to pour with rain, and that put the lid on any more cricket for the day."

lie

give the lie to = expose/prove wrong
"His table manners surely give the lie to his claim that he went to a good school."

lie at one's door = one is responsible/to blame
"I'm afraid the typing errors must lie at my door."

lie doggo/low = remain hidden/quiet
"After the bank robbery, the thieves laid low for several months and resisted the temptation to spend any of the stolen money."

lie in/through one's teeth = lie blatantly
"Len was lying in his teeth when he said he was at home ill yesterday, because I saw him in the pub at lunchtime drinking with his mates."

lie in wait = ambush/wait in order to make an attack
"The only way to catch our chairman is to lie in wait for him as he leaves one of his interminable meetings."

lie of the land = particulars of a given situation
"Let's wait and see the lie of the land before we commit to any action."

lie up = hide
"The police are after us, so let's lie up in your mother's country cottage for a couple of weeks."

live a lie = pursue a dishonest/false way of life
"I really dislike my job but I have to pretend to enjoy it; what I hate even more is having to live a lie."

take something lying down = accept something without argument/protest
"They're trying to say I didn't do my job properly, but I'm not going to take it lying down."

thumping/whacking/whopping great lie = big lie
"It turns out that Jerry's stories of his

exploits as a fighter pilot in the RAF during the last war are a whopping great lie ñ he was really a cook in the infantry."

white lie = lie told for convenience/to avoid hurting somebody's feelings
"My mother asked me how I liked this hideous new hat she had bought, so I told a white lie and said I thought it was fine."

See also: bare-faced lie; let sleeping dogs lie; make one's bed and (must) lie in it; pack of lies.

life

as large as life = present in person
"I thought Gloria had gone to America but I saw her yesterday, large as life, standing at the bus stop."

breath of life = something that enlivens/invigorates
"Glen's antics were the only breath of life in an otherwise very boring party."

breathe life into = enliven/invigorate
"The company has been moribund for a time, but perhaps the new managing director will be able to breathe some life into it."

come to life = come alive (of something non-living), or come awake (of somebody sleeping/unconscious)
"I enjoyed the sequence in the film where the boy was playing with model soldiers when suddenly they all came alive and started running across the table."
"I don't really come alive in the mornings until I've had a cup of tea."

depart this life = die
"Aunt Agatha has been very ill for a year and I don't think it will be long before she departs this life."

for dear life = very quickly (in

"When we saw the bull coming, we all ran for dear life."

for the life of one = emphasizes one's inability to do something (even if one's life depended on it)
"I can't for the life of me think where I left my umbrella"

have/lead a charmed life = have continuing good luck
"Tina fell off her bike yet again, but she seems to lead a charmed life and wasn't seriously hurt."

have the time of one's life = have a very enjoyable time
"We had the time of our lives at the disco last night."

high life = luxurious lifestyle
"We went on a cruise and lived the high life for two whole weeks."

larger than life = exaggerated
"Everything Janice wears is larger than life: hats with wide brims, long pendant earrings and shoes with six-inch heels."

lay down one's life = sacrifice one's life (for the sake of others)
"I think it is obscene that so many of the country's young men had to lay down their lives in the War."

life and soul = with total commitment
"I shall love her life and soul for ever."

life and soul of the party = somebody who is (ostentatiously) amusing/jolly
"Ric has a good fund of jokes and is usually the life and soul of the party."

life of Reilly/Riley = life without trouble/worry
"He inherited a great deal of money from his father and has been living the life of Riley ever since."

low life = criminal/disreputable people
"I don't want you hanging about with

matter of life and/or death = something that is critical/very urgent
"Please may I use your telephone ñ it's a matter of life or death."

new lease of life = opportunity for a better/longer life
"The appointment of some younger men to the board of directors has given our firm a new lease of life."

not on your life! = definitely not!
"Not on your life! You won't get me up in an aeroplane."

prime of (one's) life = age of maximum ability/fitness
"Don't worry about your fortieth birthday, Arthur, you're still in the prime of your life."

risk life and limb = endanger oneself (physically)
"Be careful. You risk life and limb every time you go out on that motorbike."

run for one's life = run as fast as possible
"Run for your life! Teacher's coming!"

See life = experience how other people live
"I want to see life before I retire so I'm taking some trips to Africa and Asia."

take one's life in one's hands = take a (grave) risk
"You take your life in your hands if you ride in that old car of his ñ the brakes are practically non-existent."

take one's own life = commit suicide
"I can't bear the pain any longer; if it continues I'm going to take my own life."

that's life! = that is the way things generally occur!
"Jeremy got the job because he was the chairman's son and not because he was the best applicant, but that's life!"

there's life in the old dog yet = I/he may be elderly, but I'm/he's still active and alert
"Jim's nearly seventy and he has just married a girl of twenty- five, so there's obviously life in the old dog yet!"

throw a lifeline to somebody = help somebody in (financial) difficulty
"I was getting deeper in debt but my father-in-law threw me a lifeline and lent some money until my financial situation improved."

time of one's life = very enjoyable time
"You should have come on the outing to Ramsgate ñ we had the time of our lives."

to save one's life = even if one's life depended on it
"I couldn't walk along that cliff path to save my life."

to the life = exactly resembling
"Is that your brother? He's you to the life."

true to life = real/closely resembling actuality
"The new portrait of Michelle is certainly true to life, even down to her numerous warts and wrinkles."

walk of life = occupation/social background
"Our social club includes people from all walks of life."

where there's life there's hope = while it is even remotely possible for an improvement in a difficult situation, do not despair
"You still need to raise another thousand pounds for the appeal before tomorrow's deadline, but don't give up yet ñ while there's life there's hope."

you (can) bet your life = certainly/surely
"You can bet your life I'll be there tomorrow."

See also: autumn of one's life; facts of

life; lead a cat and dog's life; lead a charmed life; lead a dog's life; lead a double life; seamy side of life; staff of life; variety is the spice of life.

lift

lift one's hand against = threaten (to hit somebody)
"My father was very strict but he never lifted his hand against me."

lift one's spirits = make one cheerful
"I was feeling depressed until your friendly letter arrived and lifted my spirits."

thumb a lift = signal passing vehicles for a free ride
"If we miss the last train we can always thumb a lift home."

See also: blow/lift/take the lid off; lift/stir a finger; left/bend the elbows.

light

according to one's lights = according to one's point of view
"The reintroduction of capital punishment should be made the subject of a referendum so that each person can vote according to his or her lights."

bright lights = show business and its attractions
"Let's go up to London and see the bright lights."

bring to light = discover/reveal
"The investigation into the company's affairs brought to light evidence of malpractice."

cold light of day = time when something is considered calmly/unemotionally
"We were all enthusiastic at the last meeting but the plan we devised doesn't look so attractive in the cold light of day."

come to light = emerge/be revealed
"It has come to light that somebody has been putting sugar in the headmaster's petrol tank."

give the green light to = formally authorize
"The council has given the green light to the plan to build a new maternity hospital."

go out like a light = suddenly fall asleep/unconscious
"I took two sleeping tablets and went out like a light."

hide one's light under a bushel = fail to reveal one's ability/skill
"Don tends to hide his light under a bushel; he used to play cricket for his county but he didn't volunteer for the works team."

in a bad/good light = unfavourably/favourably
"The misbehaviour of a few makes the whole group appear in a bad light."

in its/one's true light = as it/one actually is
"The minister is to appear on television to refute the story and put the matter in its true light."

in the cold light of dawn/day = when considered calmly/practically
"The plan we were all so enthusiastic about seems less attractive when viewed in the cold light of day."

in the light of = considering (information available)
"Accounting and banking have changed dramatically in the light of recent developments in computers."

light as a feather = very light
"The new racing bicycles are as light as a feather."

lighter side = less serious aspect
"There will be a talk about animal conservation and, on the lighter side, a Tom and Jerry cartoon."

light-fingered = with a tendency to steal
"Make sure you put your things away at night; some people round here are light-fingered."

light-footed = agile/nimble
"For a big man David is remarkably light-footed and an excellent dancer."

light of one's life = person whom one most admires/loves
"Tina was the light of my life ñ I don't know what I'll do now she's left me."

light upon = discover
"I was wandering through the back streets when I happened to light upon a small antique shop with some fascinating old books for sale."

make light of = regard/treat as unimportant
"Some of her remarks were quite hurtful but I decided to make light of them rather than embarrass the other people present."

make light work of = do/fulfil something with ease
"If we all help we'll soon make light work of the washing up."

red light district = part of a town that caters for sexual pleasures
"Enjoy your weekend in London but be careful in the red light district!"

see the light (of day) = happen, or accept/realize (the merit of something)
"There was a scheme for using windmills to generate electricity, but it didn't see the light of day."
"John used to be a heavy smoker but he finally saw the light and gave up smoking six months ago."

see the light at the end of the tunnel = have the end of an undertaking in sight
"We've still not finished the project, although at least we can see the light at the end of the tunnel."

see the red light = anticipate approaching danger
"I was going to criticize her work but I saw the red light and said nothing before she complained that she was given inadequate instruction."

shed/throw light on = explain/make clear
"Can anyone shed any light on how this stain came to be on the new carpet?"

shoot the (traffic) lights = drive past traffic lights when they are red
"Barry was driving too fast to stop and he shot the lights, but fortunately nothing was coming."

strike a light! = exclamation of surprise
"Strike a light! You're not going to eat all that, are you?"

See also: all sweetness and light; many hands make light work.

lighting

lightning strike = sudden bold attack
"The commandos made a lightning strike behind enemy lines and destroyed the radar station."

like greased/a streak of lightning = very quickly
"When I asked for some help with the washing up, the children all left the room like a streak of lightning."

like

I'd like to see (somebody do something) = I would be surprised if
"You criticize the performance of our athletes, but I'd like to see you run a mile in under four minutes."

if you like = if it pleases/suits you
"I'll come round and see you this evening, if you like."

I like that! = exclamation of anger/surprise
"My daughter calls me mean. I like

that! I give her ten pounds p›cket money every week!"

like anything/billy-o/blazes/crazy/mad/the clappers = very fiercely/quickly
"We can't go out yet, it's raining like billy-o."
"Terry ran like the clappers to catch the bus."

likely enough = probably
"I'll go tomorrow, likely enough, as long as it doesn't rain."

like it's going out of fashion = without restraint
"What's wrong with Colin? He's spending money like it's going out of fashion."

like-minded = of the same inclination/opinion
"We could go to the theatre this evening, if you're like-minded."

nothing like = bear no resemblance to
"That drawing is nothing like a horse ñ it looks more like a dog with a mane."

not likely! = definitely not!
"Go swimming in this weather? Not likely!"

that's more like it = that's better
"You have completed the job ahead of schedule. That's more like it, you are usually late in finishing."

the like = similar things
"The box was full of needles, cottons, pins and the like."

the likes of = such people as
"The police force would never employ somebody the likes of you!"

See also: like father, like son.

likelihood

in all likelihood = probably
"I've done the accounts up to the end of November and in all likelihood the company will make a modest profit this year."

lily

lily-livered = cowardly
"Mark is too lily-livered to dive off the high board."

lily-white = pure white
"The heroine was a tall, slim blonde with lily-white skin."

See also: gild the lily.

limb

out on a limb = exposed to danger/risk (on one's own)
"Nobody would open the bidding at the auction so I decided to go out on a limb and offer one hundred pounds."

limbo

in limbo = in a state of neglect/uncertainty
"I applied for two jobs nearly a month ago but I've had replies from neither. I hope I hear from somebody soon ñ I hate being in limbo like this."

limelight

in the limelight = at the focus of (public) attention
"Now that Norman has been made a cabinet minister, he should not be surprised that he is constantly in the limelight."

limit

within limits = somewhat/to a certain extent (but not to excess)
"Yes, I don't mind giving up time to help, within limits."

the limit = as much as can be borne (and more than which is intolerable)

"I don't mind helping occasionally, but to demand all my free time is the limit."

See also: the sky's the limit.

limpet

See: cling (on) like a limpet/grim death.

line

all along the line = at every stage (in a sequence), completely
"The accused was vindicated when the evidence proved he had been telling the truth all along the line."

bring something into line = make something correspond (with others)
"I think that local transport facilities should be brought into line with the needs of the community."

come/fall into line = agree/correspond (with others)
"Young Terry keeps breaking the rules. If he doesn't fall into line he will have to be disciplined."

draw the line (at) = set a limit (beyond which one/somebody must not go)
"I like to have a laugh, but I draw the line at crude jokes told in mixed company."

end of the line = point at which something finishes
"The cancellation of the government order means the end of the line for several small companies who were relying on it to remain solvent."

fall out of line = disagree with/move away from
"The more I hear of my children's preferences in music, the more I realize how much I've fallen out of line with modern tastes."

hard lines = bad luck
"I had hard lines last week ñ two more points and I would have won the football pools."

in line ahead = (of ships) one behind the other
"The whole fleet approached port in line ahead."

in line for = have a (good) change of obtaining (something)
"My daughter has only been working at her new job for six months and already she's in line for promotion."

in line with = in agreement with
"I have ordered more materials in line with what we decided yesterday."

in somebody's line = within somebody's competence/experience
"Linda didn't want to come on the boat with us because sailing is not in her line."

in the firing line/line of fire = vulnerable (to attack)
"You'll have a different attitude now that you've been promoted to manager and you're in the firing line."

in the line of duty = within one's obligations/responsibilities
"Maria is always willing to work through the lunch break if necessary; she regards it all in the line of duty."

lay something on the line = to risk losing something, or say something with (frank) emphasis
"I dare not make such a concession because I would be laying my job on the line."
"The boss really laid it on the line and said that we must all increase our productivity."

line one's pockets = make money/profit (at somebody else's expense)
"I suspect he's only undertaken to help so that he can line his own pockets."

line up = place/stand in line, queue
"Come on, line up and collect your tickets."

"The swallows were lined up along the telephone wires."

marriage lines = marriage certificate

"A woman needs to send her marriage lines when applying for a passport."

on the lines of = resembling

"I would like to buy a new blouse on the lines of the pink one Margaret wore at the party."

read between the lines = extract a meaning that is not explicitly stated

"Jan says the job is all right, but reading between the lines I don't think she's particularly happy with it."

shoot a line = give an exaggerated account (about oneself)

"Graham is always shooting a line about his conquests with women, but in fact he's a happily married man."

stand in line = queue, wait one's turn

"There were so many people at the reception, we had to stand in line to get a drink."

step out of line = fail to behave in the accepted/required way

"Bill stepped out of line a couple of times at work and now they've told him to look for another job."

take the line of least resistance = adopt a course of action that causes the least difficulty/trouble

"The client wanted to make yet more changes to the proposal, so we decided to take the line of least resistance and incorporate all of them without protest."

toe the line = conform/obey the rules

"I've told my children they must toe the line with regard to house rules or lose some of the freedom they presently enjoy."

See also: drop a line; end of the line/road; in one's line of country; off/on line; sign on the dotted line; story line.

linen

wash one's dirty linen in public = have an open disagreement/discussion about private difficulties

"Bringing an action for defamation may result in having to wash one's dirty linen in public."

lion

as brave as a lion = very brave

"My young daughter is as brave as a lion and will tackle any of the boys in rough-and-tumble games."

beard the lion in his den = face up to somebody in authority/power in his/her own environment

"I must beard the lion in his den and go and ask the boss for a day off next week."

lion-hunter = somebody who seeks the friendship of famous people

"Mervin is a typical lion-hunter; he gets himself invited to publishers' parties so that he can meet all the top authors."

lion's share = biggest part

"There were three of us helping but I found myself doing the lion's share of the work."

put one's head in the lion's mouth = adopt a position that is dangerous/risky

"I'll have to put my head in the lion's mouth and ask my husband if I can go to the hen party on the evening before Dora's wedding."

throw somebody to the lions = endanger somebody (to save oneself)

"The supervisor has given me extra responsibility, but warned me that if I make a mistake she'll throw me to the lions."

twist the lion's tail = defy Britain or its policies

"France seems to use many EU meetings just to twist the lion's tail."
See also: lion's den.

lip

curl one's lip = make a scornful facial expression
"I showed Tony my latest painting but he just curled his lip and said a child could do better."
give somebody lip = be cheeky
"Just do as I say ñ and don't give me any of your lip."
lick/smack one's lips = look forward to something eagerly
"I can't wait to go on holiday ñ just the thought of all those bronzed handsome men makes me lick my lips."
my lips are sealed = I will not tell anybody
"The truth about your murky past is safe with me ñ my lips are sealed."
pay lip service to = pretend to agree to something with no intention of doing it
"The machinists only pay lip service to safety regulations and one day soon there is going to be a nasty accident."
See also: bite one's lip; keep a stiff upper lip.

list

black list = list of companies/people who are (regarded as) dishonest/ untrustworthy
"We keep a black list of people who don't pay their bills and make sure we do not supply anything else to them."
enter the lists = take part in a contest
"I had to enter the lists because nobody else would state the case for our side in the dispute."
short list = list of (comparatively) few items/people, selected from a longer list, from which a final choice is made
"I still don't know which car to buy but I've got it down to a short list of three."

litter

litter bug = somebody who drops litter (in a public place)
"The council has to employ somebody to go round the park clearing up after the litter bugs."

little

little by little = gradually
"I found chess difficult at first but now my game is improving little by little."
think little of = have a poor opinion of
"Maria thought little of the exhibition, but Joan said it was marvellous."
See also: a little bird told me; little things please little minds.

live

live and learn = learn by (bitter) experience
"I bought a second-hand sewing machine and then had to pay out lots of money to replace many worn parts. You live and learn ñ it would have been cheaper to buy a new one!"
live and let live = be unconcerned what other people do, as long as they tolerate what one does oneself
"We get on well with our next- door neighbours ñ it's a case of live and let live."
live by one's wits = survive using cunning/one's mental ability (rather than, for example, by hard work)
"I couldn't get a permanent job so I had to live by my wits for a couple of years."

live from hand to mouth = to have only sufficient for one's immediate needs, with nothing for the future
"After my husband was made redundant, we had to live from hand to mouth until he found another job."

live in sin = live together as man and wife without being married
"Living in sin is no longer the social stigma it once was."

live it up = enjoy oneself (through excessive spending/indulgence)
"We always take plenty of money on holiday so that we can live it up for at least two weeks in the year."

live on one's reputation = succeed because of former achievements (without making new efforts)
"Vincent lives on his reputation these days; he doesn't go out seeking new business, it comes to him."

live rough = live in difficult conditions (with few/no amenities)
"We trekked through the jungle and had to live rough for ten days before we returned to camp."

live something down = lead a normal life until a misdeed is forgotten
"It is now three years since I got drunk at a party but my wife still won't let me live it down."

live to tell the tale = survive
"They must have been lost in the jungle for days, but unfortunately nobody lived to tell the tale."

live up to = equal a (good) example set by somebody else
"Lloyd will not be accepted as an individual until he stops trying to live up to his father's reputation."

live wire = somebody who is energetic/ enthusiastic
"Wendy is the real live wire of the department who motivates all the others who work with her."

live with = endure (something unpleasant)
"I injured a child through bad driving and I'll have to live with that fact for the rest of my life."

within/in living memory = within the lifetime of people still alive
"There has been some freak weather this year. It snowed in September for the first time in living memory."

See also: do something/live in style; live beyond/within one's means; live like a lord; live like fighting cocks; live off the fat of the land.

lively

See: chirpy/lively as a cricket

lo

lo and behold = exclamation of surprise (when somebody/something suddenly appears)
"I asked the car breaker if he had a fuel pump for a 1967 Morris Minor and lo and behold he produced one immediately."

load

a load off one's mind = relief from a worry
"I've finally paid all the income tax I owed, and that was a load off my mind."

get a load of = pay (particular) attention to
"Here comes Hal. Get a load of his new suit!"

loaded question = question inviting an answer that discredits the speaker
"The minister survived the press conference despite the fact that the journalists kept asking him loaded questions."

what a load of cobblers/rubbish! = what nonsense!

"William claims he's been climbing in the Andes. What a load of rubbish! He's never been farther than Calais."

See also: the dice are loaded.

loaf

use one's loaf = use one's common sense

"Use your loaf. You 'll never get that piano upstairs without taking the legs off."

See also: half a loaf is better than none/no bread (at all).

local

local colour = detailed information that indicates an intimate knowledge of a place

"We can write a general description using any of the guide books to the place, but we shall have to send a reporter there if we want to include some local colour."

local pub = one's nearest/regular public house

"They have ruined our local pub by installing snooker tables and video juke boxes."

See also: local rag.

lock

behind locked doors = in secret

"After the disruption caused by hecklers, the council decided to meet behind locked doors in future."

lock, stock and barrel = completely

"We sold the house and furniture, lock stock and barrel, and went to live in a caravan."

under lock and key = in a locked building/container/room

"The judge said that the convicted criminal was a danger to society and should be kept under lock and key for the rest of his life."

See also: lock the stable door after the horse has bolted.

locker

See: Davy Jones' locker.

locusts

swarm like locusts = crowd round greedily

"As soon as the food appeared all the children swarmed round like locusts."

log

See: as easy as falling off a log; sleep like a log/top.

loggerheads

be at loggerheads = disagree

"The management and unions are at loggerheads and unless they can resolve their differences there will probably be a strike."

logic

stand logic on its head = be illogical

"You can't try ski-jumping before you learn to ski ñ that's standing logic on its head."

loins

See: gird up one's loins

lollipop

lollipop lady/man/woman = somebody who is employed to control traffic where children cross the road (to and from school)

"We bought a card for our lollipop lady because it's her birthday today, and she was very pleased."

lone

lone wolf = somebody who shuns the company of others
"Glen is a lone wolf and seldom joins in the activities of the neighbourhood."

long

go a long way towards = be nearly enough for/to
"The donation from the local brewery will go a long way towards financing our anti-drink/driving campaign."

have/pull a long face = look in a disapproving/unhappy manner
"There's no need to pull a long face, you'll be seeing him again next week."

in the long run = eventually
"You can win a few pounds in a fruit machine occasionally but you always lose in the long run if you keep playing them."

long drawn out = extended (in time)
"The chairman gave this long drawn out speech about how the company is going to fight the recession."

long in the tooth = old
"Isn't Hilda a bit long in the tooth to be wearing that low-cut dress?"

long odds = a remote chance
"We have put in a bid for a government contract, but looking at the competition there are long odds on our getting it."

long shot = a guess
"They asked me the name of the inventor of dynamite. I said Nobel ñ it was a long shot, but happened to be true."

long-standing = existing for a long time
"Britain has a long-standing treaty with Portugal about mutual defence."

long-suffering = very tolerant
"Andrew can be very bad-tempered at times; my sympathy is for his long-suffering wife."

long-term = lasting for a long time
"I know you are going to take this temporary job for the summer, but what are your long-term plans?"

long-winded = boringly long (of a speaker/speech)
"I wish Mike would stop telling those long-winded jokes ñ they're seldom funny anyway."

not long for this world = on the point of death
"If those puppies keep barking like that they'll not be long for this world."

the long and (the) short of it = an abbreviated account
"We had a lot of trouble with the car and traffic, and the long and the short of it is we were six hours late arriving there."

See also: as broad as it's long; by a long chalk; the long arm of coincidence; the long arm of the law.

look

by the look(s) of/from the look of things = judging by appearances
"By the look of it, we shall have a fine day tomorrow."
"There has been an accident from the look of things."

look about (one) = look in all directions
"Look about for a new teapot while you're in town, please."

look after somebody/something = take care of/tend somebody/something
"I'm afraid I won't be able to come tomorrow, I have to look after my sick daughter."

look a gift horse in the mouth = find fault with something given free
"That shirt my mother gave me is an

awful colour, but I suppose I can't look a gift horse in the mouth."

look askance at = look at disapprovingly/suspiciously
"My family looked askance when I ordered snails as a first course in the restaurant."

look at = examine
"Would you mind looking at my eye? I think I might have something in it."

look back on = remember/reminisce
"I look back on my schooldays with horror ñ I hated them!"

look bad (for somebody) = appear to indicate trouble
"Two eye witnesses have testified that they saw the accused at the scene of the crime and things are looking bad for her."

look before you leap = be cautious/take care before acting
"You've signed that hire purchase agreement and you can't really afford the repayments. You should look before you leap."

look blue = appear to be depressed/unhappy
"What's the matter, Elizabeth? You look blue this morning."

look down (up) on = regard as inferior
"I don't like the way Trevor always looks down on the efforts of the younger members of the club."

look down one's nose at = regard with contempt
"Most people who own a pedigree dog look down their noses at somebody with a mere mongrel."

look for = search
"Please go and look for some sticks to make a fire."

look forward to = anticipate (with pleasure)
"We had a pleasant evening together and I look forward to doing it again soon."

look good = look appealing/attractive
"That roast beef looks good."

look in on = pay a brief (uninvited) visit
"We happened to be in Exeter so we looked in on my sister and her family."

look into = investigate
"Some money was stolen from work and the police are looking into it."

look here! = exclamation of protest
"Look here! That's the second time you've trodden on my foot."

look like = appear probable (that)
"It looks like being a fine day tomorrow."

look lively/sharp = hurry up/be quick
"Look lively, you'll miss your bus if you don't hurry."

look out! = beware!/take care!
"Look out! There's a car coming!"

look out for = be aware/careful of, or try to find
"Look out for pickpockets when you travel on the underground."
"I always look out for bargains in these small antique shops."

look over = look at (something large)
"We're thinking of moving and we looked over a couple of nice houses at the weekend."

look sheepish = look guilty
"I don't know who did it, but Brian was the one who looked sheepish when I accused him."

look small = appear to be foolish/insignificant
"The boss has a nasty streak in him; he always tries to make other people look small."

look the other way = deliberately ignore
"I had an extra bottle of wine but the customs officer looked the other way."

look to somebody = expect/rely on somebody (to do something)
"Jenny, you ought to know better. I looked to you to set a good example to the others."

look up = visit somebody, find an entry in a (reference) book
"Look us up any time you're in town."
"I don't know how to spell the word; why don't you look it up in the dictionary?"

look up to somebody = respect somebody
"The leader of the church should be somebody you can look up to."

not get/have a look in = be excluded/ignored
"Barry handed round some of his duty-free cigarettes but I didn't get a look in."

not like the look of something = be suspicious of something
"I don't like the look of that meat; I think it's gone bad."

not much to look at = unattractive
"Our house isn't much to look at but it's very comfortable inside."

now look what you've done! = expression of rebuke
"Now look what you've done! Spilled coffee all over the floor."

one's own look-out = something that is one's sole responsibility
"If Vicky wants to go out with Jim Smith that's her own look-out!"

See also: ask/look for trouble; black look/stare; dirty look; look at/see/view things through rose-tinted spectacles; look daggers at; look/spoil for a fight; look for a needle in a haystack; look on the bright side; look/show one's age; look snappy; look the part; not as green as one is cabbage looking.

loom

loom large = approach (of something important/significant)
"The students began to panic as the day of the examination loomed large."

loophole

loophole in the law = flaw in legislation (that allows somebody to avoid being charged with breaking the law)
"Charles was charged with speeding but was acquitted because of a loophole in the law which states that the arresting officer should have been in uniform."

loose

at a loose end = idle/unoccupied
"Why don't you come and stay with us at the weekend if you're at a loose end."

cut loose = break away (from convention), or release
"I've been travelling backwards and forwards to work in an office every day for the last twenty years ñ and I'm tired of it. I'd like to cut loose and keep a small farm, or run a seaside boarding house, or anything!"
"I tied up the boat at the jetty but somebody cut it loose and it's drifting down the river."

have a screw/slate/tile loose = be (slightly) mad
"Mike has bought a job lot of four old lawn mowers, but then I always thought he had a screw loose."

keep a loose/tight rein on = allow plenty/little freedom
"My teenage daughter is very sensible and we keep only a loose rein on her."
"What the company has to do is keep a very tight rein on its spending until the financial situation improves."

loose-leaf(ed) = having pages that can be removed/replaced
"Keep your lecture notes in a loose-leaf folder so that you can add to them during the course."

loose-limbed = lithe/supple
"You have to be very loose-limbed to do gymnastics well."

loosen somebody's tongue = persuade somebody to talk
"He shouldn't have told me really but I gave him a few whiskies to loosen his tongue."

loose off = fire (bullets/words etc.)
"The silence was shattered when one of the enemy loosed off with a submachine gun."

on the loose = behave in an unrestrained manner
"My boyfriend is looking forward to going on the loose with his mates when they go to London to see the Cup Final."

play fast and loose = deceive somebody (for selfish reasons)
"Mike is playing fast and loose by going out with Jane because it is really Pamela he likes most."

tie up loose ends = complete the final details
"The deal is nearly completed, it's just a matter of tying up a few loose ends."

lord

as drunk as a lord = very drunk
"He finally got home at midnight, drunk as a lord."

live like a lord = live in luxury
"My company booked me into a five-star hotel and I lived like a lord for a week."

lord it over somebody = adopt a superior attitude to somebody
"Why does David lord it over everybody? He's no better than the rest of us."

lord knows = I do not know
"Lord knows what made you choose to wear a pink blouse with an orange skirt!"

one's lord and master = one's husband
"My lord and master will be home soon, so I suppose I should start making his supper."

lorry

fall off the back of a lorry = be stolen
"Do you want to buy a cheap watch? It fell off the back of a lorry."

lose

fight a losing battle = attempt to do something that must end in failure
"I keep trying to get Keith to tidy his room but I'm fighting a losing battle."

lose face = lose one's reputation/respect
"The difficulty is going to be how to admit the mistake without losing face."

lose ground = retreat, lose an advantage
"For several years, Britain has steadily lost ground in the markets for manufactured goods."

lose heart = become discouraged
"Don't lose heart over failing your test ñ you're sure to pass it next time."

lose one's bottle = lose one's nerve
"We're going to scrump some apples from Farmer Jones's orchard. Why won't you come with us? Lost your bottle?"

lose one's cool/rag/wool = lose one's temper
"There's no need to lose your cool just because that other driver pulled out in front of you."

lose oneself in = become engrossed in

"I like nothing better than to lose myself in a good book."

lose one's head = panic/lose control (of oneself)

"Calm down; just because you've got the first five answers wrong there's no need to lose your head."

lose one's heart = fall in love

"I lost my heart to that spaniel puppy the first time I saw it."

lose one's marbles/reason = go mad

"Poor old Bernard has started shouting at strangers in the street; he must have lost his reason."

lose one's shirt = lose all one's money (through gambling)

"I went racing at Epsom last week and lost my shirt on the first race!"

lose one's sight = become blind

"He accidentally splashed acid in his face and he may lose his sight in one eye."

lose one's touch = lose the ability/skill to do something

"Vic usually throws a double twenty first time ñ he must be losing his touch."

lose out = fail (because of a disadvantage)

"The government has raised the duty on alcoholic drinks and it's the poorer people who lose out as usual."

lose sight of = forget/fail to pay attention to

"These grand schemes are all very well, but we mustn't lose sight of the fact that somebody has to pay for them."

lose the drift/thread = fail to understand the connection between the stages in an argument

"Sorry, would you mind repeating that point, I seem to have lost the drift of the argument."

See also: keep/lose track of; lose ground; lose one's grip; lose one's hearing; lose one's voice; lose one's way; lose sleep over; lose one's nerve; lose one's tongue; lose touch (with); what you lose on the swings, you gain on the roundabouts; win/lose the toss.

loss

at a loss/lost for words = speechless (because one cannot think of anything to say)

"When Anne said she was going to get married for the third time I was at a loss for words."

be at a loss = be puzzled/undecided

"I went to the new shop to buy a blouse but they had so many to choose from I was at a complete loss."

cut one's losses = cease doing something in order to minimize one's losses

"The weather worsened and it started to rain in the early afternoon so we decided to cut our losses and return home early."

See also: dead loss.

lost

get lost! = go away!

"Get lost! Let me read this book in peace!"

lost in admiration = very favourably impressed

"Your garden looks beautiful and I'm lost in admiration for the skill it must have taken to get it like this."

lost on somebody = have no effect on somebody

"I was telling Joseph about the joys of a day's fishing but it was lost on him, he'd rather stay at home and watch television."

See also: get lost in the wash; lost cause; at a loss/lost for words.

lot

bad lot = somebody who is disreputable
"I don't want you associating with Sarah, she's a thoroughly bad lot."

cast/throw one's lot (in) with = join somebody/something and share his/her/its fortunes
"There was a group of students going north by train and I cast my lot in with them rather than travel alone."

fat lot = very little (used sarcastically)
"There is no point in trying to light the fire with wet wood ñ a fat lot of good that will do!"

have a lot going for one = have many advantages
"I hope your plan succeeds; it certainly has a lot going for it compared with all the the other proposals."

that's your lot = that is all you are getting
"No you can't have another piece of cake; that's your lot."

whole lot = many
"That knitting is no good, you've made a whole lot of mistakes; perhaps you should start again."

See also: cast lots; draw lots; fall to one's lot; leave a lot to be desired.

loud

loud and clear = very clearly/emphatically
"All right, stop nagging. I've got your message loud and clear."

See also: for crying out loud!

love

do something for love = do something without expecting payment
"No thanks. I don't want paying for painting the club house, I did it for love."

for the love of Mike/Pete = exclamation of frustration
"For the love of Pete, haven't you finished with the photocopier yet?"

labour of love = task done for pleasure (rather than financial reward)
"I like to help young people, and painting their club house was a labour of love."

love birds = (young) lovers
"Your father and I are going out now and we'll leave you two love birds alone."

love in a cottage = marriage in which there is not much money
"Ours has been love in a cottage since my husband lost his job, but at least we've had each other."

love me, love my dog = if you like somebody, you should also like his/her family/friends
"I know you don't get on well with my brother, but if I go, he's going too ñ love me, love my dog."

I must love you and leave you = I must go
"I'm afraid I must love you and leave you now if I'm to catch the last bus home."

no love lost = great dislike/hatred
"There's no love lost between my parents and I wasn't surprised when they told me they are getting divorced."

not for love or money = not for any reward
"You wouldn't get me up in an aeroplane for love or money."

Platonic love = spiritual (non-sexual) love
"I often go out with Cynthia but it's purely Platonic love between us."

See also: all's fair in love and war; calf/

low

at (a) low ebb = at a low level
"My finances were at a low ebb so I stayed at home for several evenings rather than go to the pub."

be/get low on something = be nearly without (enough of) something
"We're getting low on typing paper, we had better order some more."

in low spirits = depressed
"Marilyn has been in low spirits ever since her mother died."

keep a low profile = (try to) remain inconspicuous
"You are new to the job so I'd keep a low profile if I were you until you become used to things here."

lay low = make ill (enough to have to stay in bed)
"Terry has been laid low with glandular fever for nearly a month now."

lie low = hide (and remain quiet)
"I think we had better lie low for a while until the Jones gang stops looking for us."

luck

as luck would have it = fortunately/luckily
"I missed the bus but as luck would have it another one came along almost immediately."

better luck next time = I hope you are more successful at your next attempt
"I'm sorry the cake you baked turned out a flop; never mind, better luck next time."

down on one's luck = suffering from misfortune/lack of money
"Can you let me have twenty pence for a cup of tea, Mister, I've been down on my luck lately."

hard/tough luck = bad luck/misfortune
"That was tough luck. Another six points and you would have beaten the club record."

hard-luck story = account of misfortune (to the teller), often to gain sympathy (and usually untrue)
"I asked Tony why he was late to work and he told me some hard-luck story about having to take his mother's ageing pet poodle to the vet because it had swallowed a chicken bone."

just one's luck = one's characteristic misfortune
"Just my luck! Three brothers to choose from and I pick the stupid one!"

luck of the devil/the Irish, *or the devil's own luck* = very good (although undeserved) luck
"Ursula has the luck of the devil. There were two hundred applicants for one place on the course so they put all the names in a hat ñ and hers was the one that was chosen."

luck of the draw = as things happen
"I have to work on Saturday three weeks running, but that's the luck of the draw."

lucky dip = choice over which one has no control
"There are three secondary schools in the town but the choice for any particular child starting at one seems to be entirely a matter of lucky dip."

no such luck = no (unfortunately)
"I sent in a correct set of answers to the quiz, but was mine one of the ones chosen? No such luck!"

push one's luck = risk a success by trying too hard to gain/profit even more
"The boss has given us a rise and an extra week's holiday each year and now you want shorter working hours

as well ñ that's really pushing your luck."

run of luck = succession of fortunate occurrences
"I won a small prize on the football pools every Saturday last month, but I broke my run of luck this week by getting absolutely nothing."

strike (it) lucky = be very fortunate (in a particular instance)
"The hotel we stayed in was excellent ñ we struck it lucky there."

take pot luck = take a chance (in a situation where there has been no preparation for one's involvement/participation)
"Why don't you and Sylvia come over to our place for the day tomorrow, although you'll have to take pot luck because I haven't told my wife that you are coming."

thank one's lucky stars = be grateful for good fortune
"You can thank your lucky stars I didn't know about it before, or I would have stopped you doing it."

try one's luck = attempt to do something (which may/may not succeed)/take a chance
"I became bored with cycling as a hobby so I thought I'd try my luck at skin diving."

with any luck = hopefully
"Bill is coming to my party and with any luck he'll bring his pretty sister with him."

worse luck = unfortunately
"We were going to visit my wife's mother on Sunday but now I find that I have to work this weekend, worse luck."

you'll be lucky = you will be fortunate (ironically)
"You'll be lucky if the bank manager agrees to extending your overdraft."

you never know your luck (unless you try) = you may be fortunate
"See that girl in the red skirt ñ why don't you ask her for a dance? You never know your luck."

you should be so lucky! = why should you be so fortunate!
"You thought you could find a taxi at this time of night? You should be so lucky!"

See also: *bad/lucky* break; lucky dog.

lull

lull somebody into a false sense of security = mislead somebody into thinking that the situation is satisfactory, in order to gain a surprise advantage
"The boss has been so pleasant lately, I wonder if he's just trying to lull us into a false sense of security before springing a nasty surprise."

lump

bring a lump to one's throat = cause one to feel deep pity/sympathy
"Those pictures of starving African children brought a lump to my throat."

if you don't like it, you can lump it = you must accept the situation whether you like it or not
"I am going to paint your bedroom pink, Tarquin, and if you don't like it, you can lump it."

lump sum = single payment (instead of a series of smaller payments)
"I decided to pay off the debt with a lump sum, rather than let the arrangement continue for the six months it still had to run."

lump together = put several (different) things into one category/group

"There are spades, forks, rakes, hoes and so on, but they can all be lumped together as garden tools."

lunatic
See: lunatic fringe.

lurch
leave somebody in the lurch = abandon somebody who is in difficulty
"Just when the company was coming into profit the principal backers withdrew their support and left the firm in the lurch."

luxury
See: in the lap of luxury.

lynx
lynx-eyed = with very keen eyesight
"You have to make sure that the unit is assembled perfectly because it has to get past the lynx-eyed scrutiny of the inspection department."

M

machine

See: cog in the machine.

mackerel

mackerel sky = thin, mottled clouds in rows

"A mackerel sky is a sure sign of rain to come."

sprat to catch a mackerel = small risk to make a large gain

"Every week I invest a pound on the football pools. It's a sprat to catch a mackerel because one day I could win a million."

mad

drive/send mad = annoy/frustrate/irritate

"I wish Linda wouldn't play that record so loud, it's driving me mad."

like mad = furiously/vigorously

"Was Bill late for work this morning? I saw him running like mad for the train."

mad about/on = very enthusiastic about

"It seems a long time ago now, but back in the sixties I was absolutely mad about the Beatles."

mad-cap = reckless/irresponsible

"Did you hear about that fool who's got a mad-cap idea about rowing across the Atlantic in a bathtub?"

method in one's madness = seemingly silly way of achieving something

"The vicar asked everyone to give him their old buttons, but there was method in his madness because he sold them to raise money for the organ fund."

midsummer madness = foolish behaviour (brought on by the heat of summer)

"I suppose it was midsummer madness, but the weather was glorious so I went out and bought an open sports car."

See also: hopping mad; mad as a hatter; mad as a March hare; mad moment; (stark) raving mad.

madam

little madam = precocious girl

"My niece is a right little madam the way she bosses everyone about."

made

be made for somebody/something = ideally suited to somebody/something

"George and Jill are blissfully happy together ñ they were obviously made for each other."

have it made = be (very) successful

"With Philip's qualifications he has it made for a legal career."

self-made man/woman = somebody who succeeds entirely through his/her own efforts

"He started work as a poor barrow-boy in the East End of London. Now, as a self-made man, he has several shops throughout the southern counties."

what one is made of = one's ability/worth

"Come on then, you bully, show us what you're made of."

See also: made of money; made to measure.

magic

wave one's magic wand = achieve something as if by magic

"My wife is always overspending. She seems to think I can wave my magic wand and get money out of the air."

work like magic = be very effective

"Have you tried that new stain remover? It works like magic."

magnitude
See: of the first magnitude/order/water.

magpie
chatter like a magpie = chatter incessantly
"No wonder my phone bills are so high. When my daughter talks to her friends she chatters like a magpie for hours."

maid
See: old maid.

maiden
maiden lady = unmarried woman (middle aged or elderly)
"I was surprised when I was introduced to the disco organizer, she turned out to be a maiden lady in her fifties."
maiden name = surname of a woman before she marries
"I do object to these official forms asking me to state my maiden name ñ I've been married for over forty years now."
maiden speech = first speech (of somebody who is newly appointed/elected)
"The newly elected member for Bristol is expected to make his maiden speech in the Commons today."
maiden voyage = first voyage of a plane/ship
"The Titanic struck an iceberg and sank during its maiden voyage in 1912."

main
in the main = generally/usually
"The were one or two minor scuffles on the terraces but in the main the match was played without any major crowd problems."
splice the mainbrace = have a celebratory drink
"We've won a prize on Premium Bonds so let's go out and splice the mainbrace."
with might and main = with all one's strength
"We tried with all our might and main to push the car out of the ditch but it wouldn't budge."
See also: eye on/to the main chance.

majority
attain one's majority = reach the age of legal responsibility
"Young people attain their majority at age eighteen these days ñ it used to be twenty-one."
silent majority = (apathetic) majority of people who support the prevailing situation
"The protesters make the most noise but their views have little or no effect on the silent majority."

make
be the making of somebody = bring out somebody's true character/potential
"I'm glad that Tom has joined the army ñ it will be the making of him."
have the makings of = have the potential to be
"Judging by its recent performances, that horse has the makings of a Derby winner."
in the making = in the process of becoming
"Now that Cynthia has lost her puppy fat she could be a beauty queen in the making."

make after = chase
"The white BMW was travelling at well over the speed limit and the police car made after it with its lights flashing."

make as if to (do something) = feign/pretend
"Peter turned round and made as if to hit me, and that's how I came to spill my drink."

make believe = pretend
"There's no scenery in this play and so you actors have to make believe that you're hiding in some bushes."

make do (with) = make best use of what is available
"If you had told me you were bringing somebody home for dinner I would have bought some extra food; as it is, we'll have to make do with what we've got in the fridge."

make fast = secure/tie up
"The tender drew up alongside the liner, made fast, and prepared to disembark the pa ssengers."

make for = aim at/move towards a particular place
"We'll start early and make for Bristol by lunchtime."

make inroads into = make a start/have an effect on something
"We worked for nearly a week before we had made substantial inroads into the job."

make it = succeed, or keep an appointment
"Gary has passed all his exams and finally made it as an accountant."
"We're having a party next weekend and I do hope you and Brian can make it."

make it up = recompense/make amends for, or settle one's differences
"You have been very kind looking after me while I was ill; how can I ever make it up to you?"
"Judging by what I saw, it seems my daughter and her boyfriend have made it up after their quarrel."

make it snappy = be quick
"Pack your bags and make it snappy, we leave in five minutes."

make no matter = do not matter
"It makes no matter to me whether you come or not."

make of = understand
"I don't quite know what to make of her remarks."

make off (with) = run away (with)
"The thieves made off as soon as the police arrived."

make out = cope/fare, or distinguish, or understand
"How did you make out on the first day in your new job?"
"I could just make out a strange figure walking through the fog."
"My son asked me to help him with an algebra problem but I couldn't make it out at all."

make over = bequeath
"My grandfather made over his gold watch to me in his will."

make much of = make a fuss/exaggerate
"She's making much of her daughter winning the local beauty contest ñ you would think she was Miss World!"

make off = run away
"The thieves made off when they heard the police car approaching."

make off with = steal
"The thieves made off with money and jewellery worth more than fifty thousand pounds."

make or break = crucial test (resulting in success or failure)
"The final assault on the summit was make or break for the mountaineers,

who were rapidly running out of supplies."

make so bold as = presume/take the liberty
"If I may make so bold, madam, would you grant me the honour of the next dance?"

make something (out) of it = cause an argument/fight
"So you don't like the way I dress. Do you want to make something of it?"

make something up = invent/lie
"The interviewer asked me some awkward questions and I had to make up the answers as I went along."
"My son claimed he had top marks in maths, but I suspect he was making it up."

make the grade = reach a required standard
"The company demands absolute dedication from its employees and anyone who doesn't make the grade will be asked to leave."

make the most of = take best advantage of a situation
"You had better make the most of the sunshine today because the weather forecast says it will rain tomorrow."

make up = invent, or complete
"I don't believe your excuse ñ you made it up."
"Ben only needs one more cigarette card to make up the set."

make up for something = compensate/supply a substitute for something
"I bought you some flowers to make up for not being able to take you to dinner last night."

make up to somebody = flatter/patronise somebody (for gain)
"It's no use trying to make up to me, you can't have any more pocket money this week."

on the make = trying to make a gain/profit
"Harry is always on the make, so be careful in any business dealings with him."

that makes two of us = so am I
"If you're going to work in Woolworth's that makes two of us ñ I start there next week."

what do you make of something? = what is your opinion?
"Professor, what do you make of the strange colouring on this sample?"

See also: get to/make first base; make a/the break; make a clean breast of; make a clean sweep; make a day of it; make advances to; make a dead set at; make a dent in; make a fool of somebody; make a fuss; make a fuss of; make a go of something; make a hash of; make a killing; make all the difference; make a meal of something; make a mountain out of a molehill; make a move; make a name for oneself; make an example of somebody; make an exhibition of oneself; make a night of it; make a packet; make a pass at somebody; make a play for; make a point of doing something; make a splash; make a stand; make a virtue of necessity; make believe; make demands on; make do and mend; make (both) ends meet; make (sheep's) eyes at; make faces; make free with; make friends with; make fun of; make good; make good time; make hay; make headway; make heavy weather of; make light of; make light work of; make merry; make money; make neither head nor tail of something; make no bones about it; make old bones; make one's blood boil; make one's blood run cold; make oneself at home; make oneself scarce; make one's hackles rise; make one's hair curl/stand on end; make one's head spin; make one's mark; make one's peace with somebody; make one's point; make one's presence felt; make one's way; make overtures; make play with; make room for; make short work of; make somebody's day; make somebody's flesh creep; make the best of (a bad job); make time for; make tracks; make up one's mind; make water; make way for; make waves.

maker

(go to) meet one's maker = die
"My father went to meet his maker ten years ago today."

male

male chauvinist pig = man with a domineering/superior attitude towards women
"My boss is a male chauvinist pig. He thinks that women are good only for clerical and secretarial work and would never employ one as a manager."

man

as one man/to a man = together/ unanimously
"I asked the team if they wanted a drink and as one man they said yes."
"I asked the team if they wanted a drink and they said yes to man."

be a man = act bravely/independently
"Why don't you be a man and stand up to him the next time he threatens you."

dead men = empty bottles
"After the part we had a dustbin full of dead men."

dirty old man = somebody with a morbid interest in sex
"A dirty old man in the park exposed himself to my daughter."

every man for himself = each person must take care of himself/herself
"The gang worked together on several robberies but when they were caught by the police it was every man for himself and they incriminated each other."

every man has his price = each person is willing to agree to something as long as the inducement is sufficient
"If he won't accept the appointment offer him more money ñ every man has his price."

every man to his trade = each person should keep to what he/she is best at
"I tried plastering a wall yesterday and made a total mess of it; now I'll have to call in an expert, which just proves that it is every man to his trade."

family man = married man (with children) who spends much of his time with his family
"We hardly see Victor in the pub these days; he's become a real family man since the birth of his second child."

front man = somebody employed to represent/divert approaches to those in authority
"The directors use the public relations manager as a front man to answer any questions from customers."

hit man = hired assassin
"Security was tight for the president's visit because the police had been informed that a hit man had been hired to assassinate him."

hit a man when he's down = add to the misfortune of somebody who is already unfortunate
"After his expulsion from the cabinet

the minister became the subject of a smear campaign. It seems the media and the public alike take pleasure in hitting a man when he's down."

I'm/he's your man = I am/he is the person you want
"If you want any help in the garden then I'm your man."

inner man = somebody's hunger/stomach
"I'm starving ñ let's go and satisfy the inner man."

like a man = resembling a brave/ resourceful person
"You're eighteen now and its time you started acting like a man."

make a man of = cause a youth to become mature/resourceful
"Come on, have a whisky ñ it'll make a man of you!"

man-about-town = socialite/somebody who is well known in society
"Roddy is a well-known man about town ñ you can't go to a party or night club without seeing him there."

man and boy = all one's life
"I've lived here for nearly sixty years, man and boy."

man in the street = average/typical person
"The new tax concessions are intended to encourage industrial investment and will have no direct effect on the man in the street."

man of breeding = somebody of high birth/aristocrat
"I don't know who he is but you can tell by the way he carries himself that he's a man of breeding."

man of his day = somebody who is famous among his/her contemporaries
"In the late sixties, Sir Alf Ramsey was the outstanding man of his day among football managers."

man of his word = somebody who i. honourable/trustworthy
"I stood bail for Roger because, as a man of his word, I'm sure he will turn up to stand trial."

man of iron/steel = somebody with great strength of character
"It takes a man of iron to resist some of the temptations that go with an important job like that."

man of letters = an author/writer
"Chaucer, Shakespeare, Hemmingway and Churchill were all men of letters."

man of straw = somebody who is cowardly/weak-willed
"The men who collaborated with the enemy during the occupation were regarded as traitors and men of straw by the members of the resistance."

man of the day/moment = somebody who has (short-lived) fame at a particular time
"The bus conductor became the man of the moment when he acted as midwife to a woman who gave birth to a baby on his bus."

man of the old school = somebody with traditional views
"The colonel is a man of the old school who thinks that all men should join the army and all women should learn needlework and embroidery."

man of the world = somebody with worldly experience, who has seen many aspects of life
"I can't help you but why not ask Mr Jones, he's a man of the world and should be able to advise you."

man of the year = somebody who achieves fame/notoriety in a particular year
"Neil Armstrong was man of the year in 1969 when he became the first person to walk on the Moon."

man to man = (honestly) on equal terms

"I would like to talk to you man to man about your intentions regarding my daughter."

marked man = somebody who is well known for a misdeed
"I'm a marked man. The sergeant caught me smoking on duty twice last week and if he catches me a third time I'll be on a charge."

may the best man win = I hope that the best person succeeds
"Let's make it a fair fight and may the best man win."

my good man/woman = impolite form of address made by somebody who regards himself/herself as superior
"My good man, can I have the wine list."

sandwich man = somebody who carries advertisement boards in front and behind
"In London the other day I saw a sandwich man with boards predicting that the world will end next year."

sort out the men from the boys = select the best members of a group from the rest
"The instructor said that the assault course the recruits were about to attempt was designed to sort out the men from the boys."

you can't keep a good man down = a determined person will succeed
"John broke his leg skiing last year but he's determined to try again this winter ñ you can't keep a good man down!"

white man = somebody who is honourable/trustworthy
"Thanks, Dave, for helping me sort out my problems, you're a white man."

See also: brotherhood of man; dead man's shoes; dead men tell no tales; every man Jack (of them); family man; girl/man Friday; hatchet man; lady's man; lollipop lady/man/woman; man in the Moon; man/somebody of few words; man of many parts; man of the cloth; no man's land; odd man out; old man; one-man band; one man's meat is another man's poison; one's own man; rich man's hobby; right-hand man; white man's burden.

manger
See: dog in the manger.

manna
See: manna from heaven.

manner
all manner of = all kinds/types of
"The banquet was spectacular, with all manner of exotic dishes."

by no (manner of) means = in no way/ absolutely not
"The chairman revealed that the company had made a loss over the year of a quarter of a million pounds but emphasized that by no manner of means was he considering voluntary liquidation."

in a manner of speaking = up to a point/ in a way
"The personnel officer said that his job was, in a manner of speaking, to keep the staff happy."

(as if) to the manner born = naturally/(as if) used to something
"My son Robert is playing Henry V in the school play and suits the role as if to the manner born."

many
a good/great many = a large number
"Sixty people were rescued from the burning ship, but a great many more

were drowned when it sank."

many a long day = a long time

"It's been many a lɔng day since I tasted a meal as good as this."

many hand's make light work = the task will be completed quicker if everybody helps

"Your mother has just made us a superb Christmas dinner, why don't you children help me do the washing up ñ after all, many hands make light work."

many happy returns (of the day) = happy birthday

"Oh Mary, I've just heard it's your birthday ñ many happy returns of the day."

many's the time = frequently/often

"Many's the time I've woken with a hangover and wished I hadn't drunk as much as I did the night before."

See also: few too many; one too many.

map

off the map = remote

"We stayed in a small village inn, right off the map."

put (a place) on the map = bring something/(somewhere) to the public notice

"The disaster at Chernobyl put the town on the map; previously, very few people outside the Soviet Union had heard of it."

marbles

See: lose one's marbles/reason.

march

get one's marching orders = be dismissed

"Some of the night shift at the factory have been caught sleeping on the job, and they're almost certain to get their marching orders as a result."

steal the march (on somebody) = gain an advantage over/get the better of somebody

"Our competitors will always be able to steal a march on us when bidding for contracts unless we can cut our production costs and improve delivery times."

See also: mad as a March hare.

mare

See: mare's nest

marines

(you can) tell that/it to the marines = I do not believe you

"If you think I'll accept that excuse you can tell it to the marines."

mark

beside/off the mark = off the point of discussion

"I agree that there are problems of overpopulation in parts of India, but that's beside the mark because we're only interested in China at the moment."

close to the mark = nearly correct

"No, I'm slightly older than that ñ but you're close to the mark."

easy mark = somebody of whom it is easy to take advantage

"If I'm short of cash I ask Dad to lend me some ñ he's usually an easy mark."

full marks = high praise

"You didn't win but full marks for trying."

get off the/one's mark = begin doing something (quickly)

"We had better get off the mark early tomorrow if we're to catch the first ferry."

make one's mark = distinguish oneself/

leave an impression
"Amelia Erhardt made her mark on aviation history by being the first woman to fly non-stop across the Atlantic Ocean."
mark (something) down/up = decrease/increase the price of something
"If you want some new bed linen go to the shop in the High Street ñ they're holding a sale and their sheets are marked down by twenty per cent."
"The cost of many manufactured goods has to be marked up by at least fifty per cent to give a profit to the manufacturer, the wholesaler and the retailer."
mark/put down to experience = be stoic about the difficulties of life
"The company whose shares I bought last month has just failed ñ I suppose I'll have to mark that one down to experience."
mark my words = be warned/remember what I say
"I can't understand why those two are getting married. It won't last, you mark my words it will end in disaster."
mark time = wait/(deliberately) take no action
"The bride's car had broken down and meanwhile the groom and wedding guests in the church could only mark time."
mark you = note what I say
"My job is well paid, but mark you I have to work very hard."
near the mark = risqué/nearly obscene
"Some of Ted's jokes are a bit near the mark."
off/wide of the mark = inaccurate/wrong
"The weather forecast was a bit off the mark = it predicted scattered showers and it poured with rain all day."
required/go too far
"Then you add a little cayenne pepper but be careful ñ it's easy to overshoot the mark."
overstep the mark = go beyond accepted limits of behaviour/protocol
"I reckon Private Jones has overstepped the mark by taking the colonel's daughter to a disco and keeping her out all night."
quick/slow off the mark = quick/slow to begin/react
"There are only a few tickets left for next week's match so you'll have to be quick off the mark if you want one."
up to the mark = up to the required standard/healthy
"Christine will not be at work for a few days ñ she's got some sort of throat infection and is not feeling up to the mark."
See also: marked man.

market
be in the market for = have an interest in buying
"We're in the market for paintings at the moment, particularly works by some of the late nineteenth- century artists."
drug on the market = something that is difficult to sell
"It's been raining all week and sunglasses are a real drug on the market."
on the market = up for sale
"I have to move nearer London so I've put my house on the market."
See also: corner the market.

marrow
chilled/frozen to the marrow = very cold
"It was a frosty morning and the wind was blowing from the north, and I was

frozen to the marrow by the time the bus arrived."

martyr

be a martyr to = suffer because of
"I'm a martyr to rheumatism this cold weather."

mass

in the mass = as a whole
"The general proposed moving the regiment in the mass to the north flank and wait for reinforcements."

masses of = plenty
"Haven't you finished yet? You 've had masses of time."

mass murder = unlawful killing of many people, genocide
"The Nazis were responsible for the mass murder of Jews during World War II."

mass survey = statistical analysis that involves questioning a large number of people
"A mass survey of parents revealed that most of them are dissatisfied with the present education system."

the masses = people in general/the population as a whole
"The rule of the tsars was so oppressive that it did not take much to provoke the masses into a revolution."

mast

before the mast = at sea (as a member of the crew)
"At one time it was common for young men to run away from home and seek adventure before the mast."

See also: at half mast; nail one's colours to the mast.

master

master mind = instigator/organizer
"The man in the dock, who was the master mind behind five armed robberies, was sentenced to twenty years in prison."

master-mind = control/organize
"The president has sent his top aide to master-mind peace negotiations between the opposing factions."

master of oneself = have oneself under complete control
"Because of the enormous responsibility they hold, it is imperative that submarine commanders are masters of themselves as well as their vessels and crew."

master-stroke = outstanding (and timely) action
"The two teams were drawing with only three minutes of play left in the Cup Final when Chelsea's centre forward pulled a masterstroke and headed the ball into the net from outside the penalty area."

See also: old master; one's lord and master; past master.

mat

See: on the carpet/mat.

match

be a match for someone = be equal to somebody in ability
"The athlete had been training hard for three years and now he was a match for any of the contenders for the gold medal."

match point = point that, if gained, wins the whole match for a competitor
"The players have won two sets each, but the champion now has match point in the final set."

meet one's match = deal with somebody who is as able/capable as oneself

"Dave is a big eater but he's met his match with Gordon ñ he eats like a horse!"

more than a match for = better than
"The captain of the destroyer prepared to engage the cruiser, although he knew the enemy's eight-inch guns were more than a match for his limited fire power."

(whole) shooting match = everything
"I sold my house, car, furniture ñ indeed the whole shooting match."

See also: needle match.

material

See: material witness; raw material.

matter

a matter of life or death = critical/urgent
"It is a matter of life or death: if the seasonal rains don't come soon the crops will fail and millions of people will face starvation."

a matter of opinion = something about which people hold different views
"Most of the sports writers predict that India will win the Test Match, but that's a matter of opinion and I still think England has a good chance."

as a matter of course = naturally routinely
"Our vet is very efficient, he sends us a reminder when the cat is due for a booster vaccination as a matter of course."

as a matter of fact = in truth (used to emphasize a statement)
"As a matter of fact I do know what it is like to be poor ñ I haven't always been a rich man."

be a matter of = be a question of what is necessary
"I know we need some extra help but it's a matter of finding the right person for the job."

be a matter of time = will happen sooner or later
"We must do something about that dead tree, it's only a matter of time before it falls down and may be injures somebody."

be the matter (with) = be the difficulty/ problem
"Something is the matter with Eric, he's been in a bad mood all day."

for that matter = concerning that
"You've got to go to Paris on Monday, and for that matter I could take a day off work and come with you."

matter in question = point being considered/discussed
"Did the matter in question occur on or about ten o'clock on the fifteenth of June?"

matter of course = something that happens naturally/routinely
"The milkman leaves us three pints a day as a matter of course."

matter of fact = the truth
"It is a matter of fact that excessive exposure to the sun's rays, especially in fair-skinned people, can cause skin cancer."

matter-of-fact = practical/prosaic
"Tim never panics, he just takes a matter-of-fact approach to each problem as it arises."

no matter = never mind/it is unimportant
"You've locked the keys in the car again? No matter, I have a spare set here."

not to mince matters = to be frank
"Not to mince matters, I don't approve of my daughter going out with you because you are a married man."

what's the matter? = what is the problem/what is wrong?
"I see you came by bus. What's the

matter with your car?"
See also: grey matter; heart of the matter; no laughing matter.

may

be that as it may = (even) having taken that into account
"I know you want adventure and, be that as it may, the Foreign Legion is not as glamorous as it appears in the films."

maybe

and I don't mean maybe = I mean what I say
"Get this room tidied up immediately ñ and I don't mean may be!"
that's as maybe = that may be so
"You demand equality? That's as maybe, madam, but this room is for gentlemen only I'm afraid."

meal

make a meal (out) of something = take excessive time/trouble in doing something
"You're making a meal out of a simple job like wiring a plug ñ here, let me do it for you."
meal ticket = provider who does not expect to be paid
"I know she's going out with Nigel but she's only using him as a meal ticket."
mealy-mouthed = hypocritical
"Some people criticize the boss, but they're too mealy-mouthed to say so in her presence."
square meal = satisfying/wholesome meal
"After eating out of packets and tins for a fortnight while camping, I'm really looking forward to a decent square meal."

mean

do you mean to say? = are you telling me?
"Do you mean to say that you've never been out of England in your whole life?"
do you see what I mean? = do you understand what I say?
"You have to connect the brown wire to the live terminal ñ do you see what I mean?"
I see what you mean = I understand
"I see what you mean ñ the colours on the wires tell you which terminal to connect them to."
mean well = be good intentioned (even if offence results)
"I know he means well, but I do wish Jack would stop cleaning the cups with scouring powder ñ I can taste it in my tea."
what do you mean by? = what is your motive/reason for?
"What do you mean by coming home at one o'clock in the morning and waking everyone up?"
See also: and I don't mean maybe; mean business.

means

by all means = of course
"Yes, by all means, call in any time you are in the district."
by no means/not by any means = emphatically not, or not entirely
"No you can't have a motorbike ñ by no means."
"I'm not by any means sure that I can do what you want."
by what means? = how?
"Even if I agree to let you go, by what means are you going to get there on a Sunday?"

live beyond/within one's means = spend more/less than one earns
"Tony is getting increasingly in debt because he lives beyond his means all the time."

means to an end = method used to achieve a desired result
"I don't really like working in the docks, it's just a means to an end because I want to get a job with one of the shipping companies."

See also: all manner of means; by fair means or foul.

meantime/meanwhile

in the meantime/meanwhile = while something is happening
"Dinner will be ready in ten minutes. In the meantime, would you and your brother mind laying the table?"

measure

for good measure = as an addition
"I bought two hundred bricks and the builder gave me a bag of cement for good measure."

get/have somebody's measure/have the measure of somebody = judge the character of somebody
"I have the measure of the man we'll be dealing with ñ he's a keen businessman and a hard negotiator."

in some measure = partly
"I agree with you in some measure but I don't approve of the way you want to do it."

made to measure = manufactured to suit a particular requirement
"Gary must be earning a good living these days; all his suits are made to measure ñ and so are his shoes!"
"This piece of wood is just the right length for that new shelf, it could have been made to measure."

measure one's length = fall full length on the ground
"He tripped over a loose slab and measured his length on the pavement."

measure up to somebody/something = reach somebody else's/a specified standard
"I'm looking forward to my new job although I may find it difficult to measure up to my predecessor, who did it for fifteen years before she retired."
"The new cruise liners are all right but they wouldn't measure up to the old Cunarders."

short measure = less than the required amount
"The brewery sacked the pub's landlord because he was giving short measures on spirit drinks and pocketing the extra profit."

take measures to = do something to ensure that
"The BMA urged the government to take measures in order to combat the spread of AIDS."

take somebody's measure = assess somebody's character
"It was the president's first meeting with the new Soviet premier and it was felt that on this occasion they would do little more than take each other's measure."

measure up somebody/something = study/get information about
"Ted invited Susan to the theatre, but she was measuring him up before giving an answer."
"Head Office wants us to handle a project in the Middle East, and I would like you to go there and measure up the situation."

See also: for good measure.

meat

be meat and drink to (somebody) = be essential/important to (somebody)
"Football is meat and drink to Jack, and he would do anything to get a ticket for the Cup Final."

one man's meat is another man's poison = something beneficial to/liked by one person may be the exact opposite to somebody else
"Business was booming for the official receiver as many companies went bankrupt during the recession ñ one man's meat is another man's poison."

See also: easy meat/touch.

medicine

dose/taste of one's own medicine = unpleasantness suffered by somebody who usually does unpleasant things to others
"For years the feudal lords ruled by terror; then after the revolution they got a taste of their own medicine."

laughter is the best medicine = cheerfulness makes one forget troubles/worry
"My arthritis can be very painful but I find that laughter is the best medicine."

medicine man = magician, wise man in primitive society
"In times of drought, the members of the tribe would consult the medicine man in the belief he could make it rain."

take one's medicine = tolerate unpleasantness (of one's own making)
"I refuse to allow you to insult my wife like that ñ come outside and take your medicine!"

medium

See: happy medium.

meet

be met with = receive
"The Pope was met with enthusiastic cheering as he stepped from the plane."

meet one's match/Waterloo = finally suffer defeat
"The world champion racing driver met his match at Le Mans when his car spun off the track and was damaged beyond repair."

meet the case = suffice
"I need something to prop open the door ñ those two books should meet the case."

See also: make (both) ends meet; meet a deadline; (go to) meet one's maker; meet one's match; meet somebody half way; meet somebody's eyes; more than meets the eye.

melt

be in the melting-pot = be changing (into something new)
"The government's plans for defence cuts are still in the melting pot and will not be announced for at least a week."

melt away/into = disappear/merge with one's surroundings
"The policeman gave chase to the bag snatcher but he just seemed to melt away into the crowd."

melt down = melt (a metal article), or melting and fire in the core of a nuclear reactor
"During the war, many ornamental iron railings were melted down to provide iron for making steel to build tanks and ships."
"The melt down of the reactor core at

Chernobyl released radioactive material into the atmosphere."

memory

burden one's memory = be remembered with difficulty
"You don't have to burden your memory with my address ñ I'll write it down for you."

commit to memory = memorize
"I understand the process when it is explained to me but find it very difficult to commit to memory."

down memory lane = in the (enjoyable) past
"Playing those 1960s records was a trip down memory lane."

if my memory serves me correct/right = if I am remembering accurately
"We were at school together, if my memory serves me correct."

See also: memory like an elephant; within/in living memory.

mend

make do and mend = improvise (using what is available)
"I hadn't got the right timber for the job so I had to make do and mend with wood from some old boxes."

mend one's ways = reform one's (bad) behaviour
"When Vic first started working here his time-keeping was very bad, but he seems to have mended his ways because he's on time every day now."

on the mend = getting better/healing
"My husband had a bad fall but after a week in hospital he's on the mend."

See also: least said, soonest mended.

mental

See: mental block.

mention

don't mention it = you need not refer to it/it does not matter (said in declining thanks)
"Please don't mention it, I enjoyed looking after your cat while you were away."

honourable mention = nonprizewinning award (in a competition)
"My effort got an honourable mention in the painting competition, whereas Joan's won first prize."

I hate to mention it, but.Ö = may I remind you that.Ö
"I hate to mention it, but you still owe me five pounds from last week."

not to mention = in addition to (introducing something important, or something trivial)
"There were many titled people at the function ñ lords and ladies, dukes and duchesses, not to mention the Prince and Princess of Wales."
"This next television programme is quite unsuitable for you to watch, not to mention that it's past your bedtime."

mercy

angel of mercy = somebody who arrives to help just when he/she is needed/a nurse
"I was late for an appointment and my car had broken down when an angel of mercy appeared ñ a passing motorist who gave me a lift into town."

at the mercy of (somebody or something) = in the power of
"The survivors of the crashed plane had no food or water and were at the mercy of the tropical heat. They would surely perish if help didn't arrive soon."

be thankful for small mercies = when in

difficulty, be grateful for any help (no matter how small)
"I needed two hundred pounds to pay for repairs to my car, when I won twenty-five pounds on the Premium Bonds ñ not enough of course, but one must be thankful for small mercies."

leave (somebody) to the tender mercies of = leave somebody to be dealt with by a cruel/unsympathetic person
"The slave trader accepted the money and gave the young girl over to the tender mercies of her new sadistic master."

merry

make merry = rejoice/enjoy oneself
"OK lads, let's make merry ñ my wife has just had twins and the drinks are on me."

make merry at somebody's expense = make fun of somebody
"The rugby team made merry at their captain's expense when they discovered that he'd once won a beautiful baby contest."

merry-go-round = frustrating/worthless activity (involving a lot of work)
"The information the police received had them on a merry-go-round until they realized they were the victims of a hoax."

the more the merrier = the more people there are, the better
"Yes, by all means bring your in-laws with you to the party tonight ñ the more the merrier."

See also: lead somebody a (merry/pretty) dance; play (merry) hell with.

mess

make a mess of/mess up = do something incorrectly/spoil something
"At my first public speaking appointment I was so nervous that I made a right mess of the whole occasion."
"I had just typed the letter when I messed it up completely by spilling coffee over it."

mess about = misbehave, or cause a nuisance (usually through inefficiency), or do something/work to no apparent purpose
"Come on children, stop messing about ñ it's bedtime."
"They messed us about on the trains last night because two drivers didn't turn up for their shift."
"Peter likes nothing better than going to the coast and messing about in his boat."

mess of pottage = something cheap/of little value
"The Russians have long regretted selling Alaska to the Americans for a mess of pottage."

message

get the message = understand (take a hint/heed a warning)
"The police commissioner said that they would deal sternly with drunk driving offenders and hoped that people would get the message and not drink and drive."

method

See: there's method in his/her/their madness.

mettle

put somebody on his/her mettle = test somebody's ability
"He has played very well in the reserve side but this chance in the first team should put him on his mettle."

Methuselah

as old as Methuselah = very old
"The chap who runs the corner shop has been there as long as anyone can remember ñ he must be as old as Methuselah."

mice

See: mouse.

Mickey

Mickey Finn = (alcoholic) drink containing a drug ("knock-out drops")
"The shore patrol carried out the unconscious sailor who had been given a Mickey Finn."

take the mickey out of somebody = make fun of somebody
"The rest of the class took the mickey out of Tony because he was the only one who couldn't answer the teacher's question."

Midas

the Midas touch = the ability to succeed (financially) whatever one does
"Harry certainly has the Midas touch; he's been involved in several business ventures and he's made a fortune out of each of them."

middle

be in the middle of (doing something) = in the act of (doing something)
"You phoned when I was in the middle of writing a letter to you."

knock somebody into the middle of next week = hit somebody very hard
"If he talks to you like that again I'll knock him into the middle of next week!"

middle-of-the-road = average/moderate
"The opposition party advocates neither total disarmament nor an increase in defence spending but a middle-of-the-road policy that would leave the situation much as it is at present."

See also: pig(gy)-in-the-middle.

midnight

See: burn the midnight oil.

midstream

halt/pause/stop in midstream = (temporarily) stop while in the act of doing something
"The chairman had just launched into his speech when the lights went out and stopped him in midstream."

See also: swap/change horses in midstream.

midsummer

See: midsummer madness.

might

See: high and mighty; with might and main.

Mike

See: for the love of Mike/Pete.

milch

See: milch cow.

mildly

put something mildly = deliberately understate something
"You have debts of over five thousand pounds ñ to put it mildly you are financially embarrassed."

mile

be miles away = be inattentive/day-dream
"Sorry, what did you say? I was miles away for a minute."

mile away/off = great distance

"It's no use trying to fool me ñ I could see your intentions from a mile away."
"I knew it was you, I could spot that hat a mile off!"

stand/stick out a mile = be obvious
"You could tell Mick was drunk ñ it stood out a mile."

talk a mile a minute = speak continuously and rapidly
"My wife was talking a mile a minute about her trip home and it was a quarter of a hour before I could tell her about my promotion."

See also: give somebody an inch and they'll take a mile; a miss is as good as a mile; not a hundred miles away; run a mile.

milk

milk and water = weak/without substance
"The press report described the minister's statement as so much milk and water and demanded that the public be told the full truth about the incident."

milk of human kindness = sincere/ sympathetic attitude towards others
"My aunt is full of the milk of human kindness ñ she's devoted her whole life to looking after stray dogs."

milk somebody = deceive somebody into parting with money
"The tenants were in a hopeless position, being milked by an unscrupulous landlord for substandard accommodation."

mother's milk = something that one especially enjoys (naturally)
"I love walking alone on the moors, it's mother's milk to me."

See also: cry over spilt milk; land of milk and honey.

mill

calm as a millpond = very calm (of water)
"We enjoyed the ferry crossing because the sea was as a calm as a millpond."

go/be put through the mill = be forced to endure an ordeal
"They really put me through the mill at the interview but I think I might have a good chance of getting the job."

mill about/around = move around aimlessly
"There were a lot of people milling around outside the station waiting to see if the trains would start running again."

the mills of God grind slowly (but they grind exceedingly small) = the punishment/reward for one's actions will eventually happen, even after a long delay
"I know you've heard nothing about that incident of six moths ago but you wait ñ the mills of God grind slowly."

See also: all grist to the mill; millstone round one's neck; run of the mill.

million

See: feel/look like a million dollars; one in a million/thousand; the 64 million dollar question.

mince

make mincemeat of = completely defeat/ destroy
"The opposition leader spoke against the chancellor's proposals and made mincemeat of them."

not mince words = speak frankly/ straightforwardly
"Not to mince words, I don't really like you and tolerate your presence

only because you're my daughter's friend."

mind

apply/give one's mind to = give attention/consideration to
"The architect said he would apply his mind to my request and make some rough sketches for approval before drawing up detailed plans."

at the back of one's mind = (always) in one's thoughts
"I've had it at the back of my mind for a long time to come and visit you."

bear/keep in mind = remember/retain in one's thoughts
"Thanks for the invitation; I'll bear it in mind and let you know tomorrow."

be/rest easy in one's mind = be calm/ unworried
"The doctor says it is just a routine minor operation so you can be easy in your mind about it."

be in two minds = be undecided
"I'm in two minds about which dress to wear for the party."

be of one/the same mind = agree/think alike
"My friend and I were of the same mind ñ we both chose Majorca for a holiday this year."

bring/call to mind = recall/remember
"I can't bring to mind the exact date when we last met, but I think it was about the end of March."
"Can you call to mind your whereabouts on the night of 21st May?"

broaden one's/the mind = provide one with new experience/knowledge
"I hope to take a trip round Europe after I finish university ñ they do say that travel broadens the mind."

cast one's mind back = remember a past event/incident
"When I look at today's youngsters I often cast my mind back to when I was their age ñ things have changed a lot in thirty years, haven't they?"

change one's mind = reconsider/decide on a different course of action
"I know I said we would have beef for dinner but I changed my mind at the butchers because lamb was on special offer."

closed mind = attitude that is not open to criticism/suggestion
"The manager has made her decision; she now has a closed mind on the subject and refuses to discuss it further."

come (in)to one's mind = be remembered
"I saw an old Austin Seven today and it came to mind that it was the first car we ever owned."

cross one's mind = occur to one
"I was in your area today but it didn't cross my mind to call and see you."

do you mind? = would you please (do, or emphatically not do, something)
"Do you mind waiting for a few minutes while I do my hair?"
"Do you mind? I don't want to hear that kind of language here!"

give somebody a piece of one's min =
be openly critical of somebody/angrily scold somebody
"If that's what Andrew said about me, the next time I see him I shall give him a piece of my mind."

go out of one's mind = become emotionally upset, or become forgotten, or become mad
"Where have you been? It's past midnight and I've been going out of my mind with worry."
"I always know what I want when I go shopping and then when I get to the

supermarket half the things have gone out of my mind."

"Our dog developed a brain tumour and went mad, so reluctantly we had to have him put down."

great minds think alike = similar ideas/ views are shared by clever people (said in a jocular way)

"I agree, that's just what I was going to say ñ great minds think alike!"

have a good/half a mind to = be inclined to

"It's beautiful weather and I've a good mind to take the day off work and go to the coast for a swim."

"There's a pretty dress in the sale and I've half a mind to buy it."

have a mind of one's own = be independent

"Thanks for your advice but I don't need you to tell me what to do ñ I have a mind of my own."

have it in mind to = have the intention of doing

"I have it in mind to move house ñ with another baby on the way this one will not be big enough."

have/keep an open mind = be undecided/ open to suggestion

"I'm not sure what to do so I'll keep an open mind about it until I have more information."

have something in mind = have an idea about something

"I'm not exactly sure what to buy Gill for her birthday, although I do have something in mind."

have something on one's mind = be preoccupied with/troubled by something

"I'm sorry I'm not very sociable tonight; I've got a lot on my mind with difficulties at work and family problems at home."

I don't mind if I do = I would like to

"Thanks for the offer of another drink, I don't mind if I do."

I wouldn't mind = I would like

"I wouldn't mind a jacket like the one Gary is wearing."

in/out of one's right mind = sane/mad

"Nobody in his right mind would pay a thousand pounds for a wreck of a car like that!"

"You must have been out of your mind to pay a thousand pounds for that wreck of a car!"

it's all in the mind = it is imaginary

"I keep getting these pains in my back but the doctor says there's nothing wrong with me and it's all in the mind."

keep one's mind on = concentrate on

"The teacher told me to stop talking in class and keep my mind on my work."

know one's own mind = be confident in one's own opinions

"My son wants to join the army when he leaves school. He's nearly seventeen and should know his own mind by now."

leap/spring to mind = become immediately/suddenly obvious

"I want to buy Mary something unusual for her birthday, but nothing springs to mind."

little things please little minds = people who are small-minded are pleased/ satisfied by petty things

"It was a sixty-page manuscript and Helen took great delight in pointing out two typing mistakes I had made. Still, little things please little minds."

make one's/the mind boggle = make one amazed/confused

"There are so many large diamonds in the Crown Jewels that they make your mind boggle."

"I tried to check the accounts but there are so many entries altered or crossed out that it makes one's mind boggle."

make up one's mind = decide

"Come on, make up your mind. Are you coming or aren't you?"

mind how you go = be careful

"Mind how you go, that ladder looks very wobbly to me."

mind out for = be careful of

"Mind out for the bottom step ñ it's loose."

mind you = all the same/even so

"I agree that politicians do not have an easy job ñ mind you, they get well paid for it."

mind your backs! = please get out of the way

"Mind your backs! This box I'm carrying is heavy."

never mind = do not worry/take no notice

"Never mind. You can take the exam again next term if you fail it this time."

never you mind = it is of no concern to you

"Never you mind, I'll decide what I'm going to wear to the party ñ not you."

put one in mind of = remind one of

"That put me in mind of the time we went to Bognor for a holiday."

put/set somebody's mind at rest = reassure somebody

"The passengers became alarmed when the lights went out on the plane, but the captain put their minds at rest when he told them it was only a minor electrical fault and it would soon be repaired."

read somebody's mind = guess what somebody is thinking

"He answered even before I'd finished asking the question ñ it was as if he could read my mind."

set one's mind on/to = be determined to (do something)

"I've set my mind on buying a new car this year."

slip one's mind = become forgotten

"I was going to phone you yesterday but it slipped my mind."

speak one's mind = give one's candid opinion

"If I may speak my mind, I think the plan is hopeless."

stoned out of one's mind/head = very drunk or drugged

"I was stoned out of my mind when I left the pub and I don't remember walking home."

take somebody's mind off something = distract somebody

"Here, have a drink; it will help to take your mind off your unfruitful day at the races."

time out of mind = for a very long time

"We've been going there every year for time out of mind."

to my mind = in my opinion

"To my mind it makes no sense at all to take a holiday in Britain in February."

See also: blow someone's mind; in one's mind's eye; mind being a blank: mind one's own business; mind one's p's and q's; of unsound mind; one-track mind; out of one's mind; out of sight, out of mind; presence of mind; peace of mind; prey on one's mind; put one in mind of; put one's mind to; put out of one's mind; small minded.

mine

mine of information = somebody who is knowledgeable

"I don't know who the nine muses

were, but ask Gill ñ she's a mine of information."

See also: gold mine.

mint

in mint condition = as new

"I'm thinking of buying this 1983 Volvo ñ it's only done twenty thousand miles and it's in mint condition."

make a mint = earn a lot of money

"Micro-electronics is the business to be in nowadays. With the right product, you can make a mint."

worth a mint = very wealthy

"He's got a private jet, five cars and a huge ranch in Texas ñ he must be worth a mint."

minute

there's one born every minute = there are many foolish people

"Bernard paid much more for his car than it is really worth ñ there's one born every minute!"

up to the minute = up-to-date, in fashion

"Janice is always up to the minute, with the latest fashions in clothes and styles in make-up."

See also: talk a mile a minute; wait a minute/moment.

mire

See: drag somebody through the mire/ mud.

mischief

do oneself/somebody a mischief = harm oneself/somebody

"Be careful with that knife ñ you'll do yourself a mischief the way your holding it."

make mischief = cause trouble/create discord

"I sent the boys to the cinema this afternoon because it was raining, otherwise they would only have made mischief around the house while their father was trying to work."

misery

put somebody out of his/her misery = put somebody out of his/her suspense/ satisfy somebody's curiosity

"I've told Ann that I've got a surprise for her, but I'll wait until after dinner and then put her out of her misery."

put an animal out of its misery = put an end to an animal's suffering (by having it humanely killed)

"Our old cat is incontinent and crippled with arthritis, and the vet has recommended that we put it out of its misery."

miss

a miss is as good as a mile = something that nearly succeeds is no better than something that is a total failure

"I failed to achieve the pass mark by only one per cent in my French exam ñ but still, a miss is as good as a mile."

give something a miss = not to do something

"I usually go to the disco on Fridays but this week I had a headache and decided to give it a miss."

See also: have a screw loose/missing; hit-or-miss; miss the boat; near miss/ thing; never miss a trick.

mist

Scotch mist = describes something that is present but thought missing/non-existent

"You say you've never seen me smoke a pipe; well what's this then, Scotch mist?"

mistake
(and) make no mistake = you can be sure
"You'll live to regret that remark, make no mistake."
there's no mistaking it = you cannot confuse it with/mistake it for something else
"The Town Hall is the large white building on the north side of the square ñ there's no mistaking it."

mister
See: Mister Right.

mixed
See: have mixed feelings about; mixed bag; mixed blessing.

mixer
a bad/good mixer = somebody who does not/does get on well with others
"I like asking Graham to our parties because he's such a good mixer."

mixture
the mixture as before = unchanged
"Wendy says she has a new way of organizing the work load, but I bet it will just be the mixture as before."

mockers
put the mockers on = spoil/ruin
"That rain has put the mockers on our plan to have a picnic this afternoon."

molehill
See: make a mountain out of a molehill.

Molotov
See: Molotov cocktail.

moment
at the moment = now
"I'm sorry, Mr Jones is very busy and can't see you at the moment."
choose/pick one's moment = select the best time to act/speak
"I've bought myself a new camera but I'll have to pick my moment before telling my wife!"
half a moment/tick = very short time
"I'll be with you in half a moment."
have its/one's moments = have occasions of outstanding ability/merit
"I'm glad you like the cake I made. I'm not a very good cook, but I do have my moments!"
in a moment = very soon
"Take a seat please, Councillor Jones will see you in a moment."
in a weak moment = a time when one easily agrees to a request
"My wife wanted a car of her own and in a weak moment I agreed she could have one."
mad moment = brief period of irrational behaviour
"I bought this purple hat in a mad moment at the January sales."
moment of truth = crucial/testing time
"Some people thought Barry was a coward, but his moment of truth came when he rescued a child from a burning house."
on the spur of the moment = impulsively/suddenly
"We happened to be looking in a furniture shop and, on the spur of the moment, we bought a new bed."
psychological moment = precise time to act for maximum effect on others
"When father came home and told us about his promotion, Tina chose that psychological moment to ask for more pocket money."

there's never a dull moment = it is always busy/interesting
"We've got so much work to do these days that there's never a dull moment."

unguarded moment = time when one is not paying attention/taking care
"George had been unfaithful and in an unguarded moment called his wife by his girlfriend's name."

See also: in the heat of the moment; man of the day/moment; wait a minute/ moment.

Monday

Monday morning feeling = general apathy (on returning to work) after the weekend
"Nobody spoke on the train today; it was obvious we all had that Monday morning feeling."

money

be made of money = be extremely wealthy
"Margaret is in the money since her divorce settlement."
"James must be made of money, judging by what he spends on clothes."

coin money = make a lot of money (in business)
"The new café on the sea front is always crowded with people ñ the owners must be coining money."

even money = equally likely
"Whether Alice or Angela get the supervisor's job is even money."

for my money = if it were my choice/if I had to bet on it
"I don't think Arsenal will win the cup this season, for my money Derby has the best chance."

get one's money's worth = derive maximum value from one's efforts/ expense
"We arrived early to get seats near the front and we intend to get our money's worth by staying to the very end."

in the money = prosperous/with (new-found) wealth
"The Jones's down the road have two new cars and are going on holiday to the Bahamas ñ they must be in the money!"

knock some money off = reduce the price of something
"I asked the salesman if he would knock some money off for payment in cash."

money doesn't grow on trees = money is hard to obtain (and must be earned)
"No you can't have a pair of new shoes ñ money doesn't grow on trees, you know.

money down the drain = wasted money
"My wife wanted a new carpet in the living room, but as we are moving in six months it would only be money down the drain."

money (is) no object = regardless of cost
"He wanted his wife to have the best medical treatment available and impressed on the doctor that money was no object."

money talks = wealth conveys advantages/privilege
"I couldn't get tickets for the Cup Final but our chairman got some easily ñ but then, money talks."

pin money = money spent on minor articles/pleasures
"My wife has a part-time job as a secretary. She doesn't have to work but likes to earn an extra bit of pin money."

pocket money = relatively small amount of spending money given by parents

to their children
"My Dad gives me five pounds a week pocket money which I spend mostly on records and sweets."

put one's money where one's mouth is = make a commitment
"You say you would like to do something to stop the nuclear arms race, so put your money where your mouth is and join the protest march this weekend."

rake in the money = prosper/do well at work/business
"If you're prepared to work long hours and live away from home, you can rake in the money by taking a job in the Middle East."
"It's Derby Day today and I bet the bookmakers will be raking in the money."

ready money = available cash/money
"The car I want to buy costs five thousand pounds. I've got three thousand in ready money, and I'll get a bank loan for the rest."

rolling in money = very wealthy
"After that shrewd investment on the stock exchange, Jim's bought a large house and is rolling in money."

spend money like water/it's going out of fashion = spend carelessly/extravagantly
"In addition to his salary, Bernard receives a large monthly allowance from his father ñ that is probably why he is able to spend money like water."
"Vic got his bonus yesterday and in the pub last night he was spending money like it's going out of fashion."

throw good money after bad = waste money in an attempt to recoup previous losses
"Robin lost five hundred pounds at the casino last night. Now he wants to throw good money after bad and return in an attempt to win back his losses."

throw money at = continue to finance a loss-making venture
"I can't understand why the government continues to throw money at the steel industry ñ last year alone it lost 140 million pounds."

throw money away = waste money
"I think that smoking is just throwing money away."

you pays your money and takes your choice = it does not matter which of several equal options one chooses
"You can get a train to Hastings from London Bridge or Victoria ñ you pays your money and takes your choice."

See also: blood money; blue one's money; conscience money; easy money; hush money; money for jam/old rope; not for love or money; see the colour of (somebody's) money; time is money.

monkey

artful/clever as a cartload/wagonload of monkeys = very crafty/sly
"The police threatened to charge Terry with receiving stolen property but he was as clever as a cartload of monkeys and pointed out that none of the items had been reported stolen."

make a monkey (out) of somebody = make a fool of somebody
"My friends made a monkey out of me. They told me it was a fancy dress party but it wasn't ñ and I was the only person who turned up in fancy dress!"

monkey business = dishonest/underhand dealings
"Two men were trying to sell cheap car radios in the pub, but the landlord warned them that he didn't want any

monkey business on his premises."

monkey with = interfere

"That engine would be running satisfactorily if you hadn't started monkeying with it."

monkey tricks = mischievous behaviour

"I'm going out to the shops for an hour, children, and while I'm away I want none of your monkey tricks."

more trouble than a cartload of monkeys = very mischievous/troublesome

"My three grandchildren are more trouble than a cartload of monkeys."

month

month of Sundays = an impossibly long time

"I need some advice ñ I'll never be able to do this job on my own in a month of Sundays."

mood

in a mood = bad-tempered

"I don't know what's upset him but Dad's in a right mood today."

in the mood (for something) = receptive (to something)

"I sometimes like listening to blues music, but I have to be in the mood for it."

See also: black mood.

moon

do a moonie = expose one's buttocks

"Glen got very drunk at the party and did a moonie in front of the vicar's wife ñ who was not amused!"

do a moonlight (flit) = move away suddenly (to avoid paying one's debts)

"Jan owed her landlord so much rent that she did a moonlight flit and got a new job up north somewhere."

moonshine = fantasy, or illicit whisky

"The party's manifesto for the forthcoming election is regarded by most of the experts as so much moonshine."

"The revenue men are trying to find the people who are making moonshine."

over the moon = very happy/ecstatic

"Fiona was over the moon when she learned she had passed all her final exams."

See also: cry for the moon; once in a blue moon.

moral

See: moral support.

more

and what's more = and in addition

"Your manner is insulting and what's more you're drunk!"

more or less = approximately, or nearly

"There were thirty people there, more or less."

"The list of names is more or less complete."

the more the merrier = the more people there are, the better will be the result

"I hope everybody we've invited comes to the party ñ the more the merrier."

See also: more fool you; more's the pity.

morning

be the morning after the night before = have a hangover

"It's the morning after the night before and I have a headache and a raging thirst."

See also: Monday morning feeling.

mortal

See: shuffle off this mortal coil.

most

at (the) most = as a maximum

"The trip will only cost you fifty pounds at most."

make the most of = take best advantage of

"I've got to go abroad on a business trip so I've decided to make the most of it by taking a week's holiday immediately afterwards while I'm still out there."

See also: for the most part.

mother

be mother = act as hostess (when pouring tea)

"Good, the tea has arrived. Shall I be mother?"

mother's meeting = group of gossiping people

"The regulars are holding a mother's meeting down at the pub to discuss the news about the doctor and his wife."

the mother and father of = the most extreme example of

"I've got the mother and father of a headache this morning."

See also: mother's boy; mother's darling; mother's milk; mother's apron strings; necessity is the mother of invention; mother tongue.

motion

go through the motions = pretend to do something, or try to do something but with no enthusiasm

"I'm convinced the new method won't work but I'll still have to go through the motions."

See also: set the wheels in motion.

mould

be cast in the same mould as = closely resemble

"You can't trust John; he's cast in the same mould as his crooked father."

mountain

make a mountain out of a molehill = make a small difficulty appear to be a large problem

"You're making a mountain out of a molehill if you think that one twinge of toothache means that you must have several teeth extracted."

mouse

the best laid schemes of mice and men = anybody's careful plans (may fail)

"I ordered a taxi to take us to the station, booked seats on the train and arranged for a friend to drive us to the airport, but then there was a train strike ñ the best laid schemes of mice and men!"

See: play cat and mouse with somebody; poor as a church mouse; when the cat's away (mice will play); quiet as a mouse/the grave.

mouth

all mouth and trousers = very talkative but reluctant to take action

"Mike is all mouth and trousers: he keeps on about what he's going to do to modernize his house but he never does anything about it."

by word of mouth = using the spoken word (as opposed to being written down or printed)

"There's no need to put an announcement on the notice board; the news will soon spread by word of mouth."

have a big mouth = talk boastfully/indiscreetly/loudly

"He has a big mouth about his abilities but is much more reluctant

when it come to actually doing something."
"If you want to keep something secret, don't ever tell Vera ñ she has a big mouth."
"Norman has a big mouth, you can hear him talking from the other side of the room."

leave a nasty taste in one's mouth = leave one with a bad/bitter impression
"The way some institutions treat old people these days leaves a nasty taste in one's mouth."

make one's mouth water = be very appetizing
"The photographs of food in that new recipe book really make my mouth water."

shoot one's mouth off = boast
"Harry is fond of shooting his mouth off about his daring exploits in action during the last war, but I happen to know he was a storeman at Colchester barracks for the whole of his time in the army."

shut one's mouth/face/trap = stop talking/refrain from speaking
"Oh shut your mouth! You don't know what you're talking about anyway."
"He was so certain he knew a short cut that I just shut my mouth and let him get on with it. Needless to say we got lost!"

See also: born with a silver spoon in one's mouth; butter wouldn't melt in his/her mouth; down in the mouth/dumps; foam at the mouth; have one's heart in one's mouth; live from hand to mouth; look a gift horse in the mouth; put one's money where one's mouth is; straight from the horse's mouth; take the words out of somebody's mouth.

move

get a move on = hurry up
"Please get a move on or we'll miss our train."

get something on the move = make something happen
"It's about time we got this job on the move."

make a move = leave
"I'd better make a move if I'm to catch the last bus."

on the move = continually moving/travelling
"Frank is always on the move, he never stays in one place for more than a few months."

See also: move heaven and earth.

much

be too much = be more than one can accept/bear
"My supervisor's personal remarks are too much and if he does it again I am going to complain to the boss about it."

be too much for somebody = be too difficult for somebody
"That thousand-piece jigsaw puzzle is too much for a child of her age."

it's a bit much = you are expecting too much
"It's a bit much when you want me to mow the lawn in the pouring rain."

make much of = exaggerate the significance of (boastfully), or make a fuss of
"Anthony makes much of the fact that he passed his O-level French exam, but so did thousands of other people."
"She always makes much of her grandchildren when they visit her."

much of a muchness = similar (and usually mediocre)
"Most modern houses are much of a

muchness ñ functional but unattractive."

not think much of = have a low opinion of

"I don't think much of June's taste in hats."

not up to much = not very good/well

"That new television series is not up to much."

"I don't feel up to much so I won't be going out this evening."

so much for something = that demonstrates how bad something is

"Sylvia told the boss I left work early yesterday ñ so much for her friendship."

without so much as = without even

"He stormed out of the room without so much as a goodbye."

muck

make a muck of something = do something badly

"The examiner asked me to set up one of the simplest experiments, and yet I made a muck of it."

muck in with = join/share with

"The place was a mess but we all mucked in and had it looking fine after a couple of hours of joint effort."

See also: common as muck.

mud

here's mud in your eye! = cheers!/good health! (a toast when drinking)

"Thanks for the drink. Here's mud in your eye!"

throw/sling mud at = insult/vigorously discredit

"The opposition find it impossible to discredit the cabinet minister in terms of his performance in office, so they are trying to throw mud at him through his private life."

See also: as clear as mud; drag somebody through the mire/mud; muddy the waters; somebody's name is mud; stick in the mud.

muddle

muddle through = achieve something despite carelessness/disorganization

"They never seem to have a proper plan but manage to muddle through somehow."

mug

mug shot = photograph of somebody's face

"The article is illustrated with mug shots of the main people involved in the affair."

no mug = somebody who is shrewd/wise

"Mary is no mug and you won't convince her with a feeble excuse like that."

See also: mug's game.

mule

See: stubborn as a mule.

multitude

cover/include a multitude of sins = include a wide variety of things

"The price excludes fixtures and fittings, which could cover a multitude of sins."

mum

mum's the word = do not repeat what I have just told you

"That is what happened, but mum's the word ñ I don't want my wife to find out about it."

murder

get away with murder = go undetected/unpunished yet do something bad

"The manager's secretary gets away with murder; she says what she likes to him and he never tells her off."

See also: (scream) blue murder.

Murphy

See: Murphy's/sod's law.

music

music to one's ears = something one is very pleased to hear

"After waiting in the rain for nearly half an hour the sound of the bus coming was music to my ears."

See also: face the music; no ear for music.

mustard

keen as mustard = eager/enthusiastic

"Why don't you give the lad a chance? He's as keen as mustard and can't do any worse than some of the older players."

muster

pass muster = be considered to be good enough

"Her work isn't the best but it will just pass muster."

mutton

See: dead as a doornail/mutton; mutton dressed up as lamb.

my

Oh my = expression of annoyance/disbelief/resignation

"Oh my, do you have to wear that bright red lipstick?"

"Oh my, you don't expect me to believe that, do you?"

See also: my foot!; my word!

N

n

to the nth degree = extremely/to an infinite extent
"Frank is confident to the nth degree that he will finish the job tomorrow."

nail

fight tooth and nail = fight fiercely
"The twins fight tooth and nail over the slightest disagreement."

hard/tough as nails = unfeeling/unsympathetic
"There's no point in asking Harry for a donation for starving children, he's as hard as nails."

hit the nail on the head = be accurate/correct
"Gill hit the nail right on the head when she said I prefer happiness to wealth."

nail-biting = causing anxiety/nervousness
"The two finalists are well matched and it should result in a nail-biting finish to the tournament."

See also: bed of nails/thorns; cash on the nail; coffin nail; nail in one's coffin; nail one's colours to the mast.

naked

See: naked eye; naked truth.

name

call somebody names = use insulting names for somebody
"I don't care. You can't hurt me just by calling me names."

clear somebody's name = prove that somebody did not commit a misdeed
"David was accused of stealing a car but he cleared his name by proving he was out of the country at the time."

have a bad name = have a bad reputation
"They have a bad name for not paying their bills on time."

have to one's name = own
"Gill is so hard up trying to bring up two children on her own that she hasn't got a decent winter's coat to her name."

in name alone/only = only by name/title, not in reality
"He's manager in name only, it's his assistant who really runs the place."

in the name of = on the authority/example of
"In the name of charity, please stop bothering me."
"Stop, in the name of the law!"

make a name for oneself = earn a (good) reputation
"Julie has made a name for herself as a talented artist."

name-dropper = somebody who habitually refers to famous people as if they were his/her friends
"I don't think he knows half the people he claims to, he's just a name-dropper."

name names = announce the names of people accused/guilty of misdeeds
"Instead of making veiled references to certain important people who are involved in the drugs trade, the time has come to name names."

no names, no pack drill = nobody will get into trouble as long as no names are mentioned
"I can tell you what took place, but no names, no pack drill."

one's middle name = one's best-known attribute
"You can always trust Roy ñ honesty is his middle name."

*or my name's not.*Ö = I am definitely sure
"That girl is wearing a wig or my name's not John Jones."
somebody's name is mud = somebody is very badly thought of
"Councillor Jones's name has been mud since he was implicated in official corruption."
somebody who shall be/remain nameless = somebody whom we all know (but not named for effect or to prevent embarrassment)
"The goal was scored by somebody who shall remain nameless."
"Somebody who shall remain nameless donated five hundred pounds."
take somebody's name in vain = cite somebody's name in an insulting/unkind manner
"I know you don't like Philip, but there's no need to take his name in vain."
what's-his/her-name (what's-its-name) = somebody/something whose name cannot be remembered
"I gave the letter to what's-her-name in the typing pool."
"Please hand me the spanner, I've got to tighten up the what's-its-name."
worthy of the name = deserving of its name/title
"Any writer worthy of the name could phrase it in a much clearer way."
*you name it.*Ö = anything you can name.Ö/no matter what.Ö
"The new shop has a very extensive stock ñ you name it, and they've got it."
"You can have anything you want, just you name it."
See also: answer to the name of; double-barrelled name; give a dog a bad name; household name; lend one's name to; name of the game; name the day; name to conjure with; not have a penny to one's name.

nancy
See: nancy boy.

nap
cat nap = brief sleep
"After working in the garden all morning, I had a cat nap before lunch."
go nap = risk everything (on a gamble)
"When I lost my job, I went nap and invested all my redundancy money in a small business venture."
See also: catch somebody bending/napping/on the hop.

narrow
narrow escape/shave/squeak = close to, but free from, danger
"I had a narrow shave yesterday when I had a puncture on the motorway, but I was able to keep the car in control until I could pull over and stop."
narrow margin = very small (amount/distance etc.)
"He backed the car into the space with a narrow margin to spare."
narrow-minded = unreceptive to other's ideas/wishes
"Mary is narrow-minded and objects to the open sale of certain types of magazines."
the straight and narrow = a lawful/moral way of life
"Ever since she came out of prison she's kept to the straight and narrow."

nasty
nasty piece of work = very unpleasant person

"Be careful of Keith ñ he's a nasty piece of work with a violent temper."

See also: cut up nasty/rough.

native

go native = adopt local customs (in a foreign land)

"After living and working among Arabs for several years, Norman had gone native ñ wearing Arab robes and even speaking the local dialect."

nature

answer/obey a call of nature = go to the lavatory

"As soon as I get on a long-distance bus I want to answer a call of nature."

in a state of nature = naked

"The window-cleaner saw me in a state of nature."

in the nature of = approximately, or resembling

"The cost will be in the nature of two hundred pounds."

"I assume those remarks are meant to be in the nature of a compliment."

in the nature of things = normal/usual

"You shouldn't scold your cat, it's in the nature of things for cats to chase birds like that."

second nature = automatic/habitual behaviour

"Mark is in trouble again; it seems that stealing has become second nature to him."

naught

come to naught/nothing = fail

"All Mike's elaborate schemes seem to come to naught."

near

a near thing = a good result that was nearly a bad one

"I just managed to pass my French exam but it was a very near thing."

near as dammit = very nearly

"It's twenty miles away, as near as dammit."

near at hand = close

"I shall be glad when we move to our new house where there are some shops near at hand."

near miss = very nearly hitting/reaching an objective/target

"I had a near miss driving to work this morning when a lorry collided with the car in front of me."

"Two airliners were involved in a near miss over Heathrow airport yesterday."

nearest and dearest = close/immediate family

"My first responsibility is to my nearest and dearest."

near thing = danger/trouble that is only just avoided

"That was a near thing ñ the teacher almost caught us!"

near the mark = bordering on indecent/risqué, or almost correct

"Some of John's comments get a bit near the mark when he's had a few drinks."

"I know he was only guessing, but Simon was surprisingly near the mark when he suggested the company might be in financial difficulties."

nowhere near = not near(ly)/well away from

"Come on, you've eaten nowhere near enough."

"The arrow was nowhere near the target."

See also: close/near to one's heart; far and near/wide; near the bone; near the knuckle.

neat

neat as a new pin = very neat/tidy
"My office is a mess yet yours is always as neat as a new pin; how do you do it?"

necessity

make a virtue of necessity = accept the inevitable (and try to derive an advantage from a disadvantage)
"It was pouring with rain so we made a virtue of necessity and tested our new waterproof clothing."

necessity is the mother of invention = inventiveness is stimulated by difficulty
"We were driving across the moors when the car's engine boiled over through lack of water in the radiator, but necessity is the mother of invention and we topped it up with two litres of lemonade we had."

neck

be breaking one's neck for = be desperate for
"I'm breaking my neck for a cup of tea."

break one's neck for = work hard/quickly
"We broke our necks to finish the job on time."

get it in the neck = be blamed/disciplined
"You'll get it in the neck if the boss finds out."

in something up to one's neck = closely involved in/with something
"The police are certain that Jacob is in the conspiracy up to his neck."

millstone round one's neck = large burden/responsibility
"I'll be glad when we can get rid of this millstone round our neck and pay off the mortgage."

neck and crop = completely
"The old machines needed constant repairs so I got rid of them neck and crop."

neck and neck = equal/level
"The Soviet Union and the United States are neck and neck in the race to send a manned spacecraft to Mars."

neck of the woods = particular location/place
"It was obvious from her accent that she didn't come from this neck of the woods."

neck or nothing = desperate
"It was neck or nothing so we sold everything we owned to buy shares in a gold mine."

risk one's neck = expose oneself to danger
"No thank you. I'm not going to risk my neck on the back of your motorbike."

stick/stretch one's neck out = take a gamble/risk
"I'm going to stick my neck out and guess that she's about twenty-five years old."

See also: breathe down somebody's neck; dead from the neck up; have the brass neck to (do something); noose round somebody's neck;
pain in the bum/neck; talk through the back of one's neck.

need

needs must (when the devil drives) = it is inevitable/unavoidable
"I ate the fish although I don't really like it, but there was nothing else and needs must when the devil drives."

need something like a hole in the head = not need something at all
"Thanks for giving me extra work to do before I go home ñ I needed that like a hole in the head!"

that's all/the last thing I need(ed)! = that is yet another annoyance/frustration
"The house was in a mess and then my mother made an unexpected call. That's all I needed!"
See also: crying need; hour of need; needs must when the devil drives.

needle
get the needle = become angry/annoyed
"Mum got the needle when she found out we hadn't done the washing up as we promised."
needle match = contest in which both contestants are very eager to win
"This year's final is a needle match between Manchester City and their old rivals Manchester United."
See also: look for a needle in a haystack; on pins and needles; pins and needles.

negative
in the negative = no
"With regard to your application for a loan, I am afraid the answer is in the negative."

neither
neither here nor there = irrelevant/unimportant
"Keep the change, it's neither here nor there."

Nellie
not on your Nellie! = definitely not!
"You won't find me going to those sorts of places. Not on your Nellie!"

nerve
bag/bundle of nerves = easily excited/frightened (person)
"By the time the dentist called me into his surgery I was a bundle of nerves."
get on one's nerves = annoy/irritate one
"That incessant background music gets on my nerves."
have a nerve = be impudent
"You've got a nerve, expecting me to clean your shoes for you."
have nerves of steel = be very calm/brave
"You have to have nerves of steel to be a steeplejack."
have the nerve = be brave/calm enough, or be impudent enough
"Very few people have the nerve to handle poisonous snakes."
"I don't know how you've got the nerve to even talk to me after what you did last night."
lose one's nerve = lack courage (to continue doing something)
"I was going to cross the stream on a fallen log but at the last minute I lost my nerve and went the long way round by the bridge."
nerve oneself to do something = summon up the courage to do something
"The cat brought in a dead mouse and I had to nerve myself to pick it up and take it outside."
touch a nerve = refer to something that angers/distresses somebody
"You certainly touched a nerve when you asked Peggy whether she had a regular boyfriend."
what (a) nerve = what impudence
"Henry has a car of his own yet he scrounges a lift from me nearly every morning. What a nerve!"
See also: war of nerves.

nervous
nervous as a kitten = very nervous
"I was as nervous as a kitten on my wedding day."

nest

foul one's (own) nest = discredit/harm oneself (through actions/behaviour near at home)
"He refuses to comply with the planning regulations and so all he's really doing is fouling his own nest."

mare's nest = something nonexistent that is claimed as a discovery
"The palaeontologist claimed that he had found a unique dinosaur fossil but it turned out to be a mare's nest."

See also: bring a hornet's nest around one's ears; cuckoo in the nest; feather one's nest; nest egg; stir up a hornet's nest.

nettle

See: grasp the nettle.

never

(well) I never did! = exclamation of disbelief/surprise
"I never did! It's John Jones, isn't it?"

never hear the end of something = be constantly reminded of something
"You'll never hear the end of it if you don't reply to your mother's letter."

never in a month of Sundays/never in the world = never
"Maria will never pass her driving test in a month of Sundays."
"Never in the world will you get all that stuff in the back of your car."

never-never land = imaginary ideal place
"The ideal of a completely socialist state is a never-never land that fails to recognize human frailty."

on the never-never = on credit/hire purchase
"I bought the car on the never-never so that I'd have enough cash left to tax and insure it."

well I never! = exclamation of surprise
"Well I never! Fancy meeting you here!"

See also: better late than never; never miss a trick; never say die; now or never.

new

brand new = absolutely new
"Jane has worn a brand new dress every day so far this week."

new blood = new member of a group (intended to invigorate it)
"Our local team needs some new blood if they're to start winning."

New World = the Americas
"The llama is a camel-like animal from the New World."

See also: new broom; new one on somebody.

Newcastle

See: carry coals to Newcastle.

news

have news for somebody = have information that will surprise somebody
"I've news for you ñ you've won the sweepstake."

news to somebody = fact previously unknown to somebody
"If the zoo has obtained another giant panda it's news to me."

break the news = inform somebody about a happening
"Congratulations on getting engaged. Have you broken the news to your parents yet?"

no news is good news = lack of information indicates that everything is well
"I haven't heard from my son since he went to New York two weeks ago, but no news is good news."

next

in(to) the next world = to death/heaven
"If you're careless with explosives they can blow you into the next world."

next door to = very nearly
"I think that borrowing pens and paper from work is next door to stealing."

next to nothing = very little
"My daughter delivers newspapers but they pay her next to nothing."

next to no time = very quickly
"Please wait, I'll be ready in next to no time."

the next man = anybody else
"You should have more confidence in yourself ñ you're as good as the next man."

what(ever) next? = exclamation of surprise
"Remember your manners! Whatever next?"

See also: next door to; next of kin.

nick

in good nick = healthy/in good condition
"I don't care what the outside of the car looks like as long as the engine is in good nick."

in the nick of time = just in time
"I arrived at the station in the nick of time, just before the train left."

night

have a good night = have an enjoyable evening's entertainment, or sleep well
"We all had a very good night at Margaret's birthday party."
"I've not been sleeping well lately but I took some tablets and had a good night last night."

make a night of it = spend all night enjoying oneself
"Let's buy a couple of bottles of wine and make a night of it."

night after night/night in, night out = continuously for several nights
"The baby's crying kept us awake night after night."

night and day/day and night = all the time/continuously
"From our house, you can hear the motorway traffic night and day."

night owl = somebody who regularly stays up late
"I'm a night owl and seldom go to bed until after midnight."

stay the night = remain overnight
"It's past midnight, so why don't you stay the night with us?"

See also: call it a night; dead of night; fly-by-night (operator); morning after the night before; one-night stand; ships that pass in the night.

nine

dressed up to the nines = wearing one's best clothes
"My wife came down to dinner dressed up to the nines, while I was still sitting around in my gardening clothes."

nine days' wonder = short-lived interesting/sensational event
"The prince's engagement was a nine days' wonder which quickly faded from the news."

nine times out of ten = more often than not/usually
"Nine times out of ten he comes home drunk at night."

nine to five = normal working hours
"I'm fed up with working overtime every week and wish I had an ordinary nine-to-five job."

right as ninepence = fit/healthy
"Brenda collapsed yesterday afternoon

yet she was as right as ninepence when I saw her that morning."

See also: on cloud nine; possession is nine points of the law.

nineteen

talk nineteen to the dozen = talk rapidly (and at length)

"My wife talks nineteen to the dozen and I hardly ever get a chance to speak."

nip

nip and tuck = equal/level

"The two runners were nip and tuck right to the finishing line."

See also: nip in the bud.

nit

nitty gritty = basic/fine details

"We are agreed in principle so let's now discuss the nitty gritty."

nit-pick = find/look for unimportant flaws in something

"I wish he wouldn't nit-pick when all we want is a general appraisal."

no

by no means = not (at all)

"By no means everybody wants an extra television channel devoted entirely to sport."

no go = absence of agreement/success

"The bank manager said it's no go, he won't lend us another penny."

no such thing = not at all, or a different thing

"We wondered if the weather would improve, but no such thing ñ it kept on raining."

"He accused me of calling him a liar, but I said no such thing."

"She said her dog was a spaniel, but it was no such thing."

no thanks to somebody = despite somebody (or his/her actions)

"We eventually finished the job, no thanks to Clive who didn't help in the least."

no time (at all) = very quickly

"Please wait, I'll be ready in no time at all."

not take no for an answer = emphasize that one wants a positive reply to a request

"Come on, I'll take you out to dinner ñ and I won't take no for an answer."

no way = definitely not

"No way will I get involved with those dubious property deals."

See also: it's no go; it's no joke; no dice; no end of; no holds barred; no man's land; no news is good news; no wonder.

nobody

See: like nobody's business; nobody's fool.

nod

a nod is as good as a wink to a blind horse = a hint is sufficient

"He says that the company has some temporary financial problems. A nod is as good as a wink to a blind horse, and I think we should not supply them with any more goods until they have paid our outstanding bills."

in the land of Nod = asleep

"Come on, children, it's time you were in the land of Nod."

nod off = fall asleep

"I think I'll go to bed, I keep nodding off."

on the nod = by (informal) agreement

"The board of directors approved the proposal on the nod."

See also: have a nodding acquaintance with.

noise

noise something abroad = make something widely known
"The company has been charged with malpractice but don't noise it abroad ñ it could be very bad for business."
See also: big fish/noise/shot.

none

have/want none of = not accept
"I want none of your excuses."
none other than = the same as
"The tramp was none other than a detective in disguise."
none the wiser = knowing no more than previously
"I've listened to your explanation for five minutes but I'm still none the wiser."
none the worse for = not harmed by
"Now I've cleaned it, the carpet is none the worse for having milk spilled on it."
none too = not very
"I'm afraid Jenny is none too bright."
second to none = the best
"My father grows roses that are second to none."
See also: bar none; none so blind.

nonsense

See: stuff and nonsense.

nook

in every nook and cranny = everywhere
"I've looked in every nook and cranny and I can't find my gold pen."

noose

noose round somebody's neck = heavy responsibility
"I refuse to buy a house on a mortgage because I don't want a noose round my neck for the rest of my life."
See also: put one's head in(to) a noose/on the block.

nose

bloody somebody's nose = hurt somebody (not necessarily physically)
"After the chief accountant had bloodied Olive's nose about errors in the figures, she took much more care over checking them."
cut off one's nose to spite one's face = suffer harm while trying to harm somebody else
"She cut off her nose to spite her face by refusing promotion because she didn't like the different office hours of the new job."
get up somebody's nose = annoy somebody
"That supervisor is so uncooperative, he gets right up my nose."
have a nose for = be good at finding
"If you want to know what's going on in the village, ask Mary ñ she's got a nose for scandal."
here's skin off your nose! = good health! (a toast)
"Thanks for the drink. Here's skin off your nose!"
keep one's nose clean = stay out of trouble
"Keep your nose clean and you'll get on well in the army."
no skin off one's nose = not harmful to one
"It's no skin off my nose if you won't talk to me."
on the nose = precisely on time
"Afteı a six-hour journey from Scotland the train arrived in London right on the nose."

put somebody's nose out of joint = displace somebody in somebody else's affections/esteem
"The boss is very attentive to the new typist, which has put his own secretary's nose out of joint."

rub somebody's nose in it = repeatedly remind somebody of his/her misdeeds
"I accept that he was caught shoplifting but there's no need to keep rubbing his nose in it."

thumb one's nose at = be defiant/show contempt
"Some of the pupils thumb their noses at the teachers now that corporal punishment has been abolished."

turn up one's nose at something = regard something with contempt/disdain
"It's no good turning your nose up at it, you've got to wear a uniform."

under somebody's nose = within somebody's sight
"He was searching for his slippers while they were under his nose all the time."

with one's nose in the air = in a disdainful way
"Ever since that incident at the party, Doris has walked past me with her nose in the air and refused to speak."

See also: follow one's nose; keep one's nose to the grindstone; lead somebody by the nose; look down one's nose at; nosey Parker; not look beyond the end of one's nose; not see beyond the end of one's nose; pay through the nose; plain as the nose on one's face; poke one's nose into; rub somebody's nose in the dirt.

not

See: as often as not; not a bit (of it); not at all; not half; not least; not to mention; not to worry.

note

somebody/something of note = famous/significant
"Nothing of note was said at the meeting."

strike the right/wrong note = be entirely appropriate/inappropriate
"That single white flower strikes just the right note with your black dress."

See also: compare notes (with).

nothing

all for nothing = with no result
"We searched for five hours and all for nothing."

be nothing to do with somebody = not be of somebody's concern
"What I do in the evenings has nothing to do with you."

count for nothing = have no effect/influence
"They have cancelled the project, so all our work of the last few weeks counts for nothing."

for nothing = free
"We had complimentary tickets so we got into the show for nothing."

good for nothing = worthless
"There are several dead elm trees nearby but their timber is good for nothing except burning."

have nothing on = be naked, or be not as good as
"Please knock before entering; you could walk in when I have nothing on."
"My new car has nothing on your old Jaguar."

have nothing on somebody = have no proof of somebody's guilt "I'm not afraid, the police have nothing on me."

have nothing to do with somebody = avoid somebody

"Promise me you'll have nothing to do with those boys who hang around outside the shop."

in one's nothings = naked
"Apparently Bronwyn likes to sunbathe in her nothings."

it is/was nothing = no thanks are needed
"Ralph tried to thank me for helping him move some furniture but I told him it was nothing."

make nothing of = not fuss about, or fail to comprehend
"I spilled his drink but fortunately he made nothing of it."
"Maggie showed me a hand-drawn map but I could make nothing of it."

mere nothing = trifle/unimportant thing
"I brought you back a small present. It's a mere nothing but I hope you like it."

nothing doing = nothing happening/with no result
"We went down town but there was nothing doing."
"I asked Kate to go out with me, but nothing doing."

nothing for it but = only possible course of action
"I've broken the machine and I suppose there's nothing for it but to go and tell the boss."

nothing if not = very
"Sarah is nothing if not honest."

nothing for it = no choice
"The car has broken down again and so there's nothing for it, we'll have to go by train."

nothing of the kind/sort = not the thing expected/mentioned
"He accused me of calling him a liar, but I had said nothing of the kind."

nothing short of = the same as/similar to
"Making a false statement to the police is nothing short of perjury."

nothing to choose between = little difference between
"I don't know whether to buy the blue shoes or the black ones ñ there's nothing to choose between them in price."

nothing ventured, nothing gained = risks must be taken to achieve something
"I've decided to emigrate to Canada and look for work there ñ nothing ventured, nothing gained."

stop at/short of nothing = do anything (however risky)
"Bill will stop at nothing to make his wife happy."

sweet nothings = trivial (whispered) conversation between lovers
"The couple sat in the corner, whispering sweet nothings to each other all evening."

there's nothing for it = there is no alternative
"It's all gone wrong and there's nothing for it but to start all over again."

there's nothing in it = the competitors are evenly matched, or there is no truth in it
"They have each won three games out of the six they have played against each other so there's nothing in it."
"Don't believe the rumours about my wife and the postman ñ there's absolutely nothing in it."

there's nothing to it = it is easy/simple
"Anybody can learn to drive, there's nothing to it."

think nothing of doing something = consider doing something as easy
"My wife thinks nothing of spending a hundred pounds on a new dress."

think nothing of it = it is unimportant
"Think nothing of it, I shall be glad to lend you my mower any time."

to say nothing of = in addition to
"He has an honours degree in chemistry, to say nothing of various A-levels and O-levels."
See also: come to naught/nothing; like nothing on earth; next to nothing; nothing of the kind; nothing succeeds like success; nothing to write home about.

notice

(at) short notice = with little warning
"I'm sorry it's such short notice, but could I come to see you this afternoon?"
give in one's notice = resign
"Pamela gave in her notice today; I assume she's got another job to go to."
give notice = announce/warn (in advance)
"I hereby give notice that the new regulations will come into force next week."
sit up and take notice = suddenly pay attention
"The boss heard that the factory inspector was going to pay us a visit, and that made him sit up and take notice."
till further notice = until some time in the future (yet to be decided)
"The cinema will be closed till further notice."

now

(every) now and again/then = occasionally
"I only see my ex-wife now and again."
just now = in the recent past, or in the near future
"Where are the scissors? I had them just now."
"Please wait ñ I'll be with you just now."
now, now = expression of sympathy or rebuke
"Now, now, there's no real reason to cry."
"Now, now, there's no need to talk to your sister like that."
now or never = this is the time to do something
"It's now or never ñ tidy your room or go without pocket money this week."
See also: here and now; now you are talking.

nowhere

get nowhere = get no result/make no progress
"I tried all my powers of persuasion but it got me nowhere."
See also: nowhere near.

null

null and void = ineffective
"The match was abandoned after half an hour and even though one team had already scored two goals the result was declared null and void."

number

get somebody's number = discover somebody's character
"I've got his number and I don't think he's trustworthy."
one's number comes up = one has good fortune
"Karl wants to buy a sports car when his number comes up."
one's number is up = one is going to be in grave trouble/die
"I knew my number was up when the boss caught me coming in late for the third day running."

one's number two = one's assistant/deputy
"I shall be on holiday next week so if you have any queries please address them to my number two, John Jones."

there's safety in numbers = a large group of people is less likely to come to harm than is an individual person
"Steve lets his daughter go on a school trip even though he won't let her spend a night away with a friend on the principle that there's safety in numbers."

See also: back number; in penny numbers; number one; one's days are numbered; opposite number.

nut

be nuts about somebody/something = enthuse about somebody/something
"Linda is really nuts about David Bowie."

do one's nut = be very angry/agitated/worried
"Where have you been? Your mother has been doing her nut for two hours wondering where you were."

in a nutshell = concisely
"I won't bore you with the details, but in a nutshell, the whole drawn-out meeting was a waste of time."

nuts and bolts = fundamental (significant) details
"The nuts and bolts of the case against her was that she was seen at the scene of the crime."

nutty as a fruit cake = silly/mad
"You can never get a sensible answer out of Charles, he's as nutty as a fruit cake."

off one's nut = mad
"Brian must be off his nut to pay that much for a shirt."

use a sledgehammer to crack a nut = use too much force/resources to bring about a small change
"Printing business cards on a thirty-inch press is using a sledgehammer to crack a nut."

See also: hard/tough nut to crack.

O

oar

put/stick one's oar in = interfere/interrupt
"The committee had nearly come to a decision when Harry stuck his oar in with some irrelevant point about the drains."

rest on one's oars = take a rest (during hard work)
"Come on, we've still got a lot of work to do ñ you can rest on your oars later."

oats

get/have one's oats = have sexual intercourse
"Graham says he doesn't need a permanent relationship as long as he gets his oats regularly."

off one's oats = unwell (and with a poor appetite)
"I've been off my oats since that recent bout of flu."

sow one's wild oats = live a carefree existence (when young and before settling down)
"I may be middle-aged now but I certainly sowed my wild oats before I met your mother and we got married."

object

no object = no restriction
"I'll buy you whatever you want ñ it's your birthday and money is no object."

See also: object of the exercise; object lesson .

obvious

See: state the obvious.

obligation

under an obligation = forced
"I feel under an obligation to repay their hospitality as soon as possible."

occasion

have occasion to = have the need/reason to
"I hope I shall not have occasion to warn you again."

on occasion = sometimes
"She has been known to take a small drink on occasion."

rise to the occasion = show ability in an emergency/unusual situation
"The disc jockey didn't arrive but Vic rose to the occasion and played a good selection of records all evening."

take the occasion to = take the opportunity to
"I would like to take the occasion to thank everybody for their kindness to me."

occur

it occurs to me = I have just thought
"It occurs to me that we could paint the walls a lighter colour to make the room look bigger."

ocean

See: drop in the bucket/ocean.

odd

against all/the odds = despite difficulties
"We were late and against all odds we still caught the train because its departure was delayed by ten minutes."

be at odds with = disagree with
"I'm at odds with my daughter over what time she should get home at night."

give/lay odds = bet/guess confidently
"I'll lay odds that the car still won't

start even after he's tinkered with the engine."

make no odds = not matter

"You do what you like, it makes no odds to me."

odd in the head = eccentric/slightly mad

"You must be odd in the head to pay a hundred pounds for a second-hand lawn mower."

odd man/one out = somebody who is left over when a group has been organized, or somebody who is different in some way

"We shall have to invite another girl to the party or Nigel will be the odd man out ñ everybody else is coming with a partner."

"Even at school Kate was the odd one out. She preferred to read books while the others were playing games."

odds and ends/sods = various small objects

"I must clear out those drawers; they're full of odds and sods accumulated over the years."

odds on = likely

"It's odds on it will rain tomorrow because I've got a day off work."

over the odds = more than necessary/normal

"Check the prices when you go to that shop, they have a habit of charging over the odds."

shout the odds = protest loudly

"No matter what the committee tries to discuss, even if it's only whether or not to paint the railings outside, Vera is always shouting the odds about the rights of women."

the odds are that = the likelihood is that

"Nobody knows what the pay rise will be, but the odds are that it will be in the order of five per cent."

what's the odds? = it is not significant

"I've run out of cigarettes but what's the odds? I'm trying to give up smoking anyway."

odour

in bad/good odour with = thought badly/well of by

"Mike has been in bad odour with his mother-in-law ever since he criticized her cooking."

odour of sanctity = (exaggerated) feeling of one's holiness/piety

"I would mind her extreme views less if she didn't always express them with such an odour of sanctity."

of

what of it? = what does it matter?

"I can wear a green tie with a blue shirt if I want to. What of it?"

off

a bit off = an unsatisfactory situation

"I think it's a bit off expecting us to work late every night this week."

badly off = poor

"We were so badly off when we first married that we could afford to heat only one room in the house."

be off with you! = go away!

"Be off with you! Can't you see I'm busy?"

fall off = decline/diminish

"Business always falls off in the winter."

get off with you = I do not believe you

"Get off with you, those shoes must have cost more than ten pounds."

go off = turn bad, or begin to dislike

"Uncooked meat soon goes off in this hot weather unless it is kept in a refrigerator."

"I went off Barry after he started telling those racist jokes."

have it away = steal something
"Don't leave your watch lying around or somebody will have it away."
have it off = have sexual intercourse with
"It's rumoured that Jack has had it off with his secretary."
in the offing = soon to happen
"Look at those black clouds. I think there is rain in the offing."
off and on/on and off = sometimes/ spasmodically
"No, I haven't seen Joe today, although he does come here off and on."
off limits = forbidden/out of bounds
"The girl's dormitory is off limits to all male students."
off/on line = not connected/connected, or not working/working
"The terminal is off line while repairs are being made to the central computer."
"The new printing presses are due to come on line next week."
off season = non-holiday period
"I like to go to the coast in the off season and have the beach to myself."
off/on the boil = inactive/active
"The community project has foundered since people's enthusiasm has gone off the boil."
"I'm bored with this old pub. Let's go to the disco where things are really on the boil."
off the rails = irrational/not sensible
"My son did go off the rails for a while in his late teens but he has settled down now and is happily married with a family."
off the record = not for publication/ unofficially
"The spokesman said that, off the record, the government is considering new legislation to catch tax dodgers."
on the off-chance = just in case (something happens)
"I called on the off-chance that you might want to come out for a drink tonight."
well off = wealthy
"When I'm well off I'll buy a Jaguar."
See also: fall off the back of a lorry; let somebody off the hook; off hand; off colour; off one's food; off one's hands; off/on one's guard; off the beaten track; off the cuff; off the map; off the peg; put off; put somebody off.

office

in/out of office = holding/not holding an official position
"The Socialists seem to make better proposals when they're out of office than when they're in power."
necessary offices = toilet facilities
"We must find a place to hold the show with the necessary offices and ample parking space."
through the (good) offices of = with the assistance of
"I was invited to the club through the offices of my father-in- law, who is a member."
See also: fill an office.

often

as often as not = about half the number of times
"As often as not I skip lunch and work right through."
every so often = occasionally
"Every so often we drive down to Devon to visit my wife's parents."
more often than not = frequently/usually
"Donald enjoys sea fishing and more often than not he catches enough for dinner."
once too often = one time too many,

resulting in failure
"You'll avoid paying your bus fare once too often and get caught by an inspector."

oil

no oil painting = unattractive
"My husband is no oil painting but I love him dearly."

oil the wheels = make something easier
"I find that a generous tip oils the wheels if you want speedy service at this restaurant."

strike oil = be lucky/succeed
"John has been trying to develop a new etching process for months and he's finally struck oil."

well-oiled = drunk
"Glen was well-oiled when he left the party and spent the night sleeping in the back of his car."

See also: burn the midnight oil; pour oil on troubled waters.

ointment

See: fly in the ointment.

old

any old how = anyhow (carelessly)
"Do the job properly, not just any old how."

a ripe old age = very old
"May you live to be a ripe old age and have dozens of grandchildren."

know somebody of old = know somebody for a long time
"You can't trust Veronica ñ I know her of old."

old boy/girl = former pupil/student
"The old boys raised a team to play the school first eleven at soccer."
"Our school is famous for its musical tradition, and there are three of its old girls in the present London Philharmonic Orchestra."

old guard/school = older/traditional members of a group/organization
"The managing director is one of the old guard, but the new young sales director seems to be getting the rest of the board to take a more up-to-date view."

old maid = unmarried woman
"I hope I soon meet somebody I want to marry, otherwise I'll finish up an old maid."

old man = father, or husband
"I inherited this watch from my old man."
"I must go now to cook my old man's supper."

old master = famous painter/painting
"The thieves broke into the manor house and stole ten old masters."

Old Nick = the devil
"Ted dreams up such crafty schemes I sometimes think he must be in league with Old Nick."

old school tie = symbol of class distinction/privilege
"The old school tie is more important than ability if you want to get a job with that company."

old timer = elderly person (with lengthy experience in a particular area)
"When I go to a first-class cricket match, I like listening to the old timers saying how the game has changed over the years."

old wives' tales = superstition
"You don't want to believe the old wives' tale that a red sunset indicates good weather; the weather forecast predicts that it will pour with rain all day tomorrow."

old woman = somebody who is fussy/indecisive, or wife, or mother
"Tim can be a right old woman when

it comes to deciding how to approach a new project."

"It's our twentieth wedding anniversary and I must buy a special present for my old woman this year."

"When we were children, our old woman used to do all the washing without the help of a machine."

See also: money for old rope; old as the hills; old boy network; old flame; old hand/stager; old hat; old thing; old sweat.

olive

See: offer/hold out an olive branch.

on

be on to a good thing = have something advantageous/profitable

"Anthony is on to a good thing: he married the chairman's daughter and was given a thirty per cent shareholding in the company."

be on to somebody = discover somebody's secret

"The customs authorities are on to me so I've got to leave the country immediately."

be on to something = discover something (that was concealed)

"If you have found a cheap solvent for carbon then you're really on to something."

dream on = entertain your wish but it will never happen

"If you want me to shave off my beard, dream on ñ I've no intention of doing so."

have something on somebody = know something incriminating about somebody

"I think Barbara must have something on Stephen the way he tolerates her insubordination."

it's (just) not on = it cannot be done

"No you can't go on holiday to France, it's just not on."

on and on = continuously

"It rained on and on for three whole days at the beginning of our holiday."

on the wagon = not drinking alcohol

"I feel much better when I wake up in the mornings since I've been on the wagon."

you're on! = I accept/agree!

"You're on! You'll give me five pounds if I can name the colours of the rainbow in their correct sequence."

See also: fall on/upon; odds on; off and on/on and off; off/on line; off/on the boil; on edge; on end; on the loose; on the receiving end; on the shelf.

once

all at once = suddenly

"All at once there was a tremendous clap of thunder that shook the whole house."

at once = at the same time, or immediately

"Don't try to talk and eat at once."

"You had better leave at once if you want even a chance of catching the last bus."

become/be made one = be united (in marriage)

"I'm looking forward to the time when you get your divorce and we can become one."

for once = for one time (and very unusually)

"For once we were all in agreement."

"Why don't you wait until last for once."

give somebody/something the once-over = quickly examine somebody/ something

"The new supervisor came round and gave everybody the once-over."
"I've found a second-hand car I want to buy and I would be grateful if you would come with me to give it the once-over."
just this once = on this occasion only
"Just this once can I borrow your hair drier?"
once and for all = finally
"Once and for all, you're not staying out until midnight!"
once in a while = occasionally
"Once in a while I go fishing, but I spend most summer weekends pottering about the garden."
once upon a time = at some time in the (remote) past
"Once upon a time I could run as fast as that, when I was much younger."
See also: once bitten, twice shy; once in a blue moon; once or twice.

one
be all one to somebody = not matter to somebody
"Give him a can of beer or lager ñ it's all one to him as long as it's booze!"
be at one with = be in agreement/ harmony with
"The students are at one with the lecturers that the college needs modernizing."
be one up on somebody = have an advantage/lead over somebody
"You're one up on your elder sister because she hasn't passed her driving test yet."
give somebody a fourpenny one = hit somebody with one's fist
"If you do that again I'll give you a fourpenny one!"
go one better = improve on something done by somebody else
"Lora ran from the school to the station in eight minutes but Doreen had to go one better and did it in less than seven."
new one on somebody = thing of which somebody was formerly unaware
"Do you know what kind of bird that is? It's a new one on me."
not be/feel oneself = feel different from normal (because of emotional upset/ illness)
"Sorry, I can't concentrate. I've just had some bad news and I don't feel myself today."
number one = oneself (to the exclusion of all others)
"You have to look after number one in the competitive world of big business."
one and all = everybody
"Happy Christmas, one and all."
one and only = (the) only one, or unique
"The fire won't light and I've already used our one and only match."
"Here he is, the one and only John Smith."
one and the same = identical
"I was surprised when I discovered that the actors who played the young boy and the old man were one and the same person."
one by one = one at a time (in a series)
"The jurors slowly filed ir o court one by one and took their places in the jury box."
one (more) for the road = a last drink before leaving
"I'll just have one for the road and then I must be going."
one-horse race = contest whose winner is known, even before it takes place
"The champion has no real competition and the contest has turned into a one-horse race."

one-horse town = place with few amenities
"We went on a mystery day trip to a one-horse town where there was nothing to do when we got there."
one in a million/thousand = great rarity
"Our son Jason is one in a million. He drove two hundred miles to pick us up at the airport because he knew we would be tired after a long trip and would not want to carry all our luggage on the train."
one-man show = event at which only one person appears to do/does everything
"Once the boss gets involved it becomes a one-man show and the rest of us might as well go home."
one-night stand = (sexual) relationship that lasts for only one evening/night
"No, I'm not still going out with Margaret. Anyway, that was only a one-night stand."
one-off = something that is unique
"We must preserve the old iron bridge. It is a one-off and there will never be anything like it built ever again."
(just) one of those things = something (unavoidable) that just happens
"If you use car parks every day, finding minor scrapes and scratches on your car is one of those things."
one or two = a few
"We could do with one or two houseplants in this room to brighten it up."
one over the eight = too much to drink
"At the party last night my husband had one over the eight and made a complete fool of himself."
one too many = too much alcohol
"I'm afraid I had one too many last night and I've got an awful hangover this morning."
one-track mind = thoughts dominated by one subject/an obsession
"All you think about is girls ñ you have a one-track mind."
one way or another = somehow
"Don't worry, I'll find the extra money one way or the other."
with one voice = unanimously
"The staff must speak with one voice if the management is to take notice of our suggestions."
you are a one! = you are amusing/cheeky/outrageous etc.
"Peter, you are a one! How can you say such outrageous things?"
See also: a hundred and one; go back to square one; one of the boys; one of these (fine) days; one in the eye for; one-man band; quick one.

oneself
by oneself = unaided, or alone
"Young Robert made that model aircraft all by himself."
"I don't like being by myself during a thunder storm."
See also: beside oneself; make oneself scarce.

onion
know one's onions = be skilled/well informed
"Why don't you ask Mary about the fault? She really knows her onions about the photocopier and can probably solve the problem in seconds."

only
if only = I wish that.Öso
"If only it would stop raining we could go for a walk."
only too = very

"Why don't you ask William? I'm sure he'd be only too happy to help."

open

blow something wide open = reveal a secret
"There was a conspiracy to hide the truth about arms exports but now the newspapers have found out and blown the whole affair wide open."

bring something (out) into the open = make everybody aware of something
"The best way to stop speculation about the company's future is to bring the whole financial problem out into the open."

come out into the open = reveal one's position/views
"Instead of making veiled criticisms, why doesn't he come out into the open and say what he thinks is wrong with the present set-up?"

in the open (air) = outside
"The Queen will greet her guests at the garden party in the open unless it rains, when the introductions will be maue in the marquee."

have/keep an open mind = be receptive to new ideas
"Even with his scientific training, Gary keeps an open mind about the possible existence of paranormal phenomena."

lay oneself open = put oneself in a vulnerable position
"The security guard who gave the thieves a duplicate key has laid himself open to a charge of conspiracy."

open and shut case = problem whose solution is incontrovertible/obvious
"Three witnesses saw her at the scene of the crime and so the police naturally thought they had an open

open door policy = national policy of trading with any country
"Germany's open door policy is being threatened by tariffs imposed by their competitors."

open-ended = with no planned finish or termination
The talks are open-ended and will continue until some sort of agreement is reached."

open fire = begin firing/start something
"If you have any questions for our guest speaker, open fire now."

open letter = letter published (in a newspaper) for general readership but addressed to a particular person
"In an open letter to the *Times* an ex-cabinet minister was highly critical of the government's economic policy."

open one's eyes to = make one aware/conscious of
"My recent visits to Bombay really opened my eyes to the realities of poverty in the Third World."

open one's heart to = confess confide in
"After a little persuasion, she opened her heart to me and told me what had been troubling her."

open secret = known fact(s) that is/are supposed to be secret
"It's an open secret that the rebels are receiving support from the neighbouring country's government."

open sesame = "magic" incantation that gives access to something that was inaccessible
"The place was full but I tipped the doorman and ñ open sesame! ñ he let us in."

open the door to = cause to happen/encourage
"I think that relaxation of the licensing laws would open the door to all kinds of abuses."

open the flood gates = remove all restrictions
"The removal of import restrictions has opened the flood gates to huge quantities of cheap goods from the Far East."
open up = confess/reveal a secret
"After hours of questioning the suspect finally opened up and told the police all he knew about the bank robbery."
open verdict = judgement of a court that acknowledges a crime may have been committed but does not apportion guilt
"The jury brought in an open verdict, but the judge immediately ordered a re-trial."
See also: keep one's options open; keep open house; open as the day; open book; opening gambit; open one's eyes to; open question; open to discussion; with one's eyes open; with open arms.

opera
See: soap opera.

opinion
be of the opinion = believe
"Bill is of the opinion that the results of professional wrestling matches are fixed."
matter of opinion = debatable/disputable
"Keith thinks that England has the best international cricket team this season, but that's really a matter of opinion."
pass an opinion = express a viewpoint
"Harry is always ready to pass an opinion on anything, particularly subjects he knows little about!"

opportunity
take the opportunity = use a particular moment/time
"I would like to take the opportunity of introducing you to my daughter Alice."

opposite
somebody's opposite number = somebody who holds a similar position elsewhere
"Would you please refer that enquiry to my opposite number in our Paris office."

option
have no option but to = be forced to
"Because of the seriousness of the offence I have no option but to request the maximum penalty."
keep one's options open = deliberately remain undecided
"One of the firms I applied to has offered me a job but I am keeping my options open until I hear from the others."
soft option = easy method of doing something
"Given a choice, Harry always picks the soft option when things get difficult."

oracle
work the oracle = be very persuasive (and get somebody to accept a proposition)
"The sales director had a difficult time but finally worked the oracle and obtained a substantial order."

order
be given one's marching orders = be told to leave

"My daughter's boyfriend started to be a nuisance so I gave him his marching orders."

in good order = healthy/working well

"I've been having trouble with my rheumatism but at least my lungs are in good order."

"The car is in perfectly good order and worth every penny I'm asking."

in running/working order = working satisfactorily

"Can you guarantee that the clock is in working order?"

in short order = quickly

"Please fetch me a spanner, and in short order."

make something to order = make something on request (to specific directions)

"My house needs a new front door but it's a non-standard size, so I'll have to get one made to order."

on order = ordered (of goods)

"I have a new car on order but it will take a month to be delivered."

order of the day = what is expected at a particular time

"Dinner jackets are the order of the day for the annual ball."

order somebody about = be domineering

"The new supervisor is annoying senior members of the staff by ordering them about all the time."

out of order = not working, or not acceptable

"My telephone was out of order so I couldn't phone you as promised."

"That last remark of yours was totally out of order."

take holy orders = become a (Christian) priest, monk or nun

"I'm seriously considering joining a monastery and taking holy orders."

take orders from = obey commands given by

"I prefer to work for myself because I don't like taking orders from anyone."

tall order = very difficult request

"Finding Easter eggs for a children's party in November is a tall order."

See also: apple-pie order; of the first order/water; order of the boot; pecking order; put/set one's house in order; (just) what the doctor ordered.

ordinary

out of the ordinary = unusual

"John's habit of putting ground black pepper on strawberries is a bit out of the ordinary."

other

a bit of the other = sexual intercourse

"They disappeared upstairs for a bit of the other."

every other = alternate items in a series

"Give a Christmas cracker to every other child, so that each pair can then pull one."

this, that and the other = things in general

"I hadn't seen my sister for months and when she came to stay we talked about this, that and the other until after midnight."

See also: all/other things being equal; in other words; look the other way; (on the one hand).Ö (and) on the other hand; the other day.

out

be out of something = to lack something

"I'm right out of sugar, could you please lend me some?"

be well out of something = be fortunate not to be involved in/with something

"There was a fight at the club last

night but I was well out of it ñ I went home an hour previously."

far out = very unusual

"Have you seen Jan's new hair style? It's far out!"

go all out = make an extreme effort

"I hear that the British team are going all out to beat the world record."

have it out with somebody = vigorously contest something with somebody

"My brother and I haven't spoken for years so I've decided to have it out with him and try to be friends again."

murder will out = a bad deed will always be revealed

"After his release he tried to start a new life in another town, but murder will out and news of his prison record soon spread through the community."

not far out = close

"Your guess that it cost four hundred pounds is not far out."

on the way out = becoming obsolete/ unfashionable

"The fashion writers say that mini skirts are on the way out."

out and about = sufficiently well (after an illness) to go out

"It's good to be out and about after spending two weeks in hospital."

out and away = by far

"This is out and away the best apple pie I've tasted for years."

out and out = absolute/total

"You should have nothing to do with him, he's an out and out scoundrel."

out for something = wanting (to obtain) something

"You should be careful in any dealings with Terry, he 's just out for whatever he can get."

out of all reason = totally unreasonable

"His asking price of five thousand for the car is out of all reason."

out of it/things = excluded/not part of a group

"I always feel out of it when they start playing quiz games because everyone is much more clever than me."

out of one's mind/tree = mad

"A third death in his family in one year was too much for poor old William and he went out of his tree."

out in the cold = excluded

"Most of the children seem to get on well together but poor Louise is often out in the cold."

out in the wilds = remote from a town or city

"I don't know exactly where he lives, except that it's somewhere out in the wilds."

out to (do something) = determined to (do something)

"I hear Glen is out to beat the world record for the number of hard-boiled eggs eaten in a minute."

out with it = say what you know/want to say

"Come on, out with it, what really happened last night?"

take it out on somebody = be angry with somebody (not necessarily with good reason)

"It's no good taking it out on me, I can't help it if the car had a puncture."

See also: down and out; edge somebody out; make out; not out of the way; odd man out; out at the elbows; out for the count; out of all proportion; out of/ beyond one's depth; out of one's element; out of commission; out of date; out of hand; out of harm's way; out of order; out of pocket; out of sight; out of sorts; out of the blue; out of the question; out of the ordinary; out-of-the-way; out of touch; out of turn; out of/within bounds; out of work; out on a limb; sit something out; truth will out.

outset

from the outset = from the beginning
"You knew what she was like from the outset so you've only got yourself to blame."

outside

at the outside = at most
"The fare will be about two hundred pounds at the outside."

outstay

See: outstay one's welcome.

over

all over = ended, or in every part
"He told me that his relationship with Pam is all over."
"We were wet all over after being caught in a shower of rain."

be all over somebody = be overfriendly with somebody
"My daughter is all over me when she wants something."

over and above = additional to
"It costs two pounds over and above the price of the goods to pay for the postage."

over and done with = totally finished
"I'll be glad when this job is over and done with and we can get back to normal working hours."

over and over (again) = repeatedly
"I'm disappointed in Jason; he makes the same mistakes over and over again."

over the top = excessive
"The price they charge for wine at that restaurant is really over the top."
"Judy's behaviour was over the top at the party last night."

See also: fall over backwards; fall over oneself; half seas over; make over; over my dead body; over the counter; over the hill; over the hump; over the odds; think something over.

overboard

go overboard = be overenthusiastic
"I know you like colourful makeup but don't you think that green and pink together is going a bit overboard?"

overture

make overtures = initiate an approach (to somebody)
"The chairman of our company thinks we should make overtures to our rivals with a view to forming a merger."

owe

owe it to oneself = feel it one's right to have
"Why don't you take a holiday? You owe it to yourself after working hard for several months."

own

be one's own man = be (totally) independent
"You won't persuade Jeremy to do anything he doesn't want to, he's his own man."

come into one's own = have the opportunity to be seen at one's best
"Janice has come into her own now that her knowledge of languages is needed to deal with overseas customers."

do one's own thing = do what one pleases
"I'm not sure it's a good idea to let

children do their own thing without some sort of guidance or supervision."

get/have one's own way = (be allowed to) do what one wants

"I see you've had to give him his own way again to prevent a scene. I think you're too lenient with that child."

hold one's own = maintain one's position (against competition/illness)

"My father is in hospital after a heart attack but the doctors say he is holding his own."

in one's own right = through one's own ability

"She helps her husband with his business, but she's also an accountant in her own right."

own somebody body and soul = control somebody completely

"I am only your girlfriend ñ you don't own me body and soul, you know."

own up = admit/confess

"If the person who wrote this owns up I shall take no further action."

See also: by one's own account; get one's own back; hold one's own; in one's own good time; in one's own time; off one's (own) bat; on one's own; the devil looks after/takes care of his own.

oyster

See: world is his/her oyster.

P

mind one's p's and q's = be careful (not to annoy somebody)
"The supervisor is all right as long as you watch your p's and q's."

pace

keep pace with = maintain position with
"I enjoy my job in research because I have to keep pace with all the latest developments."

pace out = measure a distance in terms of its length in paces (each approximating to one metre, or yard)
"The policeman paced out the distance between the car and the post it collided with."

put somebody/something through his/her/its paces = require somebody/something to demonstrate his/her/its ability
"Kay interviewed seven girls to find a good assistant and she really put them through their paces."

set/make the pace = determine/establish the speed that everyone else has to follow
"Heather is our most experienced worker. Shall we ask her to make the first two or three items and set the pace for the others?"

show one's paces = demonstrate what one can do
"Gordon played ten people simultaneously at the chess club last week and really showed his paces ñ he lost only one game."

snail's pace = very slowly
"The train went at a snail's pace because of engineering works on the line."

stand/stay the pace = continue as long as/keep up with everyone else
"We went on a pub crawl but as usual Mark couldn't stand the pace and was legless after four drinks."

pack

no names, no pack drill = no fuss/trouble will result as long as nobody is named
"The man who rescued the children from the river was a real hero but he wishes to remain anonymous ñ no names, no pack drill."

package deal = purchase/settlement involving various factors that must be accepted in their entirety
"For our new kitchen I did a package deal which included the planning, supply of equipment and units, and all the fitting."

package holiday/tour = organized holiday which includes the cost of travel, accommodation and meals
"We find the cost of travel and accommodation cheaper by buying a package holiday, even if we don't eat in the hotel but go out to various local restaurants each evening."

packed out = totally full of people
"The ground was packed out when our local team played its League Cup match."

pack it in/up = stop it
"Pack it in, you kids, or I'll bang your heads together!"

pack off = send away
"Your boyfriend is much too young for you. Why don't you pack him off to his mother?"

pack of lies = many lies (at one time)
"I believed her story of hardship but it turned out to be a pack of lies ñ she's better off than you or me."

pack up = stop doing something

"Come on, Bruce, it's nine o'clock. Time to pack up and go to bed."
pack up one's troubles = leave a difficult situation and move elsewhere
"My husband and I were always quarrelling and so I decided to pack up my troubles and return home to live with my parents."
send somebody packing = tell somebody to go away
"If Silvester comes round here again I'll send him packing!"
See also: pack one's bags.

packet
cost a packet = cost a great deal of money
"Roy's new car must have cost a packet."
make a packet = earn much money
"Harry earned a packet after the war selling surplus army blankets."
stop a packet = sustain a severe injury
"Poor John stopped a packet when his car was in collision with a lorry."

paddle
See: paddle one's own canoe.

pain
be at pains/take pains = take much trouble
"Clive took such great pains to explain why he couldn't come, I wonder if he had any intention of doing so in the first place."
for one's pains = as (inadequate) compensation for what one has done
"I spent two hours mowing her lawn and all she gave me for my pains was a cup of tea!"
on/under pain of (death) = at the risk of (severe) punishment
"Yes, you can go to the party, but you come home late on the pain of death."
pain in the bum/neck = somebody who is (always) a nuisance
"Don't tell me Christopher is coming, wherever he goes he's a pain in the neck."

paint
like watching paint dry = very boring
"Ian spent two whole hours showing us his holiday photographs; it was just like watching paint dry."
paint the town red = celebrate (by going out and enjoying oneself)
"I've just won a prize on the Premium Bonds. Let's go out and paint the town red!"
See also: no oil painting; not so black as one is painted.

pair
pair off = accompany somebody else to make a twosome
"I notice that halfway through every party, Tim always pairs off with Penny."
See also: have only one pair of hands; pair of spectacles; show a clean pair of heels.

pal
See: old pal's act.

pale
See: beyond the pale; pale as death.

palm
cross somebody's palm with silver = pay somebody (in advance for information/services)
"If you cross his palm with silver the car park attendant can always find you a place, even when the sign says full up."

have somebody in the palm of one's hand = have (total) control over somebody
"Beryl can get her husband to do whatever she wants ñ she's got him in the palm of her hand."
palm something off on somebody = (fraudulently) get somebody to take something he/she does not want
"I asked for a bottle of Scotch but the woman in the shop tried to palm me off with some imported Japanese rubbish."
See also: grease somebody's palm; have an itching palm.

pan
pan out = happen
"They were having problems but it all panned out right in the end."
See also: flash in the pan; jump out of the frying pan into the fire.

pancake
See: flat as a flounder/pancake.

pants
have ants in one's pants = fidget/be impatient
"Sit still, children, you look as though you've got ants in your pants."
scare the pants off = frighten
"He put a plastic spider in his sister's soup and scared the pants off her."
See also: bore stiff/the pants off/to tears; catch somebody with his pants down.

paper
commit to paper = write down (as a matter of record)
"I've had a good idea about how to plan the project and I must commit it to paper before I forget it."
couldn't punch his way out of a paper bag = is very feeble/weak
"Don't worry about Barry's threats ñ he couldn't punch his way out of a paper bag."
not worth the paper it's written on = worthless
"You can't rely on Robin ñ his promises are not worth the paper they're written on."
on paper = theoretically
"Although the scheme seemed workable on paper, it failed in practice."
See also: paper over the cracks; paper tiger; put pen to paper.

par
above/below par = (of stock) sold/ valued at more/less than the original price
"My original ten-pound shares are now valued at fifteen ñ five pounds above par."
"After the stock market crash, millions of pounds were written off shares as their value fell below par."
on a par with = as good as
"She is only an amateur pianist, but her playing is on a par with the best professional."
par for the course = as expected
"Nigel didn't turn up to help as he promised, but that's par for the course with him when there's work to be done."
up to par = at the expected/required standard (of health, quality etc.)
"I don't feel up to par this morning and think I'll have to take a day off work."

paradise
See: fool's paradise.

parallel

draw a parallel between = compare with (to demonstrate resemblances)
"The speaker drew a parallel between unemployment today and the depression of the nineteen-twenties."

parcel

parcel out = split into portions and share among a group
"The shopkeeper donated dozens of tins of food which we parcelled out among the old people of the village."
See also: part and parcel.

pardon

I beg your pardon = I am sorry, or I did not hear what you said, or I disagree with you
"I beg your pardon, I didn't mean to tread on your foot."
"I beg your pardon. Did you call me?"
"I beg your pardon, but you're talking a lot of rubbish!"
See also: pardon my French.

Parker

nosey Parker = somebody who pries into other people's business
"Debbie is a bit of a nosey Parker but she always knows the latest gossip."

parlour

parlour tricks = mischief
"Tina is up to her usual parlour tricks and provoking people by making outrageous comments about the Royal Family."

parrot

parrot fashion = pointless repetition
"He can repeat the rules parrot fashion but he doesn't really understand their significance."
See: sick as a parrot.

part

for my part = from my point of view
"I'm tired of trying to advise her; for my part, she can do what she likes."
for the most part = mostly
"I had a look at the items for sale before the auction began and for the most part they were rubbish."
look the part = have the appearance of whom one intends to be
"When I'm invited to dine at the Captain's table on a cruise I like to wear a dinner jacket and really look the part."
man of many parts = somebody who is versatile
"He runs his own business and acts as accountant, manager and salesman ñ indeed, a man of many parts."
on somebody's part = by/from somebody
"Let's shake hands, there are no regrets on my part."
part and parcel = inevitable/usual part
"Collecting empty glasses and cleaning the ashtrays is part and parcel of a barman's job."
part company = end an association/ partnership
"My partner and I seldom agreed about things so we decided to part company and each set up our own business."
parting of the ways = decision/departure point
"Our marriage has been unhappy for several years now and my wife and I have finally come to the parting of the ways."
parting shot = (defiant) comment made on leaving
"The chairman had a violent disagreement with the committee and

as a parting shot said that he would not be seeking re-election."

part with = give up/surrender

"I love my dog and I would never part with him."

take part in = have a share/role in

"I hear you're going to take part in the anniversary celebrations."

take somebody's part = side with/stand up for somebody

"It's not fair! Hazel always takes Edward's part whether he's right or wrong."

take something in good part = take no offence at something

"People sometimes tease Gwyneth about her accent, but she takes it all in good part."

See also: act a part; discretion is the better part of valour; part company; part of the furniture;

play a part.

party

party line = shared telephone line, or official policy as advocated by the leaders of a group/organization

"I shall be glad when we get an independent telephone; the party line always seems to be in use whenever I want to make a call."

"I don't care what your personal views are; when talking to this company's clients you must follow the party line."

party piece = somebody's favourite accomplishment

"We all had a few drinks and then Bryn did his usual party piece of balancing a pint of beer on his head."

See also: stag party; throw a party.

pass

come to a fine/pretty pass = result in a difficult/unacceptable situation

"Things have come to a pretty pass if you can't even light a bonfire without all the neighbours complaining."

in passing = do/say something casually, when the main issue concerns something else

"Howard was telling me about his work and happened to mention in passing that he was looking for an assistant. Why don't you apply for the job!"

let something pass = deliberately ignore something (rather than question/make a fuss about it)

"Karl made his usual comment about women being poor drivers, but I decided to let it pass rather than get into an argument about it."

make a pass at somebody = try to make friends with somebody (with sexual overtones)

"You need to be careful with Jack ñ I had only known him for ten minutes before he tried to make a pass at me."

pass away/over = die

"I was sorry to hear that your mother passed away last week."

pass for = be thought of as/closely resemble

"She could pass for thirty but I happen to know she's got a grownup son."

pass off = falsify/misrepresent

"Jim has a supply of old pennies which he polishes up and passes off to foreign tourists as rare coins."

pass out = graduate from an educational establishment, or faint

"Polly is due to pass out from training college at the end of July."

"It's very hot in this room. If I don't get some fresh air I think I'm going to pass out."

pass over = ignore/overlook
"Please take your time and read your statement carefully. It is very easy to pass over a mistake when you're in a hurry."

pass the time of day = have a casual conversation
"I like to go for a stroll in the park and pass the time of day with some of my old friends."

pass up = decline to accept
"I'm surprised you passed up the chance of going on holiday to Switzerland with your parents."

pass water = urinate
"Doctor, I'm having difficulty passing water."

See also: come to pass; pass by on the other side; pass muster; ships that pass in the night.

passage

work one's passage = work to earn one's fare
"I've signed on a merchant ship so that I can work my passage to Australia."

past

past it/past its best = too old to be effective
"I shall have to take the train to Scotland ñ I dare not drive that far because my old car is past it."

past master = somebody with acknowledged skill
"Why don't you ask Raymond how to fix it? He's a past master at mending these machines."

I wouldn't put it past him/her = he/she is quite capable of doing something (usually bad)
"Frank says he finished that job yesterday ñ mind you, I wouldn't put it past him to say he'd finished even if he hadn't."

pat

See: pat on the back.

patch

go through a bad/good patch = have an unsuccessful/successful period
"The business went through a bad patch earlier this year but is prospering now."

not a patch on = nowhere near as good as
"Sylvia is so proud of her painting but it's not a patch on Linda's."

patch up = re-establish a relationship (after a quarrel)
"My son and his girlfriend have had yet another row, but no doubt they'll patch it up by the weekend."

See also: bad patch.

path

cross somebody's path = encounter somebody
"I had a difficult time with Councillor Jones; I hope I don't cross his path again."

See also: beat a path to somebody's door; lead somebody up the garden path.

patience

enough to try the patience of a saint = very annoying/trying
"Waiting for my wife while she gets herself ready to go out is enough to try the patience of a saint!"

See also: try the patience of Job.

patter

good line of patter = convincing/ persuasive talk

"Beryl is one of the best sales people we have. She has a particularly good line of patter with the men and can sell them almost anything."

pause

give somebody pause = make somebody hesitate
"When he suggests we go out to dinner, ask him if he's going to pay ñ that should give him pause."

pave

pave the way for something = make something easier/possible
"Emma made a good presentation of the product, which paved the way for the sales director to clinch the deal."

pay

in somebody's pay = given money by somebody (for a favour)
"Our rivals always seem to get the best local government contracts. I wonder of they've got one of the councillors in their pay?"

not if you paid me = not in any circumstances
"I wouldn't climb to the top of that ladder, not even if you paid me."

pay off = prove to be a successful decision/investment, or settle an outstanding debt
"My decision to take the job with the lower salary but better prospects paid off when they promoted me and gave me a large increase in wages."
"This bonus will allow me to pay off what I owe on my car."

pay off an old score = get revenge/settle an account
"There were many fouls during the game, mainly through players paying off old scores."

pay one's respects = visit somebody out of courtesy
"We must pay our respects to the new vicar one of these days."

pay one's way = pay (in full) for what one has/needs
"I don't really mind how much I earn as long as I have enough to pay my way."

pay on the nail = pay immediately
"The shop will give a discount of ten per cent as long as you don't want credit but pay on the nail."

pay through the nose = pay an excessive price
"The corner shop is convenient if you forget to get something in town, although you pay through the nose for anything you buy there."

put paid to something = destroy/prevent something
"When you dropped the tray you put paid to three of my best glasses."
"Your mother's visit has put paid to my plan to take you to Paris for the weekend."

the devil/hell to pay = (serious) trouble
"We must clear up this mess before Mum gets home or there will be the devil to pay."

See also: pay attention (to); pay court to; pay dirt; pay lip service to; pay the earth for; rob Peter to pay Paul.

pea

as alike as (two) peas in a pod = exactly the same
"Our dog has just had four puppies and they're as alike as peas in a pod."

peace

hold one's peace = refrain from talking
"If you get into a discussion and you don't know what the others are talking

about, it's best to hold your peace."

keep the peace = stop people from arguing/fighting
"My parents were always quarrelling and I had to keep the peace for the sake of my younger sisters."

make one's peace with somebody = re-establish a friendship after a disagreement
"I had a violent argument with Patrick, but he had made his peace with me by the end of the afternoon."

peace and quiet = calm silence
"After working in this noisy shop all day I like nothing better than to go home for a bit of peace and quiet."

peace of mind = contentedness/freedom from worry
"For my own peace of mind I must go back home and check that I locked all the windows."

See also: dove of peace.

peacock

proud as a peacock = very proud
"Dad's as proud as a peacock of that shelf he put up ñ and it hasn't fallen down yet!"

pearl

pearls of wisdom = shrewd/wise advice
"The discussion was getting nowhere until Vic arrived and gave us all some pearls of wisdom."

peck

keep one's pecker up = remain cheerful
"Keep your pecker up. Things are bound to improve next week."

pecking order = hierarchical order of importance/precedence within group
"Ask Martin what the company's plans are; he should know, he's quite high in the pecking order these days."

pedal

soft pedal = exercise restraint about
"Thora is an avid feminist so I decided to soft pedal the issue of women's rights while she was at the meeting."

pedestal

put somebody on a pedestal = admire somebody (for being better than he/she really is)
"He put his wife on a pedestal and so was all the more hurt when he found she was capable of deceiving him."

peel

See: keep one's eyes open/peeled/skinned.

peg

bring/take somebody down a peg (or two) = humble somebody
"I'm tired of Heidi's arrogant attitude ñ she wants taking down a peg or two."

off the peg = ready to wear (of clothes)
"No, this suit isn't made to measure. I bought it off the peg at the shop in the High Street."

peg away = work steadily
"If I keep pegging away at this job it should be finished by the end of the week."

peg down = confine to a particular level/restrain
"It's time the duty on petrol was pegged down and kept at that level."

peg on which to hang something = minor topic used as an excuse for introducing a major one
"I used his point about the price of wine as a peg on which to hang a lengthy discussion of the Common Market."

peg out = die
"My old dog was twelve years old and she finally pegged out last week."
See also: level pegging; square peg in a round hole.

pelt

at full pelt = as quickly as possible
"We must work at full pelt if we're to get this finished by this evening."

pen

put pen to paper = start writing
"I have lots of ideas for stories but find it difficult to put pen to paper."
See also: slip of the pen.

penalty

pay the penalty = take the consequences (for one's actions)
"I didn't take an umbrella and paid the penalty when it started to rain ñ I got soaked!"

pencil

put lead in one's pencil = improve one's sexual prowess
"Go on, eat some oysters. They'll put lead in your pencil."
See also: blue pencil.

penny

bad penny = somebody of bad character
"I don't want you to associate with Jason, he's a real bad penny."

have one's (three)pennyworth = have one's (minor) say in a discussion
"We were nearly all agreed when Howard had to have his three pennyworth and start the argument all over again."

in for a penny, in for a pound = having made a decision, commit to it wholeheartedly.
"After some hesitation I did finally decide to buy a car, and so I bought a new one ñ well, in for a penny, in for a pound."

in penny numbers = a few at a time
"I couldn't find anyone who would buy all my books at once so I had to sell them off in penny numbers."

not cost a penny = entirely free/at no cost at all
"We went to the park and spent a happy afternoon strolling around, and it didn't cost a penny."

not have a penny to one's name = have no money
"I can't come out with you to the pub tonight because I haven't a penny to my name."

pennies from heaven = unexpected money
"I had some pennies from heaven in the post this morning ñ I received a rebate of Income Tax."

the penny dropped = somebody (finally) understood
"I tried to explain why she should be careful in her dealings with Vincent but it was some time before the penny dropped."

penny for your thoughts = what are you thinking?
"You've been staring blankly out of the window for several minutes; a penny for your thoughts."

pretty penny = much money
"He owns a big house and a yacht so he must be worth a pretty penny."

spend a penny = go to the toilet
"I wish the bus would hurry up and get to the station, I'm dying to spend a penny."

tuppeny-ha'penny (twopennyhalfpenny) = cheap/trivial

tuppenyha'penny hotel near the docks."

ten/two a penny = very cheap/common
"I'm glad I didn't buy one of those black berets ñ they're two a penny now among the girls round here."

turn an honest penny/shilling = earn money in an honest way
"At last I've found a job. It's not very exciting but I turn an honest penny."

turn up like a bad penny = (constantly) reappear
"Bill seldom goes to our pub these days yet he always turns up like a bad penny when there is free food on darts night."

See also: cut off without a penny/ shilling.

peril

at one's peril = at one's own risk
"I think it's an unsound venture and you would invest in it at your peril."

perish

perish the thought = I hope it (something unfortunate/unpleasant) does not happen
"She's not going to sing is she? Oh, perish the thought!"

person

as bad etc. as the next person = as bad etc. as anybody else
"I'm as keen as the next person, but I think we should consider the consequence more carefully before we act."

I'd be the first/last person to.Ö = I am very willing/most unwilling to do something
"If they ask for help I'd be the first person to volunteer."
but I'd be the last person to call him a liar."

in person = personally
"If you have any more trouble with the equipment, I won't send my assistant but I'll come in person to fix it."

perspective

in perspective = from a balanced/ sensible point of view
"I know you're upset about the stain on your dress but you must keep it in perspective ñ after all, you've got plenty of other dresses you can wear while that one is being cleaned."

pet

See: pet aversion; pet hate.

petard

See: hoist with one's own petard.

Pete

for Pete's/pity's sake! = exclamation of annoyance/surprise
"For Pete's sake! Can't you make less noise?"

Peter

See: rob Peter to pay Paul.

phrase

turn of phrase = manner of saying/ writing things
"Even when David is making a complaint he manages to find a neat turn of phrase that gets their attention."

See also: coin a phrase.

pick

pick and choose = choose carefully

haven't got time to pick and choose."

pick at (one's food) = eat very little of a meal
"I think something must be worrying John, he has only picked at his food for the last two days."

pick-me-up = reviving drink/medicine
"I've felt depressed since I had the flu; what I need is a good pick-me-up."

pick off = destroy one at a time
"Over the years, he's picked off his competitors so that he now has a virtual monopoly."

pick of the bunch = the best (in a group)
"They are all good typists but Maria is the pick of the bunch."

pick one's way = step carefully (between obstructions/hazards)
"There had been a gas explosion and we had to pick our way between the broken glass."

pick one's words = speak carefully (after due thought)
"Patrick is touchy on the subject of religion and you have to pick your words carefully when talking about it."

pick on somebody = bully/speak angrily to somebody, or (unfairly) select somebody for an unpleasant task
"Stop picking on me or I'll tell father."
"I know somebody has to go and fetch some more logs, but why pick on me?"

pick out = choose/select, or separate from background/surroundings
"Please get me some tomatoes ñ and pick out the ripe ones."
"If you look carefully, you'll see a deer over there. You can just pick it out from the heather."

pick somebody to pieces = be very critical of somebody
"Instead of just sitting there picking other people to pieces, why don't you get on with your own work."

pick up = get better/improve in health, or get better/increase in volume (of business), or get to know somebody/something, or collect
"Now that his temperature has dropped, I'm sure your baby will pick up."
"The hotel business always picks up in summer."
"I picked up this girl on the train and I'm going to meet her again tonight."
"Tim served no formal apprenticeship in car mechanics, he just picked it up at the garage where he works."
"If you're going to the station, would you minding picking up a parcel for me at the Red Star office?"

pick up the pieces = restore things to normal after disruption
"What annoys me is that he starts the job until it become difficult and then leaves me to pick up the pieces."

See also: bone to pick (with somebody); pick a quarrel; pick holes in; pick sides; pick somebody's brains; pick up the tab.

picnic

no picnic = difficult situation
"During World War II my uncle was at Dunkirk and he says it was certainly no picnic."

picture

get the picture = understand (a situation)
"There is quite a lot of rivalry between the people who work here, if you get the picture."

keep/put somebody in the picture = inform somebody (about a situation)
"What's wrong between your parents? You had better put me in the picture

before we go to stay with them."
See also: pretty as a picture.

pie
have a finger in the pie = have an interest/share in an undertaking
"I told him I would work for him only if I could have a finger in the pie."
pie in the sky = unattainable hope
"His plans for converting his stable into an antique shop are just pie in the sky."
See also: easy as pie; eat humble pie.

piece
all of a piece with = all the same as
"The government's policy concerning the elderly is all of a piece with their attitude to other minority groups."
give somebody a piece of one's mind = angrily complain to/scold somebody
"If she does that again I'll really give her a piece of my mind."
fall to pieces = become broken (mentally or physically)
"Nigel will fall to pieces if he doesn't stop working so hard."
"I'm sorry about your cup; it just fell to pieces in my hand."
go to pieces = lose control of one's emotions
"When he heard of his son's death he went completely to pieces."
nasty piece of work = somebody who is very unpleasant
"I wouldn't want to annoy the bouncer on the door of the night club, he's a nasty piece of work."
pull to pieces = find fault with
"I don't seem to be able to do anything these days without the boss pulling it to pieces."
say one's piece = say what one intends to say
"They were all arguing so I just said my piece and left."
See also: conversation piece; pick somebody to pieces; pick up the pieces; piece of cake; piece of skirt; piece of the action.

pig
buy a pig in a poke = buy something unseen (and thus not know its worth)
"They often have some mystery job lots at the end of the auction. You are buying a pig in a poke, but sometimes they contain some interesting items."
live like a pig in clover = live in luxury
"Silvester inherited his father's fortune and has lived like a pig in clover ever since."
make a pig of oneself = overeat (greedily)
"Maria prepared this wonderful meal and I couldn't help making a pig of myself."
make a pig's ear of something = do something badly/messily
"If that tear is supposed to be mended you've made a right pig's ear of it."
pig(gy)-in-the-middle = somebody who is (involuntarily) between two opposing people/groups
"Whenever my daughters start arguing I find myself pig-in-the-middle, and they both turn against me."
pigs might fly = it is very unlikely to happen
"He said he would pay me back the money he owes me next Monday ñ and pigs might fly!"
See also: sweat like a pig.

pigeon
stool pigeon = informer (to the police)
"The police couldn't possibly have known I was there unless they were

told by a stool pigeon."

not one's pigeon = not one's affair/business

"Don't ask me to fill in the forms. That's not my pigeon, you are employed to do that."

See also: put the cat among the pigeons.

pikestaff

plain as a pikestaff = very obvious

"Don't tell me you can't see where you've painted over the frame and onto the window, it's as plain as a pikestaff."

pile

pile it on (thick) = exaggerate

"I ate too much and had a day off work but I piled it on thick and told them I had food poisoning."

See also: pile on the agony.

pill

sugar the pill = make something that is unpleasant as pleasant as possible

"We have to make two people redundant but we can sugar the pill by giving them very generous severance payments."

See also: bitter pill.

pillar

from pillar to post = from one place to another

"I went into a big store to buy an accessory for my camera but they just passed me from pillar to post ñ nobody seemed to know which department stocked it."

pillar of society = upright/worthy member of the community

"Councillor Jones is a pillar of society, so we were all the more shocked when we found out what he had done."

See also: pillar/tower of strength.

pin

for two pins = for the slightest reason

"If he says something like that to me again, for two pins I'll hit him!"

not care/give two pins = not care at all

"I don't care two pins whether she comes or not."

on pins and needles = anxious/nervous

"Don't keep us all on pins and needles. Did you get promotion or didn't you?"

pin back one's ears = listen carefully

"Pin back your ears, I'm only going to tell you this once."

pin one's hopes on = rely on

"The shop has had poor receipts so far this year and we're pinning our hopes on the holiday season to improve turnover."

pins and needles = tingling in one's extremities

"I went to sleep with my arm draped over the edge of a chair and when I woke up I had pins and needles in my hand."

pin somebody down = force somebody to commit himself/herself

"I keep asking Ian if he wants to take part but I cannot pin him down."

pin something on somebody = incriminate somebody

"Why is it that, whenever anything goes wrong, you try to pin it on me?"

you can hear a pin drop = it is very quiet

"Like all children mine can be very noisy but you can hear a pin drop when I ask if anybody wants to go to bed."

See also: pin money; pin one's faith on/ put one's faith in.

pinch

at a pinch = if (absolutely) necessary/in an emergency

"It's really my weekend off but at a pinch I could come in and help get the job finished."

feel the pinch = be short of money

"My husband lost his job and we really began to feel the pinch when our savings ran out."

pinch and scrape = live in a frugal way/ in poverty

"My parents had to pinch and scrape to raise seven children on my father's income."

take something with a pinch of salt = doubt the (complete) truth of something

"He says he used to be a soldier in the SAS, but I take that with a pinch of salt."

pink

be tickled pink = be very amused/pleased

"I was tickled pink when I found I had won a prize in the lottery."

in the pink = in good health

"I really feel in the pink after a fortnight's holiday."

pink of perfection = best of condition

"His car is always in the pink of perfection, beautifully clean both inside and out."

strike me pink! = I am surprised!

"Strike me pink! Bill Jones! I haven't seen you for ages."

See also: pink elephants.

pip

give somebody the pip = anger/annoy somebody

"I wish you'd stop playing that record, it really gives me the pip."

pipped at the post = just beaten at the end of a contest

"Ruth nearly got the manager's job but she was pipped at the post by somebody with slightly more experience."

pipe

in the pipeline = being prepared

"The authorities won't commit to a course of action because they say there is new legislation in the pipeline."

pipe down = stop talking

"Pipe down, children, I'm trying to listen to the news on the radio."

pipe dream = unattainable ambition/ desire

"I would like to buy a villa in Spain when I retire, but with my limited resources it is only a pipe dream."

pipe up = start speaking

"What did you say? Pipe up at the back there."

piping hot = very hot

"That's what I like on a cold winter's night ñ piping hot cocoa."

put that in your pipe and smoke it! = see how you like that!

"I wouldn't come to your rotten party even if you asked me, so put that in your pipe and smoke it!"

pistol

See: put a pistol to somebody's head.

pit

pit one's wits against = compete by using one's intellect

"I entered the quiz just for fun and found myself pitting my wits against a university professor."

pitch

black as pitch/pitch black/pitch darkness = very dark

"I got home very late. It was as black as pitch and I knocked over the milk bottles, waking everyone up."

pitch in = join in/share (enthusiastically)

"For supper I got several dishes from the Chinese take-away and we all pitched in."

pitch into somebody = attack/fight somebody

"The bully was taunting Stephen, when suddenly Stephen pitched into him with fists flying."

pitch one's tent = settle somewhere (temporarily)

"I'll pitch my tent anywhere while I'm doing freelance work."

See also: at fever pitch; queer somebody's pitch.

pity

more's the pity = unfortunately

"My young daughter was going to stay with her grandmother for a week, but she's not going now, more's the pity."

See also: for Pete's/pity's sake!

place

all over the place = everywhere

"Where have you been? I've been looking for you all over the place."

be somebody's place = be somebody's duty/responsibility

"It's not your place to tell me how to do my job."

fall into place = take up its proper position

"Tina's hair is so fine and straight that you can turn her upside-down, stand her up again, and it all falls into place."

give place to = be superseded by/yield

"Over a period of only a few years, the slide rule gave place to the electronic calculator."

"The sun rose slowly over the horizon and night gave place to day."

go places = succeed

"Once I'm qualified in my profession I intend to go places."

in high places = in a position of authority/power

"Nigel usually gets what he wants, because it seems he still has friends in high places."

in (out of) place = where something does/does not belong

"The new blue vase you bought looks exactly in place among the decor of this room."

"You must admit that your T-shirt and jeans were bit out of place among the dinner jackets at that party."

in the first place = from the beginning, or the first reason is.Ö (often not followed by in the second place etc.)

"I knew Sandra would be a nuisance ñ I didn't want her to come in the first place."

"You're not eating your dinner looking like that. In the first place, I think you should go and have a wash."

know one's place = behave in a way that is appropriate to one's position

"I know my place and I wouldn't presume to tell an expert how to do his job."

pride of place = best/most prominent place

"His darts trophy takes pride of place on the mantelpiece."

put somebody in his/her place = (angrily) remind somebody of his/her position

"I'm pleased you told him off, it's

about time somebody put that young man in his place."

put oneself in somebody's place = imagine being in somebody else's position

"Put yourself in my place. What would you do?"

take somebody's place = replace somebody

"I had to go out so Jane took my place at the meeting."

take the place of something = act as a substitute for something

"Coffee has taken the place of tea as the popular drink in many homes."

See also: have one's heart in the right place.

plague

avoid somebody/something like the plague = make every effort to keep away from somebody/something

"Tony is a bad influence, and if I were you I'd avoid him like the plague."

plain

plain as the nose on one's face = very obvious

"Surely you can see what's wrong, it's as plain as the nose on your face."

plain sailing = easy progress

"The drive is plain sailing once you get out of the suburbs."

plain speaking = honest/open talk

"They are all so suspicious of each other, a little plain speaking would do a lot of good."

See also: plain as a pikestaff; plain English.

plan

go according to plan = have the intended result

"If all goes according to plan we should be in Hong Kong tomorrow."

plank

See: thick as two short planks.

plant

plant something on somebody = put something in somebody's possession to incriminate him/her

"When charged with the offence, he claimed that the police had planted the drugs on him."

plate

have something handed to one on a plate = receive something without making any effort

"She's asked me to get the materials, trace the pattern and set up the machine ñ she wants it handed to her on a plate."

on one's plate = be one's responsibility (to get done)

"You've got too much on your plate; why don't you employ an assistant?"

play

bring/call/come into play = make use of

"It was only when the reserves were brought into play that the battle turned in our favour."

fair play = even-handedness/fairness in a competitive activity

"The boys have decided to settle their differences with a fight, but I shall be there to see fair play."

foul play = crime (particularly murder)

"The police removed a body from the canal but said that they did not suspect foul play."

make a play for = attempt to get

"I hear a rumour that he's going to make a play for the presidency."

make play of/with = emphasize
"He makes much play with the fact that he served as an officer in the army before he got the manager's job."

play a part in = contribute to
"Despite all the recent advances in drug therapy and surgery, the family doctor must still play a part in community medicine."

play along with = agree to co-operate with (dishonestly/only temporarily)
"I don't think we should join his scheme but let's play along with him for the time being until we know what his plans are."

play at = do something without (total) commitment
"I wish she would take her responsibilities seriously instead of just playing at them."

play cat and mouse with somebody = tease somebody (by keeping him/her uninformed)
"I can't tolerate all the suspicion and I wish the police would stop playing cat and mouse and make a specific charge against me."

play dead/possum = remain motionless and pretend to be dead
"The young bird played dead and the cat ignored it."

play down = minimize the importance of
"The government is playing down the significance of the balance of trade figures this month."

played out = exhausted
"I'm getting too old for cycling. These days I'm played out after only a few miles."

play fair = be honest/straightforward, obey the rules
"The difficulty in bidding for contracts against foreign competition is that not every company plays fair."

play false = deceive
"Don't deal with Jones, he played us false last time."

play for time = delay in the hope of gaining an advantage
"Come on, it's your turn. Make your mind up and stop playing for time."

play hard to get = put difficulties in the way of somebody who wants to meet/talk to one
"Tina has no problems in attracting men ñ she just plays hard to get."

play it cool = remain calm/nonchalant
"No matter how agitated and upset other people get, Gill just plays it cool and gets on with her work."

play/take no part in = do not participate in
"I hope you played no part in that trouble at the club the other night."

play on words = a pun, a joke that relies on a double meaning
"Most of the comedian's jokes involved a play on words."

play (it) safe = take no risks
"I have a lot to do this afternoon so I'd better play safe and say I'll meet you at seven o'clock, not six thirty, in case I have to work late."

play somebody off against somebody else = gain an advantage by making two other people compete
"One easy, although unkind, way of dealing with two morose teenagers is to play one off against the other."

play something down = reduce something in importance
"Don't forget; we must play down any reference to price until we get them interested in the main points of our proposal."

play the field = distribute one's attentions among several people/things

"I don't have a regular girlfriend; I'm just playing the field until the right one for me comes along."

play up = be a nuisance
"My rheumatism plays up in this damp weather."

play upon = take advantage of (somebody's fears/weakness)
"Let us send Lucy to talk to him and play upon his weakness for attractive women."

play up to somebody = flatter somebody (for gain)
"Maggy has only to play up to her boss and she can get half a day off whenever she wants."

the state of play = prevailing situation
"At present, the state of play is that the committee has been discussing the matter for three hours without reaching agreement."

See also: beat/play somebody at his own game; child's play; play a waiting game; play ball with somebody; play by ear; play fast and loose; play gooseberry; play havoc with; play (merry) hell with; play into somebody's hands; play it by ear; play one's ace; play one's cards close to one's chest; play one's cards right/ well; play second fiddle; play/act the fool; play the game; play to the gallery; play with fire; two can play at that game.

please

if you please = if you would believe it (a surprising fact)
"And then, if you please, he asked me to lend him a hundred pounds."

pleased as Punch = very pleased
"My mother was pleased as Punch when I took her some flowers."

please oneself = do whatever one wants
"Please yourself, wear red shoes with a green dress if you must."

pretty please = intensifier of plain "please"
"Even if you say pretty please I won't give you any more pocket money."

pleasure

have the pleasure = meet somebody
"Who's your friend? I don't believe I've had the pleasure."

it's a pleasure = I am pleased (to help)
"I enjoyed helping you. Believe me, it's a pleasure."

take pleasure in = enjoy
"Tina takes great pleasure in teasing her sister."

with pleasure = certainly
"With pleasure. I shall be happy to drive you to the airport."

pledge

sign the pledge = promise formally not to drink alcohol
"I had such a bad hangover this morning I considered signing the pledge."

plot

the plot thickens = the situation is getting more complicated/interesting
"The plot thickens: if it wasn't Judy I saw you with last night, who was it?"

plough

plough back = reinvest
"I don't collect the interest but plough it back into my savings account."

pluck

pluck at one's heartstrings = make one feel sympathy
"Pictures of starving children always pluck at my heartstrings."

See also: muster/pluck/screw/summon up courage.

plum

have a plum in one's mouth = talk in an upper-class way

"The new manager would be better received by the workers if he didn't have a plum in his mouth."

See also: land a plum job.

plumb

See: plumb the depths.

plunge

take the plunge = take a risk

"Clara and I have been going out together for ten years and we've finally decided to take the plunge and get married."

pocket

be in somebody's pocket = be under somebody's control (because he/she pays one)

"He offered to pay me for the information, but I refused because I don't want to be in somebody's pocket."

in pocket/out of pocket = having made/failed to make a profit

"Are you sure I paid enough? I don't want you to be out of pocket on the deal."

live in somebody's pocket = live very closely with somebody

"The trouble with sharing a flat with three others is that you're all living in each other's pockets."

pocket/swallow one's pride = be forced to behave in a humble manner

"I don't like the way he talks to me but I pocket my pride because he's a good customer."

See also: burn a hole in one's pocket; dip into one's pocket; line one's pockets; put one's hand in one's pocket.

point

beside the point = irrelevant/unimportant

"Never mind the price, that's beside the point. Is it really what you want for your birthday?"

come/get to the point = reach the most significant part of a conversation/discussion

"I do wish she'd hurry up and get to the point!"

in point of fact = actually/truthfully

"I said I enjoyed the meal she had prepared when in point of fact I hate shellfish, and that's what she cooked."

make a point of doing something = make an effort to do/take care in doing something

"Whenever I'm in Canterbury I make a point of visiting the cathedral."

make one's point = state one's views persuasively

"Councillor Jones made his point well and the committee accepted his proposal."

off the point = irrelevant

"His speech was so boring because he would keep going off the point to describe his wartime experiences."

on the point of doing something = about to do something

"I was on the point of phoning you when you called me first."

point blank = directly

"I told him point blank what I thought of his behaviour."

point of no return = position/stage after which it is impossible to go back

"We've spent so much money on the project that we've passed the point of no return and we shall have to spend even more to finish it."

point of view = standpoint/way of looking at something
"We try to maintain quality but from our client's point of view the chief factor is cost."

point taken = I agree with you
"Point taken, I agree ıt needs to be done ñ but how are we going to pay for it?"

sore point = sensitive subject
"Don't mention baldness to Eddie, it's a sore point with him."

stretch a point = disregard the rules (to be helpful)
"Could you stretch a point and give me just one more week to pay what I owe?"

strong point = best feature of somebody/something
"Rose's strong point is her phenomenal memory for dates."
"The strong point of the car is that it is economical to run and maintain."

take somebody's point = accept somebody's proposal/suggestion
"I understand your reluctance and I take your point."

to the point = relevant
"I disagree with your view that the schedule is unimportant. I think that timing is very much to the point."

up to a point = so far but no farther
"Italian food is all right up to a point but I do get tired of eating pasta nearly every day."

that's the (whole) point = that is what I am trying to get you to accept/understand
"That's the whole point. You can't claim overtime if you take the previous day off."

that's not the point = that is irrelevant
"I don't care how much make-up costs these days. That's not the point, you're still not getting any more pocket money."

you have a point there = I agree with what you suggest
"You have a point there; increasing vandalism may be the result of lack of parental control."

See also: case in point; cut-off point; match point; not to put too fine a point on it; point of honour; point the finger at; up to a point.

poison

name/what's your poison? = what would you like to drink?
"What's your poison? Beer or wine?"

poke

poke fun at = derive unkind amusement from/mock
"You shouldn't poke fun at him just because he can't ride a bicycle."

poke one's nose in(to) = meddle in somebody else's affairs
"I wish your mother would stop poking her nose into our business."

See also: pig in a ,oke.

poker

stiff as a poker/ramrod = rigid/very stiff
"The rabbit had been dead for a long time because it was as stiff as a poker."

See also: poker/straight face.

pole

poles apart = widely different
"The management and the unions are still poles apart in what they each regard as an acceptable pay rise for this year."

up the pole = mad, or in trouble
"Anybody who pays hundreds of

pounds for a single postage stamp must be up the pole."
"If I don't find the money by Monday I'll be right up the pole."

polish
polish off = finish (quickly)
"If you would please help me we could soon polish off this work."
polish up = improve/revise
"If you are taking a job as a shop assistant you will have to polish up your maths."
spit and polish = elaborate (over)cleaning
"It will take a lot of spit and polish to get this room habitable again."

pond
See: big fish in a small pond.

pony
by/on shanks's pony = on foot/walking
"We went all the way across Dartmoor on shanks's pony."

poor
poor as a church mouse = very poor
"My parents were as poor as church mice and yet they managed to bring up seven happy, healthy children."
See also: poor relation.

pop
pop something on = put something on quickly/temporarily
"I'll just pop my coat on and go to the corner shop."
pop up = appear/occur
"She keeps popping up in the most unlikely places."
top of the pops = most favourite
"Of all the men in the office, Dennis is still top of the pops with me."
See also: pop the question.

port
any port in a storm = any opportunity (even if not the preferred one)
"I bought a ten-year-old Ford, but when you haven't much money you have to use any port in a storm."

pose
strike a pose = behave in an ostentatious way (to draw attention to/emphasize something)
"Here comes Graham. Watch him strike a pose by the door until everyone has seen his new suit."

possess
like a man possessed = very energetically
"I don't like going with William, he drives like man possessed."
possession is nine points of the law = the person who actually holds something is in the best position to claim its ownership
"I found this fountain pen in the street. Mike claims it is his, but possession is nine points of the law."
what(ever) possessed one? = what made one do something?
"I don't know what possessed me but I spent fifty pounds on a pair of new shoes."

post
beaten/pipped at the post = defeated at the last moment
"I got as far as the final of the quiz but was then pipped at the post."
keep somebody posted = keep somebody informed
"Please keep me posted about how the job is progressing."

See also: deaf as a post; pillar to post; pipped at the post.

pot

all to pot = confused/spoiled
"The trains are all to pot today because of a derailment farther down the line."

a watched pot never boils = an activity seems to take even longer when one is impatient for it to finish
"I have been waiting for that paint to dry for two hours now. How is it that a watched pot never boils?"

go to pot = deteriorate/become very bad
"Our team played well until midway through the game but in the second half they went to pot and were finally defeated four-nil."

in the melting pot = in a state of flux/transition
"I don't know when we will be able to make a start because the whole project has gone back into the melting pot."

pot boiler = work of art/literature created just to make money
"I wrote a book of short biographies as a pot boiler while waiting to begin work on my next novel."

pot calling the kettle black = unfair criticism from somebody who is guilty of the same fault
"He complains about my mistakes but he's always making errors himself; it's a typical case of the pot calling the kettle black."

pot shot = casual attempt/unaimed shot
"I took a pot shot at learning German but I didn't persevere with it."

See also: pot hunting; take pot luck.

potato

hot potato = somebody/something that it is risky to be involved with
"A wages policy is a real hot potato with both the government and the opposition."

pound

See: have/get one's pound of flesh; in for a penny, in for a pound.

pour

it never rains but it pours = when one thing goes wrong, other things go wrong at the same time
"I lost my cheque book, tore my jacket, and trapped my finger in a door all in one day ñ it never rains but it pours!"

pour oil on troubled waters = have a calming/soothing effect
"My parents have been arguing again so I suppose I had better go and see them and pour oil on troubled waters."

pour money down the drain = spend a lot of/waste money
"The trouble with trying to maintain an old car is that you're always pouring money down the drain to keep it roadworthy."

powder

keep one's powder dry = be prepared for immediate action
"Keep your powder dry, we'll be starting work on the new contract any day now."

power

do a power of good = do much good
"A glass of whisky will do you a power of good."

do a power of harm = do much harm
"A reputation for non-payment of debts can do a company a power of harm."

power behind the throne = actual, but

unrecognized, person in charge
"With so many successful men it is really the wife who is the power behind the throne."

powers that be = people in charge
"I don't know if I can get the day off work, I'll have to ask the powers that be."

See also: exercise one's power; more power to his elbow.

practice

in practice = actually (as opposed to theoretically)
"It is becoming increasingly difficult to follow Marxist ideals in practice."

make a practice of = do as a matter of habit/routine
"Come on, take it. I don't make a practice of giving money away!"

out of practice = stale through lack of recent practice
"Yes, I will play you at tennis, but you must remember that I'm out of practice."

put something into practice = actually do something (that was previously only planned/thought about)
"We have discussed the plan continually for several weeks now; the time has come to put it into practice."

practise

practise what one preaches = do what one tells others they should do
"You keep telling the children that their room is in a mess. Isn't it time you began to practise what you preach and tidied up the garage?"

praise

praise to the skies = give very high praise
"He's critical of my work when we are on our own, yet in front of other people he praises it to the skies."

sing somebody's praises = enthusiastically praise somebody
"Your boyfriend must be perfect, from the way you keep singing his praises."

See also: damn with faint praise

preach

See: practice what one preaches; preach to the converted.

precious

precious few/little = not many/much
"I seem to get precious few chances to enjoy myself these days."
"There's precious little point in complaining about it."

premium

be at a premium = be in short supply because of scarcity/rarity
"Experienced personal assistants are always at a premium."

put a premium on something = value something highly
"This company puts a premium on punctuality ñ so don't be late."

prepare

be prepared to = be willing to
"Councillor Jones said he was prepared to donate a hundred pounds to launch the appeal."

presence

have presence = possess an imposing bearing/impressive appearance
"It has been argued that it is more important for a leader to have presence than ability."

make one's presence felt = act/behave in such a way that makes one noticeable
"The only way you can make your

presence felt among that lot is to do something really outrageous ñ like eating peas with your knife!"

presence of mind = common sense in an emergency
"Fortunately somebody had the presence of mind to turn off the water at the main."

present

at present = now
"I am busy at present, can I phone you later?"

for the present = for now
"Wear your old jeans for the present, while I wash your new ones."

there's no time like the present = if something must be done, it might as well be done now
"If you've got toothache, I'll make an appointment to visit the dentist ñ there's no time like the present."

See also: present company excepted.

press

press ahead/on = make an effort to continue
"We can either make camp now, or press on until dark and be that much nearer our objective."

(hard) pressed for = lacking/short of
"I'm pressed for time yet I must finish this work today."

pressgang somebody into doing something = force somebody to do something
"They pressganged me onto the committee and then voted me chairman."

press something into service = improvise/make use of something when the correct item/object is unavailable
"Mixing bowls and saucepans were pressed into service to store water during the drought."

press something on somebody = force somebody to accept something
"I didn't want paying for the favour but he pressed the money on me, so I accepted it."

pressure

bring pressure to bear on somebody = attempt to compel somebody to do something
"We had to bring quite a lot of pressure to bear before he would agree to help us."

pressure group = group of people who attempt to influence those in authority
"The local council listened to objections by a pressure group who want the new by-pass to be built on the other side of the town, not along the actual route proposed by the planners."

pretence

See: false pretences.

pretty

pretty as a picture = very pretty
"My young granddaughter is as pretty as a picture in her party dress."

pretty much = more or less
"I went to visit my sick mother and found her pretty much the same as she was yesterday."

pretty well = nearly
"She's pretty well agreed to go away with me."

sitting pretty = in a favourable situation
"Now that you've got the manager's job you're sitting pretty until you retire."

See also: come to a fine/pretty pass; lead

somebody a (merry/pretty) dance; pretty kettle of fish; pretty penny.

prey

be prey to = suffer from

"I've been prey to arthritis ever since I was forty."

prey on one's mind = trouble one's mind

"A combination of financial and marital difficulties preyed on his mind and he took an overdose of sleeping tablets."

price

at a price = at high cost

"You can have the whole car repainted in bright purple if you want ñ but at a price."

at any price = under any conditions

"After the way he behaved, I won't go out with him again at any price."

beyond price = priceless

"To me, her friendship is beyond price."

fancy price = over expensive charge

"I don't like that new restaurant; they charge fancy prices for mediocre food and poor service."

price on somebody's head = reward for capturing/killing somebody

"Jake must be wary of bounty hunters now that the sheriff has put a price on his head."

price oneself out of the market = charge so much that nobody will pay the price

"He wanted a thousand pounds for his old car. No wonder he couldn't sell it, he priced himself out of the market."

what price.Ö? = what chance is there for. Ö ?

"What price power if you can't be happy?"

See also: asking price; every man has his price.

prick

See: prick up one's ears.

pride

pride and joy = object of somebody's pride

"Jason's new toy train is his pride and joy."

pride oneself on = take pride in

"Mike prides himself on his ability to do crossword puzzles."

swallow one's pride = humble oneself

"You walked out on your girlfriend after a row. Now you'll just have to swallow your pride and ask her to take you back."

take pride in = feel proud about

"There's more to life than taking pride in the fact that you can drink a pint of beer in four seconds."

See also: pride of place.

prime

cut off in one's prime = destroyed at one's peak of ability/performance

"His acting career was cut off in its prime by a car accident that left him disabled."

prime mover = initiator/instigator

"George was the prime mover in getting the firm to provide luncheon vouchers."

See also: prime of (one's) life.

principle

in principle = in theory

"They agreed with our proposal in principle, but have asked us to prepare some detailed costings."

on principle = because of one's integrity/moral values

"Sandra won't eat meat on principle."

the principle of the thing = underlying moral consideration

"I deplore fox hunting. It's not that I'm squeamish, it's the principle of the thing."

print

in/out of print = available/no longer available new for sale (of books)

"The book you want is out of print but you might find a shop that still has a copy in stock."

small print = fine details/conditions (of a contract etc.)

"The terms of the contract sound too good to be true. Are you sure you've read all the small print?"

private

See: private eye.

pro

pros and cons = arguments for and against

"Don't be hasty. Wait until you've heard all the pros and cons before you make up your mind."

probability

in all probability = very probably

"We have planned a picnic and in all probability it will rain."

problem

no problem! = that will be easy!

"You've got a puncture? No problem! I'll soon mend that for you."

profile

See: keep a low profile.

promise

ñ *and that's a promise!* = ñ and I really mean it!

"Anyone found pilfering will be dismissed immediately ñ and that's a promise!"

I promise you = I guarantee

"If you say that again you'll be in trouble, I promise you."

See also: break/keep a promise; lick and a promise.

proof

proof positive = definite proof

"He says he was at home sick yesterday but I have proof positive that he went to watch the cricket."

See also: the proof of the pudding is in the eating.

prop

See: prop up the bar.

prophet

prophet of doom = pessimist/somebody who always expects the worst

"Don't be a prophet of doom. Of course it will be sunny on your wedding day."

proportion

out of all proportion = very exaggerated

"Her reaction was out of all proportion to the remark that prompted it."

sense of proportion = balanced view

"It's all too easy to lose one's sense of proportion when discussing crimes involving children."

proud

do somebody proud = treat somebody (very) well

"We went to visit my wife's parents and they really did us proud for the whole weekend."

proud as a peacock = very proud

"June is as proud as a peacock after winning her first swimming certificate."

stand proud = project (farther than required)
"I caught my sleeve on a nail-head that was standing proud of the wooden fence."

public
See: in the public eye.

pudding
the proof of the pudding is in the eating = success is gauged by the final result
"You say you have repaired it. Go on then, switch it on ñ the proof of the pudding is in the eating."
See also: in the (pudding) club.

pull
have pull = have authority/influence
"Now that he's manager, he has the pull to get things done the way he wants."
pull a face = grimace
"There's no need to pull a face. Eat your cabbage, it will do you good."
pull in/up = halt/stop
"That's the second time the police have pulled you up for speeding this month."
"Pull in at that shop over there and I'll go in and ask for directions."
pull oneself together = regain control of one's emotions
"You're a big boy now so stop crying and pull yourself together."
pull one's socks up = improve one's performance
"Miranda will have to pull her socks up if she is to pass O-level maths."
pull one's weight = do one's share of work
"I'm going to complain to the boss if Clive doesn't start pulling his weight."
pull out = withdraw
"We were looking forward to a close race but the two best runners pulled out at the last minute."
pull out all the stops = do something as enthusiastically/vigorously as possible
"We must pull out all the stops for the Queen's visit and show her what a splendid part of the neighbourhood this is."
pull round/through = survive
"Edward has been involved in a car crash and they say he won't pull through."
pull something off = succeed
"We really need this contract; I do hope you can pull it off."
pull strings = influence people in authority
"Councillor Jones must have pulled a few strings to obtain planning permission to build himself another house in the grounds of his present one."
pull the birds/girls/women = attract women (sexually)
"This new aftershave is guaranteed to pull the girls."
pull the other one (it's got bells on) = I don't believe you
"You saw an elephant in the park? Pull the other one!"
pull together = co-operate
"If we all pull together we can finish the job by this evening."
pull over = move/steer (a vehicle) to one side
"Pull over quick. I think Tina's going to be sick."
See also: pull a fast one; pull a rabbit out of a hat; pull one's punches; pull rank; pull somebody's leg; pull the rug from under somebody(ës feet); pull the wool over somebody's eyes; pull up roots/stakes.

pulse

See: keep one's fingers on the pulse

pump

pump somebody = obtain information from somebody (by clever questioning)

"Take him out for a drink and pump him about what his company is going to do concerning the new safety regulations."

See: all hands to the pumps.

punch

beat somebody to the punch = do something before somebody else

"You should put in your offer before somebody beats you to the punch."

pull one's punches = fail to press home an attack

"She made a scathing attack on the financial director ñ and she didn't pull her punches."

punch-drunk = confused/dazed

"Incessant background music makes me punch-drunk after a couple of hours."

See also: couldn't punch his way out of a paper bag; pleased as Punch.

punishment

See: glutton for punishment.

pup

sell a pup = cheat/sell something that is worthless

"They sold you a pup when you bought that car, it breaks down at least once a week."

See also: calf/puppy love.

pure

pure and simple = and nothing but

"I admit I made a mistake, pure and simple."

pure as the driven snow = totally pure/untainted

"She's tall, blonde, twenty-three and pure as the driven snow."

purple

purple patches = florid prose

"I want you to write a simple, straightforward account of what happened ñ with no purple patches."

purpose

be/talk at cross purposes = misunderstand each other's meaning

"We were both in favour of the plan but he thought that I wasn't; as a result, we were talking at cross purposes."

put to (a) good purpose = make good use of

"Thank you for the donation. You can be sure it will be put to a good purpose."

serve a/the purpose = have a use (even if improvised)

"I can't find a screwdriver but this nail file should serve the purpose."

to no (good) purpose = with no useful outcome

"I've tried to improve his table manners but to no good purpose."

See also: accidentally on purpose; to all intents and purposes.

purse

See: hold the purse strings; make a silk purse out of a sow's ear.

push

at a push = only with difficulty

"I suppose that at a push we could see you between twelve and twelve thirty."

be pushed for = be lacking in/short of

"Do you mind if we get on quickly because I'm a bit pushed for time today."

give somebody the push = dismiss somebody from his/her job

"We're overstaffed at work now and I fear they're going to give me the push."

if/when it comes to the push = if/when absolutely necessary

"I know you're having trouble with the car, but if it comes to the push we can always walk."

pushing a particular age = nearly a particular age

"He must be pushing sixty yet he's still got all his own hair."

push off = go away

"I wish she would stop annoying us and push off."

push on = proceed with determination

"I don't want to stop yet. Let's push on to the next town."

push-over = very easy task, or opponent who is very easy to beat

"I've got a new job at the factory and it's a real push-over."

"Have you played snooker with Tim yet? He's a push-over."

See also: push one's luck; push the boat out.

put

put by = save

"I've got some money put by for my retirement."

put forward = propose

"James put forward an idea for saving the company money on its heating bill."

put in = install

"My mother has had a new central heating system put in."

put in for = apply for

"All the machinists have put in for a rise."

put it mildly = without exaggeration/ overemphasis

"Fiona is extremely pretty, to put it mildly."

put off = postpone, or distract, or deter

"Because of the rain, the match has been put off until next week."

"He was just going to hit the ball when somebody sneezed and put him off."

"Don't be put off by the price, it's worth much more really."

put one in mind of = remind one

"Your daughter puts me in mind of what you were like when you were her age."

put oneself in somebody's place = imagine what it would be like to be somebody else

"I went to the check-out and the girl added up the price of all the goods, and then I discovered I'd left my purse at home. Put yourself in my place, what would you have done?"

put one's shoulder to the wheel = make a determined effort

"You'll have to put your shoulder to the wheel if you're going to finish digging the garden before it gets dark."

put one's mind to = make a conscious effort to

"Stuart can play the piano quite well when he puts his mind to it."

put out = extinguish

"Put out that light, you should be asleep by now."

put out of one's mind = (deliberately) forget

"So you've failed your driving test. Now just put it out of your mind and concentrate on passing next time."

put somebody down as = regard somebody as
"I'd put Maurice down as a fool, but I now find he's very intelligent."

put somebody in the picture = keep somebody informed
"I've been away for a week. Can you please put me in the picture about what has happened in the last few days."

put somebody off = discourage somebody, or disgust somebody
"Michael wants to see us but I've put him off until tomorrow."
"I used to like black pudding but when I found out how it is made it put me right off."

put somebody on = to deceive somebody (as a joke)
"You were not really an officer in the SAS were you? You 're putting me on."

put somebody out = inconvenience somebody
"Are you sure we can come tonight? We don't want to put you out."

put/set somebody right = correct a false impression somebody has
"Henry thought that he was going to stay with us for the whole week but I soon put him right."

put somebody's nose out of joint = make somebody jealous
"The boss is always chatting to one of the new typists, which has really put his secretary's nose out of joint."

put somebody up to something = entice/encourage somebody to do something (wrong)
"Miranda was caught shoplifting, but she said that somebody put her up to it."

put something about = spread (a rumour)
"Somebody is putting it about that you owe a lot of money."

put something across = communicate/explain something
"I know what I want to say but I have difficulty in putting it across."

put something down to = attribute something to
"Everybody seems to have a cold, and I put it down to all this wet weather."

put something on = wear something, or falsify/feign something
"It's cold outside, make sure you put on your thick coat."
"She appeared to be really upset, but she was just putting it on."

put something right = correct a flaw/mistake
"Don't worry if you can't get all the paint off, I'll soon put it right with this special solvent."

put two and two together = draw a conclusion/make a deduction
"When I saw them holding hands I put two and two together and realized that they are much closer friends than they pretend."

put-up job = something that is contrived/falsified
"Philip claims that the charge against him is entirely a put-up job."

put up = provide/use accommodation, or offer
"He missed the last train so we put him up for the night."
"We put up at a small hotel on the outskirts of the town."
"I hear you've put your house up for sale."

put upon somebody = take advantage of somebody
"It's not fair that you should be put upon by those who don't want to do the awkward jobs."

put up with something = tolerate something
"Your wife always seems to be nagging you, I don't know how you put up with it."

stay put = remain
"You stay put here while I go back to the main road and ask somebody for directions."

See also: get/put something across; put a brave/bold/good face (up)on it; put an end/stop to; put a sock in it; put a spurt on; put on an act; put one's finger on; put one's money where one's mouth is; put one's shirt on; put/ set somebody at his/her ease; put somebody in his/her place; put somebody off his/her stride; put somebody's mind at rest; put something into practice; put that in your pipe and smoke it!; put the cat among the pigeons.

Q

quantity

unknown quantity = unpredictable person/thing
"I won my game against Clive because I know the way he plays, but the chap I have to meet in the next round is a completely unknown quantity."

quarrel

pick a quarrel = deliberately provoke an argument
"I don't care what your problem is, it's not my concern ñ so don't pick a quarrel with me."

patch up a quarrel = resume friendly relations after a dispute
"The two brothers have finally patched up their quarrel after years of bitter animosity."

quart

try to get/fit/put a quart into a pint pot = try to achieve the impossible (because there is insufficient space)
"The form requires me to give my full name, address and nationality in this tiny space ñ it's like trying to put a quart into a pint pot."

quarter

at close quarters = (very) near
"She looked quite young from a distance and only when I saw her at close quarters did I realize how old she really was."

from/in all quarters, or from/in every quarter = from all directions, or everywhere
"The enemy surrounded us and then attacked from all quarters."
"We searched in all quarters but still couldn't find it."

give no quarter = make no concession/ show no mercy
"The attackers had far superior forces but they gave no quarter and totally annihilated the defenders."

queen

Queen Anne's dead = expression to indicate that a statement is old news/ common knowledge
"Yes, I did know about your new car ñ and by the way, Queen Anne's dead."

queen it = to dominate/take control (said of a woman)
"Mrs Jones, the supervisor, really queens it over the girls in the typing pool."

queer

come over all queer = suddenly feel faint/giddy
"I looked over the edge of the cliff and came over all queer."

in Queer Street = in (financial) difficulty
"If I pay that large bill all at once I'll be in Queer Street for the rest of the month."

queer as a nine-bob/three-pound note = gay/homosexual
"The man who styled my hair was very good at his job, although he was as queer as a nine-bob note."

queer in the head = behaving strangely/ (slightly) mad
"Don't pay any attention to Brian, he's a bit queer in the head."

queer somebody's pitch = ruin somebody's chances
"He was hoping to start his own taxi business but queered his pitch by getting disqualified for drunken driving."

See also: queer/rum customer; queer fish.

question

ask a silly question (and you get a silly answer) = do not ask a question to which the answer is obvious
"I asked my father if he would change his mind and let me go on holiday with my boyfriend. I should have known better ñ ask a silly question."

beyond/without question = unquestionable/without argument
"Her suitability for the job is beyond question."
"The special army unit was so well disciplined that it obeyed orders without question."

fire off questions/fire questions at = ask questions in quick succession
"You'll have an opportunity to fire off questions at the end of the lecture."
"As soon as the film star left the theatre, reporters began firing questions at her."

in question = referred to/stated
"It couldn't have been me you saw in the restaurant because at the time in question I was on my way back from a meeting in Paris."

it's a question of = concerning/relevant to
"It's not merely a question of morality; don't you realize that your actions could be illegal?"

open question = arguable/debatable
"Whether the reintroduction of capital punishment would reduce the number of armed robberies is an open question."

out of the question = impossible
"I shall not be here on Tuesday so I'm afraid it's out of the question for me to meet you then."

pop the question = ask somebody to marry one
"It was just like a fairy story. Michael got on his knees and popped the question ñ and of course I said yes."

put a question mark against = raise doubts/query
"The weather forecast has put a question mark against the chances of doing any gliding tomorrow."

put it to the question = get somebody to state his/her opinion
"Let's put it to the question. How many people here are in favour of unilateral disarmament?"

question of the hour/moment = topical question
"My daughter has yet another new boyfriend and the question of the moment is will the relationship last for more than a week?"

rhetorical question = question requiring no answer (or answered by the questioner)
"I'm sorry, I didn't reply because I thought it was a rhetorical question!"

vexed question = controversial/difficult problem
"And now, gentlemen, we come to the vexed question of having to increase subscription charges to cover rising administration costs."

without question = undoubtedly
"Terry is without question the biggest liar I know!"

See also: beg the question; burning question; call in/into question; loaded question; the 64 million dollar question.

queue

jump the queue = go before one's turn

"Rather than wait eight months for my operation on the National Health, I jumped the queue by becoming a private patient and paying for treatment."

quick

cut somebody to the quick = badly hurt somebody's feelings
"Her unflattering remarks about my singing voice cut me to the quick."

quick and the dead = the living and the dead
"We need extra people to make up the numbers in the crowd scene. Go and find some more from among the quick and the dead."

quick one = quick (alcoholic) drink
"Let's call in the pub for a quick one on the way to the theatre."

quick/slow on the uptake = quick/slow to learn
"Gill is so quick on the uptake that you only have to tell her something once and she remembers it for ever."

quick-witted = quick to react/respond
"The bank robbers would have escaped if a quick-witted motorist hadn't realized what was happening and blocked the road with his car."

See also: cut to the quick; quick on the draw.

quid

quids in = in a position of favour/profit
"I'll be quids in if my plan is accepted and it works."

quiet

on the quiet = secretly/unobtrusively
"One of the reasons taxes are high is that people earn money on the quiet without declaring the income to the Inland Revenue."

quiet as a mouse/the grave = very quiet
"Tina is as quiet as a mouse ñ you hardly know she's there."
"There's usually something going on in town, although it's as quiet as the grave on a Sunday evening."

quit

be quits = be on a level
"He beat me in the first game but I managed to get the better of him in the second, so now we are quits."

call it quits = agree to stop arguing/fighting, or agree that there is no debt
"Why don't you boys stop fighting and call it quits."
"You bought the drinks and if I pay for the taxi home we can call it quits."

get quits with = even a score
"You wait, you bully! I'll get quits with you if it's the last thing I do!"

quite

quite a somebody/something = somebody/something that is remarkable/unusual
"The new salesman is quite an operator. He exceeded his month's quota in the first week."
"That's quite a machine. How fast does it go?"

quite a few = many
"There was a charity cricket match at the county ground today and I saw quite a few famous personalities who had come to give their support."

quite so = I agree
"Quite so, you are right ñ this is an excellent wine."

quite something = remarkable/worthy of attention

"Have you seen the new Ferrari that Gary has bought? It's quite something."

when you're quite ready/when you've quite finished = when you have stopped (doing something)

"When you've quite finished talking among yourselves, I'll continue to tell you about subtleties of neo-Classical architecture."

quote

See: quote chapter and verse.

R

r

three Rs = basics of education (reading, writing and arithmetic)

"Many of the children leaving secondary schools today are innumerate and illiterate because they were not taught their three Rs properly."

rabbit

breed like rabbits = produce large numbers of offspring

"My wife has several aunts and uncles and dozens of cousins ñ her family breed like rabbits!"

pull/produce a rabbit out of the hat = unexpectedly find an answer to a difficult problem

"I couldn't finish building my barbecue because I was six bricks short, but my neighbour pulled a rabbit out of the hat and gave me some he had over from a previous job."

See also: let the dog see the rabbit.

race

See: one-horse race; rat race.

rack

go to rack and ruin = be neglected (and so fall into decay)

"The council won't spend any money on the children's activity playground and so it's gone to rack and ruin."

on the rack = very distressed/worried

"I was on the rack because I was deeply in debt, and eventually my health suffered as well."

See also: rack one's brains.

rag

chew the rag = talk over complaints/misgivings

"A group of students chewed the rag and formed a protest committee."

from rags to riches = from poverty to wealth

"He was an immigrant boy who went from rags to riches and became chairman of his own company, owning dozens of shops throughout the country."

local rag = local newspaper

"I soon sold my old car by advertising it in the local rag."

See: glad rags; like a red rag to a bull; lose one's cool/rag/wool.

rage

all the rage = very fashionable/popular

"Mini skirts are all the rage, at least among girls who have the legs to wear them."

rail

go off the rails = behave in a foolish/not law-abiding manner

"All too many young people go off the rails during their teens but they seem to settle down after a few years."

what a way to run a railway! = what an illogical/silly way to organize things!

"To get even the smallest item from the stores at work, you have to fill in a form, get it countersigned by your immediate superior, and then submit the request to the storekeeper between ten and eleven in the morning or three and four in the afternoon ñ what a way to run a railway!"

rain

as right as rain = fit/all right

"I hear Bill has had to go to hospital. He was as right as rain when I saw him yesterday morning."

come rain or shine = whatever happens

"John has promised to come and see me again next week, come rain or shine."

it never rains but it pours = one misfortune is usually followed by others

"I broke a fingernail, laddered my tights and then missed my train ñ it seems it never rains but it pours."

put something by/save something for a rainy day = retain something until it is needed

"No matter how little you earn, you should try to save something for a rainy day if you possibly can."

rain cats and dogs = pour with (heavy) rain

"We'll have to cancel the cricket match, its raining cats and dogs."

(come) rain or shine = no matter what the weather

"We're going to Brighton on Sunday, rain or shine."

See also: rain (in) buckets.

rainbow

chase after rainbows = desire the unobtainable

"It's no good chasing after rainbows, you have to settle for what you've got in this life."

raise

raise a laugh = create amusement

"They were all looking a bit miserable but Barry soon raised a laugh by telling a few jokes."

raise a stink = make a fuss

"Dad raised an awful stink when he saw what the children's cricket match

raise one's glass to = toast (somebody's health)

"Ladies and Gentlemen, please raise your glasses to the bride and groom."

raise one's hand against = physically threaten

"Like all children, my boys were naughty when they were young ñ but I never raised a hand against them."

raise one's sights = be (more) ambitious

"Brenda's ambition is to get a supervisor's job, but I've raised my sights a bit higher than that."

raise one's voice = shout

"Don't you raise your voice to me!"

raise the ante = increase the amount of money needed to do something

"It's becoming increasingly difficult to buy a share in the venture because they keep on raising the ante."

See also: raise Cain; raise hell; raise/rear its ugly head; raise one's eyebrows; raise/take off one's hat to; raise somebody's hopes; raise the roof.

rake

thin as a rake = very thin

"Wendy has gone as thin as a rake since she stopped eating meat."

rake over the ashes = re-examine past unpleasantness

"I don't want to get into a discussion with Arnold because he'll want to rake over the ashes of my past mistakes."

rake something up = discover something (usually to somebody's disadvantage)

"I'm sure that, if we try hard enough, we can rake up something from his past that will discredit him."

rally

rally round = form a group (to help/support somebody)

"We're surprised and grateful for the

way in which our friends have rallied round to comfort us in our loss."

ram

ram something down somebody's throat = argue a case very forcefully

"I've heard the case for Communism before and don't need you to ram it down my throat."

ram something home = express something forcibly

"How can I ram home to you the importance of punctuality?"

rampage

be/go on the rampage = roam about using violence (and causing damage)

"After the match, supporters of the losing side went on the rampage and damaged several parked cars."

ramrod

See: stiff as a poker/ramrod.

random

at random = in an unsystematic way

"As a reprisal for sabotage the occupying forces chose six villagers at random and executed them."

rank

come up through/rise from the ranks = be promoted to a commissioned rank (in the services) from a noncommissioned rank, and extended to a successful person in other professions

"I've noticed that a boss is usually more understanding if he has risen from the ranks."

pull rank = use one's authority/position (to gain an unfair advantage)

"Whenever I go out with the boss he pulls rank and makes me buy the drinks."

See also: break ranks; close ranks; rank and file.

ransom

hold somebody to ransom = try to get somebody to do something by using threats

"The staff are holding the management to ransom by threatening not to finish work on a contract unless they are paid overtime or a bonus."

See also: king's ransom.

rant

rant and rave = talk angrily (and at length)

"I suppose Dad will rant and rave when he finds out about the broken window."

rap

carry/take the rap = accept the blame

"James made the mistake and I don't see why I should take the rap for him."

not worth a rap = worthless

"All Arthur's promises are not worth a rap."

rap somebody on/over the knuckles = rebuke somebody sharply

"I was rapped over the knuckles for coming in late again."

rare

See: rare animal; rare bird.

raring

raring to go = eager to begin

"Hurry up, dear, the children are already in the car raring to go."

rat

as wet as/like a drowned rat = very wet

"It started to rain and by the time I got

home I was as wet as a drowned rat."

rat on somebody = inform on/betray
"Tim Jones saw us smoking and ratted on us to the teacher."

rat race = competition in business/social life
"After Nigel left his academic post and went into business, it took him quite a while to adjust to the rat race."

smell a rat = be suspicious
"It's very unlike Harry to be so friendly and I smell a rat ñ I wonder what he wants?"

rate

at any rate = anyway, or at least/bearing in mind
"Enforced convalescence is a nuisance, but at any rate it allows me to catch up with my reading."

at that/this rate = if that were so, or if something continues in this way
"Walter is in favour of the total abolition of licensing hours, but at that rate we'd never get him out of the pub!"
"Haven't you decided on a route yet? At this rate we shall never get there."

See also: at a rate of knots; second rate.

rave

(stark) raving mad = completely mad
"He went stark raving mad and began smashing the place up."

See also: rant and rave.

raw

in the raw = in the natural/original state, or in the nude
"We drove through the downtown slums and saw life in the raw."
"Toni is a photographic model who specializes in posing in the raw."

raw material = starting material from which something can be made
"Wood and stone are the only raw materials on the island."

See also: raw deal; touch somebody on the raw.

razor

on the razor's edge = in a critical/dangerous position
"The doctor says my aunt may or may not recover; she's right on the razor's edge."

sharp/keen as a razor = very sharp (as of a blade, or mentally)
"I cut myself on a piece of plastic that was as sharp as a razor."
"The chess champion has a mind as keen as a razor."

razzle

on the razzle = out enjoying oneself (by eating and drinking)
"I met some old friends and we went on the razzle till the early hours of the morning."

reach

See: reach somebody's ears.

read

read something into something else = extract a hidden/unintended meaning from
"We must be careful not to read too much into the Prime Minister's statement."

read the riot act = angrily tell somebody to stop doing something bad/wrong
"Mother read the riot act to Dad and me for walking through the kitchen with our muddy boots on."

read up on = learn by research/study
"I must read up on Arab customs before I go to Bahrain."

take something as read = assume something to be true
"May I take it as read that you understand all the terms and conditions of the agreement?"
See also: read between the lines; read somebody like a book; read somebody's mind.

ready
at the ready = prepared for action
"I've got my pen at the ready so please tell me your address and telephone number."
ready to hand = readily available/within easy reach
"When I'm cooking I don't bother with recipes, I just use anything that's ready to hand."
See also: fit/ready to drop; rough and ready.

real
for real = genuine/true
"I tell you it's for real ñ Joan has got engaged to Archie."
in reality = actually
"Mervin says he doesn't need to wear glasses whereas in reality he's practically blind without them."
not really = expression of doubt, tending to the negative
"Am I pleased with my new dress? Not really."
oh really? = expression of surprised interest
"Oh really? And then what happened?"
the real McCoy = the genuine article
"I prefer leather gloves ñ the real McCoy, not plastic rubbish."
well, really! = exclamation of annoyance/disapproval
"Well, really! You ought to know better at your age!"

rear
bring up the rear = be last
"Ann and Julie, you go in front and we'll follow you with Tony bringing up the rear."
See also: raise/rear its ugly head.

reason
have (good) reason to believe = have evidence/justification for believing
"We have good reason to believe that you were involved in the theft of a car and would like you to accompany us to the police station."
it stands to reason (that) = logical/rational thought would indicate (that)
"It stands to reason that you cannot seat fifty people in this small room."
listen to reason = be persuaded/acknowledge common sense
"I tried to stop her going away but she wouldn't listen to reason."
ours not to reason why = we have no right to question
"The boss has asked me to dismantle all those machines you assembled last week; it seems strange, but ours not to reason why."
see reason = adopt a more sensible attitude/be persuaded
"My son has finally seen reason and given up the idea of buying a motorbike."
will want to know the reason why = will be annoyed/angry
"You had better finish your dinner or I'll want to know the reason why."
within reason = as far as common sense allows
"You can do anything you like within reason."

See also: for no rhyme or reason; lose one's marbles/reason; out of all reason.

rebound

catch somebody on the rebound = make friends with somebody while he/she is still unhappy about a previous broken relationship
"I didn't realize I'd caught her on the rebound but we became close friends once she had got over her broken marriage."

recall

beyond recall = irretrievable/ unstoppable
"I can't mend this old coat, it is beyond recall."

receive

See: on the receiving end.

reckon

be out in one's reckoning = make a mistake/miscalculation
"It's not the twenty-fifth of the month until tomorrow ñ I was out in my reckoning."

one reckons = one thinks
"Jim reckons it's going to rain. What do you think?"

reckon among = include with
"The gila monster has to be reckoned among the world's most poisonous creatures."

reckon on = expect, or rely on
"I didn't reckon on having to pay that bill this week."
"I thought I could reckon on his support, but he didn't come."

to be reckoned with = to be dealt with only with difficulty
"The trade union movement is a force to be reckoned with."

See also: day of reckoning.

record

for the record = to be formally noted
"For the record, I shall be on holiday for two weeks beginning on 4th August."

have a good track record = have experience that is to one's credit
"This applicant for the job has the best track record and I recommend that we employ her."

on record = recorded (for future reference)
"He ran the fastest race on record."

put/set the record straight = remedy a mistake
"He thought I was nearly forty but I soon put the record straight."

See also: break a/the record; off the record; track record.

red

in the red = in debt
"By the end of each month my bank account always seems to be in the red."

not have a red cent = have no money at all
"I can't come out with you till pay day because I haven't a red cent."

not worth a red cent = worthless
"She offered me a ring in exchange but it wasn't worth a red cent."

on red alert = ready for and expecting danger
"The district was put on red alert during a terrorist bomb scare."

red as a beetroot = red in the face with embarrassment/shame
"Janet went red in the face when you told that dirty joke."

red-blooded = virile

"You can't feed a red-blooded man only on salads every day."

redbrick university = any British university founded in about the last hundred years (i.e. not Cambridge or Oxford universities)

"Marilyn studied sociology at one of the redbrick universities."

red tape = official regulations (that annoy/delay)

"Because of all the red tape at immigration I missed my connecting flight."

see red = become very angry

"Cruelty to animals really makes me see red."

see the red light = be aware of approaching danger

"Harry's remarks were beginning to annoy me but he saw the red light and changed the subject."

was somebody's face red! = somebody was ashamed/embarrassed

"Was Tom's face red when the beautiful blonde he referred to turned round and proved to be a man with long fair hair and a beard!"

See also: catch somebody red-handed; have a red face; like a red rag to a bull; paint the town red; (roll out the) red carpet; red herring; red letter day; red light district.

redeem

redeeming feature = compensatory aspect/factor

"Our dog is not very pretty to look at but his redeeming feature is his friendly temperament."

redress

redress the balance = re-establish equality/equilibrium

"The visiting team were one man short and so I played for them to redress the balance."

reed

See: broken reed.

reel

reel off = recite something easily (and quickly)

"She can reel off the names of all the children in the school."

reflect

on (due) reflection = after time to consider

"On due reflection I have decided to accept your offer."

reflect on = recollect/think about

"When I reflect on my schooldays, I realize how much easier things are for today's children."

reflect upon somebody = discredit somebody

"That one silly error reflects upon his integrity as a solicitor."

refresh

refresh one's memory = remind oneself (usually by reading/being told)

"Please refresh my memory, what is your address?"

refuse

first refusal = priority offer

"Gill has offered me first refusal of the best puppy in her bitch's next litter."

See also: refuse to/wouldn't be seen dead.

regards

as regards/with regard to = concerning

"The accommodation at the hotel was good, and as regards the food it was excellent."

"I would like to talk to you with regard to the letter you sent me."

kindest regards = best/good wishes

"If you see Alan, please give him my kindest regards."

region

in the region of = about/approximately

"There were in the region of five hundred people at the meeting."

regular

regular as clockwork = very regular(ly)

"The milkman calls at seven-thirty every morning, regular as clockwork."

rein

give (free) rein to = allow complete freedom to

"I had to wait for over an hour at the hospital, giving rein to my worst fears."

keep a tight rein on = keep under strict control

"George keeps a tight rein on his children, but they still seem to get into trouble regularly."

take the reins = assume control

"The business has thrived since Norma took the reins."

relation

poor relation = inferior member of a group

"Belgium is no longer the poor relation of the Common Market."

relieve

relieve oneself = urinate

"I was late because I had to stop and relieve myself on the way."

relieve somebody of something = steal/take something from somebody

"While I was trying to help a woman who had fainted, a pickpocket relieved me of my wallet."

remember

something to remember one by = a beating/tirade of abuse

"If I ever see him again I'll give him something to remember me by."

render

render an account = give somebody a bill (for payment)

"I had a nasty surprise when my solicitor rendered his account for the work he did when I bought my new house ñ I didn't expect it to cost so much."

repeat

not bear repeating = too unpleasant to repeat

"Tony told us a joke that does not bear repeating."

repeat oneself = say something more than once

"I'm tired of repeating myself, so pay attention this time."

resistance

See: take the line of least resistance.

resort

as a/in the last resort = as a final attempt/method

"I've written and telephoned without success, so as a last resort I thought I'd come round in person to see you."

resources

leave somebody to his/her own resources = allow somebody to do what he/she likes or find his/her own way out of a difficulty

"We must keep Tina busy because left

to her own resources she usually gets up to mischief."

respect

be no respecter of persons = remain independent of the importance/status of others

"Glen is no respecter of persons ñ he won't compromise his behaviour or the way he dresses no matter where he is."

in respect of/with respect to = concerning

"I am writing in respect of the complaint you made last week."

"With respect to the complaint you made last week, we are looking into the matter."

with all (due) respect = expression of polite disagreement

"With all respect, I think you have added the figures incorrectly."

See also: pay one's respects.

rest

a change is as good as a rest = if one cannot do nothing (to take a rest) one should do something completely different

"I took a week off work but instead of going on holiday I repainted the outside of my house. Still, a change is as good as a rest."

at rest = not moving, or dead

"The old mill has been at rest for nearly a hundred years."

"My father has been at rest since I was a girl."

come to rest = cease moving

"After the collision, the car came to rest on its side."

(why don't you) give it a rest! = stop doing it!

"You've been playing records all evening. Please, give it a rest!"

last resting place = grave/tomb

"For many young men in World War I, their last resting place was in Flanders."

lay to rest = bury (in a grave)

"Our dog was twelve years old when he died, and we laid him to rest under a tree in the garden."

put/set somebody's mind at rest = reassure somebody

"Please phone David and tell him that his missing wallet has been found, to set his mind at rest."

(you can) rest assured = you can be sure

"Rest assured that misbehaviour will not go unpunished."

rest on = depend on

"One theory about the existence of extraterrestrial life rests on the presence of carbon compounds in meteorites."

rest with = be the duty/responsibility of

"Putting the children to bed rests with the babysitter."

See also: rest on one's laurels; rest on one's oars.

retreat

See: beat a (hasty) retreat.

return

answer by return = reply to correspondence immediately

"This is the third time I have written to you about my complaint and I would appreciate a reply by return."

in return for = in exchange for

"I'll give you two of my sweets in return for a piece of your chocolate."

many happy returns = may you have many more happy birthdays

"Many happy returns. What's it feel like to be twenty-one yet again?"

See also: point of no return; return the compliment; return to the fold.

reveal
See: reveal/show one's hand.

rhetoric
See: rhetorical question.

rhyme
be without/have no rhyme or reason = be illogical/lacking in common sense
"I can't follow these instructions because they seem to have no rhyme or reason."
for no rhyme or reason = without cause
"This man turned round and hit Peter for no rhyme or reason."

rib
stick to one's ribs = satisfy one's hunger
"I like stew with dumplings. It really sticks to your ribs."
tickle somebody's ribs = amuse somebody
"The thought of Big Dave playing the part of the Christmas fairy really tickled my ribs."
See also: Adam's rib; dig somebody in the ribs.

rich
rich as Croesus = very wealthy
"He has a country mansion and runs a yacht and a private aircraft ñ he must be as rich as Croesus."
strike (it) rich = obtain a lot of money
"Ursula struck it rich when she married a stockbroker."
that's rich = that's ridiculous/unbelievable
"Harry has been put in charge of all company transport? That's rich ñ he can't even drive a car!"
See also: richly deserve; rich man's hobby.

riddance
good riddance to = I am glad to be rid of
"My boyfriend has walked out on me and good riddance to him!"

ride
along for the ride = for the company/to make up the numbers (without taking part)
"The rest of the group wanted to go to a disco. I didn't mind whether I did or not but I went along for the ride."
give somebody/have a rough ride = submit somebody to/receive harsh treatment
"The auditors gave the accountant a rough ride because of errors in the figures."
"He went before the disciplinary committee and had a really rough ride."
let something ride = let something continue without interfering
"She began to make personal remarks but I just let them ride."
ride something out = tolerate a difficulty until it is over
"We are very short of money but we'll be all right as long as we can ride it out until pay day."
ride up = move up gradually (from the normal position)
"I have to wear a petticoat under this skirt to prevent it from riding up when I move."
ride roughshod over somebody = bully somebody
"Harry rides roughshod over anybody who gets in the way of his business plans."
riding high = successful

"Anthony has been riding high ever since he changed jobs."

take somebody for a ride = cheat somebody, or murder somebody

"That salesman really took us for a ride, these goods are very shoddy."

"Anyone who informs on the crime syndicate risks getting taken for a ride."

See also: ride for a fall.

rig

rig up = make a (temporary) construction (from materials easily available)

"See if you can rig up some sort of tripod so that we can hang the cooking pot over the fire."

right

be/get/keep on the right side of somebody = be on/establish/maintain friendly relations with somebody

"Our teacher is all right as long as you keep on the right side of her."

be on the right track = acting/thinking in a way that will lead to a correct conclusion

"No, that is not the correct answer ñ but you're on the right track."

by right(s) = according to the law/rules

"By rights, you shouldn't leave work before five o'clock."

dead to rights = with no excuse

"The police caught him dead to rights breaking into the shop."

get it/something right = correctly understand something

"You've had six lessons now and it's about time you got it right."

go right = happen correctly/successfully

"It was one of those days when nothing seemed to go right."

in one's right mind = sensible/sane

"He couldn't have been in his right mind when he paid fifty pounds for that old vase."

in the right = correct (legally or morally)

"You may be in the right, but what you said to Susan was very hurtful."

keep on the right side of somebody = be careful not to anger/annoy somebody

"Our teacher is all right as long as you keep on the right side of her."

Mister Right = a woman's perfect (marriage) partner

"Prudence will never have a boyfriend if she keeps waiting for Mister Right to come along."

put/set somebody right = correct a mistaken idea/impression

"Ann thought I was Scottish but I soon put her right."

put/set something right = correct a wrong, or repair something

"I gave you too much change but I'll put it right the next time you buy something."

"The trunion sprocket has come off the pinion, but don't worry ñ we'll soon put that right."

right away = immediately

"Please go to the shop right away."

right-hand man = trusted deputy

"I was glad I had Lester as my right-hand man when I was incapacitated with influenza and couldn't get in to work."

right in the head = sane/sensible

"You can't believe everything old Walter says these days because he's not quite right in the head."

right you are = certainly

"Right you are, sir, I'll drive you to Victoria station."

see somebody right = ensure that somebody is paid/rewarded

"I'll see you right if you help me to move this pile of bricks."

serve somebody right = be what somebody deserves
"It will serve him right if his wife finds out."
too right!/true! = I agree totally
"Too right! This is the best steak I've eaten since leaving Australia."
See also: as right as rain; bit of all right; get/start off on the right/wrong foot; give one's right
arm (for); have one's heart in the right place; I'm all right, Jack; in one's own right; (my) right arm; put/set somebody right; see somebody right; strike the right note; take something in the right spirit; two wrongs don't make a right.

ring
have a hollow ring to it = seem false/ insincere
"I'm suspicious of her promises ñ they have a hollow ring to them."
have a ringside seat = be a nearby witness
"I happened to be in the typing pool, so I had a ringside seat when the new girl told the supervisor what she could do with the typing job."
have a true ring to it = seem meritorious/worthy
"I really like Stephen's plan for improvements, it has a true ring to it."
make/run rings round somebody = defeat easily
"I played chess with my young nephew and he ran rings round me."
ring off = deliberately end a telephone call
"When I asked if I was speaking to Councillor Jones he simply rang off."
ring true = sound as if true
"His excuse about the train being late doesn't ring true to me."
See also: dead ringer (for somebody); ring a bell; ring down the curtain; ring the changes; three-ring circus; throw one's hat into the ring.

riot
run riot = do something in an uncontrolled way
"The Virginia creeper we planted last year has run riot and covered half the wall."
See also: read the riot act.

rip
let something rip = allow something to go as fast as possible
"We'll soon see of the engine runs better now ñ go on, let her rip."

ripe
See: ripe old age.

rise
give rise to = originate
"A cross between a greyhound and a collie gives rise to a lurcher."
rise above oneself = think one is better than one really is
"The trouble with Wilma is that you pay her a few compliments and she immediately rises above herself."
rise and shine! = get up! (out of bed)
"Come on boys, rise and shine! We've got to make an early start today."
take a/the rise out of somebody = tease/ play a joke on somebody
"The whole family took the rise out of Dad when he first tried to cook the Sunday dinner."
See also: rise from the ranks; rise to the bait; rise to the occasion; rise/get up with the lark.

risk
at one's own risk = be unable to claim for any damage/loss

"Customers leave their coats here at their own risk."

run the risk of = do something involving a risk

"I had to use my car but I ran the risk of being prosecuted because it wasn't taxed."

See also: risk one's neck; run/take the risk.

river

sell somebody down the river = betray somebody

"I would have got away with coming in late if Harry hadn't sold me down the river and told the foreman."

rivet

See: rivet one's attention.

road

get the show on the road = get something started

"Come on, the tea break is over; let's get this show on the road."

in/out of the road = in/out of the way

"The trouble with having a big dog like an Alsatian in a small flat is that it always seems to be in the road when you're carrying a tray of glasses."

"Please get out of the road, I'm coming through with a tray of dishes."

on the road to recovery = getting better (after being ill)

The patient is out of intensive care and well on the road to recovery."

on the road to ruin = heading towards (financial) disaster

"The company cannot pay its bills and is on the road to ruin."

road hog = (dangerously) discourteous driver

"I had to swerve when some road hog overtook me and cut in front."

take to the road = become a tramp

"I've a good mind to sell all my possessions and take to the road."

See also: end of the line/road; middle-of-the-road; one (more) for the road.

roar

do a roaring trade = do much business

"It started to rain and one market stall did a roaring trade in collapsible umbrellas."

rob

rob Peter to pay Paul = use money intended to pay for one thing to pay for another

"The only way I can settle the gas bill is to rob Peter to pay Paul and use the money I've put by for the electricity."

rob somebody blind = deceive/cheat somebody into parting with his/her money

"Be careful doing business with Paul ñ he'll rob you blind if he can."

See also: daylight robbery; fair exchange is no robbery.

robin

round robin = petition (originally with signatures in a circle, so that nobody could be seen to have signed first)

"We sent a round robin to the boss asking him to change the shift system."

Robinson

See: before you can say Jack Robinson.

rock

go off one's rocker = become mad

"Look at the clothes Barry is wearing. I think he's really gone off his rocker this time."

on the rocks = in financial difficulty (of a person or business), or served with ice (of a drink), or breaking down (of a marriage)
"Simon's business has been on the rocks for some time and I understand he's going into liquidation."
"Frank always drinks bourbon on the rocks."
"Their marriage is on the rocks and they've decided to split up."
See also: rock bottom; rock the boat; steady as a rock.

rocket
give somebody a rocket = reprimand somebody
"Dad gave me a rocket for denting his car."

rod
rule with a rod of iron = be very strict
"There was never any problem with discipline at my school because the headmaster ruled with a rod of iron."
spare the rod and spoil the child = strict discipline is good for children
"They gave their daughter complete freedom and she was caught shoplifting ñ spare the rod and spoil the child."
See also: make a rod for one's own back.

rogue
rogues' gallery = collection of photographs of criminals used by the police for identification purposes
"I had a brief glimpse of one of the robbers and had to go to the police station to look through their rogues' gallery."
See also: rogue elephant.

roll
have/make somebody roll in the aisles = make an audience laugh very much
"The after-dinner speaker had us rolling in the aisles."
roll in = come in large quantities
"If you offer a ten per cent discount for cash money will come rolling in."
rolling in money = wealthy
"Ted's just bought yet another new car ñ he must be rolling in money."
roll on (the day) = may it/the day soon come
"Roll on June ñ that's when I take my holiday."
"Roll on the day when I've finished working and can retire to the country."
roll up = arrive, or come here, or a hand-made cigarette
"Michael rolled up half an hour early."
"Roll up, have a look at these pictures."
"Would you like a roll up or are you having a cigar?"
roll up one's sleeves = be prepared for hard work
"Come on, let's roll up our sleeves and get this place cleaned up."
See also: heads will roll; keep/set/start the ball rolling.

Rome
Rome wasn't built in a day = it takes time to complete something that is difficult/important
"No I haven't finished the job yet, but Rome wasn't built in a day you know."
when in Rome, do as the Romans do = follow the example of people around one
"Most of the other girls on the beach were topless so I took my blouse off ñ

when in Rome, do as the Romans do!"

See also: fiddle while Rome burns.

romp

romp home = win easily

"The competition wasn't very strong and the champion romped home in record time."

roof

bring the roof down/raise the roof = make a lot of noise

"The disco party nearly brought the roof down."

"The disco party raised the roof until the early hours of the morning."

have a roof over one's head = have somewhere to live

"The family is destitute and they haven't even got a roof over their heads."

shout something from the rooftops = tell something to everybody

"I know I was convicted for speeding, but there's no need to shout it from the rooftops."

See also: hit the roof.

room

make room for = create (a) space for

"All move up and make room for Ken."

See also: bugged room; elbow room; no/not enough room to swing a cat.

roost

come home to roost = be affected by a previous (bad) action

"You cannot keep treating people like that without your unkindness one day coming home to roost."

rule the roost = be head of a group

"Grandmother rules the roost in our household."

root

be rooted in = originate in

"His attitude to ownership is rooted in Communist ideology."

pull up roots/stakes = move somewhere else from a place one has lived in for some time

"After Donald's wife died, he decided to pull up roots and go to live near his daughter in Scotland."

put down roots = become established/settled in a place

"During my early career I frequently changed jobs and moved from place to place, but now I want to put down roots and raise a family."

root and branch = totally

"The company needs reorganizing root and branch."

rooted to the spot = unmoving (although capable of doing so)

"I could see the horse galloping towards me but I was so frightened I just stood there rooted to the spot."

root for somebody = support somebody

"I want you all to root for the Labour candidate in the election."

root out = discover (and destroy)

"The new president has pledged to root out corruption wherever it exists."

take root = become established

"I don't know how such a peculiar idea took root, but most people seem to believe it."

See also: grass roots.

rope

give somebody enough rope = allow somebody freedom to continue a foolish/wrong course of action until he/she suffers the consequences

"I suspect Terry has been pilfering goods from the stores. Give him enough rope, and we'll catch him doing it one day."

know the ropes = be experienced/know how to do something
"When you know the ropes this job is quite straightforward."

on the ropes = on the verge of collapse/ruin
"The shop is on the ropes and must surely have to close soon."

rope somebody in = persuade somebody to (join a group to) do something
"I went with my wife to the theatre club and got roped in to paint scenery."

See also: at the end of one's rope/tether; money for jam/old rope; on a tightrope.

rose

a rose by any other name (would smell as sweet) = a name/title does not matter in itself
"The council calls its rat catcher a rodent operator, but a rose by any other name.Ö"

everything's coming up roses = everything is going well
"Everything's coming up roses now that we've got our first few business contracts."

look at/see/view things through rose-tinted spectacles = be very optimistic
"You're bound to be disappointed one day if you persist in looking at the world through rose-tinted spectacles."

roses all the way = free from difficulty/uncomplicated
"You've got off to a good start but life won't be roses all the way, you know."

See also: bed of roses.

rotten

See: rotten apple (in the barrel).

rough

be rough on somebody = treat somebody harshly, or be unfortunate for somebody
"Don't be too rough on her, she's only a child and didn't know she was doing wrong."
"It was rough on David having to bring up two children on his own after his wife left him."

cut up rough = behave in an aggressive/unpleasant way
"The boss is bound to cut up rough when he hears what has happened here."

feel the rough edge of somebody's tongue = be talked to angrily
"John was late for work this morning and felt the rough edge of the manager's tongue."

live rough/rough it = live without modern comforts/conveniences
"I enjoyed living in a tent on holiday and roughing it for a change."

rough and ready = usable but not finely finished
"Dinner is a bit rough and ready I'm afraid, but at least it's filling."

rough and tumble = horseplay/scuffle
"My daughter would rather join in a rough and tumble with her brothers than play with dolls."

rough something out = plan something in broad outline (but not in detail)
"Let's rough something out so that you can make a start ñ we can plan the details later."

sleep rough = sleep in the open, without proper shelter
"I wouldn't like to be a tramp sleeping rough in this cold weather."

take the rough with the smooth = accept the disadvantages along with the advantages

"My job is well paid although I sometimes have to work at weekends ñ still, you have to take the rough with the smooth these days."

See also: dirty/rough end of the stick; give somebody/have a rough ride; ride roughshod over somebody; rough diamond.

round

daily round = routine occurrences of life

"It is difficult getting back to the daily round after a fortnight's holiday abroad."

do the rounds = go from person to person/place to place

"When I stay with my parents I have to do the rounds and visit all my other relatives in the district."

get round somebody = get one's way by flattering/persuading somebody

"Tina can always get round her father when she wants something."

get round to = find time to

"I must get round to mowing the lawn this weekend."

go the rounds = be passed from person to person/place to place

"The rumour soon went the rounds and reached the ears of the boss."

in the round = three-dimensional, visible from all round

"Photographs do not do it justice, it has to be seen in the round."

round about = approximately, or near

"I'll catch a train at round about ten o'clock."

"There are few jobs available round about here."

round down = decrease an awkward number to the nearest convenient one

"Please measure those lengths of wood, ignore the inches and round down the figures to the nearest foot."

round off = to complete

"We had a nightcap before bedtime to round off a perfect day."

round on somebody = attack somebody (verbally)

"I'm sorry I made a mistake, but there's no need to round on me like that."

round the bend/twist = mad

"He's gone completely round the twist since his mother died and left him to fend for himself."

round trip = return journey

"With cheap day tickets it costs less to pay for the round trip than to buy an ordinary single."

round up = collect together, or increase an awkward number to the nearest convenient one

"The cowboys rounded up the steers and herded them into a corral."

"Ignore the pennies and round up all the prices to the nearest pound."

talk somebody round = persuade somebody

"Don't worry if your father says no, I'll soon talk him round."

See also: in round figures; round robin; round the clock; round the corner; square peg in a round hole.

roundabouts

what you lose on the swings, you gain on the roundabouts = disadvantages in one area are balanced by advantages in another

"I got less than I wanted when I sold my car but I made a good profit on the caravan ñ what you lose on the swings, you gain on the roundabouts."

row

in a row = consecutively

"It rained for four days in a row."

rub

not have two ha'pennies/pennies to rub together = be very poor
"When your grandmother and I got married we didn't have two ha'pennies to rub together."

rub along with = be friendly with
"I find it difficult to rub along with Paul, he's so unpredictable."

rub down = smooth (using friction)
"Make sure you rub down the window frames before you repaint them."

rub off on(to) = be acquired through close contact
"Donald is a compulsive liar and I'm afraid it has rubbed off onto his children."

rub one's hands = show pleasure
"My father rubbed his hands when he found out how much his antique clock is really worth."

rub shoulders with = be in close company with
"My wife likes going to Ascot to rub shoulders with the gentry."

rub somebody up the wrong way = annoy/irritate somebody
"Dad's all right as long as you don't rub him up the wrong way."

rub somebody's nose in it/the dirt = degrade somebody
"He's always belittling me and I wish I had a chance to rub his nose in the dirt."

rub something in = continually remind somebody of something
"My wife is a good driver but I failed my test ñ and doesn't she keep rubbing it in!"

there's the rub = that is the difficulty/problem
"We can get there easily but we can't get back ñ there's the rub, because there are no trains on a Sunday."

See also: rub salt into the wound; rub shoulders with; rub somebody's nose in it.

rubber

rubber stamp something = agree/approve of something one has not formally considered
"With any luck the committee will merely rubber stamp our application without discussing it in detail."

rude

See: rude awakening.

ruffle

smooth somebody's ruffled feathers = calm somebody (who is offended)
"Eileen was upset by your remarks and it took me a long time to smooth her ruffled feathers."

ruffle somebody's feathers = offend/upset somebody
"I know he's careful with money, but calling him mean was bound to ruffle his feathers."

rug

pull the rug from under somebody('s feet) = suddenly place somebody at a disadvantage
"We were on the point of signing a lucrative contract when the bank pulled the rug from under our feet by withdrawing their financial support."

See also: snug as a bug in a rug; sweep something under the carpet/rug.

ruin

mother's ruin = strong drink (usually gin)

"I must admit I like a nice glass of mother's ruin before I go to bed."
See also: go to rack and ruin; on the road to ruin.

rule

as a rule = usually
"As a rule ī catch the seven o'clock train to work so that I can be sure of getting a seat."
ground rules = basic rules
"Let's establish the ground rules so that everybody knows what to expect."
rule of the sea/road = accepted "laws" governing ships/road vehicles
"A powered vessel should give way to sail ñ it is an unwritten rule of the sea."
rule of thumb = practical (rather than theoretical) method
"I haven't been taught the finer points of carpentry, I just make things by rule of thumb."
rule out something/rule something out (of court) = exclude something
"We must allow sufficient time for the journey because you can never rule out the possibility of traffic jams at that time of day."
"The committee ruled Nigel's proposal out of court because it was too expensive."
work to rule = pay strict attention to working regulations (and thus slow down work)
"The union has ordered its members to work to rule, rather than call a total strike."
See also: golden rule; rule the roost; rule with a rod of iron; the exception proves the rule.

rumour

ugly rumour = rumour that is nasty/unpleasant
"I heard an ugly rumour that they are going to shut all the pubs on Sundays."

run

dry run = rehearsal
"We will have a dry run in the morning and make the actual presentation in the afternoon."
have a (good) run for one's money = get (good) value for one's expenditure
"It's a pity the holiday is over but we did have a good run for our money."
have the run of the house = be free to go anywhere in a house
"Our dog spends most of the day outside but we give him the run of the house at night."
in/out of the running = having/not having a chance of being successful
"Several people have applied for the job but I think I'm out of the running because of my lack of experience."
make the running = set the pace/standard
"Maria makes the running in the maths lessons but I am better than her at French."
on the run = having escaped from custody
"The escaped prisoners have been on the run for two days now."
run across somebody = meet somebody by accident
"I ran across my old headmaster the other day."
run along = go away
"Run along and get ready for bed."
run a mile = run quickly away (in panic)
"If my girlfriend sees a spider she runs a mile."
run away with = win easily, or accept unthinkingly
"Sue's champion dachshund runs

away with all the shows it enters."
"He ran away with the idea that I was a German, and started speaking to me in that language."

run down = exhausted/in poor health, or in a poor condition
"I really was run down after working a whole year without a break."
"The business was neglected and is now run down."

run for it = escape/run away
"The thieves had to run for it when the police arrived."

run into somebody = meet somebody accidentally
"I went to Paris for the weekend and ran into my brother whom I haven't seen for years."

run-of-the-mill = ordinary
"I would rather have a pair of run-of-the-mill jeans than some of these fancy trousers that are fashionable nowadays."

run on something = great demand for something
"There has been a run on coffee since a large price increase was forecast."

run out = be ended/expire
"Come in now, Jane, your time has run out."

run out of = be used up/have no more of
"The car has run out of petrol."

run out of steam = expend all one's energy
"I cycled for nearly ten miles before I ran out of steam."

run out on somebody = desert somebody
"Is it true that Mary's husband has run out on her?"

run somebody down = criticize somebody
"It isn't fair to run him down when he's not here to defend himself."

run somebody in = arrest somebody
"I hear the police have run in Helen for shoplifting."

run somebody through = pierce somebody's body with a sword
"The swordsman disarmed his opponent and ran him through."

run somebody/something over = knockdown/drive over with a road vehicle
"My sister's cat got run over by a lorry."

run something in = run a new machine until it is working properly
"My new car has done five thousand miles and is just about run in."

run something into the ground = consume/use something until it is exhausted/no longer functioning
"I won't be able to sell this old car so I'll just run it into the ground and then give it away for scrap."

run/take the risk = do something involving risk
"If we smuggle this brandy we run the risk of being caught and fined."

run the show = be in control
"Harry can be very helpful but I wish he didn't always want to run the show."

run through something = rehearse, or go through from the beginning
"Let's have a last run through our lines before the performance this evening."
"Please run through those names again from the top of the list."

run to something = have (enough of) something
"Do you mind having your coffee in a mug? I'm afraid we don't run to cups in this office."

run up = make in a quick (but approximate) way, or allow to accumulate

"I'll ask my mother if she can run up a fancy dress costume for me to wear at the party."
"You can soon run up a big bill if you buy goods on credit."
run up against = encounter
"Every time we try to get the scheme going we seem to run up against yet another problem."
run wild = behave in an undisciplined way
"I wish they would set free all zoo animals and let them run wild in their natural habitats."
(go) take a running jump (at yourself) = go away
"I've told you three times I don't want to buy double glazing. Why don't you take a running jump?"
trial run = first test of something new, a rehearsal
"You cannot judge the quality of a car on a two-mile trial run, you really need to drive it for a whole day."
See also: also-ran; cut and run; fall/run foul of; go/run to seed; in the long run; run a tight ship; run counter to; run in one's blood; run in the family; run its course; run/rushed off one's feet; run riot; run short; run somebody/something to earth; run somebody to ground; run the gauntlet; (run) true to form; run with the hare and hunt with the hounds; still waters run deep.

rush
give somebody the bum's rush = throw somebody out
"And tell him that if he ever comes round here again I'll give him the bum's rush."
See: rush hour; rush off one's feet; rush one's fences.

rustle
rustle up something = obtain something quickly (using improvisation)
"No matter when we visit my mother unannounced, she always manages to rustle up a meal for us."

rut
in(to) a rut = in a monotonous manner
"The trouble with commuting to a nine-to-five job is that it is all too easy to get into a rut."

S

sack

get the sack = be dismissed from a job
"Pete got the sack for punching the foreman on the nose."

give somebody the sack = dismiss somebody from a job
"They gave Pete the sack for punching the foreman."

hit the sack = go to bed
"Come on, folks, it's eleven o'clock ñ time to hit the sack."

wear sackcloth and ashes = be contrite/penitent
"I broke a vase and my wife made me wear sackcloth and ashes for a week!"

sacred

swear by all that is sacred = give a solemn undertaking/vow
"He swore by all that is sacred that he had never even been to the shop, let alone stolen from it."

See also: sacred cow.

sacrifice

make the supreme sacrifice = give up one's life (for a cause/friend), or surrender one's virginity
"Thousands of young men made the supreme sacrifice during World War I."
"I agreed to go and stay with him for the weekend but I'm not going to make the supreme sacrifice, at least not yet!"

saddle

in/out of the saddle = in/out of control
"Business has improved greatly since Margaret has been in the saddle."

saddle somebody with something = pass on a difficulty/responsibility to somebody
"I went to the church fete and the vicar saddled me with the job of selling raffle tickets."

safe

be on the safe side = do something to avoid danger/risk
"The weather forecast says it will be fine but I think I'll take my umbrella to be on the safe side."

better (to be) safe than sorry = caution is better than taking a risk
"We'll take your parents to our usual restaurant, not the new one we haven't tried yet ñ it's better to be safe than sorry."

safe and sound = unharmed
"Our cat stayed away for three days but came back safe and sound."

See also: play (it) safe; safe as houses; there's safety in numbers.

said

after/when all is said and done = after everything has been considered
"Her painting is not brilliant but when all is said and done she's only twelve."

no sooner said than done = something will be done immediately
"You've only got to ask Ken for a favour and it's no sooner said than done."

sail

plain sailing = easy
"I thought the exam might be difficult but it turned out to be plain sailing."

sail against the wind = take an opposite view to most people
"All the young lads have short haircuts these days, but Kevin sails

against the wind and grows his shoulder-length."

sail close to the wind = be risqué

"You sailed close to the wind when you said Martin's wife has put on a bold front."

sail into somebody/something = tackle somebody/something with force/ vigour

"The boss sailed into me for leaving the office unlocked when I went to lunch."

"Alice sailed into her dinner ñ it was as if she hadn't eaten anything for a week!"

sail under false colours = pretend to be what one is not (to gain an advantage)

"He claims to be a chemist but he doesn't even know the basics about acids and alkalis ñ I suspect he's sailing under false colours."

set sail = start a voyage

"We're going on a cruise and we set sail next Saturday."

trim one's sails = modify one's actions/ views to suit the circumstances

"The council has had to trim its sails and postpone plans for a new car park because of lack of funds."

See also: take the wind out of somebody's sails.

saint

enough to make a saint swear = very annoying/frustrating

"These regular delays on the trains are enough to make a saint swear."

saints alive!/saints preserve us! = expression of (exasperated) surprise

"Saints preserve us! Aren't you ready yet?"

See also: my giddy/sainted aunt; try the patience of a saint.

sake

(just) for old time's sake = because of pleasant memories

"We hadn't seen each other for years so we went and had a drink for old time's sake."

for the sake of = in the interests of, or without justification

"I didn't reply to his remarks for the sake of keeping the peace."

"You can't still be hungry, you took another cake just for the sake of it."

(just) for the sake of argument = as a basis for discussion/hypothetically

"Just for the sake of argument, let's assume that you inherited a million pounds."

See also: for God's/goodness' sake.

salad

See: salad days.

Sally

See: Aunt Sally.

salt

above/below the salt = in/not in a position of honour/privilege

"I went to a reception at the embassy but I was of course only sitting below the salt."

put salt on somebody's tail = apprehend/ catch somebody

"The next time he comes near this house I'll put salt on his tail."

salt a mine = introduce something valuable among worthless things to make all of it seem worth more than it really is

"The auctioneer salted the mine by putting one valuable plate among a job lot of old crockery."

salt something away = store something for the future

"I've got plenty of logs salted away for the winter."

take something with a grain/pinch of salt = be disinclined to believe something

"Bill says he was delayed because there was an elephant loose in the street, but I'm inclined to take that with a pinch of salt."

worth one's salt = be conscientious in one's work (and thus be worthy of one's pay)

"Louise always does a good day's work and is certainly worth her salt."

See also: like a dose of salts; rub salt into the wound; salt of the earth.

Samaritan

See: good Samaritan.

same

all/just the same = make no difference, or nevertheless

"I would prefer tea to coffee, if it's all the same to you."

"I told him he need not pay but he insisted just the same."

at the same time = nevertheless

"You may not like Anne but at the same time you have to admit that she's good at her job."

be all the same to = (do) not matter

"If it's all the same to you I'd rather have coffee."

much the same = unchanged/very similar

"I hadn't been to my home town for years but it was much the same as I remember it."

not in the same street as = cannot be compared (favourably) with Richard has bought a new Japanese motorbike but he says it's not in the same street as his old Triumph."

same again = another dish/drink the same as the previous one

"Same again, Philip? I'll pay for the drinks this time."

same as ever = consistent/unchanged

"I see old Harry is the same as ever ñ miserable and unfriendly!"

same here = I agree wholeheartedly

"Same here, I too think we should have another drink."

same old story = recurrent happening

"My job's the same old story ñ too much work and not enough pay."

(and) the same to you = I wish you the same

"And the same to you! How dare you call me that!"

See also: be of the same mind; by the same token; in the same boat; in the same breath; one and the same.

sand

build on sand = initiate something without proper foundation

"The business was built on sand because it has insufficient capital, and it soon failed."

happy as a sand boy = very happy

"Dad's as happy as a sand boy since he retired, pottering in the garden or sorting out his collection of stamps."

the sands (of time) are running out = time is getting short

"We must hurry this job along, the sand of time are running out."

See also: bury one's head in the sand.

sandwich

See: knuckle sandwich.

sardine

packed (in) like sardines = packed together very closely/tightly

"We were packed like sardines in a train that became stuck in a tunnel for nearly half and hour."

sauce

I want none of your sauce = do not be cheeky

"Get on with your homework ñ and I want none of your sauce."

See also: what's sauce for the goose is sauce for the gander.

sausage

not a sausage = absolutely nothing

"I helped him all day, and what did he offer me for it? Not a sausage!"

save

save somebody's skin = rescue somebody/save somebody's life

"The girl was trapped in the overturned boat but the rescuers saved her skin by making a hole in the hull and pulling her through."

save something for a rainy day = retain something for lean times/an unfavourable situation

"My mother taught us always to save some of our pocket money for a rainy day."

See also: saved by the bell; save face; save somebody's bacon; save the day; saving grace; save your breath; scrimp and save; to save one's life.

say

and so say all of us = we all agree

"He's the best manager we've ever had, and so say all of us."

as they say/as the saying goes = expression emphasizing that an idiom/saying has been used

"It was a case of the blind leading the blind, as they say."

"It never rains but it pours, as the saying goes."

as you say = I agree

"As you say, something will have to be done about the problem of unemployment."

don't say.Ö = expression of annoyance/surprise

"Don't say you've broken another cup."

have no say (in) = have no authority/opportunity to express one's point of view

"Ken wanted to paint the room green but his wife had already chosen pink and he had no say in the matter."

have nothing/something to say for oneself = be unable/able to account for one's actions/behaviour

"You were driving at ninety miles an hour. Have you anything to say for yourself?"

have one's say = express one's point of view (forcefully)

"I went to the meeting and the committee wouldn't change its policy ñ but at least I had my say."

I can't say = I do not

"I can't say I want to go and visit your mother this weekend."

I couldn't say = I do not know

"I couldn't say how long the job is likely to take."

if I may/might say so = if you want to know my point of view

"I don't believe in miracles, if I may say so."

I'll say! = emphatically yes

"Does Tony like whisky? I'll say he does!"

I mean to say = expression used to draw attention to a statement already made

"I didn't want to work late every evening ñ I mean to say, would you?"

I'm not just saying that/this = I really mean it

"Sylvia is the best typist round here, and I'm not just saying that."

I must say = I must emphasize
"I must say I prefer your red dress to that blue one."

I say = expression of surprise, or to attract somebody's attention
"I say, I haven't seen you for years."
"I say, isn't that the Duke of York sitting over there?"

I wouldn't say = I do not mean exactly
"I wouldn't say she's ugly, just unattractive."

it goes without saying = you can assume it/it need not be mentioned
"It goes without saying that I will give you my complete cooperation."

I wouldn't say no = I would gladly agree
"If you're making some tea I wouldn't say no to a cup."

I wouldn't say that = I disagree
"I wouldn't say that. I think Everton is a much better team than Liverpool."

say no more = I do not need to be persuaded
"Say no more, I'll come round straight away."

(just) say the word = say what you require
"Just say the word and I'll be glad to help."

says you! = according to you!
"Says you! I don't believe a word of it!"

that is to say = in other words
"There will be four of us at the meeting, that is to say Gill, Ursula, Vic and me."

there's no saying = one cannot even guess
"We should send out written invitations to the party or there's no saying how many people will turn up."

they say that = it is rumoured that
"They say that the government is going to raise the duty on petrol."

what would you say to? = would you like?
"What would you say to a weekend in Paris?"

you can say that again = I agree with you
"You can say that again, she's the prettiest girl in the room."

you don't say? = is that a fact/true?
"You don't say? Has Jenny really had triplets?"

(do) you mean to say? = do you really mean?
"Do you mean to say it will cost me forty pounds just to repair one small dent in my car?"

See also: I dare say; never say die; say when; suffice it to say; to say nothing of; to say the least.

scales

remove the scales from somebody's eyes = make somebody aware of the (unpalatable) truth
"I felt it my duty to remove the scales from Thora's eyes and tell her about her husband's past."

tip/turn the scales = be the small additional factor that precipitates an action/decision
"The candidates were well matched but Lorna's better qualifications tipped the scales in her favour."

scarce

make oneself scarce = run/stay away
"The children had been naughty and they soon made themselves scarce when their father returned home."

scare

scare somebody out of his/her wits/scare somebody stiff = greatly frighten somebody

"Spiders scare me stiff."

"I was scared out of my wits when the police arrived."

scare (the) hell out of/pants off somebody = greatly frighten somebody

"My brother jumped out from behind a tree and scared hell out of me."

"The horror film on television last night scared the pants off me."

scarlet

See: scarlet woman.

scatter

scatter to the four winds = spread widely

"The Ming dinner service has been split up and the various pieces scattered to the four winds."

scene

arrive/come on the scene = arrive

"You can always expect trouble when Glen and his friends come on the scene."

be one's scene = be what one likes/excels at

"I don't like orchestral concerts ñ discos are more my scene."

behind the scenes = out of public view

"The government presents a unified image but I wonder what goes on behind the scenes at cabinet meetings."

create/make a scene = make a (noisy) fuss

"Please be quiet ñ don't make a scene in front of all these people."

set the scene = establish/talk about the background to something

"Actors in period costumes strolled among the crowd to set the scene before the pageant began."

scent

on the (right) scent = having a clue/ information about what one seeks

"The police haven't yet caught up with the fugitives but they claim that they are on the right scent."

put/throw somebody off the scent = divert somebody's attention or mislead somebody

"He seemed to know quite a bit about our secret project so I told him it had been cancelled to throw him off the scent."

schedule

according to schedule = as planned

"Despite earlier delays, the project is now proceeding according to schedule."

ahead of/behind schedule = before/after the planned time

"The train arrived five minutes ahead of schedule."

on schedule = on time

"Since the appointment of a new traffic manager the buses have been running on schedule."

school

of the old school = belonging to an old-fashioned/traditional group

"Harry is one of the old school and still writes all his business letters in longhand."

tell tales out of school = break a confidence/reveal a secret

"I shouldn't tell tales out of school, but do you know who I saw coming out of Gerald's flat?"

See also: old school tie.

science
See: blind with science.

score
know the score = be acquainted with the facts
"Roy shouldn't be surprised at the price, he knows the score regarding the costs of materials and labour these days."
have a score to settle with somebody = have reason to avenge oneself
"I should avoid Patrick, he says he has a score to settle with you."
on that score = for that cause/reason
"Pam is perfectly capable of looking after herself, so you needn't worry on that score."
score (points) off somebody = do/say something that makes somebody else look foolish
"Normally Harry is quite cooperative but he will try to score points off me in committee meetings."
settle a score/old scores = avenge oneself (for past wrongs)
"I'm glad Mick has arrived, I've a score to settle with him."
See also: know the score.

scot
See: scot free.

scrape
scrape along/by = just manage (financially)
"My husband hasn't a well-paid job but we manage to scrape along with difficulty."
scrape through = just succeed
"My son passed his French exam easily but only scraped through maths."
See also: scrape (the bottom of) the barrel; scrape up an acquaintance with.

scratch
be/come up to scratch = be of the required standard
"I'm afraid this product doesn't come up to scratch."
do something from scratch/start from scratch = begin something (again or with no previous experience/ preparation)
"The tiles I put on my wall are all crooked so I've decided to take them down and start from scratch."
scratch one's head = think hard
"I had to scratch my head to remember his name."
scratch somebody's back = do somebody a favour
"I don't mind scratching her back because she's done me several favours in the past."
(only) scratch the surface = tackle only a small part of a problem
"The government is making a million pounds available for research into AIDS, but it is enough only to scratch the surface of the problem."
See also: start from scratch.

screw
put the screws on somebody = apply pressure/use force to get somebody to do something
"If he doesn't confess soon we shall have to put the screws on."
See also: have a screw loose; muster/ pluck/screw up one's courage.

scrimp
scrimp and save/scrape = spend as little as possible

"I've scrimped and saved all year for this holiday ñ now I'm going to enjoy myself."

sea

(all) at sea = bewildered/confused

"My new hi-fi has so many lights and switches that I was all at sea when I first tried to use it."

stranger things happen at sea = even more unusual things can occur

"David may even turn up on time for once ñ you never know, stranger things have happened at sea."

worse things happen at sea = the present difficulty could be even worse (intended as consolation)

"Don't worry about breaking the glass ñ worse things happen at sea."

See also: arm of the sea; between the devil and the deep blue sea; find/get one's sea legs; half seas over; there are plenty more fish in the sea.

seal

put/set one's seal on = agree/authorize

"Just ask the under manager for permission ñ he'll set his seal on anything."

set the seal on something = ensure that something will happen

"Sir Robert's financial backing has set the seal on the success of the venture."

See also: my lips are sealed; seal somebody's fate.

seam

come/fall apart at the seams = collapse/ become ruined

"The trouble with much modern furniture is that it falls apart at the seams after you've had it only a couple of years."

"When I told him of his daughter's death he just fell apart at the seams."

seamy side of life = nasty aspects of life

"You see the seamy side of life when you visit some of the inner city slums."

search

search high and low = look everywhere (to find somebody/something)

"Where were you? I've been searching high and low for you."

search me = I do not know/do not ask me

"Search me why the show has been cancelled."

See also: look/search for a needle in a haystack.

season

silly season = time (when there is little news, during late summer) when the news media devote time/space to trivia

"The front-page story is about a dog that can ride a bicycle ñ it must be the silly season."

See also: compliments of the season; off season.

seat

have a good seat = ride (a horse) well

"Miranda has a good seat and can ride any horse she's given."

hot seat = difficult position/ responsibility

"Nancy is in charge of the group and in the hot seat if anything goes wrong."

take a/one's seat = sit down

"If you will all take your seats, I'll serve the dinner."

See also: have a ringside seat; in the driver's seat; take a back seat.

second

get one's second wind = find new resources of energy after being tired/ exhausted
"When I work all night, I become very tired by three o'clock but then I get my second wind and can work on quite easily."

second-class citizen = underprivileged member of a group/society
"It's unfair that, in many ways, unmarried mothers are regarded as second-class citizens."

second-rate = inferior
"You cannot expect a good response to an advertisement if you place it in a second-rate magazine."

second sight = clairvoyance
"My Mum must have second sight ñ she knew where I'd hidden the biscuits."

second thoughts = change of mind/ revised opinion
"I was going to sell my car but I've had second thoughts and decided to keep it until its road tax expires in five months time."

split second = very brief moment of time
"For a split second I thought you were my sister."

See also: at second hand; just a minute/ moment/second/tick; play second fiddle; (come off) second best; second childhood; second hand; second nature; second to none.

secret

See: open secret.

see

as far as I can see = according to my judgement/understanding
"As far as I can see, you've got nothing to worry about."

as I see it = in my opinion
"As I see it, there's a good chance she'll say yes."

do you see what I mean? = do you understand?
"You hold the lower nut with one spanner while you undo the top nut with another one ñ do you see what I mean?"

have seen better days = be less attractive than formerly/be worn
"My old car still keeps going although it has seen better days."

I'll be seeing you = goodbye
"Thanks for the tea, I'll be seeing you."

I'll see (about that) = I might
"I might go to London tomorrow. I'll see."

I see (what you mean) = I understand
"I see, you need two spanners to do the job."

let me see/let's see = I am trying to calculate/decide/remember
"Let me see now, that will be two pounds twenty please."
"Let me see, I think it's nearly three years since we last met."

see about something = deal with something
"You sit down, I'll see about the washing up."

see double = see (or think one sees) two images of the same object
"That bang on the head made me see double for a while."
"Your twin girls are so alike that whenever they come here I think I'm seeing double."

see here! = exclamation of anger/ annoyance
"See here, young woman! When are you going to serve me?"

seeing is believing = only a sight of

something is real proof of its existence
"Incredible as it may seem, there was a snake with two heads ñ I saw it, and seeing is believing."

seeing that.Ö = because/considering that.Ö
"Sceing that it's raining hard, the f‚te will probably be cancelled."

seeing things = having a hallucination/ observing a visual illusion
"I didn't know your brother was back from Australia and when he walked into the room I thought I was seeing things."

see into something = investigate something
"Sorry, I don't know why your order hasn't been delivered but I'll see into it right away."

see one through = last/persist
"I've bought enough potatoes to see us through the week."

see over something = inspect/view something
"Our house is too large for just the two of us and so we spent part of the weekend seeing over some flats with a view to buying one."

see somebody off = beat somebody/chase somebody away, or go with somebody to where he/she starts a journey
"William challenged me to a game of snooker but I soon saw him off."
"A game warden saw off the poachers before they could kill any of the animals."
"I have to go and see my mother off at the airport."

see somebody out = outlive, or go with somebody to an exit
"My grandfather is over eighty but he says he'll see me out if I don't begin to take things easier."
"Here are your coat and gloves. I'll come downstairs with you and see you out."

see somebody right = ensure that somebody is paid/rewarded for his/her work
"I'll see you right if you help me move this pile of bricks."

see somebody through = help somebody overcome a difficulty
"My religious faith has seen me through my grief."

see something through = persist in doing something
"When Hal makes a commitment, he sees it through no matter what happens."

see the last of = see for the very last time
"Sally was an unpleasant character to work with, and I hope we've seen the last of her."

see through somebody/something = realize that somebody/something intends to deceive
"The inspectors soon saw through his scheme to avoid paying income tax."

see to somebody/something = attend to/ deal with somebody/something
"Would you mind seeing to the milkman, he's called for his money."
"I must see to that broken window."

see to it that = make sure that
"The manager has asked me to see to it that all the shelves are fully stocked before we open the shop in the morning."

see you later = goodbye
"I must go now ñ see you later."

so I see = that is obvious
"You said you'd made a mess ñ so I see!"

when you've seen one you've seen them all = they are so alike that seeing any one of them is all that is needed
"I'm not interested in art so I didn't go

to the gallery ñ when you've seen one painting you've seen them all."

you see = I told you so
"You see! I said it would break if you kept on hitting it like that."

See also: glad to see the back of somebody/something; I'd like to see (somebody do something); not see beyond the end of one's nose; not see the wood for the trees; not to see somebody for dust; refuse to/wouldn't be seen dead with; see daylight; see eye to eye; see how the land lies; see life; see one's way (clear) to; see red; see stars; see the colour of somebody's money; see the light (of day); see the world; see the writing on the wall; see which way the wind blows; see with (only) half an eye; wait and see.

seed

go to seed = become shabby through lack of care
"Old Freddie seems to have gone to seed since his wife died and he's been living on his own."

seize

seize on something = eagerly accept something
"The committee seized on Councillor Jones's idea for a party in December with a professional Father Christmas ñ to be paid for out of the budget for entertaining overseas visitors."

seize up = stop functioning (because of jamming/sticking)
"I bent over to pick up a twopenny piece and my back seized up ñ couldn't straighten it properly and I was in agony."
"The enquiry found that the light aircraft crashed after its engine seized up through lack of coolant."

self

self-made man = somebody from a humble background who has become wealthy/important entirely by his own efforts
"Harry is a self-made man: he started with nothing and now, after many years of hard work, he is fairly rich."

self-possessed = confident and unflappable
"Everyone tended to panic except Irene, who remained self-possessed and calmly dealt with the emergency."

self-righteous = overconfident in one's own moral standards/superiority
"Charles thinks he's better than the rest of us, the self-righteous prig!"

self-willed = wanting to have one's own way in all things/very uncooperative
"A few weeks' community service can make self-willed teenagers into co-operative and caring members of society."

sell

be sold on something = be convinced of something's worth
"I'm not totally sold on the idea of painting the ceiling deep pink."

sell off = sell at a low price
"The shopkeeper had too many cucumbers and had to sell them off cheap to get rid of them."

sell-out = betrayal, or an organized event with a full attendance (all tickets sold)
"The only way the enemy could have known of the plans was through a sell-out by one of our own men."
"The concert by Queen was a sell-out six weeks before the event."

sell out = sell a share in a business
"I've decided to sell out and go and live in the country."
sell short = present as less good than in reality
"You were selling it short when you said that the restaurant was quite good ñ it's excellent."
sell up = sell what one owns
"I shall have to sell up to pay all my debts."
sold out (of) = out of stock
"The shop has sold out of bread and won't have any more until tomorrow."
See also: go/sell like hot cakes; sell a pup; sell one's soul for something; sell somebody down the river.

send

send away/off for something = order something by post/mail order
"Mum has sent off for some new jeans for me ñ I hope they fit."
send somebody down = expel somebody from university
"Three students were sent down for dealing in drugs."
send somebody/something up = parody somebody/something
"Some comedians who send up the establishment do it to make a political point."
See also: drive/send somebody up the wall; pass/send/take the hat round; send chills/shivers up somebody's spine; send flying; send somebody about his/her business; send somebody packing; send somebody to Coventry.

sense

bring somebody to his/her senses = make somebody use common sense/reason
"Glen used to behave very irresponsibly until that recent brush with the police brought him to his senses."
come to one's senses = regain consciousness, or realize the truth
"Doreen was knocked unconscious in a fall from a horse and it was three days before she came to her senses."
"It's about time Julia came to her senses and realized what Nigel is really like."
in a sense = to some extent
"In a sense she was misled by the advertisement's claims, and expected too much of the product."
in one sense = regarded from one point of view (but not another)
"In one sense you were right to object to the wording of the advertisement, but you have to see it also from the manufacturer's point of view."
out of one's senses = mentally unbalanced/mad
"You must have been out of your senses to let Harry treat you like that."
sixth sense = extrasensory/paranormal feeling
"It was pitch black but some sixth sense told me that there was somebody in the room."
See also: horse sense; sense of proportion; take leave of one's senses.

separate

separate the men from the boys/separate the sheep from the goats = separate the better members of a group from the rest
"Many people can answer questions on their own special subject, but it's general knowledge questions that separate the men from the boys."

sepulchre

painted/whited sepulchre = somebody who hides his/her misdeeds behind a pretence of goodness/piety
"Although Frank always volunteered to help with any of the church's fund-raising campaigns, he turned out to be a whited sepulchre with two convictions for fraud."

serious

you can't be serious = you cannot really mean it
"You can't be serious. Did you really pay a hundred pounds for that?"

servant

what did your last servant die of? = why don't you do it yourself?
"No I won't go and get your book from upstairs ñ what did your last servant die of?"

serve

serve its turn = act as a (temporary) substitute for/suffice for a particular purpose
"The bolt is worn and not an exact fit but it will serve its turn until I can buy a new one."

serve one right = be what one deserves
"It will serve you right if you get stomach ache after eating all those apples."

serve one's time = remain in a job for the full allotted period
"My father served his time in the navy before opening a shop in the High Street."

serve time = be imprisoned
"Neil was convicted of fraud and is serving time in Wormwood Scrubs."

See also: first come, first served; if my memory serves me (right); serve a/the purpose; serve somebody right.

service

at one's service = available for use/to help
"My telephone is at your service until yours is repaired."

be of service to somebody = assist/help somebody
"Just ask if I can be of any service to you."

have seen good service = have had long/satisfactory use
"These shoes have seen good service but they cannot be repaired yet again and the time has come to throw them away."

See also: pay lip service to; press something into service.

sesame

See: open sesame.

set

all set = prepared/ready
"We'll leave in five minutes if you're all set."

be set on something = keenly desire something
"I'm set on going up the Eiffel Tower when I go to Paris."

make a dead set at = determinedly approach/attack somebody
"As soon as I walked in the room my next-door neighbour made a dead set at me."

set about somebody = attack somebody
"The youth threatened the old lady so she set about him with her walking stick."

set about something = start to do something (purposefully)
"It was a fine afternoon so we decided

to set about tidying up the garden."

set aside = save money
"I try to set aside something every week towards my holiday."

set in = become established
"The talk was so boring that torpor set in and some of the audience actually fell asleep."

set off = begin a journey
"We set off at dawn so that we could get to the coast before lunchtime."

set somebody against somebody (else) = foment hatred between two people
"My husband's mother is always trying to set him against me, probably because she's jealous."

set somebody/something on somebody = allow somebody/something to attack somebody
"Don't you dare come round here again or I'll set the dog on you!"

set something off to advantage = display something to show it at its best
"The black velvet dress sets off your diamond brooch to advantage."

set to = (begin to) do something purposefully
"We can tidy the room in a few minutes if we all set to."

set up = establish
"The police have set up an incident room near the scene of the crime."

well set up = secure/well provided for
"His father's money left Jim well set up for life."

See also: have one's mind set on something; keep/set/start the ball rolling; put/set somebody right; put/set something right; put/set the clock back; set a thief to catch a thief; set one's cap at; set one's face against; set one's heart upon; set one's seal on; set one's sights on; set one's teeth on edge; set somebody by the ears; set somebody by the heels; set somebody (back) on his/her heels; set/make the pace; set the record straight; set the wheels in motion; set to work.

settle

settle down = establish oneself in a place, or begin to do something
"After working abroad for several years, Gill wants to settle down to a permanent job in Britain."
"I like to settle down and read a book after dinner."

settle for something = accept something reluctantly/as a compromise
"I would like a Jaguar but can't afford it, so I've settled for a Skoda."

settle on = choose
"There were so many curtain materials to choose from, but we finally settled on a green fabric with bright pink flowers on it."

settle something on somebody = (formally) donate something to somebody
"My father's company settled an annual pension of five thousand pounds on him."

settle up with somebody = pay off a debt
"We had an excellent meal and were surprised how little it cost to settle up afterwards."

See also: an account to settle; settle an old score; settle somebody's hash; settle/square an account with somebody; when/after the dust has settled.

seven

See: at sixes and sevens; seventh heaven.

sew

sewn up = completed/finalized
"Our holiday arrangements are all sewn up ñ we leave next Saturday."

sex
See: fair sex.

shack
shack up with somebody = live with somebody
"I've been turned out of my lodgings so I'm going to shack up with my boyfriend for a while."

shade
put in the shade = make seem less important/significant
"I enjoy cooking but the dishes Margaret makes put mine in the shade."
shades of = reminiscent of
"Our boss has a very dictatorial attitude to the staff ñ shades of Hitler there!"

shadow
be afraid of one's own shadow = be timid/easily frightened
"Don't worry that Stephen might be aggressive ñ he's afraid of his own shadow."
shadow of one's former self = much less energetic/healthy than formerly
"Arthur has finally come out of hospital after four weeks but he's only a shadow of his former self."
worn to a shadow = made tired/thin through working hard
"Weeks of hard work refurbishing his guest house in time for the first summer visitors had worn David to a shadow."

shaggy
See: shaggy dog story.

shake
in two shakes (of a lamb's tail) = very soon
"Please sit down and I'll be with you in two shakes."
no great shakes = not very good/well
"I went to see that new film last night but it was no great shakes and I don't recommend it."
shake in one's shoes = tremble with fear
"Policemen always make me shake in my shoes, even when I've done nothing wrong."
shake like a jelly/leaf = tremble with fear
"When the head teacher called me into her study I shook like a jelly in case I had done something wrong."
shake off = get rid of
"The fugitive was unable to shake off the dogs that were following his trail."
shake one's fist = express anger/threaten (by waving ones clenched fist)
"He was so angry he couldn't speak; he just shook his fist under her nose."
shake one's head = indicate disagreement/sorrow
"When I asked if I could help she just shook her head in silence."
shake up = enliven
"It needs somebody to shake them up out of their complacency."
See also: shake a leg; shake hands on it; shake somebody to the foundations; shake the dust from one's feet.

shame
put somebody/something to shame = make somebody/something appear to be inferior (by being much better)
"Hal's writing is so neat and legible that it puts mine to shame."
shame on you! = you ought to feel ashamed!
"Shame on you! You know better than to argue with your mother."
what a shame! = how unfortunate/ unlucky!

"What a shame! You've broken your favourite vase."

See also: crying shame.

shanks

See: shanks's pony.

shape

get into shape = get fit

"I haven't taken much exercise during the winter but I must get into shape before the beginning of the cricket season."

in any shape or form = at all, or no matter what form something takes

"Sandra is a strict vegetarian and won't eat meat in any shape or form."

in good shape = satisfactory, or (physically) fit

"After getting that rise my finances are finally in good shape."

"William is in remarkably good shape for a man of his age."

in the shape of = in the form of

"Retribution struck in the shape of my mother-in-law."

knock into shape = make something conform to a requirement

"The storeroom is an untidy mess but I'll soon knock it into shape."

shape up/take shape = develop (towards a particular form)

"How is your autobiography shaping up?"

"The project will soon take shape when we get more people working on it."

See also: all ship-shape and Bristol fashion; lick into shape.

share

go shares with = share (usually cost/ money)

"If you give me a lift to London in your car we can go shares with the cost of the petrol."

share and share alike = share equally

"Here are some sweets for you, children; make sure you share and share alike."

share of the gravy = share of the proceeds/profits

"I think we should ask the boss for a rise. We do all the work, so it's only fair for us to have a bigger share of the gravy."

See also: lion's share.

sharp

have a sharp tongue = talk angrily/ sarcastically

"I usually get on well with my father, although he can have a sharp tongue occasionally."

look sharp (about it)! = be quick!

"Look sharp! Here comes the boss!"

"Get those boxes moved, and look sharp about it!"

sharp practice = dishonesty (in business dealings)

"Just because we underbid our rivals and got a major order, they have accused us of sharp practice."

sharp's the word! = be quick!/hurry!

"Sharp's the word! We've only got ten minutes to get to the station to catch the train."

See also: keen/sharp as a razor.

shave

See: close call/shave.

shed

See: shed/throw light on.

sheep

count sheep = keep counting to oneself in an attempt to fall asleep

"I've tried a hot drink at bedtime and counting sheep, but I just can't seem to get to sleep these days."

See also: black sheep (of the family); make (sheep's) eyes at; might as well be hung for a sheep as a lamb; separate the sheep from the goats; wolf in sheep's clothing.

sheet

between the sheets = in bed

"I'm tired after all that walking and I can't wait to get between the sheets."

sheet anchor = somebody/something that provides long-term support

"Lady Dorothy's financial support and encouragement was the sheet anchor of the drama society in its early days before it became really established."

three sheets to the wind = drunk

"Tom was three sheets to the wind and couldn't walk across the room without stumbling."

with a clean sheet/slate = with no faults/misdemeanours recorded against one

"Henry has apologized for his bad behaviour and should be allowed to rejoin the group with a clean sheet."

See also: white as a sheet.

shelf

left on the shelf = unlikely to get married (because of age or unattractiveness)

"She's only twenty-five and yet she's worried about being left on the shelf."

shell

come out of one's shell = become less shy/more confident

"Pam used to be quite shy but she's really come out of her shell since she got engaged."

go into one's shell = behave in a timid/shy way

"Laura is very shy and goes into her shell whenever a boy comes into the room."

shell out = pay

"We've been invited to the mayor's reception and so I shall probably have to shell out for a new dress for my wife."

shift

See: shift one's ground.

shilling

See also: cut off without a penny/shilling; turn an honest penny/shilling.

shine

take a shine to somebody = form a liking for somebody

"Rachel seems to have taken a shine to the boy who has come to live next door."

take the shine off/out of = cause to appear inferior/less important (than formerly regarded)

"Any one of our workman could take the shine off the new foreman."

See also: come rain or shine; make hay while the sun shines; rise and shine!

ship

run a tight ship = maintain strict control

"We have little freedom at work because our manager runs a very tight ship."

ships that pass in the night = people who have only one (accidental) meeting

"Most people one makes friends with on holiday turn out to be ships that pass in the night."

spoil the ship for a ha'porth of tar = fail to complete something valuable by omitting an inexpensive detail/

finishing touch (ha'porth is short for halfpennyworth)
"The old pine dresser had been lovingly restored but they spoiled the ship for a ha'porth of tar by fitting it with cheap plastic handles."
when one's ship comes in = when one becomes wealthy
"When my ship comes in I intend to take a year's holiday travelling round the world."
See also: all ship-shape and Bristol fashion; ships that pass in the night.

shirt
put one's shirt on = bet all one's money on
"We went greyhound racing last night and I was losing steadily until I put my shirt on a dog in the last race ñ and it won at odds of ten to one."
stuffed shirt = somebody who is humourless/pompous
"Our boss is such a stuffed shirt ñ he'll never come to any of the office parties, although he's always invited to them."
work in one's shirt sleeves = work without wearing a coat/jacket
"It is still very formal in our office; we can't work in our shirt sleeves even in the hottest weather."
See also: keep one's hair/shirt on.

shiver
give one the shivers = evoke a feeling of horror
"I hate snakes ñ even a photograph of one gives me the shivers."
send shivers down/up one's spine = cause a feeling of excitement/ revulsion
"Whenever I merely hear his name it sends shivers down my spine."
"Snakes and spiders send shivers up my spine."

shoe
be in somebody's shoes = be in somebody's place/position
"Charles is going out with the new secretary ñ I wish I was in his shoes."
on a shoestring = at minimum cost
"We've been living on a shoestring since my husband lost his job."
step into somebody's shoes = succeed somebody (to a job/position)
"Mandy has done very well since she stepped into the manager's shoes."
where the shoe pinches = what causes financial problems
"Trying to save for a holiday is where the shoe pinches."
See also: dead man's shoes; fill somebody's shoes; lick somebody's boots/shoes.

shoot
shoot ahead = rapidly progress/take the lead
"The Russian runner shot ahead right from the beginning of the race."
shoot up = grow/rise rapidly
"You son has shot up since I last saw him six months ago."
the whole bang shoot = the lot/ everything
"Please empty that cupboard and throw everything away ñ I want to get rid of the whole bang shoot."
See also: shoot a line; shoot down in flames; shoot one's bolt; shoot one's mouth off; (whole) shooting match.

shop
all over the shop/show = scattered/ spread everywhere

"Two aircraft collided in mid air and pieces of wreckage landed all over the shop."
"I went rifle shooting yesterday but my shots went all over the show and I didn't hit the bulls eye once."
set up shop = start a business
"I've decided to set up shop as a consultant."
shop around = compare things before buying/choosing one of them
"If you want a puppy don't buy the first one you see, but shop around until you find the right one."
shut up shop = stop working (temporarily or permanently)
"It's getting late; let's shut up shop and finish the job tomorrow."
"Arnold can't get a decent job in England and so he's decided to shut up shop and emigrate to Canada."
talk shop = talk about one's job
"I don't usually go for a drink with my partner after work because he always talks shop, and I prefer to forget about the job until the next day."
See also: closed shop; cop shop; like a bull in a china shop.

short

at short notice = with little warning
"Would you like to go to a concert this evening? I'm sorry it's such short notice but I was only given the tickets today."
bring somebody up short = make somebody suddenly stop what he/she is doing
"Ann was strolling along aimlessly when I brought her up short by calling her name from the other side of the street."
caught/taken short = have the (sudden) desire to urinate
"Why is it that my children always seem to get taken short on the motorway when there are no services for miles and miles."
cut a long story short = recount something briefly
"I forgot to send for a new cheque book, I've lost my cash card, and ñ well, to cut a long story short, can you lend me ten pounds until Monday?"
for short = in abbreviated form
"Our dog's kennel name is Owenbank Figaro Godelpus but we call him Figgie for short."
give somebody short shrift = devote little time to somebody (and in an abrupt manner)
"Gerald tried to borrow another ten pounds from me, but I gave him very short shrift."
go short = have too little of something
"We went short of luxuries when we were first married because we had so little money."
in short = stated briefly
"Without going into details, I think that the plan is, in short, rubbish."
in short supply = scarce
"The red pens are in short supply; will a blue one do?"
in the short term = over a short amount of time
"The new import restrictions should help the country's balance of payments in the short term, at least until our trading partners take reciprocal action."
little short of = nearly the same as
"When my children say they will leave me in peace if I let them go to the pictures it is little short of extortion."
make short work of = complete/conclude quickly

"The champion made short work of the challenger and knocked him out in the first round."

nothing short of = (exactly) the same as
"I think that the factory farming of calves for veal is nothing short of murder."

run short = not have enough
"You can't have a drink of milk with your supper because we're running short and must keep some for tomorrow morning's breakfast."

sell somebody/something short = fail to present somebody/something to best advantage
"She sold herself short at the interview by failing to mention her previous experience."

short and sweet = brief and to the point
"I asked the boss for a rise and his reply was predictably short and sweet!"

short change somebody = give somebody insufficient change (when paying for something)
"Be careful in that shop ñ they have a habit of short changing you."

short-circuit = omit usual formalities to hasten a procedure
"It can take ages to get a licence when you apply in writing, but you can short-circuit the system by applying at the office in person."

short for = abbreviation of
"NATO is short for North Atlantic Treaty Organization."

short-handed/short-staffed = with insufficient helpers/staff
"We are short-handed at work because so many of the staff are on holiday."

short head = small amount/distance
"I contacted the council as soon as I heard the land was for sale, but my neighbour beat me by a short head and got his bid in first."

short of = except/without going as far as, or not as far as
"I'll do anything to get some more money ñ short of stealing it."
"The shells landed a few yards short of our trenches."

short of breath = breathless/panting
"I must lose some weight ñ I get short of breath just walking up the stairs."

short on something = lacking in something
"He's a nice lad but he's a bit short on brains."

short-tempered = easily angered
"My father gets increasingly short-tempered as he gets older."

short weight = less than the proper weight (as required/paid for)
"The coal doesn't seem to last as long as it used to; I wonder if we're getting short weight."

stop short of = not go as far as
"I may not like her but I would stop short of calling her names."

See also: as thick as two short planks; cut short; fall short; have somebody by the short and curlies; in short order; the long and (the) short of it; short cut; short list; short measure.

shot

get shot of = get rid of/dismiss
"The new employee was useless and so the management got shot of him after only a week."

like a shot = eagerly/quickly
"If I had a chance to go to the United States I'd take it like a shot."

shot across the bows = warning
"The chairman's comments were a shot across the bows and I think we had better improve our performance."

shotgun wedding = enforced marriage (usually because the bride is pregnant)
"My parents had a shotgun wedding and had only been married a few months before I was born."

shot in the arm = fillip/stimulant
"The new player was a shot in the arm for the team, which played noticeably better."

(all) shot to pieces = destroyed/spoiled, or very distressed
"Our plans for the future were shot to pieces when I lost my job."
"Glenda was shot to pieces by the news of her mother's death."

See also: big fish/noise/shot; call the shots/tune; leap/shot in the dark; long shot.

shoulder

have broad shoulders = be able/willing to accept much responsibility
"George must have broad shoulders ñ he's taken on the job of secretary of the tennis club as well as being treasurer of the cricket club."

put one's shoulder to the wheel = start hard work
"The only way we'll complete the job on time is for everyone to put their shoulders to the wheel."

shoulder to cry on = somebody who listens to one's troubles sympathetically
"My daughter has been married for ten years yet she still comes home to see me when she wants a shoulder to cry on."

shoulder to shoulder = close together (in mutual support)
"We must stand shoulder to shoulder and resist any attempt to negotiate with us individually."

shrug one's shoulders = display indecision/lack of interest
"I asked Jack if he wanted to come but he just shrugged his shoulders and said he would think about it."

straight from the shoulder = directly/without compromise
"I want to know what's wrong with me, Doctor; please tell me straight from the shoulder."

See also: chip on one's shoulder; cold shoulder; have a good head on one's shoulders; head and shoulders above; old head on young shoulders; rub shoulders with; shoulder the blame/responsibility.

shout

shout one's head off = shout loudly
"All right, I heard you ñ there's no need to shout your head off."

shout somebody down = make so much noise that a speaker cannot be heard
"The minister started to speak but students in the audience shouted him down."

See also: all over bar the shouting; shout one's mouth off; shout something from the rooftops.

shove

shove off = go away
"It's about time we shoved off and let you get on with your work."
"No, I won't give you any money for a cup of tea. Shove off!"

See also: shove it up one's jumper.

show

for show = for appearance sake only
"The shutters by those windows are just for show ñ they're fixed to the wall and won't close properly."

give the show away = reveal a confidence/secret
"Don't tell Mildred about the surprise party, she'll only give the show away."
good show! = well done!, or I am pleased
"You passed all your exams? Good show!"
"Good show, dinner is ready."
on show = displayed for everyone to see
"One of Norma's paintings is on show at the local library."
show (good) cause = provide good reason
"Can you show good cause why you let it happen?"
show off = display one's possessions/ talents in order to impress somebody
"Mike has only driven to the pub to show off his new car ñ he usually walks!"
"Jenny, don't show off. Any girl your age can do cartwheels so we're not impressed."
show of force = demonstration of power
"NATO troops are holding an exercise on the German border as a show of force to the Warsaw Pact countries."
show of hands = vote made by people raising their hands
"The motion was passed on a show of hands, although voting was close and the opposition asked for a recount."
show somebody up = make somebody appear foolish/inept, or accompany somebody upstairs
"Barry knows I'm a poor darts player; he only challenged me to a game to show me up."
"When Councillor Jones arrives, please show him up to my office."
show up = arrive, or reveal faults/feature
"Isn't it about time the bus showed up?"
"My wrinkles really show up unless I wear heavy make-up."
"The oblique sunlight shows up the rough texture of the wall."
steal the show = attract the most attention/praise (away from somebody/something else)
"All the acts were good but an unknown young comedian stole the show."
to show for (it) = have as recompense
"I worked in the garden all morning but all I've got to show for it is blisters!"
See also: all over the shop/show; get the show on the road; give the game/show away; hoist/show/wave the white flag; look/show one's age; run the show; show a clean pair of heels; show a leg; show fight; show one's face; reveal/ show one's hand; show oneself in one's true colours; show one's paces; show one's teeth; show somebody the door; show the flag; show the white feather.

shrift
See: give somebody/something short shrift.

shrink
See: shrinking violet.

shrug
shrug off = dismiss/regard as trivial
"I've told my husband he smokes too much but he just shrugs it off and says they're his lungs and he'll do what he likes with them."
See also: shrug one's shoulders.

shuffle
See: shuffle off this mortal coil.

shut

shut one's eyes to = deliberately ignore
"You can't shut your eyes to the fact that those watches are so cheap they are probably rubbish or stolen."

shut the door on/to something = make something impossible
"The management's refusal to raise the pay offer has shut the door to further negotiations."

shut up = stop talking etc.
"Please shut up, I'm trying to listen to the radio."
"Can't you make that dog shut up? The neighbours will be complaining."

See also: open and shut case; shut one's eyes to; shut one's mouth/face/trap; shut/slam the door in somebody's face; shut up shop; with one's eyes closed/shut.

shutter

put up the shutters = cease business activity
"We'll get no more customers today, so let's put up the shutters and go home."

shy

have a shy at = make an attempt
"I've never played snooker before but I'll have a shy at it."

See also: fight shy of; once bitten, twice shy.

sick

fall sick = become ill
"I spent most of my holiday in bed because I fell sick two days after we arrived at our hotel."

make one sick = cause one to be angry/upset
"Micky is always boasting about his sporting achievements ñ he makes me sick."

sick and tired of = very tired of
"I'm sick and tired of hearing her voice."

sick as a dog = very sick (vomiting)
"No you can't have any more ice cream; you'll be as sick as a dog if you do."

sick as a parrot = very disappointed/envious/upset
"Barbara is sick as a parrot about losing her ring."
"Harry is really jealous of my new car ñ he's as sick as a parrot."

worried sick = very worried
"Where have you been until this time? We've been worried sick about you."

See also: sick at heart; sick joke; sick of the sight of somebody/something; sick to death of.

side

from/on all sides = from/in all directions
"Missiles were hurled at him from all sides."
"The theatre had a central stage with seats on all sides."

let the side down = perform badly to the cost of other members of one's group
"Dan's very slow rate of work has let the side down and the whole shift has lost its productivity bonus as a result of him."

on every side = in all directions/everywhere
"The proposal met with opposition on every side."

on the old (etc.) side = fairly old (etc.)
"Your new girlfriend is very attractive but isn't she a bit on the old side for you?"

"My new shoes are on the tight side but should be all right after I have worn them a few times."

on the right/wrong side of = nearly/just more than
"I doubt if she's on the right side of forty."
"I bet she's on the wrong side of forty."

on the side = in addition to one's regular job
"Bob augments his income by doing window cleaning on the side."

pass by on the other side = ignore somebody in trouble
"I went to help this drunk but he merely hurled abuse at me ñ I wish I had passed by on the other side."

pick sides = choose members of each team before a contest
"There are enough of us to pick four sides and hold a knock-out competition."

put on side = pretend to be what one is not
"I like Norma because she's a genuine person and never puts on side."

put something on/to one side = postpone something
"I must get on with the accounts ñ I can't put them to one side any longer."

side by side = close beside/neighbouring
"Her two dogs walked obediently side by side."
"They demolished the old house and on the site built two new ones side by side."

side with somebody/take somebody's side = favour/support somebody in a dispute
"In any competition John sides with the weaker contestant."
"In any argument John always takes my side."

split one's sides = laugh heartily/violently
"The clown's antics made us split our sides."

take sides = favour/support one party in a dispute
"A parent shouldn't take sides when children start quarrelling with each other."

take somebody on/to one side = talk to somebody privately (away from others)
"You'll have to take David to one side and tell him the bad news."

(on) the other side = (life after) death
"I've been a widow for ten years, ever since my dear husband crossed over to the other side."

to be on the safe side = as a contingency/for reassurance
"It doesn't look as if it's going to rain, but I think I'll take my umbrella to be on the safe side."

See also: bit on the side; brush aside/to one side; get on the wrong side of somebody; get out of bed (on) the wrong side; have one's bread buttered on both sides; keep on the right side of somebody; know which side one's bread is buttered; laugh on the other side of one's face; like the side of a house; look on the bright side; on the side of the angels; on the wrong side of the blanket; on the wrong side of the tracks; other side of the coin; seamy side of life.

sidelines

sit on the sidelines = observe something without taking part in it
"When the two main political factions start arguing at our committee meetings I just sit on the sidelines and

sideways

knock somebody sideways = confuse/shock somebody
"The news of his father's death knocked him sideways."

sieve

See: have a head like a sieve.

sight

catch sight of = start seeing, or get a glimpse of
"As we reached the brow of the hill we caught sight of the church tower in the distance."
"I just caught sight of my mother as she disappeared into the shop."

do something on sight = do something immediately/without hesitation
"I saw this pretty blouse and bought it on sight."

get out of my sight! = go away!
"Get out of my sight, and don't come back until you've had a good wash."

in one's sights = in one's range of vision, or in one's awareness (with a view to possession)
"I've had that bird in my sights ever since it flew down from the tree."
"I haven't yet got a manager's job but I keep it in my sights."

in sight of = close enough to be seen
"It was five days before the ship sailed in sight of land."

keep/lose sight of something = remain aware/unaware of something
"That is irrelevant; we must keep sight of the main purpose of this meeting."
"You seem to have lost sight of the main purpose of the meeting."

keep something in sight = stay within visual range of something
"The aircraft climbed so rapidly it was difficult to keep it in sight."

know somebody by sight = recognize somebody (to whom one has not been introduced)
"I know that woman by sight; doesn't she sometimes read the news on television?"

not be able to stand the sight of somebody/something = have a strong dislike for somebody/something
"I wish he'd go away, I can't stand the sight of him."
"I'm glad that vase has finally been broken ñ I never could stand the sight of it."

out of sight = excellent
"The rock concert was out of sight."

out of sight, out of mind = what one cannot see will (easily) be forgotten
"My husband is very attentive when he's at home, but when he's away on business he never even thinks to phone me ñ out of sight, out of mind."

second sight = ability to foretell the future
"Hilda's mother has second sight and correctly predicted the date on which Hilda met the man she eventually married."

set one's sights on = try to obtain
"My wife has set her sights on a holiday in Greece this year."

sick of the sight of somebody/something = very tired of seeing somebody/something
"Is that boyfriend of yours here again? I'm getting sick of the sight of him."
"I've done so much driving this week I'm sick of the sight of the car."

sight unseen = without having been seen/examined
"There was a second-hand washing machine advertised in my local paper

for only ten pounds, so I bought it sight unseen."
See also: at first sight; lose one's sight; sight for sore eyes.

sign
sign of the times = characteristic of now (the present)
"The large increase in sexually transmitted diseases is, I'm afraid, a sign of the times."
sign on the dotted line = make one's signature on a (legally binding/ official) document
"The contract is complete, all you have to do is sign on the dotted line."
sign the pledge = promise/undertake not to drink alcohol
"The doctor said that if I don't sign the pledge my liver condition will definitely get worse."
See also: sign somebody's death warrant.

signal
give somebody a/the signal = indicate when somebody should do something
"When you want me to start pulling on the rope, just give me the signal."

silence
silence is golden = it can be best to say nothing (in a difficult situation)
"When the sergeant asks if there are any complaints, silence is golden."

silent
as silent as the grave = very quiet
"I expected there to be someone at home, but when I returned it was as silent as the grave."
See also: silent majority.

silk
make a silk purse out of a sow's ear = make something good out of bad/poor quality materials
"I was hoping I could repair my old car and make it roadworthy, but it turns out you can't make a silk purse out of a sow's ear."
take silk = become a Queen's Counsel
"He took silk after being a barrister for only ten years."

silly
play sill beggars = behave in a foolish manner, or deliberately annoy/obstruct
"Stop playing silly beggars and give me my pen back."
"My solicitor has still not returned the contract; I wish she would stop playing silly beggars and get on with it."
See also: silly season.

silver
See: born with a silver spoon in one's mouth; cross somebody's palm with silver; every cloud has a silver lining.

simple
the simple life = way of life that lacks extravagance or luxuries
"I would like to give up this hectic city living and retire to the country and the simple life."
See also: pure and simple.

sin
for one's sins = as an annoyance/ punishment
"I wanted to go shopping on Saturday but I can't because I've got to work overtime for my sins."
See also: cover/include a multitude of sins; live in sin; ugly as sin.

since
See: ages since.

sing

sing for one's supper = perform a favour/service in return for something one needs

"Let me help you decorate the room for the party ñ I might as well sing for my supper."

See also: sing somebody's praises.

sink

be sunk = be in a hopeless situation

"We're sunk if Dad comes home and catches us."

sinking feeling = feeling of apprehension/dread

"Whenever I think of going to the dentist I get that sinking feeling."

sink or swim = commit to success or total failure

"I have said I can solve all their problems, so sink or swim I am committed."

sink to somebody's level = be/perform as badly as somebody else

"Just because Glen gets drunk at parties, there's no need to sink to his level."

See also: everything but the kitchen sink; hook line and sinker.

sit

sit back = relax

"Now that we have organized the party, we can sit back and enjoy it."

sit for = pose for an artist/photographer, or take an examination

"Louise has agreed to sit for me in return for copies of the photographs."

"It's only a week before I have to sit for my finals."

sit in on something = be present (without taking part)

"I don't want to contribute to the discussion, but I would like to sit in on the meeting."

sit on = deliberately take no action, or be a member of a board/committee etc.

"Get your application in early because the council will sit on it for weeks before doing anything about it."

"I have been invited to sit on the entertainments committee."

sit out = not take part in a dance, or stay to the end

"That dance has made me breathless, I think I'll sit the next one out."

"The supporting film was awful but we had to sit it out before the main feature started."

sit something out = wait until something (usually unpleasant) is over

"We ran aground on a sandbank and had to sit it out until high tide."

sit tight = be unwilling to move, or to change one's point of view

"You sit tight, I'll get the food."

"They tried to get me to join the union, but I decided to sit tight until it became compulsory."

sit up (and take notice) = pay attention/take notice

"I told him about his father's affair with my daughter ñ that made him sit up."

sit up and beg = grovel/be subservient, or not go to bed

"She may be the Warden, but we pay for her services so why should we sit up and beg?"

"We sat up until midnight to watch the snooker final on television."

sit up for = wait for somebody to come home

"Now Linda has her own key, we don't have to sit up for her any more."

See: sit at somebody's feet; sit in judgement; sitting duck; sitting pretty; sitting target; sit on one's hands; sit on the fence.

six

(all) at sixes and sevens = confused/disorganized
"They were all at sixes and sevens when they were told that the Queen was going to visit them."

knock/hit somebody for six = defeat somebody completely, or surprise somebody
"He picked up a heavy stick and knocked his attacker for six."
"The news that she had won the lottery really hit her for six."

six of one and half a dozen of the other = equal
"When my two children quarrel I never know who to blame because it's usually six of one and half a dozen of the other."

six of the best = a caning
"There was no detention at my old school ñ we got six of the best for breaking any of the school rules."

sixth sense = intuition/understanding not based on any of the normal five senses
"It was pitch black but some sixth sense told me that there was somebody else in the room."

sixty

See: the 64 million dollar question

size

be (about) the size of it = describe something
"We're hopelessly outnumbered and that's about the size of it."

how's that for size?/try that on for size = what do you think of that?
"Here's the ten pounds I said I would give you next week. How's that for size?"
"I replied to his query with a complete set of statistics. Let him try that on for size."

size somebody/something up = decide what somebody/something is like
"The salesman had an aggressive manner and I soon sized him up."

See also: cut down to size.

skate

get one's skates on = hurry
"Come on, get your skates on or we'll be late."

skate over = ignore/consider only superficially
"Helen told me about her past, although I notice she skated over the time she was living in Paris."

See also: skate on thin ice.

skeleton

skeleton staff = minimum number of people to work someth˙ g
"During the rail strike we kept the office open using a skeleton staff of people who lived nearby."

See also: skeleton in the cupboard.

skid

put the skids on/under = hasten
"Now that we have the new contract we can put the skids under the plan to move to larger premises."

skin

by the skin of one's teeth = only just
"I caught the last train by the skin of my teeth."

get under one's skin = be annoying
"I wish Peter would stop whistling ñ he knows the noise gets under my skin."

have a thick skin = be insensitive (to people's remarks)
"Harry's got a thick skin and you can say what you like to him, he won't mind."

save somebody's skin = rescue somebody
"I was in debt when my father gave me five hundred pounds and saved my skin."
skin deep = superficial
"She claims to be co-operative but her co-operation is often only skin deep."
skin somebody alive = punish somebody severely
"If I find out who did this I'll skin him alive!"
soaked to the skin = very wet
"We were caught in a sudden shower of rain and soaked to the skin."
See also: here's skin off your nose; keep one's eyes skinned; no skin off one's nose; slip on a banana skin.

skip
skip it = forget/ignore it
"No thanks, I don't want any payment ñ skip it."
skip off = go away/leave
"Where's Linda? She always skips off when there's work to be done."

skirt
piece of skirt = young woman
"Did you see that nice piece of skirt who just came in the room?"

skittle
See: all beer and skittles.

sky
sky high = very high
"Unless inflation is checked, prices will rise sky high."
the sky's the limit = there is no upper limit
"When I entertain a pretty girl I don't mind how much I spend ñ the sky's the limit."
See also: mackerel sky; pie in the sky; praise to the skies.

slagheap
on the slagheap = discarded/of no further use
"There are so few jobs around here that a man can find himself on the slagheap when he's fifty."

slam
See: shut/slam the door in somebody's face.

slang
slanging match = argument in which the parties insult each other
"I don't want to discuss the matter with Roy because it will only turn into another slanging match."

slap
slap and tickle = sex play
"I see no need to get married as long as I can have a bit of slap and tickle."
slap in the face = action that greatly discourages/frustrates
"I'd worked there for more than fifteen years, so being made redundant came as a real slap in the face."
slap on the back = congratulations
"The supervisor gave Belinda a slap on the back for finishing the work so quickly."
slap on the wrist = minor punishment/scolding
"Overall Janet's work was good but she deserves a slap on the wrist for a few silly mistakes."
slap-up = excellent/expensive
"If you pass your exam I'll treat you to a slap-up meal."
See also: slap in the face.

slate

wipe the slate clean = cancel/ignore previous debts/misdemeanours
"Once you have served your sentence you can wipe the slate clean and start a new life."

put something on the slate = buy something on credit
"I had no change to buy my paper this morning but the newsagent put it on the slate and said I could pay him tomorrow."

See also: have a screw/slate/tile loose.

slave

slave driver = somebody who makes people work very hard
"Our boss is a real slave driver ñ we don't even get a tea break!"

sledgehammer

use a sledgehammer to crack a nut = use unnecessarily powerful forces/resources
"Employing an experienced chef to make sandwiches is using a sledgehammer to crack a nut."

sleep

get one's beauty sleep = have sufficient sleep to wake totally refreshed
"My daughter is bad-tempered all day if she doesn't get enough beauty sleep."

lose sleep over = worry
"I don't know how I'm going to pay for a new outfit, although I shan't lose any sleep over it."

put an animal to sleep = humanely kill an animal
"Our old cat developed leukaemia and we had to have her put to sleep."

put somebody to sleep = anaesthetize somebody (causing unconsciousness)
"The only way I will have teeth extracted is if the dentist puts me to sleep."

sleep around = be promiscuous
"I hear that Ruth sleeps around ñ she has a new boyfriend nearly every week!"

sleep in = oversleep
"My alarm clock failed to go off and I slept in for nearly an hour."

sleeping partner = associate who contributes money but takes no part in the running of a business
"Harry doesn't make any decisions, he's just my sleeping partner."

sleep like a log/top = sleep deeply/soundly
"I drank a couple of brandies before going to bed and slept all night like a log."

sleep off = recover while asleep
"Vic had too much to drink last night and is sleeping it off."

sleep on something = postpone making a decision about something
"It's a major decision, so why don't you sleep on it and give me your answer in a day or two."

sleep together = have (regular) sexual intercourse
"Janet and John are not engaged but I believe they are sleeping together."

sleep with somebody = have sexual intercourse with somebody
"I didn't sleep with my wife until after we were married."

See also: let sleeping dogs lie; sleep rough.

sleeve

have an ace up one's sleeve = secretly retain something for use at the best

"Richard hasn't made any sort of objection yet ñ I bet he's got an ace or two up his sleeve."

have/keep something up one's sleeve = keep something secret (for later use)
"I know exactly what happened, but I'm keeping it up my sleeve for now."

See also: in one's shirt sleeves; laugh up one's sleeve; roll up one's sleeves; wear one's heart on one's sleeve.

slice

See: best thing since sliced bread; slice of the cake.

slide

let something slide = neglect to do something
"My wife has had to let the housework slide since she injured her arm."

slight

not in the slightest = not at all
"I don't care in the slightest whether you come or not."

slink

slink/slip away = leave in a guilty/surreptitious way
"After being told off he just slunk away."

sling

See: sling one's hook; throw/sling mud at.

slip

Freudian slip = speaking the wrong word, which indicates an unconscious idea
"She called the hydrogen bomb the ultimate detergent ñ an obvious

give somebody the slip = evade/elude somebody
"The escaped prisoners gave their pursuers the slip during the night."

let something slip = say something accidentally, or miss an opportunity
"Frank let slip that he is looking for another job."
"I had a chance of going to the United States, but I let it slip."

slip of a boy/girl = young (slender) boy/girl
"She's much too young to go out with him ñ she's just a slip of a girl and he's a fifty-year-old man."

slip of the pen = mistake in writing
"I'm sorry I spelled your name incorrectly, it was a slip of the pen."

slip of the tongue = something said by mistake
"He definitely said that he thought she was unattractive but then claimed it was a slip of the tongue."

slip one over on somebody = cheat/deceive somebody
"The barman slipped one over on me and gave me a foreign coin in my change."

slip somebody something = give somebody something unobserved
"She slipped me a note while the teacher wasn't looking."

slip up = make a mistake
"The exam went well but I think I slipped up on a few maths questions."

there's many a slip 'twixt cup and lip = do not depend on a plan until it is completed
"I hope to go to China later this year but I'm not depending on it ñ there's many a slip ëtwixt cup and lip."

See also: slink/slip away; slip one's mind; slippery as an eel; slip through

slog

slog one's guts out = work very hard

"I slog my guts out and get paid only a hundred pounds a week."

slope

slope off = leave surreptitiously

"Where's Charlie? I didn't see him slope off."

slot

slot in = accommodate/fit (in)

"The vet said he could slot us in at the end of tonight's surgery."

slow

go slow = deliberately work slowly

"The tanker drivers are going slow and as a result petrol is in short supply."

in slow motion = much more slowly than usual

"The empty car rolled down the hill in slow motion and nobody could do anything to stop it."

slow(ly) but sure(ly) = slow and effective (progress)

"The procession made slow but sure progress along the main street."

See also: quick/slow off the mark; quick/slow on the uptake.

sly

on the sly = deceptively/secretly

"I believe that Malcolm is meeting his secretary on the sly after work."

See also: sly dog.

smack

See: smack in the eye.

small

feel small = feel humiliated, inferior

"The teacher pointed out my mistakes to the rest of the class and really made me feel small."

in a small way (of business) = with little capital/stock

"She is a picture-framer in a small way."

it's a small world = what a coincidence

"We went to Scotland for the weekend and found that our former neighbours were staying in the same hotel ñ it's a small world!"

make small talk = have an unimportant conversation

"We stood around making small talk until the guest of honour arrived."

no small = considerable/large

"Cycling to work every day at her age is no small achievement."

small-minded = lacking imagination/ tolerance

"My father is so small-minded he won't even let us listen to pop music on the radio when he's around."

small-time = doing something on a small scale

"He's a small-time operator dealing in antique silver."

small wonder = as expected

"It's small wonder you got burned, staying out in the sun all that time."

See also: small beer; look small; small fry; (wee) small hours; small print; small talk; still small voice.

smart

look smart = hurry

"Look smart or you'll miss your bus."

See also: smart Alec(k).

smash

smash-and-grab = robbery in which a thief breaks a shop window to steal displayed goods

"Two men made a smash-and-grab raid on the camera shop."

smash hit = very successful book/song/ show etc.
"His latest record was a smash hit within a week of being released."

smear

smear campaign = systematic attempt to discredit somebody (using accusations in articles/speeches)
"One of the Sunday papers ran a smear campaign against the Prime Minister's son."

smell

See: smell a rat; smell of the grease-paint.

smile

be all smiles = be very happy
"She was all smiles when she announced her engagement."

come up smiling = remain cheerful after coping with a difficulty
"That's the third accident Gerald has had this year but he still comes up smiling."

keep smiling! = do not worry!
"Keep smiling! Things are bound to getter better soon."

smile on somebody = favour somebody
"You will get on well as long as the boss smiles on you."

See also: wipe the grin/smile off somebody's face.

smoke

go up in smoke = quickly disappear
"He won a large sum of money in the national lottery but it soon went up in smoke."

smoke somebody/something out = discover something/somebody, or force somebody out of hiding
"Our rivals have a new process and I want somebody to smoke it out."
"There's an informer among us and the chief is determined to smoke him out."

put up a smokescreen = do something to hide one's intentions
"They have asked for a completely itemized invoice but I think they're merely putting up a smokescreen because they don't want to pay our bill yet."

See also: put that in your pipe and smoke it!; there's no smoke without fire.

smooth

See: smooth somebody's (ruffled) feathers; take the rough with the smooth.

snail

See: snail's pace.

snake

snake in the grass = somebody who is deceitful/untrustworthy
"Some snake in the grass has told the manager that I was late for work this morning."

snap

snap at/up = eagerly buy/take
"I offered to sell Gary my car and he snapped at it."
"I saw a car advertised at a bargain price in the local paper but it had already been snapped up when I phoned the seller."

look/make it snappy = hurry
"Please bring me those books and look snappy about it."
"Make it snappy. I can only stay a few minutes."

snap one's fingers at = treat with contempt

"Professional car thieves just snap their fingers at the police these days."

snap out of it = cease being depressed/moody etc.

"Don't be so miserable ñ come on, snap out of it."

snap somebody's head off = reply very abruptly/sharply

"I only asked if I could help ñ there's no need to snap my head off."

sneeze

not to be sneezed/sniffed at = not to be ignored/missed

"I have an offer of a job that pays another five thousand pounds a year, and that's not to be sneezed at these days."

sniff

sniff out = discover

"If there's any news June will soon sniff it out."

See also: not to be sneezed/sniffed at.

snook

See: cock a snook.

snow

snowed in = unable to leave a building because of accumulated snow

"We went to Scotland for the skiing and were snowed in at our hotel for three days."

snowed under = overwhelmed with tasks to do

"I can't meet you at any lunchtime this week because I'm snowed under and will have to work through my lunch break on every day."

See also: cat's/snowball's chance in hell; pure as the driven snow.

snuff

snuff it = die

"I hear old George snuffed it last week."

snug

snug as a bug in a rug = very comfortable

"With the curtains drawn and a nice big fire we were as snug as a bug in a rug."

so

and so forth/on = et cetera

"We need to buy some cups, plates, and so forth."

"My wife wants to employ somebody to do the washing, ironing, an so on."

how so? = why?

"You didn't come last night as you said you would. How so? Didn't you feel well?"

is that so? = really?

"Is that so? You actually saw somebody taking a fox for a walk on a lead?"

it is so! = yes it is!

"It is so! I did see somebody taking a fox for a walk on a lead."

or so = approximately

"There were twenty or so people at the party."

so-and-so = somebody/something one dislikes (strongly), or somebody/something whose name one cannot remember

"My boss is a right so-and-so these days ñ always complaining about something."

"What do you call the so-and-so that's used to clamp a hose onto a pipe?"

so be it = I accept/let it be

"If that's your attitude, so be it ñ but I don't like it."

so far, so good = progress up to now is satisfactory
"I've assembled the main frame. So far, so good ñ now let's put the wheels on."
so-so = average/mediocre
"Mandy's work is only so-so these days, I wonder if something is worrying her?"
so there! = exclamation of emphasis
"Well I've got a new bicycle, so there!"
so what? = what of it?
"My girlfriend has left me, but so what? There are plenty of other girls around."
See also: ever so; just so; so much for something; so to speak; without so much as.

soak
See: soaked to the skin.

soap
get on one's soap box = firmly state one's (known) point of view
"Walter got on his soap box and told us yet again what he thinks about the government's wages policy."
soap opera = long-running radio/ television serial about the daily lives of a group of people
"The only television programmes in the early evenings seem to be soap operas."
See also: soft soap.

sob
sob story = account of somebody's misfortunes, related to obtain sympathy
"Arthur was late for work yet again and told some sob story about being unable to find a plumber to deal with a burst pipe in his flat."
sob stuff = sentimental account meant to arouse sympathy
"The local newspaper is full of sob stuff about lost dogs and children."

sober
sober as a judge/stone-cold sober = completely sober
"Last night I was stopped by the police, who were checking for drunken drivers. Fortunately I was stone-cold sober."
sobering thought = aspect/factor that makes one consider something seriously
"That's a sobering thought ñ when you're the age I am now, I'll be eighty years old!"

sock
bless one's (little) cotton socks = expression of affection
"Your baby wants his dinner, bless his little cotton socks."
put a sock in it = be quiet
"Put a sock in it, I'm trying to listen to the news on the radio."
sock it to somebody = speak in a forthright/impressive way
"Eric really socked it to them at the sales conference and stimulated the enthusiasm of all the salesmen."
See also: pull one's socks up.

sod
not care a sod = not care in the least
"I don't care a sod whether I go or not."
See also: Murphy's/sod's law; odds and ends/sods.

soft
be soft on somebody = be (sentimentally) in love with

somebody, or be lenient towards somebody
"Bill has been soft Helena for years and they have finally got engaged."
"Mick is too soft on his boys and doesn't tell them off when they are badly behaved."
have a soft spot for = have an affection for
"My grandfather left me a gold watch in his will, but then he always had a soft spot for me."
soften up = reduce resistance
"Artillery shelled the enemy-held town to soften it up before the infantry went in."
soft job = occupation that is easy to do
"Malcolm has a soft job somewhere in the civil service."
soft option = an easy choice (among more difficult alternatives)
"Many science students think that a language course is a soft option at university."
soft pedal = deliberately fail to emphasize the importance of something
"Somebody is stealing stock from the warehouse but I'm going to soft pedal until I know who the culprit is."
soft soap = flatter/flattery
"It's no good trying to soft soap my father, he's a miserable old devil."
"You can try soft soap on him, but I don't think it will work."
soft touch = somebody who is easy to convince/deceive
"Brenda says her boss is a soft touch and will always give her a day off work when she wants one."
See also: soft in the head.

soil
See: dirty/soil one's hands.

sold
See: sell.

soldier
come the old soldier = act in a more experienced/superior way, or malinger
"I wish my manager wouldn't come the old soldier with staff who are older than him."
"A slight cold is no excuse not to go to work, so don't come the old soldier with me!"
game of soldiers = something one does not want to do
"Charles has asked me to sweep up the office but blow that for a game of soldiers ñ I'm not employed as a cleaner."
soldier of fortune = somebody who (travels and) lives by his/her wits, or a mercenary
"Keith lived in Africa for three years as a soldier of fortune."
soldier on = persist despite difficulties
"The relief workers keep soldiering on, although they are desperately short of help and supplies."

something
be/have something to do with = be associated with
"That chain is something to do with the timing mechanism, I think."
"Gary has something to do with stock broking."
make something (out) of it = cause an argument/fuss, or make something appear more significant than it is, or understand
"So I spilled your drink. Do you want to make something of it?"
"I've only been out with Rose twice and already her mother is trying to

make something out of it."

"It is a very poor photocopy but you should be able to make something of it."

make something of oneself = become successful

"Jenny should make something of herself one day if keeps working hard."

or something = or some other thing (largely meaningless)

"Why don't you come round for a drink or something one evening?"

see something of somebody = meet somebody

"Now that we've re-established contact I hope to see something of you more often."

something like = approximately, or resembling

"There were something like a thousand people in the audience."

"I would like a house something like the one my parents own."

something like it = excellent

"You've passed your driving test? That's something like it!"

something of = to some extent

"Marion is something of an artist."

something of the kind = something similar

"Can you find me a large stone or something of the kind to put behind the wheel of the car."

something tells me = I believe/suspect/think

"Something tells me it's going to rain."

you know something? = I'm going to tell you something (important)

"You know something? I think I've found a way to make a lot of money."

son

every mother's son (of them) = everybody

"It started to rain and every mother's son of them got very wet."

son of a gun = (popular) man

"I hear you're getting married again, you old son of a gun."

See also: like father, like son; his father's son.

song

for a song = cheaply

"Charles bought an old cottage for a song and completely renovated it."

make a song and dance about something = make a fuss about something

"It is only a small cut and there's no need to make such a song and dance about it."

See also: swan song; wine, women and song.

soon

as soon as maybe = quickly/as soon as possible

"Please authorize payment of these invoices, and as soon as maybe."

no sooner said than done = done immediately

"You wanted a cigarette? Here you are, no sooner said than done."

sooner or later = eventually

"We've had three weeks of drought but it's bound to rain sooner or later."

the sooner the better = as soon as possible

"Our manager's announced his retirement ñ and the sooner the better, as far as I'm concerned."

speak too soon = assume something will happen before it is certain

"I think I have got the job, but I mustn't speak too soon."

sore

stick out like a sore thumb = be very obvious

"That one modern house sticks out like a sore thumb in a street of Victorian villas."

"You can tell William doesn't like women, it sticks out like a sore thumb."

See also: (like a) bear with a sore head; sight for sore eyes; sore point.

sorrow

more in sorrow than in anger = sadly rather than angrily

"Helen has finally sued her malingering husband for divorce, but I think she did it more in sorrow than in anger."

See also: drown one's sorrows.

sorry

feel sorry for somebody = pity somebody

"I feel sorry for any young couple trying to buy their first house these days."

See also: better (to be) safe than sorry.

sort

after a sort = not totally

"Our new car is all right, after a sort ñ it's certainly better than out old one."

a good sort/not a bad sort = somebody who is kind/pleasant

"Kate is a good sort; she fed my cat every day while I was away on holiday."

"My father is not a bad sort really, just a bit grumpy at times."

bad sort = somebody who is dishonest/unpleasant

"That chap is a real bad sort ñ he's been in prison twice for assault."

it takes all sorts (to make the world) = one should tolerate everybody

"I saw a girl with green hair today, but it takes all sorts I suppose."

of a sort/of sorts = of a kind

"He wears a jacket of sorts with patches at the elbows."

out of sorts = (slightly) ill

"Please phone the office and tell them I won't be at work today because I'm feeling out of sorts."

sort somebody out = attack/reprimand somebody, or discover what is troubling somebody

"If he says that again I'm going to sort him out."

"My daughter keeps having bouts of depression and I think she needs professional help to sort her out."

sort something out = find a solution to a difficulty, or select from a miscellany

"Don't worry about your finances, I'm sure the bank will help you sort something out."

"I promised my mother I would sort out some old clothes for her church jumble sale."

See also: nothing of the kind/sort.

soul

bare one's soul = reveal personal details/facts

"I didn't realize that Anne was so unhappy until she got slightly drunk one night and bared her soul to me."

God bless my soul!/upon my soul! = exclamation of surprise

"God bless my soul! Where did you get that hat?"

not able to call one's soul one's own = be in somebody else's control/power

"The trouble with holiday camps and other organized holidays is that you can't call your soul your own."

not a soul = nobody

"We advertised the event but not a soul came."

the soul of = a good example of

"The Mother Superior is the soul of compassion."

sell one's soul for something = do anything to obtain something

"Harry is so addicted to alcohol that he'd sell his soul for a bottle of whisky."

soul-destroying = disappointing/onerous

"We had the soul-destroying task of clearing up all the mess afterwards."

soul-searching = analysis of one's own motives/reasons for doing something

"After much soul-searching I decided to break off my engagement."

See also: keep body and soul together; life and soul; life and soul of the party; own somebody body and soul; with all one's heart (and soul).

sound

sound in wind and limb = physically fit

"My father is nearly seventy but he's still sound in wind and limb."

sound off = talk loudly

"John's always sounding off about the extremely poor quality of the beer at our local pub."

sound somebody out = attempt to find what somebody is planning/thinking

"We'll have to sound out the opposition before we decide what action to take."

See also: clear/sound as a bell; safe and sound.

soup

in the soup = in trouble

"You'll be right in the soup when your father finds out."

souped-up = with a more powerful engine

"She rides a souped-up Honda motorbike."

sour

See: sour grapes.

sow

sow the seeds of = initiate/originate

"The charge hand is deliberately sowing the seeds of discontent among the workers."

See: silk purse out of a sow's ear; sow one's wild oats.

space

in the space of an hour/minute/moment = in an hour's/minute's/moment's time

"I had twelve phone calls in the space of an hour."

See also: breathing space.

spade

call a spade a spade = be very frank

"I like doing business with Victor because he calls a spade a spade and you know exactly what he wants."

doubled in spades! = even more so!

"The old trains were uncomfortable and so are the new ones ñ doubled in spades!"

spade work = basic/initial work

"Once the spade work is over and the scheme is running, the job will soon become quite routine."

See also: black as the ace of spades.

Spain

See: castles in Spain/the air.

span

See: spick and span.

spanner

throw a spanner in the works = frustrate/sabotage

"When they announce their plan I'm going to make an official objection and throw a spanner in the works."

spare

go spare = become angry/emotional
"The boss will go spare when he finds you have damaged the company van."
spare tyre ñ fat round one's waist
"Jane had developed a spare tyre since she stopped smoking and started eating sweets."
to spare = more than needed
"We got to the airport with half an hour to spare before we had to check in for our flight."
See also: spare somebody's blushes; spare the rod and spoil the child.

spark

spark off = begin/initiate
"I don't want to talk to her because it will only spark off a row."
make the sparks fly = cause an argument/trouble
"Wait till Barry sees Mick chatting up his wife ñ that will make the sparks fly."
See also: bright spark.

speak

be on speaking terms with somebody = be casual friends with somebody
"My new neighbour moved in last weekend and already we're on speaking terms."
generally speaking = in general/on average
"Generally speaking, I prefer lamb to pork."
know somebody to speak to = know somebody quite well
"She lives in our road but I don't know her to speak to."
nothing to speak of = nothing worthy of attention
"I had a look round the new shop but it's nothing to speak of."
speak as one finds = for a point of view based on personal experience
"You always praise Brighton and you must speak as you find, but I think it's a dreary place."
speak for somebody = express somebody else's point of view
"I can't speak for my wife but I would like to go."
speak for yourself = I disagree with you
"Speak for yourself, but I think you're totally wrong."
speak out = express one's views boldly
"I am going to speak out against the committee's decision."
speaks for itself = be self-evident
"The scheme speaks for itself ñ it's far too ambitious and expensive."
speak the same language (as somebody) = have the same views (as somebody)
"I always enjoy talking to Mike about music because we speak the same language."
speak up = talk more loudly
"His talk is interesting but I do wish he'd speak up."
speak volumes = be significant
"He must like her ñ the money he spends on presents speaks volumes."
speak well of = praise
"I saw your old boss the other day and he still speaks well of you."
speak with a forked tongue = lie
"Jack says he didn't go to work because he was ill but I think he speaks with a forked tongue."
strictly speaking = being exact/precise
"Strictly speaking, a slow-worm is a kind of reptile."
to speak of = worthy of attention

"We just strolled around the streets and did nothing to speak of."

See also: actions speak louder than words; in a manner of speaking; plain speaking; so to speak; speak one's mind; speak/talk of the devil; speak/talk the same language as somebody; speak too soon.

spec

on spec = on the chance that something might happen

"We didn't have tickets but went to the theatre on spec in case it was not fully booked."

spectacles

pair of spectacles = batsman's score of zero in both innings of a cricket match

"The opening batsman was out of form and got a pair of spectacles in the county match."

See also: look at/see/view things through rose-tinted spectacles.

spell

spell something out = describe something in detail

"The job is straightforward and I shouldn't have to spell it out to a person of your experience."

under the spell of = fascinated/influenced by

"My daughter is completely under the spell of this man she met on holiday."

spend

spend a bomb/packet = spend a lot (of money)

"We spent a bomb on new carpets for the whole of the ground floor."

See also: spend money like water; spend a penny.

spice

See: variety is the spice of life.

spick

spick and span = neat/tidy

"Harry always makes sure he looks spick and span before he goes to meet anyone."

spike

on the spike = put aside for possible use later

"I don't need all this material to write the article, but I'll put the unused notes on the spike in case I have to add information to lengthen the article later."

spike a drink = add spirits to a weaker drink

"They spiked his drink by putting a vodka in his lager."

See also: spike somebody's guns.

spill

See: cry over spilt milk; spill the beans.

spin

spin a yarn = tell an (untrue) story

"He spun some yarn about the trains being delayed to account for being late."

spin something out = make something last longer

"There was very little to discuss but the chairman still managed to spin out the meeting for two hours."

See also: flat spin; make one's head spin.

spine

See: send shivers down/up one's spine.

spirit

be with somebody in spirit = think about somebody when one is unable to be with him/her

"Good luck with your exams ñ we'll

be with you in spirit."

in high/low spirits = cheerful/miserable
"Everyone was in high spirits and the party was a great success."
"My father has been in very low spirits since his accident."

moving spirit = somebody who initiates/is active in an undertaking
"The local vicar is the moving spirit in our youth club."

out of spirits = depressed/unhappy
"I've been feeling out of spirits for some time, and I think I need a holiday."

public spirit = a feeling of wanting to benefit society
"Councillor Jones displayed much public spirit by donating five hundred pounds for a new bus shelter by the old people's home."

spirit away = remove secretly
"The accused man was spirited away from the court before the waiting crowd or reporters and cameramen realized it."

take something in the right spirit = not take offence at something
"The children made fun of my father's accent but he took it in the right spirit."

the spirit is willing (but the flesh is weak) = one's desires cannot always be achieved physically
"I would like to climb Snowdon, but at my age the spirit is willing but the flesh is weak."

spit

dead spit of = identical to
"That vase is the dead spit of one I have at home."

spit and polish = fastidious/thorough cleaning
"... polish on the house ready for her mother's visit at the weekend."

spitting image = exact replica
"Your daughter is the spitting image of her mother."

spit it out = say it
"Spit it out! How much do you want to borrow this time?"

See also: be spitting feathers; within spitting/striking distance.

spite

in spite of oneself = even though one would rather/should not
"I couldn't really afford these new shoes but I bought them in spite of myself."

See also: cut off one's nose to spite one's face.

splash

make a splash = attract much attention
"His book made quite a splash when it was first published."

splash down = landing of a spacecraft in the sea
"The astronauts splashed down in the Pacific Ocean."

splash out (on) = spend much money (on)
"We've decided to splash out on a holiday abroad this year."

spleen

vent one's spleen = display anger
"After a bad day at work he often vents his spleen on his poor wife."

splice

See: splice the mainbrace.

splinter

splinter group = small group that has broken away from a larger one extremists have formed a splinter group outside the main party."

split

do the splits = drop/sit on the floor with one leg straight forwards and the other backwards
"The acrobats finished their act by doing the splits in turn."

splitting headache = severe headache
"Mildred phoned to say she has a splitting headache and won't be coming to work today."

split on somebody = betray somebody (to the authorities)
"I would have got away with it if you hadn't split on me."

split second = very short time
"My attention wandered for a split second and I nearly collided with the vehicle in front."

See also: split hairs; split one's sides; split the difference.

spoil

be spoiling for something = be eager/ keen for something
"Joe is a nuisance ñ he's always spoiling for an argument."

spoil sport = somebody who spoils somebody else's enjoyment
"Don't be a spoil sport, come and be my partner so that we can all play bridge."

See also: spare the rod and spoil the child; spoil the ship for a ha'porth of tar.

spoke

put a spoke in (somebody's wheel) = place difficulties/obstructions in somebody's way
my job but I'll soon put a spoke in his wheel."

put one's spoke in = interrupt (to express a point of view)
"We were having a quiet discussion until Mary had to put her spoke in as usual."

sponge

sponge off/on somebody = scrounge (money) from somebody
"Old William usually sponges a drink off somebody in the pub."

throw in/up the sponge = give in/ surrender
"I can't finish this puzzle, I'll have to throw in the sponge."

spoon

spoon feed somebody = deny somebody independent action/thought
"You won't be spoon fed all your life and it's about time you began to think for yourself."

wooden spoon = prize awarded to somebody who does least well in a contest
"I came last in the tournament and was awarded the wooden spoon."

See also: born with a silver spoon in one's mouth.

sport

See: blood sport; fighting/sporting chance.

spot

blind spot = gap in one's knowledge/ understanding
"I have a fair knowledge of most biological sciences but I have a blind spot when it comes to botany."

high spot = best/most important
"The cabaret was the high spot of the

in a spot = in trouble
"I wonder if you could help me ñ I'm in a spot and need to raise a hundred pounds in cash by tomorrow."
on the spot = in the place required, or immediately
"A newspaper photographer happened to be on the spot and took some spectacular pictures of the fire."
"He offered me ten pounds for it so I sold it on the spot."
put somebody on the spot = cause somebody difficulty
"The teacher put me on the spot and made me explain by actions to the rest of the class."
spot cash = ready money
"He said I could have it for ten pounds spot cash."
spot check = random/surprise check
"We can't test all the items all the time so just do a spot check on three or four from time to time."
"The police stopped my car for a spot check on the condition of the tyres."
spot of = little
"We're having a spot of bother with the new machine."
spot on = exactly correct
"Those gloves you bought me were spot on ñ they match my dress perfectly."
tight spot = difficult situation
"The soldiers were in a tight spot, under fire and short of ammunition."
See also: have a soft spot for; knock spots off; rooted to the spot.

spout
up the spout = spoiled/ruined, or pregnant
"The French air traffic controllers are on strike so my trip to Paris is up the spout."
"Bill is worried because he thinks his girlfriend is up the spout."

sprat
See: sprat to catch a mackerel.

spread
spread like wildfire = spread very rapidly
"There was an outbreak of chickenpox at my son's school which spread like wildfire until nearly half the children caught it."
spread oneself = be indulgent/lavish
"We decided to spread ourselves and stay in the best hotel."
See also: spread one's wings.

spring
spring a leak = let in water
"The boat sprung a leak and we had to row back to shore quickly."
spring somebody from custody/jail = arrange for a prisoner to escape/be released
"His gang members bribed a warder to spring him from jail."
spring something on somebody = surprise somebody
"I've got to go away for a week on a training course ñ the manager sprang it on me this morning."
where did somebody/something spring from? = where did somebody/something suddenly appear from?
"Suddenly there was a policeman among us but I don't know where he sprang from."
See also: full of the joys of spring; no (spring) chicken.

spur
spur somebody on = encourage somebody to try harder

"It was bitterly cold walking home tonight but the thought of a hot drink in a nice warm house spurred me on."

win one's spurs = achieve recognition
"The young cricketer won his spurs when he scored eighty not out in his first county game."

See also: on the spur of the moment.

spurt

put a spurt on = go faster
"Come on, put a spurt on or we'll never get there."

spy

spy on somebody = secretly observe somebody
"Close the curtains because I don't want the woman over the road spying on us."

spy out the land = make a preliminary investigation
"You go and spy out the land and see if there are any vacant seats near the front."

square

all square = equal/even/level
"At the end of the first half the football teams were all square with two goals each."

be (a) square = be dull/unfashionable
"Oh, Dad, don't be a square; please let me have my hair dyed."

go back to square one = return to the beginning
"The attempt failed and we had to go back to square one."

have square eyes = suffer the effects of watching too much television
"You've been watching TV for hours non-stop ñ you'll have square eyes if you're not careful."

square bashing = basic training in the armed forces
"As soon as you join the army you have six weeks square bashing."

square meal = meal that is nourishing/sufficient
"When you join the army at least you'll get three square meals a day."

square up with somebody = pay (a debt to) somebody
"If you lend me ten pounds I'll square up with you when I get paid."

square up to somebody = face an attacker/critic
"The Prime Minister squared up to his critics in parliament and won them over to his point of view."

square up to something = face a difficulty/problem with resolution
"It is about time you squared up to the fact that you have a drinking problem."

square with = agree with
"Ask him what happened and see if it squares with what you saw."

See also: fair and square; settle/square an account (with somebody); square deal; square peg in a round hole.

squeak

See: narrow escape/shave/squeak.

squeeze

in a tight squeeze = in (financial) difficulties
"I can't afford to come with you because I'm in a tight squeeze this month until pay day."

squib

See: damp squib.

stab

have a stab at = make an attempt at
"I think I'll have a stab at learning French."

See also: stab in the back.

stable
See: lock the stable door after the horse has bolted.

stack
See: stack the cards against somebody.

staff
staff of life = bread
"I hate this supermarket bread; give me a good crusty loaf ñ the staff of life."

stag
stag night/party = celebration (of a forthcoming wedding) for men only
"Are you going to Jim's stag party on Friday evening?"

stage
set the stage for = prepare for
"We have sent out invitations to set the stage for a family reunion on my parents' silver wedding day."
stage fright = anxiety/nervousness felt before appearing in public
"I often feel stage fright before I give a lecture, although I'm usually all right once I've started speaking."
stage-manage = organize
"The display was stage-managed perfectly and went off without a single delay."
stage whisper = loud whisper (that is meant to be heard by others)
"My wife said she was cold in a stage whisper that was intended to make them turn the heating up."

stairs
below stairs = servants' accommodation
"It's cook's birthday and I've permitted the servants to have a small party below stairs."
work below stairs = work as a servant
"My grandmother used to work below stairs as a housemaid when she was young."
See also: by the back stairs.

stake
at stake = at risk
"If you do that you are putting your whole career at stake."
go to the stake for = accept criticism/ unpleasantness for what one does/ believes in
"I hold few strong views but I would go to the stake for the campaign against child pornography."
have a stake in something = make an investment in something
"Money spent on education is a stake in our children's future."
stake out = observe carefully/carry out surveillance
"The police thought the robbers must have staked out the bank to learn the staff's routine."
See also: pull up roots/stakes; stake a claim.

stamp
stamp/on out = eliminate/put down
"We must stamp out vandalism in this town once and for all."
See also: rubber stamp something; stamping ground; stamp one's foot.

stand
as matters/things stand = in the present circumstances
"As matters stand, the company should begin to make a profit in two month's time."
know how/where one stands = be aware of one's position/status

"I'll be glad when we get all the exam results so we know where we stand for next year's course of study."

leave somebody standing = progress much faster than somebody else

"I thought I was a quick typist but Silvia leaves me standing."

make a stand against = defy/resist

"It's about time somebody made a stand against the rise of violent crime in Britain."

on stand-by = in reserve and ready

"We should have enough people to finish the job on time, although I do have two others on stand by in case they are needed."

stand alone = be unique, or be without help

"W. G. Grace stood alone as the best cricketer of his time."

"In the early years of World War II, Britain stood alone against the might of Germany."

stand aside/by = observe passively/fail to see

"The crowd just stood aside while the two thugs attacked a policeman."

stand by = be ready for action, or be supportive, or observe passively/fail to see

"Stand by men, it is time to begin the attack."

"Jim stood by his wife throughout her drugs problem."

stand corrected = accept that one has made a mistake

"I stand corrected ñ it was in 1972 I got divorced, not 1971."

stand down = cease to be ready for action, or withdraw from a contest

"The enemy will not attack during daylight so I have told the defenders to stand down."

"The player Henry was drawn against has stood down so he has a bye in the first round of the chess tournament."

stand fast/firm = be unyielding

"She stood firm and would not change her testimony, despite aggressive cross-examination."

stand for = represent, or tolerate

"The initials BBC stand for British Broadcasting Corporation."

"Janet's husband gets drunk most evenings ñ I don't know why she stands for it."

stand in for = substitute for

"The supervisor is going away for a week and I have to stand in for her."

stand in somebody's way = prevent somebody from doing something

"If you really want to join the army, I won't stand in your way."

stand-offish = with a superior/unfriendly attitude

"Brenda is a very friendly girl but her parents are a bit stand-offish."

stand one in good stead = be available when needed

"This old umbrella has stood me in good stead for more than ten years."

stand or fall by something = be committed to something (whether it succeeds or fails)

"That's my opinion and I stand or fall by it."

stand out = physically protrude, or be more noticeable than other things

"Thyroid disease can make a patient's eyes stand out."

"His was the best drawing and it stood out among the others."

stand/stick out for = persist in a request without compromise

"The management has offered the workers another five pounds a week but they are sticking out for ten pounds."

stand over = supervise/observe closely
"His work is acceptable only if you stand over him and make sure he does it properly."
stand somebody up = fail to keep an appointment
"I'm angry with Graham because he agreed to meet me outside the cinema but he stood me up."
stand to lose/win = be able to lose/win
"If Pete's next choice of horse in the accumulator comes first, he stands to win over a thousand pounds."
stand up and be counted = make one's views known to everyone
"People who disagree with the decision should not grumble among themselves but stand up and be counted."
stand up for = champion/support
"You should stand up for what you believe in."
stand up to = resist
"Don't let him treat you like that ñ stand up to him!"
"I don't think this cheap carpet will stand up to much wear."
take a stand on = positively state (and be prepared to defend) one's point of view
"Nuclear disarmament is an issue I'm willing to take a stand on."
See also: hold/stand one's ground; it stands to reason (that); last ditch stand; not be able to stand the sight of somebody/something; stand a good/ fair chance of; standing joke; standing on one's head; stand on ceremony; stand one in good stead; stand on one's dignity; stand on one's own (two) feet; stand/stick out a mile.

star
see stars = apparently see flashing lights (after a blow to the head)
"When that branch fell on my head, I saw stars for several seconds."
star-studded = with many famous entertainers
"The play opened with a star studded cast and was an immediate success."
star turn = high-quality performance/ performer
"The manager's presentation was the star turn of the sales conference."
thank one's lucky stars = regard oneself as very fortunate
"I thank my lucky stars I bought my house when I did ñ I couldn't afford today's prices."
See also: (one's star is) in the ascendant.

stare
See· staring one in the face.

stark
See: (stark) raving mad.

start
for a start/to start with/for starters = in the first place
"No you can't come to the pub ñ for a start you're not old enough."
"I'll have the car and here's a hundred pounds' deposit just for starters."
get off to a bad start = begin something badly
"The British runner got off to a bad start but had caught up with the leaders by the third lap of the race."
get off to a good/flying start = begin something well
"A major order ensured that our business got off to a good start."
head start = initial advantage (in a contest)
"Nigel's father is company chairman, which gave him a head start when he joined the firm."

make a fresh start/start from scratch = (re)start from the beginning
"I would like to move to another town and make a fresh start."
"The new paint won't adhere to the walls so I'll have to strip it all off and start from scratch."
start life = begin one's working life
"She started life as a shop assistant and now she has her own boutique."
start out as = begin as
"I go to pottery classes and I made this ashtray ñ although it really started out as a vase!"
See also: false start; get/start off on the right/wrong foot; in fits and starts; keep/set/start the ball rolling.

state
get in(to) a state = become (emotionally) upset
"You couldn't help spilling the ink so there's no need to get into a state about it."
state of the art = present status/stage of development
"This is the best result you can expect at the present state of the art in dry cleaning synthetic fabrics."
state the obvious = say something that everybody already knows
"I don't want to state the obvious, but shouldn't we move back up the beach now that the tide is coming in?"
See also: in a state of nature; the state of play.

station
above one's station = above one's accepted position in life
"She married well above her station ñ I think her husband is an earl."
See also: action stations.

statistics
vital statistics = (a woman's) measurements
"She has a good figure ñ her vital statistics are 36-24-38."

status
status symbol = possession that indicates somebody's high position (socially)
"A holiday abroad is no longer the status symbol it once was ñ today everybody has one."

stay
stay put = remain in one place/position
"That window keeps rattling in the wind; I must fix a wedge in it to make it stay put."
"You stay put here while I go and buy the tickets."
See also: stay one's hand; stay the course; stay the pace.

stead
See: stand one in good stead.

steady
go steady = not be excessive/ extravagant, or have a regular friendship with somebody of the opposite sex
"Yes, I would like another drink but please go steady ñ only a small one this time."
"Janet and John have been going steady for nearly a year now."
steady as a rock = very steady/reliable
"The tower is a steady as a rock even in gale-force winds."
"You can always rely on Gary ñ he's as steady as a rock, particularly when you need somebody to confide in."
steady on! = do not be so aggressive/ angry/excessive

"Steady on! There's no need to use bad language!"
"Steady on! I said I only wanted a small drink."

steal
steal somebody's heart = acquire somebody's love/affection
"That puppy we bought last week has completely stolen my heart."
steal somebody's thunder = rob somebody of the chance to receive credit/praise
"I did all the hard work but my boss stole my thunder by announcing the discovery as his own."
steal up on somebody = move unnoticed towards somebody
"He stole up on her and gave her a fright."
See also: steal a march (on somebody); steal the show.

steam
full steam ahead = at maximum speed
"We have finally raised the finance so it's full steam ahead with the new project."
get (all) steamed up = become angry/ upset
"I know you are disappointed with your exam results but there's no point in getting all steamed up about it."
get up steam = summon up vitality
"I don't think I could get up steam to walk all the way ñ let's take the car."
run out of steam = become exhausted
"The challenger was outclassed and ran out of steam long before the end of the fight."
under one's own steam = by oneself/ unaided
"Fred took the last available seat in the car and so I had to get there under my own steam."
See also: blow/let off steam.

steel
See: man of iron/steel; steel one's heart against.

steep
a bit steep = unreasonable
"It's priced at fifty pounds, and I think that's a bit steep for a second-hand lawn mower."

steer
bum steer = false information/poor advice
"The advice to invest in those shares turned out to be a bum steer ñ their value has fallen steadily since I bought them."
steer a middle course = compromise (between extremes)
"The government is trying to steer a middle course between extra spending on defence and total disarmament."
See also: steer clear of.

step
in/out of step = conforming/not conforming
"I find it increasingly difficult to keep in step with the rapid changes of fashion these days."
"The landlord of our local is completely out of step with what his younger customers expect of a modern pub."
retrace one's steps = go back along the route just travelled
"I dropped my keys and had to retrace my steps for nearly a mile before I found them."
step by step = gradually/sequentially
"Take it step by step and you'll soon

learn how to use word processor."

step down = resign

"After the scandal over misappropriated funds the chief accountant was asked to step down."

step in = interrupt/intervene

"Mike stepped in to stop a fight between two lads and they both turned on him."

step in the right direction = contribution towards what is desired/required

"The jumble sale did not yield nearly enough money to pay for repainting the church hall, but at least it was a step in the right direction."

step on it = hurry

"Step on it or we'll miss the beginning of the show."

(ask somebody to) step outside = challenge somebody to a fight

"I object to your personal remarks ñ step outside!"

step/tread on somebody's toes = offend somebody

"I'm sorry if what I said offended you ñ I didn't mean to step on anyone's toes."

step up = increase

"The company has decided to step up the output of umbrellas because of the unusual demand created by the continuing rainy weather."

take steps = take action

"I have asked the safety officer to take steps to ensure that such an accident can never happen again."

watch one's step = be (very) careful

"Watch your step, the boss is in a particularly bad mood today."

See also: false step; fill/step into the breach; follow in somebody's footsteps; step into somebody's shoes; step out of line.

Stephen

See: even Stephen(s).

stew

get in(to) a stew = become agitated/upset

"David won't make a good driver until he learns not to get into a stew every time he makes the slightest mistake."

See also: stew in one's own juice.

stick

dirty/rough end of the stick = unfair/harsh treatment

"Petty criminals in the eighteenth century got the rough end of the stick when they were transported to Australia for what we would now regard as minor offences."

give somebody stick = harangue somebody

"My father will give me stick when he sees what I have done to his car."

give something (some) stick = push something to its limit

"Come on, give it some stick ñ let's see how fast this car can go."

on a sticky wicket = in a difficult situation

"I was on a sticky wicket when I claimed for a new camera on my insurance because I lost the old one entirely through my own carelessness."

stick at something = persist in doing something

"I like to get rid of unpleasant tasks by sticking at them until they are done."

stick in one's craw/gullet/throat = be unacceptable

"What sticks in my gullet is the way he always takes the best seat."

stick something out = endure a difficult/unpleasant situation

"There was no heating during the electricity strike and we had to stick it out by wearing extra clothes."

stick together = remain together (loyally)

"My parents have stuck together despite many difficulties in their marriage."

stick up = rob using firearms

"Two men with shotguns stuck up our local post office."

stick up for = support

"More and more men are sticking up for the rights of women."

stick with which to beat somebody = (confidential/damaging) knowledge about somebody used to put pressure on him/her

"He used his knowledge of my prison record as a stick with which to beat me and force me to give him money."

wield a big stick = use authority/power to control somebody

"Whenever the boss wields a big stick, productivity actually falls because people resent it so much."

See also: cleft stick; come to a sticky end; get hold of the wrong end of the stick; have light/sticky fingers; put/stick one's oar in; stand/stick out a mile; stand/stick out for; stick in one's throat; stick in the mud; stick one's neck out; stick out like a sore thumb; stick to one's guns; something that sticks in one's gizzard.

stiff

See: bore stiff/the pants off/to tears; keep a stiff upper lip; scare somebody stiff; stiff as board; stiff as a poker/ramrod; worried stiff.

still

still waters run deep = somebody can be more emotional/knowledgeable than he/she first appears

"I thought that Candy was totally unemotional until she became so upset over the death of her kitten, proving that still waters run deep."

sting

sting in the tail = something unpleasant revealed only in the final outcome

"Having my car off the road for a week while it was being repaired was bad enough, but the real sting in the tail was what it cost!"

take the sting out of something = reduce the severity/unpleasantness of something

"The garage gave me twenty-five pounds for trading in my old car battery, which took a little of the sting out of having to buy a new one."

stink

like stink = to excess/the maximum limit

"We had to run like stink to get away from the bull."

See also: cry stinking fish; raise a stink; smell/stink to high heaven.

stir

stir the blood = inspire one

"The sound of a military band always stirs the blood."

See also: lift/stir a finger.

stitch

a stitch in time saves nine = the correction of a minor fault promptly prevents the development of many other (possibly major) ones

"There are one or two places where flying gravel has chipped a small flake of paint off my car. I must re-paint them before they go rusty ñ a stitch in time saves nine."

in stitches = laughing very much/ uncontrollably
"We were in stitches watching the antics of the chimpanzees at the zoo."

not have a stitch on = be totally naked
"This girl then walked on stage and she hadn't a stitch on."

stock

lay in a stock of = obtain a supply of
"We must remember to lay in a stock of coal before the cold weather."

on the stocks = incomplete but in the process of being completed
"The new formula one car is still on the stocks but it should be finished well in time for next month's Grand Prix."

somebody's stock rises = somebody's status/reputation increases
"His stock as an actor rises every time he wins another award."

stock in trade = something that is standard/usual
"Part of a representative's stock in trade is a collection of the latest jokes."

stock up on/with = obtain/store a supply of
"You had better stock up with sugar because they say there is going to be a shortage."

stock still = motionless
"We remained stock still and watched the wild birds feeding their young."

take stock of = review
"We must take stock of our finances before deciding about going on holiday this year."

See also: laughing stock; lock, stock and barrel.

stocking

See: blue stocking.

stomach

have a strong stomach = be difficult to disgust
"You need a strong stomach to be able to watch some of these horror videos."

have no stomach for = be most disinclined to
"She has no stomach for professional competition these days, and will only appear as an amateur."

turn one's stomach = make one (feel) disgusted/sick
"The state of her kitchen was enough to turn your stomach."

See also: butterflies in one's stomach/ tummy; on an empty stomach.

stone

cast the first stone = be first to condemn/ criticize
"You can do as you like, but I've made similar mistakes myself and I'm not going to cast the first stone."

leave no stone unturned = try every possible way (in a search)
"The customs officials left no stone unturned in their search for contraband."

stone dead = (completely) dead
"He fired at the charging buffalo and killed it stone dead with the first shot."

stone deaf = completely deaf
"Ever since Tony was involved in that explosion at his works he has been stone deaf."

stone me/the crows! = exclamation of disbelief/surprise
"Stone me! Is that the time?"
"Stone the crows! Can't you do better than that?"

stone's throw = short distance
"The hotel claims to be a stone's throw from the beach."
stony broke = with no money at all
"After a day at the races I was left stony broke."
See also: get blood out of a stone; fall on deaf ears/stony ground; have a heart of stone; kill two birds with one stone; stone cold; stone-cold sober; stoned out of one's mind/head.

stool
See: fall between two stools; stool pigeon.

stop
come to a dead stop = halt abruptly
"The horse came to a dead stop and threw its rider over the gate."
come to a full stop = stop totally
"The scheme to divert the river has come to a full stop because of lack of money to finish it."
full stop = and that's final
"I won't do it, full stop."
stop a tooth = insert a filling into a tooth
"One of my fillings has fallen out ñ I'll have to get the dentist to stop the tooth again."
stop dead = come to an abrupt halt
"For some reason, at ten o'clock my watch stopped dead."
"The pickpocket stopped dead when he saw the policeman."
stop off/over = interrupt a journey (to stay somewhere for a short time)
"James is going to stop off at Rome for a few days on his way back from the Middle East."
stop short of doing something = not go as far as doing something (dishonest/illegal/immoral)
"I may withhold the truth at times, but I stop short of actually telling lies."
See also: pull out all the stops; put an end/stop to; stop at/short of nothing.

store
in store = on its way
"The weather forecasters say that there's rain in store for the weekend."
set/lay (great) store by something = value something (highly)
"I set great store by his judgement."
See also: cold storage.

storm
bend/bow before the storm = yield to a (verbal) attack
"The speaker had to bow before a storm of abuse from the audience."
storm in a teacup = disproportionally large fuss about something trivial
"The outcry about the proposed changes to the design of the pound coin turned out to be a typical storm in a teacup."
take somebody/something by storm = make a great impression on somebody/something
"He took her out every evening and gave her lots of presents ñ he really took her by storm."
"Five thousand rock fans arrived for the festival and took the small town by storm."
weather the storm = endure/survive throughout a difficult situation
"If I can weather the storm until payday, I should be able to settle all my debts."
See also: any port in a storm.

story
cut a long story short = give an abbreviated account
"I missed the last train, I haven't

enough money for a hotel, it's freezing cold ñ to cut a long story short, can I stay with you for the night?"

likely story = unbelievable account (meant ironically)
"Philip says he's never late for an appointment ñ a likely story!"

same old story = repeated/boring account
"My job is the same old story ñ too much work for too little pay!"

story line = thread of a narrative/piece of fiction
"His book contained so many plots and sub-plots it was impossible to follow the main story line."

success story = account of how somebody succeeds in life
"His autobiography is a success story about a man from a humble background who became the owner of an international company."

tall story = exaggerated/unlikely account
"Graham's description of his night in Soho is probably just one of his tall stories."

that's (quite) another/a different story = that is (very) different
"Norman is very good with words and their meanings, but give him any numerical problem to do and that's quite a different story."

*the story is/goes that*Ö = the excuse/general opinion is that.Ö
"If you're asked, the story is that we need more time to finish the work."
"The story goes that there is to be a large increase in the price of petrol."

the story of my life = what always happens to me
"I had another puncture yesterday ñ that's the story of my life!"

See also: cock and bull story; shaggy dog story.

straight

get something straight = ensure that something is accurate/true
"We must get this straight ñ is it my turn to pay or yours?"

go straight = lead an honest life (after formerly not doing so)
"After three convictions for shoplifting, Martha has finally decided to go straight."

know something straight off = know something without thinking
"He knew straight off that I was a newcomer."

straight away/off = immediately
"Certainly, Madam, I'll do it straight away."

straight out/up = frankly/honestly
"Tell me straight out, will I ever recover?"
"Straight up? Is that what really happened?"

straight talk = frank/honest discussion
"I had a straight talk with my daughter about what she is going to do when she leaves school."

the straight and narrow = honest/moral way of life
"With all these temptations around him, Jim found it increasingly difficult to keep to the straight and narrow."

See also: (straight) from the horse's mouth; keep a straight face; set the record straight; straight answer; straight as a die; straight from the shoulder.

strait

strait-laced = of a rigid/strict point of view
"I couldn't tell that joke to my wife's parents because they are too strait-laced."

strain
See: straining at the leash.

strange
be a stranger to = be unaccustomed to/ unfamiliar with
"I studied arts and I'm a complete stranger to science."
"I suspect Terry is no stranger to the inside of a prison cell."
little stranger = newborn baby
"Jane went away for six months and when she came back she brought a little stranger with her."
strangely enough/strange to tell = curious/surprisingly
"I work in a brewery but strangely enough I never drink beer."
"Strange to tell, our cat had kittens and we thought it was a male."
stranger things have happened = even more unusual things are possible
"She may even apologize ñ stranger things have happened."
See also: stranger things happen at sea.

straw
choose/draw the short straw = be selected from among others for an unpleasant task
"Oliver Twist drew the short straw and had to go and ask for a second helping."
straw in the wind = something trivial that may signify something significant in the future
"The workers' non-cooperation is a straw in the wind that might indicate widespread industrial strife to come."
straw poll = sample of people's views
"A straw poll indicated that most of the group are in favour of the proposal."
See also: clutch at a straw/straws; last straw; make bricks without straw; man of straw.

streak
be on/have a winning streak = win successively (at gambling)
"I don't want to finish playing yet, not while I'm on a winning streak."
do a streak = run naked in public
"Did you see that girl do a streak across the cricket pitch at Lords?"
See also: like greased/a streak of lightning.

stream
swim against the stream = hold a view opposite to most others
"Most of the girls in my daughter's class are learning cookery and office practice, but she is swimming against the stream and studying carpentry and motor mechanics."

street
be on the street(s) = have nowhere to live
"If I don't find a job soon I'll be on the streets."
Fleet Street = the (London) newspaper business
"My son is determined to have a career in Fleet Street."
go on the streets = become a prostitute
"Many girls who run away to London eventually go on the streets."
not in the same street as = not nearly as good/the same as
"Our amateur sportsmen are not in the same street as some of those from the American universities."
streets ahead = much better than/ superior to
"That wine you brought is streets ahead of the stuff I make myself."

(just/right) up somebody's street = well suited to somebody
"When Linda comes to stay make sure you play only pop music ñ that's right up her street."
Wall Street = American big business
"The fall in the dollar's value worldwide sent tremors through Wall Street."
See also: Civvy Street; in easy circumstances/on easy street; in queer street; man in the street; the old lady of Threadneedle Street.

strength
at full strength = undiluted, or having the required number/complement
"The best way to get stains off collars is to use liquid detergent at full strength."
"The Home Secretary said that the Metropolitan Police had not been at full strength for ten years."
give me strength! = exclamation of annoyance/frustration
"Give me strength! That's the fourth time he's asked for a glass of water since he went to bed."
go from strength to strength = continue to improve
"The company has gone from strength to strength since it was established ten years ago."
in strength = in force/large numbers
"Send for reinforcements ñ the enemy are attacking in strength."
on the strength = as a member of the staff/workforce
"The paperwork in the sales department has moved much more quickly since they took a qualified accountant onto the strength."
on the strength of = because of (something demonstrated previously)
"On the strength of my forthcoming salary increase I have decided to buy a better car."
pillar/tower of strength = somebody on whom one can rely for help/ encouragement
"My mother has been a tower of strength during my husband's long illness."
strengthen one's hand = make one's position better (in a contest)
"Before entering the chess tournament he strengthened his hand by getting extra coaching from a grand master."
See also: trial of strength.

stretch
at a stretch = without stopping, or in the extreme
"After travelling for three days I slept for twenty hours at a stretch."
"I can lend you five pounds or, at a stretch, ten."
at full stretch = using maximum energy/ resources
"We cannot accept any more orders because were working at full stretch to complete the existing ones."
do a stretch = serve a prison sentence
"Alfred has done a stretch in Chelmsford Prison."
See also: by no stretch of the imagination; stick/stretch one's neck out; stretch a point; stretch one's legs.

stride
get into one's stride = attain one's usual rate of doing something
"I'm sorry I've made such a slow start but I'll be much quicker once I get fully into my stride."
make great strides = make good progress

"They've made great strides in building the new school since I was here last month."

put somebody off his/her stride/stroke = spoil/interrupt what somebody is successfully doing
"The lecture was going well until the projector broke down and put the professor off his stride."

take something in one's stride = achieve something without difficult/worry
"That's the second time they have asked Jeremy to move office already this year but he seems to take it all in his stride."

strike

it strikes me = it occurs to me
"It strikes me that it's time to go to bed."

strike an attitude = express a (strong/inflexible) opinion
"Harry claims to be an anarchist, but he's really only striking an attitude to be provocative."

strike camp = (take down tents and) move from a temporary resting place
"We struck camp at dawn to make an early start on the next part of our journey."

strike fear/terror into (the heart of) somebody = terrify somebody
"The ghost story struck fear into the hearts of the children."

strike home to somebody = have an impact on somebody
"It was only after his wife left him that it finally struck home to him how much he relied on her."

strike out in another direction = begin a new course in one's business/life etc.
"I was getting nowhere selling cars so I thought I would strike out in another direction and open a dry cleaning business."

strike somebody all of a heap = astonish/astound somebody
"When I heard the news I was struck all of a heap."

strike somebody off = remove somebody's name from a list/register
"The doctor was struck off for unprofessional conduct."

strike up = begin
"He struck up a conversation with the girl sitting next to him."

strike while the iron is hot = act while the opportunity exists
"My neighbour wanted to sell his car in a hurry so I struck while the iron was hot and bought it at a very cheap price."

wildcat strike = sudden unofficial strike (i.e. without trade union sanction)
"Car production stopped because of a wildcat strike by workers in the body shop."

See also: lightning strike; strike a balance; strike a bargain; strike a blow for/against; strike a chord; strike a light!; strike a pose; strike (it) rich; strike (it) lucky; strike me pink!; strike oil; strike the right note; strike terror into somebody; strike while the iron is hot; within striking distance.

string

have somebody on a (piece of) string = control somebody
"Watch Clive come running when Angela calls him ñ she's got him on a piece of string."

hold the purse strings = be in control of money/spending
"We all give our wages to mother ñ she's the one who holds the purse strings in our family."

keep somebody on a (piece of) string = make somebody wait for a decision
"They have been keeping me on a string for two weeks and still haven't said whether or not they accept my offer."

string along with somebody = accompany/join in with somebody
"I met John and Janet on holiday and strung along with them for the rest of my stay."

string somebody along = retain somebody's affection/friendship (without returning it)
"Mike still occasionally goes out with Lorna but I think he's just stringing her along."

string somebody up = hang somebody
"I think that all rapists should be strung up."

(all) strung up/highly strung = agitated/ nervous
"There's no need to get so strung up about a job interview."
"Nigel is temperamental but he's very highly strung, you know."

with no strings attached = without conditions
"It's a straight cash deal with no strings attached."

See also: another/two string(s) to one's bow; pull strings; tied to one's mother's apron strings.

strip

strip off = get undressed
"We all stripped off and went for a midnight swim."

tear a strip off somebody = harangue/ rebuke somebody
"The boss will really tear a strip off you if he finds out what you've done."

stroke

at a (single) stroke = in only one go
"At a single stroke the professor gave an answer to the question that had been puzzling the students for an hour."

on the stroke of = exactly at
"The firework display will begin on the stroke of midnight."

See also: put somebody off his/her stride/stroke.

strong

(still) going strong = continuing to function well
"My old watch is still going strong after twenty years."

somebody's strong suit = something that somebody is good/best at
"Bill's strong suit is being able to eat more than anybody else."

strong-arm tactics = physical violence
"The demonstrators would probably have dispersed quietly and there was no need to use strong-arm tactics."

See also: (using) bad/strong language; going strong; have a strong stomach; strong point.

struck

be struck on somebody = like somebody very much
"My daughter is really struck on the boy she met at the youth club."

See also: strike.

stubborn

stubborn as a mule = very stubborn
"You won't get Glenda to change her mind, she's as stubborn as a mule."

stuck

be stuck for something = be without something

"I couldn't finish making the box because I was stuck for the right screws and all the shops were closed."

be stuck on somebody/something = be attracted to or like somebody/something

"My son is really stuck on the girl who lives next door."

"When I was sixteen I was stuck on the music of the Beatles."

be stuck with somebody/something = be unable to get rid of somebody/something

"I went out for a walk with Julie but we got stuck with her little sister."

"Why is it I am always stuck with the job of making the tea?"

get stuck in = begin eating, or begin working (hard)

"Get stuck in, there's plenty more food where that came from."

"If we get stuck in we can finish this job by tonight."

stuck up = snobbish, feeling superior

"Marcia is too stuck up for the likes of us."

See also: stick.

stuff

do one's stuff = demonstrate what one can do, or do what is expected of one

"You should see Martin doing his stuff on the computer keyboard."

"I'm glad Sarah is on the team ñ you can always rely on her to do her stuff."

know one's stuff = be knowledgeable/skilful (in a particular subject)

"Billy really knows his stuff when it comes to football."

stuff and nonsense = utter nonsense

"That's stuff and nonsense, of course I can juggle with three balls at once!"

that's the stuff (to give the troops) = that's just what is required

"That's the stuff, give it another push and it will be in the right place."

See also: bit of skirt/stuff; hard stuff; hot stuff; kid's stuff; knock the stuffing out of somebody; stuffed shirt.

stumble

stumble across = accidentally find

"I stumbled across this silver bracelet in the junk shop down the road."

stumbling block = obstruction to progress

"The chief stumbling block to his promotion is his lack of qualifications."

stump

be stumped = be at a loss/not know

"I was totally stumped and couldn't remember the man's name."

stump up = find/pay some money

"If we all stump up a pound we'll have enough for a round of drinks."

stump somebody = ask somebody something he/she cannot do/does not know

"I stumped George by asking him who won the Cup Final last year."

style

do something/live in style = do something/live in an extravagant manner

"We decided to do it in style and hired a chauffeur-driven car to take us to the reception."

See also: cramp somebody's style.

subject

be subject to = be conditional on, or be likely to be affected by

"Our departure is subject to the time of the high tide."

"My husband is subject to hay fever in the early summer."

change the subject = alter the topic of conversation

"I want to talk to you about your time-keeping ñ and don't change the subject!"

subject somebody to = force somebody to experience/undergo

"It was extremely unkind of you to subject him to the embarrassment of pointing out his errors in public."

success

nothing succeeds like success = success once/in one area is likely to be followed by more success

"Each time William reinvests the proceeds of one property deal in another one, he makes even more money ñ but nothing succeeds like success."

See also: success story.

such

such-and-such = somebody/something unnamed

"How did you get on with old such-and-such the other day?"

"If you ask her how much it is she says such-and-such, and then you haggle and she reduces the price."

such as it is/they are = it/they are poor/unsatisfactory

"Here's your supper, such as it is."

suck

suck up to somebody = fawn on/flatter somebody (in the hope of a favour)

"Tommy Jones is always sucking up to the teacher."

See also: blood sucker; teach one's grandmother to suck eggs.

sudden

all of a sudden = suddenly

"All of a sudden a piercing scream broke the silence."

suffer

on sufferance = tolerated (unwillingly)

"I had little in common with the others and it soon became obvious I was only there on sufferance."

See also: not suffer fools gladly.

suffice

suffice it to say (that) = one need say only (that)

"Suffice it to say Wendy was the last to arrive as usual."

sugar

See: sugar daddy; sugar the pill.

suit

suit oneself = (selfishly) do what one likes

"Suit yourself, but I had hoped that you would come and help."

See also: birthday suit; follow suit; somebody's strong suit; suitcase economy; suit one's book; suit somebody down to the ground.

sum

sum total = complete total

"We worked in the garden for two hours and the sum total of all our efforts was only one flower bed weeded and tidied."

summer

Indian summer = summery weather in autumn

"I had to take my holiday late but fortunately we had an Indian summer

and the weather was splendid."
See also: one swallow doesn't make a summer.

sun
catch the sun = become sunburned
"Glenda went on the beach for the first time this year and caught the sun all down her back."
touch of the sun = illness/slight madness caused by overexposure to the heat of the sun
"Since he came back from India, the Colonel has been suffering from a touch of the sun."
under the sun = anywhere/worldwide
"There is no place under the sun as beautiful as Britain in the spring."
See also: make hay while the sun shines.

Sunday
Sunday best = one's best (formal) clothes
"Dad wore his Sunday best to visit the bank manager."
See also: month of Sundays.

sundry
See: all and sundry.

sunk
See: sink.

supper
See: sing for one's supper.

supply
in short supply = scarce
"Because of very wet spring weather, apples will be in short supply this year."

suppose
I don't suppose you could.Ö = please could you.Ö
"I don't suppose you could help me with the washing up?"
I suppose so = I agree (reluctantly)
"Can I lend you some money? Well, I suppose so."
what do you suppose? = what do you think?
"What do you suppose would happen if we turned that switch?"
"What do you suppose this is? A bar of gold?"

sure
a sure thing = a (near) certainty
"An increase in the duty on petrol is a sure thing in the next budget."
be sure and/to = ensure that/be certain to
"Be sure and let me know when you're next in town."
don't be/you can't be/you can never be too sure = one cannot be certain
"Don't be too sure, you haven't got the exam results yet."
"I should take a raincoat and an umbrella, you can't be too sure."
"You can never be too sure if my old car will start in damp weather."
for sure = certainly/definitely
"Do you know for sure exactly what happened?"
make sure = ensure/make certain
"Please help the driver by making sure you have the exact money for your bus fare."
sure as hell = certainly
"He's sure as hell going to kill himself on that motorbike one day."
sure-fire = certain
"I've bet on the dog in trap four ñ its a sure-fire winner."
sure of oneself = confident
"I wish I had Graham's confidence, he's always so sure of himself."
sure thing = emphatically yes

"Sure thing! I'll be there at ten o'clock."

that's for sure = that is certain
"She won't dare do that again, and that's for sure."

to be sure = of course
"To be sure it's expensive, but look at the quality."

See also: sure as eggs is eggs; sure enough.

surface

See: scratch the surface.

surprise

catch/take somebody by surprise = confront somebody unexpectedly
"I caught him by surprise while he was having dinner with his secretary."
"The arrival of the police took them completely by surprise."

much to one's surprise = causing one astonishment/great surprise
"Much to his surprise, Ted won first prize in the raffle."

suspicion

above/beyond suspicion = not even considered as possibly guilty
"The victim described his assailant as a white man and so Smith, who is a black West Indian, is above suspicion."

swallow

one swallow doesn't make a summer = one good omen/sign does not make a good forecast
"The first sample of orc from the trial boring is very promising, but we should remember that one swallow doesn't make a summer."

See also: swallow one's pride.

swan

swan around = go around (selfishly) indulging in pleasurable activities
"The boss came to France with us to install the equipment, but while we worked through the weekend to get the job finished he just swanned around sampling the local food and wine."

swan song = somebody's last performance/work
"She appeared in the tile role of ëCarmen' as her swan song."

sway

See: hold sway.

swear

swear black and blue = assert adamantly/emphatically
"I thought I saw Silvia with a man in the nightclub but she swears black and blue that she's never been there."

swear black is white = assert a falsehood
"Norman says he hasn't had a drink since last month, but he'd swear black is white if it suited him."

swear by = trust/rely one completely
"My grandfather swears by his cutthroat razor for giving him a close, comfortable shave."

swear like a trooper = habitually use swear words
"Joe is by far the best car mechanic we have, but he swears like a trooper and sometimes upsets our women clients."

swear somebody in = formally install somebody into an office/position
"Several deputies were sworn in the assist the sheriff to hunt down the wanted men."

See also: swear blind; sworn enemies.

sweat

in a cold sweat = apprehensive/ frightened

"I was in a cold sweat in case the policeman noticed that my car tax was out of date."

no sweat = no bother/trouble

"No sweat, I'm happy to change shifts with you if you want Friday afternoon off."

old sweat = somebody who is experienced/long serving

"What we need is an old sweat with experience of working these ancient machines."

sweated labour = people who work for very poor wages (and often for long hours)

"The mill owners used sweated labour to earn them fortunes."

sweat it out = remain throughout a difficult/unpleasant experience

"We were stuck in a lift and had to sweat it our until help arrived."

sweat like a pig = sweat copiously

"In the sunny weather I was sweating like a pig by the time I had finished mowing the lawn."

See also: by the sweat of one's brow; sweat blood.

sweep

See: make a clean sweep; sweep somebody off his/her feet; sweep something under the carpet/rug; sweep the board; sweep the deck; sweep/ wipe the floor with.

sweet

all sweetness and light = apparently friendly and good-tempered

"Our supervisor is always having arguments with us about our work, but when the boss comes round she is all sweetness and light."

be sweet on somebody = be (slightly) in love with somebody

"Ann is always fussing around her boss and I think she's a bit sweet on him."

have a sweet tooth = like eating sweet foods

"I have a sweet tooth and can't resist eating chocolate and ice cream."

the sweets of = the rewards of

"The champion revelled in the sweets of his triumph over the challenger."

See also: short and sweet; sweet dreams; sweet nothings.

swell

feeling swell = feeling happy/healthy

"I've been feeling swell since the doctor prescribed those tablets."

See also: swollen-headed.

swim

go swimmingly = proceed successfully/ well

"The bride looked beautiful and the whole wedding went swimmingly."

in the swim = up-to-date/involved with the latest trends

"I'm looking forward to the end of my convalescence and getting back to work and in the swim of the business world."

swim against the tide = act/behave in a way that is opposite to most other people's

"We all agreed to vote Conservative but Peter insisted on swimming against the tide and voting Labour."

See also: sink or swim.

swing

get into the swing of things = adopt an (existing) routine

"The job is not as complicated as it appears, and you'll soon get into the swim of things."

go with a swing = occur successfully/ without difficulty

"We gave them all a glass of punch when they arrived and that ensured that the party went with a swing."

in full swing = happening vigorously

"The party was in full swing by the time we arrived."

See also: no/not enough room to swing a cat; swinging the lead.

switch

be switched on = be aware (of current trends)

"My father hates modern fashions ñ I don't think he'll ever get switched on."

switch from/over = change

"He can switch from being nice to nasty in a couple of seconds."

"I've decided to switch over from the buses to the underground because it is more reliable."

swollen

See: swollen-headed.

swoop

at/in one fell swoop = simultaneously

"The children said they were still hungry so I put a plate of cakes on the table and at one fell swoop they vanished."

sword

cross swords with somebody = have an argument/disagreement with somebody

"Barry has a nasty temper and I would hate to cross swords with him."

double-edged sword = something that can cause damage in two different ways

"The law on assault is a double-edged sword: it can be applied to an attacker or to somebody who is defending his property."

sword of Damocles (hanging over one) = disaster that could happen at any time

"The possibility of being made redundant has been a sword of Damocles hanging over me for several months now."

symbol

See: status symbol.

sympathy

in sympathy with = in agreement with in principle

"I'm in sympathy with what you want to do, but I don't know how you're going to get the money to do it."

system

all systems go = let us begin

"The food is on the table ñ all systems go!"

get something out of one's system = reveal/get rid of something that has been occupying one's thoughts

"I can't forget what it was like when Janet and I still lived together ñ I think I'll take a holiday and try to get her out of my system."

T

t

to a T = exactly
"Your new dress fits you to a T."
See also: dot the i's and cross the t's.

tab

keep tabs on = continually check/watch/be informed
"As the job gets more complicated, I find it increasingly difficult to keep tabs on what's going on."
pick up the tab = pay the bill
"We had an expensive lunch, but fortunately Andy picked up the tab."

table

drink somebody under the table = drink more (and remain conscious) than somebody else (who does not remain conscious)
"Glen claims he's a big drinker, but even my daughter could drink him under the table."
turn the tables on somebody = seize the advantage from somebody by reversing the situation
"In the previous darts competition Mike beat me two-one, but I turned the tables on him today by winning all three games."
See also: lay/put one's cards on the table; round table conference.

tablet

keep (on) taking the tablets = reply to a crazy action/statement
"You've put the cake to cook in the fridge and the ice cream in the microwave! Never mind, just keep taking the tablets!"

tack

change tack = alter a course of action
"It's not going to work this way, we'd better change tack and try another approach."
on the right/wrong tack = making a correct/incorrect assumption
"She thinks I'm going out with Jeremy but she's completely on the wrong tack."
See also: get down to brass tacks.

tag

tag along = follow or accompany somebody (perhaps when not wanted)
"We can never get rid of young Chris, he always tags along wherever we go."

tail

keep/stay on somebody's tail = tenaciously follow somebody
"Keep on the suspect's tail and don't let him out of your sight."
tail off = diminish
"The skate board was popular for a while but interest in it eventually tailed off."
turn tail ñ turn back and leave in the direction one came
"As soon as he saw me approaching he turned tail and walked away."
with one's tail between one's legs = in a sad/ashamed manner
"He didn't seem at all sorry, but he went away with his tail between his legs after I made him apologize in front of everyone."
with one's tail up = carefree/happy
"Jenny really had her tail up after she won the competition."
See also: hang on somebody's coat tails; in two shakes (of a lamb's tail); like a

dog with two tails; make neither head nor tail of; put salt on somebody's tail; sting in the tail; tail wagging the dog; twist somebody's tail.

take

be able to/can take it = be/is able to tolerate pain/trouble etc.
"Don't bother with a local anaesthetic, I can take it."
"Tina is always teasing her brother and unfortunately he can't take it."

be taken with somebody/something = find somebody/something attractive
"I didn't like many of the exhibits in the museum, although I was quite taken with some of the Renaissance bronzes."

I take it (that) = I assume (that)
"Do I take it that you disapprove?"

it takes one to know one = you are the same as the person you describe
"Jim called Gerald a liar ñ well, it takes one to know one!"

take after somebody resemble somebody
"Your son certainly takes after his father, he has the same red hair and blue eyes."

take it from me = believe me
"Take it from me, we're going to have a severe winter this year."

take it from there = carry on without help/planning/supervision
"I'll introduce you to the audience and you can take it from there."
"After you've shown her once how to do the job she should be able to take it from there."

take it or leave it = accept or refuse something
"I'll offer you five hundred pounds for the car ñ take it or leave it."

take it out of one = exhaust/tire one
"My father can still cycle up the hill but it takes it out of him."

take it out on somebody = direct one's anger/displeasure at somebody else
"Whenever she gets annoyed she takes it out on her children."

take off = suddenly improve/succeed
"Sally had the idea of opening a boutique for children and it's really taken off."

take one back ñ cause one to remember
"The smell of pipe tobacco always takes me back to the time I used to sit on my grandfather's knee."

take on the appearance of = resemble
"In the half light, the Alsatian took on the appearance of a wolf."

take somebody for somebody else = mistake one person for another
"I took you for your sister; are you twins?"

take somebody in = cheat/deceive somebody, or admit somebody to one's home
"I was taken in by the salesman ñ the car turned out to be uneconomical and unreliable."
"Bruce was evicted from his flat so we took him in until he found somewhere else to live."

take somebody off = imitate somebody
"The impressionist was marvellous at taking off film stars and politicians."

take somebody up on something = accept an offer
"Bill offered to give me a lift to work and I quickly took him up on it."

take something back = retract a statement
"How dare you call me that! Take it back at once!"

take something in = understand something, or include something
"He gave the explanation so quickly that I couldn't take it all in."

"When you compile the list, make sure you take in all the references on the attached page."

take something over = take control/ possession of something

"I appreciate Tom coming to help but I do wish he didn't always try to take over."

take something upon oneself = accept/ take responsibility for

"The filing system was in a mess so I took it upon myself to sort it out."

take something up with somebody = bring up/discuss a topic with somebody

"If you cannot help me I shall have to take the matter up with your superior."

take to something = come to like something, or adopt something (habitually)

"She thought she would be nervous looking after the horses but she soon took to them."

"Now we have renovated our old bathroom my husband has taken to having a shower every morning."

take up with somebody = associate/make friends with somebody

"My son has taken up with the Jones boys who live down the road."

See also: be taken aback; bring/take somebody down a peg (or two); caught/taken short; go take a running jump (at yourself)!; run/take the risk; take cover; take effect; take heart; take holy orders; take it easy; take off one's hat to; take one's cue from; take one's medicine; take one's time; take sides; take somebody for a ride; take somebody on/to one side; take somebody's mind off something; take somebody's name in vain; take somebody's place; take somebody's point; take somebody to one's heart; take somebody to task; take something as read; take something into one's head; take something to heart; take steps; take the edge off; take the floor; take the place of something; take up arms; take up the cudgels.

tale

dead men tell no tales = one cannot be incriminated by somebody who is dead

"The gangster killed the only witness to his crime, on the principle that dead men tell no tales."

tell its own tale = be self-evident

"The meat had disappeared from the kitchen and the cat's paw prints on the table told their own tale."

tell tales about somebody = inform on/ reveal confidences about somebody

"I don't want to know what your brother did, and I'm tired of you telling tales about him."

tell tales out of school = indulge in gossip

"I don't want to tell tales out of school, but did you know that Mary is having an affair with David?"

thereby hangs a tale = the account could be continued further

"Judy always wears a different outfit every day but this morning she came to work in the same clothes as she wore yesterday ñ and thereby hangs a tale."

See also: live to tell the tale; old wive's tales.

talent

See: budding talent.

talk

do the talking = be spokesman

"You all keep quiet and let me do the talking."

idle talk = gossip/useless conversation
"I've heard that we're going to get a pay rise, but it may be just idle talk."

know what one is talking about = be expert/knowledgeable
"I prefer Doctor Smith because he seems to know what he's talking about."

now you're talking! = what you are saying now is really relevant
"Would I like another drink? Now you're talking!"

pillow talk = conversation between lovers (in bed)
"A former model wrote a hilarious novel based on pillow talk with her many male friends."

(make) small talk = (have a) trivial/polite conversation
"There was a delay before the car came to collect us so we made small talk in the meantime."

sweet talk somebody = flatter somebody (for gain)
"My daughters can usually sweet talk me into giving them what they want."

*talk about.*Ö = that is a perfect case of.Ö
"Talk about noise! You couldn 't hear yourself speak!"

talk back to somebody = answer somebody in an impolite/rude way
"It annoys me the way the children talk back to you like that."

talk down to somebody = talk to somebody as if he/she were less intelligent/important
"Harry is quite good in meetings but he must learn not to talk down to people."

*talking of.*Ö = now that subject has arisen.Ö
"Talking of Debbie's party, how are we going to get there?"

talk of the town = something that everybody is discussing
"The modern sculpture outside the new library is the talk of the town."

talk somebody into/out of something = persuade/dissuade somebody
"Dennis didn't want to go at first but I managed to talk him into it."
"Dennis is determined to go and nobody can talk him out of it."

talk somebody round = persuade somebody
"Dad has said I can't wear makeup yet ñ but I'll soon talk him round."

talk something over = discuss something (at length)
"Before you make your final decision, let's talk it over."

you can talk = you are not in a position to criticize
"You think Simon is a fool because he gave money to a beggar? You can talk, you've done some pretty foolish things yourself!"

See also: money talks; speak/talk of the devil; talk big; talk nineteen to the dozen; talk shop; talk somebody's head off; talk the hind leg off a donkey; talk through one's hat; talk through the back of one's neck; talk to somebody like a
Dutch uncle; talk turkey.

tall
See: tall order; tall story; walk tall.

tan
See: tan somebody's hide.

tangent
go/fly off at a tangent = suddenly diverge from the path/subject
"We were discussing last night's concert when Anna went off at a

tangent and started talking about her new flat."

tap

on tap = available for (immediate) use
"I have my own word processor and printer at home, so that everything I need is on tap."

tape

have/get something/somebody taped = have a good knowledge of the nature of somebody/something

"I suspect that Bob is trying unfairly to influence the outcome of the enquiry, but I've got him taped."

See also: red tape.

tar

See: spoil the ship for a ha'porth of tar; tarred with the same brush.

target

See: sitting target.

tart

tart somebody/something up = make somebody/something superficially more attractive (in a tawdry way)
"Old Mrs Jones was all tarted up for the vicar's garden party."
"My car is getting old; I think I'll tart it up with a respray and try to sell it."

task

hard task-master = somebody who makes one work hard
"Our boss is quite pleasant, although she can be a hard taskmaster at times."

take somebody to task = criticize/ discipline somebody
"I had to take William to task over the way he behaved last night."

taste

develop/have a taste for = acquire/ possess a liking for
"I've developed a taste for African music since my trip last year to Nigeria."

to taste = in the amount preferred
"For that extra spiciness, add powdered nutmeg to taste."

to one's taste = such as to give one pleasure
"Modern paintings are not to my taste."

See also: acquired taste; dose/taste of one's own medicine; in bad taste; leave a nasty taste in one's mouth; no accounting for taste; taste blood.

tat

See: tit for tat.

tea

not for all the tea in China = not at all/ ever
"You wouldn't get me to wear a mini-skirt for all the tea in China."

See also: another cup of tea; nice (old) cup of tea; not one's cup of tea; storm in a teacup.

teach

that will teach one/somebody = what happened is (just) retribution for what one/somebody did
"That'll teach him to try and light a cigarette with a red-hot poker."
"That will teach John to be cheeky to Wendy ñ she just got up and slapped his face!"

See also: teach one's grandmother to suck eggs; teach somebody a lesson; you can't teach an old dog new tricks.

tear

dissolve in(to) tears = begin to cry copiously
"When the little girl saw the dead bird she dissolved into tears."

reduce somebody to tears = make somebody cry
"He gave her such a scolding that he reduced her to tears."

tear oneself away = force oneself to leave
"I couldn't tear myself away from the beautiful display of flowers."

See: bore stiff/the pants off/to tears; crocodile tears; tear a strip off somebody; tear one's hair out; wear and tear.

teeth

armed to the teeth = carrying many weapons, or possessing as much as possible to give one an advantage
"Suddenly we were confronted by two bandits who were armed to the teeth."
"I wanted to impress them so I went armed to the teeth with copies of articles and papers I had written."

bare/show one's teeth = reveal one's intention to fight/resist
"After days of inactivity, the enemy finally showed its teeth by a frontal attack on our position."

draw somebody's/something's teeth = cause somebody/something to be less of a danger
"I knew that Harry could be aggressive in negotiations, so I drew his teeth by taking him out for a boozy lunch first."

get one's teeth into something = make determined effort in doing something
"All I do all day long is to check invoices; I wish they would give me a job I could really get my teeth into."

give one's eye/back teeth for something = do anything to obtain something
"I'd give my eye teeth for a chance to go to Australia."

gnash one's teeth = feel/show angry frustration
"It makes me gnash my teeth to see so much food deliberately destroyed or wasted when there are people starving in Africa."

grit one's teeth = hide one's feelings
"Mr Jones called me incompetent but, as he was the boss, I had to grit my teeth and accept it."

in the teeth of = against/in conflict with
"We persevered even in the teeth of organized opposition."

make one's teeth chatter = cause the jaws to shake and the teeth to knock rapidly together
"The room was so cold it made my teeth chatter."

teething troubles = initial difficulties
"Like all new machines, it had a few teething troubles but it is working well now."

See also: bit between one's teeth; by the skin of one's teeth; cut one's teeth on; fed up (to the back teeth); in the teeth of the wind; kick somebody in the teeth; lie in/through one's teeth; set one's teeth on edge.

telegraph

See: bush telegraph.

tell

as far as one can tell = as far as one knows/is aware
"As far as I can tell Sylvia has split up with Mark."

I can tell you = I assure you
"Emma can be very bad-tempered, I can tell you."

I told you so = I predicted it would happen
"If you've cut yourself with that knife I can only say I told you so."
tell me another = I do not believe you
"You won first prize in a talent contest? Tell me another!"
tell on somebody = inform on somebody, or cause somebody to feel exhausted/strained
"My mistake won't be discovered as long as nobody tells on me."
"Working on the night shift is really beginning to tell on Colin, he's looking very tired."
tell somebody (where to get) off = scold/reprimand somebody
"Mum told me off for wearing my best shoes for playing football."
"If Brian uses my parking space again, I'll really tell him where to get off."
(I'll) tell you what = I propose/suggest
"Tell you what, why don't we have a picnic this afternoon?"
there's no telling = one cannot know
"I cannot say how many people will come ñ there's no telling."
to tell the truth = to be perfectly honest
"Thanks for the drink, but to tell the truth I prefer tea to coffee."
what did I tell you? = what I said was true
"Liverpool did win. What did I tell you?"
you never can tell = it could happen
"You never can tell, you might win a fortune on the football pools."
you're telling me = I agree
"You're telling me, the price of beer is ridiculously high!"
See also: all told; live to tell the tale; tell apart; tell its own tale; (you can) tell that/it to the marines; tell tales about somebody; tell tales out of school.

temper
keep/lose one's temper = conceal/show one's anger
"In professional competition you have to learn to keep your temper."
"The motor mower wouldn't start so Dad lost his temper and kicked it."

ten
ten to one = it is very probable that
"Ten to one it will rain on the Bank Holiday."

tender
See: leave somebody to the tender mercies of; of tender age; tender trap.

tenterhooks
be on tenterhooks = be (very) anxious about the possible outcome
"The tightrope walker had us on tenterhooks until he reached the safety of the other side."

term
in terms of something = define/describe with reference to something
"But what do the changes to the schedule mean in terms of extra work?"
on bad/good terms with = unfriendly/friendly with
"I've been on bad terms with Stephen ever since he jilted my sister."
See also: be on speaking terms with somebody; blanket term; come to terms with; contradiction in terms; on easy terms; terms of abuse.

terror
strike terror into somebody = make somebody very afraid/fearful
"Warriors wore those African masks to strike terror into their enemies."

See also: holy terror.

test

put somebody/something to the test = test somebody/something
"Peter claims to be an expert on football, although asking him to name all the clubs in the first division put him to the test."
"The model glider looks fine, although the only way we can really put it to the test is to see if it will fly."
See also: acid test.

tether

See: at the end of one's rope/tether.

thank

have only oneself to thank for = be the sole cause of
"You wouldn't listen to advice so you've only yourself to thank now that it's in a mess."
I'll thank you to = please (used when annoyed)
"I'll thank you to park outside your own house, not outside mine!"
thanks for having me/us = thank you for your hospitality
"We've had a splendid evening and thanks for having us."
thanks to/no thanks to = because of/in spite of
"We only found your house thanks to a policeman who gave us directions."
"We finally found your house, but no thanks to the policeman who directed us the wrong way."
thank you/thanks for nothing = I am not pleased
"You've broken my pen ñ thanks for nothing, I could have done that for myself!"
See also: thankful for small mercies; thank one's lucky stars; vote of thanks.

that

and all that = and all (the rest of) that sort of thing
"There was plenty of ice cream, jellies, cream cakes, and all that, but nothing savoury."
and/so that's that = that is the decision/result
"You're not having one, and that's that!"
"Our team has been knocked out of the championship, so that's that."
at that = as well, or whereupon
"The Joneses have bought a new car, and a large one at that."
"Mick shouted an insult and with that walked out of the door."
in that = because/since
"His request is unreasonable in that he knows we cannot afford it."
is that so? = expression of questioning surprise
"Is that so? I thought he was going last night."
(just) like that = without hesitation
"When I asked her she said yes, just like that."
that's about it = that is more or less all
"That's about it for today's output, let's see of we can produce more tomorrow."
See also: be that as it may; how's that for; that will do; that's done it!; that's the way it goes; you do that!

then

(every) now and then = occasionally
"I like to smoke a big cigar every now and then."
See also: there and then.

there

so there = expression that emphasizes a (supposed) advantage
"My house is bigger than yours ñ so there!"

there and then/then and there = at that very time (and place)
"He accepted my price and wrote out a cheque there and then."

there again = alternatively
"I could wear my blue blouse, or there again my white one."

there are (somethings) and (somethings) = there are good and bad examples of something
"If you have some spare cash you could buy a camera, although there are cameras and cameras, and you have to be careful which one you buy."

there you are = it is inevitable, or I said that would happen, or that is what you need/requested
"I've got to pay for my daughter's wedding, but there you are ñ that's what fathers are for."
"There you are! I knew you'd get it right in the end."
"There you are, two teas and a coffee."

there you go = here you are
"There you go, two bars of chocolate as you requested."

See also: (not) all there.

thick

a bit thick = slightly stupid, or unjust/unfair
"The new office boy is a bit thick but he's very willing to help."
"There is no ticket left for me? That's a bit thick, considering I was the one who helped to organize the whole outing."

in the thick of something = in the most active/dense part of something
"There's a labour dispute at work and as shop steward I'm right in the thick of it."

thick and fast = many and often/quickly
"The questions came flying at me thick and fast."

thick as thieves = very close/friendly
"Lionel and Mandy were thick as thieves until Lionel changed his job, now they hardly see each other."

thick as two short planks = stupid
"Mark is as thick as two short planks ñ I still don't understand why you employed him here."

through thick and thin = despite all adversity/difficulties
"My wife has stood by me through thick and thin."

See also: blood is thicker than water; box somebody's ears/give somebody a thick ear; have a thick skin; lay it on thick/with a trowel; pile it on thick; the plot thickens; thick/thin on the ground.

thief

set a thief to catch a thief = the best way to discover/outdo a wrongdoer is to use another wrongdoer
"James was habitually late until I put him in charge of signing in people as they arrive at work, now he has to be there before everybody else ñ set a thief to catch a thief!"

See also: den of thieves; thick as thieves.

thin

thin edge of the wedge = insignificant start of a worsening situation
"He asked me to work an extra twenty minutes, but it's the thin edge of the wedge ñ next time it will be half an

hour and after that probably a whole hour!"

thin on top = balding
"You know who I mean ñ he's tall, with glasses, and ginger hair a bit thin on top."

See also: into thin air; lean/thin time; out of thin air; skate on thin ice; thick/thin on the ground; thin as a rake.

thing

a daft/silly/stupid etc. thing to do = a daft etc. action
"If you bit your own tongue that was a daft thing to do."

a/the good/sensible/wise etc. thing to do = a good etc. action/decision
"Investing in those shares turned out to be a wise thing to do."

all things to all men = adaptable/suited to everybody
"Graham should make up his mind what his viewpoint is and stop trying to be all things to all men."

and another thing = moreover
"And another thing, what about that money you owe me?"

do the handsome thing = be chivalrous/generous
"We had a slight argument but Hugh did the handsome thing and apologized."

for one thing = as just one example/reason
"No you can't go out ñ for one thing, it's too late."

have a thing about = have a special affection for/interest in/obsession about etc.
"Barbara has a thing about the Beatles."
"He has a thing about girls in black stockings."
"I have a thing about bats ñ Iím terrified of them."

it's a good thing = it is fortunate/lucky
"It's a good thing your wife doesn't know what you've been doing."

make a good thing of something = make something profitable/successful
"He's made a good thing of selling souvenirs to tourists."

make a thing of something = overemphasize something
"It really doesn't matter, so there's no need to make a thing of it."

no such thing = on the contrary, or something different/non-existent
"I thought Nora would help, but no such thing ñ she left it all to me."
"She said she was an experienced secretary but she was no such thing, just a mediocre typist."
"There seems to be no such thing as a decent loaf of bread these days."

of all things = from all the possibilities
"I offered to help with the staff party and of all things they want me to dress up as Father Christmas!"

old thing = form of address to a colleague/friend
"I say, old thing, can you lend me a cigarette?"

on to a good thing = involved in something beneficial/profitable
"They run the only shop in the district that caters for vegetarians so they're on to a good thing."

poor thing = object of pity/sympathy
"Poor thing, her husband has left her with three children to bring up."

sure thing = certainly
"Sure thing! I'll be happy to help."

taking one thing with another = considering everything
"They've offered me a job, and taking one thing with another I think I'll accept it."

the thing is.Ö = the problem/question is.Ö
"The thing is, how are we going to get there?"
the very thing = exactly what is required
"A brandy and port is the very thing for a hangover."
(have) too much of a good thing = (do) something in excess
"You'll be sick if you eat any more ice cream ñ you can have too much of a good thing, you know."
See also: all/other things being equal; all things considered; do one's own thing; first thing; first things first; hearing things; I've never heard of such a thing; just the thing; know a thing or two; near miss/thing; not know the first thing about; (just) one of those things.

think

get/have another think coming = be mistaken
"If he thinks I'm going to say yes he's got another think coming!"
good thinking = a good idea
"Remember you suggested altering the spring tension? That was good thinking ñ it solved the problem immediately."
I should think not/so = I agree that is incorrect/correct
"You don't intend to leave your wife after all? I should think not!"
"You intend to remain faithful to your wife after all? I should think so too!"
I shouldn't/wouldn't think of doing something = under no circumstances would I do something
"I wouldn't think of going to a bullfight ñ it's degrading and cruel."
that's what you think = that is your opinion
"I should get a new suit? That's what you think ñ I can't afford it."
think no end of = regard very highly
"Lily has met this American boy and she thinks no end of him."
think no more of = forget
"It's all over now so think no more of it."
think something out/over/through = plan something mentally, or consider something (carefully)
"She says she wants to think it over before deciding."
"I can't tell you yet because I haven't thought it through."
think twice = consider carefully
"I'd certainly think twice before buying a car that is more than five years old."
"He wouldn't think twice about taking somebody else's money."
think something up = devise/invent something
"I've got to think up something to wear for the fancy dress party."
think tank = group of specialists who meet to produce ideas/solutions to problems
"We should form all the managers into a think tank to suggest some new products for development."
think twice = consider carefully
"I'd certainly think twice before spending that much on a holiday."
who does he/she think he/she is? = he/she has an inflated opinion of himself/herself
"William said I would look younger if I shaved off my beard. Who does he think he is, telling me what to do?"
See also: great minds think alike; not think much of; put on one's thinking cap; think little of it; think nothing of doing something; think nothing of it;

think on one's feet; think the world of somebody/something; wishful thinking.

this

this and that/this, that and the other = various trivial things

"I spent a lazy morning just doing this and that around the house."

"We spent a whole hour talking about this, that and the other."

this is how it is = this is the situation

"This is how it is ñ we have to get the roof repaired."

Thomas

See: doubting Thomas.

thorn

See: thorn in one's flesh.

thought

train of thought = sequence in which one's thinking runs

"I was interrupted by a phone call and lost my train of thought."

See also: food for thought; penny for your thoughts; perish the thought; second thoughts;
sobering thought.

thousand

I believe you, thousands wouldn't = I (reluctantly) accept what you say

"You say your train was late because there was an escaped elephant on the line. Well I believe you, thousands wouldn't!"

See also: one in a million/thousand.

thrash

thrash something out = discuss and resolve difficulty/problem

"We finally solved the problem, but it took us several hours to thrash it out."

thread

pick up the threads = resume one's line of reasoning/way of life after a break

"I've just gone back to work after being off ill for a month and I'm finding it difficult to pick up the threads."

thread one's way = move between obstructions/through openings

"The policeman had difficulty threading his way through the crowd."

"We got there quicker by threading our way through the back streets."

See also: hang by a thread; lose the drift/thread.

three

See: three Rs.

thrill

thrills and spills = alternating success and failure

"Since I graduated, I miss the thrills and spills of college life."

See also: thrilled to bits.

throat

at each other's throat(s) = fighting/quarrelling

"Those children are at each other's throat again."

*words stick in one*ε *s throat* = be unable to speak because of nervousness/reluctance

"I wanted to say how sorry I was to hear of his bereavement but the words stuck in my throat."

See also: cut one's own throat; cutñ throat competition; frog in the throat; jump down somebody's throat; ram something down somebody's throat; stick on one's craw/gullet/throat.

throe

in the throes of = in the process of (usually something difficult)

"My parents arrived unexpectedly while we were in the throes of redecorating the living room."

throne

See: power behind the throne.

through

be through (with) = be finished (with)

"I'll be glad when we're through with this project."

"Rose and I are through."

through and through = thoroughly/ totally

"The dog was a champion through and through."

See also: fall through; pull round/ through; see through somebody/ something.

throw

throw a party = organize (and pay for) a party

"I'm throwing a party to celebrate my daughter's engagement."

throw a wobbly = have a tantrum

"Just because you can't do what you want there's no need to throw a wobbly."

throw oneself at somebody = try to gain somebody's affection/love by openly demonstrating one's affection for him/ her

"John is very attractive and I understand why you've fallen for him, but there's no need to throw yourself at him."

throw one's weight about = be domineering (using one's authority/ power)

"I'm tired of him throwing his weight about, who does he think he is anyway?"

throw somebody over = end a friendship/ relationship with somebody

"Ian threw over his girlfriend when he found she had been seeing another man."

throw something in = add something (as an afterthought/gift)

"They didn't know what to do that day so I threw in the suggestion that we all should go for a walk."

"Because I had bought fifty hedging plants the salesman threw in a couple of rose bushes free."

throw something off = get rid of something

"They couldn't throw off their pursuers."

throw something open = make something accessible

"He then threw the discussion open to members of the audience."

throw something together = assemble/ make something hurriedly

"I'm glad you liked the meal ñ it was just something I threw together at the last minute."

throw up = abandon/surrender, or vomit

"Rod has decided to throw up playing squash because he's getting too old for it."

"Just the thought of eating snails makes me want to throw up."

See also: dive/throw somebody in at the deep end; throw a spanner in the works; throw caution to the winds; throw good money after bad; throw in one's hand; throw in the towel; throw in/up the sponge; throw money at; throw money away; throw oneself at somebody's feet; throw out the baby with the bath water; throw somebody out on his/her ear; throw somebody to the dogs; throw somebody to the lions; throw somebody to the wolves; throw something in someone's face.

thumb

give the thumbs up/down = give approval/disapproval
"The authorities have given the thumbs up to our planning application."
"You can ask your father, but I think he'll give it the thumbs down."

thumb-nail sketch = small, rapidly drawn picture, or brief description
"He made a thumb-nail sketch to show me where he lived."
"Please tell me what happened ñ not in detail, a thumb-nail sketch will do."

twiddle one's thumbs = do nothing
"He kept me waiting for nearly an hour while I twiddled my thumbs."

See also: all fingers and thumbs; rule of thumb; stick out like a sore thumb; thumb a lift; thumb one's nose at; under somebody's thumb.

thunder

go like thunder = progress quickly/vigorously
"He jumped over the wall and then went like thunder to get away."

thunder box = lavatory I must go and use the thunder box."

See also: blood and thunder; steal somebody's thunder.

tick

give somebody a ticking off/tick somebody off = scold somebody
"If you do that again you'll get a good ticking off."

on tick = on credit
"By the time we had paid for the house, we had to buy the carpet on tick because we had no more money."

tick over = run gently (without needing attention)
"The engine ticks over at a thousand rpm."
"The company is not doing a great deal of business but keeps ticking over."

what makes somebody tick = what motivates somebody
"Harry is a strange fellow and I sometimes wonder what makes him tick."

See also: half a moment/tick.

ticket

that's the ticket = that is the correct/required thing
"That's the ticket. Kick harder with your legs and you'll soon learn to swim."

work one's ticket = obtain one's release from a job before the contract of service has expired
"He worked his ticket by pretending to be mentally ill, and got discharged from the navy."

See also: just the job/thing/ticket; meal ticket.

tickle

See: be tickled pink; catch/take/tickle somebody's fancy; slap and tickle; tickle somebody's
ribs; tickled to death.

tide

tide somebody over = help somebody to overcome a difficulty
"My neighbour lent me a loaf to tide us over until I go to the shops."

See also: swim against the tide; time and tide wait for no man.

tie

be tied up = be busy/occupied, or (inseparably) joined to, or confused by

"I can't start the job for a couple of days because I'm tied up doing the accounts."

"Nearly all my money is tied up in savings certificates."

"I can't understand this article ñ I always get tied up with such long words."

tie somebody down = make somebody decide, or restrict somebody's freedom

"I can't tie them down to a fixed estimate of what it is likely to cost."

tie in with = be logically associated with

"Your account of what happened does not tie in with what three other witnesses have said."

See also: have one's hands tied; old school tie; tie somebody (up) in knots; tie the knot; tied to one's mother's apron strings; with one hand tied behind one's back.

tiger

paper tiger = somebody who appears forceful/strong but is really feeble/ineffective

"The managing director has the nominal power but he is a paper tiger, and it is his assistant who actually runs the company."

tight

on a tight-rope = finely balanced

"The patient is in a coma and on a tightñrope between complete recovery and severe mental disability."

See also: in a tight corner; in a tight squeeze; keep a tight rein on; run a tight ship; sit tight; pull one's belt in/tighten one's belt.

tile

on the tiles = out (at night) enjoying oneself

"We got home at dawn after a night on the tiles."

See also: have a screw/slate/tile loose.

till

See: catch somebody with his/her fingers/hand in the till.

tilt

(at) full tilt = (at) speed

"The car ran full tilt into a tree."

"When they saw the shark, the bathers swam at full tilt to the shore."

See also: tilt at windmills.

time

about time = the appropriate time, or late

"It's about time you had a new coat."

"You're here at last ñ it's about time, I've been waiting for half an hour."

ahead of one's time = with an idea/invention that is too advanced for one's contemporaries

"Brunel's atmospheric railway was ahead of its time; with the benefit of modern synthetic materials it would probably have succeeded."

all in good time = as soon as is/seems appropriate

"You can have a new bicycle all in good time."

any time = no thanks are necessary

"I know you're grateful, but that's all right, any time."

at one time = at some time in the past

"At one time you could go to the pictures for half a crown (12 pence)."

do time = serve a prison sentence

"Barry will cope with the sentence, he's done time before."

for the time being = meanwhile
"For the time being I'm going on a diet."

from time to time = occasionally
"I walk to school from time to time instead of catching the bus."

gain time = create enough time to do something (by causing a delay)
"You keep them talking to gain time while I look up the figures."

half the time = often
"He's never there half the time."

have a time of it = have difficulties
"We had a time of it at the shops because Gill just couldn't find the kind of shoes she wanted to buy."

have no/not much time for somebody/something = have a strong dislike for somebody/something
"I've no time for Gerry since he insulted my girlfriend."
"Dad hasn't much time for my pop records."

in good time = with time to spare
"Make sure you get there in good time or you won't get a seat."

in one's own good time = at whatever time suits one
"Leave him alone, he'll finish in his own good time."

in one's own time = at whatever rate suits one, or in one's non-working time
"Please answer the questions in your own time."
"I wrote the article entirely in my own time."

in one's time = at some time in one's past
"In his time, Joe was one of the best darts players around here."

keep (good) time = synchronize, or display the time accurately
"We have to order stock carefully to keep time with seasonal demands."
"I've had this watch for twenty years and it still keeps good time."

long time no see = it is good to meet you again
"We haven't met for ages, long time no see."

make good time = travel more quickly than expected
"I made good time and got here in less than an hour."

not before time = only just in time
"I'm glad you've decided to have your hair cut ñ and it's not before time."

one/two etc. at a time = singly or in specified groups
"Make sure you wash the plates one at a time."
"You'll finish quicker if you carry them two at a time."
"Lucy was eating several sweets at a time."

take one's time = do something at the (slow) rate one prefers
"You don't have to rush off to work this morning so why don't you take your time and have some breakfast before you go."

lean/thin time = time of difficulty (because of lack of money)
"We had a lean time when we first got married because your father was out of work for nearly a year."

time after time/time and again = repeatedly
"The challenger wouldn't admit defeat and came back for more punishment time after time."

time and tide wait for no man = procrastination is inadvisable
"By the time he had made up his mind it was too late and the opportunity was lost, proving once again that time and tide wait for no man."

time flies = time passes more quickly than one realizes

"It's nearly midnight ñ how time flies when you're enjoying yourself."

time is getting on = it is getting late

"Time is getting on and we had better be going home."

time was = there was a time (in the past)

"Time was when a girl could walk alone at night without worrying about being attacked."

See also: a stitch in time saves nine; at the same time; behind the times; bide one's time; big time; fall on bad times; from time immemorial; have the time of one's life; high time; in the fullness of time; in the nick of time; kill time; mark time; old timer; play for time; serve time; serve one's time; there's no time like the present; time out of mind.

tin

See: little tin god; put the (tin) lid on.

tinker

See: not care a tinker's cuss/damn; not worth a tinker's cuss/damn.

tinkle

give somebody a tinkle = telephone somebody

"Give me a tinkle and let me know what time the show starts."

have a tinkle = urinate

"I must stop work for a minute and go and have a tinkle."

tip

tip somebody off = inform/warn/give a hint to somebody

"Jan tipped me off that the boss is going to make an inspection tomorrow."

tip the balance = be the factor that precipitates an action/decision

"The contestants are well-matched and practically anything could tip the balance."

See also: on the tip of one's tongue; tip of the iceberg; tip/turn the scales; tip somebody the wink.

tire

See: dog tired; sick and tired of.

tit

tit for tat = repayment of a defeat/hurt by defeating/hurting the other party

"Bill beat me at chess last week and I beat him tonight ñ so we're tit for tat."

to

to and fro = backwards and forwards

"I went to and fro to the shops three times today."

toing and froing = moving backwards and forwards (without making any progress)

"Apart from a lot of toing and froing between union headquarters and Downing Street, there is nothing to report about the strike."

toast

See: warm as toast.

tod

on one's tod = alone

"I didn't go out last night. I sat at home on my tod watching television."

today

here today and gone tomorrow = ephemeral/present for only a short time

"It's difficult to find a windowñcleaner who will call regularly ñ they all seem to be here today and gone tomorrow."

toe
on one's toes = alert/ready
"A policeman has to keep on his toes all the time he's on duty."
tread on somebody's toes = offend/upset somebody by interfering with/ usurping what he/she is doing
"There are so many committees and subcommittees around here that it is almost impossible to do anything without treading on somebody's toes."
turn up one's toes = die
"My grandfather was over ninety before he turned up his toes."
See also: from top to bottom/toe; toe the line.

toffee
not do something for toffee = be unable to do something
"I don't go sailing because I can't swim for toffee."

together
together with = in the company of, or also/and
"They sent me the goods, together with an invoice."
"I bought a new dress, together with a hat and gloves."

token
by the same token = moreover/similarly
"The bus failed to arrive on time and by the same token several people were late for work."

told
See: all told; tell.

toll
take its toll = be very harmful
"The Great Plague took its toll of the citizens of London."

Tom
any/every Tom, Dick and Harry = anybody/everybody
"Make a list of about ten people you would like to come, but remember you just can't invite every Tom, Dick and Harry."
peeping Tom = somebody who derives (sexual) pleasure by spying on others who are undressed/undressing
"The police are trying to find a peeping Tom who has been annoying people on our housing estate."

tomorrow
as if/like there's no tomorrow = as if it is the last opportunity (to do something)
"My wife went to the shops and was spending money as if there's no tomorrow."
tomorrow is another day = there will be another opportunity (said in consolation for a disappointment)
"Don't be too upset you didn't win a prize, tomorrow is another day."
tomorrow never comes = what is not done now is unlikely to be done at all
"You mustn't put that phone call off any longer ñ remember, tomorrow never comes."
See also: here today and gone tomorrow.

ton
See: like a ton of bricks; weigh (half) a ton.

tone
tone down = lessen the extremeness of
"I've drafted a very strong letter of complaint; do you think I should tone it down a bit?"

tong
See: like hammer and tongs.

tongue
anything else while your tongue's warm? = have you anything else to say?
"You've already asked me to fetch your slippers, make you some tea and turn on the television ñ anything else while your tongue's warm?"
find one's tongue = begin talking (after being nervous/shy)
"Wendy was very shy when she first arrived although it didn't take her long to find her tongue."
give somebody the rough side of one's tongue = talk to somebody in a harsh/scolding manner
"The lad was cheeky to me so I gave him the rough side of my tongue."
give tongue to = begin talking about (enthusiastically/vigorously)
"After the chairman had read the statement, various members of the audience gave tongue to a whole series of objections."
have a tongue in one's head = be able to speak
"Usually Melvin never complains but you should have heard him today ñ at last he's got a tongue in his head."
have/with one's tongue in one's cheek = insincerely/not meant seriously
"I suggested that Andy should captain the rugby team, although I did say it with my tongue in my cheek!"
lose one's tongue = become speechless (through nervousness/shyness)
"Come on, speak up! What's the matter ñ lost your tongue?"
mother tongue = native language
"Karen speaks English without a trace of an accent ñ you'd never think her mother tongue was Estonian."
on the tip of one's tongue = not quite remembered
"I can't remember the name of the place we stayed in, although it's on the tip of my tongue."
wag one's tongue = talk indiscreetly/excessively
"I asked the milkman in for a cup of tea ñ that will make my neighbours wag their tongues!"
with one's tongue hanging out = be very thirsty
"My tongue was hanging out by the time we had climbed to the top of the hill."
See also: cat get one's tongue; civil tongue (in one's head); have a sharp tongue; hold one's peace/tongue; slip of the tongue; speak with a forked tongue.

too
See: none too.

tool
down tools = stop working
"The typists have downed tools and are refusing to work overtime unless they are paid extra for it."

tooth
See: fight tooth and nail; have a sweet tooth; long in the tooth; teeth.

top
be/get on top of = dominate/overcome
"The garden in our new house was in a mess but we're getting on top of it now."
be (the) tops = be (the) best
"Among seaside resorts, I still think Exmouth is tops."
come out on top = succeed (eventually)

"Competition was fierce at this year's flower show but my Dad's roses came out on top as usual."

from top to bottom/toe = thoroughly/ overall

"We gave the house a good clean out from top to bottom."

"The bride looked beautiful from top to toe."

take it from the top = start again at the beginning

"No, that was no good; let's take it from the top and go through the whole routine again."

on top of that = in addition to that

"For being late home you will have to stay in tonight ñ and on top of that you can tidy your bedroom."

over the top = excessive

"Her combination of a punk hairstyle and a traditional wedding gown was a bit over the top, don't you think?"

top of the pops = currently in favour

"Christine is top of the pops with Mervin since she helped him with his typing."

top somebody up = overcharge somebody

"That repair was very expensive, I think they topped me up."

top something up = completely fill something that was partly empty

"We should top up with petrol before we drive onto the ferry."

See also: at the top of one's voice; blow one's top; cap/top it all; off the top of one's head; on top of the world; (not) out of the top drawer; sleep like a log/ top; thin on top; top brass; top dog; top of the ladder; top of the tree; top the bill.

torch

See: carry a torch (for somebody).

torn

torn between (two things) = in a dilemma

"I'm torn between the red dress and the blue one, and I don't know which one to buy."

that's torn it = that has spoiled/ruined something

"That's torn it! He's called the police!"

See also: tear.

toss

it's a toss up = it is not certain

"They may be pleased or they may not ñ it's a toss up."

toss something off = make something quickly with ease (although not necessarily to a high standard), or drink something quickly

"Helen can toss off two of those paintings in a day."

"Harry tossed off the whisky in a few seconds."

toss up = spin a coin to decide something

"They tossed up to see who would start the game."

win/lose the toss = guess correctly/ incorrectly which side of a tossed coin will show

"The other team won the toss and put us in to bat."

See also: argue the toss.

touch

finishing touches = final details (which complete something)

"Mary is just putting the finishing touches to her flower arrangement."

get in touch (with) = contact/ communicate (with)

"Now that my mother has a telephone, it's much easier to get in touch with her."

keep in touch (with) = maintain contact/ communication (with)
"I'll see you again next month but in the meantime let's keep in touch."

lose touch (with) = be unable to communicate (with)
"I lost touch with my brother when he emigrated to Australia."

lose one's touch = lose the ability/skill to do something
"I used to be able to play darts quite well but I seem to have lost my touch recently."

out of touch (with) = not in communication (with), or lacking (latest) information (about)
"It was a surprise to hear from my cousin again ñ we'd been out of touch for several years."
"If you don't read the trade journals regularly it's easy to get out of touch with the latest developments."

touch and go = very uncertain
"I may have just passed the exam, but it's touch and go."

touch down = land, or score (at various football games)
"Our plane touched down half an hour early."
"One cf our rugby players touched down in the first minute of the game to score a valuable try."

touch somebody = persuade somebody to lend one money, or evoke an emotional response in somebody
"Last night my son touched me for fifty pence."
"I was really touched by the get well cards people sent me."

touch somebody on the raw = say something that angers/embarrasses somebody
"I don't know why Harry left his last job but it touched him on the raw when I mentioned voluntary redundancy."

touch something off = initiate something
"Michael's comments touched off a discussion about religion."

touch something up = make small improvements in the appearance of something
"I must touch up the chipped paint on my car."

touch upon something = mention something briefly
"He told us about his early career, although he only touched upon his service in military intelligence."

See also: easy meat/touch; common touch; Midas touch; soft touch; touch bottom; touch wood; wouldn't touch somebody/something with a bargepole.

tough

See: hard/tough as nails; hard/tough luck; hard/tough nut to crack; (tough as) old boots; tough/ugly customer.

tow

have somebody in tow = have somebody with one
"Wherever Elizabeth goes she has her mother in tow."

towel

throw in the towel = surrender
"We're never going to persuade them so we might as well throw in the towel now."

tower

See: ivory tower; pillar/tower of strength.

town

go to town = be extravagant/thorough

"You ordered a new cooker, fridge and washing machine? You really went to town!"
"I only asked him to tell me briefly how it works but he went to town and spent a quarter of an hour explaining it in the minutest detail."

on the town = enjoying oneself with food, drink, entertainment, etc.
"I spent last night on the town ñ no wonder I've got a headache this morning."

See also: ghost town; man-about-town; paint the town red; talk of the town.

traces
See: kick over the traces.

track
in one's tracks = where one is (located)
"I was so surprised it pulled me up in my tracks."

keep/lose track of something = have/not have knowledge about (the location of) something
"As a doctor, James has to keep track of the latest developments in medicine"
"I've lost track of how many boyfriends my daughter has had."

make a track/tracks for = move in the direction of
"He suddenly got up and made a track for the door."

make tracks = leave
"Come on, it's late ñ time we made tracks."

(hard) on somebody's track = following/looking for somebody
"The Fraud Squad are hard on his track and he's trying to get out of the country."

on the right/wrong track = moving in the correct/incorrect direction
"That is not exactly the correct answer, but you're on the right track."
"He was looking for my office and went to Carlisle Street instead of Carnaby Street, so he was on the wrong track altogether."

on/from the wrong side of the tracks = from a socially inferior background
"Although he came from the wrong side of the tracks his sheer ability earned him the respect of all his colleagues."

on the track of somebody/something = looking for/pursuing somebody/something
"Charles says he's on the track of a chap who would be ideal for the vacant manager's job."
"I'm on the track of a rare stamp I need to complete the set."

track record = account of one's previous achievements
"What we require is somebody with a proven track record who can take over the job immediately without having to be trained."

track somebody/something down = follow/look for somebody/something until he/she/it is found
"I'm trying to track down my old Aunt Maud."
"Paul has tracked down an early recording of Scott Joplin playing one of his rags."

See also: cover one's tracks; off the beaten track; one-track mind.

trade
trade something in = surrender something in part-exchange when buying something else
"The gas company is offering fifty pounds off a new cooker if you trade in your old one."

trade something off = exchange one thing for another/barter
"In negotiations with the trade union, the management traded off an extra fifty-five pounds a week in wages for a reduction in the length of tea breaks from twenty minute to ten minutes each."

trade on something = take (unfair) advantage of something (to gain sympathy)
"She traded on her disability to get preferential treatment wherever she went."

See also: jack of all trades; trick of the trade.

trail

hard/hot on somebody's trail = following close behind somebody
"Mary has gained the most points so far but Belinda is hard on her trail."

See also: blaze a trail; hit the road/trail.

train

in train = happening (on schedule)
"The testing of the prototype machine is complete and modifications are in train."

See also: get on/join the gravy train.

trap

tender trap = state of being in love
"As soon as he saw Julie he was caught in the tender trap."

See also: death trap; shut one's face/ mouth/trap.

traveller

See: armchair traveller.

tread

tread under foot = conquer
"The small band of resistance fighters were soon trodden under foot by the occupying forces."

See also: follow/tread in somebody's footsteps; fools rush in (where angels fear to tread); skate/tread on thin ice; tread on eggs; tread on somebody's corns; tread on somebody's heels; tread on somebody's toes; tread water.

treat

treat somebody like (a piece of) dirt = show contempt for somebody
"I don't know how Jill puts up with her husband ñ he treats her like dirt."

will do a treat = is (exactly) what is required
"That new large pan you bought will do a treat for cooking chips."

See also: Dutch treat; treat somebody like a dog.

tree

top of the tree = highest position in a career
"Hal is a business genius and had reached the top of the tree before he was twenty-five."

See also: bark up the wrong tree; family tree; money doesn't grow on trees; not be able to see the wood for the trees; out of one's mind/tree; up a gum tree.

tremble

See: in fear (and trembling).

trial

trial and error = try to do something in various ways until the correct one is found
"I lost the instruction book and so I had to find out how to use the machine by trial and error."

trial of strength = contest to determine the stronger/strongest

"The FA Challenge Cup match is a trial of strength between the winners of the FA Cup and the Football League Cup."

trial run = a test of something by doing/using it for the first time

"We gave the machine a trial run before using it on the production line."

"Let's have a trial run and see if everybody knows what to do."

triangle

See: eternal triangle.

tribute

be a tribute to = be in recognition of the worthiness of

"This award is a tribute to Walter's twenty years of dedicated service to the company."

trick

do the trick = do what is required

"I'm very nervous before boarding a plane but usually a couple of stiff brandies do the trick and calm me down."

"I need something to hold the door open; that big book should do the trick."

how's/how are tricks? = how are things going (with you)?

"Good morning, Dave, how's tricks?"

"How are tricks in the grocery trade this week?"

never miss a trick = do not fail to take advantage of an opportunity

"Harry never misses a trick when it comes to doing business."

trick cyclist = psychiatrist

"Harry's been acting very strange lately ñ I think he should go and see a trick cyclist."

trick of the trade = helpful inside/special knowledge associated with a trade

"A photographer friend told me a trick of the trade is to keep one's stock of unexposed colour film in the fridge, to stop it deteriorating in storage."

up to one's (old) tricks = displaying one's usual (deceitful/mischievous) behaviour

"Robert has been up to his old tricks again; he was courting two different girls at once until one of them found out and straightaway told the other one."

See also: bag of tricks; confidence trick; dirty trick; you can't teach an old dog new tricks.

trigger

trigger-happy = too willing to make use of weapons

"The last thing we want is a trigger-happy general at the disarmament talks."

trip

trip the light fantastic = dance

"You should have seen Auntie Joan and Uncle Harry tripping the light fantastic at the wedding reception."

See also: ego trip.

Trojan

See: work like a horse/Trojan.

trooper

See: swear like a trooper.

troops

See: that's the stuff (to give the troops).

trot

on the trot = continually moving, or consecutively

"I'm really tired this evening ñ I seem to have been on the trot all day."
"No wonder Harry is drunk, he's had six doubles whiskeys on the trot."

trot something out = easily/habitually exhibit or say something
"Just mention the war to my grandfather and he trots out his old medals."
"Sarah is very keen on athletics and can trot out the names of all the leading runners and their record times."

trouble

ask/look for trouble = be provocative (inviting a violent response)
"A teenager in a leather jacket jostled his way through the crowd, looking for trouble."

get somebody into trouble = make somebody pregnant
"Bill had only been going out with Jan for a few months before he got her into trouble."

go to the trouble of doing/take the trouble to do something = make a special effort to do something
"You shouldn't have gone to the trouble of making more coffee just for me."

no trouble! = that will be easy!
"No trouble! I'll give you a lift to the station any time."

there's trouble brewing/in store = difficulty/trouble is likely to occur
"There's trouble brewing and the crowd of demonstrators is getting very restless."

trouble one's head with = bother about
"Don't trouble your head with it now ñ you can let me have it tomorrow."

trouble–shooter = somebody brought in to solve problems
"Peter is a good trouble-shooter and he will soon find out what is wrong with the machine."

See also: fish in troubled water; pack up one's troubles; pour oil on troubled waters; teething troubles.

trousers

wears the trousers = (be a woman who) makes family decisions
"Mum wears the trousers in our house and we all have to do what she tells us."

See also: all mouth and trousers; catch somebody with his pants/trousers down.

trowel

See: lay it on thick/with a trowel.

truck

have no truck with some. ody/something = avoid association/involvement with somebody/something
"I've had no truck with Mark since he was convicted of theft."
"I want no truck with any of your dubious schemes."

true

out of true = out of alignment
"It annoys me to see a row of pictures hanging on a wall with one or two of them out of true."

See also: come true; ring true; (run) true to form; show oneself in one's true colours; too right!/true!; true blue; well and truly.

trump

turn up trumps = be efficient/kind and help somebody in difficulty
"We couldn't afford a holiday but my father came up trumps and let us have

the use of his cottage in the country for a fortnight."

See also: one's best/leading/trump card; trump somebody's ace.

trumpet

See: blow one's own trumpet.

trust

take somebody on trust = believe what somebody says without proof

"She claimed she was qualified for the job and we took her on trust."

take something on trust = accept something without checking

"Joe said that the delivery was late because his lorry broke down, and I took his reason on trust."

trust one to.Ö = as expected, one has.Ö

"Barry tried to mend the machine? Trust him to get it wrong!"

truth

arrive at the truth = find out what (really) happened

"The police interviewed several witnesses before finally arriving at the truth."

home truth = true (but unpleasant) comment addressed to the person it concerns

"It's time somebody told Don a few home truths about the way his sarcastic comments often upset people."

naked truth = absolute truth

"A witness under oath is expected to tell the naked truth."

truth will out = the true facts will (inevitably) emerge

"You didn't expect me to find out what you had done, but truth will out, you know."

See also: have a true ring to it; home truth; moment of truth; ring true; to tell the truth.

try

try it on (for size) = do something that is unlikely to be accepted, to determine whether it will be accepted

"The unions have asked for a twenty per cent pay rise for their members, but they're just trying it on for size."

try one's hand at = attempt to do something new/for the first time

"While I was there I tried my hand at skiing, and thoroughly enjoyed it."

try something (on) (for size) = try something to find out whether it fits/suits one

"I'm sure this coat will suit you, madam, why don't you try it on?"

"You said you couldn't find a good book on dahlias ñ why don't you try this one of mine for size?"

try something out = use something to find out whether it is suitable/works

"This car would be ideal for you, sir, why don't you try it out?"

"I found this light bulb in a drawer. I'll try it out in the table lamp to see if it works."

tuck

take a tuck in = economise/reduce something by omitting part of it

"You'll have to take a tuck in that estimate to bring it down to a cost I can afford."

tuck in(to) = eat heartily

"Dinner's ready ñ come on, tuck in."

"The early morning walk had made us hungry and we all tucked into our breakfast."

tuck somebody in/up = make somebody comfortable in bed (by wrapping them tightly in the bedclothes)

"Mummy, please come and tuck me in."

tucker
See: best bib and tucker.

tug:
tug at one's heartstrings = appeal to one's emotions/sympathy.
"Those old films about the child and his lost collie dog always tug at my heartstrings."

tumble
tumble to something = (suddenly) realize something
"I had gone bald and grown a beard since Tim and I last met, and it took him some time to tumble to who I was."
See also: rough and tumble.

tummy
See: butterflies in one's stomach/tummy.

tune
in tune with somebody/something = have an affinity for somebody/something
"I support the campaign because I'm in tune with its aims."
to the tune of = to the total of
"The cost of the repairs came to the tune of a hundred pounds."
See also: call the shots/tune; change one's tune.

tunnel
See: see the light at the end of the tunnel.

tuppence
not care tuppence = not care at all
"Jane is infatuated with Stephen but he doesn't care tuppence for her."

turkey
See: talk turkey.

turn
as it turned out = as things transpired
"We hadn't got enough people to make up a team but as it turned out it started to rain and the match was called off."
at every turn = at every stage
"Progress on the project is slow because the client raises problems at every turn."
do somebody a good turn = do somebody a favour
"Being made redundant actually did me a good turn because I soon found a much better job."
in turn(s) = in sequence
"Please come up in turn to collect your books."
on the turn = (of the tide) at the stage of turning, or (of milk) on the point of going sour
"We must go back to the causeway because the tide will soon be on the turn."
"This tea tastes nasty ñ I think the milk must be on the turn."
out of turn = out of order/sequence
"Bill should have laid one of his cards next ñ you've played out of turn."
take a turn for the better/worse = improve/deteriorate
"I hope the weather takes a turn for the better before the barbecue on Saturday."
"Despite the warning to do better, Jack's work hasn't improved ñ indeed it's taken a turn for the worse."
take (it in) turns = alternate
"We've had a lot of calls this morning and Janet and I have been taking (it

in) turns to answer the phone."

turn against somebody/something = change from liking somebody/ something to disliking him/her/it
"Jeremy and I used to be friends but he turned against me when he learned of my views on fox hunting."
"A former supporter of Arsenal, Vic turned against the club after it came bottom of the league."

turn of phrase = manner of saying/ writing something
"Why don't you ask Hal to help you write the application? He usually has a good turn of phrase."

turn of speed = fast rate of movement
"The lorry is very economical on fuel and yet has a good turn of speed when required."

turn on a sixpence = turn in a very tight circle
"London taxis are easy to park because they turn on a sixpence."

turn out = come to pass/happen, or prove (to be), or assemble
"It all turned out right in the end."
"As it turns out you were wrong to think that she was inefficient ñ she's the best secretary I've ever had."
"A huge crowd of people turned out to watch the fireworks."

turn somebody down = refuse an application/request from somebody
"Walter applied for the night watchman's job but we had to turn him down because he's too old."

turn somebody in = hand over a criminal/fugitive to the police
"James is so mercenary he'd turn in his own mother for the reward money."

turn somebody off = cause somebody to dislike somebody/something
"He is fairly good looking but his bad breath turns me off him."
"That bout of food poisoning has turned me off oysters for life!"

turn somebody on = arouse somebody
"I'm not turned on by modern pop music."
"That new barman at the club really turns me on."

turn something down = refuse an offer of something
"I sent Sarah an invitation to the party but she had to turn it down because she's going away for the weekend."

turn something in = stop doing something
"I've had enough of work for today; I'm going to turn it in and go home."

turn up = appear/reappear, or find
"I turned up at the address he gave me but the house was empty."
"Our cat was missing for days but eventually it turned up, looking a bit thinner than before."
"Please see if you can turn up any information on the proposed by-pass scheme."

turn up for the book(s) = unexpected occurrence
"Catching German measles at my age was quite a turn up for the books."

whatever turns you on! = whatever interests you! (although it does not interest me)
"Go fishing if you must ñ whatever turns you on!"

See also: come/turn up trumps; do a turn; not turn a hair; put/turn the clock back; serve its turn; tip/turn the scales; turn a blind eye to; turn a deaf ear; turn an honest penny/shilling; turn one's hand to; turn one's head/brain; turn one's stomach; turn on one's heel; turn on the heat; turn over a new leaf; turn the corner; turn the tables; turn to (good) account; turn to advantage; turn turtle; turn up one's nose at something; turn up one's toes; U-turn.

turtle

turn turtle = turn upside down

"The deck cargo made the ship top heavy and it turned turtle."

twice

once or twice = a few times/occasionally

"I've only been there once or twice."

See also: once bitten, twice shy; think twice.

twiddle

See: twiddle one's thumbs.

twinkle

in a/the twinkling of an eye = immediately/quickly

"I'll be with you in the twinkling of an eye."

"He finished his drink in the twinkling of an eye."

twist

round the twist = slightly mad

"You must have been round the twist to walk across the electric railway tracks."

See also: get one's knickers in a twist; twist somebody's arm; twist somebody round one's little finger.

two

put two and two together = deduce

"Belinda is always going out with Sean, and putting two and two together I think they're probably more than just good friends."

there are no two ways about it = there cannot be two opinions about the matter

"She's got to go ñ and there are no two ways about it!"

two's company (but three's a crowd) = two friends may resent the intrusion of a third person

"Susan and I were having a private conversation when Nigel insisted on joining us. I tried to hint that two's company, but he would not go away."

two–time somebody = deceive one's (sexual) partner by simultaneously associating with somebody else

"I was livid when I found out that my boyfriend Philip had been two-timing me."

See also: as alike as (two) peas in a pod; another/two string(s) to one's bow; be in two minds; for two pins; in two shakes (of a lamb's tail); kill two birds with one stone; not have two ha'pennies/pennies to rub together; one or two; one's number two; take two bites at the cherry; two a penny; two can play that game; two heads are better than one; two of a kind; two wrongs don't make a right.

tyre

See: spare tyre.

U

U

U-turn = reversal of direction/policy
"The government denied that it would make a U-turn in its economics policy."

ugly

ugly as sin = very ugly
"I was commissioned to take photographs of various cosmetics so I asked the agency for two attractive models, but the ones they sent were as ugly as sin."
See also: tough/ugly customer; ugly duckling; ugly rumour.

unaccustomed

unaccustomed as I am (to public speaking) = I am not used to (speaking in front of an audience)
"Unaccustomed as I am, it gives me great pleasure to propose a toast to the bride and groom."

uncle

(well) I'll be a monkey's uncle = I am really surprised
"Well I'll be a monkey's uncle! You got the puzzle right first time!"
Uncle Sam = (government of) the United States
"The people would have starved if Uncle Sam hadn't sent dozens of aircraft carrying tons of grain."
See also: Bob's your uncle; talk to somebody like a Dutch uncle.

under

come/fall under = be grouped with
"I know this is Basingstoke but anything to do with your telephone system comes under the Guildford exchange."
down under = Australia (and sometimes New Zealand)
"I could tell from Sheila's accent that she came from down under."
take somebody under one's wing = guide/protect somebody
"He felt out of place at the new school until one of the older pupils took him under his wing."
under the weather = unwell
"I don't think I'll go to work today because I feel under the weather."
under somebody's thumb = dominated by somebody
"Poor old Arthur has been under his wife's thumb for the whole of their married life."
under way = in progress
"After weeks of waiting, I'm glad that the project is at last under way."
See also: keep something under one's hat; take somebody under one's wing; under a cloud; under age; under consideration; under cover; under one's breath; under one's own steam; under somebody's nose; under somebody's thumb; under the counter; under the hammer; under the influence.

understand

come to an understanding = make an agreement
"The unions have finally come to an understanding with the management."
give somebody to understand = cause/lead somebody to believe
"We were given to understand that this train stops at Watford."
on/with the understanding that = on (the agreed) condition that
"You can go to the disco on the understanding that you get home by eleven o'clock."

unknown

into the unknown = into an area about which nothing is known

"Yuri Gagarin, the first Soviet cosmonaut, was travelling into the unknown."

See also: unknown quantity.

unsound

of unsound mind = mad

"He must be of unsound mind to pay so much for a house that is practically falling down."

unstuck

come unstuck = fail

"Arnold's scheme to breed rabbits for both fur and meat has come unstuck."

up

be one up on = have an advantage

"We were persuaded to enter the pub's pools tournament and at least I'm one up one Mary ñ she's never played before and I have."

be/come up against = have to contend with

"When I entered the competition I didn't know I'd be up against the club champion."

"Ever since we started this job we have come up against one problem after another."

come up with = give/offer

"We still hadn't quite enough money and then David came up with ten pounds."

it's all up with = there is no hope for

"Our cat has a terminal disease and I'm afraid it's all up with him."

on the up-and-up = improving

"Since his operation, father has been on the up-and-up."

up against it = be in difficulties

"If we run short of time we'll be really up against it."

up a gum tree = in (serious) difficulties

"I ran out of petrol at two o'clock in the morning and was really up a gum tree."

up-and-coming = promising

"The leading part had been given to a young up-and-coming actress and she should play it very well."

up and doing = active/busy

"I like to be up and doing by seven o'clock in the summer."

up and down = first in one direction and then in the opposite one

"I'm getting tired of travelling up and down to town to work."

ups and downs = times of good and bad fortune/health

"The company has its ups and downs but on the whole it is doing very well."

"My mother keeps remarkably well for her age, although naturally she has her ups and downs."

up to a point = to a certain extent

"I don't mind football up to a point but the game I like best is cricket."

up to somebody = the duty/responsibility of

"You must please yourself, it's not up to me to tell you what to do."

up to something = able to do something, or involved in something dishonest/ mischievous, or of the quality/ standard of

"You'll have to go fishing on your own because I don't feel quite up to it today."

"Those children are very quiet ñ I bet they're up to something."

"This cake is very good, but it's not up to the one you made last week."

up with somebody = at the same level as/ equal to somebody, or be troubling somebody

"If you keep practising like that you'll

"There must be something up with the baby, she shouldn't keep crying for no apparent reason."

up with somebody/something! = success to somebody/something!

"Up with temperance! Down with drink!"

"Up with Thatcher! Vote Tory! "

up with you = get up/get out of bed

"Come on, up with you, it's time to get ready for school."

well up on something = well informed/ knowledgeable about something

"Why don't you ask Gill? She's well up on dog breeding."

what's up with him/her? = what is troubling him/her?

"Lisa is crying. What's up with her?"

See also: be one up on somebody; do up; end up; in something up to one's neck; not up to much; one's number comes up; one's number is up; up in arms; up the creek; up the pole; up the spout; up the wall; up to date; up to no good; up to one's elbows; up to the hilt; up to the mark; up to the minute.

upper

on one's uppers = with very little/no money

"I'll be on my uppers if I don't find a job soon."

See also: gain/have the upper hand; keep a stiff upper lip; upper crust.

upright

See: bolt upright.

upside

turn something upside down = confuse/ jumble something

"You've turned that cupboard upside down looking for your tennis racket ñ now tidy it up again!"

uptake

quick/slow on the uptake = quick-witted/ slow-witted

"You only have to tell Tina once, she's very quick on the uptake."

"Robert is so slow on the uptake you have to tell him everything ten times before he gets it right."

use

come in useful = be of use in the future

"Keep that piece of wood, it may come in useful."

get used to = become accustomed to

"I haven't tried draught Guinness before but I think I could very soon get used to it."

have no use for somebody/something = dislike/hate somebody

"Ian is idle and lazy and I have absolutely no use for him."

"Would you like to have this lighter? I have no use for it now that I've given up smoking."

it's no use = it is hopeless/impossible, it is no good

"It's no use, we'll never find our way out of this maze."

"It's no use asking, he'll never agree."

make oneself useful = give help

"You can make yourself useful by taking the dishes to the kitchen."

make (best/good) use of something = use something to (best/good) advantage

"I suggest that investing in National Savings Certificates will make best use of your money."

no use to man or beast = useless

"This new tin-opener is no use to man or beast."

V

vacuum

create/leave a vacuum = leave a gap
"When Silvia leaves the company it will create a vacuum that will be very difficult to fill."

vain

(all) in vain = ineffectively/unsuccessfully
"Every attempt to save the drowning dog was in vain."
See also: take somebody's name in vain.

valour

See: discretion is the better part of valour.

value

place/put/set a (high) value on = estimate the (high) worth of
"He puts a high value on integrity."
See also: face value.

van

in the van = at the front
"The cooks will march in the van and set up a field kitchen as soon as we arrive."

vanish

vanish into the blue/thin air = disappear completely
"There were two pens on my desk yesterday but now they have both vanished into thin air."

variety

variety is the spice of life = changes in one's activities/situation make life interesting
"I know that Graham is going out with three different girls, but they say that variety is the spice of life!"

veil

See: draw a veil over.

velvet

See: iron hand/fist in a velvet glove.

vengeance

with a vengeance = excessively/thoroughly/violently
"Since Henry's wife left him he's been drinking with a vengeance."
"Bill has never liked the scheme and when they asked for his opinion he told them with a vengeance."

vent

give vent to = freely express
"She finally broke down and cried and gave vent to her emotions."
See also: vent one's spleen.

venture

See: nothing ventured, nothing gained.

verdict

See: open verdict

verge

verge on = be close to/nearly
"Her dress was a very dark blue verging on black."

verse

See: quote chapter and verse.

very

all very well = acceptable/all right
"That may be all very well for you, but what am I going to do?"
the very thing = just what is required

"That piece of wood is the very thing I need to make a shelf in my garage."

vested

vested interest = something that gives one a personal/selfish advantage
"Allen is the chief objector to the proposed by-pass, but he has a vested interest because it would take most of the trade from his garage."

vex

See: vexed question.

vicious

See: vicious circle.

victory

Pyrrhic victory = success at such a cost it is rendered worthless
"He proved his point by exposing malpractices by the directors, but it was a Pyrrhic victory because they made him redundant immediately afterwards."
See also: landslide victory.

view

come into view = in sight/visible
"As we turned the corner the village green came into view."
have in view = be planning/thinking about
"What we have in view is redecorating the lounge and then buying a new carpet."
in the long view = considering well in advance
"The police are coping with the problem at the moment, but in the long view the government will be forced to bring in new legislation."
in full view = completely in sight
"She removed her blouse in full view of everybody."
in one's view = in one's opinion
"You may think it was amusing, but in my view it was in very poor taste."
in view of = because of/considering
"In view of your age the court has decided to be lenient and impose a fine rather than imprisonment."
take a long view = consider well in advance
"We could patch it up, but it is better to take a long view and make a proper repair."
with a view to = with the intention of
"I'm having the outside of my house painted with a view to selling it."
See also: birds eye view; point of view; take a dim view of; view with a beady eye.

villain

the villain of the piece = somebody who acts/behaves badly
"They have charged two men with stealing metal from the stores but the real villain of the piece is the person they sold it to."

vine

clinging vine = somebody who monopolizes one's attention/time
"She's a very nice girl most of the time but I do wish she wasn't such a clinging vine."

violet

shrinking violet = somebody who is shy
"She was quite a shrinking violet until she left home and went to university."

virtue

by virtue of (the fact that) = because of
"We won't reprimand you this time by virtue of the fact that you've admitted your mistake."

vital

See: vital statistics.

voice

at the top of one's voice = as loud as one can
"I called at the top of my voice but she still didn't hear me."

give voice to = express (publicly)
"Mary was silent during the early part of the discussion but then finally gave voice to her opinions about the subject."

have a voice in = be in a position to state one's opinion
"I can attend the meetings as an observer but I have no voice in their discussions."

in good voice = singing/speaking well
"The tenor was in good voice and sang the solo beautifully."

lose one's voice = be unable to speak
"My wife had laryngitis and lost her voice for several days."

lower/raise one's voice = speak quieter/louder
"Please lower your voice when you go into the church."
"Don't you raise your voice to me, young lady!"

voice crying in the wilderness = (somebody with a) minority point of view
"I tried to persuade the demonstrators not to cross the barriers but I was just a voice crying in the wilderness."

wee/still small voice = conscience/reasonableness
"I was going to take some bricks from the building site but a wee small voice stopped me from doing it."

with one voice = in total agreement/unanimously
"With one voice the committee rejected the proposal."

void

See: null and void.

volume

See: speak volumes.

vote

put to the vote = obtain a decision by voting
"Shall we all go to Paul's house or John's? Let's put it to the vote."

vote of confidence = vote that determines whether a ruling body still represents the views of the majority
"The opposition demanded a vote of confidence over the government's defence proposals."

vote of thanks = request for appreciative applause/thanks
"At the end of the various speeches, I want you to propose a vote of thanks to the bride's parents."

See also: vote with one's feet.

W

wade

wade into somebody/something = unhesitatingly tackle somebody/something
"The boy waded in with both fists."
wade through = move laboriously through
"I've got to wade through all these reports before I can go home."

wag

See: tail wagging the dogÖ

wagon

on the wagon = not drinking alcohol (although formerly doing so)
"No thanks, I won't have a beer ñ I'm on the wagon."
See also: climb/jump on (board) the bandwagon.

wait

everything comes to he/him who waits = somebody who is patient will eventually get what he/she wants
"I hooked the fish at ten o'clock and it took me more than two hours to land it ñ but everything comes to he who waits."
wait and see = await a decision/the outcome
"I know you want to go to the park this afternoon but you'll just have to wait and see."
wait a minute/moment = I wish to say something, or please wait a short time, or exclamation of surprise
"Wait a minute ñ I don't think that's true."
"Wait a minute and I'll tell him you're here."
"Wait a moment! Aren 't you the man who called yesterday?"
waiting in the wings = waiting for an opportunity
"The manager is soon to retire and Margaret is waiting in the wings to take over the job."
wait up = not go to bed (until somebody arrives)
"You go to bed and I'll wait up for your father."
(just) you wait = a threat (of discipline/punishment)
"Just you wait! I'll tell my Dad of you!"
See also: lady in waiting; lie in wait; play a waiting game; wait on somebody hand and foot.

wake

in the wake of = following after/behind
"The children scampered along in the wake of their parents."
"There were a lot of fallen trees in the wake of the storm."
See also: enough to wake the dead.

walk

walk all over somebody = be totally inconsiderate of somebody's dignity/feelings, or convincingly defeat somebody
"Don't let Tony walk all over you like that, why don't you assert yourself more?"
"I played my son at snooker and he walked all over me."
walk away with/walk it = win convincingly/easily
"Jane beat everybody in the competition and walked away with first prize, as usual."
"If Jane has entered the competition, she should walk it."

walk off with = steal
"Somebody has walked off with my raincoat."
walk on air = be extremely carefree/happy
"Malcolm has been walking on air since he was offered that job he has been trying so hard for."
walk tall = feel proud and confident
"You can walk tall now that you've qualified and gained your first professional appointment."
walk the streets = earn a living as a prostitute
"She was penniless and in desperation had to walk the streets."
walk through one's part = do what one has to do in an indifferent/disinterested way
"I'm bored with my job and I just walk through my part these days."
walk out on = abandon
"After nearly ten years Jill's boyfriend has walked out on her."
walk out with = have as a boyfriend/girlfriend
"I see your Susan is walking out with that young man from the grocer's."
See also: cock of the rock/walk; walk off one's feet; walk of life.

wall
drive/send somebody up the wall = make somebody very annoyed/frustrated
"The constant squeaking of that machine is driving me up the wall."
go to the wall = become bankrupt
"He has debts of several thousand pounds and his business has gone to the wall."
walls have ears = one might be overheard
"No, don't tell me here ñ remember, walls have ears."
(see the) writing on the wall = indication (that something bad may happen)
"Bill saw the writing on the wall and resigned his job before he was dismissed."
See also: back to the wall; bang/knock one's head against a brick wall; fly on the wall.

wand
wave one's magic wand = achieve something difficult as if by magic
"I had been arguing with their accounts department for weeks until I wrote to the financial director, who waved his magic wand and got the matter resolved in an hour."

want
be found wanting = be discovered lacking
"Trevor was given a chance to play in goal in the first team but long before the end of the game he was found wanting."
for want of = because of an absence/lack of
"The rain came in for want of a tile on the roof."
somebody (just) didn't want to know = somebody was not interested
"None of the workers signed the petition ñ they didn't want to know."
want for = need/require
"We didn't want for apples after this year's bumper crop."
you want to.Ö = you should.Ö
"You want to see my roses this year ñ they're splendid."
"You want to be careful with that knife."

war
be in the wars = be (slightly) injured

"After Tina fell off her bike she looked as though she'd really been in the wars."

carry the war into the enemy's camp = counter-attack an opponent in order to pursue one's aims/argument
"I told him it didn't matter what I said to my wife, and carried the war into the enemy's camp by demanding why he thought he could speak to her in the way that he did."

on the warpath = (angrily) looking for trouble
"Barry is on the warpath looking for the person who let down the tyres on his bicycle."

war of nerves = conflict involving threats etc. but no actual fighting
"I'm involved in a war of nerves with the Inland Revenue about how much tax I owe them."

See also: all's fair in love and war; declare war.

warm

warm as toast = comfortably warm
"We curled up on the sofa in front of the fire and were as warm as toast."

See also: warm the cockles of one's heart.

warrant

See: sign somebody's death warrant.

wart

warts and all = including all blemishes/faults
"We decided to buy an old country cottage, warts and all."

wash

(all) come out in the wash = eventually have a satisfactory outcome
"Don't worry about a few mistakes, it'll all come out in the wash."

get lost in the wash = unaccountably disappear (while among other things)
"The accounts are only in error by two pence. Don't worry, that will get lost in the wash."

it/that won't wash = it/that is an unconvincing reason
"The excuse that you overslept because your alarm clock did not go off just won't wash ñ you said that yesterday."

take in somebody else's washing = help somebody by doing part of his/her work
"We prefer to fulfil our own projects, although we do take in other people's washing and do just part of a job."

washed out = very pale, or abandoned (because of rain)
"Have you been ill? You look all washed out."
"Because of heavy overnight rain, racing was washed out for the day."

(all) washed-out/-up = failed/finished
"Since that incident over the petty cash, Ben is all washed up with this company."

See also: wash one's dirty linen in public; wash one's hands of.

waste

go/run to waste = be wasted
"Eat some more cake, it's a pity to let it go to waste."

waste not, want not = do not waste anything and a need will not occur
"Please write on both sides of the paper ñ waste not, want not."

See also: lay waste; waste one's breath.

watch

be on the watch for = be observant for/look out for

"I'm on the watch for a second-hand typewriter, have you seen one for sale recently?"

watch it/out = be careful

"Watch it, there's some broken glass on the floor."

"You'll be in trouble if you don't watch out."

watch one's step = take care

"You have to watch your step when you're talking to Colin when he's had a lot to drink."

watch over = care for/guard

"My mother came to live with us so that we could watch over her in her old age."

watch somebody like a hawk = observe somebody very closely

"Dennis is a very unreliable worker and needs watching like a hawk."

See also: a watched pot never boils.

water

make water = urinate

"The doctor asked me to make water to provide a specimen for analysis."

muddy the waters = (deliberately) confuse the issue

"The directors are probably going to recommend that we accept the take-over bid, but we can muddy the waters by asking detailed questions about the company accounts."

tread water = remain upright and afloat (by moving one's feet in the water), or bide time/wait

"The crew of the capsized yacht had to tread water until the rescuers arrived."

"I'm short of money and just about treading water until pay day."

turn on the waterworks = cry profusely (and perhaps deliberately)

"When my daughter wants something from her father she has only to turn on the waterworks and he gives it her."

water something down = dilute something

"The original proposal was very watered down in the version finally accepted by the directors."

water under the bridge = past event (and no longer important)

"There's no need to refer to what happened last year, it's all water under the bridge now."

See also: blood is thicker than water; cast one's bread on/upon the waters; come hell or high water; dull as ditchwater; go through fire and water; hold water; in deep water; in hot; water; keep one's head above water; like a fish out of water; like water off a duck's back; make one's mouth water; milk and water; of the first magnitude/order/water; pass water; pour oil on troubled water; pour/throw cold water onto something; spend money like water; take to something like a duck to water; throw out the baby with the bath water.

Waterloo

See: meet one's match/Waterloo.

wave

make waves = cause difficulties/trouble

"I would like to change several things about my new job but it's too early yet to make waves."

on the same wavelength (as) = sharing an interest/opinion etc. (with)

"Keith and I are on the same wavelength when we're talking about sailing."

wave aside = dismiss (as irrelevant/unimportant)

"He waved aside all my protests."

wave down = signal with the hand in order to stop a vehicle
"See if you can wave down a taxi."
See also: on the crest of a wave; wave one's magic wand.

way

by the way = incidentally
"By the way, how did you get home last night?"
by way of = via, or as/for
"We returned home by way of Paris."
"He bought me a beer by way of payment for giving him a lift home."
get into/out of the way of doing something = adopt/break a routine
"The machine looks a bit complicated but you'll soon get into the way of using it."
give way (to) = let past, or collapse/subside, or be followed by, or express/release one's emotions, or concede/submit
"Will vehicles going down the hill please give way to any coming up."
"The ladder gave way and he fell to the ground."
"The Socialist government gave way to a Conservative one."
"After the shock wore off she gave way and cried for an hour."
"We refuse to give way on a matter of principle."
go a long way to(wards) = be very helpful in
"This bonus will go a long way towards paying off my overdraft."
go one's own way = act independently
"They keep asking me to join their social club but I much prefer to go my own way."
go out of one's way = take trouble to
"Frank went out of his way to help me with research for my project."
go the way of all flesh = cease to exist/die
"My old car has finally gone the way of all flesh ñ I had to scrap it last week."
have a way with one = have an attractive/friendly personality
"Tony has a way with him and should make a good salesman."
have a way with somebody/something = be good at dealing with/using
"My grandmother has a way with young Sam ñ he never cries when she's looking after him."
"Robin is an excellent journalist, he really has a way with words."
have/get (everything) one's own way = do what(ever) one wants
"You'll spoil that child ñ he always gets his own way."
have it both ways = have the advantage of two mutually exclusive options
"You've ended up with neither wife or girlfriend, but you would try to have it both ways."
in a way = in one respect
"The holiday was all right in a way, but the food at the hotel was awful."
in/out of somebody's way = obstructing/not obstructing somebody, or within/out of reach
"Whenever he comes to my workshop he gets in my way."
"You should keep all medicines out of the children's way."
lead the way = go first
"I'll lead the way and the rest of you can follow."
lose one's way = become lost
"We lost our way in the dark."
make one's way = go, or succeed
"It's after midnight and time for me to make my way home."
"Pamela is determined to make her way in the hairdressing business."

make way for = move aside (and leave room) for
"Make way for the Queen!"
"Jack has decided to retire and make way for a younger man."

not out of the way = acceptable
"I thought that a price of twenty pounds was not out of the way."

one way and another = considering everything
"One way and another it was a very successful meeting."

on the way = coming/expected, or on route
"I hear that Sarah has another baby on the way."
"Let's make an early start and have breakfast on the way."

on the way out = becoming unfashionable/obsolescent
"With many young people, rock ën roll music is on the way out."

(be) on your way = leave/move away
"Be on your way, and don't let me see you round here again."

(well) on the way to = nearly
"Sir Peter has been so successful inthis new business that he's well on the way now to being a multimillionaire for the second time."

out-of-the-way = little-known/remote
"I know of an out-of-the-way restaurant we could go to."

put in the way of = help to obtain
"Charlie often puts me in the way of new business."

see one's way (clear) to = be able willing to
"Do you think you could see your way to letting me borrow your bicycle for the afternoon?"

step this way = please follow me
"Step this way, sir, and I'll show you to your room."

that's the way it goes = that is the (inevitable) situation
"I told Peter I would go to his party but the boss says I have to work that evening ñ still, that's the way it goes."

there are no two ways about it = it is indisputable
"That music was rubbish, and there are no two ways about it."

way out = very fashionable/up-to-date, or not close to requirement
"Have you seen Sharon's hair-do recently? It's way out!"
"Those measurements you gave me must have been way out, this skirt will never fit."

See also: couldn't punch his way out of a paper bag; elbow one's way; fall by the wayside; in a bad way; in a big way; in the family way; look the other way; meet somebody half way; mend one's ways; no way; out of harm's way; parting of the ways; pave the way for something; pay one's way; that's the way the cookie crumbles thread one's way; under way.

weak

have a weakness for = have an (irresistible) fondness for
"My daughter has a weakness for tall boys with dark hair."

weak as a kitten = very weak
"After a week in bed with flu I felt as weak as a kitten."

weak-kneed = easily frightened/ intimidated
"He's just a weak-kneed coward."

See also: in a weak moment; soft/weak in the head.

wear

wear and tear = gradual deterioration through use

"The stair carpet gets a lot of wear and tear and will soon need replacing."
wear down = gradually reduce
"His resistance was worn down by constant nagging from his wife."
wear off = diminish/fade
"We had better put him to bed until the effects of the whisky wears off."
See also: if the cap fits, wear it; wear one's heart on one's sleeve; wear the trousers; worse for wear.

weather
lovely weather we're having = we are having very bad weather (meant ironically)
"Lovely weather we're having this week ñ it hasn't stopped raining for three days!"
See also: dirty weather; fair-weather friend; keep a weather eye open; lovely weather for ducks; make heavy weather; under the weather; weather the storm.

weave
get weaving = begin moving/working
"Get weaving or you won't finish the job today."

wedding
See: shotgun wedding.

wedge
See: thin end of the wedge.

weed
weed something out = remove something that is unwanted (from among others)
"We must weed out the traitors in our midst!"
widow's weeds = (black) mourning traditionally worn by a widow
"The street was empty apart from two women going to early mass in their widows' weeds."

week
See: any day of the week; dirty weekend; knock somebody into the middle of next week.

weep
See: cry/weep buckets.

weigh
weigh (half) a ton = be very heavy
"What have you got in this suitcase? It weighs a ton!"
weigh in = join in enthusiastically/vigorously
"We were all arguing and even Stephen weighed in with his comments."
weigh something up = consider/evaluate something
"I think we should weigh up the situation carefully before committing ourselves."

weight
See: carry weight; pull one's weight; throw one's weight about; worth one's weight in gold.

weird
weird and wonderful = strange but clever
"My neighbour has this weird and wonderful machine that can peel potatoes, dice vegetables, make pastry and grind coffee."

welcome
be welcome to = be (willingly) allowed to
"You are welcome to borrow my computer whenever you want to."

"Did you say you are going to Paris? You're welcome to it!"

outstay one's welcome = remain too long
"I think it is time Brian went home; doesn't he realize he's outstaying his welcome?"

(as) welcome as the flowers in May = very welcome
"We called on my parents-in-law completely unannounced and they made us as welcome as the flowers in May."

you're welcome = I need no thanks/I was pleased to do it
"That's all right, you're welcome."

well

be as well = be advisable/prudent
"It would be as well to order an extra pint of milk when your mother comes to stay."

be well out of = be fortunate not to be involved in/with
"There was a fight after we left the pub last night so we were well out of it."

do well out of = profit by
"He sold his house for twice what he paid for it so he did well out of the deal."

(all) well and good = acceptable
"Finding the carpet you want is all well and good, but how are we going to pay for it?"

well and truly = thoroughly
"I was well and truly ashamed when I realized what I had done."

well I never did = exclamation of surprise
"Tracy has finally married him? Well I never did!"

well off = in a fortunate situation, or wealthy
"Maria is a wonderful person, and yet Glen treats her very badly ñ he just doesn't seem to know when he's well off."
"Jack has just bought another new car, he must be very well off."

well out of = lucky not to be concerned with
"There has been a lot of trouble in Iran since you returned from there ñ you're well out of it."

well up in/on something = well informed about something
"Why don't you ask Roy? He's well up on Japanese art."

See also: all very well; just as well; well-heeled.

west

go west = cease to be of use/exist
"My old vacuum cleaner has gone west at last and I'll have to buy a new one."

wet

wet one's whistle = have an (alcoholic) drink
"Dad wants to stop at the next pub and wet his whistle."

See also: talk wet; wet behind the ears; wet blanket; wet the baby's head.

whale

have a whale of a time = enjoy oneself
"The children had a whale of a time playing in the sand pit."

what

and what have you/and what not = and so on
"The table was piled with sandwiches, jellies, cakes, and what have you."

give somebody what for = punish/scold somebody
"Our teacher found Tim smoking in

"the toilets and really gave him what for."

have (got) what it takes = have the necessary abilities/qualities
"Greta has got what it takes to become a great actress."

I know what = I have an idea/suggestion
"I know what, why don't we paint it bright green?"

know what's what = be experienced/ prudent
"When you talk to David about motorbikes you can tell he knows what's what."
"You'll leave here at once, if you know what's what."

or what = or what the cause/reason is
"These plants keep dying, and I don't know whether it's lack of warmth, lack of water, or what."

what about? = would you like? or what do you think about?
"What about a game of darts?"
"What about that gorgeous blonde over there?"

(well) what do you know! = exclamation of surprise
"What do you know! It's stopped raining at last."

what in the world.Ö? = (emphatically) why?
"What in the world made you buy shoes that colour?"

what of it? = what concern is it of yours?
"What of it? I'll buy purple shoes if I want."

what's all this?/what's up? = what is happening
"What's all this? Has nobody made the tea yet?"
"What's up? Why is everyone shouting?"

what's-his-name = somebody whose
"I saw you with old what's-his-name in the pub last night."

what's it to you? = what is your interest in it?
"So I'm going out with Mandy ñ what's it to you?"

what's yours? = what would you like to drink?
"I'm going to have a brandy. What's yours?"

what with = because of/owing to
"What with the dry weather and a plague of greenfly, my roses are very disappointing this year."

See also: and what's more; for what it's worth; so what?; what did I tell you?; what on earth?; what price.Ö?; what's cooking?; what's eating you?; what's the odds?

wheel

behind the wheel = in control
"The company will have no problems while this chairman is behind the wheel."

set the wheels in motion = make a start to a (usually slow) procedure/process
"It will take ages for the council to grant planning permission for our house extension so I'd better set the wheels in motion now."

take the wheel = take control
"My father is thinking of retiring from the family business and letting somebody else take the wheel."

wheeling and dealing = doing business in a clever but often underhand way
"Karl only keeps his business going by wheeling and dealing with the East Europeans."

wheels within wheels = complicated set-up in which small parts affect the other parts around them

council's various committees and subcommittees is almost impossible because there are wheels within wheels."

See also: oil the wheels; put a spoke in (somebody's wheel); put one's shoulder to the wheel.

when

say when = please tell me when I have poured you enough drink

"How much whisky do you want? Say when."

where

where it's at = place of most excitement/interest

"I don't go to the pub any more, I go to the disco ñ that's where it's at."

whet

whet somebody's appetite = stimulate somebody's eagerness/interest

"I showed the sales director a preview of the proposal to whet his appetite for the main advertising campaign."

while

worth somebody's while = worth somebody making the effort/spending the time

"It's very late and not worth your while going home now. Why don't you stay the night with us?"

"If you would help me to carry these boxes into the house I'll make it worth your while."

See also: once in a while; while away the time; while the going is good.

whip

have the whip hand over somebody = have the advantage/control over somebody

"Even when she gives me a twenty-point start, Gill always seems to have the whip hand over me when we play Scrabble."

whipping boy = somebody (likely to be) punished/reprimanded for somebody else's errors

"I have to collect everybody's work and take it to the manager while he goes through it, but he then makes me a whipping boy for any mistakes."

See also: crack the whip; fair crack of the whip.

whirl

give something a whirl = try something

"I've never eaten squid before, but I'll give it a whirl."

"The car looks fine. Do you mind if I give it a whirl before I decide whether to buy it?"

whisker

by a whisker = by a very narrow margin

"The car came round the corner and missed me by a whisker."

See also: cat's pyjamas/whiskers.

whisper

See: stage whisper.

whistle

whistle for something = ask for something but with no prospect of getting it

"If those children want their ball back out of our garden they can whistle for it!"

See also: blow the gaff/whistle on somebody; clean as a whistle; wet one's whistle; whistle in the dark.

whit

not a whit = not at all

"The judge listened to the defence argument but said he was not a whit convinced."

white

give somebody a whitewash = beat an opponent (at a game) before he/she has scored at all

"I played Victor at darts and it was a whitewash ñ he beat me three games to nil."

white as a sheet = very white

"What frightened you? You 've gone as white as a sheet."

See also: bleed (somebody) white; in black and white; hoist/show/wave the white flag; show the white feather; swear black is white; white-collar worker; whited sepulchre; white elephant; (great) white hope; white lie; white man; white man's burden.

whiz

whiz kid = somebody who is intelligent/keen and progresses rapidly in his/her job

"David is quite a whiz kid; he went from assistant salesman to sales manager in just over two years."

whole

on the whole = considering everything

"There were one or two unsatisfactory moments, but on the whole our holiday was very enjoyable."

See also: go the whole hog; the whole bang shoot.

whoop

whoop it up = have a boisterous/enjoyable time

"The rugby team likes to whoop it up after a match, especially if they win."

why

whys and wherefores = explanation/(all) the details

"Tell me the result ñ never mind the whys and wherefores."

wick

get on somebody's wick = greatly annoy somebody

"My neighbour's dog keeps barking and it's really getting on my wick."

wicket

See: sticky wicket.

wide

See: far and near/wide; give a wide berth (to); off/wide of the mark.

widow

See: grass widow; widow's weeds.

wife

See: old wives' tales.

wild

be wild about = be very enthusiastic about, or be angry about

"I'm wild about their new record."

"I'm wild about losing my gold fountain pen."

See also: out in the wilds; run wild; sow one's wild oats; spread like wild fire; wild goose chase; wild guess; wild horses wouldn't.

wilderness

See: voice crying in the wilderness.

will

at will = when one wishes

"I keep most of money in a current bank account so that I can draw some out at will."

"Load your rifles and fire at will."

with a will = with determination and energy

"The waiter brought the food and we started eating it with a will."

with the best will in the world = no matter how much one tries/wants

"I haven't got any more so I couldn't give you any, even with the best will in the world."

See also: willing horse.

willies

give one the willies = make one feel frightened/uncomfortable

"He looks quite normal but there's something about him that gives me the willies."

win

win somebody over = persuade somebody (to give help/support)

"Your father doesn't approve of motorbikes so if you want to buy one you'll have to win him over first."

win through = persevere and succeed

"It's going to be hard work but we'll win through in the end."

you (just) can't win = it seems one always fails

"Every time I block a hole in the fence to keep the dog in he gets out somewhere else ñ I just can't win."

See also: carry/win the day; win by default; win hands down; winning streak; win one's spurs; win/lose the toss.

wind

get/have the wind up = become anxious/ frightened

"My wife gets the wind up whenever she has to go to the dentist."

get wind of something = learn indirectly about something

"Mike got wind of our forthcoming engagement and laid on a surprise party for us."

in the teeth of the wind = with the wind against one/in one's face

"The sailing boat could make little progress in the teeth of the wind."

in the wind = being planned (secretly)

"I hear that some drastic changes are in the wind."

like the wind = very quickly

"The horse ran like the wind along the top of the ridge."

put the wind up somebody = make somebody anxious/frightened

"Two men blocking the path put the wind up her."

see how/which way the wind blows = postpone a decision until one has more information

"I'd like to see which way the wind blows before deciding whether to accept their offer."

take the wind out of somebody's sails = take away somebody's advantage/ confidence

"James was going to tell us all about his trip to Hong Kong but we took the wind out of his sails by telling him we had been there a few months ago."

tilt at windmills = struggle against imaginary/trivial opposition

"Old Fred still wants people to inform on fifth columnists in our midst, but he's only tilting at windmills."

wind somebody up = deliberately make somebody agitated/anxious

"Don't worry about what Colin says, he's only trying to wind you up."

wind something up = bring something to a conclusion

"We didn't wind up the party until two o'clock in the morning."

See also: broken-winded (horse); free as the air/wind/a bird; get one's second wind; it's an ill wind; sail close to the wind; sound in wind and limb; straw in the wind; three sheets to the wind; throw caution to the winds.

window

window dressing = presenting something in the best possible way by revealing only its good features

"They have painted the living room and tidied the garden in order to sell the house, but it's really only window dressing because the roof needs attention and the electric wiring is still unsafe."

window shopping = looking at goods in shop windows with no intention of buying

"We walked along Oxford Street but we were only window shopping."

wine

wine and dine somebody = treat somebody to an expensive meal

"One of the directors has offered to wine and dine me so he is probably looking for a favour or trying to sell me something."

wing

clip somebody's wings = reduce somebody's influence/power

"Paul has gone back to live with his parents and he has to be home each night by eleven o'clock ñ that will really clip his wings!"

spread one's wings = begin to act independently

"My daughter wants to spread her wings and find a flat of her own."

take somebody under one's wing = guide/protect somebody

"He felt out of place at the new school until one of the older pupils took him under his wing."

See also: waiting in the wings.

wink

not have/sleep a wink = have no sleep at all

"I was worried about you and didn't sleep a wink all night."

tip somebody the wink = give somebody (secret) advantageous information

"I'm looking for a cheap, reliable car so tip me the wink if you hear of one."

See also: a nod is as good as a wink to a blind horse; forty winks.

wipe

wipe something out = cancel/destroy something

"The money I won on the football pools has wiped out all my debts."

"All four aircraft were wiped out by missiles fired from the ground."

wipe the grin/smile off somebody's face = reduce somebody's confidence/pride

"Peter thought he was the club's best tennis player but my daughter beat him in straight sets ñ that soon wiped the grin off his face!"

See also: sweep/wipe the floor with somebody; wipe off the face of the earth.

wire

get/have one's wires crossed = misunderstand (each other)

"I think we must have got our wires crossed ñ I was talking about the daughter, not the mother."

See also: live wire.

wise

be wise to somebody/something = know about (the implications of) somebody/something

"Brenda wants me to help her decorate her living room, but I'm wise to her ñ she'll want me to paint the whole house!"

put somebody wise = inform somebody

"Arnold can be an difficult person to deal with so I thought I had better put you wise about his strange ideas before you go to see him."

See also: be wise after the event; none the wiser; wise guy.

wish

wishful thinking = hoping for what is very probably unattainable

"My ambition is to enter parliament as an independent MP, but it's only wishful thinking."

See also: wish somebody joy.

wit

have/keep one's wits about one = be alert/careful

"If you're going to hitch-hike through Turkey, you had better keep your wits about you."

to wit = that is to say (as follows)

"I need three tools ñ to wit: a hammer, screwdriver and bradawl."

See also: at one's wits end; live by one's wits; scare somebody out of his/her wits.

witch

witch hunt = persecution of somebody whose beliefs/opinions are unaccepted by the majority

"He became the subject of a witch hunt because of his outspoken views on homosexuality."

with

be with somebody = support somebody, or understand somebody

"I agree, I'm certainly with you on that point."

"You go straight over at the crossroads and then turn left at the traffic lights ñ are you with me so far?"

with it = aware of modern trends/fashion

"Mum, just because you're forty there's no excuse not to be with it."

witness

eye witness = somebody who is present at and sees an incident

"None of the eye witnesses could remember the colour of the car used in the bank robbery."

material witness = witness (in a court of law) whose evidence is crucial to the case

"The prosecution's case collapsed when a material witness failed to appear in court."

without

See: be without/have no rhyme or reason; without so much as.

woe

woe betide one = one will be sorry

"We're leaving at ten o'clock, and woe betide you if you're late!"

woe is me = I am (very) unhappy

"Woe is me! Everyone else has got the day off and I've got to go to work!"

wolf

throw somebody to the wolves = allow somebody to take the blame, or deliberately place somebody in danger/difficulty

"Harry is flattered to have been given the manager's job, but if he makes one mistake they'll throw him to the wolves."

See: cry wolf; keep the wolf from the door; lone wolf; wolf in sheep's clothing.

woman

make an honest woman (out) of = marry

"John has been living with Janet for over ten years and now he's decided to make an honest woman of her."

scarlet woman = adulteress/prostitute

"Because Wendy has so many men friends, she has gained the reputation of being a scarlet woman."

See also: my good man/woman.

wonder

I shouldn't wonder = I would not be surprised

"I shouldn't wonder if it rains this afternoon, the clouds look very black."

it's a wonder = it is surprising

"The way Kevin treats that dog, it's a wonder he hasn't been bitten."

I wonder if you'd mind (doing something) = please would you (do something)

"I wonder if you'd mind waiting a few minutes."

no wonder = I'm not surprised

"No wonder you can't cut the wood, that chisel you're using hasn't been sharpened properly for years."

wonders (will) never cease = I am very surprised at what has happened

"Wonders will never cease ñ my son has washed the car without being asked."

See also: nine days' wonder; small wonder.

wood

not be able to see the wood for the trees = be over-attentive to details and fail to realize/understand the main issue

"Henry insists on knowing exactly what everyone is doing minute by minute, but he can't see the wood for the trees and fails to keep the whole project on schedule."

out of the wood(s) = out of difficulty/danger

"We may have solved a few of the problems but we're still not out of the woods yet."

touch wood = hopefully/with luck

"June should have got her exam results by now and know that she's passed, touch wood."

See also: dead wood; neck of the woods; wooden spoon.

wool

wool-gathering = day-dreaming.

"Don't sit there wool-gathering, come and help me tidy up."

See also: dyed-in-the-wool; pull the wool over somebody's eyes.

word

be as good as one's word = keep one's promises

"If John has said he'll do it, he will ñ he's always as good as his word."

break/keep one's word = fail to keep/keep a promise

"I have promised to take my wife out tonight, and I dare not break my word."

famous last words! = so you claim/say!

"You're sorry and you'll never do it again? Famous last words!"

have a word with somebody = talk briefly to somebody

"Mary probably knows, why don't you have a word with her?"

have the final/last word = make the final comment in an argument

"Linda will agree with you eventually, as long as she has the last word."

have words = quarrel

"John and Janet have had words and he's gone off and left her."

in a word = in (brief) conclusion

"You've asked me what I think about their new record ñ in a word, it's rubbish!"

in other words = putting it another way

"Michelle has several boyfriends at once ñ in other words, she's promiscuous."

man/somebody of few words = somebody who says little

"The ship's captain was a man of few words yet his intentions were always perfectly clear."

my word! = exclamation of surprise

"My word! How you've grown!"

not be the word for it = be an understatement

"They kept me waiting for half an hour ñ annoyed wasn't the word for it, I was livid!"

not in so many words = not exactly

"He didn't ask me to leave in so many words, but he made it clear he didn't want me there."

operative word = most significant word

"Please leave quietly ñ quietly being the operative word."

put in a good word for somebody = praise/recommend somebody

"If you're having lunch with the boss, put in a good word for me."

take the words out of somebody's mouth = anticipate what somebody is about to say

"That's correct, you took the words right out of my mouth."

take somebody at his/her word/take somebody's word for it = believe somebody without question

"I can't prove it, you'll just have to take me at my word."

"He said he didn't do it and I could only take his word for it."

word for word = exactly as spoken/written

"That's word for word what she told me."

words fail me = I am unable to find words to express my feelings

"You have been so stupid about the whole thing, words fail me."

See also: actions speak louder than words; by word of mouth; eat one's words; exchange words; from the word go; have a word in somebody's ear; man of his word; mark my words; mum's the word; not get a word in edgeways; play on words; (just) say the word; the last word; words fail me; words stick in one's throat.

work

give somebody the works = let somebody have everything that is available

"My nephew wanted a special ice cream so the people in the café gave him the works: three kinds of ice cream with fruit and all the trimmings."

"Go on Paul: you can beat him. Give him the works!"

go to work on something = begin working on something

"I'll have to go to work on that carpet and try to remove the stains."

gum up the works = cause something to stop working

"The process was working perfectly until the manager changed the system and gummed up the works."

have one's work cut out = have a difficulty to be overcome.
"We'll have our work cut out to get there before nightfall."

many hands make light work = a task is easier when one has help
"We'll help you with the washing up ñ many hands make light work."

out of work = unemployed
"Patrick has been out of work and on the dole for more than six months."

set somebody to work = get somebody to start working
"The gardener has arrived and I've set him to work on the lawns first."

set to work = begin working
"The coffee break is over, it's about time you set to work."

(all) worked up = anxious/excited
"It was an accident ñ there's no need to get all worked up about it."

work like a horse/Trojan = work very hard
"I went to see about a job at the local factory but they pay only sixty pounds a week and expect you to work like a horse for it."

work of art = paint/sculpture or anything requiring great artistry/craftsmanship
"The wedding cake was a real work of art."

work off = get rid of by exercising
"At the end of a busy day I like to work off my frustrations by playing a game of squash."

work out = come to a happy/successful conclusion
"After a difficult start the project worked out well."

work-out = session of physical exercise
"Are you coming with me for a work-out at the gym?"

work something out = calculate/solve a problem
"The sum is in old pounds, shillings and pence and I've forgotten how to work it out."
"Don't worry, darling, we'll work it out together."

See also: all in a day's work; dirty work; donkey work; give somebody the works; in running/working order; make short work of; nasty piece of work; the business/works; throw a spanner in the works; work like a dog: work one's passage; work one's ticket; work something to death.

world

a world of = very much
"There's a world of difference between a labrador and an alsatian."

for (all) the world = for anything
"I wouldn't hurt you for all the world."

for all the world like = exactly like
"He walked in out of the rain looking for all the world like a drowned rat."

on top of the world = very happy
"It's a lovely day and I'm feeling on top of the world."

out of this world = very good/unusual
"I think the flavour of fresh strawberries is out of this world."

(all) the world and his wife = many people
"We went down town to do some Christmas shopping and all the world and his wife were there."

the world is one's oyster = all the good things in life are available to one
"I was young once and the world was my oyster; now that I'm older my ambitions are few."

think the world of somebody/something = be very fond/have a high opinion of somebody/something

"My mother's dog is only an old mongrel but she thinks the world of him."

what/why in the world? = emphatically what/why?

"What in the world do you call that thing?"

"Why in the world did you marry him in the first place?"

See also: dead to the world; get/have the best of both worlds; have the world at one's feet; it's a small world; it takes all sorts (to make the world); man of the world; New World; not long for this world; not the end of the world; with the best will in the world.

worm

even a worm will turn = even somebody who is very tolerant/patient may one day decide not to be

"He used to bully his secretary without mercy, but even a worm will turn and one day she walked out and left her job without even saying goodbye."

worn

See: worn to a shadow.

worry

no/not to worry = there is no need to worry

"I've run out of butter but not to worry, we can use margarine instead."

you should worry = you certainly have no reason to worry

"You can't find a boyfriend? You should worry, with your good looks!"

worse

worse for wear = in a bad state because of prolonged effort/use, or drunk

"I've had my washing machine for ten years and its getting worse for wear."

"Terry drank six pints of beer and was a little worse for wear."

See also: none the worse for; worse luck.

worst

at (the) worst = regarding a situation in the least optimistic way

"Don't worry about your driving test. At worst you'll fail, and then you can always take it again."

come off worst/get the worst of something = suffer more than somebody else

"Jack picked a fight with Barry and came off worst."

"I collided with a fence, but fortunately the fence got the worst of it."

do one's worst = (try to) be as bad as one can

"He can't harm us now ñ let him do his worst."

if the worst comes to the worst = if the most unpleasant thing possible happens

"Even if the worst comes to the worst, we can always sell up our business here and start again somewhere else."

the worst of it is that = the most unfortunate/unpleasant thing about the situation is that

"We were stranded in the car all night and the worst of it was that we didn't have anything to eat or drink."

worth

for all one is worth = with all of one's energy/vigour

"The car wouldn't start so two of us got behind it and pushed for all we were worth."

for what it's worth = if it is worthy of consideration (usually said by somebody who thinks it is important)
"For what it's worth, I overheard them planning a robbery."
not worth a tinker's cuss/damn = worthless
"I found an old coin in the garden and took it to an expert for valuation, but he said it wasn't worth a tinker's cuss."
See also: worth one's salt; worth one's weight in gold; worth somebody's while; worthy of the name.

wound
See: rub salt into the wound; wind.

wrap
keep something under wraps = keep something secret
"I hear there's going to be a price increase soon, but keep it under wraps or everybody will buy them up."
wrapped up in = engrossed with
"It's no good trying to talk to Vic, he's too wrapped up in that book."
wrap something up = complete something
"If we hurry, we can wrap up this job by this evening."
wrap up! = be quiet!
"Wrap up! I'm tired of hearing your problems!"
See also: wrap somebody (up) in cotton wool.

wrist
See: slap on the wrist.

write
write something off = accept that something is permanently lost, or destroy something
"He's never going to pay that money so I suppose we must write it off."
"Barry drove his car off the road and wrote it off."
write something up = (neatly) write a description of
"Ian witnessed the incident and he's been asked to write it up for the local paper."
"Ian has to go to the police station to write up his statement."
See also: (see the) writing on the wall.

wrong
don't get me wrong = do not misunderstand me/do not take offence at what I say
"Don't get me wrong, but shouldn't you have finished that job by now?"
get on the wrong side of somebody = cause somebody to dislike one
"Colin's all right as long as you don't get on the wrong side of him!"
get something wrong = misunderstand, or make a mistake
"No you've got it wrong ñ I'm Jane, this is June."
"I don't mind knitting jumpers, but I always seem to get the cuffs wrong."
go wrong = make a mistake, or cease to function/work properly, or become dishonest/immoral
"I made this model aircraft, but I went wrong somewhere with the fuselage."
"Our washing machine is always going wrong."
"Mark went wrong in his early teens and has been in and out of prison ever since."
in the wrong = culpable/guilty
"Whenever we have an argument, how is it that I always seem to be in the wrong?"

two wrongs don't make a right = a second error does not cancel the first
"Ignoring her after insulting her won't help ñ two wrongs don't make a right."

what's wrong with that? = why not?
"If I want to dye my hair pink, what's wrong with that?"

See also: get/start off on the right/wrong foot; get hold of the wrong end of the stick; not put a foot wrong; on the wrong side of the blanket; on the wrong track.

Y

yard

in somebody's own back yard = located near somebody/in the neighbourhood
"James is having an affair with somebody at work; you'd think he'd look farther than his own back yard!"

like a yard of pump water = very thin
"Rick is six foot four tall and like a yard of pump water."

the Yard = Scotland Yard (headquarters of London's Metropolitan Police)
"Inspector Jones has been promoted and transferred to the Yard."

yarn

spin a yarn = tell a long (untrue) story
"I won't accept your excuse ñ you've spun that yarn before!"

year

all the year round = throughout the year
"I prefer an evergreen hedge because it has leaves on all the year round."

getting on in years = becoming old
"My old dog is still lively, although he's getting on in years now."

the year dot = a long time in the past
"Old George has been with this company from the year dot."

year in, year out = continuously (every year)
"We have been going to the same holiday hotel year in, year out ever since we got married."

See also: for donkey's years.

yellow

have a yellow streak/stripe down one's back = be cowardly
"You can't rely on him when things get tough because he's got a yellow stripe down his back."

yen

have a yen for = desire/want
"I really have a yen for a nice, juicy apple."

yes

yes and no = answer that agrees in one respect but disagrees in another
"Would I like to go to a disco party? Yes and no. I like the company but all that loud music gives me a headache after a while."

yesterday

See: not born yesterday.

yet

as yet = up till now
"There have been no phone calls as yet."

you

(strictly) between you and me = confidentially (with only us knowing)
"Between you and me I think that new supervisor is a twit."

you and yours = you and (all) your family
"Would you and yours like to come to lunch next week sometime?"

you and your something = something belonging to somebody else of which one disapproves
"You and your great idea for boiling eggs in the microwave. Look at the mess they've made!"

young

not as young as one used to be = getting

"I notice Nora generally drives to the shops these days instead of walking. Still, she's not as young as she used to be."

young at/in heart = with a young person's outlook although no longer young

"My mother is nearly eighty but she's still young in heart and enjoys the company of her grandchildren."

you're only young once = the opportunities of youth are available for only a short time

"I'm determined to have a good time before I settle down and get married ñ remember, you're only young once."

See also: young blood.

your

your actual = the real

"So this is your actual home computer, is it."

yours truly = me

"And guess who won first prize ñ yours truly."

See also: what's yours?; you and yours; you and your something.

Z

zero

zero in on = accurately aim at

“We shouldn’t be vague, we should zero in on the cause of the problem.”

See also: zero hour.